ART AS THE
EVOLUTION
OF VISUAL
KNOWLEDGE

ART AS THE

OF VISUAL

EVOLUTION
KNOWLEDGE

CHARLES BIEDERMAN

135

CHARLES BIEDERMAN, RED WING, MINNESOTA

I DEDICATE THIS BOOK
TO ALL ARTISTS PAST
AND PRESENT WHOSE
WORKS HAVE EXTENDED
THE HORIZON OF MAN'S
VISUAL EXPERIENCE

EGYPTIANS	VAN DOESBURG	DONATELLO	MONDRIAN
DAGUERRE	CONSTABLE	MASACCIO	LEONARDO
SEURAT	CEZANNE	CHARDIN	COURBET
TITIAN	PEVSNER	WRIGHT	VERMEER
GRIS	DÜRER	GABO	MONET
UCCELLO	INGRES	MANET	GOYA
VELASQUEZ	RUBENS	ALBERTI	SULLIVAN
MALEVITCH	GREEKS	ROMANS	GAUGUIN
VAN GOGH	GRIFFITH	PISSARRO	HOGARTH
PALEOLITHICS	REMBRANDT	VAN DER ROHE	GIORGIONE

The old is at bottom a habit; the new an adventure. 299

James Harvey Robinson

There are two ways to slide easily through life: Namely, to believe everything, or to doubt everything; both ways save us from thinking. 178

Alfred Korzybski

. . . thinking, is an adventure; it essentially involves an element of chance, an experimental element. 173

Cassius J. Keyser

Man is born in ignorance, not in sin. 311

Porter Sargent

LEONARDO DA VINCI   JEAN CHARDIN   GUSTAVE COURBET

To my mind one should not substitute oneself for the past, one has
merely to add a new link. 66
                    Paul Cezanne

In art as in biology there is heredity but not identity with the ancestors. 188   Juan Gris

One has only to continue what has
been done. 230   Piet Mondrian

CLAUDE MONET · CAMILLE PISSARRO · PAUL CEZANNE

Art books generally fall into one of two types—those advocating the Academician's view and those advocating the ''Modernist's'' view. Art As The Evolution Of Visual Knowledge is a history that rejects both of these views because both have outlived their usefulness. In general, each group is trying to escape the responsibilities of the present, the former by contending that only the past can show the artist how to make his art, the latter by presuming that the artist is free to do anything he pleases. Meanwhile the radically altered conditions of the present demand the most crucial revisions ever undertaken in evaluating and in making art. It is precisely because of the general lack of courage to attempt these revisions that we find such chaos in the world of art today.

Art As The Evolution Of Visual Knowledge assumes that a fundamental analysis of art begins with the fact that artists, like everyone else, must live in the world of reality. To this reality, like it or not, they orient themselves with both conscious and/or unconscious assumptions. The manner in which this orientation is realized supplies us with the key for achieving adequate evaluation of any art in relation to its own times, to its past or to its future.

In other words, art does not, as many imagine, free men from bondage to objective

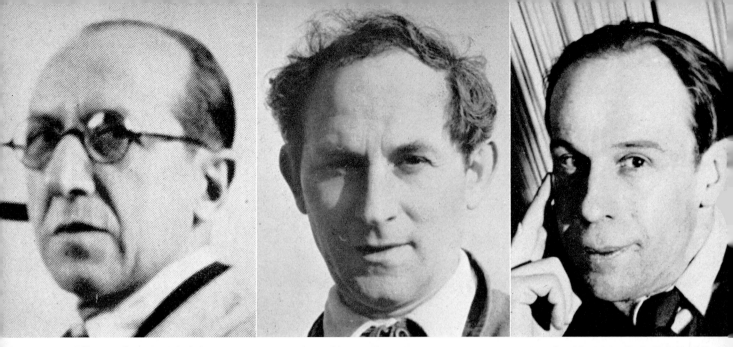

PIET MONDRIAN   NAUM GABO   THEO VAN DOESBURG

reality. It is rather one of the most profound means at man's disposal for comprehending reality, and thus constitutes one of the major records of how humans of other times saw and sought to utilize the experience of the reality about them.

Nor is art, as many imagine, in bondage to some particular past orientation to reality, however fruitful it was in the past. On the contrary, the orientation of art to reality is constantly changing, not by choice, but by necessity.

Our studies demonstrate that the history of art is inescapably a series of statements about reality, and that every great forward step has been realized by an effort to eliminate fantasy and supplant it with ever greater correspondence to the potentialities of the actual world. It should not be thought that such an approach inevitably justifies the old "realistic" theory of the Academician as the final goal of art. Nature reveals far more possibilities to the artist than will ever be contained in any theory of absolutes —or, for that matter, in any theory of irresponsibility. As with our comprehension of nature, art is a never ending process of new discovery and new realization—a matter of development, growth—a natural growth.

Our analysis, therefore, views art history as essentially a process of scientific development, a process in which ever greater insight has been gained into the natural laws of the world and how best to utilize them for making a useful art. From this point of view

LOUIS H. SULLIVAN   MIES VAN DER ROHE   D. W. GRIFFITH

nature remains the greatest teacher of the artist, who continues, as in the past, to penetrate ever further into the natural laws that govern the world from which his art inevitably originates.

It is extremely important to realize that our understanding of these laws is constantly changing because human consciousness of them is always changing. To comprehend these laws adequately it is necessary to examine the process by which knowlege of them came into existence.

Living as we do in a period when the relationship of the artist to the objective world is one of bewildering confusion (to put it mildly), it would appear that such a study as we propose is most urgently needed.

Consequently, the historical analysis in the pages following is primarily concerned with how man as an artist has oriented himself to the world in which he exists, and how this mode of orientation has progressed and/or regressed from the Paleolithic period into our own times. Such an approach avoids the all too prevalent necessity of resorting to verbal obscurity as a substitute for consciousness of one's responsibility as an artist, a critic or a user of art. In this way we can become adequately aware of the particular stage of art development which presents its challenge to the artists of today as well as to those for whom art is made. New York 1938—Red Wing 1948

C O N T

E N T S

IMITATION TO INVENTION

PICTOGRAPHS TO PHOTOGRAPHS

Man has long found solace in good talk to offset bad conduct. 300

James Harvey Robinson

Speech gave man a unique power to lead a double life. He could say one thing and do another. 300

James Harvey Robinson

Any advance in our knowledge of nature is strictly connected with new languages of similar structure which reflect the structure of the world. 179
                              Alfred Korzybski

Underlying all communication . . . are the rules . . . of symbolism.
Some of these are obvious enough when stated, but, perhaps for this reason, have been generally neglected. 246   C. K. Ogden and I. A. Richards

I WORDS AND THINGS

I believe that, with sufficient caution, the properties of language may help us to understand the structure of the world. 303*
Bertrand Russell

But it has long been recognized that language is far more than merely a vehicle for the expression of thought. It is a vehicle so built up out of man's experience that it is, historically speaking, to some extent a record of his experience in all its manifold aspects, social, industrial, scientific, mechanical, artistic, moral, religious, governmental or what not. 45
James Henry Breasted

That languages, as such, all have some structure or other is a new and, perhaps, unexpected notion. Moreover, every language having a structure, by the very nature of language, reflects in its own structure that of the world as assumed by those who evolve the language. In other words, we read unconsciously into the world the structure of the language we use. 179
Alfred Korzybski

Still another difficulty is due to the magic of words. We are still far from free of this influence and are therefore forced to think that when there is a word there must be a thing corresponding to it and also forced to think of the wording as necessarily meaning what it usually has meant in our experience. 354
William A. White

Those who seek freedom must make the effort to free themselves from the trammels of language, which are also the trammels of thought. 131
Charles Glicksberg

Freedom of speech . . . is the prerequisite of the freedom of action. And the science of semantics is that vigilance which is the price of freedom of thought. 217
Bronislaw Malinowski

There are those who will assume that it is irrelevant to begin a book on art with a discussion of language. The reversal of this assumption will bring us much closer to the facts. Consider for a moment the present state of affairs between the *non*-verbal level—the actual art—and the verbal level—what is being said and written about art. In recent decades as the amount of material written about art constantly increases, there appears to be a corresponding increase in the efforts of writers to prevent their readers from discovering what, if anything, they have to say about art. We are, therefore, compelled to consider, if only briefly, the medium by which we must communicate with each other—namely, language.

Most of us are unconscious of the fundamental operations of the language we use. We think that if we are devoted slaves of grammatical rules, know how to spell words, and know what the

* The source of all quotations not directly within the text may be found by referring to the number in the bibliography which corresponds to the number after each quotation.

dictionary says the words are supposed to mean, then we know all that is necessary about the utilization of language. This problem has been very clearly stated by Wendell Johnson: "He [the student] learns grammatical correctness reasonably well, because that is emphasized. But so long as the student's primary anxieties are made to revolve around the task of learning to spell, punctuate, and observe the rules of syntax, he is not likely to become keenly conscious of the fact that when he writes he is, above all, communicating. If he is to learn to communicate effectively, he must realize that his first obligation to his reader is not to be grammatically fashionable, but to be clear and coherent. One does not just communicate, one communicates something to someone." [1] In short, language, whether written or spoken, serves the primary function of communicating not words, but *experiences,* via the medium of words. Any investigation of language must recognize the implications of this basic function.

Words signify far more than most of us realize. In recent years various kinds of scientists have demonstrated the large degree to which we are unconscious of the operations of our nervous system. And since language is our paramount mode of expression, an activity everyone exercises, then certainly these unrecognized operations of our nervous systems must be operating also in our language. Indeed, it has been demonstrated from numerous avenues of scientific inquiry that hidden motives lurk in our "truthful" utterances. Towards a similar end as the old Socratic maxim, "Know thyself," we could well say, "Know thy language."

Freud, for example, devoted a great deal of energy to the study of the words we use and their relationship to particular nervous disorders; many others in the field of psychology and psychiatry etc., have continued the study. Among the more recent and advanced researches into the functional structure of language are the works of Alfred Korzybski, which he calls "general semantics." [2]

Korzybski maintains that in order to understand the basic function of anything, we need to hunt down its fundamental structure, in language as in any scientific field. Here, we cannot undertake anything like an adequate study of the functional structure of language, but can only touch on a few important points in a manner necessarily oversimplified. It is strongly urged that the reader pursue the problem further in the works of Korzybski. [3]

We approach this subject by making a distinction between two interrelated levels of human activity—the objective and the verbal. The objective level is the world-of-things and is *unspeakable* because it IS-NOT-words. It is *on* this level that we actually live our lives. For example, you can fly an airplane, but you cannot fly the name-word which we give to this machine. The verbal level, on the other hand, is the world-of-words and is speakable only, because it IS-NOT-things. Words are a collection of marks or sounds which human beings have created to serve as symbols for the things and happenings they appear to experience on the objective level. It is *with* this level and particularly these kinds of symbols that it becomes possible for us to live according to human as distinct from animal types of orientation. Words serve the primary purpose of achieving communication with others about what happens inside our skins when we react to what exists outside our skins on the objective level.

Unconscious or ignorant of these two levels of human activity, certain artists have nevertheless utilized a set of verbalisms, which might seem at first glance to be based on the above distinctions. That is, when the artist is speaking about art, and the fallacy of his reasoning processes is exposed, he commonly resorts to a very handy statement to the effect that words are after all quite useless in explaining art, because art is not words. On the other hand, the same artist may be quite willing to speak about art so long as nothing happens to disturb his usual irresponsible indulgence in word-noises; but if you question the logic of his words, he then tries to convince you that words are useless anyway where art is concerned, so why be fussy?

It is true that art obviously is not words, but neither, as we have just noted, is anything else

1. Wendell Johnson: "You Can't Write Writing," *Etc.,* 1:26, August, 1943.

2. Alfred Korzybski: *Science and Sanity: An Introduction to Non-Aristotelian Systems and General Semantics.* The Science Press Printing Co., Lancaster, Pa., 1933. The notions we express here are based on the theories of Korzybski.

3. See also the works of Oliver L. Reiser, Wendell Johnson and others.

that we use words for. If one examines the function of language, he will discover that the words we use are *never* ANY of the *things* we speak about (except when we are talking about words, and even here words are never things!). *Therefore, in this respect, the visual arts are not any different from any other field of human effort as concerns the use of verbal symbols.*[4]

Now, since words are not things and things are not words, the problem becomes one of finding the relationships between them so as to be able to use these symbols properly for purposes of communication. This connecting link, as Korzybski clearly demonstrates, is one of STRUCTURE; that is, our symbols or words *must be similar in structure to the structure of the objective level* which we are symbolizing. For example, the symbols on a restaurant menu *are not* food, but they generally correspond in their symbolic meanings to the food that may be had at the particular restaurant. The menu with the food makes a "word-fact" relationship. There is a correspondence in structure between the symbol and the fact symbolized.

Word-fact relationships are explained in another way by Korzybski. If we have a map showing New York between San Francisco and Chicago, and if we follow such a map in trying to go from Chicago to New York, obviously we will fail to arrive at our destination. The map is not *similar in structure* to the structure of the territory mapped. The same holds true of language; when our symbols do not correspond structurally to the facts symbolized, we run into trouble, just as when we travel by a false map. Since the map IS NOT the territory and the words ARE NOT objects, then the only connecting link between them is a similarity or a correspondence in structure. Unfortunately most of us use language like a map-maker who diagrams the territory his map is supposed to represent without proper regard for the observable characteristics of the territory being mapped or symbolized. (Later on we shall see how much that is said about art has little or no relationship to the actual art.)

We may say, "But this is all very obvious—so what?" Perhaps its very obviousness makes it difficult to see; otherwise most of the population of the world would not follow those false map-makers, the propagandists. In short, because of the very obviousness of such situations, we are often incapable of meeting them properly.

But the propagandist knows more about language than most of us, at least he knows how to use it destructively. He knows that he can count on our making an automatic assumption to the effect that a word invariably represents the "facts" as they actually are on the objective level, since most of us are unconscious of (or at the very least confused by) the important distinctions between words and things. He knows that few realize the possibilities of using language in such a way as not only to misrepresent the facts, but also to lead us altogether into a world of fiction. And so the propagandist has no qualms about using language to make things appear other than they actually are. This can be seen especially in propaganda as totalitarians use it. In fact, Hitler wrote: "Propaganda's task is . . . not to evaluate the various rights, but far more to stress exclusively the one that is to be represented by it. It has not to search into truth as far as this is favorable to others, in order to present it then to the masses with doctrinary honesty, but it has rather to serve its own truth uninterruptedly."[5]

It follows, therefore, as Horace Kallen points out, that, "In Nazi usage 'honor' means ambush, 'loyalty' betrayal, 'justice' serving your own interest, 'peace,' the waging of undeclared war; 'truth' reckless lying; 'war-mongering,' resisting Nazi assault; 'freedom,' obeying the 'leader' blindly and unquestioningly; 'science,' scholastic conformation to Nazi dogma; 'art,' the portrayal of life by means of forms, images, sounds and symbols whose qualities contradict and compensate for all that life in Nazidom actually is."[6]

4. We shall discuss this problem in more detail in a more extensive context later in our studies.

5. Adolf Hitler: *Mein Kampf*, p. 236, Houghton Mifflin Co., New York, 1939.

6. Horace M. Kallen: *Art and Freedom*, Vol. 2, p. 877. Reprinted by permission of the publishers, Duell, Sloan and Pearce, Inc. Copyright 1942 by Horace M. Kallen. Substitute the word "communist" for "nazi" and we bring the statement up to date. Since this was first written, World-Civil-War II has been concluded and the deceptive semantic devices have been somewhat altered. For example: "Moscow and its agents have said that they were bringing freedom, but they really brought subjugation. They daily talk of democracy, but they took away what democracy the Balkan peoples had. Each 'free election' of which they boast is mass intimidation. Their 'people's rule' is imposed by force upon unwilling peoples. Their term 'anti-Fascist' merely means pro-Communist, 'democracy' means Communism, 'Fascist' means anti-Communist. They call the best democrats Fascists. 'Rule by the people' means rule over the people." ("Russia in the Balkans," p. 3, by Reuben H. Markham, published by *The New Leader*, December 21, 1946, Vol. XXIX, No. 51.)

And Erich Fromm comments: "Never have words been more misused in order to conceal the truth than today. Betrayal of allies is called appeasement, military aggression is camouflaged as defense against attack, the conquest of small nations goes by the name of a pact of friendship, and the brutal suppression of the whole population is perpetrated in the name of National Socialism. The words democracy, freedom, and individualism become objects of this abuse too." [7]

In other words, the propagandists know the power of the magic-of-words, and therefore in their use of language they have reverted completely to primitive practices. Primitive man regarded words as things—which led to the belief in the magic-of-words. A striking example of this is seen in the belief among Primitives that the name is a part of one's body; in some tribes an individual's original name is never uttered, since then a part of the self can escape and so get into the possession of others who can do one harm. And, make no mistake, then as now, word-magic produced results. For example, the Primitive after the proper rituals could shake the hand of his enemy and utter, "I give you the handshake of death"; investigators have seen this actually produce death. While this identification of words with things is most pronounced among Primitives and the "mentally" ill, today the propagandists, in their manipulation of word-magic, serve as tribal priests in a return to primitivism.

But in our times, when the art of deceit with word-magic has been perfected, the opposite drive has also appeared, so that perversions of language can be exposed and we can learn to use words in a more sane manner. Korzybski has shown the crucial need for avoiding the "identification" [8] of words with things and anything with anything else. He has shown the imperative necessity for replacing the general practice of identification with the habit of differentiation, since the world reality process is a dynamic, ever-changing, never-repeating continuum of occurrences. By releasing the potentialities of differentiation inherent in the highest degree in the visualization process, our observations are not nullified by the false, frustrating reports that result from identification.

Identification is well illustrated by the aforementioned prevalent tendency of artists to assume that because words cannot be the art, then it becomes futile to speak about art with words. Yet imagine the cry that would go up if artists were denied by law the right to speak about art. It would appear, therefore, that the problem is how to speak properly about art, not whether or not we can "speak" a painting. After all the purpose of language is not to reproduce a painting, but rather to communicate about our experiences with it. These experiences are not in the painting, since they occur within our nervous systems, and merely showing the painting will not tell another person what we have specifically experienced.

The problem of identification has become a vital factor for semantic investigation. If we are conscious of the dangers of identification, we then become aware automatically of many disastrous pitfalls which await us in our use of language. To avoid identification is to avoid the disease of verbal paralysis. Thus Korzybski writes: "We live in a four-dimensional space-time manifold which, on all levels, consists of absolutely individual events, objects, situations, abstractions etc., and we must conclude that structurally we live in an *indefinitely many-valued* or infinite-valued world, the possibilities of which follow in principle the laws of combinations of higher orders. The above statement represents a description of a structural observation about the empirical world, independent of our pleasure, and can be contradicted only by exhibiting empirically, actual 'identity' or 'absolute sameness' etc., of different events, objects, or situations etc., which exhibiting becomes an impossibility if we decide to investigate facts more fully." [9]

Another important factor in the functional structure of language has to do with the many-valued meanings of our most fundamental terms, such as "democracy," "human rights," "freedom," "equality," "art," etc. As a result of the vicious verbal habits of assuming only one meaning rather than many potential meanings for these *multi-valued* terms, we become canalized (verbal paralysis) in our reactions to and use of them. Consequently when someone else with different canalizations uses these terms, trouble begins.

7. From ESCAPE FROM FREEDOM, by Erich Fromm, p. 274. Copyright 1941 by Erich Fromm and reprinted by permission of Rinehart and Co., Inc.

8. The Korzybskian sense of this term is "absolute sameness," "sameness in all respects."

9. Korzybski, op. cit., p. 462.

This was well illustrated by the various public figures who shouted about "democracy" in connection with the recent war. They all used the term in their public utterances, although their other actions disclosed wide differences in their notions of democracy. Can a Lindbergh mean the same thing as a Bertrand Russell? We are still witnessing today how disastrous the non-recognition of these multi-valued terms can be in the behavior of "primitive" mentalities who hide their barbaric intentions behind a halo of sacred terms such as "free enterprise," "rugged individualism," "Americanism," etc.

Korzybski calls this phenomenon the "multi-ordinal" character of language. All terms which are of this multi-valued character are, to begin with, *undefined,* in that, whatever meanings they can have, can arise only *when such terms are put into a definite or particular context.* By being conscious of the multi-orientational potentialities in our use of the most important terms, it becomes possible to adjust them to the structure of the dynamic variabilities of the actual facts.

Thus we can see how harmful it is to take the view that, "There are no new terminologies or meanings permissible in a discussion with me that do not bear the sanction of the dictionary . . ."[10] Anyone who has bothered to give even a cursory examination to the history of words realizes that word-meanings change and expand, etc., for the simple reason that man's experiences in this world are undergoing constant change and expansion; and since the purpose of words is to communicate experiences, they are thus periodically if belatedly adjusted to these ever changing conditions. If one fails to realize this changing character of words, and the multi-ordinality or plurality of important key terms, he will then automatically assume that such terms must have an absolute and limited meaning. If someone else uses these terms otherwise, it will be assumed that he does so because he is ignorant of *the* meaning of these terms. But in a dynamic world structure we need a dynamic structure for our language and not a static, frozen one as the above dictionary zealot would insist. The question is are men to be the slaves of words, or words the slaves of men.

In the case of the term "art," *we allocate* it each time we use it into a particular context which automatically prescribes the particular meanings we are using at a *particular time.* Thus the term becomes flexible enough to be given meanings that correspond to the objective level where man's activities as an artist exist. That is, there is not some one kind of art, BUT MANY KINDS OF DIFFERENT ARTS. In fact, there are as many different arts as there are things labelled as such by human beings. Hence, in actuality we are not confronted by the problem of whether this or that is or is not art; the problem is rather of the *kind* of "art."

By recognizing the multi-ordinality of the word "art," we can apply it accurately in the many references we shall make to the various arts in man's history. In other words, the *functional structure* of this term can be adjusted to the structural character of that aspect of the objective level we are talking about, the actual visual arts. To communicate successfully whatever we may mean by "art," we must always put it into a definite context which will indicate to what aspect we are referring. By recognizing the *plurality* of the meanings of key terms in our language, we can then cover the wide variability of actual life situations without inventing new terms.[11] In this way the term "art" can be varied in its meanings to cover the differences between any of the many works of a single artist, and differences between any of the many works of two or any number of artists in the same culture, or the differences between any of the artists of any of the different cultures of similar or *dissimilar* historical times, etc.

The usual practice, however, is to tack a definition to the term art and then use this definition as an absolute for measuring what is or is not supposed to be art. This may simplify our job of evaluating art, but since our job is not that simple, the consequences are that such evaluations complicate our real life experiences in a highly destructive manner. We constantly bump into occurrences on the objective level which do not fit into these *a priori* notions, and so our otherwise neat definitions are an endless source of disturbance.

Here we would like to note briefly a few examples of the misuse of language in the field of art.

10. Evelyn Marie Stuart: "Consult the Dictionary," *The Art Digest,* 19:25, February 1, 1945.

11. Therefore, to facilitate the proper operation of multi-ordinal or multi-dimensional terms, to remind the reader that the meanings of such terms are created by the context in which they are placed, we shall use quotation marks occasionally for such terms.

From the publicity for the opening of a new gallery we are informed that, *"all types* and *kinds* of *art forms* and of *art personalities* find a place on our walls and in our organization." (emphasis ours)[12] But a few paragraphs later we find: "In short, the movement which the Associated American Artists spearhead is a movement of the artist back to his proper place in society, and a movement of society back to its proper appreciation of the artist. This movement is trying to reestablish for contemporary American art the conditions which prevailed before art became an aesthetic cult."[13] Obviously the owners of the "Associated American Artists" have not the slightest intention of permitting "all types and kinds of art forms and of art personalities" to enter and be accepted by this organization. And so it is false to claim, as they do, that, "We sponsor no school, no aesthetic ideology at the expense of another."[14] How false these statements are can easily be ascertained by the simple process of examining the artists who are ballyhooed. There we see that the Association collects and sells a very distinct type of art and certainly not "all types and kinds." But above all it should be pointed out that one is compelled to "sponsor" some school or schools at the expense of another school or schools, unless one is in favor of *all* schools or against *all* schools and either attitude is, to say the least, obviously nonsensical.

An artist writing to uphold something he calls "Modern art" furnishes another example (and here we find that little word "all" again), "All copying of subject as seen by the physical eyes (Naturalism) is craft, not art."[15] This same writer claims in the very next sentence, however, that "copying has existed only in a few decadent periods in the long history of art . . ."[16] (In other words, copying *is* art and it is also not art!)

Of course, such statements are enough to raise the blood pressure of any Academician; in fact in the very same journal, we find one Academician denying the "Modernist" the right to call his painting a "picture." Thus: "There never was or can be such a thing as a non-representational *picture*."[17] Denying the "Modernists" the privilege of calling their paintings "pictures," does not whittle down the value of their paintings; it only whittles down the functional span of our language. If they wish to call their paintings "pictures," and we happen to be one of those who object to their "pictures," then it would simply be necessary to distinguish between different kinds of pictures. As a matter of fact the same writer with this adamant view on "pictures" elsewhere actually does use the term when referring to the art of the "Modernists."[18] In other words, the actual world of facts compels us to resort to more extensive meanings than our neat petrified definitions would permit. Thus a paradox is inevitable and we find that the old Academician's art *is* and *is not* art, and the Modernist's pictures *are* and *art not* pictures.

Such wrangling as this makes a solution impossible. It serves only to cultivate all kinds of word blockages that prevent coherent thinking and unnecessarily and destructively complicate our use of language. How much simpler and more constructive the whole issue becomes, when the term "art" is permitted to cover all such manifestations that humans generally so label, while at the same time distinctions are made between DIFFERENT KINDS of art. In this way the futile "this-is-art-and-this-is-not-art" kind of arguments are avoided. The latter either-or attitude usually reduces discussion to mere word-noises or "chin-music," and destroys the useful function of language by limiting one's range of reasoning to two- or few-valued modes of logic. By recognizing the multi-ordinal character of the key terms we employ, our language is made into a useful, functioning instrument, since we thus increase the range of our ability to reason usefully. In short, *words are not things. The word art IS NOT "art."*

Therefore, as Korzybski explains: "We see that we can reach . . . an important conclusion;

---

12. R. Lewenthal: "What the Associated American Artists Stand For": from brochure issued by Associated American Artists Galleries, 1945.

13. Ibid.

14. Ibid.

15. R. M. Pearson: "A Modern Viewpoint: What Is Modern Art?", *The Art Digest,* 19:22, February 15, 1945.

16. Ibid., p. 22.

17. Evelyn Marie Stuart: "Consult the Dictionary," *The Art Digest,* 19:25, February 1, 1945.

18. See p. 10, *The Art Digest,* Vol. 18, October 1, 1943.

namely, that, first of all, we must distinguish between words, symbols which symbolize something, and noises, not symbols, which have no meaning (unless with a pathological meaning for the physician); and, second, that if we use words (symbols for something), all disputes can be solved sooner or later. But, in cases in which we use noises as if they were words, such disputes can *never* be settled."[19]

It may be imagined, however, that whatever the linguistic state of the artist, this need not have any effect upon his art. This of course is delusionary. One of the main objectives of this book will be to show the crucial interdependence that exists between what man thinks and says and what he experiences and makes as an artist.

19. Alfred Korzybski: *Science and Sanity,* p. 82.

Demetrius was wont to say that there was no difference between the words and speech of the unskilled and ignorant and the sounds and rumblings caused by the stomach being full of superfluous wind. This he said not without reason for as he held it did not in the least matter from what part of them the voice emanated, whether from the lower parts or the mouth, since the one and the other were of equal worth and importance. 212

Leonardo da Vinci

What has gone, has gone forever. 357
Alfred Whitehead

It is not really sufficient to direct attention to the best that has been said and done in the ancient world. The result is static, repressive, and promotes a decadent habit of mind. 358
                    Alfred N. Whitehead

Past, Present, and Future—these cannot be understood singly and separately—they are welded together indissolubly as one. 178   Alfred Korzybski

2 HISTORY FOR WHAT?

The old drags us down like a chronic disease—and
its nature has hitherto been badly diagnosed.
This is obviously but one aspect of man's fate. The
old is the indispensable foundation of the new.
Without it no advance in knowledge and human
improvement would be possible. Father Time is the
benefactor to whom we literally owe everything,
but he is exceedingly jealous of his established
scheme of things. Wisdom will come as we learn to
recognize vividly our abject dependence upon him
and at the same time invent more ingenious ways
than those hitherto discovered for exposing and
overcoming his inveterate prejudices. 301

James Harvey Robinson

The foundation of all understanding of sociological
theory—that is to say, of all understanding of
human life—is that no static maintenance of perfection is possible. This axiom is rooted in the nature
of things. Advance or Decadence are the only
choices offered to mankind. 358

Alfred N. Whitehead

Perhaps, neurologically, animals feel similarly as we
do about 'time', but they have no neurological
means to elaborate linguistic and extra-neural means
which alone allow us to extend and summarize the
manifold experience of many generations (time-
binding). They cannot pass from 'time' to 'times'.
Obviously, if we do not, we then renounce our
human characteristics, and copy animals in our
evaluating processes, a practice which must be
harmful. 179

Alfred Korzybski

Of all the forms of human inquiry which can lead us to knowledge about human existence and the world
in which it is activated, history is among the most important. Properly employed, it can be one of the most
fruitful sources of knowledge concerning man's behavior not only in the past but also in the present. Yet
the historical approach has been one of the most neglected by those who wish to move on to needed change,
and the most abused by those who want things to "stay put."

In spite of the numerous "history" classes, this situation is especially true in the field of art.
These classes are such a source of nonsense, such a monotony, that most art students flee from the subject
at the first opportunity, never to return to it again. In a great measure it is such unpleasant and futile experiences that generate the opinion that it will always be impossible for us the living to understand why
those in the past did as they did.

But failure, as such, is not proof that failure is inevitable. The record so far has been one of
defeat because history has been the tool largely of those who falsify the past, either deliberately or under the
guise of "objective" history.

It may be of some significance that in recent years many historians are insisting that there should
be a more strict surveillance over the collecting of so-called facts so that more accuracy and less falsehood

might result. It is naive to assume, however, that insistence upon more accurate facts will invariably achieve less falsehood, since it is quite possible to present a collection of "truthful facts" which will nevertheless give a false impression of the actual events because other facts were omitted.

In the 19th century such a pursuit of "facts" by the historian *was* an innovation, a revolutionary affair, in contrast to the then usual practice of gross distortion and manipulation of "facts" to serve the ends of those in power. But like all revolutions, it has been followed by still others, so that the mentality which was revolutionary in the 19th century is today a reactionary one. Hence in the context of the present, historians of the old school are obsessed with the magic of the term "facts," as though they were something superior, complete and replete with truth. As H. E. Barnes has pointed out, "The naïve assumption of many historians that there are concrete and integral entities known as historical facts lying about in profusion in our collections of historical sources is actually an animistic vestige."[1]

Another sacred word, second only to "facts" among the old school historians, is "chronology." Regardless of the merits of chronology, it is generally made to seem so very important in itself that the student is apt to suppose that he has attained historical knowledge in its fullest sense when he succeeds in memorizing names, dates and places in their chronological order. Thus he is prevented from investigating, with the modern tools of inquiry such as science offers, the basic significance of the chronology which appears in history.

Actually both chronological and non-chronological methods are necessary and each is indispensable to the other. Chronology if used properly is of aid in discovering the asymmetrical order, and so structure, of the evolution of human history. Non-chronological approaches if used properly make possible comparisons of similarities and the very important differences within similarities, which are uniquely illuminating in the critical examination of human evolution. Hence it is our contention that historians who insist *only* upon the chronological approach, or *only* upon the non-chronological approach, end up by inadequately comprehending and utilizing the method to which they happen to be partial. The either-or attitude makes this inevitable.

Today many new avenues of knowledge have been discovered which throw new light upon the observation of history. New responsibilities have appeared which the older historian is loath to accept. The newer thinkers realize that the field of history must function as an interdependent part of man's activities as-a-whole. Mere collecting of facts, no matter how well done, is not enough.

The pertinent question to ask ourselves is: what are the factors which prompted our ancestors to adopt particular modes of action resulting in the manifestations we label "facts"? Were not these particular modes of action the result of their particular beliefs about, or interpretations of their environment?

In the past, as now, the recognition of facts as facts was the result of certain basic beliefs about the world in which man lived; these beliefs were passed from one generation to the next. Each new generation took over these notions *in toto,* then gradually modified them. In this manner each of our ancestors acquired the "mental" tools which determined his method of interpreting and evaluating the so-called factual world. In other words, each of our ancestors inherited some system of beliefs for distinguishing a so-called fact from a so-called non-fact; for distinguishing "reality" from non-reality. On the basis of these beliefs, then, our ancestors would proceed to interpret the world and other men, and to manipulate their environment. Thus they shaped their culture according to beliefs that came from the past. Each generation slightly modified certain beliefs and then passed these on to their successors. Therefore, the conclusion is inescapable that what we are so fond of calling "facts" resulted from particular beliefs or basic assumptions, beliefs which were altered from time to time as experience provided information which was shown to offer better survival values. Thus, for example, "facts" will appear very different to us according to whether we believe in the doctrines of Christianity or those of modern science. The term "fact" is not a *thing,* but a *label* which covers various attitudes towards things and beliefs about things. "Truth does not lie in the mere accumulation of facts," remarked Einstein, "but in an attitude of mind, and a mode of life and action, that must be renewed from generation to generation."[2]

---

1. From *A History of Historical Writing,* p. 267, by Harry Elmer Barnes, copyright 1937 by University of Oklahoma Press, Norman.

2. As quoted by Porter Sargent in *War and Education,* p. 269, P. Sargent, Boston, 1944.

We do not deny that the "fact" collectors have their useful value, but the time has come when enough facts have been collected to make it not only possible but imperative to approach the far more fundamental task of unearthing the interrelationships which bind all these facts to each other into some kind of structural, experiential sequence, a sequence that will reveal the significance of the past. Theories without facts or facts without theories are useless. We need both theory and fact, since each factor is part of a single problem. In actuality we cannot separate these two factors, but unfortunately we can reason that it is possible to do so. The result of the latter is to decrease the exactitude of our interpretation of history.

One of the curious paradoxes of man's behavior is that few objections are raised to thinking in evolutionary terms about phenomena which *seem* to deal only with things outside man—such as the formation of the earth or the development of man's mechanical progress. However, when one adopts the evolutionary attitude towards the examination of what obviously goes on *inside* man, his reasoning behavior, his art, which reflects his method of reasoning, etc., objections are hurled immediately, and evolution of any kind is, by the vast majority, emphatically denied.

That historical attitude which entails thinking about the thinking behavior of our predecessors and the consequences of that thinking behavior, invariably makes us face the difficult situation of thinking about our own thinking, of doubting and reconsidering that which we have habitually accepted from the past without questioning its value. Few indeed have the courage to examine the process by which we have acquired our most "cherished convictions," convictions for the maintenance of which millions are periodically murdered.

In brief, we are generally willing to search out asymmetrical relationships in any field except those that make us face ourselves—face the problems of why man has done as he has done and why he does today as he does. For thus he must judge his own actions instead of putting it off till the alleged day of judgment arrives. Men fear this responsibility: they prefer to impose it on anything or anyone, out-there, up-there or anywhere except in-here, in themselves. Men fear whatever forces them to change present behavior, even though vaguely knowing that change is inevitable. We all "know" in one way or another that we need to change and that things change whether we like it or not; but in the most important things we are always finding excuses for putting off the changes that should be made.

It is primarily such an excuse that comprises the function of "objective," "factual," "chronological," etc. histories. As Harry Elmer Barnes has pointed out, their purpose is "to leave things as they are," thus implicitly denying change in a world where never-ending change is a *natural*, inescapable inevitability. In this light we can understand why the advocates of objectivity make such evaluations as the following: "A history should only give the facts and thus each reader is left to make his own interpretations of them." In other words, each one is free to satisfy his own particular prejudices without being interrupted by the disturbing interpretations of others. It is precisely the type of history one expects to find in a laissez-faire society.

The objective historians are apt to contend that to go further than accurate reporting is not only dangerous, but harmful. And they are correct, in the sense that it *is* harmful to their notions of history, since once historical inquiry passes beyond the mere presentation of chronological "facts," the historian immediately becomes involved in the task of investigating and evaluating human activity (including the activity of historians who presumably avoid going beyond chronological facts!).

And so we cannot escape the conclusion that those who consider a description of the wars, wealth, power, inventions, and the like of our ancestors as the only real, factual aspect of the past, and who maintain that anything that goes further can only be mere conjecture, are at best rationalizing their ignorance. This amounts to a refusal to face the basic responsibilities of inquiries into history as befits one living in the 20th century. As a rule such types of history have become convenient subterfuges for the *status quo,* institutional opportunism of the crassest kind. As Porter Sargent has ably put it: "Presidents and trustees of our universities and colleges, who have to keep open their pipelines to the great financial centers, see to it that teachers of history and other social subjects are selected with care, then conditioned and kept in a proper state of subservient timidity. The system results in men once liberal and independent becoming, with exceptions, tame stooges."[3]

3. Porter Sargent: *War and Education,* p. 445, P. Sargent, Boston, 1944.

In short, "objective history" is not the affair its sponsors wish it to appear. Since a human being is a subjective-objective continuum, it is impossible for anyone to be as objective as "objective historians" imagine they are. It is not only futile but false to regard the past as though it were a matter of nothing but "facts," and to assume that we are neutral in our observation of it, however we may record history. On this subject H. E. Barnes has pointed out that: "In the first place, modern psychology has completely undermined the assumptions of those who uphold the ideals of complete historical objectivity. It has shown that no truly excellent piece of intellectual work can be executed without real interest and firm convictions. The notion that the human intellect can function in any vital form in an emotionless and aimless void is obviously contrary to the most elementary teachings of psychology. The assertion of the erudite school that we must approach historical problems with no preconceived notions, *actually means that we should have no unorthodox notions.* Members of the erudite school are replete with *preconceived notions,* but they are the opinions and dogmas that are currently received and approved by the historical guild." (emphasis ours)[4] And in speaking of this problem, Erich Kahler has written: "the breakdown of the unity of history is so complete that modern historians do not dare to assume that there is such a thing as history, or a consistent human evolution. They manifest the deepest distrust toward any claim of meaning in history and regard any interpretation of history as unfounded speculation. In reality, there is no presentation of facts without interpretation. The choice of facts in itself constitutes an interpretation, whether it is determined consciously or subconsciously, whether the material is deliberately chosen to back up an argument or whether it appears to impose its own arrangement."[5]

With this advanced orientation to history, a new type of historian is emerging. Robert Lynd has pointed out that specialists in particular fields will be writing their own histories rather than waiting for the conventional historian to do so: "It may be that the historian, instead of continuing to be a historian first and a specialist secondarily, will in the future more commonly reverse that order. He may secure his primary training in a specific field, and utilize history as a method rather than as an independent subject-matter."[6] As a matter of fact, in recent years specialists in particular fields have become interested in contributing to human knowledge with the "historical" point of view. They see it as a necessity, as a responsibility which the conventional historian is loath to assume. For the new kind of historian, history offers a *method* for securing unique knowledge about his own field of specialization and its relation to mankind at large. He regards neither his special field nor historiography as fields all to themselves, as has been the custom; rather, each field is related to the other and to *all* other fields of any kind. It is these men, not the "objective" historians, who will discover the *new* "facts" about history.

But what, one may well ask, must the historian accomplish if he is to make his job a useful one? He must be capable of being a sort of receptacle for the records of man's various achievements and failures and then of putting this material into a coherent structural order, evaluating the significance of the relationships as he finds them. His analytical interpretation of those records will result from an effort to understand the function of the changes in the development of mankind from the very remote past to the very near future. Such an approach is indispensable if one's purpose is to comprehend the past as it applies to the present, in order finally to increase the human capacity to become more human in the future.

Since each generation inherits the culture of the generation preceding, there must then be some relationship between all cultures of some kind or other. To establish the basic character of this interdependence is a fundamental task. The purpose of such a procedure is to discover eventually why these relationships have evolved into the type of culture now extant and why we interpret the reality of the world as we do today.

Above all the historian must be aware of the basic assumptions by which he determines the structural order of the events he analyzes. His task is two-fold: he must ascertain the assumptions which were used in the past to interpret the phenomena of the world, and, equally important, he must be con-

4. From *A History of Historical Writing,* p. 266, by Harry Elmer Barnes, copyright 1937 by University of Oklahoma Press, Norman.

5. Erich Kahler: *Man the Measure,* p. 6, Pantheon Books, Inc., New York, 1943.

6. R. S. Lynd: *Knowledge for What?,* p. 174, Princeton University Press, Princeton, 1940.

scious of the kinds of assumptions he himself employs for accomplishing the same purpose in his own culture, since these latter will affect *his* interpretation of the past.

Thus the historian's task becomes the evaluation of the structures that comprise change and those that frustrate it. These two opposing factors are found operating in every individual and culture and race and nation, and their totality comprises the subject matter of history, just as the totality of man's knowledge comprises the tools for the analysis of history. Used in this way, history *can* teach us, in a most emphatic manner, that it is non-sensical to try to make things as they once were or keep them as they are: history *can* teach us that unless human life moves on to ever greater progress, ever greater regression results.

Anyone adequately acquainted with the literature on "Modern" art today is well aware that the writers of it are not only far from being constructively historical in their analyses, but many of them deliberately attempt to avoid or even condemn such an attitude. The prevalent practice of explaining Modern art by itself without disclosing its basic relationships with the past *as-a-whole* has invariably failed to produce a coherent and satisfying analysis of what is occurring in present day art. The continued and increasing confusion that exists today, after hundreds of books dealing with Modern art have been published, attests to this failure. In general, these books have dealt with works produced during the last hundred years or so, and with the art of Primitives. The arts of recent years are usually "explained" in the form of poetic biographies, from Cézanne to Picasso. The Primitive arts are included in order to justify and rationalize the particular kind of reverence popularly paid to the art produced since Cézanne; hence the Primitive's activities are erroneously compared (identified) with those of supposedly civilized modern adults.

The histories of the Academicians are also usually composed of biographies, not so much "poetic" as "objective," but dealing mainly with artists from the Renaissance up to around the time when the Camera was invented. And where the Modernist rationalizes with the Primitive for his criterion, the Academician employs the arts of Greco-Roman and/or Renaissance times.

Neither of these groups achieves an outlook which could rightly be called historical in the more advanced sense. The Academician's "consciousness" of and interest in art begins 2,000 years ago with the Classical Greeks. Ordinarily it ends at that point where it is abruptly interrupted by the appearance of the Impressionists. The "Moderns" are particularly interested in the art *before* Classical Greece and *after* the Impressionists. Neither group ventures to produce a structural synthesis, an as-a-whole comprehension of all the main phases of man's art. They merely pick out those scattered portions of history which seem to fit comfortably into their *a priori* conclusions and all the rest is labelled as error.

Actually there is little essential difference between the two groups. Both are trying to escape the basic problems before the artist today. The Academicians, who never grew out of the past, are hypnotized by it and thus they seek escape from the present. The majority of Modernists have never understood coherently how to grow out of the past; they are hypnotized instead by their own private world. They seek escape from the difficulties of the reality about them by fleeing into a delusional art world of their own making. It is imperative that we clearly understand these two general methods of observing history in order to see the false consequences which inevitably follow. It is precisely this historical impasse which prevents any resolution of the arguments between those who uphold the old or those who see the need for a new art.

Fortunately, however, men are beginning to learn that both the dictatorship of the past over the present and of the present over the past are impossible. Experience indicates that a modified combination of both these views is necessary. The past, the present, the future are intertwined, interdependent. Not only does the past influence the present and future, but the present and yet-to-come future influence our notions and formulations of the past. Our approach, therefore, will lead us to a positive examination of *both* the areas which have been separately considered by the above-mentioned groups. In other words, we shall try to understand the basic relationships of all arts to each other. Our attitude is expressed in the following by G. E. Partridge: "Genetic psychology assumes as an ultimate fact, and as a background for all its principles, an endless process of time, stretching out into an infinitely remote past and pointing towards an infinitely remote future. Every thing, and every event, must be regarded as the completion of an infinitely long process of development, in terms of which it can be explained; and also as germinal of a future, of which it is in turn to be the cause or genetic origin. Development and change are continuous and unbroken. Nothing is stationary, and man himself is in a stage of active evolution toward a higher form."[7]

While our conclusions may indicate certain apparent sympathies with both the Academician's and so-called Modernist's points of view, our basic conclusions will be far different from either, due to our difference in *attitude towards and method of historical analysis.* Many notions, both past and present, heretofore considered incompatible with each other, will be seen as having an interrelated significance in the formation of the history of "art." Certain trends, upon which most of our nervous Modern friends have looked with utter contempt, will find very important places in our history—for example, the literal recording of nature; Impressionism; and Cubism, upon which both the reactionaries and the Moderns have looked with heated anxiety. Naturally in drawing together seemingly divergent viewpoints, we shall considerably transform these notions (and their functions) from what they have commonly been held to be.

Our interest in the past will not be simply the desire to know how those in the past lived and made art. We intend to study the efforts of our predecessors in order to profit from their successes and errors. The object of our inquiry is to understand what basically comprised each main period of man's art, and why, in order to find what events led to the chaos of the present. Above all, the purpose of our history is to analyze the past in order to comprehend adequately the present, so that we may be able to see where we are going in the future and what the value of going there may or may not be. If we succeed, we shall then be in a position to evolve order where confusion now reigns under the guise of progress.

Many attempts have been made previously to discover the relationships which exist between all the arts produced throughout the history of man. A time-honored division into Archaic, Classical and Decadent periods has been frequently made. Others employ the Spenglerian interpretation, using the age phases of man—childhood, manhood and old age. Then there is the notion that art is the same, always and everywhere, when it is so-called "great" art.

Many of these systems lead to varying degrees of truth, but they tend to result in an anthropomorphic analysis of art. Each culture is regarded as a single organism passing from birth or beginnings to maturity or achievement and then finally decadence and death. While from one point of observation such as arrangement might seem justified, it becomes crucially inadequate for purposes of comprehending the broader vista of art history as-a-whole. It does not take into account sufficiently, if at all, the place of each culture within the greater, fundamental whole of the entire history of art.

Nevertheless, such an approach may be utilized, providing we extend it so that it encompasses the relationships between all arts—namely, *by considering the entire history of art as a single "organism"* OF AGE AS OF TODAY! Many great artists and art cultures have been born, have lived and died, but art has been born only once and as yet has never died. Thus we consider it as a single organism many thousands of years old, and the result of efforts of untold millions of artists; an organism which has not been developing in some arbitrary fashion, but in a definite and specific direction, as specific as the operation of the organisms that produced the art. It is necessary that we become coherently conscious of the particular stage of this development as it exists in our century, if progress in art is to be continued.

History is one of our most important sources of knowledge about any kind of human behavior, including art, but it must be history in the larger sense of the term in which the historian uses all the knowledge he is able to bring to the inquiry regardless of whether or not such knowledge is traditionally accepted as bearing on the comprehension of history. We should worry less about the preservation of anachronistic definitions and more about the purpose of actual human activities.

Hence, our history of art will be preoccupied with the "problems of reality" as they have

7. From G. E. Partridge: *Genetic Philosophy of Education*, p. 20. Copyright 1912 by The Macmillan Company.

appeared throughout man's existence. Although man did not become *directly* conscious of any problem of reality until the Classical Greek period, nevertheless such problems had existed for all previous cultures. In our history we shall attempt to read art as a form of language, a form of communication about the world reality; as a record which reveals the beliefs of our ancestors about human life and the reality in which it is lived.

Art, it should be understood, produced the *first* forms of recorded language, a language just as reliable for making investigations of human development as is that with which we are familiar in the remains of Egyptian cultures, etc. As a matter of fact, art is one of the more revealing, but at the same time the most neglected, sources for studying the history of man's general development. For it is in art that man has literally pictured his notion of the world; and it is in art that mankind has left the largest number of records. A great deal of effort has been given to the translation of the writings of man from Egyptian times to the present, but we have almost totally failed to "translate" the symbols of visual communication that are to be found in the earliest arts of man. It is necessary that we regard the art that preceded what we commonly recognize as writing, with the same degree of importance we give to the study of the written records of man if we are to comprehend adequately the evolution of human culture.

Our concern with the development of the problem of reality in art will obviously lead us into other branches of human activity because of the overlapping character of all forms of knowledge. Hence we shall be concerned with problems and factors ordinarily but erroneously considered as outside the province of the analysis of art.

However, if we were to write a complete history about any one subject, we would have to write a history about every subject, about all forms of knowledge, all forms of human enterprise, about everything that man has ever done, and everything that happened before man stepped out of the trees. But naturally to write such a history is beyond the capacity of a single or even many individuals or cultures. In short, it would seem that what we propose is impossible of realization. This is quite true, but the reality of the world does not always conform to man's desires.

One might ask why we advocate such complex views, since obviously a single individual cannot produce such a history. We do so because the implications of this awareness of the actual problems of history are of crucial importance; so important that we want the reader to remember it; to remember, in short, *that one cannot say ALL about anything!*

Thus we can realize that absolutes about art comprise false knowledge, that "art" knowledge must move on like life itself; we must revise past knowledge, discover new knowledge potential to and crucially necessary for the adequate comprehension of the times in which we are now living and building. Art, like all things, is a dynamic affair; only the latest, not the final discoveries can be realized. Our knowledge of history must evolve into a new consciousness of the past, as well as of the present.

But regardless of the impossibility of attaining perfection in the writing of history, this is the direction in which we are compelled to work, like it or not. We reach towards perfection, knowing full well it is unobtainable, simply because we have no other choice. We know that if we do not accept this viewpoint, we shall fail to achieve anything worthwhile. Constant realization that this is the great problem would be a tremendous factor in avoiding ancient pitfalls of absolutes. Instead we would comprehend the fact that what we aim at *can never be completely achieved,* and that it is naive to delude ourselves into assuming that *it has ever been achieved.* In the words of Cassius Keyser: ". . . absolute rigor is an ideal, to be, like other ideals, aspired unto, forever approached, but never quite attained, for such attainment would mean that every possibility of error or indetermination, however slight, had been eliminated from idea, from symbol, and from argumentation. We know, however, that such elimination can never be complete, unless indeed the human mind shall one day lose its insatiable faculty for doubting."[8]

8. Cassius J. Keyser: *The Human Worth of Rigorous Thinking*, p. 47, 3rd edition, Scripta Mathematica, Yeshiva College, New York, 1940.

Light is the most important messenger bringing us news from the outside world. What does it really tell us? We think we actually see things, their outlines and colors. In reality the light merely reports this: "I come from such and such a direction, vibrate with such and such an intensity and such and such a velocity, and I have entirely forgotten what happened to me on the journey on which I set out just after my birth and which ends here on your retina with my death." Everything else, such as our perception of colored objects, is not like a newspaper reporter's "copy", but is an unconscious combination by the editorial department (the brain) of thousands and thousands of these reporter's messages, depending on impressions derived from all the senses taken together. 40

Max Born

Evolution did not stop with the development of the visual sense as a super-tool and super-connection between human beings and the external world. The human being still had to develop the ability to see. 208
                    Matthew Luckiesh & F. K. Moss

3 ART AND VISION

That stimulation of the eyes by light is necessary for the development of the optical centers is shown by Claparede's report, that the visual centers of cats whose eyelids were sewn together at birth were arrested in their development. 176

Kurt Koffka

. . . the question whether the empirical or the nativistic theory of eye-movements is right—whether these movements take place according to inherited laws, or whether they must each be learned by individual experience—now assumes an entirely different meaning. Since the visual phenomena themselves, or at least their physical correlates, regulate eye-movements by virtue of their specific qualities, it follows that in the course of development eye-movements must depend upon the phenomena which go with them. Progress in any performance, such as visual fixation which we have been discussing, will therefore be partly conditioned by the progress made in the act of seeing itself. 176   Kurt Koffka

. . . a number of isolated facts does not produce a science any more than a heap of bricks produces a house. The isolated facts must be put in order and brought into mutual structural relations in the form of some theory. Then, only, do we have a science, something to start from, to analyse, to ponder on, criticize, and improve. Before this something can be criticized and improved, it must first be produced, so the investigator who discovers some fact, or who formulates some scientific theory, does not often waste his time. Even his errors may be useful, because they may stimulate other scientists to investigate and improve. 179   Alfred Korzybski

Fundamentally we shall study the development of art as related to the evolution of man's visual organs and of his ability to reason. Art, we shall find, is inseparably related to man's growing faculty to visualize and reason about himself and his environment in an ever more accurate manner. Art history has been approached from almost every angle; but this more fundamental one, the development or evolution of human vision and its relation to man's maturing capacity to reason about the world and himself, has been little recognized. For centuries writers have been discussing what we are supposed to see, feel, and think in art, but almost nothing of consequence has been said about *what we see with* and *how we see with it.*

Looking at art is not enough, for we must learn to *think properly* about what is looked at. Art is a *looking-thinking* experience. For this reason the remainder of this book deals largely with what humans from "prehistoric" times to the very present have *thought* about the art they have *looked* at.

Oliver L. Reiser has shown[1] that the unreflective person makes "no distinction between *appearance* and *reality* and a thing is asserted to be in fact what it appears to be." This was the attitude, more or less, of humans up to about the 5th century B.C., when man first began to be *conscious* of "problems of reality."

1. From Oliver L. Reiser: *Philosophy and the Concepts of Modern Science*, p. 71. New York, 1935. By permission of The Macmillan Company, publishers.

Today, as Reiser has pointed out, those reflective persons who deny the "validity of the principles of naive realism" try to show that, "the world we live in arises out of two factors, the *environment* and the *organism*. Our perceptions of, and beliefs about, reality are a function not only of the external world as such, but also of the human individual. In other words, what we call reality cannot be completely described in terms of external objects alone. Here is an analogy for the two-term relation we have in mind: the tides of the earth cannot be explained in terms of the earth alone nor in terms of the influence of the moon alone. The tides are a function of the inter-relation of the earth and the moon, and neither must be neglected or reduced to terms of the other." [2] This indivisible relationship between the organism and the environment is seen with especial clarity in the study of the various arts of man, for the artist and the objective world are inseparably interdependent (in spite of what some present day artists maintain!).

Art in its various forms constitutes the principal evidence of man's past efforts at visualization, and when studied in this way should produce data of inestimable value to many of the other sciences which deal directly or indirectly with the development of man's vision in relation to the phylogeny of the human nervous system.

As each of us on the ontogenetic level is born with a yet to be developed capacity to visualize, so on the phylogenetic level the earliest members of the human race were similarly (but not identically) handicapped. This can be observed in the actual arts made by Pictographic man.[3] The earliest men who began human culture did not inherit visual experiences from preceding cultures as a foundation for their education. They had to start from the very beginning—they had to "invent" culture.

While Pictographic man's art tells us a good deal about how his ability to visualize developed, we can also get some insight into the evolution of vision from an inquiry into what is known about the infant's visual growth. Naturally, we are not born with our three-dimensional or stereoscopic visual capacities operating at full efficiency. The abilities for seeing, hearing, feeling, and thinking are there, but in an undeveloped form.

In the early stages, the infant, as far as visual activity is concerned, first relies on the sense of touch in order to confirm any information which the eyes appear to indicate. Touch is employed as a check upon vision, while the eyes are being developed into what will later become the dominant and most accurate contact with the outside world.

Watch an infant when he perceives his image in the mirror; he touches it and to his apparent surprise strikes a flat plane which prevents him from reaching the form he believes he is seeing. The touch information in this case contradicts what he has experienced when previously seeing and touching similar appearing phenomena. Finally he reaches behind the mirror or else crawls around to the back, as though he expects to find there the child he thought he saw.

Kurt Koffka speaks of this in the following: "The behaviour of children in response to reflections in a mirror is of especial interest. Preyer describes his son's development in this respect very

2. From Oliver L. Reiser, *Philosophy and the Concepts of Modern Science,* p. 72. New York, 1935. By permission of The Macmillan Company, publishers.

3. In future references to "prehistory," we shall employ the term Pictographic, in order to use more accurate terminology. H. E. Barnes, who employs the term "preliterary" for his purpose, has pointed out, as many others have, that the term "prehistory" is a contradiction of the facts. The archeological findings from the earliest times *are* obviously historical material, since they produce factual evidence of the cultures in question. Thus it should prove crucially beneficial to discard the term "prehistory," if for no other reason than to prevent the further identification of those periods as *pre* historic and therefore something separated from later times. (See H. E. Barnes: *An Intellectual and Cultural History of the Western World,* p. 1, Reynal and Hitchcock, New York, 1941.) It is naive to claim that history began only at that time at which historical documents and records began to be kept in the form of written language as we know it today. This kind of material is only one kind of historical data. All through the Pictographic period man left behind documents of a historical nature, which can be just as revealing as any written ones of later times. The most important "historical documents" which these earliest men left behind were art! We must learn to *read* the art of Pictographic man as well as we have learned to read a slab of writing left behind by the Egyptians. Once we have learned to read pictures as well as we are able to read letters, a more comprehensive knowledge of early man can begin. In the words of Robinson: "What was not long ago called prehistory has become honest-to-God history, for few question now that implements, pottery, decoration, ornaments and curiously arranged stones are quite as authentic sources of knowledge as inscriptions. They are indeed more fundamental than writing." (See J. H. Robinson: "Newer Ways of Historians," *The American Historical Review,* XXXV:248, January, 1930.)

thoroughly. At first the image was not seen at all, later it was smiled at and grasped at, then it was apprehended as if it lay *behind* the mirror, and finally movements of avoidance were observed; for the child looked away when the mirror was held up before him. At this stage of development the reflection apparently frightened him, as something which did not fit into any of his patterns. . . . But development proceeds rapidly with a child. In two weeks' time after the sixtieth week of life all shyness before the mirror had been overcome by Preyer's son, and some preparation, at least, had been made for a correct understanding. Yet the child still grasped for and, indeed, struck at, his image. But soon this behaviour also ceased and the child employed the mirror thereafter just as we do."[4]

Many interesting questions arise: does the child, at first, know that he sees his own image, and if not when does he? Probably something like the following happens: in the beginning stages the child sees something that appears to have the forms he has experienced before with other human phenomena, but upon investigation the sense of touch is contradicted, not to mention the fact that he obtains no sound or other responses which were also a part of such previous experiences. This lack of correlation between previous experience and the mirror, the frustrating absence of form and sound, etc., make the mirror image appear disquietingly different to the child. This may well account for his successive reactions: the initial pleasure and reaching out to make a contact, followed by shyness and even fear, in turn replaced by the anger of frustration.

Of course, when the child appears to employ the mirror "just as we do," this may be only an acceptance of the phenomenon as such, with no recognition as yet that the image is his own. We must remember that the child has first to learn that he is seeing his own image. Therefore, he is in no position to recognize it automatically. Only with further experience is he able gradually to discover this—by observation of corresponding actions between himself and his immediate environment and the visual data of the material in the mirror image.

However, the essential point is that here we have an excellent example of the growing organism confronted with the problem of comprehending the *image* of an object as distinct from the *forms* of the object; we shall see that it took mankind thousands of years to be able to realize a coherent distinction between the two.

Visual development with the child involves a very detailed and complicated process. As we have mentioned, in the early stages the sense of touch is paramount, first with the mouth and then with the hands. This touch stage passes through various developments, and there occurs gradually a transition from the dominance of the sense of touch to the dominance of the sense of sight, the latter becoming the major means of contact with the outside world. The first situation is eventually reversed, with vision becoming the principal check for touch and other senses.

When the child begins to direct his eyes toward points of interest, it is toward stationary objects first, then toward slowly moving objects, and later toward rapidly moving ones. In the matter of movement of the eyes, the horizontal sweeps are developed before the vertical.

We have touched upon only a few of the many factors in the process under discussion, but they give us some notion of the ramifications involved in visual development. Ontogenetically speaking, the visual development follows a *natural order*. This is important, as recognition of this fact will play a major role in our investigations into the development of art.

Medical histories of congenitally blind individuals, whose vision has been restored by surgery, also supply us with very important data. From these cases we can learn further about the structure and operation of vision. Harvey A. Carr gives us some highlights from reports on such a case. He writes: "The following brief digest of Latta's account [of one of his patients] is given for illustrative purposes. Latta's account is based mainly upon the notes of the ophthalmologist in charge of the case.

" 'The patient was afflicted with congenital blindness due to cataracts. He was extremely active and inquisitive throughout life. He was accustomed to roam about the village and adjacent country at will. As a young man, he worked as a gardener, and as a grocer's assistant. He ran errands, and worked

4. Kurt Koffka: *The Growth of the Mind,* pp. 341-342, translated by Robert Morris Ogden, Harcourt, Brace, and Co., Inc., New York, 1924.

in the harvest field. He apparently guided himself largely by means of audition. He was not greatly handicapped by his defect.

"'He was unable to distinguish ordinary objects by means of vision, but he could readily distinguish night from day, and he reported that he could easily perceive a light and locate it accurately. This amount of vision and the locality attitude developed toward it must be taken into account in interpreting the case.

"'He was operated upon at the age of thirty years. The operations on the two eyes were a week apart. The eyes were first protected by dark glasses instead of bandages, and these naturally permitted some vision.

"'For ten days he appeared dazed, and experienced much difficulty in interpreting what he saw. He was extremely inquisitive and learned quickly by asking questions of his fellow patients. The first object seen was the face of the house surgeon. He did not know what it was, but he finally identified it after the surgeon *spoke* and while he at the same time *felt* of his own face. He failed to identify a red blanket that was thrown across the foot of his bed. He identified a bunch of daffodils on the basis of their odor with which he was quite familiar. Later he identified objects hung on the walls of the room as pictures because of his previous knowledge of the usual location of such objects.

"'He continually reported that objects looked much larger than he expected them to be on the basis of his previous tactual knowledge of them. Visual objects did not seem to be located close in front of the eyes as is often reported by such subjects, but their distance was apparently much less than that of normal vision. When he first looked out of the window at the pavement below, he felt that he could easily touch it with a stick. However, the actual distance of the pavement is not reported by the author. The patient was tested about a month later by Latta and Rivers, and they found no evidence of any perception of stereoscopic effects.'" [5]

In the case of Latta's patient attempting to orient himself visually to the surgeon's face, we witness the initial steps similar to those taken by the infant—the use of touch to confirm what is being seen. Since this patient was blind from birth and was seeing for the first time, it was only natural that he started from the beginning of the visual learning process. Until the surgeon restored his sight, he understood the world primarily with the sense of touch, sound, and smell, while his visual experience was of the lowest possible order, namely, the perception only of light or its absence. The results of his gaining sight illustrate the difference between the sense of vision and all the others. Previous to the operation this man "knew" about faces and streets, but having experienced these two factors, this "knowing," only through the medium of his ears, hands, feet, walking stick, etc., his three-dimensional sense was of an entirely *different order of relations* from that which appeared once the eyes began to function. Previously when he had contacted pavement, it was within reach of his stick or feet. Previously when he had contacted a face, he felt it with his hands. Hence, when he gained vision, both of these canalized and more familiar means of bodily orientation had to serve as a sort of check upon the data produced by the newly found, uncanalized and unfamiliar experiences of vision. He used his more experienced senses to learn about the new one. With the attainment of vision the patient was compelled to reorient himself to think out anew the phenomena of three dimensions and "space," because of the new factors about these phenomena which vision disclosed. When he *imagined* that he could touch the pavement with his stick, just as a child expects to reach the moon with his hand, he revealed the type of visualization he possessed at the time. Like the infant, he also had to go through the preliminary adjustments of a complicated world of vision. Once the latter is operating adequately, the individual is able to learn the projection mechanism, to learn to see the image in his eyes as though it "appeared" out-there, at its proper place in space where the source of visual stimuli presumably exists. In the stages reported, the Latta subject had as yet learned this only to a partial extent; that is why he supposed he could touch the pavement with his stick.

Matthew Luckiesh mentions another case of congenital blindness in which sight had been

---

5. H. A. Carr: *An Introduction to Space Perception*, pp. 16–17, Longmans, Green and Co., New York, 1935.

restored. He "appeared to think that external objects 'touched' the eyes." [6] In such a case the individual is actually receiving a more accurate report about the location of the image than the "normal" individual obtains or is conscious of. For the images produced by our eyes are *not* in the external world as they *appear,* but inside our own heads. However, we learn to *project* the image in order to obtain useful survival. In the earliest stages of the evolution of human eyes, it may be that men considered the image to be in the eye; only by experience with the outside world did the human organism eventually acquire the ability to "project" the image.

In order better to understand our analysis of the earliest efforts of man to be an artist, the non-artist reader ought by all means to try, whether he feels capable or not, to make a recording of a human figure. (The human figure is suggested as a subject because the points we are to discuss will be brought out more strongly than in drawing a simple object where mistakes might not be so apparent.) Notice during this experiment the difficulties in the actual seeing, *regardless* of one's inability to draw. The model will "appear" to be a well proportioned human form; but in the first attempt to record it, all the parts will be very badly done, especially in their relationships to each other. The various features of the head will not have their proper proportions; one foot may be longer than the other and so on. The whole drawing will be out of proportion and lack the oneness of organization that is otherwise *felt* in observing the model. Failure to grasp this as-a-whole relationship of the parts is due not only to a lack of technical skill, but also, and far more important, to the lack in ability to observe and grasp *consciously* the as-a-whole visual structure. The beginner is untrained in this respect and so unable to cope adequately with the problem. In other words, he consciously sees only a partial, very generalized amount of data essential for the success of his recording, even though all necessary visual data are otherwise being recorded on the eye-brain. And, most important, notice not only the inability to *see* the model correctly, but also the inability to *think* out how to achieve this act of seeing. In short, we must learn to see!

In order to arrive at a satisfactory comprehension of the visualization process in "art," we must become cognizant of the fact that seeing is not an isolated activity of the organism, but is determined by the particular type of integration of the seeing-thinking development. Once the student achieves that degree of development which secures for him adequate co-ordination, he becomes able to observe characteristics which have been registering on his eye-brain before, but which, because his nervous system was untrained or inexperienced, did not previously register upon his consciousness.

Koffka refers to this problem in a slightly different way: "Many adults, too—as for instance the author and his wife—if called upon to draw things which are not quite easy, like a chair, will do exactly the same thing [as a child] . . . Again and again one tries to draw the back and seat of the chair as rectangles, and when the drawing fails to look right, one resorts to all manner of intellectual tricks; because to perceive only a certain aspect of anything is a task which can be achieved by many persons only after the greatest effort and practice. It is different with those who possess some talent in drawing; for they learn with relative ease, some perhaps even without external aid; yet a correct apprehension of the *appearance* of a thing is certainly neither a natural nor an original propensity. At first each thing has actually but one phenomenal appearance or, perhaps, in some cases a small number of appearances; and these succeed in maintaining themselves despite all changes of perspective." [7]

Here we have a good example of what we have been discussing: the *kind and degree of consciousness* involved in seeing. Like the child, most adults are not conscious of the laws governing the assimilation or the production of visual imagery. Thus when one attempts to transpose the *object* chair into a recording on a flat surface, he is compelled to reduce his notion of that object to its most "primitive" terms. That is, his "visual" consciousness consists of reducing the chair to linear sections; the seat is square, the legs and back are at right-angles to the seat, etc. Such depictions are an attempt to record the known tactile character of the chair. The consequences are that the unity of the visual image transmitted by light becomes confused or completely destroyed because the particular situation involved requires a

6. Matthew Luckiesh: *Visual Illusions,* their causes, characteristics and applications, p. 18, D. Van Nostrand Co., New York, 1922.

7. Koffka, op. cit., pp. 295–296.

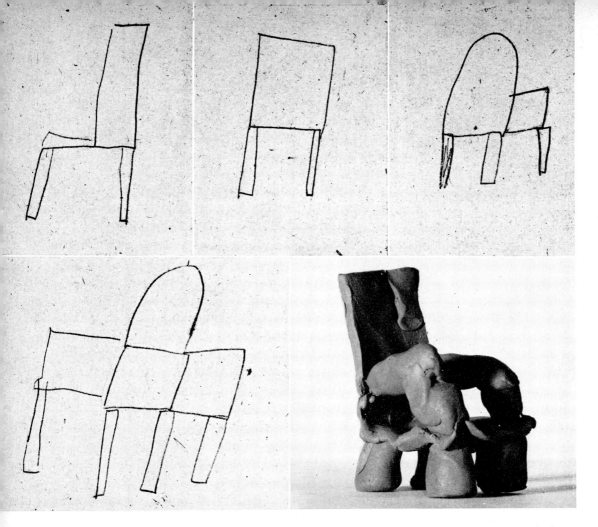

1. Drawings and sculpture of a chair by a six-year-old child. Above left, *a;* above center, *b;* above right, *c;* below left, *d;* below right, *e.*

recording not of the tactile characteristics of the object, but of the image resulting from light bouncing off the object. Hence, the unity peculiar to the forms of objects when conveyed by light is not attained, since an effort is being made that requires the production of a visual image and not a tactile recording. At the same time the unity of the tactile character of the object also becomes confused, or completely destroyed, because such a recording objective requires another medium of art for its realization — sculpture.

In short, we are in the confusing situation of trying to force tactile consciousness into a visual context, a confusion of which we are unconscious. Or we might put it this way: such a situation represents a sculptor's consciousness being subjected to a task that requires a painter's consciousness.

It follows that under these circumstances it is inevitable that one will fail in comprehending the chair as-a-whole in terms of the particular unity which characterizes the *laws of vision.* Our difficulty lies in our inability to *translate or transpose the tactile knowledge of the object into the laws which govern visual images produced by light striking and then reflecting from the object into our optical process.* The lack of this ability to translate the tactile knowledge results in the formation of a "primitive" kind of visual consciousness which compels us to see the chair in a series of linear sections put in various linear relationships, often (in the more naive cases) having no semblance to the appearance of a chair. Consequently our visual recording activity is forced to operate under the confusing dominance of non-visual, or *tactile* laws. But we can record the chair from only one visual point of view at any one time, or in any one drawing, whereas, to depict the chair as it actually exists tactilely would require the impossible feat of simultaneously depicting the many different visual points of view which represent each aspect of the tactile character of the chair. Obviously, it is impossible to make such a depiction on a linear surface and still produce a recording having the appearance of a chair. Under the circumstances, the best we can do is what the child does: make various relationships of rectangles, a case of flattening out or unfolding the various gross aspects of the chair (figure 1). Here the tactile intention has been forced into a transformation by the linear or non-tactile medium employed. Result: we are presented with a compromise between sculpture and linear art.

Therefore, the difference between an untrained person's attempt to depict a chair on a linear surface and that of a trained artist, is that the former will try to draw the chair as he "knows" it actually appears to tactile experience, while the latter draws the chair as he knows it actually appears to his consciousness of visual experience. The untrained person is really trying to draw the *chair itself;* the trained person draws that which appears to human vision as a light-report of the chair's appearance. The former individual is not conscious that, in order to succeed in depicting a visual symbol having the appearance of a chair, he must record its special character in terms of light-reports rather than in terms of the chair as such. The trained artist is conscious of these problems of visual experience in relation to the medium employed.

This explains why the naive realist cannot produce a drawing that *looks* like a chair. He is not drawing the chair as it appears and is registered by his *visual* receptors. Since humans cannot see things as they actually "know" them to exist, they must learn to visualize objects in that manner which most efficiently utilizes the only available means for seeing. Hence, we must recognize that we do not visualize the chair only in its own terms, but also in human terms!

This whole problem is radically altered when one works with sculptural or tactile material. Then the problem of recording visual images as such—the problem of recording light-rays on a flat surface—does not exist. Thus, if Koffka had tried to make a chair with clay or wood, he could have been far more successful in making a "recording" that *looked* like a chair. In such circumstances it is possible for the naive realist to do what he mistakenly tried to do in making a visual image, or visual recording— namely, make an actual chair, because the laws of visual imagery are *not operating in the production* of such a "depiction." For now the naive visualist can make rectangles and make these rectangles in their proper, tactile, three-dimensional relationships.

This has been clearly demonstrated to the author in the following simple experiment. (See figure 1.) A six-year-old girl was asked simply to draw a chair; she chose a side-view, *a*. She was then directed to draw the chair from any position in the front; with some hesitation she produced *b*. When a chair was placed before her so that she would see a three-quarters view, she at once noted factors which were missing in her two previous drawings. She was asked if she could make a drawing including them. Reluctantly she did so, this time choosing a back-view of the chair for the attempt. The right side of the drawing was done last, showing an arm and "another" leg—*c*. Finally she was asked to draw the chair again from any position in the front and she reluctantly drew *d*.

Throughout all these attempts to *draw* the chair, the "artist" was conscious of the discrepancy between the object and her renditions of it. None satisfied her. But when she was asked to make a chair with plasticine, no hesitancy or irritation occurred. She set to work methodically, making four stumps for the legs, a flat square piece for the seat, a similar but larger piece for the back, and finally two arms— result *e*. Here the "artist" was working in a medium which permitted adequate realization of her particular *level* of recording "knowledge."

The author has made many such experiments with children between the ages of 4 and 8. Although many interesting differences have been noted, the general pattern of events prevailed: namely, difficulty and reluctance to cope with the problem of drawing the chair—the visual image; confidence in making a chair with form-material—the tactile "image."

In short, the problem of producing, or "reading," visual images is a problem of the ability to translate or transpose tactile knowledge into visual knowledge and then the ability consciously to translate the visual back to the tactile. This the naive visualist can do only partially and in some cases not at all.

So in the case of children and the majority of adults, the visual activity involved when trying to record objects is *over-empirical.* It is low-order seeing. The process of visualization is not understood as a *joint phenomenon of the observer and the observed,* and so we fail to realize that the object visualized, and the visualization of the object, are two extremely different but related events.

In order to see things not only as we actually see them, (as light-rays report them to us) but to see them in the most efficient manner possible for human needs, we must visualize in that manner called "perspective." In the childish, over-empirical method, the observed is everything, it dominates consciousness, and the observer is nothing. In the more developed attitude, one is conscious of the needs and function of the observer as well as his relation to the observed.

Consciousness of visualization—this is the crux of any kind of seeing. For example, if one is a doctor, he may be able to observe at once that a particular person is ill with a particular disease; or, if one is an auto-mechanic, that a motor is at fault at a particular place or places. But the observer who is unfamiliar with the particular visual structures involved in each case, will probably see only a sick person or a defective machine, although all the visual data available to the doctor and the mechanic are present for the untrained observer. The situation is similar for the beginning art student in the life-class. He too "knows," he senses that his figure is badly drawn, but does not know why. The reasons must be pointed out to him by his instructor until he is able to do this for himself. The layman is unconscious of the significance of the data that are before him; if anything, it will probably confuse him. The trained expert knows *how and what to look for*. Visual activity makes special demands in art as in other fields, in that it requires special training in the cortical area. It is not simply a matter of "feeling," as so many artists and others unfortunately assume.

From the time that we are born all of us develop, in varying degrees, the ability to visualize. Initial attempts to draw from a model, however, make us realize how little we develop our capacities in those aspects peculiar to art. This is not meant to imply that only the artist possesses a high order of visual acumen but rather that the majority of us are able only to visualize well in some restricted aspect, usually that demanded by our vocation.

In early cultures the majority of humans were oriented to the experiences of developing their visual capacities on that level peculiar to art. In more recent cultures, however, we find that only a small part of the human race engages in such visual experiences, while the rest are utterly lost; this is in evidence not only in what the latter hang on their walls, but also in what they hang or tie upon their bodies. Hence the majority of individuals are canalized to the most vulgar forms of art produced by the worst types of artists extant today. We refer to magazine and advertising art, and, of late, to political or nationalistic art, which canalize people to respond with *signal*-reactions, resulting in a low level of cortical activity.

Unfortunately for most of us, once we become adults we lose to an appalling degree the initial visual curiosity we possessed as infants and children. This is indeed a tragedy, considering that there is so much more necessary visual experience and knowledge to be acquired in adult life. But once we attain adulthood we become practically unconscious of tremendous areas of our visual life, especially in art. Consequently there is an enormous amount of visual material of which we are not aware (although it constantly impinges in a disturbing manner upon our senses), while beneficial visual experiences are generally passed by or not recognized. Failing to advance, we are compulsively drawn to the most harmful experiences that repeat the familiar, that call for no disturbance to our visual lethargy.

But art *can* teach us how to secure visual sanity, so badly needed. When we come to the analysis of the present, our studies will show that art is now in a particular stage of development which makes it possible to radically alter the prevalent low level of visual behavior. Recent innovations in art have already begun here and there to bring healthful visual benefits to the general population, and can continue to do so by spreading the effects of art throughout all our lives.

Pictographic man's art discloses that the ability to visualize evolved very slowly, as did his other activities. Human life passed through thousands of years before artists finally emerged who could record nature's reality with great accuracy. But this remarkable degree of visual accuracy can now be acquired in the short space of a single lifetime. This is possible because each generation gained a little more ability in recording than had its predecessors; then each passed on to the next the accumulated knowledge it had acquired.

This transmission mechanism, which Korzybski calls *time-binding*,[8] is unique with humans

8. See Alfred Korzybski: *Manhood of Humanity: the Art and Science of Human Engineering*, E. P. Dutton and Co., New York, 1923.

32

and distinguishes them from animals. The latter repeat more or less what previous generations have done, but human beings are able in each succeeding generation to move on to higher orders of development. A part of this process, perhaps the most important part, goes on in the development of our visual organs, evidence of which we shall observe in actual works of art.

As a result of this "time-binding" evolution, an individual can, within the span of a single life-time, learn complicated forms of mathematics or record complicated forms of nature's appearances. Obviously we are not born with all these accomplishments, but rather acquire them through educational knowledge, which has been inherited from the labors of all the human beings who have preceded us. Hence, before we can see usefully, we must learn to see by conscious methodology, in a similar way that a musician must learn to hear. However, unless we are sufficiently conscious, unless we comprehend the structural significance of those thousands of years in which man has been evolving his ability to see, then we shall continue to fail in our attempts not only to understand *adequately* the art of the past, but the art of our own times as well. By discovering the road along which "art" has previously travelled, we can find out where that road is leading in the present. This knowledge is crucially important for us in view of the fact (as our history will make clear) that we are passing from one epoch of art to another of a greatly different nature.

But before we begin to examine directly the works themselves which past artists have left behind, we must stress a crucial factor—the necessity and *responsibility* on the part of the reader to *translate what he reads into visualizations. Since words are not the things we are going to speak about, the reader must translate the word-symbols into the things they represent. This permits the very necessary non-verbal or visual experience to result from our discussions.* It will be of no use either to the reader or the author to have the material we are about to present either accepted or rejected merely on the verbal level. Whatever may be the reader's eventual evaluation of this history, it is imperative that he experience it on the *unspeakable* level where, after all, what we shall talk about exists.

II INVENTION OF THE ARTS

The magical ideas of primitive races and their views on sorcery largely depend on the incomplete development of the psychic mechanisms governing imaginal projection. For primitive man, a thought may be as good as an act, a word as an object, a subjective imitation as a real enactment. 180

Ernst Kretschmer

As long as we assume that their minds [primitive mentality] are orientated like our own, that they react as ours do to the impressions made upon them, we assume, by implication, that they should reason and reflect as ours do with regard to the phenomena and entities of the known world. But we agree that as a matter of fact they neither reason nor reflect thus . . . 195   Lucien Levy-Bruhl

4 PRIMITIVE ORIENTATIONS

To follow primitive mentality in its course, to un-
ravel its theories, we must, as it were, do violence
to our own mental habits, and adapt ourselves to
theirs. It is an effort which it is almost impossible
to sustain, and yet without it their minds are likely
to remain unintelligible to us. 195

Lucien Levy-Bruhl

To the primitive mind . . . the other world and this
one make one and the same reality only, a reality
both imagined, felt and lived. 196

Lucien Levy-Bruhl

To the primitive mind, however, everything is a
miracle, or rather, nothing is; and therefore everything is credible, and there is nothing either impossible or absurd. 196

Lucien Levy-Bruhl

. . . if we trace their actions back to the group-
ideas and sentiments upon which these depend, we
find that their behavior is by no means foolish; it
is, on the contrary, the legitimate consequence of
these. 195

Lucien Levy-Bruhl

Magic, the technique of animism, clearly and unmistakably shows the tendency of forcing the laws
of psychic life upon the reality of things . . . 117

Sigmund Freud

The more we study the history of the past the
more deeply are we impressed by the painful slowness of his [primitive man's] progress. What seems
simple and easy to us, looking back along the road
he travelled, was to him most difficult and perplexing . . . in his mind there was but little light
of past experiences, and he was faced on all sides
by the darkness of the great unknown. 322

H. G. Spearing

In the previous chapter we reviewed evidence which indicates that the process of seeing or visualizing is
an emergent, developmental affair. The organs of vision, together with the rest of the nervous system of
the new-born child, for example, are undeveloped. With the development of the entire organism-as-a-
whole the child through *experience* gradually acquires the ability to release the potentials inherent in the
visual receptors.

We have also noted that one cannot split seeing from thinking, that we always "see-think" our
seeing. In this chapter we shall examine the reasoning processes of the Primitive mentality in order that
we may properly evaluate the early efforts of man to see and record his seeing of the world around him.

Ernst Grosse, as long ago as 1902, pointed out that a scientific comprehension of more recent
art must rest upon an analysis of the art of Primitive nations. With this we emphatically agree.

Yet most of us, when we observe and evaluate Primitive behavior, are not adequately conscious
of our own way of knowing the world. We forget, if we ever knew, why our "knowing" of the world is
the kind it is and not some other kind. We project our attitudes upon the Primitive, instead of *projecting*

ourselves into the Primitive's life. Then, when we invariably fail in our efforts to push the Primitive into our patterns of reasoning, we come to the conclusion that something must be wrong with his thinking rather than with our own. If we are to discover how the Primitive comprehends reality, we must first become aware of our own position in this respect. We have to be sufficiently conscious of our own methods of reasoning to be able to comprehend any interpretation of reality different from our own.

The solution is not, however, as some investigators have advocated, to forget all that we know in order to understand the Primitive. For we "forget" only on the conscious level, while that which we suppress continues even more freely on *sub*conscious levels. If we wish to avoid projecting and so imposing upon the Primitive our way of knowing and understanding the world, if we wish to see his method more clearly, it is vitally necessary that we do the opposite of forgetting, that is, be very conscious of our own way of comprehending the world. Only then does it become possible to keep our orientation to reality from interfering with our comprehension of the Primitive's method of orientation. Moreover, our way of knowing, our *kind* of consciousness is exactly the tool which makes it possible for us to comprehend Primitive mentality, providing we use it as such, instead of mixing up the Primitive's reasoning processes with our own.

Erwin H. Ackerknecht has written in regard to a similar problem in the study of the history of medicine: "our medicine is not *the medicine* nor our religion *the religion,* and there is not one medicine but numerous and quite different medicines in the different parts of the world and in the past, present and future. Measuring everything with our everyday standards, we will never understand either the past or the future. . . . This method of seeking in primitive medicine only for what it has in common with ours and of projecting into primitive medicine our categories leads to somewhat strange results." [1] This attitude is just as applicable to the study of art.

In order to understand the Primitive adequately, we must always keep in mind why and how magic arose and then how it developed into what we see today in extant Primitive cultures. As man began to be conscious of the world about him, beyond the simple awareness-demands of the animal stage, he encountered many things which were terrifying and incomprehensible. All these unknown quantities had to be accounted for somehow if man was to survive "mentally" with his higher cortical action in contradistinction to the animal's. In an effort to cope with this threatening, omnipresent continuum of fear, our early ancestors began to seek explanations which would dispel it. Gradually Pictographic man devised a system of magic which turned the *unknown into the known* and thus fully accounted for the surrounding phenomena and his relationship to them.

Field workers among extant Primitive tribes still observe and report this fear of the unknown. For them, Lévy-Bruhl tells us, everything that is unknown is suspicious;[2] and so it was in the beginning only more so. It is possible today to observe only the concluding results of a system of behavior which had its beginning in the very earliest times and has now reached the end of its developments. It is imperative, therefore, that we constantly keep in mind the distinction between the extant Primitive cultures, those at the starting point, and those which comprise the various stages of development between the two extremes. We must remember that the Primitive cultures observed today in Africa and elsewhere have a history *as old as our own*: in fact, their history is also our history, a history which began many thousands of years ago in early Paleolithic times when the notion of magic was invented and developed until it encompassed every phenomenon. It is this latter stage which we observe in recent and extant Primitive peoples. These Primitives exhibit a behavior based upon the canalizations of generation after generation which have believed the occult to be everywhere in everything. The original fear which was responsible for the invention of this system of reasoning was perpetuated by the basic consequences of the system, keeping alive, as it did, the fear of anything unknown or different. Whenever anything strange did arise, the system immediately accounted for it in some way, usually by destroying the individuals connected with the new phenomenon.

1. E. H. Ackerknecht: "Problems of Primitive Medicine," *Bulletin of the History of Medicine,* XI:503, May, 1942, The Johns Hopkins Press.

2. Lucien Lévy-Bruhl: *Primitive Mentality,* p. 387, translated by Lilian A. Clare, George Allen and Unwin, Ltd., London, 1923. See especially Chapter XII, "The Primitive's Dislike of the Unknown."

Lévy-Bruhl tells us that to the Primitive the concealment of stillbirth is related to the lack of rain.[3] When the native is asked for the connection or relationship between these two events, "he will reply that his ancestors always thought thus, and he will wonder, not at the fact, but at the question." [4] Quite probably in the early formative periods of magic, it was observed once (or a number of times) that there was a lack of rain after the occurrence of stillbirth. Any event which is out of the ordinary, such as twins, or a baby's having upper teeth before lower ones, is held suspect by the Primitive. It is upon these types of events that the Primitive hangs a great deal of his magic. (Contrary to popular belief, the Primitive's actions do not always lead to the conservation of the tribe's health. Often the sick are spared and healthy ones killed because of some unusual characteristic of the latter, such as the cutting of upper teeth before the lower ones.)[5] Such experiences are automatically considered as a message of displeasure from the occult powers; from then on they are accepted as such without reservation.

Thus although the original stage of fear is no longer apparent, fear nevertheless continues from one generation to the next in a form somewhat analogous to the original stage which led to the invention of magic; namely, not only a fear of anything that threatens to disrupt the system of reason which has made all things known, but a fear of the known as still being the unknown. In other words, for their ancestors, who preceded the invention of magic, everything was practically unknown and so feared. This led to man's inventing a system that gradually accounted for everything, in order that he might have some security in the mystery that surrounded him and that was within him. Subsequent Primitive peoples, however, have come to fear anything that jeopardizes their all-knowing system and so threatens to return them to the old, "original" fear. *The originators of the notion of magic devised it in order to dispel the unknown; succeeding generations maintained it in order to prevent the return of the unknown!*

Rasmussen reports the following explanation from a "wizard":

"We fear!

"We fear the elements with which we have to fight in their fury to wrest out food from land and sea.

"We fear cold and famine in our snow huts.

"We fear the sickness that is daily to be seen amongst us. Not death, but the suffering.

"We fear the souls of the dead, of human and animal alike.

"We fear the spirits of earth and air.

"And therefore our fathers, taught by their fathers before them, guarded themselves about with all these old rules and customs, which are built upon the experience and knowledge of generations. We know not how nor why, but we obey them that we may be suffered to live in peace. And for all our angakoqs and their knowledge of hidden things, we yet know so little that we fear everything else. We fear the things we see about us, and the things we know from the stories and myths of our forefathers. Therefore we hold by our customs and observe all the rules of tabu." [6]

In the end, therefore, the original state of fear which gave rise to the invention of magic remains. Magic is not so much an explanation of the unknown as it is the means for obtaining protection and getting along in a world filled with its potent force. It gives man confidence that he "may live untroubled." So it might be a little more correct to describe the magic view of world reality as essentially made up of the known-unknown.

Again we must emphasize that a consideration of how the empirical level is observed and utilized will permit us to discover the source of the Primitive's notions. All beliefs of all times have originated in some kind of *basic assumptions,* whether they consist of magic, religion, or science. It is these assumptions, often unconscious, which determine the interpretation of reality adopted by those in

---

3. Ibid., p. 266.

4. Ibid., p. 266. How similar all this is, and the following, to the conservatism in our own or any times! "In the Congo region 'the most progressive men,' says Bentley, 'are the first to be destroyed. When the india-rubber trade commenced, the first to sell it were killed as witches; so, too, with every innovation.' There is nothing more dangerous than not to do as others do, to do better, or above all, to do something which has never been done before." (As quoted by Lévy-Bruhl in *Primitive Mentality,* p. 395, from *Pioneering on the Congo,* by Rev. W. H. Bentley, i, p. 278, (1900).)

5. Lévy-Bruhl, *Primitive Mentality,* p. 156.

6. From *Across Arctic America,* by Knud Rasmussen, pp. 130-131. Courtesy of G. P. PUTNAM'S SONS, New York, 1927.

any particular culture. For the Primitive, of course, there exists no conscious problem of reality as such. Rather, early man first saw the world primarily in terms of undifferentiated-visual-reality data, in the sense that there did not exist for him as for us, problems of reality and non-reality. By identification he saw everything not as parts of a whole, but as a oneness.

This well known tendency of Primitives to see the world not as a series of causes and effects, but as a oneness, may have originated from certain early experiences in the development of the human eye-brain. Abstracting from admittedly scanty data on visual evolution (e.g., Luckiesh's report of the congenitally blind person whose sight had been restored by surgery and who thought that objects *touched* the eyes; and the well known inability of children to distinguish between "thought and body" and between a "sign and the thing signified"[7]), it seems reasonable to speculate that the earliest of human specimens, sometime during the initial transitions from the animal to the human stage, had not yet learned to *project* upon the outside world, where the visual phenomena originated, the image reports which occurred in their eyes. That is, to the earliest of humans the images may have appeared to be within the eyes themselves, where, incidentally, they do exist. Since the human eye naturally functions in such a way that the image occurs in the eyes, and not outside, it therefore seems reasonable to assume as suggested in the previous chapter that it is not innate or natural that we are able to *project* the visual image, or at least make it appear to be projected. This had to be learned and acquired.

If this is true, then it throws some new light upon the genesis of magic. If there was no image projection, the objective world would not have been seen in terms of "out-there"; rather everything in a sense would have been seen as only "in-here" experience, in the eyes or the head of the organism. Not only reports from the objective world, but also the visual phenomena seen in dreams, hallucinations and illusions—*all would have been regarded as equal-valued visual experiences; no difference in the visual reports would have been recognized as far as reality differentiation was concerned*. Hence in these early stages of human development, the Primitive "mentality" inevitably would have regarded sensory experience as a single *oneness* without differentiation. The distinction, if any, was nebulous. In fact, the inability to make a distinction, when humans became conscious of a vague out-there as well as in-here, one way or the other, led to the conclusion that both were *one,* since everything appeared to be both in-here and out-there.

Thus dreams, illusions, etc., and "reality" are all visual material, and so of equal value to the Primitive. In fact, if anything, dreams, visions, etc., are more important to the Primitive than the visual material emanating directly from the objective level. Lévy-Bruhl writes: "To the primitive mind, as we know, the seen and the unseen worlds form but one, and there is therefore uninterrupted communication between what we call obvious reality and the mystic powers. Nowhere perhaps is this more directly and completely brought about than in dreams, in which man passes from the one world to the other without being aware of it." [8]

For the Primitive then there is no clear distinction between seen and unseen worlds; he *sees* the so-called dead in his dreams and visions. Omens, divinations, etc., are *seen* also. Thus, "To the Tanala, ghosts are thoroughly individualized and entirely real. Every native will report seeing ghosts and talking with them. It is very often difficult for the people to distinguish between dream states and waking states. Hearing ghosts talk to one is so common an experience that natives often will not pay attention to you if you call them only once." [9]

Indeed dreams are astounding phenomena. The things the Primitive sees in his dreams are actually, say what else you will, just as visual as any of the objective visualizations he experiences. In fact, as we have just mentioned, dreams seem a greater reality than the "objective" one. A dream is thought to reveal things that are happening. For the Primitive past, present and future all come to much the same thing, in the sense that there is no distinction between them. What the omen says, *already is*. And so the

7. Jean Piaget: *The Child's Conception of the World,* p. 55, translated by Joan and Andrew Tomlinson, Harcourt, Brace and Co., London, New York, 1929.

8. Lévy-Bruhl, op. cit., p. 98.

9. Ralph Linton in *The Individual and His Society,* by Abram Kardiner, p. 269, Columbia University Press, New York. 1939.

revelation of dreams is adhered to, no matter how contradictory it may appear on the objective level or what risks are involved in obeying it.

Lévy-Bruhl relates this example of a dream that was "fulfilled": "in his sleep one night [a man] saw ten men plunging into a frozen river, entering it by one hole made in the ice, and coming out by another. On awaking, the first thing that he did was to prepare a great feast and invite ten of his friends. They all accepted, and soon began to make very merry. . . . Thereupon he related his dream, which did not surprise them in the least, for they all prepared to put it into execution immediately. They therefore went to the river, broke the ice, and made two holes, about fifteen feet from each other. The divers removed their garments, and the first led the way; jumping into one of the holes, he had the good luck to come out by the other; the second did the same, and all the others with the exception of the tenth, were equally fortunate; he, however, paid the penalty for all, since he could not manage to emerge, and perished miserably under the ice." [10] *The greatest risk of all was to disregard the dream.*

Certainly the Primitive has every reason for considering dreams as even more important than or dominant over the world of objective visual experience. *For in dreams he can do things which are impossible under any circumstance in reality!* Are not dreams, as the rest of his magic, the means by which he is able to close the gap between contradictory phenomena? The Primitive's so-called disregard for the "law of contradiction" (such as the differences between life and death, animate and inanimate, the real and the unreal, and so on) is possible because he lives in a world of consciousness where these are *not* contradictions! It is no contradiction, for example, that a dead man lives when he has often been seen alive and well by many people in their dreams and has exerted his influence upon the community on numerous occasions. And it is no contradiction that a dead man can be seen in many places at the same time, since he has been seen in the form of a snake, basking in the sun over his grave, by one; in the form of a spider in the hut of a relative by another; in the shape of a log floating down the river by still another. As a matter of fact, to quote Kahler, "In New Guinea, people remember a time when the dead and the living were not separated from one another but lived together peacefully." [11]

Furthermore, according to his system of magic, the Primitive can easily make the transition from the living world to the world of the so-called dead. This is accomplished by visiting them through the medium of dreams. While he thus visits, he is himself one of the living-dead, who returns to this world upon waking. Thus the dead can visit in the living world as well as the reverse. The so-called dead merely experience a different *kind* of living. Consequently a dead man continues to own his property and govern it by making his demands known through the dreams, visions of the "living," etc. He may also take the form of an actual live human by means of a living substitute. [12]

As the researches of Lévy-Bruhl [13] make clear, it is the Primitive's very distinction between what we call the real and dreams that makes it possible for him to consider dreams as "real" as the real. For the world of dreams is related to the other-world, the world of the "dead," the occult world in general, which he considers as real as the world of the "living." But, since this occult world is, in certain respects, unlike the world of the living, it is only natural that its perception is obtained by means other than those usually employed. In this sense, the dream is a consistent method of perceiving one aspect of all that the Primitive assumes to comprise reality. This theory holds good even where the dream involves matters dealing with the living rather than with the dead; for via the dream he is able to transport himself to other places and experience what has happened or is about to happen. Therefore, the Primitive makes distinctions (between what *we* call the real and the dream), but never on the basis of whether one is more real than another, or one is real and another not. For him, in brief, everything is real!

Actually it is not a bit more naive and inconsistent for the Primitive to assume this attitude than it is for the Christian to assume that the art images picturing *his* other-world represent a reality as real as the here-world. The Christian has, after all, visions and dreams which are pure reality to him. The authenticity of the imagery information in both cases is arrived at in a similar manner; but it is necessary

10. Lévy-Bruhl, op. cit., pp. 117-118 (from *Relations des Jésuites*, xlii, pp. 150-152, 1655-6).

11. Erich Kahler: *Man the Measure*, p. 46.

12. Lévy-Bruhl, op. cit., pp. 80-81.

13. Lucien Lévy-Bruhl: *How Natives Think,* p. 60, translated by Lilian A. Clare, G. Allen and Unwin, Ltd., London, 1926.

to realize that although in both cases each is equally real, they are not identical. Hence it is only natural that the sensory channels through which each world is experienced must differ. Thus the dream medium for the Primitive, and the image-art medium for the Christian, both offer images and channels of images differing from those used to perceive the here-world directly.

In all cultures where man has believed in superior, immortal beings, (with minor exceptions) he has managed to make such beings visible. And whenever man has added to or replaced the actual world with another, he has always been forced to depict and see this other-world in terms of the actual—simply because he knows no other.

Thus man gives his invented worlds some kind of visual face, and a great part of his art has served this function, since it is well suited for the purpose of making visible that which otherwise could not be.

The Primitive has a wide range of visual-magic-channels by which to make seen the whole complexity of what we call the unseen. It is possible for him to make his magic adequately meet (at least for him) the complexity of objective experiences. He must, in fact, employ a number of channels (sound, visual, olfactory, etc.) for his magic, so that it will cover all contingencies in the environment. Dreams, divinations, taboos, omens, ordeals, etc., are parts of a complex system designed to utilize and meet the demands of a complex world of experience. Therefore everything in the Primitive's world is knitted together as one. By identification he sees not unique parts within a whole, but undifferentiated oneness.

Thus man began his first major steps toward civilization with the general basic assumption that the world was governed according to the arbitrary powers of magic. It was magic which made things operate as they did and not the structure of the things themselves and their functional relationship with each other. On this problem Kurt Koffka has written: "Since everything that exists for a people at this stage of civilization possesses mystical qualities which are much more important to them than 'natural' characteristics, our distinction between the living and dead, the animate and the inanimate, can have no meaning to them. Rivers, clouds, winds, even the main directions of space, to mention but a few examples, all have their mystical powers. The distinction, therefore, between animate and inanimate, is a product of development; at the beginning no such question could possibly arise, since everything, even including directions, names, and words in general, possesses its active principle as an imminent attribute." [14]

On this basis, it is little wonder that empirical observations of causes and effects are given no credence as explanations of what we consider "chance" or accidental phenomena. To the Primitive all must be explained by some activity of occult forces.

Lévy-Bruhl gives excellent examples of how this functions. A man throws a spear, it ricochets, hitting and killing a man standing on the ground.[15] The thrower of the spear is immediately accused of deliberately seeking to kill the man, because witchcraft has taken possession of him and commanded him to kill that particular individual. The fact that it was apparently an accident has no effect upon these decisions. Another typical case is that of a tree falling on and killing a man.[16] The Primitive is quite willing to accept, as he often has in such a situation, the empirical evidence that the tree was rotted and weakened and so bound to fall. But he is not satisfied with this explanation, even granting these obvious facts; he insists upon knowing why the tree was rotted, why it fell just at the moment a man was standing by it. He will contend that a witch had made the tree rot as a part of his plan to make it fall at just the moment it did; otherwise why did the tree not fall a little before or a little after the man was standing by it, and so on. The Primitive mentality gives prime credence to what is for him the magical function of reality and regards the empirical order of reasoning with an incredulity similar to that which most of us today hold for magic. It is true that he does many things, such as hunting, which depend on a successful regard for empirical reasoning. Yet investigation discloses his assumption that all such activities are controlled by occult powers. The success of a hunter does *not exist* until granted by the powers of the magic world.

Another striking example of the disregard which Primitives hold toward relationships of causes and effects is the custom that an individual accused of stealing must drink poison to prove whether he

14. Kurt Koffka: *The Growth of the Mind*, p. 340.   15. Lévy-Bruhl, *Primitive Mentality*, p. 44.   16. Ibid., p. 45.

is innocent or guilty.[17] If guilty, he will die. In some instances an individual may become so irritated at being repeatedly accused of theft that he will decide voluntarily to take the poison test and clear up the matter once and for all. If the absurdity or the danger of this test is pointed out, he becomes either *indifferent* or *angry* and insists on going through with it. In such a case we see evidence of an unshakable belief in the superiority of the occult forces which the Primitive believes cannot be altered. To him, as Ackerknecht puts it, the "natural is supernatural but the supernatural quite natural. . . ."[18] Poison does not consist of chemical properties and their inevitable actions, as we understand it; it is considered merely a vehicle for mystical forces. For that matter how is the Primitive to assume that harmless looking stuff like poison, without some powerful outside assistance, could possibly kill a man? But if the chemical solution is not recognized as the principal operative, you may reason, why not use water or any other liquid? Because the Primitive has found, *by experience,* that occult forces evoke death only through particular agencies. One dies because witchcraft gives poison the power to kill. Witchcraft is the grand catalyst for the Primitive mentality, making all things operate as they do. Thus an innocent individual who volunteers to take poison "knows" it is perfectly safe for him to take it. (Although innocent, the poison kills him, but at the same time it eliminates the only witness to that truth!)

But we may ask: "Why doesn't the Primitive reserve his supernatural explanations for only those events which are obviously difficult to grasp? Why does he use them for occurrences which he shows evidence of understanding by more empirical methods?" We ask this because we consider it sane and sufficient to employ reasoning processes based on the observation of verifiable empirical data. But for the Primitive, the *reverse* of this process is true. So, "if, instead of attributing to them [the primitives] our own habits of mind, we try to adapt ourselves to their mental attitude, indifferent as this is to the most obvious causal relation, and solely occupied with mystic and unseen forces, we shall find that their way of thinking and acting is the natural and even necessary outcome of this."[19] Quite "logically," it would be ridiculous and even stupid for him to recognize as very significant the empirical method of observation and reasoning. When he compares our explanation of events to his, ours appears altogether uninteresting. However, he *is* able to "understand" simple, empirical relationships of causes and effects, just as we are able to "understand" his way of reasoning; but he does not understand how we can attach much credence to such picayune observations in a world which is filled to the brim with the fantastic and powerful happenings of the occult!

Lévy-Bruhl sums up the difference between our system and the Primitive's thus: "Our experience is the sum-total of a comparatively small number of data and an infinitude of inferences. That of the primitive mind on the other hand contains but a small proportion of inferences; but it contains many direct data to which we deny objective value, although in the primitive's eyes they are as real as, even more real than, those afforded by the senses."[20]

And think what we will of magic, its practice is astoundingly effective, and its results are especially significant to the Primitive "mentality." These amaze us when we hear of them for the first time, *as they naturally amazed the Primitive himself.* Let the reader project himself into this world where one can shake the hand of his enemy and the enemy dies![21] There are numerous examples of severe

17. Ibid., pp. 220-221.

18. Ackerknecht, "Problems of Primitive Medicine," p. 505. But, as Lévy-Bruhl points out, they do not think of two worlds, but of one. He further makes clear, as does Ackerknecht, that we on the other hand are compelled to think of their one world as two because we can only reach their world in terms of our own understanding of that world. If the Primitive were to verbalize this problem—which he finds no need to do—he would only speak about *a* world and certainly not about "worlds." However, it seems futile to decry these disadvantages, since the advantages we otherwise possess are the very means by which we can achieve our prime objective. After all, we do not wish to become a Primitive, nor can we, in order to comprehend their mentality. If that were possible, however, it would only mean that we would fail to achieve our objective. Our purpose is to project ourselves into the Primitive's milieu without throwing overboard our tools of investigation, namely, our particular "mental" equipment. But in the projection it becomes necessary to avoid as much as possible the identification of the Primitive's mentality with our own. Only thus does it become possible to reach forward to our objective.

19. Lévy-Bruhl, *Primitive Mentality,* p. 223.

20. Ibid., p. 61.

21. See chapter 1, p. 8.

illness and death brought on by transgressions of taboos. Frances Densmore writes of a Sioux Indian, Chased-by-Bears, who sold to her through her interpreter his sacred stone, although he did not have its "helper." (Only if one possessed the "helper" or "brother" of a sacred stone was it considered proper to sell it.) "But misfortune followed his action. After a few weeks the writer on returning to the reservation was informed that Chased-by-Bears had suffered a stroke of paralysis, which was attributed to his sale of the sacred stone and its song. Mr. Higheagle was requested to visit Chased-by-Bears and ascertain whether the report were correct. It was found that Chased-by-Bears seemed to be in danger of death."[22] However, after being reassured that the stone would be returned, he began to improve, and soon after it was actually returned, he recovered his health.

We need always to keep in mind that the results produced were due in great part to the particular attitude which the Primitive adopted. These attitudes inevitably entailed certain consequences.

In addition to this, however, much of the magic is centered around practices and observations which have a well-grounded basis in fact, even though the Primitive may not be conscious of it. In the following M. C. Burkitt relates one of many remarkable instances of this: "A tradition exists among the local Bantu natives to-day which connects this cave at Domboshawa with the production of rain. In fact the place is really a sacred spot and, until recently, in times of drought pilgrimage was made there to obtain rain. The method of procedure was to bring offerings to the cave and wait there for some time until the sign that the offerings had been accepted and therefore that rain would come appeared. The sign took the form of smoke issuing from the top of the great round granite dome of the hill itself, in the side of which the rock-shelter opens. The mechanics of the phenomenon would seem to have been due to the following circumstances. At the back of the rock-shelter are the beginnings of a huge fissure which apparently continued through the rock right away to the top of the hill, forming, as it were, a sort of chimney. Under certain conditions the smoke from a fire lit in the cave would be drawn up this fissure or chimney and would issue out of the top of the mountain. This would only take place when the wind was blowing from a particular direction, i.e., from the east whence the rain normally came. This explains why the suppliants often had to wait a considerable time before their requests were granted, even when all the necessary ritual performances had duly taken place. They had to wait, indeed, till the wind went round to draw the smoke up to the top of the mountain, and incidentally, to bring up the clouds."[23] Here we see that the conclusions of the Primitive are based on valid observation although the basic assumption of magic power is false. The point is, nevertheless, that we ourselves make a false assumption if we regard magic as so much ineffective hocus-pocus. On the contrary, its effectiveness is such that we have yet to learn much about it. For instance, many of the directions in which the Primitive reasoned are only recently being rediscovered as having some valid reference on factual grounds. We in the 20th century are just beginning to comprehend the value for human life of attitudes which had their origin with Primitive cultures. One could give endless examples to show that we have something to learn from the knowledge-efforts of the Primitives.

Modern scientists tell us that accident and chance are not such arbitrary factors as most of us assume. Modern psychologists have shown that dreams are not mere fantasy but have some reference to reality. Psychologists further demonstrate that our intentions may be unconsciously and basically of a destructive nature, while on the surface they may appear to be most benign. Recall the example of the spear-thrower accused of witchcraft, which implies the theory that death may have been intentional, even though the spear-thrower was not conscious of his true intention.[24] Of course the Primitive attributes this to witchcraft, we to the function of the individual's subconscious.

Among the greatest advances in modern knowledge has been the realization of the unity of the human organism and its environment. Primitive man, in principle, regarded these factors as one; for him there was no split between "body," "mind," "environment." Moreover his consideration of the past, present and future as a oneness has also been shown in a sense to be valid. The difference lies in the

22. Frances Densmore: *Teton Sioux Music,* p. 213, Smithsonian Institution: Bureau of American Ethnology, Bulletin 61, Washington, D. C., 1918.
23. M. C. Burkitt: *South Africa's Past in Stone and Paint,* pp. 119-120, Cambridge University Press, 1928.
24. Lévy-Bruhl, *Primitive Mentality,* p. 44.

44

fact that he sees past, present and future as one in terms of *identification*. Modern scientists, on the other hand, while retaining this oneness, regard the past as distinguished from the present, the present from the future and all as a series of unique (non-identification) interdependent events, each with its series of unique points in time-space.

We have previously explained how early man probably was unable to distinguish between the subjective and objective. This would account for the thorough oneness which pervades his every reaction to what we consider as distinct entities in interdependent relation to one another, and gives the basic clue to why he reasons as he does. Reality becomes a problem of *undifferentiated* oneness—identification.

We must not forget that in addition to all this, the Primitive dared not risk, by accepting a new way of reasoning, the terrifying punishment at the hands of the omnipotent and arbitrary demons of the occult world. But, we may well ask, why fear death—the usual punishment—if such a state were considered little different from pre-death existence? Death is feared by the Primitive unless he can die under the proper circumstances. There is such a thing as a "bad death," to use Lévy-Bruhl's expression, and this has to be avoided if one is to make the transition successfully to a desired after-life. Therefore, his fear is not of death as such but of the *kind* of death, the "bad death" that deprives him of proper burial and a desirable rather than a disastrous after-life.[25] Quite possibly the relationship between the living and the dead is the key to the Primitive's belief in his control of mystical forces. This is suggested by John Layard: "For, just as the dead depend for their well-being on the continued sacrifices made to them by the living, so also do the living depend on the dead for their power over the unseen forces that rule their existence. . . ."[26] Since the dead return to the world of the occult, as they once came from that world at birth, and since they are dependent upon the living, they are thus compelled to be the channel by which the living negotiate with the all-decisive force of the occult.

Recall that magic was invented principally for coping with man's fear of the unknown. These experiences with fear naturally set up canalizations which persisted and grew deeper through thousands of years. These, as we have suggested, were the more powerful factor in the later stages of Primitive culture, and were responsible for the continued hold of magic upon the Primitive mentality. But the original fear of the unknown is different from the later variety. Early man feared everything around him because he was handicapped by complete ignorance; yet he possessed a brain which demanded answers to the vast mystery which surrounded him; in late Primitive cultures, when magic had become a closed, completed system, having reached the end of its possible development, the Primitive fears primarily *what has never been done before*. It is his greatest fear because it extends beyond his already completed comprehension of the total significance of the universe. In such problems we are dealing with phenomena which pervade all history.

For example, in the beginning of a specific epoch of culture we find the creative mentality in the fore, inventing, discovering and performing daring enterprises. Eventually this activity evolves into some completed system. Once this occurs, the conservative mentality comes to the fore; it is characterized by a fear of discovery, invention and of daring enterprise. It is a non-creative activity. The former attitude advances human knowledge, while the latter endeavors to prevent advance. It seems reasonable to assume that the European Paleolithic Primitives were by necessity much more flexible in their practice of magic than extant Primitives; otherwise there never would have been a progression on the Paleolithic scene from magic to the religious stage of Egypt, and finally to the higher types of civilization. For the modern Primitive's ancestors were ours too. Magic became a closed, finished system among certain offspring of European Paleolithic man, e.g., Eskimos, Africans, etc. These were the peoples who left the European continent to settle in the more extreme climates of hot or cold.

In the following chapter, we shall be concerned with *creative Primitive mentality*; creative, because it began the first steps in man's effort to comprehend himself and the world environment in which that self operated. We shall not speak of development, however, as a physiological affair, but in a broader social sense. By the time man began the rudiments of culture, he had already a more or less physiologically developed nervous system and visual organs. Whatever developments followed were mainly concerned

25. Ibid., p. 274.
26. John Layard: *Stone Men of Malekula,* p. 50, Chatto and Windus, London, 1942.

with discovering the potentialities inherent in the operation of the human nervous system. Up to about Cro-magnon man the development has been largely physio-biological. After Cro-magnon man, development is largely psycho-biological. The first stage was concerned with the development of the human organism as such—the means by which human culture was to be achieved; the second stage was mainly concerned with a further evolution of the now physically developed organism—the achievement of human culture.[27] By analogy, the physiological stage of development is like the prenatal period of human growth while the second stage is like the postnatal period when the psychic forces comprise the important developments.

27. See Oliver L. Reiser: *The Promise of Scientific Humanism*, p. 19, Oskar Piest, New York, 1940. By permission of Creative Age Press, New York.

. . . . since the time when skeletons of homo sapiens first appeared in the geological record, perhaps 25,000 years ago, man's bodily evolution has come virtually to a standstill, though his cultural progress was just beginning. "The physical difference between men of the Aurignacian and Magdalenian cultures on the one hand, and present-day man on the other, is negligible, while the cultural difference is immeasurable." Progress in culture has, indeed, taken the place of further organic evolution in the human family. 76

V. G. Childe

. . . . the human organism is still in process of evolution. It is a curious thing that although psychologists of the twentieth century pay lip service to Charles Darwin and his doctrine of biological evolution, they have never really taken the idea of evolution seriously, in the sense that they realize that the human type is still "on its way" and that evolution has not yet completed its work. 286

Oliver Reiser

We know that the period of our human childhood has been inconceivably long; we know that in the far distant time, the first specimens of human-kind —the initial members of the time-binding race of man—were absolutely without human knowledge of the hostile world in which they found themselves; we know that they had no conception of what they themselves were; we know that they had neither speech nor art nor philosophy nor religion nor science nor tools nor human history nor human tradition; we know, though we to-day can hardly imagine it, that their sole equipment for initiating the career of the human race was that peculiar faculty which made them human — the capacity of man for binding time; we know that they actually did that work of initiation, without any guidance or example, maxim or precedent; and we know that they were able to do it just because the power of initiation—the power to originate—is a time-binding power. 178   Alfred Korzybski

Since the day when man first began scratching pictographic ideographs on his cave walls some 25,000 or more years ago, he has been refining his methods of recording and diffusing ideas. 154
P. B. Horton

. . . . there can be no question that this art [Paleolithic] was subject to the law of evolution, both in regard to technique and mastery of color, and in reference to refinement and perfection of form and figure. 244   Hugo Obermaier

What is Art? . . . many definitions have been given, none of them altogether satisfying. Let us discuss its origins; perhaps they will help. . . . 322
H. G. Spearing

Pictographic man began his career as an artist with a nervous system and visual organs little developed as far as their *inherent potentialities* were concerned. In the early stages of human life, preceding the invention of art, man was not accustomed to or capable of seeing reality for purposes of depicting it. He had to start from scratch. And, as we shall see, he probably started by *actually scratching*. Our analysis must begin with an attempt to reconstruct the probable preliminary visual experiences of our earliest ancestors, for these experiences eventually led to their first conscious efforts at art. The earliest artists certainly did not start to sculpt and draw out of a clear sky. In subsequent cultures the artist has had the examples of the art of previous peoples. But the *first* artists had the momentous task of beginning the beginning of art! This must be constantly kept in mind if we are to appreciate and comprehend adequately the initial struggling efforts of these earliest of all human artists.

By necessity much that we have to say about the beginnings of art will be speculative, since there is very little evidence of the first and earliest steps. When we reach the period of representational art, we shall base our discussion largely on examples that have been found in excavations of Paleolithic sites in

France, Spain and Africa and shall, in general, follow the chronological order worked out by Breuil, Obermaier and others. But speculations on earlier beginnings must be derived largely by abstracting backwards from the mass of available evidence of later times. We shall try to posit what we would expect to find in the genesis of art as a result of what we do find later on in Paleolithic times; we shall be helped also by evidence available in extant (or recently extant) Primitive tribes, and, in some cases, in children's behavior.

However, here and there we shall find bits of evidence from Tertiary times and in the Mousterian or early Paleolithic period which would appear to enforce our analysis. And if our theory of the genesis of art is correct, then we shall have to place the beginning of art considerably farther back in time than we now do, just as not long ago new discoveries supplanted Egypt with the Old Stone Age.

When we speak about the "beginning of art," we do not wish to rule out the possibility that art began in more than one place, perhaps at different times. We are simply referring to the beginning of art in Europe in the sense that there it appears to have not only begun but to have successfully evolved through many thousands of years to the climax seen in the so-called Magdalenian period. In short, we are concerned with a beginning of art that survived into a high degree of achievement. Later in our analysis we shall be able to state more specifically why this event occurred in Europe and nowhere else.[1]

We do not maintain that the various stages of art development necessarily occurred in the uninterrupted order in which we present them. That is, a particular stage of development may have been achieved in one area or time before it was achieved in another area at another time; moreover, these particular stages may have been developing in different ways. What we are contending is that wherever the various developmental stages which we present occurred, it was always in a certain general order; that is, a higher stage of development did not precede a lower stage, except in the case of regressions. As far as times are concerned, a higher stage of art may have occurred in one part of the world before it occurred in another part of the world, but in neither place did a higher stage of art precede a lower one.

It is quite likely that any of the stages of art development which we have posited may have occurred in a number of places in various times. But for one reason or another, the group of humans carrying these developments degenerated or disappeared; probably many such cases remain to be discovered. Recall that four ice glaciers swept back and forth across the greater part of Europe. Consequently one group of humans carrying the highest order of art development extant at a certain time could have been destroyed and other groups at lower stages of development who survived would in time have again realized these higher developments. No doubt the entire Paleolithic period of art development was characterized by ups and downs similar to those that occurred in the history of Egyptian culture.

> In the archaic thinking of a prelogical kind, found among primitive savage races, the vividness of the images is greater than among more highly developed races, and the effect produced in the observer is projected and believed to be an inherent attitude of the object, which thus acquires a "demonic" character. 354   William A. White

Examples of two- and three-dimensional art have been found among the earliest works of man. From this it would appear (but not prove) that these two mediums emerged, relatively speaking, together. But since these two methods of art are extremely different, there exists the possibility that two separate approaches led to their discovery and invention as well as their development. This would suggest the possibility that they did not originate at the same time or develop in the same way or at the same rate of progress. Our analysis will attempt to point out the reasons for this.

We shall attempt first to trace the sculptural developments. It was in this medium that man realized his first major achievements in the field of *representational* art. However, when we come to the

1. The author regrets that he has never been able to view the European originals of Paleolithic art, an admittedly serious handicap. However, every effort has been made to see as many reproductions as possible, especially photographs of the linear arts and casts of the sculptural arts.

analysis of linear art, we shall find that the first important achievements were *not* representational. It is our contention that the actual inception of representational art implies a *development from lesser or preliminary levels of visual activity and interest*. Actual evidence indicates that there were such preliminary activities. Our analysis will show that representational art is already a high order of art activity which requires preceding development from a genesis consisting of a non-representational type of activity.

We begin by asking ourselves: what would be the most likely *visual* experience in nature which would attract human organisms not yet adapted to the type of seeing required for the direct making of representational art? A number of factors suggest that stones, just as they were found in nature, must have served a major role in this capacity. Pictographic man could experience stones more easily perhaps than any other object in nature, because of their very simple visual structure and because experiencing them stimulated the then preponderantly important tactile sense as well as the visual. Stones were visually simple and tactilely satisfying in more ways than one (e.g., the highly important role of tools) to a Primitive whose ability to see and comprehend was as yet undeveloped.

The entire early period of man's culture is commonly known as the Old Stone Age because the principal tools and implements of existence were largely fashioned from stone. We should not assume, however, that upon seeing stones, man, without further experience, immediately made tools and art. The first sculptural art and tools, as we shall see, were found, not made! That is, the simple structure of stones made them suitable for immediate use; they were more or less ready-made art objects and tools. In the latter capacity they could be easily grasped in the hand and hence directly employed for grinding, pounding, throwing, etc.

When man began to *invent* the shape of his tools he used flint; we believe, however, that the grainless variety of stones must have engaged his earliest interest. These may be found in all kinds of simple, curved shapes, and supply man with a variety of "ready-made" tools adaptable to use by the human hand. It may be assumed that all kinds of stones were used from the beginning, i.e., both the smooth, grainless variety and the naturally chipped flint, but just as man had first to discover that he could use stones, so he must have had to pass through a gradual process of necessity for and discovery of ever more complex uses of stones as tools.

Subsequent to the use of ready-made, nature-shaped stones of the grainless variety, must have come the discovery that the nature-shaped *flint* stones could be used in a greater variety of specialized directions. The natural, grainless varieties were limited to pounding, grinding and the like, while the natural flint tools, because of the sort of surfaces and edges left when broken by natural processes, offered the possibilities of cutting, scraping, etc., and so extended and refined the tool-kit of man.

The earliest chipped flints have been designated as eoliths; there has long been a dispute as to whether they are the products of nature or of man. Those who believe that eoliths are the products of nature have convincingly shown by controlled experiment that such stones can be and are produced by natural processes.[2] But this does not prove that man cannot or did not make such stones, but only that they can occur in a natural state. It is reasonable to assume that early man's first flint tools *were* ready-made, that those flint stones fortuitously chipped by natural processes were actually used. No experts, to our knowledge, deny that such flints could have served as tools and there seems to be good reason for assuming that man did use them — unless we wish to deny that such a notion could occur to him. Hence we can say that some so-called eoliths were made by a natural process and probably served as "ready-made" tools. But at some time when the natural supply was inadequate, some genius hit upon the notion that he could make such tools himself, whenever he needed them, by simply employing the methods of nature. Thus there is also the possibility that some eoliths are not the result of natural processes but are man-made copies of the natural process! In short, some are results of natural processes, some are artifacts, and both were used as the early flint stone tools of man. From such experience and knowledge there ensued the discovery that flint stones could be worked into an even greater variety of different shapes than those produced by the natural processes and so further extend the tool-kit of man.

2. See especially Hugo Obermaier: *Fossil Man in Spain,* pp. 10-18, translated by Christine D. Matthew, with an introduction by H. F. Osborn, Hispanic Society of America, New York, 1924.

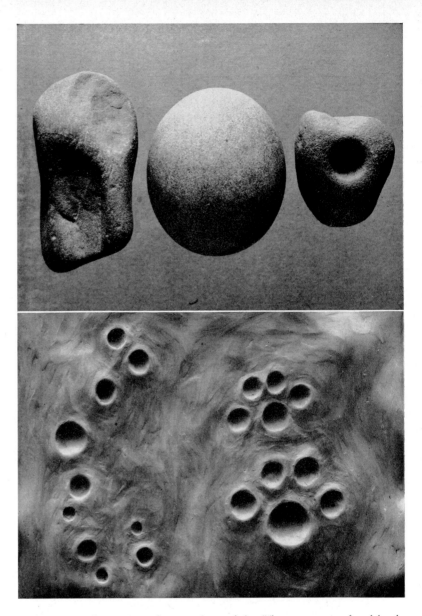

2. Above, natural stones, curved, geometric. cup-hole. (These stones were found by the author and his friends. They were collected in the countryside expressly to serve as examples of the problems discussed in this chapter.) Below left, Mousterian cup-stones (copied in clay after Sollas, after Capitan and Peyrony); right, Aurignacian cup-stones (copied in clay after Sollas, after Didon; see biblio. No. 320).

R. R. Schmidt has made the interesting observation that the "first shaped tool is proportioned to its prototype, the human hand. . . ."[3] In this respect it is interesting to note the general development. Early Paleolithic tools were mainly manufactured to fit the grasp of the *complete* hand. But in later Paleolithic tools we see considerable changes. Now there is greater variety of shapes, sizes and functions. Now man is manufacturing tools for much finer operations, tools that are made for a greater variety of hand grips. In these he has passed from the early stages of tools made for various grips of the hand, to more refined uses where the fingers play a more developed role as part of the tool "socket." And just as the preceding use of "ready-made" tools reached its highest point in the finding of those stones that most readily suited various grips of the hand, so the beginning of the next epoch—the direct manufacture of stone tools—began with the hand as the prototype of the shape for the tool. Development then continued into the recognition of the role played by the fingers until such refinement was achieved that the fingers gripped the instrument, or

3. R. R. Schmidt: *The Dawn of the Human Mind*, p. 96, translated by R. A. S. Macalister, Sidgwick and Jackson, Ltd., London, 1936.

3. Natural stones fortuitously resembling animal, bird and human heads (found by author and friends).

that handles were invented, further increasing the power and accuracy of the hand in operating the tool.

   Just as early man first selected certain stones for hunting or self-protection, so we can imagine him beginning his career as an artist by picking up the very simplest of the grainless varieties of stones in an idle moment of curiosity, just as we ourselves do today. But once stones became the tools of man, curiosity in them was no longer an idle one but an intensely serious affair. And, as his interests developed through experiences and experiments with them, he may have eventually become increasingly selective about various kinds, and so have collected them for various purposes—magic ornament, monument, etc. Thus Obermaier speaks of "the enthusiasm for 'collecting curiosities' . . . among the customs of the Early Palaeolithic. These treasures consisted of round pebbles, variegated stones, beautiful minerals, fossils, etc."[4] Of course the collections of natural stones by man in early Pictographic times would be difficult to distinguish from other natural stones unless they were found with other evidence.

4. Obermaier, op. cit., p. 127.

But just as we assume that the earliest tools were not invented but were natural products used as found (only their function being invented), so likewise we assume that the first manifestations of "sculptural art" consisted of collections of natural stones as well as other natural objects. Nature at first supplied ready-made the principal tools and sculptural art; only later did man discover ways to manipulate and so direct and extend the natural processes and eventually create products directly from nature's raw materials. (As a matter of fact, we shall find that the Mimetic and Inventive factors are never found alone throughout all of man's "art." It has always been a question of degrees and kinds.)

An early development in the use of stones probably occurred in making arrangements and groups, in some way such as occurred on a larger scale in the Megalithic cultures of Neolithic Europe and in other parts of the world. Of great importance was the fact that stones, the simplest visual phenomena to comprehend and use, aside from their important practical function, seemed unchanging, as though they would endure forever. These and other similar factors had a psycho-physiological effect upon early man. The use of stones to ward away illness and death, to make decisions endure, to comprehend and prophesy events, etc., actually constituted what was Primitive man's earliest forms of psycho-logics, what we commonly refer to as magic or mysticism.

It would seem quite probable that most extant Primitive cultures are continuing practices which originated in Paleolithic times. Although these are now somewhat elaborated and more rigid, nevertheless they give us some notion of how stone-magic was used in the earliest periods of human culture. Frazer gives numerous examples of this, such as the following: "But while a general magical efficacy may be supposed to reside in all stones by reason of their common properties of weight and solidity, special magical virtues are attributed to particular stones, or kinds of stone, in accordance with their individual or specific qualities of shape and color."[5]

". . . . the old Danish historian Saxo Grammaticus tells us that 'the ancients, when they were to choose a king, were wont to stand on stones planted in the ground, and to proclaim their votes, in order to foreshadow from the steadfastness of the stones that the deed would be lasting.'"[6]

"At initiation a Brahman boy is made to tread with his right foot on a stone, while the words are repeated, 'Tread on this stone; like a stone be firm'; and the same ceremony is performed, with the same words, by a Brahman bride at her marriage."[7]

"In the Banks Islands there are some stones of a remarkably long shape which go by the name of 'eating ghosts,' because certain powerful and dangerous ghosts are believed to lodge in them."[8]

". . . . in the Babar Archipelago tired people will strike themselves with stones, believing that they thus transfer to the stones the weariness which they felt in their own bodies."[9] And in Frances Densmore's *Teton Sioux Music,* we find this: "To dream of a small stone was regarded by the Teton Sioux as a sign of great import, indicating that the dreamer, by fulfilling the requirements of his dream would become possessed of supernatural power, in the exercise of which he would use the sacred stones. This power would be shown in an ability to cure sickness, to predict future events, and to tell the location of objects beyond the range of his natural vision."[10]

Thus we have seen how earliest man fashioned from his experience with stones, his tools, his art and his magic. But these three factors were not isolated in the life of the Primitive; they were linked together as *one*.

In the beginning of stone-magic culture, all kinds of curved shapes were probably used, but gradually more and more perfectly geometric, smooth stones were sought, the perfection of shape allowing more importance to be attributed to them, both in the material and magical sense. Densmore cites the very

5. From J. G. Frazer: *The Golden Bough,* p. 33, New York, 1934. By permission of The Macmillan Company, publishers. Abridged edition.

6. From J. G. Frazer: *The Golden Bough,* p. 33. By permission of The Macmillan Company, publishers.

7. From J. G. Frazer: *The Golden Bough,* p. 33. By permission of The Macmillan Company, publishers.

8. From J. G. Frazer: *The Golden Bough,* p. 190. By permission of The Macmillan Company, publishers.

9. From J. G. Frazer: *The Golden Bough,* p. 540. By permission of The Macmillan Company, publishers.

10. Frances Densmore: *Teton Sioux Music,* pp. 204-205.

interesting report of the symbolism of sacred stones for the Sioux Indians, as related by Chased-by-Bears: "The outline of the stone is round, having no end and no beginning; like the power of the stone it is endless. The stone is perfect of its kind and is the work of nature, no artificial means being used in shaping it. Outwardly it is not beautiful, but its structure is solid, like a solid house in which one may safely dwell. It is not composed of many substances, but is of one substance, which is genuine and *not an imitation of anything else.*" (emphasis ours)[11]

When it becomes possible to investigate more adequately the earliest periods of stone culture, we shall probably find that the stones selected for magic purposes were, like the tools, comprised of many stages, some of which (suggested from the evidence in ancient as well as recent Primitive cultures) could possibly have been as follows (see figure 2):

(1) The use of various shaped stones, i.e., all kinds of curved stones.

(2) The seeking for and use of particular shaped, smooth, geometric stones, perfection of shape implying perfection of tool and art-magical power. Thus, for example, the stones considered sacred or magic by the Teton Sioux Indians, "were the native brown sandstone, usually spherical in shape, though oval stones and stones slightly flattened were also used, the principal requirements being that they should be regular in outline and *untouched by a tool.*" (emphasis ours)[12]

(3) Attempts to copy and thus multiply the stone shapes of the geometric period. A probable example of the latter is this material mentioned by Sollas: "At La Quina [Mousterian period] many spherical balls [35-90 mm. in diameter] of limestone, shaped by the hand of man, have been found."[13]

(4) Interest in and use of that type of stone with a hollowed out hemisphere or "cup-shape" on one of its surfaces (a frequent phenomenon in natural stones); this would gradually develop from an interest in variously shaped stones to those quite perfectly shaped both in the interior of the cavity and on the exterior surfaces.

(5) Increasing the quantity of such stones by copying them and then carrying them to further developments. A good example of this, again in Mousterian "art," would be the "cup markings" on rocks, of which Burkitt has written: "a trench had been dug in a Mousterian deposit and in it the bones of a child had been laid, the skull towards one side of the trench, the limb bones towards the other. The little trench itself had been covered by a large rock purposefully placed in position on which were cut cup markings."[14] It is of interest to note that the "cup markings" of Aurignacian times show a marked advance over the earlier Mousterian. The latter exhibit a more arbitrary arrangement in the relation of one cup hole to another on the stone surface, as compared to the former, which are definitely arranged in geometrical relations (see figure 2).

(6) Engraved and painted stones, also passing from a variety of curved to a variety of geometric stone periods. The Azilian painted pebbles, as they are called, although found in the deposits of a period subsequent to the close of the Paleolithic period, nevertheless serve as an example. The Tasmanians of Australia, for instance, are reported to have used small painted stones in their ancestor-magic; Sollas places their culture within the Mousterian level.

11. Ibid., p. 205.

12. Ibid., p. 205.

13. W. J. Sollas: *Ancient Hunters,* pp. 211-212, Macmillan and Co., Ltd., London, 1924. It is of interest to find that certain of the "eolithophiles" claim, regarding the Tertiary and Early Quaternary periods, "the existence of Eolithic ornament and art. According to them, the stony alluvial deposits afforded ... 'geometric' stones of the most varied forms...." (Obermaier, *Fossil Man in Spain,* p. 9.)

14. M. C. Burkitt: *The Old Stone Age,* p. 128, Cambridge University Press, 1933.

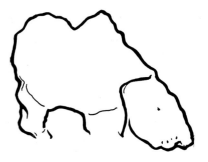
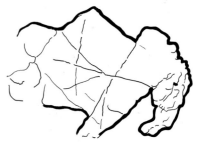

4. Natural stones fortuitously resembling relief carvings of animal figures. Above, bear (?) or rhinoceros; below, mammoth. (Found by author and friends.) Recognizability of this material is diminished in the photograph; therefore, beside each one a few suggestive guide lines have been indicated.

56

5. Horse from rock-shelter frieze, Cap-Blanc cave, Dordogne region, France; Magdalenian period. Courtesy, Chicago Natural History Museum.

Thus far we have observed two general types of art activity, the Mimetic and the Inventive, but the Mimetic has been confined to copying inanimate nature, as in the stone examples to which we have already referred. The concern has so far been largely with the shape of the stones as such, first in the natural state and then in the man-produced state. The latter would represent the inanimate Mimetic stage of behavior; that is, inanimate nature comprised the subject-matter of the earliest form of Mimetic art activity. The tactile aspect of stones must have predominated in man's initial contacts with them, but the visual would have gained ever more importance as man tried to copy first the natural stones and then developed mimetically and inventively the subsequent steps in his stone-art-tool magic, until artists reached the stage of copying animate subjects. Hereafter the concern was largely with the shape of the stone as a representation of some other object than the stone, namely, animals, first in the natural state, i.e., stones that fortuitously took on the appearances of animals, and then in the man-produced state, i.e., stones deliberately carved into animal shapes. Thus the earlier visual experiences of man aided his development to the point where he had become a more acute observer of the surrounding world, and could see, particularly in the rough stones of nature, certain resemblances to forms in nature. MacCurdy has written: "There is some evidence that even proto-Neandertal man was attracted by natural objects which fortuitously resembled familiar animal forms. These were picked up as curiosities. . . . Primitive man might well have been attracted by suggestive natural forms just as we are today. Imagination has always played an important role in art and was, no doubt, the chief attendant at its birth."[15]

Here again, as with the problem of eoliths and the collecting of natural stones, it would be difficult to ascertain those that were collected for their resemblances unless other evidence were obtained to verify it. Accidental resemblances in stones, etc., were, after all, being produced by natural processes long before there were men to see them, not to mention the fact that men did not see them until they were both able and needed to see them. Furthermore, man probably copied some of these natural resemblances in order to increase the supply. (See remarks on the Pueblo Indians, p. 58.) It would also be difficult to distinguish these from the natural formations. In that case we cannot be sure which were made by man, which naturally. It would seem reasonable to assume, however, that early efforts to collect naturally shaped stones appearing to resemble animals, as well as early efforts to copy such stones, had already begun during the height of what we posited as the inanimate period of Mimetic art. For man tends to begin the new while the old continues, an occurrence that is seen throughout art history. The old and the new overlap before the latter reaches dominance. Therefore, the order in which we place the various stages of art

15. G. G. MacCurdy: *The Coming of Man*, p. 108, The University Society, Inc., New York, 1935.

6. Venus of Willendorf, Aurignacian period. Vienna State
Museum of Natural History. Photo, The Bettmann Archive.

development is not meant to imply that each stage appeared only after the preceding one had been concluded.

Once man had definitely entered the profession of the hunter, he became more and more familiar with the appearances of animals and was in a better position to recognize accidental resemblances in naturally shaped stones. At first he probably saw only resemblances to the animal in *general;* later he was able to recognize the *particular,* the specific animal. (Reproduced are such stones, see figures 3 and 4.) Considering the importance of animals to the Primitive, now primarily a hunter, one can easily imagine the magical potency that he would attribute to stones in which he discovered miraculous resemblances to animals.

In a conversation Frances Densmore told the author that the Pueblo Tribes in southwestern United States have "hunting dogs"—bits of turquoise stone which have a faint, natural resemblance to dogs. Because of what is considered their miraculous resemblance, they are thought to give success in hunting expeditions. The Primitive's primary concern is his existence in a world of magic and the resemblances found in stones untouched by man can only be comprehended as products of the mystical powers, not as accidents. Hence they have great magical import.

Thus in the development of animate "sculptured" art, we can now distinguish a further step: namely, the renewed interest in irregular-shaped stones, for in them man began to discover resemblances to recognizable objects (whereas "perfect" stones—in the very apt words of the Indian, Chased-by-Bears— were not an "imitation of anything else").

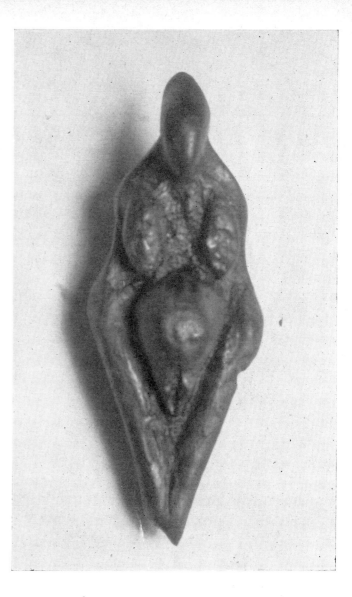

7. Mentone Venus, Aurignacian period. Photo, Musé des Antiquites Nationales, St. Germain-en-Laye.

This was naturally followed by efforts to increase the recognizability of an object discovered in stones, that is, the Primitive artist incised the natural shape so as to make it more distinct. As MacCurdy put it, "He soon learned to supplement nature's work, for example in a nodule of flint, by strengthening the likeness to an animal." [16] Or he might have done it in another way, as in the following example (also given by MacCurdy) concerning a visit to newly discovered caverns: "Two red spots were pointed out as being the only bits of color as yet noted in the caverns; the author at once recognized them as representing a pair of eyes, the head of the animal being formed by the projecting rock." [17]

We would also expect that the natural supply might have been increased by copying the natural stones. This is precisely what the Pueblo Indians, mentioned above, do: in addition to the naturally-shaped hunting dogs they also fashion similar ones out of clay, and both kinds are worn together on a string as a necklace.

Finally man was able to carve directly into the stone to make whatever object he desired, regardless of what the original stone shape might have looked like. Now he was able to control the production of his art resemblances not only in quantity but in kind and no longer needed to depend upon natural accidents or copying of accidents. *Man had now embarked upon his career as a SCULPTOR!*, in the sense that we commonly understand that term today, i.e., *sculpting of recognizable forms directly from the raw material.*

16. Ibid., p. 108.
17. G. G. MacCurdy: *Human Origins*, Vol. 1, pp. 237-238. D. Appleton-Century Co., New York, 1924.

We have explained why discovery of the possibility of recording the animal world did not begin with the beginning of man's art and culture, as is commonly assumed. Man's culture had to pass from lower to higher levels before animal depictions could be attempted. Human experience had first to evolve to a point calling for a culture of magic built around the animal world. Only then did man pass into the more highly developed stage of animal-magic art. Even if we posit the animal as of the greatest importance to man from the very beginning of his emergence as an artist (which we are inclined to doubt), still we must consider the fact that he could not abruptly construct such a highly developed art and culture as is implied by animal magic. It seems more reasonable to assume that simpler forms of magic preceded the use of animal images in magic. This whole point revolves around the question of whether or not at the beginning of human culture man was *primarily* carnivorous. We cannot ignore the fact that the human being is not equipped with natural tools to attack and kill animals. He had to develop artificial means of offense and defense against the rest of the animal world, and not until he was able to do so was he in a position to become primarily dependent upon animals for his food. During such a period, therefore, a non-animal art would be formed; man must have then been primarily a food-gatherer rather than a food-hunter, living on eggs, plants, shell-fish and other food that could be caught or gathered with the bare hands.

Moreover, we should not forget that all this time the function of man's visual receptors was also evolving, another necessary adjunct to the birth of animal-recording magic. What one sees is determined not only by what he can see, but by what he wants to or thinks is most important for him to see, because the latter determines to a great extent *how* he will see, and the "how" implies limitations. But when new needs arise, man begins to change the "how"; he is then released from the limitations of the previous ways of seeing-thinking, new discoveries follow, and once more he begins to transform his culture. Of great importance in this process is the environmental factor.[18]

Eventually, when man's life became predominantly that of a hunter, the animal form became the major subject-matter in the Mimetic stage of art. Only a very few recordings of the human form have been found. The majority of human figures so far discovered are in three dimensions or very high reliefs and are largely confined to the Aurignacian period; at least it was in this period that human sculpture in Paleolithic times reached its highest development. Animal sculpture is found in Aurignacian and Magdalenian times.

Examples of both human and animal sculpture are reproduced (see figures 5, 6, 7). As will be seen, more accuracy in detail was achieved with the animal form than with the human. But in both cases, there are lacking examples of earlier beginnings which must have preceded these. Obermaier suggests that this may be because earlier sculpture was done in less durable material. Also missing are examples of the stages that must have come in between the various examples that have been found.

The scarcity of human depictions can be partially accounted for by the probable belief that dangers were involved in doing so; of this we shall have more to say later when we come to an extensive discussion of the magic function of this art. The animal form as a subject predominated and first reached a high state of development, not only because it was so important to survival, but also because the demands of magic necessitated its portrayal.

Although, as we have already pointed out, the earliest representational artists of the animal form experimented with both two- and three-dimensional mediums, it was in the sculptural medium, the more simple, direct path, that the *first major development* in *representational* art was achieved. Man became a highly developed representational sculptor, primarily of the animal form, long before he became a highly developed representational linear artist; this is attested to by the scientifically ascertained chronology of Paleolithic art. Hence, while Pictographic sculptural works were probably not the *first* form of art, as some investigators have thought, they were certainly the *first medium to reach a high degree of representational development*. It is most important to realize that the three-dimensional factor could be seen and experienced more easily by men who were in the beginning stages of learning to visualize; especially when we consider the fact that the physio-tactile sensory level played a necessarily dominant role in the early stages of visual

18. A good example was the situation at the end of the Paleolithic period when the ice receded and trees, plants, etc., replaced the frozen tundra. The result was a terrific upheaval in human culture.

art. With the three-dimensional medium the artist was able to "feel" his way with his hands as he made attempted duplications of the forms of nature. The tactile sense in the linear arts, on the other hand, was, for all practical purposes, eliminated—hands could not touch and feel the actual forms as they were being built up. For these reasons, accidental resemblances of three-dimensional objects on a relatively flat surface were also less likely to have been discovered in the early stages. It was natural that the artist should first be able to recognize those accidental resemblances in stones which possessed the principal characteristic of three dimensions, of actual form in actual space. In other words, stones were *similar in structure* to that which they resembled—there was a three-dimensional, physio-tactile correspondence.

Representations of nature in two-dimensional (linear) mediums require a far greater degree of visual development: here the artist must learn how to depict forms *without actually realizing any forms at all!* In sculpture what the eyes see the hands can actually feel; in drawing and painting, what the eyes see the hands can never actually feel. Without the assistance of the tactile factor, the individual must possess a greater degree of visual acuity before he is able to record on a flat surface and produce illusions of the third dimension. In achieving such ability, man must have passed through a development in many ways analogous to that which occurs in the infant's ontogeny (see chapter 3), a development from the combined activity of the tactile and the visual to ever greater dominance of the latter. In this regard the following remarks by Reiser are of interest: "It is generally recognized that in the evolution of organisms old structures will disappear, losing their functions, and new structures will appear with new functions to take the place of the older ones. Thus in the evolution of the nervous system it is known that the lower organisms are dependent upon what are called the 'contact senses,' such as touch and taste, for their knowledge of the external environment, but that with further specialization of the 'distant receptors,' involving vision and audition, have become more important, eventually assuming dominance over the other senses. In connection with these changes it is important to note that one main difference between man and the lower vertebrates is the extent to which the visual centers in the brain, and the subcortical visual tracts, have developed."[19] In the case of the early Primitive's art this increased importance of the visual level is evident in the long evolution in achieving two-dimensional representational art.

On the whole, H. G. Spearing has an excellent understanding of the difficulties in which these first artists were involved. But in one place he writes: "Let us try to put ourselves in the position of these pioneers. How were they to know that a certain arrangement of lines would represent an animal or a man to other men? In fact, it is extremely unlikely that these lines did succeed at first in conveying any impression to their less gifted fellow-men. It was only by slow transitions from the actual carved model to flatter and still flatter carvings that ordinary men came to see that a thin flat form might have some resemblance to a real solid animal."[20] We would take issue with Spearing's contention that the two-dimensional arts evolved by the gradual linearization of the sculptural medium. Such a procedure reverses the *natural order of development* persisting throughout the art history of man. Furthermore, to assume that Paleolithic man made his sculpture flatter and flatter until he realized linear art, is to assume that he began this process knowing ahead of time the end toward which he was striving; but in that case there would have been nothing to prevent him from making linear art directly. But be that as it may, still it seems unreasonable to suppose that the early artist would gradually remove the very factor which permitted sculpture to perform its function as sculpture, namely, the third dimension. Linear art, as our analysis will show, was probably arrived at in a far more natural and direct manner. Moreover, the fact that linear recording art has been found which is just as old as sculpture of similar subjects demonstrates the probability that both mediums were in the process of evolving before sculpture itself had become a developed art. This Spearing also recognizes when he writes that: "discoveries have been made of drawings which are quite as old as the sculptures. As these drawings are not nearly so good as the carvings, the real conclusion seems to be that primitive man had been tentatively striving in various ways to represent natural objects, and had

19. From Oliver L. Reiser: *Philosophy and the Concepts of Modern Science,* pp. 198-199. By permission of The Macmillan Company, publishers.

20. H. G. Spearing: *The Childhood of Art,* p. 56, Kegan Paul, Trench, Trubner and Co., Ltd., London, 1912. By permission of Ernest Benn, Ltd., London.

made much more rapid progress in carving than in drawing . . . The strange superiority of sculpture over drawing . . . becomes intelligible if we regard representation on the flat as possible only for men whose perceptions have been strengthened by long use or who have developed a desire for expressing ideas which cannot conveniently be embodied in a carving."[21] For, as Spearing says elsewhere, "They [the 'pioneers' of art] had to learn to look at it [the flat depiction] only from one point of view. It is quite likely that at first they always wanted to turn the strange thing around and look at the other side, and that is why we get those *contours decoupés* or silhouette carvings with the details fully worked out on both sides."[22] In pointing out that the linear artist had to learn to look at his flat art from one point of view, Spearing is referring to a problem similar to the one which Koffka discussed in relating his difficulties in drawing a chair (see chapter 3). A sculptor is able, relatively speaking, to record each form as it actually appears to occur in reality. Whereas the difficulty for the linear artist arises from his having to maintain a stationary point of view, not to mention that of making forms appear where only a flat surface continues to exist. *His problem is to record the object as it appears to his eyes; i.e., he has to record the appearance of the IMAGE of the object and not the appearance of the object, as such; the latter is what the sculptor does.* This is no mean accomplishment. For instance, if Koffka had attempted to *sculpt* a chair rather than draw it, he would have found it considerably less difficult to make his result look considerably more like a chair. As we have said before, linear representations require a higher level of visual ability than do sculptured ones.

In the following we shall attempt to reconstruct the probable general development of events that led to the discovery of linear recording art. At the same time we shall seek further understanding of the relationships between the two principal art mediums of man. Although the "known" examples of earliest art in both mediums are reported as of similar age, this would not necessarily prove that the genesis of both mediums occurred together. It is possible, considering the *technical ease* with which the invention of the line could have occurred, that this may have been the very first form of art. For with most anything at hand, the line could be easily discovered by accidental or deliberate experiment, i.e., with any piece of wood, bone or shell scratched across the earth, with a finger or shell drawn across the clay floor or wall of a cave, with any piece of stone scratched across another, and so on. At first lines were probably significant only as lines having their own meanings, and not as depictions of anything else.[23]

With the invention of the line a factor would appear that is of no small importance. Of all other possibilities in the genesis of art, it involved man in the direct and complete act of creation; this may very well have led him to consider it an achievement on the order of a miracle. This may seem highly unreasonable unless we keep in mind the level of human behavior with which we are dealing.

In any case, the ease with which the linear medium could be manipulated, the fact that it allowed for a complete act of creation or invention of art, could have made it possible to serve as a guide for the pre-animate stages of sculpture. In the linear art the line and its arrangement were both invented, whereas in sculpture only the arrangement and not the forms were invented. In other words, man probably learned first to make arrangements with lines, which could then have suggested the arrangement of stones. The next step in linear art development would quite naturally lead to the discovery that lines could be used for Mimetic purposes. Where the natural stones had served as "ready-made," three-dimensional objects of art, (their natural variety suggesting the Mimetic direction of development, e.g., copying the spherical stones of nature) so in the linear medium, scratches made by one rock falling over another, or marks left by great glacial sheets as they scraped their way over rock and earth, marks left by the turtle as it came out of the water and crawled across the wet beach—phenomena such as these may well have led to the discovery of the Mimetic possibilities of the linear medium. Such observations not only suggested the mediums to employ, but also the direction for developing this aspect of art. And even in the Mimetic pre-animate direction, linear art would seem to have held the dominant position. Recall that at this stage

21. Ibid., pp. 30-31.

22. Ibid., p. 57.

23. There have been reports of such lines found in Tertiary deposits, but it has not been proven that they were made by man, rather than by animals or other natural causes.

8. Sacred drawings of Aboriginal Australians. After photograph taken by Spencer and Gillen for *Native Tribes of Central Australia*. Courtesy of Macmillan and Co., Ltd., London.

of culture man had not yet completed the fabrication of his artificial weapons of defense and offense so that he could surpass the weapons with which animals are born; under these circumstances various animate objects, such as shells, eggs, nuts, plants, etc., offered him his chief sources of supply as a food-gatherer. These, therefore, would also supply the subjects and even the objects of his magic art. Now objects of this sort did not need to be sculptured, since the originals were perfectly suitable for use, something not possible in sculpture when the animal became the dominant subject. Thus a string of shells, nuts, etc., were made into a necklace, or were placed in a circle upon the ground, etc. In such ways they could be used for magical purposes. Therefore, the actual three-dimensional objects of nature would have taken the place of Mimetic sculptural activity of this sort. Sculpture would be restricted to the making of spheres, cup-holes, and the like, as has been described. As for the linear arts the situation would appear to have been quite different. Here Mimetic activity was largely directed towards imitation of linear marks left by natural occurrences, as we have described above. However, the major part of linear art would consist of invented symbols which were given "subjective" rather than objective or representational meanings. Where "art" dealt with the actual objects of nature, in this earliest stage of culture, it was the actual objects themselves which were employed, while Mimetic activity in both mediums was largely confined to geometric shapes, cavities and lines seen in nature.

The major point we make is that this first epoch of art was probably restricted to what we are now habituated to calling "decorative" or "ornamental." Decoration, as we are employing it here, however, has to do with the genesis of the effort to create and to imitate with *art for magical,* i.e., practical purposes. Hence, our use of the term refers to the presence of a functional content; we reject the notion that "decorative" or "ornamental" art is simply pleasing or meaningless. In this epoch must have originated and evolved various types of ornament such as necklaces, scarification and painting of the human body. Charms, amulets, scars, etc., placed upon the body gave one strength and protection, insuring "proper" survival. Along with these would occur the "decoration" of other objects—shells, stone, bone, wood, etc. Thus we advance the theory that the birth and formation of the first epoch of art consisted of that kind commonly misunderstood as "decorative" or "ornamental." In other words, this first stage consisted largely

63

9. Aboriginal Australians with bodies decorated for a ceremony. After photograph taken by Spencer and Gillen for *Native Tribes of Central Australia*. Courtesy of Macmillan and Co., Ltd., London.

of invented symbols which man created as magic protection. In contrast to the next stage of culture, where man employed largely Mimetic magic ("objective") symbols for his survival, the first stage consisted largely of invented ("subjective") symbols.

Things that man invented, such as those called "ornament"—necklaces, bracelets, etc.—and "decoration"—such as painting or scarification of bodies or objects with non-representational material—and clothing, pottery, monuments, etc., all had very specific, and important meanings of a magic nature in early civilizations. But as the original meanings have vanished until most of them are completely lost, we have come to assume, especially today, that the majority of such inventions served simply to please human vision. But, as Lévy-Bruhl has written: "It is the same with clothing as with food: the mystic element plays an important part, and in certain cases preponderates over utilitarian considerations. Many 'savage' tribes, before coming into contact with white men, wore no garments of any kind, but there were none among whom there were no adornments: feathers, beads, tattoo marks, painting, and the like. Now, as we know, these adornments are not mainly, nor solely, decorative. They have a mystic character, and possess magic power. The eagle's feather assures him who wears it the strength, piercing sight and wisdom of the bird, and it is the same with other things." [24] The attitude implicit in Lévy-Bruhl's remarks will help us greatly to formulate a more basic comprehension of this early period of art.

In this "Decorative" period the linear forms of art must have occupied the dominant place. However, once the animal recording stage was reached, it was the sculptural medium which took over the leading role, because, as we have pointed out, with sculpture there was a similarity in structure to the objects being recorded; hence it was more readily possible to achieve a high degree of accuracy.

The Aborigines of Australia represent a culture such as one would expect to see between the "Decorative" and the animal recording stage of art. Here we find painting predominates in nearly all the tribes and is found everywhere, whereas sculpture is rare aside from the manufacture of tools and weapons.[25]

24. Lévy-Bruhl, *How Natives Think*, p. 297.

25. See D. S. Davidson: "A Preliminary Consideration of Aboriginal Australian Decorative Art," *Memoirs of the American Philosophical Society*, IX, 1937.

In such a "Decorative" period every family must make their own "art" and so each man and woman was an artist. As D. S. Davidson says of the Australian Primitive: "Hence, in a general way each and every family must not only provide its own food but manufacture its own weapons and tools and *decorate its own possessions."* (emphasis ours)[26] Thus in the earliest cultures nearly all were artists, just as in the ontogenetic history of us all. Gradually, however, as art developed it became more and more specialized, the product of fewer individuals.

We can now, perhaps, posit the following similarities and differences involved in the genesis of the two main art mediums:

(1) The line offers the simplest and most direct possibility for man's discovery of a medium and invention of a method of art. Following upon the invention and arrangements of lines, came the Inventive arrangement of "ready-made" stone forms found in nature. In the first phase of Mimetic art, the linear medium occupied the dominant role, sculpture being limited in its Mimetic activity to the imitation of geometric stones. But if the line was a direct invention, the material on which it was made was not, since it was ready-made by nature; whereas the first stone forms that were used were not invented, but were ready-made; what was invented here was the use to which they were put and the organizations into which they were placed for magical functions. In this period of so-called "Decorative" art, which functioned as the earliest magic of man, *the major activity was primarily Inventive, the minor Mimetic.*
(2) In the next epoch, art activity was primarily representational, particularly of the animal, but also of the human form. Now the sculptural medium occupied the dominant role since it offered the simplest and most direct path for achieving the goal of the times, the representation of animals. For this reason a high degree of development in representing the animal in art was achieved with the sculptural medium long before it was reached with the linear. While the line was easy to invent and manipulate in the technical sense, it was far more difficult to develop for representational purposes. On the other hand, the advanced stage of sculpture in which stones are carved (not merely manipulated into arrangements of "ready-mades" or simply engraved or painted), was considerably more difficult to invent and manipulate technically; yet it became the simplest to develop once the primary object of art was to record the animal form. In other words, linear art began with a line and largely remained in the simple stage of lines until later Paleolithic times (Aurignacian); for linear art, though simple to make in the technical sense, was fraught with the tremendous problem of *representing actual forms without the use of any actual forms.* As for sculpture, the great difficulty was to invent and perfect a method for carving forms in hard, resistant materials. There is of course the probability that these early artists worked considerably in clay or wood, a few examples of which have survived. The great advantage of the sculptor, however, was that he was able to work with forms in the effort to make forms; whereas the linear artist had to learn to "make" forms without using any at all. Finally, we note that linear art began with the direct act of *invention* while sculptural art began with the direct act of *recording* nature.

The earliest manifestation of the linear arts was the single line; subsequently arrangements of many lines appeared (see figure 10), from simple to ever more complex organizations as man progressed. It probably took thousands of years, from the time man first discovered that he could invent lines, before he developed these arrangements and combinations to the point where he realized he could use them to depict animate objects.

Thus the linear artist began by putting lines together, producing groups or arrangements of them which were at first the result of invention. In the process he must have come to attribute to them

26. Ibid., p. 4.

10. So-called Macaroni, copied in clay after G. B. Brown (see biblio. No. 49).

symbolic meanings, even before he discovered that they could be converted to *representational* functions and meanings. Eventually he made the great discovery that lines could be so arranged, *put into such an order* that the result had the appearance of inanimate and, much later, animate objects. M. C. Burkitt has written of the beginnings of linear art: "The first manifestation of engraving art is the so-called 'Macaroni.' This consists of a series of more or less parallel sinuous lines. They were probably made at first with the fingers in clayey walls and later with an instrument on harder surfaces. Their meaning is of course quite unknown. Following on these and not far different in age come the first simple animal figures."[27]

It will be noted that Burkitt says the "Macaroni" lines are not far different in age from those of the first animal figures. This could have been due to the persistence of the former because of magical significance that had come to be attributed to them over thousands of years. To comprehend this we must realize Primitive man's intense surprise and delight in this newly found ability to make lines, and the solemnity of their significance for him. We must also realize that he attributed meanings to all his actions, that everything was alive, in that he did not recognize the inanimate, death, and the like as we do. This was especially true in the extremely important function of art, since it was his principal contact with the great, powerful forces that animated the natural world about him. For with it he built a language that became his principal tool for manipulating and communicating with the world of the occult, the only world he knew.

These first artists experienced reactions not encrusted with thousands of years of canalization as to what IS art (e.g., art IS the copy of nature-appearances or it IS NOT art), and thus when they first produced lines and then arrangements of them, they were able to respond directly, and hence experience a conscious awareness of distinct emotional reactions.

27. M. C. Burkitt: *Prehistory,* p. 210, Cambridge University Press, 1925.

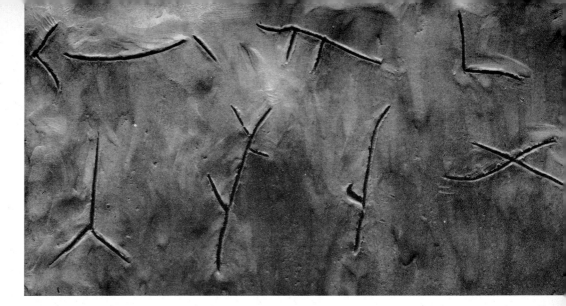

11. So-called enigmatical signs on cave walls at Altamira. After G. B. Brown (see biblio. No. 49).

Granting that these "Macaroni" lines were given magical meanings, the important ones would be retained, even after the new symbology of animal representation was already in the process of being developed. Here again there was no complete break between the old and the new; one overlapped into the other. The "Macaroni" lines symbolized "reality" in a far different manner than did the representational arts, in the sense that the latter could not symbolize the experiences of man in the same way that the non-representational lines did. Each supplied a method of symbolization not possible with the other, yet each supplemented the other. A more developed example of this will be found in later cultures—that is, the word-record as distinct from the picture-record. We shall go into the details of these symbolization problems in a later chapter.

Now specifically, what could lines as such represent for the earliest as well as subsequent Paleolithic cultures? First occurred the invention of line, the source of which would primarily originate from within rather than from without the organism of man, symbolizing the reaction of man to the world. Mimetic art, on the other hand, primarily originates in the world outside of man; that is, the *things* that man reacts to are recorded. For apparent reasons, each supplies a different channel of communication. As for Mimetic art, it begins with copies of otherwise natural lines; for example, those lines made by the scraping of great sheets of ice across the rock faces of the earth or the claw marks of animals, etc. These lines left on the surfaces of rocks would have had meanings in some way connected with man's observation of and reaction to their natural causes. Such powerful manifestations of natural forces would provide the impetus to magic beliefs, or meanings that these copied lines would have for man. In short, these stages are comparable to (but by no means identical with) the two stages, in later cultures, represented by highly abstract forms of word-writing on the one hand and picture-writing on the other. These two general kinds of symbols have continued to exist in some degree throughout all human culture. The one (Pictography) *predominantly* tells us how man *"SEES"* "reality"; the other (abstract writing) *predominantly* tells us how he *"THINKS"* about "reality." But since seeing and thinking are interdependent affairs that cannot be split apart, then we must comprehend them as *one* if we are to understand how man "see-thinks" reality.

Relevant is the following comment by George G. MacCurdy: "The inanimate world is represented by club-shaped and tent-shaped figures; by spirals, circles, chevrons, frets, volutes, wave ornaments, and alphabetiform signs, of which some at least were derived from animate objects through processes of conventionalization."[28] There is a long-standing controversy as to whether these line-symbols were derived from nature forms or invented directly. Baldwin Brown, concerning such signs in early Magdalenian times, writes that Abbé Breuil, "formerly regarded these conventional patterns of early Magdalenian origin as

28. MacCurdy, *The Coming of Man*, p. 60.

having been arrived at by a process of degeneration from drawings founded on nature, but as his knowledge of the history of Magdalenian art went deeper he had come to recognize the early origin and the independence of an irreducible stock of original geometrical designs, that existed and developed quite apart from the great naturalistic art of the caves."[29] In other words, it would seem that both theories are correct in different instances. As we have just explained, it seems quite reasonable to assume that in the earliest stages of art there were two kinds of lines, the one Mimetic (primarily symbols emanating from the "objective" world), the other Inventive (primarily symbols emanating from the "subjective" world), with possible overlappings. The former developed into the Pictographic or picture form of writing; the latter were the beginnings of the more modern or alphabetic kind of writing. Some of the symbols referred to in the above quotations are undoubtedly the result of the continued use in later Paleolithic times of early attempts to record inanimate nature and then the animate world. In any case both would naturally appear very "conventionalized," since they were highly generalized representations of nature. Some of these early symbols continued into the animal representational period because there probably existed no adequate substitutes for the meanings and functions they had acquired. Just as the non-representational symbol could not serve the function of a representational one, the latter could not replace the function of the former, and so both were retained (as they are to the present day). Also the early stages depicting the animate world were still practiced after more realism could be achieved because they offered a convenient form of "shorthand" Pictography and/or because of their "ancient" meanings. Moreover, it is probable that all these different kinds of symbols were gradually modified while others were dropped out and new ones added, and that this process went on right through the very realistic Magdalenian periods of art. It was these signs which were actually the inception (but not the realization, as some erroneously assume) of what was much later to become an alphabet.

Let us now briefly review the early stages of linear art, reduced to this general order:

(1) Man's discovery that he can invent a line and then organizations of lines.

(2) Man's copying of lines seen in "accidents" and other manifestations of nature, e.g., the straight lines resulting from the scraping of one hard surface against another; curved lines found in shells, etc.

(3) Man's realization that he could invent his own geometric shapes independent of natural shapes.

(4) Man's discovery of, then the copying of, geometric shapes seen in nature. These four stages would deal with a form of orientation built around a world dominated by occult forces.

(5) The next step would begin the transition from the predominant concern with the inanimate to the higher forms of animate existence. In the accidental occurrences of the natural world some rock surfaces were scratched in such a way as to resemble animals in general. There are very surprising accidents of this kind, so lifelike that merely a detail need be added here and there to make them complete, which is precisely what the Paleolithic artist did. But these very realistic accidents were probably not seen until man was able to see them; until then more simple types of accidents were discovered and noted by his eye-brain. Also collections of lines or shapes resembling recognizable objects could have been accidentally produced during the non-representational periods of art, particularly in stages 3 and 4.

(6) When these were later recognized, man found that he himself could depict the animal and human forms and need not depend upon accidents either of nature or those that occurred in earlier art activities. The preliminary attempts probably appeared little different from the so-called accidental type; there would then follow a transition from geometric or formalized to organic or particularized types of recordings.

29. G. B. Brown: *The Art of the Cave Dweller*, p. 192, John Murray, London, 1928.

In his excellent study of Paleolithic man, R. R. Schmidt speaks of the artist's experiments with the so-called "Macaroni" lines.[30] He points out how the artist must have recognized accidental resemblances which occurred in them, such as in Schmidt's example (set figure 12, left). These lines, he says, were recognized as the back of an animal, to which the artist simply added a few strokes to represent the legs in order to complete the animal. In this way he suggests that the imitation of nature was born. But, as we have just discussed the problem, we believe that man began imitating the "appearances" of inanimate nature long before he copied animals. If we are correct, then it is possible that by the time artists reached the Mimetic animate stage, the activity of copying was already a familiar experience. Hence, what would be discovered in these accidents would not be the notion of copying, but rather the possibility that a new subject could be copied. Furthermore, we would expect first a more geometric series of depictions of the objective world (somewhat similar to the evolution we find in children's art in which there are various stages from the line to lines). This would be followed by an attempt to produce shapes which gradually evolved into various stages of geometric arrangements of lines and shapes, such as we posited as the "Decorative" stage of art. These lines and shapes are eventually converted to representational devices (as occurs in the case of children's art).

The Australian Aborigines represent one of the more primitive cultures that has been investigated. The art of these people would seem to be analogous to early stages in children's art; that is, geometric arrangements of lines and shapes and the first beginnings of conversion to the higher forms of representational subjects.

An example of how geometric arrangements could be directly converted into representational devices is illustrated by the following: in his *Ancient Hunters,* W. J. Sollas shows a reproduction of an aboriginal Australian work of art (see his figure 152). Here we see representations of (a) trees, (b) men dancing around the trees, (c) the sticks which are beaten together in order to keep the time of the dance.

(a) is thus [figure] (b) by the addition of two rows of small circles, [figure] (c) simply [figure].[31]

In other words, the first stages of conversion of geometric lines into higher forms of representational functions would be more or less like the ground plan symbols of Architects.

The next step after "ground plan symbols" must have been some sort of effort to depict an object in elevation. The so-called "enigmatical signs" on cave walls, such as those reproduced (figure 11) from the cave at Altamira, could well be just this type. For example, the upper left marks could represent a horned animal—side-view of the body, top-view of the horns; the upper center marks could represent an animal or a bird—we can see head, body, legs; the upper right marks could be a seated figure or a bird in flight. All those made with crossed and vertical lines (bottom row) could be walking, dancing, standing (male), running human figures. For each of these signs we have suggested some of the many possible subjects that might be represented. We say "might be," because they have a good many representational possibilities. Some, if not all, might have been meant as non-representational signs. But some such attempts must have been made in the early stages of Mimetic activity.

A probable development subsequent to this may be seen in Schmidt's example already referred to (figure 12). Here we believe that the artist was attempting to reproduce the organic character of the animal with organic lines. Hence we would be inclined to consider it as no accident but rather a deliberate effort in which the artist was depicting a horned animal. The curved lines tangent to what is presumably the end of the head appear to be a top-view depiction of horns. The downward turn of the spine lines indicates the back legs while the front legs are attached underneath the beginning of the spine.

Figure 12 (from G. B. Brown) furnishes an example of what would comprise the next step—an effort to depict the shape or area of the animal's body, at first with somewhat geometric or conventionalized methods. Although we see here no further details beyond those in Schmidt's example (i.e., contour of

30. R. R. Schmidt: *The Dawn of the Human Mind,* p. 131.

31. As a matter of fact, these early attempts to depict more complex objects would appear not far different from early attempts to depict simpler visual phenomena which we posit for the Mimetic efforts in the first or "Decorative" stage of art, such as circles, chevrons, spirals, etc.

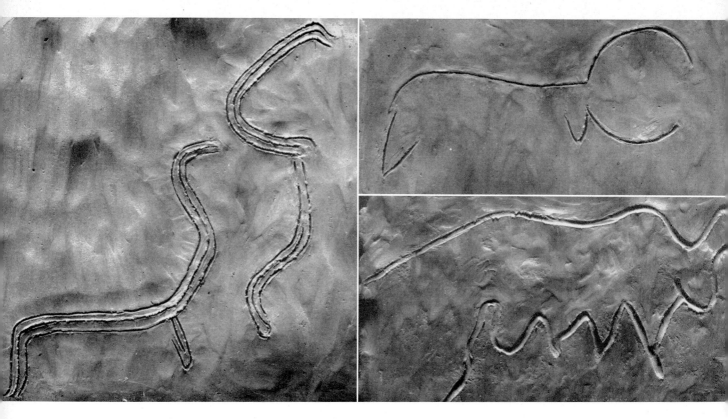

12. Left, colored lines, early Aurignacian period. Copied in clay after R. R. Schmidt, after Breuil (see biblio. No. 312). Above, right, finger drawing, early Aurignacian period. Copied in clay after G. B. Brown, after Count Begouen (see biblio. No. 49). Below right, early Aurignacian engraving from La Clothilde cave, Spain. Copied in clay after Pijoan, after del Rio and Breuil (see biblio. No. 270).

the back, front and rear legs and likewise the top-view of the antlers), nevertheless, in this case the *shape* rather than the outline is suggested, an advance over the mere single line drawing. A more advanced example of this stage might be such as that seen in the geometrically conventionalized female figure engraved on ivory (figure 13), in which the completed area of the linear shapes is finally achieved. It would appear that here the artist switched to a ground-plan view of the breasts, as the artists above did with the antlers, in order to avoid the difficulties of perspective or foreshortening.

In the next step we should expect to find an effort to depict the animal again with organic shapes, such as we see in the examples from La Clothilde (figures 12, 13). Here instead of an organic *single line* drawing, there has now been achieved the organic character of the *shape*.

In certain of the very early examples it is difficult to determine what specific animal is represented. It was only natural that the form in general of most animals, rather than particular or specific animals, was at first produced. Only after attempts to make the general form of animals, could the artist pass by gradual stages to the depiction of individual animals.

We have already discussed the fact that Pictographic artists first became adept in the recording of the animal with the sculptural medium, and that this form of representational art made the most rapid strides because it allowed the most direct (i.e., the shortest and least difficult) approach in man's initial attempts to familiarize himself with the particular problem of recording. In other words, it was easier to record the *form* than the *image* of an object. This experience with the "round" of nature pressed its influence upon the early efforts of linear artists to depict the animal. This can be seen in early simple drawings in which only the profile of the animal is indicated. By showing only the general outline of the form (actually a cross-section of the third dimension) the artist was using the most direct, primitive, linear method of indicating the *entire form*. As yet he had not hit upon the discovery that he could make the form by means of illusions. In the next step he tried to do this latter by lines crossing the area indicated by the outline. The next step probably consisted of painting the whole area in one color. After these

70

13. Left, early Aurignacian engraving on clay from La Clothilde cave, Spain. Copied in clay after Schmidt, after del Rio and Breuil (see biblio. No. 312). Right, female figure engraved on mammoth ivory, Predmost, Czechoslovakia. Copied in clay after Schmidt, after Absolon (see biblio. No. 312).

two-dimensional attempts to achieve form, artists returned to concentrate upon the line drawing again in the effort to secure a more satisfactory solution. Then the lines began to indicate, in increasing degrees, the form of the animal. Finally he discovered the device of shading, a more adequate solution than that supplied by his early attempt to represent the form.

According to Breuil, who scientifically established the chronology of the various two-dimensional arts of Pictographic times, the earliest examples show the animal only in profile, with two legs and the very simplest indications of contour. At first these were done in clay; later rock engravings appear. These latter are deeply incised and crudely cut with flint into the rock face. Of this early stage H. F. Osborn says: "That the powers of observation were only gradually trained is shown by the fact that details which in later drawings are well observed are here overlooked; . . ." [32]

In the second stage of line engraving, which is still deeply cut, there now appears a greater accuracy. All four legs are sometimes indicated, as well as the hooves, previously omitted. This develops until the incisions become less deep and more cleanly cut; details such as the hairy portions begin to appear. Burkitt points out that at this time natural form projections were used. The latter could be easily converted to represent some form aspect of an animal the artist wished to depict.

In the third stage the engravings become reduced in size and not as deeply cut. This is the high point in the development of the engraved type of art.

In the fourth stage engravings had declined as a medium of importance. This was due to the fact that the painting medium had now become highly developed, especially in the modelling of three-dimensional illusions with color, so that its use was far more desirable than that of engravings. Engravings of course are not a true linear medium, in that the incision method results in a relief technique and is

32. H. F. Osborn: *Men of the Old Stone Age,* p. 320, Charles Scribner's Sons, New York, 1915.

14. The La Gréze Bison, Aurignacian period. After photo by G. B. Brown (see biblio. No. 49).

actually a compromise between sculpture and painting. The development of linear art is definitely limited with this method, whereas painting, the direct method of linear art, permitted illusions of form. However, before such illusions could be achieved, painting also had to pass through many developmental stages, i.e., from line to form illusions.

Obermaier tells us that painting materials consisting of red and yellow ochre have been found in the oldest Mousterian deposits, but he is of the opinion that these were used only for decorating the human body.[33] Why, he does not say. We believe it is entirely possible that such coloring material may have had many other uses. The Photographic records which Spencer and Gillen secured of the art of the Australian Aborigines show that they not only decorate their bodies with scars, paint, bird and plant down of various colors and in various designs for ceremonial purposes, but also make large paintings on flat, smooth ground similar to those on the body, but far more complicated. While the culture of these Aborigines has been shown to be a mixture of many different stages, from Mousterian to Neolithic, so that an exact analogy cannot be made, nevertheless such practices do suggest the various uses of paint that could have been attempted in Mousterian times of which no traces would have survived (figures 9, 16, 17).

Regarding early efforts at painting, Burkitt writes: "Amongst the earliest paintings would seem also to be a species of 'Macaroni,' as in the case of the engravings. These are found at the La Pileta. . . ."[34] He also points out that there were, "In the beginning, simple black, red or yellow line or dot tracings; rarely representing anything recognizable."[35] Obermaier places among the "earliest manifestations," "Spiral tracings with the finger on clay. Hands silhouetted in red and black. Coarse rows of colored dots or discs."[36]

The fact that the "dot" appeared among these early symbols is of interest, since some Paleolithic paintings of the animal form were made by the dot method, which may have been a continuation of early dot practices. There is also the possibility that in some later cases when animals were to be depicted, they were first laid out with dots and then these were connected with a continuous line. In this connection also it is perhaps of some significance that the art of the Central Australians shown by Spencer and

33. Obermaier, op. cit., p. 211.   34. Burkitt, *Prehistory*, p. 210.   35. Ibid., p. 210.   36. Obermaier, op. cit., p. 237.

15. The Browsing Reindeer, from Limeuil at St. Germain, Magdalenian period. After photo by G. B. Brown (see biblio. No. 49).

Gillen indicates that often entire surfaces of objects will be decorated in circles or zig-zags by the use only of dots, simply by leaving openings to indicate such designs.[37] In other instances "decoration" will consist only of dots covering all of a certain part of the body.[38] In such as the latter there is not so much an attempt to make a design as to produce simply a dotted area.

In this connection, observation of the Pictographic arts seems to indicate that the fingers were the first *principal* engraving tool; that is, they were drawn through the clay. Similarly the index finger was probably the first painting tool. Fingers were the most simple, direct, and familiar tools available. In engraving the next development would consist in the use of a tool made of flint, and in the paint medium, a brush of some kind replaced the finger. Spencer and Gillen report that the Aborigines they studied make a brush by cutting off one end of a twig and then chewing it into a brush-like affair. They also grind their pigments by first chewing them.

It is easy to understand why hand silhouettes should appear among the earliest manifestations of animate painting. Hand prints could have first been suggested to Pictographic man when he observed the impressions left by his hand on a clay wall or floor. The human hand was the first animate object to be recorded with paint, not only because of the ease with which it could be done, but also because of its great importance. Its impress was probably considered the same as the actual hand. Another source of the hand print might have been the accidental prints made by the hunter's hand while it was covered with the blood of an animal during the slaughtering process. Think in magic terms of the significance of this hand print, made with the blood of the important animal!

These prints, where the hand was used both as a stencil and printing block, have been found in numerous Paleolithic sites. There are also a good many reports of hand-paintings among extant Primitive tribes. For example in the following we find that, "the tribes of Yucatan have the custom of printing the impress of the human hand, dipped in a red-colored liquid, in the walls of certain sacred edifices. . . .

". . . on Australian pictographs . . . 'In very many places there are representations of a human hand imprinted or delineated upon the rocks or in caverns . . . The representations of hands are made in two ways. In one the hand is smeared with red ocher and water, and impressed upon the rock surface.

37. See Baldwin Spencer and F. J. Gillen: *The Northern Tribes of Central Australia,* plate 11, London, 1904.
38. See ibid., figure 57, p. 201.

16. Aboriginal Australian ceremonial ground drawing and performers. After photographs taken by Spencer and Gillen (see biblio. No. 323). Courtesy of Macmillan and Co., Ltd., London.

In the other the hand, being placed upon the rock, a mouthful of red ocher or pipe-clay and water is squirted over it. The hand being then removed there remains its representation surrounded and marked out by the colored wash.' " [39]

We shall have more to say about the significance of these hand silhouettes presently.

It is to be expected that painted "Macaroni" passed through an evolution similar to that already described for the engraved examples of "Macaroni." Hence the next stage is seen in the simple, early attempts to depict the outline of animals. Following this stage the art became more accurate, more details, showing more than the mere contour were added, and shading was begun. Towards the close of this phase both engraving and painting were employed in the individual work. Another technique found in this period, according to Obermaier, was that of "interrupted grouped lines, or of continuous rows of dots" in the formation of animal recordings; after this shading appears.[40]

The next stage in which contours are filled in entirely with one color is considered by most investigators to be a regression. But according to Burkitt some of these paintings possibly date from the first stage of what, in his arrangement, is the latter part of "Phase I." [41] If this is true, this type of painting makes sense, at least in those cases where it preceded any attempts at shading the animal form. By this means, as we have previously suggested, the artist was actually making a preliminary effort to indicate the entire surface area of the three-dimensional animal, just as later the Egyptian placed a single color over his figures in sculpture and painting. This effort would appear to be similar to those early stages of outline drawing or engraving which we evaluated as the artist's attempt to show the entire form of the animal by drawing its outline only. We should keep constantly in mind that linear artists were predominantly governed in their efforts by tactile orientations; the earlier the art the more dominant the tactile factor. Therefore in the early stages of the attempt to show a *round* object on a *flat* surface, the

39. Garrick Mallery: *Picture-Writing of the American Indians*, p. 712, 10th Annual Report of the Bureau of Ethnology (1888-1889), Washington, 1893.

40. Obermaier, op. cit., p. 238.   41. Burkitt, *The Old Stone Age*, p. 188.

17. Aboriginal Australians preparing a ground drawing in connection with a black-snake totem ceremony. After photographs taken by Spencer and Gillen (see biblio. No. 323). Courtesy of Macmillan and Co., Ltd., London.

artist quite naturally attempted to draw the form of the object by surrounding it with an outline—not merely indicating the "outline" of the object. He did the nearest thing he could do to showing the *form* of the object by cutting out its contour with his finger in the clay or painting the contour with his finger. Perhaps the next stage for the engraved outline, the cross-hatching of the interior, gives an even better parallel to the painter's attempt to indicate the animal as-a-whole by filling in the outline with a single, all-over wash of color. The immediate result in both cases was to distinguish the animal from the surrounding areas as well as to indicate the animal as-a-whole. But this technique of an over-all wash made it possible also to take advantage of some accidental effects, since the wall on which the painting was made was very rough and thus lent itself readily to accidental suggestions of form. This must have helped the artist to discover that he could produce an illusion of form in his linear art by modulating the entire over-all color. Thus we would account for the function of the all-over wash in the early stages of representational art.

Now according to the findings of those who have scientifically ascertained the chronology of Paleolithic art, these flat wash paintings occur also after the shading of the animal form begins. We suggest three possible reasons: (1) This type of art could have been continued into times when more developed forms of art were achieved, just as the dotted or "punctuation style" extends from Aurignacian to Magdalenian times, because of a reluctance to discontinue magical powers "known" to have been possessed by the older art forms. (2) It may be that every now and then, as throughout all history, there was a tendency to revert to older forms of behavior during times of crisis, in the hope of reviving prosperity that was presumed to have existed or actually did exist in the past. (3) The all-over color wash could be an attempt to pass from mere shading (i.e., production of form illusion) to the achievement of the over-all *color* of the animal. Then it was possible to begin the development of the complexity of shading-color effects until eventually the climax of late Magdalenian polychrome painting was achieved.

In any culture we must look for the simplest, most direct approach to the solution of a problem, the line of least resistance. This was the way man could utilize most fully the natural order of development. It is from this point of view that the one-color, all-over wash painting appears as the natural transition to the more extensive polychromatic period. In short, the artist first indicated the *whole general form* of the animal with a *single color* and later, by gradual stages, was able to modify it more and more in order to record the various *particular color-forms within the general form*. The artist learns to modulate light and shade first, then color as light and shade.

Finally when polychrome painting reached the height of its Paleolithic development, it assumed the major role in art. The more powerful, more complete recording by color-modelling now took command in the quest for ever more accurate representation of nature. In its development we observed the progression from line to shading, then flat color wash to color-form modelling, i.e., a progression from monochrome to biochrome and finally polychrome. Thus there was a definite development, entailing definite relationships between the qualitative and quantitative factors, first in the rise of sculpture, then of engraving and finally of painting. Each medium rose in quantity and quality and then receded in both aspects as the next medium or art method rose to dominance over the others.

In the depiction of animals, sculpture matured much sooner than the linear medium, as has been shown; but the former did not exert any considerable influence upon the latter until the linear artist had begun to make the effort to depict the third dimension on a flat surface; in other words, when the painters became "sculptors" (if we can stretch the meanings of words for the moment), they were able to learn from the sculptors' methods. Thus while linear art was probably invented before sculpture and was a guide for it until the animal recording stage of art was reached, nevertheless, hereafter the situation was reversed. As we have explained, the linear artist's approach to recording animals was a tactile one imposed by the dominance of the sculptural art. What the linear artist then tried to accomplish in his medium was to make more perfect "sculpture" or tactile depictions of animals and to this superiority was attributed superior, magic power; hence they were probably considered more desirable than sculptural products. However, the majority of Pictographic works so far discovered are actually a compromise between sculpture and painting; they are engravings or "reliefs." But most of these compromises favor the linear rather than the sculptural medium. Since wood was quite probably employed for sculptural purposes, it may be that the majority of Paleolithic sculpture has disappeared forever.

We have thus traced the development of two-dimensional art to the point where a developed art of painting dominates the scene. The evolution has been from engraving, to combinations of outline engravings and paintings. There was a progression from shading to silhouettes, biochromes and at last polychromes, so that finally the animal is modelled in three-dimensional illusions with various colors. Throughout, one can trace a general transition from the less flexible and harder materials of clay, wood, bone and stone engraving to the more flexible material of painting. The two-dimensional medium has emerged from the early, simple cross-section engravings of animals to the much more complex, three-dimensional illusions of painting. MAN HAS NOW BECOME A PAINTER! in the sense that we understand the term today.

It was an achievement of no small proportions when man discovered a method for recording forms on a flat surface, for he had no previous experience and no knowledge to inherit from previous artists. To appreciate this achievement it is also necessary to realize that he had to comprehend the notion of making forms appear on a flat surface *without actually producing any forms at all*. In this situation another difficulty had to be overcome, in that the tactile sense could no longer be *literally* employed to assist the artist in realizing forms, as it could be in the sculptural medium. Hence, greater visual acuity was demanded of the painter than had been achieved by the sculptor. These Pictographic painters achieved the first great step in recording not the object but the *image* of the object! Backgrounds, perspective, motion, foreshortening devices were experimented with, but it took thousands of years more before these aspects of image-recording were successfully accomplished.

It will help us to comprehend the subtle transformations through which man's "visual" activity continued to develop, if we understand that although the *physio*-tactile element was eliminated in linear art (especially in the case of painting as distinct from engraving), nevertheless a *psycho*-tactile influence remained. This influence, in fact, predominated (but less and less the more art was developed), as the determinant for the laws governing visual recording on a flat surface until the 15th century A.D., when man's efforts at linear art came to be substantially dominated by the visual-image. It is this psycho-tactile influence that explains the *contours decoupés,* of which Spearing wrote.[42] He also relates an interesting incident bearing on this problem: "A friend tells me that a very small girl, for whom he had drawn a picture of a bird in profile, immediately asked why it had only one eye. He tried to explain, but he could not satisfy her. Finally she seized the pencil, turned the paper around and gave the bird its other eye on the back of the drawing."[43] This child treated the problem of visual-image recording as if it were actually a problem of "sculpting" the object—a problem of dealing with an object comprised of forms. Perhaps it would be more correct to say that such orientations are a combination, or a confusion of both the image and the object.

The author observed another instance, quite a different kind, of the influence of the tactile upon the visual problem of recording. A six-year old girl, when shown a drawing of a table depicted in correct perspective, looked at it a few seconds, and then picking it up and standing it vertically on the drawing table exclaimed, "Yes, *now* it looks like a table!"

In Pictographic art, then, the transition from sculpture to painting, from the making of actual forms to the making of illusions of those forms, meant that the new art could be made and experienced only on the actual visual level, since the physio-tactile factor had been completely eliminated.

But if the Pictographic artist did not develop sculpture beyond a certain point, how could he have developed the more difficult linear medium to such an extent that it came to replace the three-dimensional one? Actually only a certain degree of development was accomplished in painting also. As the sculpture of these times did not reach the perfection of later times, e.g., Roman sculpture, so painting did not reach the perfection, for example, of the Renaissance. Compare any sculpture or painting done in Paleolithic times with works of later cultures, and it will be seen that the Pictographic artist had by no means exhausted either medium in its potentialities for achieving accurate recording. This was of course inevitable since the human "visual" receptors were likewise in an early stage of development. The sculptural medium, like the painting, was developed, not as far as possible, but as far as it could be under the particular visual limitations of the early artists.

The Pictographic painter could supersede the sculptor largely because of the factor of color and the apparent advantages of illusionary methods of producing form. Once painting reached a stage of development where it offered advantages not to be secured in sculpture, the development of the latter was neglected.

Perhaps the most important factor that made painting achieve dominance was precisely its lack of *actual* dimensions. Once painters were able to create illusions of the third dimension, the very fact that one could make form where no form existed may have given it a superior magical significance and power. One can well imagine that the realization of forms (i.e., illusions of forms) on a relatively flat surface, which heretofore had only been done in actual sculptured form, compelled men to look upon this achievement in the linear medium as having even greater magical powers than the sculptural one. (In fact many a layman today is awed by the painter's ability to make forms appear on a surface that is perfectly flat!)

It is also of great importance that once linear art reached sufficient development, it became a more suitable medium for recording objects such as the hairy form of the animal (the most important subject of the Paleolithic artist), as compared to the solid, more or less smooth effect that one is restricted to in sculpturing; this medium is actually more suited to representing the smooth surface of the human form.

Thus although painting superseded sculpture in those respects which were the particular advantages of the linear medium, nevertheless, it was not yet possible to carry even painting to the end of its potentialities. In fact, the usefulness of both sculptural and painting mediums in depicting both the animal and human forms was not exhausted until thousands of years later. A factor that certainly put an end to the development of animal painting beyond the stage it reached in Paleolithic times, was

42. See p. 62 where we quote Spearing on this matter.

43. H. G. Spearing: *The Childhood of Art,* p. 57, Kegan Paul, Trench, Trubner and Co., Ltd., London, 1912. By permission of Ernest Benn, Ltd.

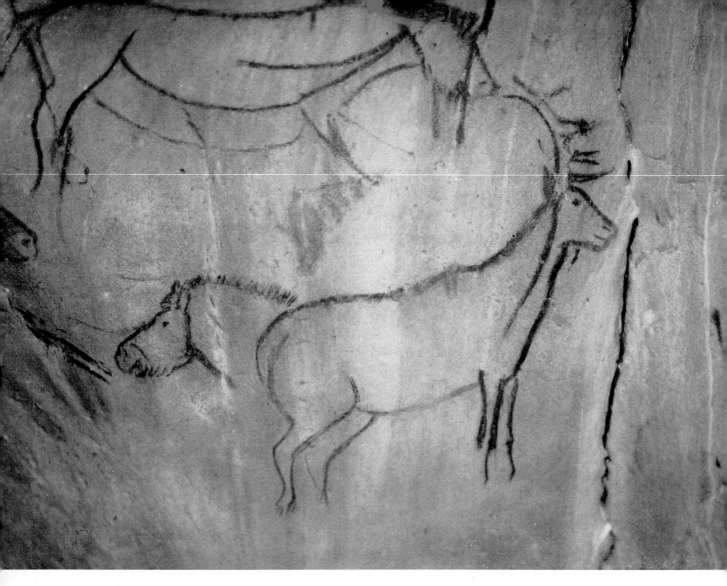

18. Cave drawings, Niaux, France, late Magdalenian period. Courtesy, Chicago Natural History Museum.

the climate change brought about by the recession of the last glacier and hence the great change in the environment. This naturally created an upheaval in the art-magic.

We have already discussed the theory that the art of Pictographic man served the vital function of magic. There are writers who dispute this theory and maintain that the true purpose of most, if not all, of Pictographic art was "disinterested activity," "art for art's sake," merely "decorative," and the like. Thus according to G. B. Brown, Grosse maintains that the "aesthetic" or "artistic" activity of this early period was not "entered upon as a means toward an end"; and Yrjö asserts that if this art served a "utilitarian, non-aesthetic" purpose it must not be considered a "genuine work of art." For "True art has its one end in itself, and rejects every extraneous purpose. . . ." [44]

After reading the contentions of those who hold to this view, one is impressed with the fact that "art for art's sake" enthusiasts of Paleolithic works are more concerned to produce a theory of meaningless art than to unearth what meanings such art served. Let us be clear on this point: there is nothing in the entire history of art that is not "entered upon as a means toward an end." It is quite impossible that this should be otherwise; there is no such thing as "art for art's sake," in the beginnings of art or at any other time since. Such a phrase posits a meaningless art and is as non-sensical as if we

44. G. B. Brown: *The Art of the Cave Dweller*, p. 140.

78

19. Cave drawings, Niaux, France, late Magdalenian period. Courtesy, Chicago Natural History Museum.

were to say that man manufactures "electricity for electricity's sake"! "To be is to be related"! Even a glacier scraping lines on a rock as it moves along its course produces lines of meanings—ask the geologist. Are we to assume that such a complex structure as the human nervous system produces meaningless lines? On the contrary, we maintain that all art has some purpose, is in some way functionally related to everything that man does. It is impossible to avoid this, even should the artist try. This is just as true of Paleolithic man's art as it is of the art of any other culture. As a matter of fact, there is so much evidence of the magic function of this earliest art that it seems incredible that anyone should have denied it. If any art, no matter what kind, appears meaningless to us, this is not proof of its being meaningless, but only that we are ignorant of its meanings! Writers who doubt that Paleolithic man's art was made for purposes of magic seem to have no reason for doing so except that they prefer their art to come that way. Paleolithic man, however, was forced to live in a practical world; and we use the word "practical" advisedly.

During Paleolithic times, as we have already pointed out, humans largely depended at first upon food gathering and later mainly upon hunting for their existence. Especially in the latter period, of which we possess many remains, we would expect to find their magic beliefs and art based predominantly upon the great importance of the animals in their lives. And in painting, as in sculpture, we find the animal predominating as subject-matter.

79

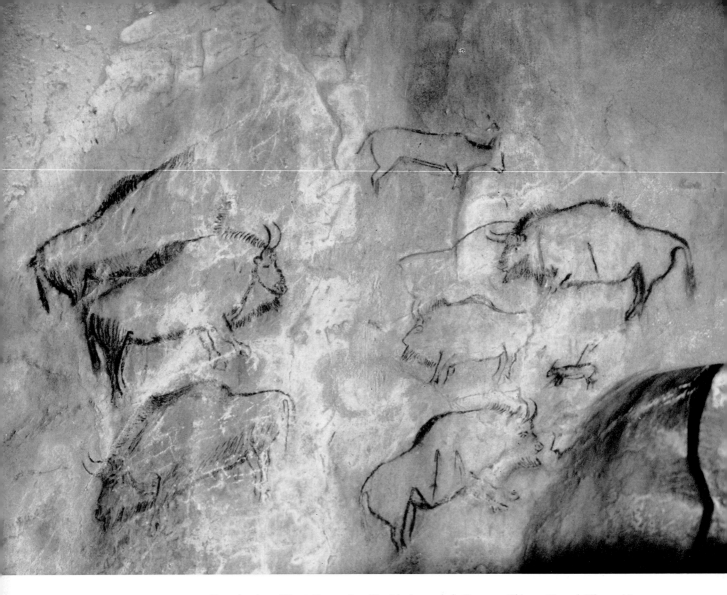

20. Cave drawings, Niaux, France, late Magdalenian period. Courtesy, Chicago Natural History Museum.

Frazer says in *The Golden Bough* [45] that the Primitive's worship of animals falls into two general classes: those which are neither killed nor eaten and those which are killed and eaten. The former class is depicted to secure protection from or derive some sort of assistance from the animal: the latter class to insure a food supply.

An example of the former class of depictions would be those animal forms (which may well represent the totemic protection of the tribe to which the hunter belonged) sculptured on one end of the hunting tools, such as harpoons. This presumably gave the harpoon a magic power so that its user was assured of being able to capture what he hunted. Similarly, "batons" may be predecessors of the totem pole. There is a good deal of evidence that sculptural and linear depictions were used in symbolic ceremonies of the hunt.[46] The effigy of the animal was made in clay, drawn on the ground or painted on the wall. The clay effigy was shot with darts or whatever instrument was generally employed in the

45. J. G. Frazer: *The Golden Bough,* p. 532.

46. See Norbert Casteret: *Ten Years under the Earth,* pp. 15 and 18, translated by Barrows Mussey, The Greystone Press, New York, 1939; D. C. Fox: "Prehistoric Rock Pictures in Europe and Africa," p. 5, *Bulletin of the Museum of Modern Art,* Vol. 4, April, 1937; Leo Frobenius and D. C. Fox: *Prehistoric Rock Pictures in Europe and Africa,* pp. 22-23, The Museum of Modern Art, New York, 1937.

21. Cave drawings, Niaux, France, late Magdalenian period. Courtesy, Chicago Natural History Museum.

actual capture of the particular animal; the painted animal had darts or arrows painted on its side. After the animal had actually been captured, it would appear that it was often necessary to return to the effigy and render its "soul" or occult power harmless so that it could take no vengeance upon the hunters. This might have been done sometimes by destroying the image in its entirety or only in certain parts that were considered the key to its power of retaliation.

Clay models found in Paleolithic caves often indicate that they have been shot many times; some still have arrow heads in them, others show what might be mutilations, i.e., the head has been broken off.[47] Although this has been attributed to natural causes, it is possible that Pictographic man destroyed the head once the animal had actually been captured in order to render it harmless as far as its soul was concerned. For with the head removed it could no longer see or hear! Observation had indicated that such an operation upon the actual animal rendered its physical part harmless; the same operation

47. In this regard it is interesting to note that among the engraved arts of Africa, some types are found in which the contour of the animal is filled in with pock marks; it may be possible that this is a practice similar to one exercised with sculptural idols among recent or living African peoples. That is, they stick nails or pointed objects into the belly of the wooden sculpture in order to get the favors which the object can supply. Perhaps the engraved pock marks were made prior to each hunting expedition for a particular animal, thus insuring its capture by first capturing it symbolically. This technique is also in evidence in some of the Francocantabrian arts, but here the pock marks are dotted paint marks.

upon the art would render similar results upon the feared psychical or soul-object. This was necessary since the image of the animal was also *the* animal; art and reality were an identification. Therefore the soul of the animal would be captured in art, then the "physical" animal would be captured, and finally the soul would be rendered harmless in operations both upon the actual animal and upon the art. Such a practice would not necessarily have been confined to all animals; some were probably more feared than others and their attributes of occult power would vary accordingly.[48] This attitude towards the head would be comparable to the practice of not showing the features in sculpture of the human form. (In the Paleolithic painting-art of Africa, the head of the animal is frequently left blank within the contour, although the rest of the figure may be detailed. When we come to examine the art of south-eastern Spain we will find both the animal and human forms rendered, with rare exceptions, entirely in silhouette, few details if any being indicated.)

In some cases the hand silhouettes, already mentioned, seem to have been placed directly upon the animal's depiction to symbolize possession of or power over it. There are numerous reports from extant Primitive tribes indicating that these hand images are still utilized for similar purposes. Those investigators who have maintained that these hand silhouettes "in no sense can . . . . be considered as 'art,' in the strict sense of the word," [49] are involved in verbal definitions of "what *is* Art," and this in turn is bound to lead to difficulties in the proper evaluation of the significance of these phenomena. It seems most probable that the early artist was more concerned with the purpose and efficiency of his art-magic than with some obscure notion of "Art." He believed that by employing the actual hand to make a depiction of it, he thus achieved far greater magical potency. By the time these artists were able to depict animals they were quite capable of making "free-hand" depictions of hands, as they probably did in some cases. The Primitive's assumption that everything was bound together by the occult guided his decisions in the making of art, not any notion of "art for art's sake." What Obermaier, and others, are telling us is that *they* do not consider it art; but from the Paleolithic artist's point of view, hand prints were certainly nothing less than his other recordings. He was concerned with creating the best results for his *magic* activities. Among these activities, natural results, such as accidental resemblances in nature, were of the greatest importance. Hand prints were probably considered a similar phenomenon. In the Primitive's eyes, the important factor was that a natural object—the hand—"made" the print.

It is of interest to note that not all linear or sculptural recordings indicate that the animal has been symbolically wounded or captured. However, as Frazer points out, there are two classes of animal worship.[50] Hence there would be two corresponding classes of art: (1) dealing with the capture of the animal; (2) dealing with the propagation of the animal.

Depictions of the female, both animal and human, are far more common than those of the male. Some investigators believe this to be due to the fact that homage was paid to the female as the symbol of procreational activity. Such a theory seems reasonable (and has been observed among more recent Primitive peoples), in view of the fact that Paleolithic man had not yet learned to control the production of his food supply by means of the domestication of plants and animals. Since the human

---

48. The following from Frazer is relevant to this problem: "But after all the resurrection of dead game may have its inconveniences, and accordingly some hunters take steps to prevent it by hamstringing the animal so as to prevent it or its ghost from getting up and running away. This is the motive alleged for the practice by Koui hunters in Laos; they think that the spells which they utter in the chase may lose their magical virtue, and that the slaughtered animal may consequently come to life again and escape. To prevent that catastrophe they therefore hamstring the beast as soon as they have butchered it. When an Esquimau of Alaska has killed a fox, he carefully cuts the tendons of all the animal's legs in order to prevent the ghost from reanimating the body and walking about. [Certain African tribes remove the nerve from the end of the tusks when they have killed an elephant.] But hamstringing the carcass is not the only measure which the prudent savage adopts for the sake of disabling the ghost of his victim. In old days, when the Aino went out hunting and killed a fox first, they took care to tie its mouth up tightly in order to prevent the ghost of the animal from sallying forth and warning its fellows against the approach of the hunter. The Gilyaks of the Amoor River put out the eyes of the seals they have killed, lest the ghosts of the slain animals should know their slayers and avenge their death by spoiling the seal-hunt." (From J. G. Frazer: *The Golden Bough*, pp. 529-530. By permission of The Macmillan Company, publishers. Also see p. 230, "The Head Tabooed.")

49. Obermaier, *Fossil Man in Spain*, p. 234.   50. See p. 80.

female is the means of reproduction, and since there was in a sense no distinction between men and animals, and since animals are often men reincarnated, etc., the human female could also easily be considered as capable of increasing the animal supply through magical rites.

The belief that an image gave its maker control over the creature depicted helps account for the fact that Pictographic artists (except those in the Levant) made only a few images of humans; at any rate only a few recordings of the human form have been found. This scarcity of depictions of the human form can be partly accounted for by a study of beliefs among living Primitives, quite generally considered to be survivals from those of early man. Most Primitives today believe that if a person's likeness is mutilated, the result will be transmitted to that person's body. The Primitive fears, in other words, that a depiction of himself can be used to harm him. Hence we find numerous reports of his objection to being Photographed. Often he will run away from the Camera or shield his face, and some investigators have risked their lives insisting upon taking the Primitive's picture. Casteret explains this phenomenon very well: "By getting your portrait I acquire your double, in the magical sense of the word, and I am then able to bewitch you, and work all sorts of mischief upon you.

"Prehistoric men, who after all were the creators of magic, knew this perfectly well; and so they carefully avoided reproducing the human figure except under special circumstances, and then with elaborate precautions." [51]

This same author puts the depiction of humans into three classes "all characterized by evident intent never to show the face without deforming it." [52] In the first group are those which, though executed quite realistically, have no faces or but vaguely indicated ones: "all the thirty known Aurignacian statues are without face." [53] The second group is made up of those with the features exaggerated. "These, it seems, are men in masks. This explains the curious human profiles in certain caverns, characterized by enormous eyes, a nose like a beak or muzzle, and huge ears." [54] Casteret further points out that: "The mask among primitive peoples is seldom a plaything; it is used for ritual, war, or the chase. It is indispensable to the negro witch-doctor; with its help he assumes a frightful appearance which spreads dismay among the audience at his magic ceremonies and incantations." [55] In the third group are very "grotesque" figures, concerning which there was until recently doubt as to whether they were animal or human. Casteret says of them, "They are men masked and completely disguised." [56] Their bodies are camouflaged with various parts of different animals and a mask covers the face. Such figures are considered to be depictions of magicians;[57] through the animal disguise the magician not only takes on the courage and prowess attributed to the animal parts which cover him, but also gains protection from the harm that would undoubtedly come to him if his actual appearance alone were shown. Casteret describes such a figure in the following: "The most interesting picture of a prehistoric magician is that discovered by Count Begouen and his three sons in the cave of the Trois-Frères, near Saint-Girons (Ariège).

"The wizard, whose body is painted with ritual red and black, is shown dancing naked, but, as Count Begouen describes him, 'He has gloved his hands in the skin of a lion's paws, with sharp claws; he is hidden behind a mask with the beard of a bison, an eagle's beak, the eyes of an owl, a wolf's ears and a stag's antlers. He has fastened a horse-tail to the base of his spine. Thus he believes he has taken on all the magic power, all the physical qualities of the animals: the bravery of the lion, the sharp sight of the eagle by day and of the owl by night, the hearing of the wolf, the endurance of the bison, the speed of horse and stag.'

51. Norbert Casteret: *Ten Years under the Earth*, p. 58.

52. Ibid., p. 58.

53. Ibid., p. 59. There are only a few exceptions known to the author, an example of which we shall discuss later.

54. Ibid., p. 58.

55. Ibid., p. 60.

56. Ibid., p. 58.

57. Precisely such a magician was recorded in a drawing made of an Indian by George Catlin. See reproduction in his *Manners, Customs and Conditions of the North American Indians*, London, 1850.

22. Left, relief, male figure, so-called spear thrower of Laussel, Aurignacian period. Right, relief, Venus of Laussel. Photos on this and opposite page by courtesy of the family of Dr. Gaston Lalanne.

"This sorcerer is engraved and painted ten feet above the floor at the end of a hall 1625 feet from daylight. He has the place of honor in a natural amphitheater; ranged at his feet is a long procession of animals engraved on the rock: lions, tigers, reindeer, bison, bears, dziggetai, which are marked with wounds, arrows, clubs, in a word with all the paraphernalia of hunter's witchcraft. On the clay floor one may still see (now religiously preserved) the bare footprints of the men who once went through their ceremonies here.

"In the light of these relics we can reasonably imagine the arrival of the sorcerer. By the pale light of a stone lamp, its moss wick dipped in animal fat, he would come to the sanctuary in his frightful disguise, and perform the mysterious rites of his religion.

"He attempts with his incantations and his spells scratched on the rock to draw to his tribe the good will of occult forces. He prays after his fashion that his people may be protected from tigers, from lions and bears, that they may never lack the meat of bison, horse and reindeer, that their warriors may triumph in combat and in the chase." [58]

It would appear that among the males only the magician could risk making an appearance before occult forces, since all male figures depicted with the linear medium wear magician-like disguises. It would seem that the male form, in the shape of the magician, symbolized protection from harm and assured success in hunting; in short he had to do with the survival of the living. The female form, in addition to her function of reincarnating animals, may have been an important symbol in beliefs about the "dead"; such symbols are known to be thus used in later cultures. The fact that woman gave birth to all human beings could easily have led to her being more directly related to the "dead," who were reincarnated and again born of woman; this belief also is common among living Primitives. That very early there existed a concern with the dead is evidenced by the careful burials which began to appear in Mousterian times. In any case, whether the human form was depicted in two or three dimensions,

58. Casteret, op. cit., pp. 60-61.

23. Relief, female figure, Laussel.

these early artists were extremely careful to disguise the face. Or else, in the case of the engraved male figure of the Aurignacian period, the head was broken off (figure 22). This latter may be a significant lead by which our problem will be answered; since the head is an important part of both animal and human forms, as previous observations have indicated, perhaps the only linear depictions of the human form to be made without disguises were for the purposes of destructive magic, a form of magic comparable to the well known practice among extant tribes of harming or killing another by doing precisely that to his image. Such works of art would thus have been "mobile" types; they could be destroyed in order to effectuate their magic function in a ceremony that might have often taken place away from the caves, thus accounting for the fact that so few human figures in the linear medium have been found. This might also account for the absence of sculptured male forms; they were probably destroyed in magic ceremonies.

Another point of interest is the fact that among the sculptured human forms in northern arts, it is mostly the female forms which are "protected" by the absence of facial features. There is a partial exception in the so-called Brassempouy female head (figure 24), in which the eye sockets and nose are indicated. Interestingly enough, here we have only the head—the body is missing; perhaps it was intentionally broken off. The problem may be just opposite to that of a male relief figure with the head missing; this relief (the "spear thrower" from the shelter of Laussel) seems to be the only undisguised male form, and it has no head. This seems to be further indicated by the Brassempouy headless female torso in ivory (figure 24). All this strongly suggests destructive magic as differentiated from the Willendorf female (figure 6) and other sculptures (figures 7, 22, 23) where the entire figure is present with the exception of facial features. This latter type probably had some positive magic function.

Further evidence that these Pictographic artists were not concerned with "art in itself," is to be found in the persistent superimposition of one drawing or painting over another; sometimes many animals are thus depicted. Apparently the main concern was to get the object depicted for some purpose other than art "for art's sake." It seems probable that superimposition was deliberate, that it was not

24. Brassempouy female head and Brassempouy headless female torso, Aurignacian period. Archives Photographiques: Paris.

done (as some writers contend) merely because it made no difference to the artist or for lack of space on the cave wall. Could it have been that the artist [59] was striving to increase the magical potency of his own animal depiction by tying it, so to speak, to the magic of the older ones, especially to those drawings that were thought to have proved very effective for their original author? It is difficult to believe that the Primitive artist would be so careless where magic is involved as to be totally unconcerned with the fact that he was placing his depiction upon older *magic*. If nothing was to be gained by superimposition, why do we find such practices even in places where there actually was space for new depictions? Sollas reports that the Bushmen would not dare to interfere with the polychromes of an artist so long as he was alive, nor for that matter even as long as his memory lasted.[60]

The arrangements of animals found within superimpositions would incline one to the theory that some deliberate purpose was involved. If these superimpositions had no relation to each other, why does each figure seem to fit with the other? For example, one figure will be drawn to such a size that it fits within the contour of another; the next figure will be drawn so that the hind quarters of another animal are utilized for it. In a number of other examples we find a reindeer partially superimposed upon a horse upside down. If all the superimpositions were scientifically investigated with the above assumption in mind, it might be possible to discover certain significant relationships. Perhaps, as was suggested, the practice of superimposing one drawing over another was the Pictographic artist's way of appropriating the magic of the older arts. This would seem especially probable in cases where some art object was thought to have produced very excellent results. It is similar to the fisherman who wants to fish where the other fellow is having better results.

59. At this stage of Pictographic art, we may speak of "the artist"—for now only specialists, not everyone, as in the Decorative stage, would have been producers of art. And the artist now was probably a tribal priest.

60. W. J. Sollas: *Ancient Hunters*, p. 480.

If any further evidence of the magical function of this art is needed, it may be pointed out that a great deal of the major works have been discovered hidden in "dark and remote recesses" of caves.

Burkitt and others have made clear that the caves were lived in only at or near the mouth or entrance, and that with rare exceptions the art is found far in the interior, frequently in places difficult to detect or reach. In fact, Obermaier points out that many of the engravings "are actually invisible and were designed by their makers for the eyes, not of men, but of the gods." [61]

Luquet advances a convincing argument for the theory that the art was not restricted to the deep interiors, and that it was a common practice to make art at the entrance to the cave.[62] Even if he is correct, however, this does not mean that the art made deep in the interior of the cave did not serve the magical function other writers attribute to it. If it was a common practice to put art at the entrance, this may have served a different magical purpose. We would suggest, for example, that the art placed at and within the entrance of the cave may have functioned as magic for the protection of the cave's occupants from animals that might attempt to enter. Obermaier says: "We must . . . . dismiss any idea that the purpose and character of these paintings are merely decorative, and this conclusion is further strengthened by the fact that in many cases they are limited to the remotest crannies and clefts, wrapped in utter darkness, and only to be found with the greatest pains." [63]

Now some authors, such as Luquet, are willing to admit that art served a magic function in the more developed forms of Paleolithic art, particularly the Magdalenian period, but prior to that time they assume that the function of art was "purely artistic" or "disinterested activity." [64] To support this contention they point out that in the art of the Aurignacian period there are no arrow heads piercing the animal and other such apparently magical manifestations as are found in Magdalenian art.

Luquet, however, has been willing to speak of the *gradual development* of man's *tools,* from the lower to the higher Paleolithic, and their relationship to the development of man's orientation to his existence. But he assumes that art has developed as a sort of meaningless pastime until the last phase of the Paleolithic period, when, according to him, the notion of magic suddenly pops into the picture to give the art some meaningful relation to men's lives.

It would appear that the error of those writers who oppose a magic function for part or all of Paleolithic art, is similar to the error commonly made in our times. Some of us are quite willing to speak of the invention and development of mechanical things in human history, but not of the development of the human beings that produced them. We are quite willing to speak of the development of nearly everything, even of man's cranial volume, but not of the use of that cranium. We need to remove this method of evaluation from our consideration of Paleolithic culture and magic, to recognize that magic must have an origin and development like anything else, since after all magic concerns the origin and development of the mentality of Paleolithic man. It is just as reasonable to speak of the invention and development of magic as it is to speak of the invention and development of tools and art; actually all three fields should be considered as an interdependent development in the beginnings of human culture. Thus the absence of certain indications of magic function from Aurignacian art would be due to the fact that magic, like tools and art, had to be developed by gradual stages before "perfection" was achieved. As in the early art and the early tools, so in early magic, factors are absent which will appear in later, more developed forms. Art, tools, magic developed as a oneness!

Even a cursory study of magic amply indicates that it was a vital, practical necessity for Primitive man's survival. We have pointed out already the terrifying and complex world he faced. He had not only to devise the very beginnings of art but of human knowledge as well. He had to inaugurate consciousness of the self and the world around man. This consciousness began with a world which repeatedly aroused questions—questions which brought with them an accompanying "emotional" impact: trees struck by lightning, floods, ice sheets, rain, the struggle between one animal and another; night and day; the mysterious process of women giving birth to their own kind and the equally mysterious

61. Obermaier, *Fossil Man in Spain*, p. 260.
62. G. H. Luquet: *The Art and Religion of Fossil Man,* translated by J. T. Russell, Jr., preface by G. G. MacCurdy, Yale University Press, New Haven, 1930.
63. Obermaier, op. cit., p. 260.
64. Luquet, op. cit., p. 113.

process of their kind being suddenly frozen in what we today call death. Imagine the tremendous problem earliest man faced regarding his need for knowledge of all these mysterious processes. Probably the first important product of man's dawning consciousness was a fear of so much that was unknown; hence the necessity of magic certainly existed with the beginning of man's consciousness.

Therefore it seems reasonable to assume that the needs for magic arose along with all other *human* needs and that it was begun and developed gradually along with tools and art, all as a oneness of orientation!

For earliest men the act of art creation, both non-representational and representational, was a momentous, magical experience, one which continued to be so throughout the Paleolithic period. The "ready-made" objects discovered in the accidents of nature were like a miracle for early as well as later men, and even more miraculous perhaps were his achievements of representations without the assistance of natural accidents. Early Paleolithic artists who discovered and began the development of representational art used natural formations that suggested objects they wished to represent. Later they learned that with a few cuts here and there they were able to increase and perfect the likeness to the original. The likeness found in the natural, ready-made object was not only of great magical import—here was an animal already magically made!—but it also served as a help to an artist who was at first unable to carve anything in its entirety. But the fact that the Magdalenian artist (who was otherwise well able to create an entire figure without the aid of a ready-made natural object to start with) still would often use such natural assistance, only tends to further substantiate the great importance attached to the miracle of natural formations suggesting animal objects. Hence, later artists were simply continuing the earlier practice because of the great magical import that had come to be attached to finding their subjects suggested in natural formations.

But even Luquet, who insists that Aurignacian art was a "disinterested activity," writes of children's art: "When they gradually arrive at the understanding that they have themselves also produced a resemblant drawing (or one so judged by their obliging imagination) it is to them the revelation of an ability at once creative and miraculous which, by these characters, partakes of magic." [65]

With all this in mind, imagine the terrific psychological impact of the function of magic, as it was experienced in the furthest depths of the cave interior. Imagine Pictographic man as he records his animals upon the wall. There before him, within the small circle of light from the lamp he holds in his hand, stands the completed image. How "real" it appears to the artist and his people: the rough surface of the cave wall catches the light in patches; the animal actually moves as light and shadow are thrown into movement each time the source of light is moved. But above all we must see the psychological effect of the image surrounded by the subtly blended circle of darkness, a pitch-black darkness, the darkness of the beginning out of which emerged the light of human knowledge; the darkness of the mysterious and omnipotent world of the occult surrounding the circle of light in which reposes the powerful image of a bison. The image within the circle of light, surrounded by the circle of darkness, was the only condition under which this particular art was ever seen! Thus through the light on the image Primitive man established a contact with occult forces. In such a way, by gradual stages, the fear of the "unknown" was conquered to an extent not possible in the beginning of human consciousness. By thus attempting to make the unknown known, the greatest fear of all was removed, the fear of that which cannot be comprehended. We can imagine the potent symbolical role which light played as a force in the magic beliefs of mankind.

When first discovered, the art of Paleolithic times was ridiculed to lengths that today seem fantastic; its authenticity was denied since it was thought that artists of such early times would have been incapable of such "realism." In recent years there has been an inclination among most "Prehistorians," artists and laymen to over-evaluate the realism of this art.

We are rightly impressed with the confidence with which Pictographic man was finally able to depict animals under the most difficult of conditions. But the boldness of his simple execution is so powerful that it tends to capture us in a hypnotic visual embrace. To such an extent is this the case that we are unconscious of replacing the actual reality characteristics of the animal portrayed with the

65. Ibid., p. 148.

particular degree or kind of "realism" indicated by the depictions of the artist. Under the "spell" of especially the most realistic examples, nature is identified with the art and so it appears as a miracle of recording accuracy. But nature, and *not* the art of *any* artist (as so many unconsciously assume), is the original source for securing a criterion of reality in art. Pictographic man did not develop his recordings of animals beyond a certain point. One need only observe animal sculpture or painting of later times to see this clearly. In every case the recordings of the early artists were over-simplified. Most of the linear works were confined to side-views of the subject; other points of observation were rarely tackled. Hence many characteristics were avoided or not realized at all.

Another factor of this problem should not be overlooked: most of the reproductions of Paleolithic art are far different from the originals. Very few seem to have been Photographed. The copies are made on smooth, machine-made paper, while the originals were made on a rough rock or clay surface. In some cases the forms of the animal were made up of actual forms that occurred in the natural wall or ceiling surface. G. Baldwin Brown has correctly remarked that "many scientific students may feel constrained to doubt, first, whether these twenty-thousand-years-old drawings can really be made out, and, secondly, whether the draughtsman, being human, has been able to keep himself from unconsciously completing, and a little beautifying, the representations." [66] While some of the copies may be what for want of a better word we call "improvements," comparison of copies with Photographs reveals that in many cases the copies are very inferior to the originals.

The "Prehistorian," whose visual art experiences are usually limited, tends to be extremely enthusiastic about the realism of Paleolithic art. Most people, in fact, who have little training in visual activity tend to consider many kinds of depictions realistic which are actually full of inaccuracies. This tendency among "Prehistorians" is probably also a part of a general tendency to over-evaluate the behavior of the Primitive (or the child, for that matter), when it is suddenly discovered that he can do considerably better than was expected of him.

M. C. Burkitt even goes so far as to propose the possibility of art schools, preliminary sketches as models, etc., in Paleolithic times: "It would seem unlikely that even the artist-medicine-man-priest should have been able so incredibly skilfully to paint the animals in the caves from memory only. Even if he had instruction as to the technique of his craft, the results are so surprisingly life-like—take for example the ceiling at Altamira where each bison has a character of its own, no two being alike in this respect—that it would seem reasonable to suggest the possibility that he first made sketches from nature and that these were afterwards used in the production of the cave drawings. The modern artist starting to-day on a big canvas will often make such a small sketch first. Some of the drawings found in the homes may be these sketches. As we have already noted, at Hornos de la Peña in north Spain, the engraving of a horse can be seen near the entrance; within a few yards of it in an Aurignacian deposit there was discovered an engraving on bone of the hind quarters of a horse amazingly similar in its lines to that engraved on the cave wall close by.

"Finally, as we have spoken much about schools for the artist, we must not omit to remember that at such places we might expect to find the practice 'slates' of the budding draughtsmen. These would be likely to take the form of pieces of bone or stone covered with attempts at engravings. It is significant that, while at a site like La Madeleine only finished products occur, at Les Eyzies there are any number of such crude attempts. Are we to consider that at the rock-shelter of Les Eyzies there used to be so many thousands of years ago a prototype of our artistic academies of to-day?" [67]

It is readily understandable why the non-artist would suppose that Paleolithc artists must have had sketches to work from in order to produce the results they did. But one suspects that such a supposition arises from a projection upon Paleolithic man of the behavior of present day artists and the greater demands that the copying of nature makes upon the latter. It seems extremely doubtful that such a method was ever needed or even occurred to Paleolithic artists. Like the child artist of today,[68] he

66. G. B. Brown: *The Art of the Cave Dweller*, p. 5.

67. Burkitt, *The Old Stone Age*, pp. 215-216.

68. See Helga Eng: *The Psychology of Children's Drawings*, p. 33, Harcourt, Brace, and Co., Inc., New York, 1931.

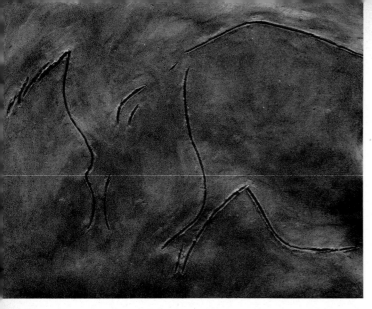

25. Two drawings of the hindquarters of horses, copied in clay
after Burkitt, after Breuil, from Hornos de la Peña
(see biblio. No. 57).

probably had more security if he relied on *visual memory,* than if he worked directly from nature. Working directly from the original model would have made more complex demands upon his ability than would the visual memory image, because the latter conveyed only what he was able to accomplish in his particular eye-brain stage of development. It may be that the eidetic ability is a probable answer to this problem. Moreover, considerable evidence has been collected by field workers to show the extraordinary visual memory among extant Primitives: his ability to find his way in the jungle and to map out large tracts of land from memory.[69] In fact, so strong is the visual factor with Primitive peoples that their language is principally an effort to picturize the subjects of conversation.

In any case it would seem more profitable to find out how living Primitives produce their art than to strive to see a parallel between the Paleolithic and present day artist. Burkitt's assumption that the artist drew a sketch from nature on a fragment of material and then copied the result on a wall, appears to be an incorrect inference. The two examples he gives we have reproduced together (figure 25) for comparison purposes. Our objection is this: both examples are from the very early phase of Aurignacian art when the engravings consisted of the outlines or profiles of the animal. And in all such art, especially where the same animal is concerned, there would inevitably occur a great similarity, since the style or stage of art is similar. In the same way, children at similar age levels produce works of art which *appear* very similar, especially to the layman. In other words, the Burkitt examples are easily taken for being very much alike. But in doing so, we mistake one drawing as a copy of the other, when actually there is only a great degree of similarity in the level of drawing ability of the artists concerned. Actually the differences between the two drawings are very great; for example, the one animal appears to be walking, the other to be standing still. But these differences may not be easily apparent, just as they are not in the case of children's art, unless one has developed the experience of seeing the *differences within similarities.*

Although it is true that if one were a copy of the other, they would naturally be in a similar style, nevertheless, drawings done in the same stage of art development by a number of different artists would appear just as similar also. It is for this reason that depictions of animals from France, Spain and Africa also appear to have been done by the same artist!

We think it more likely that the medicine-men-artists were individuals who gave some natural manifestation of their capabilities for this work.[70] Furthermore, the so-called sketches such as Burkitt and others have offered as examples might actually be the broken parts of some particular object (on the order of the "batons" for example) or they might have been made directly on broken materials or, (and this seems the most likely) deliberately broken for some special magic purpose.

That each of the bison "has a character of its own" on the Altamira ceiling does not show

69. See Lévy-Bruhl, *How Natives Think,* p. 109.

70. W. J. Sollas: *Ancient Hunters,* p. 152.

that the artist (or artists) captured the individual character of each bison; after all such a great difference as is observed in the art would not be likely in actual reality. This difference can be more reasonably explained by the inability of the artist (or artists) to do precisely what Burkitt assumes has been done. Moreover, it is possible to employ considerable variation in the drawing of animals, and, unless one is an acute observer, he is not apt to notice the lack of accuracy or correspondence to reality. There is, as a matter of fact, no better example of this than the Altamira ceiling. If instead of bisons, a great number of human figures had been painted by artists with the same degree of recording ability, we would be more likely to see the great discrepancy between reality and the art. The reason we make this error to a greater degree in the case of animals is that the human form is more important to us, hence we are more familiar with it and exercise greater discrimination. The reason the Paleolithic artist made this error was his lack of ability to observe and record the animal more accurately, even though it was of great importance to him.

G. Baldwin Brown goes to even further extremes in over-evaluating Paleolithic art. He credits Paleolithic artists with an attitude that had its inception with the Greeks: "Nature he dominated instead of bowing before her as her bondsman, and he presented before nature the typical forms she was to materialize at his bidding."[71] Here the Greek notion of the "ideal" is implicitly attributed to even Paleolithic artists. It would thus appear that practically all the arguments since the Greeks over the problem of art were unnecessary, since great art from the very beginning consisted of the imposition upon nature of some perfect ideal concocted by the omnipotent artist! Moreover, Brown goes even further: he claims that in the recumbent bison of Altamira, "everything is anticipated for which, after forty or fifty thousand years, the modern Impressionists are contending as an entire revolution in art." And, "the artist gives a more convincing appearance of movement than the camera."[72] Casteret also would have it that practically all 19th and 20th century revolutions in art were anticipated by artists of Paleolithic times. According to him, they invented Futurism, Pointillism, Cubism and the practice in general of distorting reality![73] And as though this were not enough, he insists that after achieving these "modernistic" inventions they proceeded to outdo the "Modernists" by having "the taste to go back at once to sane and natural representations of the animals of their times." When we have concluded our examination of Photography and art from Impressionism to Cubism, it will readily become apparent how utterly erroneous are those who contend that the Paleolithic artists not only anticipated but outdid both the Camera and all the innovators of "Modern art" as well. We shall find that their great error consisted in making too much out of slight or far-fetched similarities.

Such views among "Prehistorians" are usually encouraged by "authorities" in the art world today. Alfred Barr, for instance, claims that, "the art of the 20th century has already come under the influence of the great tradition of prehistoric mural art which began around the 200th century B. C."[74] From one point of view such remarks may appear impressive; however, in later discussions of the influence of Primitive art upon "Modern" art we shall make clear that these influences are actually more of a commentary upon the decadence rampant in the majority of art today than an explanation for a legitimate contents of 20th century art.

This attitude widely prevalent among artists and art critics today of extravagant, indiscriminate praise for Paleolithic art, is largely due to the fact that distortion of reality is now a general practice. Most artists have become so canalized to distorting reality that they no longer possess the visual acuity to detect the varying degrees of recording accuracy present in any art. In fact, it has come to be considered quite an accomplishment to be indiscriminately opposed to any kind of "realism," past or present.

It cannot be emphasized too often that nature is the criterion of reality, not the art-recording of it; the latter is merely the criterion by which to measure the *degree* and *kind* of visual ability of the artist

71. G. B. Brown: *The Art of the Cave Dweller*, p. 270.

72. Ibid., p. 230.

73. Casteret, *Ten Years under the Earth*, pp. 54-55. Only one of these has *slight* justification; one Paleolithic artist represented a boar with eight legs to show motion—one of the devices employed by the Futurists.

74. Preface by Alfred H. Barr, Jr., in *Prehistoric Rock Pictures in Europe and Africa*, by Frobenius and Fox, p. 9.

as a respondent to the objective world. That Pictographic artists achieved amazing results is not to be denied; but it is necessary to realize that the problems of "reality" and art are considerably more complex and interesting than either "Realists" or "Distortionists" seem to suspect.

As for the "realism" which the Paleolithic artists achieved, it would be erroneous to assume that it appeared to them as it appears to us. We must remember that they were in the beginning stages of art-visualization. There is, in fact, as we have previously noted, some similarity between their position and that of an art-student today who starts out to develop his ability to draw. Crude results are inevitable at first, but there is a gradual gain in accuracy. But the artist of today can in a single lifetime gain the ability to do very accurate recordings because of eye-brain knowledge which has, over thousands of years, come down to him from his predecessors. This advantage the earlier artists did not have; they were engaged in the very important and difficult task of laying the foundation of man's art. It was a long, slow, difficult process.

As we penetrate farther and farther into history we shall realize that artists of almost every culture, with exceptions that we shall note later, supposed that their art had reached the pinnacle of perfection in the recording of nature, when, as a matter of fact, artists in each culture succeeded at best only in recording *what they were able to see;* thus the results appeared to them as perfect depictions of reality. Artists in Primitive cultures were particularly susceptible to this error, since they did not consciously recognize any "problem of reality."

We shall find that few artists in any period of art suspected that what they saw in the objective world was only a *part* of what was to be seen. It was these few, however, who were the ones to further extend man's visual knowledge. Not until more recent times did man clearly realize that he might not be seeing *all* that was to be seen. But particularly as a result of modern science, there is gradually being born in human awareness the absolute necessity of never being absolute about what we "see-think" about the objective world. Today the old attitude is reversed: we now maintain that what we see is only a part of what there is to see, and hence discoveries always remain to be made.

Our history will show that non-allness-seeing was the only type of visual activity any of our ancestors were ever able to exercise, regardless of what they otherwise assumed; just as non-allness-seeing is the only type of visual activity *we* today can exercise. The difference between ourselves and Pictographic man (or any of our predecessors for that matter) is one of degrees of visual acuity.

If we expect to achieve adequate comprehension of the various kinds of seeing, it becomes imperative that we avoid identifying our ability to see with that exercised in other periods. The observations of field workers among Primitives, for instance, have often been distorted by the assumption that Primitives see and think as we do, when as a matter of fact, they see differently and for different purposes, and *naturally* so!

There are a number of experiences related by field workers among Primitive tribes which give us some insight into how the Primitive sees. For example the following: "Thus, though some Australians are capable of making rude drawings of animals, etc., others, on the contrary, as Oldfield tells us, 'seem quite unable to realize the most vivid artistic representations. On being shown a large colored engraving of an aboriginal New Hollander, one declared it to be a ship, another a kangaroo, and so on; not one of a dozen identifying the portrait as having any connection with himself. *A rude drawing, with all the lesser parts much exaggerated, they can realize.* Thus, to give them an idea of a man, the head must be drawn disproportionately large.'" (emphasis ours)[75] There have also been reports that Bushmen are unable to recognize their own Photographs.

These incidents give us a clue to the differences between the visual ability of the Primitive and our own. In both cases Primitives were confronted with accurate, even Photographic records, but they were unable to recognize the content as "having any connection" with themselves. In the former case only a depiction reduced to very simple visual terms with certain characteristics exaggerated could be recognized. It is interesting to note that investigators of children's drawings have found a similar phenomenon: children tend to recognize objects in other children's drawings more readily than those accurately drawn in perspec-

75. Sir John Lubbock: *The Origin of Civilization and the Primitive Condition of Man,* p. 45. New York, 1882. Permission of D. Appleton-Century Co., Inc.

tive.[76] In other words, it would seem that Primitive people (in fact any people) are not able to comprehend a depiction which produces a higher degree of realism than their own level of visual development. We would be inclined to presume, however, that if a Primitive such as those referred to by Oldfield were shown a *life-size* Photograph in color of himself, he would probably react to it with immediate recognition, just as he might to a mirror reflection.

However, it is necessary to expect differing degrees of visual ability even among various levels of Primitive cultures.

But what are we to say to the fact that Primitives consider their art as though it were as real as the reality? Is this due to an inability to discern the differences between art and reality? Lévy-Bruhl, to mention but one writer, is inclined to disagree. He points out that the mystic view of reality is projected on the art and in this fashion it becomes as real as its original. In fact the art is considered as a distinct part of the original in the same way that Primitives regard a name as part of a person. With this we certainly agree; however, he prefaces this notion by first pointing out that, "If primitives view the pictured resemblances differently from ourselves, it is because they view the original otherwise also."[77] But this of course is precisely the point; beyond mere identification on the mystic level between the art and its original, there is still another factor involved in this type of eye-brain orientation. With us the "problem of reality" in representational art is to secure as much correspondence as possible between these two factors. But this is not the Primitive's conscious "problem of reality"; his is one dealing primarily with the mystic factor which permeates everything. Hence, things having characteristics in common (the differences being ignored) must therefore have mystical qualities in common. And, to be mystical is to be "real." Therefore, if the image is injured, the original is likewise injured. Consequently we here are dealing with a level of art behavior where a *correspondence of similarities* has prime importance; hence the perceiving of differences between art and reality is comparatively little developed. But, to repeat, this inability would vary according to the stage of Primitive orientation involved.

Art is the main barometer of man's visual development. Each stage in that development releases further potentialities which are inherent in the "cortical" development of stereoscopic vision. We have abundant evidence of this evolution in man's art. As artists developed their visual ability they were able to record nature ever more accurately. In short, the evolution of "vision" and "art" proceed hand in hand, until in the case of Paleolithic artists they were able to produce quite accurate visual records of *certain* natural objects.

It is true that artists in nearly all cultures that followed produced an art further developed. But only the earliest Paleolithic artists have the distinction of being the inventors of art and of having discovered that man could record the appearances of nature. In looking back over the entire Paleolithic period in France and northern Spain, we find that not only was art invented, but that the main mediums and subjects of the future had also made their appearance. For there was both sculpture and painting, both human and animal subject, and the invention of signs or symbols of communication, both Mimetic and non-Mimetic.

In conclusion: we have advanced the assumption that tools in the earliest cultures of man were predominantly natural products and were first used as found. Through his own efforts man learned to increase these natural products and finally to improve upon them. We have seen that man invented methods for recording certain aspects of the objective world and for making various tools and instruments. We have found no basis for the possible existence of something called "non-utilitarian" art. Thus we have not only sought the function of Pictographic arts but have found it necessary to regard as art things generally not so considered—the limestone balls and the cup markings of Mousterian times; the hand silhouettes of later periods. These we have found to be important evidence throwing light upon the genesis of art.

Unfortunately, the term "art" has all too often come to signify something precious and above the earthly affairs of life. Removal of such verbalistic fictions would release us tremendously from our present inability to observe, experience and speak about art like reasonable men conscious of living in the 20th century.

76. Helga Eng, op. cit., p. 153, quoting Passy. In this regard it has been observed by the author that children are, as a rule, far quicker than adults to discern resemblances in very primitive arts as well as in natural formations which suggest certain subjects.
77. Lévy-Bruhl, *How Natives Think*, p. 49.

This jungle valley of Egypt lying athwart the eastern Sahara
not only gathered between its contracted rocky walls the
prehistoric hunters scattered along the North African coast,
but it also held them together in the possession of all the
resources necessary for the unhampered development of
human life under conditions so favorable that the once local
communities were slowly consolidated into the first great
society of several million souls, swayed by one sovereign
hand and in possession of the leading fundamentals of civilization. Thus in the centuries between 5000 and 3500 B. C.
arose the first great civilized state at a time when Europe
and most of Western Asia were still inhabited by scattered
communities of Stone Age hunters.   45
James Henry Breasted

. . . . the mechanism of culture contact and the process of give and take . . . . has been taking place ever since mankind began to create civilization. For no cultured people has ever been able to develop in isolation. Nations do not flourish in watertight compartments. Diffusion of culture has been taking place throughout the whole history of civilization. Giving and receiving, both of material and ideas have been the vital factors in effecting progress. 314

G. Elliot Smith

6 THE IMAGE OF MAN REPLACES THE ANIMAL

The Nile Valley is for us . . . the earliest social
arena, where we may observe man victoriously
emerging from an age-long struggle with nature,
and entering this new arena of social forces, to begin the baffling struggle of mankind with himself—
a struggle which has hardly passed beyond its beginnings at the present day. 45

James H. Breasted

In Egypt, as in every other country—epochs of high
civilization . . . are preceded by periods of preparation and of slow development, during which the
ground is rendered suitable for all that is to follow. 277

Hermann Ranke

The Paleolithic period in Europe closed with the retreat of the last great ice sheets, which for thousands of years had periodically sprawled over the greater part of the continent. With this change the Magdalenian culture gradually disappeared; the period in which the animal was the predominant element of art-magic had finally come to an end. At first there were efforts to depict an effect of great masses of animals, which, as Schmidt points out, were probably last desperate attempts here and there to bring back the abundant supply as of old.[1] Paleolithic culture and its art terminated with the disappearance of the environmental conditions that had literally "fed" it. The gradual loss of the old animal supply brought on the gradual dis-appearance of the old art in its developed polychromatic form. Emerging now were new orientations to meet new conditions that increasingly appeared as the ice receded ever farther to the north. The particular kind of animal life which had previously formed the basis of man's economic existence, his art, his beliefs and his culture, probably retreated with the ice to the north, as some tribes of humans may have also done; at any rate a similar milieu appeared eventually in Scandinavia and elsewhere in the north.

Forests, more abundant vegetation, and new kinds of animals—in short, an entirely different kind of environment—replaced the old arctic conditions in western Europe. Those peoples who did not retreat with the ice to the north were compelled to make a very decided readjustment. But for thousands of years in post-Paleolithic Europe man's culture was apparently not carried beyond the hunting and food-gathering stage. The change from a land of ice to a land of forests, great as it was, was not the kind to force men to leave the hunter stage, and so we find merely a transition from one kind of hunting and food-gathering culture to another kind. It would appear, as we shall later explain, that the earlier stages of man's evolution occurred in those places where the natural environment forced him to make drastic changes. Thus we must look elsewhere than Europe for the next great advance in the evolution of culture.

But to consider this problem we must first examine another Paleolithic culture which appears to have played a transitional role in the eventual continuation of human evolution beyond the hunter stage. We refer to the people whose art is found on the open rock-shelters of eastern and southern Spain. A similar art, which we shall consider presently, has been found scattered throughout Africa. The cultures north of the Cantabrian mountains are referred to as "Francocantabrian," as distinct from the Levant cultures south of the mountains.

Abstracting principally from evidence that appears to be implied in the evolutional indications of the art, we find that that of the Levant is an emergent development from and beyond the attainments of the Francocantabrian art. The Levant art would seem to have branched off from the Francocantabrian during Aurignacian times. For the earliest stages of art development, that would necessarily take place

---

1. R. R. Schmidt: *The Dawn of the Human Mind*, p. 166.

before the earliest Levant examples could be attained, have been found only in the Francocantabrian area (e.g., "Macaroni" and earliest organic outlines of animals). Moreover, of the northern cultures, it was the Aurignacians who depicted the human form more frequently; this is another link with the Levant art, since here the human form also predominated. (It is rather odd that nowhere in the Levant or Francocantabrian areas have early stages in linear depictions of the human form been found which are comparable to those early steps in the development of the linear depictions of animals—unless the "enigmatical signs" are the remnants of such art. This may have been due to the use of perishable materials during early developments.)

In any case, our analysis inclines us to consider Levant art as essentially an offshoot and a progression from the Francocantabrian culture. We find, as we remarked before, that the most developed subject of the latter, the animal, was the most developed subject in the Levant; but in the Levant, it was not as detailed in treatment as in the north, mainly because of the greater importance of the human form. In short, the human form was the minor subject in the north and the major in the Levant.

Obermaier, who sees significant similarities between the arts of the Francocantabrian and the Levant, writes that: "The close relationship of the art of both regions is further confirmed by the fact that in all essential points their artistic manifestations have followed a parallel course of evolution, which also goes to show that these were contemporary . . . . the earliest art of both regions consists of rather clumsy and primitive figures, followed by monochrome linear designs. Later come paintings in uniform plain color, or partly in line shading; and, finally, the semipolychrome and polychrome representations."[2]

He thus points out two kinds of similarities in their arts: (1) The increasing ability to record the subject in each new phase more accurately than in the last; (2) the evolving manner in which paint was used, i.e., from monochrome to biochrome and finally to polychrome paintings. One other similarity that Obermaier mentions is very important: "The animal pictures common to both regions betray the same realism, the same artistic conception, the same style and finish—similarities which could hardly be a coincidence."[3] In general we agree with this statement. However, there are certain differences within these similarities which are significant. "The same realism" is not quite correct; the Levant animal paintings never approach the *detailed* recording accuracy of the northern arts. In both form and color they are treated more simply. This is significant, because the Levant animals indicate that the artists who made them would have been quite capable of achieving, if they had wished to, the detailed recording level of the northern artists—as occasionally they did. That they did not do so as a general practice was perhaps because their culture did not put as great importance and emphasis upon the animal for subject-matter as upon the human form, now becoming a more important theme of culture.

The reader may well ask: if this was true, then why were the human forms not done more realistically? This will be taken up when we come to the discussion of the possibility of sculpture having existed in this culture; here we shall only point out that in sculpture considerably more realism could have been obtained, while in the linear medium the artist strove to achieve as much realism as he could in what was a more difficult, more slowly developed art. Still another important factor concerning this point, which will be discussed more extensively later, is the operation of the magic upon the development of the art. The requirements of magic imposed certain standard practices in order to realize particular results, e.g., disguise of the human form in one way or another frustrated further development of recording until some crisis released this staticizing grip of magic.[4]

The fact that the predominant subject in Levant art was the human form, while in the Franco-

2. Hugo Obermaier: *Fossil Man in Spain,* pp. 254-255.

3. Ibid., p. 254.

4. In the Levant arts we see that there was still a concern with devices for protecting the human form, as well as the animal, in that they were largely indicated in silhouette. One is tempted to speculate on the exceptions to this general rule and to wonder if these do not indicate an exceptional practice, such as painting a silhouette over a drawing after its magic function had been realized; or whether in some cases later peoples put black silhouettes over earlier red ones. In any case, during Francocantabrian times the figure in the linear arts was protected by being clothed with various powerful magic parts of animals; in the Levant this is no longer true except perhaps for masks; the figure is simply clothed in the protective darkness of the silhouette. Later this advance was carried to the final step, when the curtain of darkness was raised and the human form appeared in the daylight, disguised now in the shape of the ideal.

cantabrian it was the animal, is what we consider to be the most significant link between the two cultures; this can be made more clear as our discussion develops.

We list below what seem to be the most significant differences between the arts of the two cultural areas of Paleolithic Europe:

(1) With the Levant culture the human form, a more difficult subject to record, was the chief subject-matter of the art. This we have shown to be an advance over previous efforts.

(2) The Levant people painted their art upon open rock-shelters, as compared to the Francocantabrians who painted inside cave-tunnels.

(3) In the Levant almost all subjects were depicted in motion, whereas, in the Francocantabrian arts nearly everything was depicted statically, as though the subject had posed for the artist; for this reason some writers refer to these depictions as "portraits." [5]

(4) The Levant arts indicate that the general magic view of existence was far more advanced in the sense that they not only recorded the human form frequently but also depicted themselves at their everyday activities, such as hunting, dancing, fighting. Here was a world where man, not the animal, dominated. In short, a higher level of orientation to the world outside seems to be indicated.

(5) The Levant arts show some deliberate effort to compose or arrange the subjects, an activity that is naturally implied in any attempt to depict groups. The Francocantabrians made such attempts, but only in a very limited sense where either a group or a row of animals is sometimes shown, or in the superimpositions.

Each of the above five points indicates that the art of the Levant cultures was developing beyond that of the Francocantabrians. Hence it is the differences within the similarities as well as the similarities within the differences that tend to indicate that the one culture may have stemmed from and was a development over the other. The question will arise as to why the Levant culture, presumably contemporaneous with the Francocantabrian, should have made these further advances. The main factor would seem to have been the climate, since southeastern Spain was never covered by ice, and different temperatures, vegetation, animal life, etc., inevitably led to particular changes when the cultural elements of the north were brought across the Cantabrian mountains.

Another difference between the two cultures which has often been remarked upon (and which we believe to have been more apparent than real) is the fact that although sculpture of the human as well as animal form has been found in the north, none has been found in any sites of the Levant cultures. As far as the present author is concerned, it is highly probable that sculpture was made in the southeastern Spanish cultures of wood or clay—most likely largely of wood, and hence has not survived. In fact some of their painting seems to contain depictions of sculpture. If we abstract from the kind of environment involved, we find that these people would have greater access to wood than their neighbors to the north. Doubtless they preferred the wood medium, as do the present inhabitants of Africa, and for a similar reason: it was a plentiful material. That they probably worked in perishable materials may account for the fact that sculptural art is the one not found at all.[6]

Every culture usually possesses "fixed" art (by which we mean art that could not be moved, such as murals), along with "mobile" art (by which we mean objects such as individual pieces of sculpture that could be moved). In the Francocantabrian cultures both are found together, the one on the walls, the other on the floor-beds of the caves. This arrangement is also found in ancient Egypt, with the great difference that the walls and the caves, so to speak, were artificial, man-made. But in the case of the Levant and African Paleolithic cultures we find only the fixed variety of art. One can see how the particular climate and vegetation produced these differences. That is, in the predominantly bleak, snow-covered arctic country

5. To be sure these artists often enough depicted the animal in motion, but it is the rigidity that one finds in the frozen depictions of motion in sculpture.

6. Even as regards the present examples of wood sculpture from Africa, experts are inclined to believe that none of it is over a century old, since the medium could scarcely have survived for a longer period.

of the Francocantabrian cultures, and in the bleak, sand-covered country of the Egyptian cultures, man was compelled to find or to make permanent shelters for himself and to make his art and perform at least the major part of his rituals in his natural or his man-made "caves."

Conditions were entirely different with the Levant peoples and non-desert Africans. For them the climate and the vegetation were such that permanent shelters were not necessary. They could lead a more "mobile" life in all its various phases than would be possible in a very cold snow-covered (Francocantabrian) or very hot, sand-covered, barren country and climate (Egypt). Therefore, in the Levant, it seems reasonable not to expect to find sculpture and the linear arts together. The environment would have allowed man to be more "mobile," and we should thus expect that there would have been more "mobile" art.

A good example of the mobility of a people's rituals in such an environment is to be found in the account of the Witchetty grub totem people of Central Australia, as reported by Sollas from the works of Spencer and Gillen.[7] We shall mention only some of the points which are pertinent to our discussion here. At the Witchetty grub ceremony the members who perform the rituals of the particular totem, leave the rest of the tribe and encamp at a rocky gorge. (On the wall of this gorge, interestingly enough, there are a number of grouped, straight parallel lines, as far as one can make out from the Photograph. See figure 8.) The next day the men leave, the leader with a wooden bowl, the rest with Eucalyptus twigs, one in each hand. They arrive at a sacred cave in which there is a large stone surrounded with pebbles. Here a brief ceremony takes place with the stone and the pebbles, and the wooden bowl and twigs. They then leave this cave for a large rock nearby called "The Decorated Eyes." Here some of the cave pebbles are thrown in a particular direction, then later collected and returned to the cave. This ceremony is repeated at some ten separate caves. Although this is far from the end of places visited before this particular ritual is over, we have described enough to show how much territory is involved in one of these mobile affairs. For the same reason the "art" objects connected with it are also spread over a wide area. Caves, of course, play a part in the magic ceremonies of many kinds of Primitive tribes, as they may have also with the Levant people. However, they do not play such a major role for peoples living in warm climates as they would have in the case of the Francocantabrian people who carried their art deep into the earth's interior. In short, when we speak of whether or not a culture has a mobile or permanent art we can only speak of what predominates.

A factor which suggests the type of sculpture that the Levant and African Paleolithic peoples might have made is suggested by inferences from the Egyptian arts subsequent to these Paleolithic cultures. In the Egyptian's "fixed" linear arts we notice that the contents deal with the everyday activities of the people. The sculptured medium, on the other hand, was *mainly* reserved for the most important depictions of individuals, gods, kings, etc., along with small images of slaves who accompanied the deceased to the land of the dead. Similarly in the linear arts of the Levant and Africa, we notice a parallel in that these also dealt mainly with everyday affairs of the people. In the Egyptian arts, however, such scenes concerned preparations for the continuation of life after death, whereas it is quite likely that in the Paleolithic Levant and African cultures such scenes were part of magic rituals aimed *mainly* at continuing their everyday life successfully.[8] Again in all the *linear* arts of the Levant and Africa, just as in Egypt, animal-headed, human-

---

7. W. J. Sollas: *Ancient Hunters*, p. 308.

8. We do not mean this to imply that these people had no beliefs about an after-life, since such beliefs appear to have existed as far back as Mousterian times. It would seem, however, that until the development of Egyptian culture, man's art was largely, not entirely, devoted to the maintenance of everyday life. It was only after magic had developed far enough into its second stage, i.e., when the occult power had been transferred from the animal to the human form and thus magic had become "religion," that man's art was given over largely to the problem of after-life. As a matter of fact, we see something of this gradual transformation process in the Egyptian's art where animal- and bird-headed humans continued for a time before the completely humanized figure dominated the scene. In other words, the first great stage of human orientation to the objective world, that of magic, was given over largely to making man feel secure in his life existence in the face of the great unknown with which he felt himself surrounded; whereas, the second stage, the religious orientation, was given over largely to making man feel secure in meeting the end of life existence, i.e., death, the great unknown into which he must enter after earth-life. Until man conquered his environment enough to feel his emerging dominance, he must have been *largely* tied to art-magic dealing with everyday existence. Only later when he directly controlled the production of his food supply did he turn *largely* to after-life with what is now his art-religion. This is symbolized in the transformation of the dominant position of the human over the animal form in the art of man.

100

shaped gods are comparatively rare. In Egypt these are more frequent among the sculptured objects, which is to be expected, since it was the then more important medium, and this may have been the case in whatever sculptural activities existed in the other two cultures.

In the history that follows we shall learn that the first developed achievements in the depiction of the human form, just as in the development of the animal form, were realized in the realm of sculpture. The reasons for this sequence of events in the case of the human form are similar to those already explained in animal depiction developments. This would seem to add a further argument to the existence of sculptured human figures having accompanied the linear art development of the human form. In brief, it seems likely that the Levant cultures had not only a thriving sculptural art but one far more developed in recording accuracy than is apparent in surviving linear arts.

According to our theory, where low order linear recordings exist there is generally present a higher order of recording in the medium of sculpture (as we witnessed in Francocantabrian art and as we shall also find in Egypt and elsewhere); we can thus quite reasonably assume that not only did the Levant and African peoples possess sculptural arts, but that it was also superior in recording achievement to their linear arts and all *previous sculpture of the human object*. This assumption would especially make sense if we consider the art situation in Africa today among those peoples who have never passed out of the Primitive stage of development and where we see the great role of sculpture in art. It seems reasonable to abstract back into the past from such evidence. Thus, although so far no sculpture has been found in the Levant or African areas, some evidence of it may one day appear.

Up to this point we have given our reasons for assuming that the Levant art is an offshoot of the North. We now come to the problem of the relationships between the Levant art and that to the south of it in Paleolithic Africa. The striking similarities between these two art areas have been written about at length and have been the basis for the assumption that the Levant culture was an offshoot of the African. However, here again the differences will be our main concern.

The first striking fact that meets us in considering the differences between the Levant and African cultures is the consistent, compact development of the Levant arts as compared to those in the African area, where we see only sections of the Levant developments. This has been demonstrated by an analysis of the general order of various superimpositional examples found in Africa. The inconsistencies revealed by the superimpositions are so pronounced in the African arts that they cannot be ignored.

Regarding the problem of where and when and how migrations may have occurred between Spain and Africa, it is significant that the Levant art appears not to have been interrupted, as one would expect if any extensive, influential migration had occurred during the upper Paleolithic period from Africa into Spain. In the latter area the art seems to have progressed steadily; there are no indications of upheavals or interruptions by migrating Africans. At least we can say that the migrations, if they occurred, were ineffective in altering the process of the Levant arts.

But when we look to the arts of Africa we do not find this to be the case. Here we get the appearance of a people frequently interrupted as though by waves of cultural migrations; so that however often and whatever the direction of the migrations, it would appear that Africa was more affected than Spain. Furthermore, it is quite possible that the end or high point of the Levant culture migrated to Africa when the climate changed as a result of the recession of the ice. This would not have been as severe a change for the Levant culture as for the Francocantabrian (whose accustomed environment was moving ever northward), for the environment in Africa was relatively similar to that which had supported the people in southeast Spain.

Since the Spanish arts show a consistency throughout, while the African specimens show considerable interruption and variations in their evolution, this would tend to enforce the theory that the basic source of this evolution was in Spain and not Africa. It is quite possible that there were repeated waves of migrations from Spain to Africa. Sollas, who accepts such migrations, points out that the art becomes increasingly recent the further south we go from France to southern Africa.[9]

Another important aspect of this problem is that the highest development of the type of art found in the Levant areas seems unmistakably to have been eventually realized not in Spain but in Africa and this in turn seems to be the forerunner of the Egyptian kinds of art. Here we find more developed depictions of the human form, far superior composition, due to more complex, magic-religious beliefs apparent in the African art. Consequently we see the more frequent employment of large and small figures to distinguish between the more important individuals in the culture; we see burial scenes, rain ceremonies, and animal-headed humans, all very suggestive of the Egyptian culture. In short, the more developed orientations to the objective world are indicated in the now emerging anthropomorphic beliefs that African art represents. Just as the Levant arts are a development from and beyond the Francocantabrian, so the African are a development from and beyond the Levant on the way to the Egyptian stage of evolution. And this serial order reminds us that the Spanish arts were the next door neighbors of precisely that kind of art and culture (where animal magic predominated) which one would expect to be the predecessor of just the stage of cultural evolution found in the Spanish arts, where the human form takes a predominant place in the magic beliefs.

With this theory we do not mean to rule out the possibility that art of the human form could have occurred without a cultural inheritance such as has been posited for the Levant peoples; our view is that where such conditions do not exist, the main steps of evolution are not successfully realized. In other words, a similar type of art may arise in many areas independently, but the highest degree of evolution of a particular stage occurs only in some particular culture. Thus there exist *parallel* efforts among various cultures, but *diffusion* of necessary, preceding cultural experience must occur before any significant advance becomes possible in any one culture.

As for the question of Egypt and its place in the evolution of recording art, we find three significant relationships: (1) The Francocantabrians brought to a high state of development the preliminary order of animate depiction, specifically the concentration upon the animal form in art. (2) The Levant artists began the transition to the next order of the depiction of animate objects, the human form. (3) The Egyptians brought to a high state of development the depiction of the human form.

Considering further relationships, we find the following: The Levant art shows definite connections with the Francocantabrian; it possessed as its most developed form of visual recording that which comprised the most developed recording in the latter, i.e., the recording of the animal form. Moreover, Levant art exhibited a definite cultural advance from and beyond the Francocantabrian; it was characterized by the transition from the predominance in quantity and importance of the animal form, to a predominance in quantity and importance of the human form. And finally the Egyptian art definitely exhibited a development from and beyond the art and culture of the Levant; that is, the transitional character of the Levant, with African developments as the link, was brought to a higher stage of development in the art accomplishments of the Egyptians. This will become more clear when we have concluded our examination of Egyptian art in the latter part of this chapter. In this way then, Levant art, along with that of Paleolithic and post-Paleolithic Africa, operates as a transition between Francocantabrian and Egyptian.

Such an assumption as we have made is not the accepted theory among "prehistorians" and archeologists. However, it is not wholly without substantiation, as may be seen in the following quotations: V. G. Childe reports that E. S. Thomas made a detailed comparison between the more conventionalized elements of the later Spanish cave art and the signs on Egyptian vases and found "so many coincidences that it is clear that Early Predynastic Egyptian art was not only inspired by the same ideals but also developed along the same lines as that of East Spain."[10] Leo Frobenius is a strong advocate of the theory

9. Sollas, op. cit., pp. 493-494.

10. V. G. Childe: *New Light on the Most Ancient East,* p. 83, Kegan Paul, Trench, Trubner and Co., Ltd., London, 1934. (D. Appleton-Century Co., New York, 1934.)

that Egyptian culture showed a "lineal descent" from the Stone Age, and Douglas C. Fox, one of his colleagues, has pointed out the links between Spain and predynastic Egypt which he has found in Africa: "there were two types of pictures, [in Inner Fezzan] one depicting wild animals, among them giraffes eighteen feet high, the other human figures sometimes with animal heads. . . . The style in which the human figures were depicted was apparently related on the one side to that of the Levant art of Spain and on the other to that of early Egyptian art. There were, for instance, no less than four representations of the Egyptian god Bes.

"In the second compositions (human figures), among them the Barth pictures, there often occurred the pictures of cattle which sometimes, Frobenius says, 'bore disks between their horns, just as in Egypt. This reminded us that in the Sahara Atlas were pictures of rams with disks between their horns and that Georg Schweinfurth had already posed the question of whether or not these could be the ur-pictures of the Egyptian ram god, Jupiter Ammon.'

"A year later (Diafe XI) Frobenius found in the Libyan Desert rock paintings which were quite clearly those of the Egyptian god Set, something which tended to confirm him in the belief, first suggested by Schweinfurth, that the ideas embodied in the figures of many gods which we know as Egyptian came from the west, that these ideas travelled slowly eastward across the wastes of what are now the Sahara and Libyan Deserts, which were then dry countries, as in South Africa, but by no means so desolate as they are today, and that these ideas were renovated and remodeled by the Egyptians, who finally gave them the historical stamp with which we are familiar."[11]

". . . . [at Wadi Sora] we have human figures in the most lively movement: bowmen in every possible position, acrobats, dancers, swimmers and people in costumes, one next to the other, and even the 'handprints' which occur in the Francocantabrian caves. Some of these pictures are so similar to those of Eastern Spain that Professor Obermaier holds the style of both to be practically identical. On the other hand, there are also pictures which in subject (the jackal-headed god, Set) and treatment (exaggerated shoulders and narrow waist) indicate the possibility of a relationship with Egypt. The rich finds we made of stone artifacts of various types lead us to believe that these pictures were painted in the late Old Stone Age (Late or Upper Paleolithic)."[12]

Both Childe[13] and Winkler[14] have pointed out the stylistic agreements between the art found in the Uwenat Oasis in southern upper Egypt (below ancient Egypt proper) and that of southeastern Spain. Winkler says we do not know whether this art came from the Mediterranean to Africa or from Africa to the Mediterranean. But, as Petrie has pointed out, there is nothing in "prehistoric" Egypt to compare with the art of the cave men of Europe.[15] It would seem logical to assume, therefore, that the principal evolutionary movement was not from Africa to Spain, but in the opposite direction. As Wilhelm Worringer says: "scientific research continually gives more substantial shape to the picture of a cultural connection of high value in the Stone Age extending with a movement from West to East from the South of France and Spain through North Africa and the Northern Sahara region as far as the Nile district and beyond."[16]

Our general theoretical basis for assuming a serial progression in the arts from the Francocantabrian to the predynastic Egyptian cultures is as follows: In the previous chapter we posited as the first stage of culture a "Decorative" period, a sort of preparatory period to the building up of the high point of magic culture which occurred in the subsequent animal-magic stage. These magic beliefs comprised man's first highly organized interpretation of the objective world. They were formulated in his efforts to cope with and combat a world his uninformed mentality found strange and fearful. His orientations to the world were determined by his first conscious reactions to it (explained in chapter 4), and were such as to make it possible for him to survive those very reactions. Just as man had to realize physical

11. Leo Frobenius and D. C. Fox: *Prehistoric Rock Pictures in Europe and Africa,* pp. 39-40.

12. Ibid., pp. 42-44.

13. Childe, op. cit., p. 35.

14. H. A. Winkler: *Rock Drawings of Southern Upper Egypt,* Vol. 2, p. 37, H. Milford, Oxford University Press, London, 1938-1939.

15. W. M. F. Petrie: *Arts and Crafts of Ancient Egypt,* p. 13, A. C. McClurg and Co., Chicago, 1910.

16. From *Egyptian Art,* p. 1, by Wilhelm Worringer. Courtesy of G. P. PUTNAM's SONS. New York, London, 1928.

survival, so he had also to realize psycho-logical survival. It was a matter of psycho-physiological survival needs. Under the initial conditions of the beginnings of human culture, the notion of magic was indispensable and natural to man's first structuralized orientation to the objective world and himself. When the subjects of the art produced by a particular culture exhibit an extensive concern with the animal form, this is evidence that we are dealing with cultural developments already of a high order; this is even more true when the human form becomes important. Thus in a comparatively more advanced and more recent culture like the Egyptian, we see the transition from the animal-human-form concern to the predominant human-figure emphasis. Compare such a culture with the Francocantabrian in which the animal dominated the consciousness of man. The Egyptian obviously expresses a considerably higher order of human development and orientation than does the latter.

Hence if the Francocantabrian is accepted as a considerably lower order of human cultural orientation and development than the Egyptian, then the Levant and African Paleolithic arts, as the subject-matter indicates, would appear to lie between these two cultural levels operating as a transition from the one level to the next. In short, the Francocantabrian stage of development had to evolve before art could *successfully* reach a stage of predominant concern with the human form. Accordingly we posit the Levant as an offshoot of the Francocantabrian, the African as an offshoot of the Levant.

Only after man had developed to the point where he began to achieve dominance over the animal world (i. e., domestication), did he achieve sufficient security to begin to picture occult forces in what became the more powerful human form. That man had to feel secure by dominance over the animal both "mentally" and "physically," as a prerequisite before the human form could dominate art, is well demonstrated by the art of the Francocantabrian cultures which shows definite evidence of fear in depicting the human form.

As man developed his knowledge through increasingly improved observation of the objective world, he was able to realize ever more developed potentialities; in other words, he obtained ever increasing control over the psycho-physiological events which determined his existence. In this way he passed from a dependence upon an uncontrolled food supply to control of it; i.e., he domesticated the plants and animals that made up his food needs. With this transformation there gradually occurred an increase in his belief in his kind, and so we see that the most powerful forces of the occult world were no longer clothed in forms of the animal (which now became minor forces of magic) but rather assumed a human form. The human form was placed at the apex of the world of the occult. Thus religion came into being, the more advanced and final stage of magic!

From here on man's image dominated visual consciousness. The darkness which the Paleolithic man of northern Europe feared was now pierced by the blazing light of the Sun. Man's consciousness had thus passed from the darkness of the earth's caves to the light of the Sun. The Sun stood over the heads of men and reigned over all things on the earth. Man had taken a great step forward, for the gods of Darkness were now dominated by the god of Light! If the realization of the first developed stage of human culture occurred in a world covered with ice and cold, then the second great stage of evolution formed in a world covered with sand and heat!

It will already have become apparent to the reader that we consider it incorrect and misleading to speak of Egyptian culture as the "dawn of history," the "dawn of civilization," and the like, as many writers do. Human history and civilization had their beginnings in the beginning of human culture many thousands of years before the Egyptians made their appearance. The historical theorists of the 19th century believed that Egyptian culture began in a developed state, although the only evidence for this belief was a lack of evidence to prove or disprove it. Since then evidence has been amassed by researchers in various fields which shows conclusively that the formation of Egyptian civilization was the result of many cultures preceding it; it represents the focal point and continuation of these preceding cultures, literally and developmentally.

104

26. Above left, portion of the fresco in La Cueva de la Vieja, Alpera, Spain, after Breuil. Above right, red figured pottery jar, predynastic period, about 3500 B. C. Courtesy of The Metropolitan Museum of Art. Below, rock painting, hunting scene, southwest Africa. Frobenius-Institut, Frankfurt-am-Main.

We have already presented our arguments for the hypothesis that there was a serial development from the art of the Francocantabrians to that of predynastic Egypt. Here we shall not examine other preceding and contemporary cultures, particularly those from the East, which also influenced and were influenced by Egypt. The study of these other arts would prove highly valuable but in the main they exemplify some achievement which is but a facet of what is to be found in a more highly developed state in Egypt. Thus the study of Egypt serves our purpose, since we are primarily concerned with those cultures that molded the main stem of the development of man's art.

So far we have been concerned with cultures primarily regulated by a Primitive level of magic, dealing first with plants, etc., then with animals and later with human beings. In the latter two forms of magic, however, we can already see the beginnings of a transition to a higher order of magic — religion. This transition was carried further by the Egyptians, whose civilization exhibited many remnants of past beliefs along with new ones which were formed by the transitional process. The old mingled with the new, but as time moved on the new became dominant. Hence in Egyptian sculpture there were animal-headed or animal-bodied human forms, characteristics of combined animal and human beliefs inherited from Paleolithic predecessors. But the human form rose more and more into the dominant position; and from this point on until our own century, the artist's concern was largely with recording

27. Above, painting in the tomb of Rekh-mi-re, at Thebes, showing sculptors at work on a red granite statue of Thutmose III, Dyn. XVIII. Courtesy of The Metropolitan Museum of Art. Below, Workmen at their tasks; upper part shows sculptors at work. Relief from the tomb of Ti, Dyn. V. Courtesy of Professor George Steindorff.

this subject. Thus by the time of the Greek and Roman cultures, Primitive magic, although still persisting, no longer occupied the dominant place in the affairs of mankind. In short, if the new begins in the far distant past, the past persists into the far distant future of the new.

Naturally the transition from a hunting to a farming culture, which involved a transition from the magic of animism to the religion of anthropomorphism, implied changed environmental factors upon which man now assumed he was dependent. In the earliest cultures the hunter depended primarily upon the *uncontrolled* propagation of animals; art and its magic were his only means of influencing animal procreation. But when man took a direct hand in the reproduction of animals and plants by the more practical means of domestication, he became dependent upon the sun, the earth, rain, etc. And so it was to these things that he transferred his magic rituals. Moreover, these elements of nature came increasingly to be embodied in human form symbols.

In Frazer's *Golden Bough* we find many examples of Egyptian rituals concerning the changes of seasons and the accompanying changes of the Nile River. The kings, for instance, in ancient times walked around the temple in order that the sun would be able to make its daily journey around the sky without any accident (such as an eclipse) to interrupt it. And "after the autumnal equinox the ancient Egyptians held a festival called 'the nativity of the sun's walking stick,' because, as the luminary declined daily in the sky, and his light and heat diminished, he was supposed to need a staff on which to lean." [17]

Thus the entrance of agriculture and its development by man brought many new symbols into the arts.

That the art of Egypt had a direct lineal descent from Paleolithic Europe can readily be observed by comparing paintings from rock shelter walls in Paleolithic east Spain and Africa, with paintings on predynastic Egyptian pottery. In each there appears a similar manner of drawing animals and humans; the great difference is in the ordering or arrangement of the subjects. In the Spanish and African examples the contents are arranged somewhat in the manner of a child, as compared to the Egyptian example, where we see the beginning of more advanced arrangement, i.e., the contents are placed in ordered, geometric divisions. Egyptian art indicates more conscious control in the structuralization of the contents. In these three examples we see the relationships between the linear art of three different cultures. It would be equally interesting to find out the sculptural relationships that occurred, especially since the sculptural medium dominated the Egyptian scene; but at present this is not factually possible.

Before examining first the linear and then the sculptural arts of Egypt in some detail, certain preliminary considerations must be presented.

While undeniable advances were made by Egyptian artists in two-dimensional depictions, most of us are familiar with the fact that in the linear arts a set formula (in the case of the human figure, head and legs in profile, shoulders square to the front, front-view of the eye) for recording reality was employed, a formula never drastically changed throughout most Egyptian art. Different explanations for this phenomenon have been advanced, depending usually on which school one adheres to—Academic or "Modern."

The Academicians have contended that the Egyptian artist was simply unable to rise beyond a primitive level of linear recording. While these Academicians were in power (up until recent years), Egyptian art was considered inferior and of no great consequence in comparison to the great achievements of the Greeks. But since the advent of "Modernism," there has been a swing to the other extreme: and now all kinds of far-fetched notions are attributed to the Egyptian artist to account for his distortions of reality. The Moderns argue, e.g., that as a result of the "free winds of expressionism" we today realize that the Egyptian linear artist's distortions are "artistically right" and that the Realists' need for intellectualizing art has spoiled our appreciation of Egyptian works.[18] We propose a modification of these either-or views.

The Academicians' explanation might be true of the very early linear artists of Egypt. But indisputable evidence indicates that early in dynastic history the linear artist was simply forbidden to draw a correctly recorded, realistic side- or front-view of the human form. As Margaret Murray has

17. From J. G. Frazer: *The Golden Bough*, p. 78. By permission of The Macmillan Company, publishers.
18. See Sheldon Cheney: *A World History of Art*, p. 85, Viking Press, Inc., New York, 1937.

28. Painted limestone stele showing an official, his wife and two servants. 2475-2000 B. C. Courtesy of The Metropolitan Museum of Art.

explained it: "By a conservative people like the Egyptians the conventions in art were preserved long after increased knowledge had made many of them unnecessary. Here also religion stepped in, and insisted that the archaic was in accordance with the divine will. As all art was for religious purposes, the Egyptian artist had no choice but to comply. . . ."[19] Moreover, we have inescapable proof that from quite early times the linear artist was capable of drawing at least a profile correctly. This proof constitutes an exception to the rule that the linear artist was forbidden to draw correctly and is found when sculpture is indicated in a two-dimensional recording. In such instances the artist invariably realized a correct side-view of the entire figure, with the exception of the eye (figure 27). Once such a recording was accomplished, then at least from that time on the linear artist must have been quite conscious of the differences between reality and his particular manner of depicting it in recordings of non-sculptured subjects. It would appear that he was consciously, deliberately following a set method for linear depictions.

But why the insistence upon making this distinction? Why not record sculpture as any other subject? Observation indicates that when such personages usually represented by the sculptor were also recorded by the linear artist (that is when the linear recordings of such subjects were not copied from the sculptural) the artist invariably employed the usual linear formula. Therefore the reason for this difference is simply that it conveyed to the observer the distinction between sculptured and non-sculptured subjects. In this way the observer could always tell when he was presented with a linear recording of a sculptured object. The conveyance of this distinction was of great importance for the Egyptian since, as

19. Margaret A. Murray: *Egyptian Sculpture*, p. 8, Gerald Duckworth, London, 1930.

we shall presently see, sculptured products occupied a different religious function from that of the linear arts.

Therefore we can say that from the moment that the Egyptian linear artist displayed an ability to record the sculptured human form on a linear surface correctly, he was deliberately restricting himself to the primitive linear formula whenever he used it.

Many "Modernists" may be disconcerted by the fact that the Egyptian (like his Paleolithic predecessor) was essentially concerned with very practical objectives, and not with "art for art's sake." Egyptian art served a purpose fundamentally like that of the cave artist, since in both cases art was thought to have a magic power. Magic functions exerted a great control over the character of the art and tended for the most part to keep it within the limits of a formula not to be broken until some crisis appeared which precipitated new developments or regressions.

Actually the whole course of Egyptian art history appears to be a case of periodic lessening and tightening of religious restrictions upon the way in which the artist might make his recordings. The best known illustration is the religious revolution of the XVIIIth Dynasty when there were attempts (although slight) to model with color and shading two-dimensional depictions of the human figure.

When we come to the study of another period of art dominated by religion, the Christian, we shall realize more fully that religion, like its magic forerunner, is essentially conservative behavior. Hence the more primitive the religious powers are, the more difficult it is to inaugurate change, even change that remains religious, as is well illustrated in the case of Akhenaten, who attempted to establish monotheism. Thus if Egyptian culture represents man's first great step in controlling *environmental* nature, on the other hand we witness here a new frustrating force to human culture arising, namely, man himself— the beginning of the great problem of how to control *human* nature.

All this reminds us that in observing any art it is necessary to avoid taking too literally what *we* see in that art, as though it were simply a question of "visual" activity or any other single factor. We must not lose consciousness of the cultural milieu, which may deter or encourage the development of the visual factor involved.

It appears that the factors which account for the distortions in the linear arts of Egypt, rather than being either a concern for greater "artistic reality," as some would have it, or an inability to draw correctly, as others see it, were actually something like this: (1) Egyptian linear art passed through a period of development until the linear formula of recording already referred to was achieved. (2) At this point the religious powers restricted any further extensive development, a restriction that was broken through at times but never completely abandoned. Linear depictions of front- or side-views were correct only in the depiction of sculptured subjects; or when guidelines were drawn on the solid stone block preparatory to cutting actual sculpture.[20]

Therefore, in the following explanation of how the linear formula of recording arose, we shall be concerned only with an analysis of the formation of this formula before the religious powers made laws which forbade any further radical changes. Obviously, art had to pass through a period of development before the recording stage of this formula could be realized.

Like the Paleolithic artists, the Egyptians engraved the contours and then applied color with paint. While color was used, there was apparently little attempt (with minor exceptions such as painting under Akhenaten) at realism or modelling. No concerted effort was made to depict the color modulations which occurred as a result of changing color tones in light and shade. (This was true in sculpture also, but to a considerable extent it was not so necessary, since light falling on the actual forms changed and modulated the all-over color.)

At first only the single or a few figures were depicted and then groups. There was also a development from a single row of figures to more complicated groups which involved a further problem of showing one group of figures behind others on a flat surface. The linear artist first tried to accomplish this by placing each row of figures completely above the other. This can be noted in scenes where several rows of workmen are shown pulling a sled with a statue upon it. The bottom row is the nearest group

20. Ibid., p. 2.

and each row "recedes" as it goes up. The next step towards more realism was to place each row partly behind as well as above the preceding row.

The Egyptian linear artist, however, never discovered the laws of perspective which would have permitted him to model three-dimensional illusions on a two-dimensional plane; hence he was compelled to resolve all his problems in terms of two-dimensional reasoning and observation. Forms were flat, and so was space, so to speak. If, for example, the linear artist had to depict objects in different places on a body of water, he would show the top-view of the water surface and the waves in the conventional side-view manner. If one boat was in back of another, each was drawn side-view, one above and partly behind the other. If fish were shown, they were indicated side-view on a top-view of the water. In other instances the artist might have been concerned only with showing the depth or side-view of the water, e.g., in scenes where a water-bucket was being lowered into a pond. Here a cross-section of the water was more informative than a top-view. In short, the artist linearized everything either as top or elevational views, according to which gave the most complete record of what was being reported.

We find a similar type of reasoning in the depiction of human forms; here the head is almost invariably side-view, as are the legs, while the torso appears to be, and the eyes are always shown front-view. In the female figure we generally see that where the breasts are indicated (usually only one is shown), they were always depicted in side-view. In brief, it would seem that the artist chose those linear views of the figure which would most impressively and completely depict it on a two-dimensional plane. This choice was due to the fact that tactile laws rather than those governing visual images dominated the recording efforts of early Egyptian linear artists. One has the very decided impression that the Egyptian, realizing the obvious advantages which sculpture has over the linear arts (but not yet realizing that the latter is potentially superior in other respects), therefore concluded that the linear medium was simply an imperfect tactile or sculptural medium. And, in order to overcome its handicaps he devised a formula for depicting the human form in order to get as great a tactile effect as was practically possible.

Now granting the dominance of the tactile laws over the efforts of the linear artists, let us examine their works more in detail. We may find figures depicted in what at first appears to be a complete profile. But if we look closely, we shall find that they are actually front-view torsos with the arms stuck on the side underneath the chin. (See figure 27, tomb of Ti.)

In the more common depictions of the profile figure we find a particular formula. The eye, the *area* of the torso and *one contour* of the torso, sometimes one or both arms, all these were generally shown in front-view recordings. The head, excepting the eye, one contour of the torso, the breast (male and female), the buttocks, the legs, and sometimes one or both arms—these were generally shown in side-views. The exception to front- or side-views was the abdomen, generally indicated by a three-quarters front-view, as evidenced by the position of the navel. Regarding these remarks on the contours and area of the torso, observe figure 28. Notice that the side-view contour of the torso, in both males and females, is indicated on that side which has a side-view of the breast. This contour is the one generally under the chin on that side of the torso which comprises the front side of the figure. As regards the other contour of the torso, this would appear to be varied—a front-view contour in some cases, at times evidenced by an indication of the junction of the pectoral and biceps muscles, and in other cases a back-view contour, depending upon the pose or action of the body. Another variation occurs in cases in which both hands were doing something similar, e.g., swinging a stick down on cattle; here both hands were clasped next to each other at the end of the stick. In such poses both arms were attached to that side of the torso which is under the chin; that is, they were attached on that side which represented the side-view contour of the torso, the other contour being a correct side-view of the back (figure 27, tomb of Ti). These are only some of the poses and formulae employed.

As for the rendition of the head, the reason it was usually in profile, rather than full-face which would have given *more* of the tactile area, was that this was the only way it could be depicted in linear art so that its attention could be properly directed to the scene in which it was involved.[21] But on the cther hand, why did the artist draw the eye front-view? Not because he could not attempt a side-view,

21. The front-view of the face appears to have been mostly reserved for the gods. This may have been the basic reason for not using the front-view more frequently, even after artists were able to make a fairly good attempt at it.

for to depict the side-view of the eye would be only a little more difficult, but because the important eyes were more completely and effectively shown tactilely in a front-view. (In later times we do find attempts to depict the side-view of the eye, but even here the eyeball remained in front-view.)

Now the question may be asked, why were the linear arts used at all, if they were considered to be, as we remarked earlier, a sort of lower order sculpture? This problem will be extensively considered in the section dealing with Christian art. Here we need merely point out that the distortions that ensued in early phases of linear art development produced particular psycho-logical effects which were retained because of religious value, even after discoveries of greater realism had been achieved. And religion, it is necessary to remember, is not concerned with actual reality but with the "reality" of another world. (Or, to put it another way, religionists are concerned with transforming the real world into another world.) In short, the religious element suppressed the full development of realism in both linear and sculptured art; that this is so is borne out by actual documents that have come down to us from the Egyptians, indicating restrictions placed upon art. Thus we account for the use of realism in this art only up to a certain point, after which only slight changes occur.

Still another aspect of the important function of the linear arts in Egypt, was their operation as part of the art of writing: they supplied the *descriptive visual* aspect of that being written about. The sculptured representations of gods, kings, etc., functioned as the *actual* "soul" or thing depicted. Hence a greater degree of realism (not unrestricted realism) was demanded in those sculptured images directly concerned with preserving the body of the dead. The religious function of Egyptian art held back the development of realism in both mediums, but it operated to a lesser degree in the sculptural arts. Throughout the times of Egyptian culture, sculpture was the most important medium of art.

We have already noted that artists of Paleolithic times discovered and invented all the basic art tools and mediums, and that these continued to be employed by all artists until our own century, little modified from their original Paleolithic forms. The human form, however, instead of the animal, became the overwhelmingly dominant subject of Egyptian art; and although the Egyptian inherited the visual recording experiences of his predecessors, he nevertheless passed through similar medium evolutions experienced by European Paleolithic peoples, because he was concentrating upon the depiction of the human figure, a far more difficult form to record. The Egyptian sculptor was continuing what had been begun by those Francocantabrian sculptors of the human form and probably developed further by the Levant and African cultures. As we have already explained, sculpture affords the artist the most direct release and approach to the realization of preliminary steps in tackling a new subject. The more difficult linear method, as we shall see in later studies, reached maturity only at a much later period as regards the human subject, just as had occurred in the case of the animal form. Our investigations will make clear that whenever painting displaced sculpture as the *major* medium it was for purposes of concluding what had been begun in, and carried as far as possible with, the sculptural medium. This will occur in the Renaissance. But when sculpture displaced painting as the major medium, it was always for purposes of beginning a new epoch, the old having been concluded by the linear. This happened in the Egyptian culture and quite likely at an even earlier period in the Paleolithic human-form culture of southeast Spain.

For in the beginnings of a new period and new art content, artists are able to achieve their first developed successes in depicting the *actual* forms of nature, not illusions of those forms. Sculpture, the medium similar in *tactile structure* to the form-structure of nature, makes possible the most simple, direct approach to a new, more difficult subject. (This evolution which we find appearing in history is further evidence for the assumption that sculpture was perhaps the major art of the Levant and African Paleolithic cultures.) In other words, each new epoch of art begins with a new subject-matter, and achieves its first major recording success with the tactile medium of sculpture; once this medium reaches the epitome of its potentialities in a particular stage of art development, then sculpture forms are gradually transformed on the linear surface by the two-dimensional artist, until these forms emerge more and more into the realization of the recording of a visual image as distinct from the recording of tactile or sculptural form. *Thus in each epoch success is achieved first in tactile correspondence and then in visual image correspondence!* But the sculptor never passes beyond tactile effort, except when he compromises his medium with the linear one in the form of relief methods. The linear artist, however, begins his art efforts by first

29. Left, Anubis, the jackal-headed god. Courtesy of The Metropolitan Museum of Art. Right, statue of the seated Lady Senuwy, Dyn. XII. Courtesy, Museum of Fine Arts, Boston.

compromising his medium with the sculptor's, in that he tries first to achieve sculpture-like recordings and only later realizes that his task, given his particular medium, is to record not the forms but the *image of the forms of objects.*

There is another reason why sculpture was so important to the Egyptians; namely, the sculptured *forms* functioned as substitutes for the body of the dead. Concerning the tenacity of the Egyptian's belief in the life after death, Breasted has the following interesting notion: "the conditions of soil and climate resulted in such remarkable preservation of the human body as may be found under natural conditions perhaps nowhere else in the world. . . . The surprisingly perfect state of preservation in which he found his ancestors when the digging of a new grave may have disclosed them, must have greatly stimulated his belief in their continued existence, and aroused his imagination to more detailed pictures of the realm and the life of the mysterious departed." [22]

However, when the Egyptians began to bury their dead in coffins or tombs rather than in the sand, the bodies were not so well preserved (hence the coffin was called "sarcophagus" meaning "flesh-eating"), and so portraits of the deceased, made in stone, wood or plaster and then painted, were interred with the departed.

These stone images of the dead, buried with their own bodies, would thus additionally assure them of having their original body intact in the other world. In fact it was a better body, since the sculpture had the benefits of idealizations. These were times when man was largely what we might call an unconscious logician, and so it was very easy for him to identify similarities as had been done in the Paleolithic past. For example, it was not at all difficult for him to assume that since his image was made of a lasting material, such as stone, his own body would also endure.

Thus the sculptor, along with those who practiced the art of mummification, participated in the most important of all functions—the preservation of the body of the dead so that its owner might possess it intact in the next world. As a matter of fact, G. Elliot Smith informs us that a sculptor was called a "vivifier," and that the word for "to carve" was "to give birth," "to create," "to give life." [23]

In the early dynasties we find, to quote Petrie, that art "searched for the truth, it carefully observed anatomy. . . ." [24] After this, although there were periodic attempts throughout Egyptian art to increase sculptural realism in an effort to produce something approaching a portrait, the dominant effort was to make only a stereotyped depiction. So much was this the case that in some instances it was generally impossible to tell one king from another by the visual evidence of the art alone. Consequently, it was a common practice for one king to take over the statues of another to serve as his own, merely by changing the name.

Nevertheless we note that even though portraiture was restricted in its development, still there was a steady increase in the accuracy of portraying the general human form. [25] At intervals the priests attempted to interrupt and reverse this direction. But until the final regression set in, Egyptian artists were following the natural order of development in depicting the human form, just as had the early Paleolithic artists in their depictions of the animal form. Thus it was necessary first to achieve static depictions before dynamic figures could be represented; [26] and it was also necessary first to achieve the

22. J. H. Breasted: *The Dawn of Conscience,* pp. 45-46, Charles Scribner's Sons, New York, 1934.

23. G. Elliot Smith: "The Wonder of the Mummy," p. 554 in *Wonders of the Past,* Vol. 1, edited by Sir J. A. Hammerton, Wise and Co., New York, 1937, published by G. P. PUTNAM'S SONS.

24. Petrie, *Arts and Crafts of Ancient Egypt,* p. 15.

25. Petrie suggests, p. 41, *Arts and Crafts of Ancient Egypt,* that the revolution under Akhenaten in the XVIIIth dynasty was only a culmination of the naturalistic tendency that had been growing during the preceding reigns.

26. There is one exception to this rule, and that is the Levant art, which produces dynamic human figures in battle and in the hunt. Here it was possible because the simple formula for depicting humans offered no great difficulties for dynamic poses; whereas once artists were concerned with the anatomical recording of the figure, a certain degree of development was required before this anatomy could be put in a pose indicating motion. In fact, observation of the Levant art indicates that the simplest depictions produce the most convincing sense of movement. Not until developed Greek art appears do we see this degree of movement effectuated in accurate linear and sculptured depictions.

30. Left, portrait head of Chephren, Dyn. IV. Courtesy, Museum of Fine Arts, Boston. Right, portrait head of a priest, Dyn. XXVI-XXX. Courtesy, Museum of Fine Arts, Boston.

recording of the human form as such before it became possible to realize the further, more developed ability of perceiving and being able to depict the human form in particular—the individual or portrait. This is the very natural serial development through which every student in a "life class" must pass. First he achieves the ability to record the general human form and then he is able to portray an individual.

But, as we remarked before, the artist's ability to record is not simply a case of visual development, since the operation of this factor is severely bound up with all other activities, with man's beliefs and with his general reasoning development. These other factors can stimulate or retard the development of the visual factor, just as the results of visual development can delay or stimulate human behavior in general. For this reason efforts at realistic portraiture occur throughout Egyptian history, but are not consistently pursued.

Thus the fact that portraiture was not completely or consistently realized by Egyptian sculptors was due not only to their lack of ability but also to the fact that Egyptians as a whole did not feel the need for it, and thus did not allow their artists to develop their potential ability. These were communal times—the individual as such was of no importance; what was important was that which the individual represented in the generalized experiences of the culture. Thus everything was *mainly* depicted as generalization, not individualization.

There would appear to be, excluding the primitive periods, three different types of sculpture throughout the history of Egypt, as far as the rendition of the head is concerned. These are: (1) The direct idealization of the human head with no intention of depicting a literal portrait (figure 30, head of Chephren); (2) idealization in which the general characteristics of the person's head are retained but idealized to a large degree; (3) little or no idealization, in which a predominant effort is made to depict a literal portrait of the actual person (figure 30, head of a priest). Throughout the history of Egyptian

114

art each of these three types was gradually perfected. As for the rest of the human figure, it was consistently more or less idealized into a fixed, frontal (mostly standing or sitting) pose.

Another aspect of this problem of restricted realism is to be seen in the fact that idealizations were more particularly retained in the case of depictions of gods and kings, in order to set them apart from others, to heighten their dignity, their power, their divinity.[27] There was far greater freedom exercised in the depiction of lesser figures, such as servants and workers in general. They were shown in more familiar, life-like poses and activities, while animals, interestingly enough, were done the most realistically in both two and three dimensions.

But in any case, no matter what the subject, the Egyptian sculptor never turned the head nor the torso of a human figure on its base. In the linear arts, as we have seen, the head was almost always turned to one side or the other, but in sculpture it was never turned to either side.[28] The figures might be seated or standing, and figures of lesser importance might bend at the waist and the like, but in almost all cases the human figure was frozen into a front-view. Any extreme action occurs only in the linear arts, and there it is generally action petrified. The Egyptian sculptured figures are like transfixed blocks of stone stuck in space. It was the Greeks who finally turned and twisted into space the sculpture of the human form.

The Greek and Roman sculptors succeeded many times in making one forget that their sculpture was of stone, but it would seem as though the Egyptian sculptor intended that one never forget that his figures were made of STONE. If the developed sculptural art of Greece invites you to walk around the human form, the Egyptian sculpture *forbids* you to stand at the side, *commands* you to stand in front! And in the front you meet an impassive face, the eyes of which look beyond you as though you were but a grain of sand. In fact, one cannot imagine the religion of Egypt existing without stone, without the power of stone to back it up, without stone to give it strength.

This brings us to the problem of Egyptian Architecture, which was, in a sense, inseparable from stone sculpture. Egypt achieved the first highly developed stone Architecture. Particularly the pyramids and obelisks are the earliest examples of a developed and precise effort to erect monuments of stone in which the Architecture is completely shaped by man. We believe that this problem is in some way connected with the problem of the megaliths—admittedly an extremely controversial subject. Surviving megaliths, regardless of their age, are the most primitive examples of stone monuments and Architecture, and are to be found in various parts of the world (figure 31).

Some writers are inclined to explain these monuments as a development from Paleolithic cave burials.[29] This does not seem unreasonable, considering that man very early in his evolution seems to have exhibited decided beliefs about stones and the dead—there is evidence of burial rites from as far back as Mousterian times. We can imagine that the importance of these burials would have prompted man also to mark the graves. The early markers were probably of the most simple type, passing through a development somewhat similar to the stone stage we posited for sculpture in its inception. At first it sufficed merely to place any single stone as a marker.[30] Later more stones would be used and arranged in particular

27. In our analysis of the Christian arts we shall go into detail regarding the psychological function of the deliberate idealizations or distortions of reality by which religious phenomena are generally set apart. What we say there will bear on the Egyptian practices of generalizing or idealizing the human forms of their officials, kings and gods.

28. The author has been able to find only a few instances in which the Egyptian sculptor breaks the frontal law.

29. See Worringer. *Egyptian Art,* pp. 39-40.

30. See reference to Mousterian graves, page 55.

31. Megaliths, France. Courtesy, Chicago Natural History Museum.

ways. Gradually larger stones would be used and their arrangements become more complex.[31] Perhaps none of these early phases of stone marking of burial places consisted of stones large enough or permanent enough in construction to enable them to survive, as did the massive megalithic monuments found later in Europe and elsewhere. The possibility of small monuments of this kind is suggested by the findings of John Layard among the stone culture people of Malekula. There dolmens ranged "from six inches to four or five feet high. . . ."[32] Small obelisks have also been found from quite early times. Early stone monuments were probably comprised of stones just as they were found in their natural state, and so it would be difficult to recognize early monoliths, even if one saw their fallen remains lying about.

On the other hand, the earliest development of stone monuments and Architecture beyond the natural state occurred in Egypt, where little so-called megalithic material is found. Childe has mentioned a few examples from very early times which are suggestive of the dolmen type of megalithic monuments. Concerning an early tomb at Hierakanpolis excavated by Petrie, he wrote: "the chamber was formed by three upright slabs of desert sandstone roofed by a fourth after the manner of a dolmen. More often the chambers were roofed with wood, till under the Second Dynasty the corbelled roof of mud-brick began to replace timber work."[33] However, it would appear that in general the Egyptians, instead of increasing the size of the megaliths as was done in Europe, passed more quickly and directly into what we know today as Architecture.

31. In connection with this problem the following by Sollas is of interest. In discussing the Bushmen funeral customs, he writes that after the grave was filled with earth, "stones were thrown on it by the mourners, and afterwards a stone was contributed by every passer-by till a cairn was raised." (*Ancient Hunters*, p. 478.)

32. John Layard: *Stone Men of Malekula*, p. 700.

33. Childe, *New Light on the Most Ancient East*, p. 109.

In any case, in some way similar to the early beginnings posited in Paleolithic Europe, from the use of single and then complex arrangements of stones, there could have been developed the invention of the mastaba as an outgrowth of the grouped and piled stones; the mastaba in turn, as many writers have pointed out, led to the making of the pyramids. Similarly from the early, more primitive monolith the obelisk might have evolved.

Some such early beginnings for Egyptian stone Architecture are suggested by further data from the stone people of Malekula. John Layard has shown, in the myths and rituals of these people, inescapable connections with the "megalith-builders," whose origin was in "Western Asia." [34] These beliefs suggest still further that "stone-magic" was one of the principal influences in the initial formation of Egyptian culture. Thus Layard speaks of: "Dolmens and 'altars' in the Small Islands and Malo called by names indicating 're-birth.' " [35]

"The fundamentally religious nature of all these monuments, both dolmens and 'altars,' is strikingly shown by the fact that all the words just cited [see preceding quotation] are derived, according to Dr. A. Capell, from the Indonesian *batu,* meaning 'to appear,' or 'to be born,' and so also 'to be born again' or 're-born,' clearly brought out in the Vao symbolism by virtue of which the large dolmen erected during the Maki rites represents the womb." [36]

In describing the various types of monoliths Layard writes: "in the first three steps in this rank only plain monoliths are erected, while in the fourth and fifth the monoliths that are put up are furnished with a vertical groove, and it is not till the sixth step is reached that we find the monolith carved to represent the human figure. This highest rank, according to yet another native characteristic of always trying to 'go one better' even than the best, is then capped by two supernumerary ranks, for which the right is acquired of erecting monoliths carved with three, or even four, faces.

". . . . We thus find that in the center of the monolithic area the chief monument erected for the most important rank is a carved monolith representing the human form. As Deacon has abundantly shown, all such monuments are said to be the habitation of ancestral ghosts. . . .

"In the highest rank of all, then, we find the erection of a stone statue which is a kind of collective representation of all those who have taken that rank. In the preparatory stages conferring the same title we find in descending order, firstly, stones carved only with a vertical groove, and lastly, perfectly plain, uncarved monoliths. There can therefore, I think, be no doubt that the plain monolith in the earlier steps in fact also represents a statue, from which, for the reasons stated above, the carving has been omitted." [37] In such a way we see the early stages of monoliths, dolmens, etc., becoming the habitation and the means for "re-birth" of the dead. It was exactly for such a purpose that the pyramids and statues of the Egyptians were made. Such beliefs probably had a long history before they appeared in Egyptian culture and hence became a part of its genesis; such a past history of the use of stone could help to explain the tremendously powerful character of the Egyptian's belief in the efficacy of his various stone monuments to the dead as securing an after-life.

It would seem therefore, that the European continent, which remained in a very primitive state during post-Paleolithic times, also remained in a primitive state of monument and Architecture; while Egypt, because of a more favorable climate, peculiar geographical conditions, and influences from both the West and the East, continued the development of human culture during post-Paleolithic times and exhibited precisely the type of developments we would expect from such a beginning as that with which stone monument practice undoubtedly began.

In brief, just as man had discovered and created the art of sculpture by beginning with the natural stones as he found them, and then developed through various stages until he was able to record

34. John Layard: "Maze-Dances and the Ritual of the Labyrinth in Malekula," *Folk Lore,* xlvii: 123-170, June, 1936.

35. Layard, *Stone Men of Malekula,* p. 705. Recall that the Egyptian word for sculptor was "the vivifier," "to give birth," etc.

36. Ibid., p. 705.

37. Ibid., pp. 698-699.

the forms of nature in the stone material, likewise a similar process resulted in the discovery and creation of the art of Architecture in stone, a process that began in the beginning of culture with the ready-made stone products of nature and proceeded to evolve until stone took precedence over wooden and brick man-made shelters as well as natural ones for the dead and the living.

If this is correct, we can now posit three factors found in earlier levels of culture which can be found in a more developed form in the art of Egypt:

(1) There was a further development of the linear depiction of the human figure, mostly a combination of engraving and painting, as had also been done in the cave arts of Europe.

(2) The stone sculpture of the human form, which was evolved particularly in Aurignacian times (and we believe continued in wood in the Levant and African Paleolithic cultures), became the foremost subject of Egyptian arts.

(3) Early natural stone monuments developed into stone Architecture, the outstanding examples being the pyramids and obelisks, the former dealing with the dead, the latter with the sun! The function of the first example is apparent; that of the latter is suggested by the fact that some of the obelisks were plated with metal and thus reflected the sun.

Judging by the evidence of predynastic art, it would appear that a very primitive culture was contacted by a far more advanced Paleolithic culture. For we see predynastic arts which are far more primitive than the Paleolithic and then examples which represent a similar level of development. Finally the Egyptian artists swing into action on their own, no longer beginners but leaders in art and culture in general. In short, it would appear that Egyptian history passed through steps of development similar to those we shall later find in Greece, Rome, etc. That is, first we see a primitive beginning, primitive by comparison to the more advanced contemporary culture; then the latter is contacted, amalgamation takes place, and so our once primitive culture now steps off as the precursor of future advances.

Thus step by step the Egyptians developed the human capacity to see-think out the various problems which secured still another major achievement in man's ability to interpret and record objective reality.

We have seen, however, that artists and what they produce are bound to culture as a whole. In the case of the Egyptians, their priests periodically suppressed the very direction that was necessary to the continued evolution of art and even religion. Art is bound to everything, as everything is to art; whatever happens affects art, as art affects the rest of human culture. But even though Egyptian art did not present one unbroken wave of progress, in the long run Egyptian artists succeeded in periodically recapturing the impetus to move forward towards ever greater accuracy in the recording of nature.

The main characteristics and achievements of Egyptian artists were formed very early in the history of their culture, and all further development was very gradual. Early in their history, Egyptian artists displayed a great degree of recording ability. Had they had the necessary amount of freedom of opportunity to develop, great accuracy in realistic recording could perhaps have been realized very much earlier in history. As it was, the development of Mimetic art was delayed some two thousand years and did not occur until Greco-Roman times.

Perhaps the fact that Egypt was surrounded and protected by natural barriers made possible the extremely slow-changing character of its culture. Yet the great progress achieved in art by the Egyptians was not superseded by other nations and peoples contemporary with them, who lived in environments more open to the outside world; at least this was not true until Egypt had passed its high point of development and Greece began its rise among the leading cultures of man.

Sculpture continued as the dominating medium of art after the downfall of Egypt, since it had yet to be exhausted in its potentialities for further development. It was the Greek artists who used this medium to secure further evolution in art. They concluded one aspect of the task begun by the Egyptian artists, and began another. It was from the Egyptian's highly developed generalized depictions of the human form that the Greeks took the art of sculpture to yet a higher level of development, further perfecting this objective as embodied in the notion of an "ideal." However, this trend first appeared with the Egyptians rather than with the Greeks. What the Greeks originated was a far greater perfection, both visually and theoretically, of the ideal. Therefore, the Egyptians were actually the forerunners of that which forms the first major, developed era of Greek art. In fact we shall find that the Greeks and Romans bring to a more consistent, complete development the two main aspects of Egyptian art—Idealism and Realism.

But of far greater importance than the question of the influences the Egyptians received, is what they have given to other nations, not only to the civilizations of the Near East, which under the New Kingdom monarchs were completely subject to the influence of Egypt, but also, and most important of all, to the Greeks, who in their 'archaic' period received valuable inspiration from Egypt and whose art has had a decisive and transforming influence on everything which has been created in Europe since their time. 277   Hermann Ranke

Art imitates nature. 59

Aristotle

In the history of Occidental philosophy the problem
of reality did not make its appearance until the time
of the early Greek philosophers, about the year five
hundred B.C. 285
                                    Oliver L. Reiser

Since the objects of imitation are men in action, and these men must be either of a higher or a lower type (for moral character mainly answers to these divisions, goodness and badness being the distinguishing marks of moral differences), it follows that we must represent men either as better than in real life, or as worse, or as they are. It is the same in painting. Polygnotus depicted men as nobler than they are, Pauson as less noble, Dionysius drew them true to life. 60

Aristotle

Greek art, like Egyptian, started from very primitive beginnings and gradually progressed towards more and more realism. When the Greeks eventually came into contact with the more developed art of their predecessors, particularly the Egyptians, they assimilated these previous advances and then assumed the leading role in achieving further developments in the evolution of art, a role which the Egyptians had formerly held.

One of the outstanding developments in Greek art, as compared to that of Egypt and previous cultures, is to be seen in their treatment of the human form. There were no longer those creatures of fantasy, partly animal or bird and partly human; the major and important subject was the human form as such, and particularly the male form, gods and heroized humans.

The principal problem of artists, up to and including the 5th century B. C., continued to be one of developing more and more accurate recordings of the general appearance of the human form. From the earliest times to the 5th century B. C., artists, when they portrayed the human form, had concentrated *mainly* on its general characteristics. With each progressive step in man's visual development more accuracy in this type of recording was gained. That is to say, for every culture up to and including the Classical Greek, there always remained a further aspect of the generalized reality for the artist to discover and record.

Our studies have shown that in Egyptian sculpture of the human figure, the most extensive degree of realism was achieved (when it was achieved) in the treatment of the head, while the body was consistently idealized. Throughout their three-dimensional art there can be seen an ambivalence between this sort of treatment of the human figure and that kind in which there was a consistent idealistic treatment for the entire figure including the head. It was this latter direction which the Greeks took up from the Egyptians and developed to the greatest perfection that has ever been achieved by artists before or since (figure 32). Where the Egyptians had been ambivalent between the real and the ideal, the Greeks pushed the ideal (i.e., the general shape of the human form) to its highest degree of realism and achieved more realism than any Egyptian work of art reveals. There was more realism not only in the recording of the human form but also in the fact that the Greeks freed the human form from the block of stone and activated it in the third dimension. The Egyptian frontal position was completely broken; the Greek figures ask the observer to go all around them.

Thus the Classical (5th century) Greek artists perfected the three-dimensional depiction of the human form *in general,* an achievement indicating that man now had a higher degree of ability to visualize reality than ever before. In this respect the Greeks began the consistent resolution of the problems that operated in Egyptian art. That is, in the art of the Egyptians we do not find a consistent effort to achieve a perfection of the human form as such; there was rather an effort at complete idealization in some cases, and in others an idealization that strove to retain the particular characteristics of the individual. Hence there existed a great *diversity* of idealized types. Consequently in the art of Egypt, there appears to be an ambivalence between the ideal and the real, while in the art of the Greeks one sees an effort to achieve a perfected type of the human form as such, more or less a particular ideal for all individuals.

123

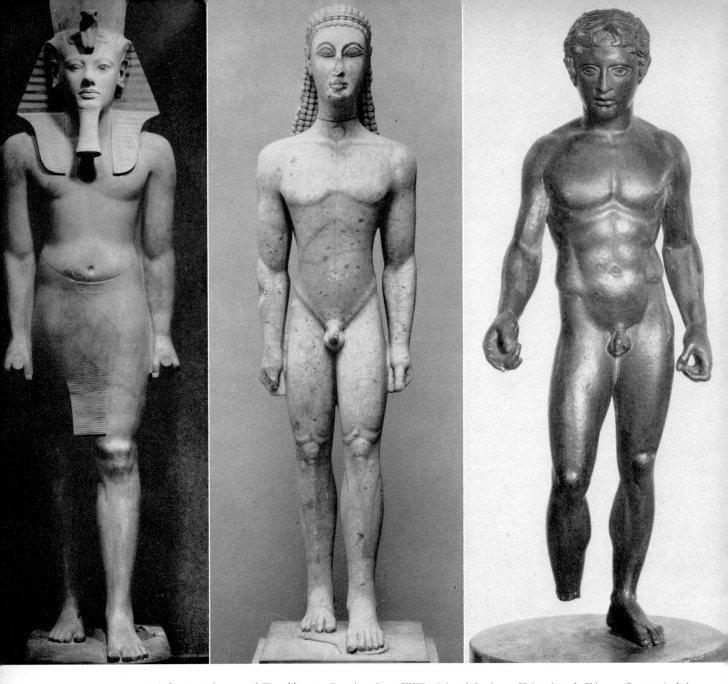

32. Left, restored statue of Tutenkhamon, Egyptian, Dyn. XVIII. Oriental Institute, University of Chicago. Center, Archaic Apollo, Greek, 6th Century B. C. Courtesy of The Metropolitan Museum of Art. Right, Statuette of a Youth, Greek, 5th Century B. C. Courtesy of The Metropolitan Museum of Art.

As a matter of fact, the Classical Greek sculptor deliberately avoided the depiction of the human form as a particular individual, at least on the visual level. A name was attached to the sculpture to indicate whom it was supposed to represent, since this could not always be determined by the visual level alone. Portraits of individuals were at first forbidden. It is reported that Phidias was accused of sacrilege and imprisoned because he introduced portraits of himself and his friend, Pericles, the head of the Athenian state, on the shield of one of his statues of Athena.[1] The important meaning of an individual was what he represented of the community, not what he actually looked like, and so he was depicted as a general symbol. Thus Kahler tells us: "there was a very definite restriction imposed on all attempts at a too radical characterization and individualization. The demand for portraits increased as people dedicated their

1. G. M. A. Richter: *The Sculpture and Sculptors of the Greeks,* p. 162ff., Yale University Press, New Haven, 1929.

124

pictures to deities—a residue of primeval offerings. Statues or busts of famous statesmen, thinkers, Olympic prize-winners, were erected in halls of honor. We hardly know, however, how Pericles, Plato or Sophocles really looked, for all preserved portraits are more or less types in the manner of divine representations, they are, as we would say, idealized. All youths look a little like Apollo, all men with a beard, a little like Zeus, all women like Hera or Athena. Only Socrates is an exception. His ugliness is faintly indicated, although it, too, is somewhat like that of a Satyr." [2]

Even the depiction of classes of human beings was avoided by these 5th century Greek artists, or at least considerably minimized. The attempt was made to transform all reality into a perfection of the human form in general. P. A. Sorokin describes this well when he says: "before us are immortals or idealized mortals; old age is rejuvenated; the baby is depicted as grown up; the women have little that is specifically womanish and appear like perfect athletes; there are no concrete landscapes. The postures and the expressions are free from any violent or debased or too human emotion and distorting passion. They are calm, serene, imperturbable like the gods. Even the dead shine with the same calmness and serene beauty. All the statues have a 'Greek' profile; not because the Greeks were such, as Winkelmann thought, but because it was the profile thought to be perfect." [3]

Thus the art of the Classical period did not depict either the very old or the very young, but a medium between these two extremes in order to produce perfect, eternal youth (figure 34, center). There was even an attempt to avoid the depiction of specific sex; instead there appeared a combination of both male and female characteristics. Every phase of life depicted in the art turned towards some supreme, central ideal of all humanity.

Mathematics played a major role in the art of Classical Greece; the artists used it in creating the rules for securing ideal depictions of the human form. In fact, as Philoaus tells us, "All things which can be known have numbers; for it is not possible that without number anything can be either conceived or known." [4] The artist would select perhaps ten models; from each he would choose those parts of the figure which he found to be the most perfect and then combine them into a single, ideal representation of the human form.

As a result of the art developments of the 5th century B. C., there eventually appeared the first conscious, theoretically worked out awareness that artists were concerned with the depiction of the perfect human form in general. This the theoreticians called the "universal" or "ideal," and the formulation of such a notion was the direct result of man's consciousness of a "problem of reality," as we shall explain. This ideal, as Aristotle explained it, is inherent in but seldom if ever achieved by nature. It is the artist's task to perceive and achieve this ideal towards which nature strives. [5]

These notions of art were the crystallization of what had been going on for thousands of years in man's art history. The Greeks, whose culture represented the natural culmination of preceding human activity, seem to have been the first men who were coherently aware of their ability to rationalize the phenomena of the universe, both in their logical systems and in their art. Before Classical Greek times, men had tried to give some reason for considering and depicting reality as they did; but the Greeks were conscious, to a degree at least, of the *reason for reasoning* as they did, and thus they achieved what has since become man's most important characteristic: his ability to think about his method of thinking, to manipulate *consciously* his ability to reason, to rationalize. In the field of art this meant that the artist thought about the way in which he saw, the method by which he visualized nature's reality. Thus, it was no accident that the Greeks realized a consciousness of man's inherent ability to reason and abstract (a consciousness of reality as a problem) at about the same time that they achieved perfection in recording the general appearance of the human form. For once man achieved in his art an accurate likeness to the general appearance of the human form, he was also in a position to become conscious of the fact.

2. Erich Kahler: *Man the Measure,* pp. 282-283.

3. P. A. Sorokin: *Social and Cultural Dynamics,* Vol. 1, p. 291, The American Book Co., New York, 1937.

4. From Tobias Dantzig: *Number: The Language of Science,* p. 43, 2d ed. New York, 1933. By permission of The Macmillan Company, publishers.

5. The detailed discussion of Aristotle's theories is reserved for a later chapter.

We can perhaps make this problem more clear by considering for a moment the two general levels with which the human organism contacts and evaluates the objective world—"feeling" (thalamus) and "thinking" (cortex)—and their bearing on early man's activities as well as those of the Classical Greeks. These two levels are interdependently related in their function, but "feeling" (thalamus) predominates in the Primitive's behavior.

Keeping this in mind, we observe again that very early attempts at recording the animal form in Pictographic times were, comparatively speaking, very inaccurate and crude. Yet it would appear that early man experienced and so considered his representations to be as real as the corresponding object in nature. How, we might ask, could these early men have considered their art, crude as it was, to be as real as nature? It was possible because of the predominance of the feeling or thalamic level in their functioning. The discriminatory activity of the cortex did not operate to any high degree because of its predominantly unconscious function; thus the Primitive was not especially impressed by the differences between his art and reality. It was *similarities, not differences,* that were of the greatest importance. And since the Primitive concentrated upon similarities and largely ignored differences, there was therefore identification: if he saw in his art certain characteristics similar to an animal form, it was enough for him to consider the art as the real animal. All he needed on the conscious level was to see that two or more objects had certain features in common; they then automatically became the same. Thus it was possible for the Primitive to accept consciously as absolute reality his crude art recordings.[6]

Of course, both "thalamic" and "cortical" experience operate in all art for all peoples; but when the "feeling" level of similarities dominates in determining conscious art experiences, discrimination and differentiation, which necessitate extensive use of the cortical level, operate at a minimum and are *largely unconscious.* In order to comprehend how any progress is made, therefore, we must also analyze the unconscious level, whence differentiation gradually evolved.

Now regardless of how real the Primitive artist might consciously have thought his art to be, when he viewed reality in comparison to his depiction of it, he very gradually discovered discrepancies in his art. These experiences originated on the unconscious level. It was this unconscious differentiation, eventually becoming conscious, which gradually made possible ever more accurate recordings of nature's reality. As each small difference was pushed into consciousness, it was incorporated into art.

This gradual developmental process can be observed in the child artist's evolution as he becomes more and more aware of the reality. Observe him when he corrects his drawing; he does not do so through any extensive analysis; it is simply a case of suddenly seeing a difference between the art and reality, which he incorporates into his drawing without a moment's hesitation. The very nature of this process accounts for the long period required for the evolution of man's early art, particularly as regards the Paleolithic period.

However, as man evolved, the cortical level gradually rose to ever higher degrees of conscious operation, and in proportion to this rise there was a development of man's ability to differentiate in his observation and analysis. Finally the cortical level became dominant with the Greek artists of the 5th century B.C. and they were able consciously to observe and analyze differences, as well as similarities, between nature and art. This ability to differentiate on high levels enabled man finally to achieve the perfected recording of the general character of the human form (figure 33). Only such an ability would allow artists to hammer out the differences in their art to such a degree that the general form of the human figure could be as perfectly recorded as it was by the Greek Idealists.

Primitive man, therefore, largely dominated by the thalamic ("emotional") level, was able to accept the similarities between his art and the reality by ignoring the differences between them; by identifying on the basis of similarities he accredited the reality of reality to his art.[7] But by the time of the Greek Idealists, man's behavior was dominated by the cortical level and so a highly developed ability

6. This analysis applies to even more developed recordings of later times. For thousands of years the function of art was such that man was compelled to regard it as the reality. Even in Greek times statues were put on trial for murder and convicted, and the like.

7. In order to comprehend this type of orientation to art and reality it is necessary that we in turn avoid identifying our reaction to this situation with the Primitive's. We must project!

33. Left, Venus of Willendorf, Paleolithic. Photo, The Bettmann Archive. Center, wooden female figure from Dier-el-Bersheh. Egyptian, Dyn. XII. Courtesy, Museum of Fine Arts, Boston. Right, Aphrodite of Kyrene, Greek, 1st Century B. C. Terme Museum, Rome. Photo, The Bettmann Archive.

to differentiate. Thus the Greek artists were able to achieve a greater similarity between their art and nature by using this differentiational ability to see the general differences between the two and gradually eliminate them. In short, differentiational activity was used to achieve *more similarities* between the general form of nature and that of art. The Primitive artist was only concerned with gross similarities; the differences between his art and reality were ignored. The Greek artist was concerned with eliminating these differences in order to achieve a similarity between art and reality, at least on the generalized level.

Therefore, we regard the development of art as mainly a record of the transition from an *un*conscious process of slight differentiation to one of extensive *conscious* differentiation. This was a part of the general trend of man's evolution for thousands of years, characterized by an ever-increasing cortical activity which finally dominated consciousness. With the Classical Greeks man's cortex began to play a dominant role in the production of art and in general human behavior. "Laws of thought" were formulated and categories established; there was no longer a reliance largely on unconscious, low-order cortical activity. Instead man's thinking about his thinking played a major role in determining the manner in which he saw the world.

34. Left, the Emperor Caracalla, Roman, 3rd Century A. D. Courtesy of The Metropolitan Museum of Art. Center, head of an athlete, Greek, 2nd half of 5th Century B. C. Courtesy of The Metropolitan Museum of Art. Right, Roman head, 1st Century B. C. Courtesy of The Metropolitan Museum of Art.

Cassius J. Keyser, speaking of the change from the world of "feeling" to that of consciousness of thought, has written as follows: "How long our human ancestors, in remote ages, may have groped, as some of their descendants even now grope, among the things of *sense,* in the hope of finding *there* the desiderated good, we do not know—past time is long and the evolution of wisdom has been slow. We do know that, long before the beginnings of recorded history, superior men—advanced representatives of their kind—must have learned that the deliverance sought was not to be found among the objects of the *mobile* world, and so the spirit's quest passed from thence; passed from the realm of perception and sense to the realm of concept and reason: thought ceased, that is, to be merely the unconscious means of pursuit and became itself the quarry—mind had discovered mind; and there, in the realm of ideas, in the realm of spirit proper, in the world of reason or thought, the great search—far outrunning historic time—has been endlessly carried on, with varying fortunes, indeed, but without despair or breach of continuity, meanwhile multiplying its resources and assuming gradually, as the years and centuries have passed, the characters and forms of what we know today as philosophy and science and art. I have mentioned the passing of the quest from the realm of sense to the realm of conception: a most notable transition in the career of mind and especially significant for the view I am aiming to sketch. For thought, in thus becoming a conscious subject or object of thought, then began its destined course in reason: in ceasing to be merely an unconscious means of pursuit and becoming itself the quarry, it definitely entered upon the arduous way that leads to the goal of rigor." [8]

The first repercussion of this change was that man overevaluated the importance of his new found ability to reason about reality and art. The Greeks' realization of their ability to record the general

8. Cassius J. Keyser: *The Human Worth of Rigorous Thinking,* pp. 46-47, Scripta Mathematica, Yeshiva College, New York, 1940.

128

appearance of the human form with accuracy was a useful and necessary development in art. But then they overdid it; they began to think that they could achieve something superior to nature—indeed, that they actually had. They assumed that this perfection of the recording of the general human form was actually a perfection of the forms of nature, a perfection which nature presumably sought but seldom if ever achieved. What they had actually perfected, of course, was not the human form of nature but the ability of man to depict the general character of the human form.

Something similar happened with man's newly discovered ability to reason about reason, to produce consciously, various systems of logic. It was decided that the human mind and its products ruled supreme as an independent power over all the universe. The extreme of this view is to be found in Plato's theory that "ideas" are manifestations of the divine power and as such are the only legitimate source of "truth." He considered the empirical level as the most imperfect source of truth; the divine "idea," like the ideal in art, transcended empirical reality. It is an indication of Plato's totalitarian leanings that he had a higher regard for the art of Egypt than for that of his own country. For here was an art completely controlled and dictated by the religious powers. Here the "divine idea" was supreme and art as well as everything else was but its servant.

Aristotle, although holding to notions similar to Plato's philosophy, differed considerably in that he did not degrade the empirical level to oblivion, but regarded it as an important source of knowledge. Hence he devised a link between the empirical level and the divine. For him the former was not a mere shadow of the latter, but a definite, even if still a lesser, part of the manifestation of the divine.

Thus Aristotle rejected Plato's nihilistic attitude towards art. He took the opposite view and regarded artists as able to foster particular benefits to humans with their abilities to "imitate" nature. Subsequent events have proved that Aristotle was more correct than Plato. For Aristotle, however, the term "imitation" had more than one meaning, as can be seen in the quotation at the head of this chapter. Moreover, he was particularly partial to one of these meanings, although he seems to have been reticent to say so frankly: namely, that the proper subject for the artist's imitation was the general ideal towards which nature strove, but seldom if ever achieved. According to him the imitation of this "ideal" was the supreme task of the artist, who thus completed the process allegedly initiated by nature.

This conscious awareness and analysis of problems of reality in art by the Greeks brought about radical changes which must be considered if we are to analyze adequately all subsequent art. First of all the *consciousness* of the reasoning process man employed in his interpretation and recording of reality was now directly influencing the formation of what he saw. That is, since the Classical Greeks assumed that nature strove for an ideal, they were bound to see and comprehend nature in a very different manner than would be the case if they abided by theories calling for a literal recording of nature. In short, man's consciousness of what he thought and why he did so, now played a great role in determining what he felt and saw in the world of experience. The consequences of this consciousness of reasoning were crucially different from those in previous cultures where the process was largely restricted to the unconscious level. With the Primitives, the peoples of magic, such a restriction was natural, since they were unable to go further. With the Egyptians, it was not natural, but a man-made situation, in the sense that if religion was to survive with totally undisputed power, it was necessary for the priests deliberately to impose restrictions upon man's consciousness of reasoning and seeing.

The Greek artist of the Classical period, however, as an Idealist, still continued to ignore differences, although of another kind than in previous art times. Earlier artists had largely ignored the differences between their art and the general form of nature; only similarities were important, as we have pointed out. But the Greek Idealist with his art generalizations ignored the differences to be found between every individual human form. Hence their rationalizations of reality became limited and static.

But once the grip of the ideal notion was broken, it was possible for the Greek artist to enlarge the scope and further perfect his awareness of the many *more* factors which constituted reality; in short, he could seek the particulars in the general form of nature. Since artists were now able to visualize in a *consciously* directed manner in the search for the ever more accurate perception of nature's reality, they were also able to incorporate this into their art recordings. Once again, just as Egyptian artists had attempted on numerous occasions, artists struck out to secure more realism, a greater correspondence with reality.

35. Left, standing Venus, Greek, 1st Century B. C. In the collection of the Minneapolis Institute of Arts. Center, Old Market Woman, Greek, Hellenistic period. Courtesy of The Metropolitan Museum of Art. Right, Agrippina "the Younger," mother of Nero, Roman, 1st Century A. D. In the collection of the Minneapolis Institute of Arts.

Thus, after Classical times in Greece, there was a gradual rise in the artist's ability to depict the particulars in reality. Old people were made to appear old (figure 35, center), infants to look babyish, women were more commonly depicted and there was more emphasis on sex differentiations. However, the Greeks did not engage in any large-scale attempt to record those particulars which would have resulted in literal portraiture. This was to be the principal task of the Romans. The quest for the particular among Greek artists, in the major portion of their art, went only as far as was necessary for depicting the various classes in their society: the aged and the infant, the poor and the rich, the lame and the healthy, the scholar and the wrestler, etc. Artists were more interested in showing that a certain person belonged to the class of the poor rather than that he was a particular individual in the poor class.

Only towards the end of Hellenistic times did definite attempts at portraiture appear. But on the whole most of these were a further development of one aspect of Egyptian sculpture, i.e., the idealization of the particular form of a particular individual. Only a few seem to be a direct effort at literal portraiture, but even in these there was never achieved the degree of realism that was to be found later in Roman sculpture.

Nevertheless, Lysippos, a late 4th century artist, was reported to have boasted that he took nature herself as a model.[9] In other words, nature as it appeared to his eyes was becoming the artist's "ideal," so to speak. If there was as yet no striving for complete, literal realism, at least more of it was sought than in the preceding Greek period. "If before mortals were depicted like the immortals," says Sorokin, "now the gods tend to be depicted like mortals." [10] One aspect of this increasing realism is seen in the fact that after the Classical period, the Greeks, with few exceptions, depicted the human form more

9. Richter, op. cit., p. 218.   10. Sorokin, op. cit., p. 299.

130

or less in its natural life-size, thus symbolizing their regard for man as a man—a human being, instead of a deity. Compare this, for instance, with the colossal size of many of the hieratic and royal representations of the Egyptians.

Moreover, from the middle of the 5th century B.C. on, artists came to be recognized as specific individuals for the first time in history, at least on any large scale.[11] Thus the works of artists were no longer anonymous. It was perhaps inevitable that recognition of individuality should appear at the time a high degree of realism was attained. Each artist was attempting to secure his individuality by working in a particular, personal style. If the ideal was not completely dispensed with, it was, nevertheless, no longer the dominant factor. Heretofore the culture had dictated to the artist what he should express in his art, and in the Classical period there had been conformity to severe, inflexible, mathematical formulations in order to achieve the general or ideal depiction of the human form. But after the Classical period there occurred the inception of that modern venture of the artist's expressing his personal attitude towards his culture. Gradually each individual artist became free to choose his own manner of art; the old rules were no longer the order of the day. Individual originality gradually replaced mass conformity to a single cultural style, although the full effects of such a change were not to be seen until the times of the Renaissance. The accusation of plagiarism eventually became something to be avoided, whereas in the earlier times each artist had worked more or less like the others in his particular culture. Now originality, imagination, invention of an individual kind became the order of the day.

Thus after the Classical period of the 5th century B.C. there appeared in Greek art a Romantic trend, which in its broader aspects released the evolution of art. For the artist was thereby absolved from uselessly continuing the already accomplished task of depicting the human form in general, and could move on to further progress—to the recording of more particulars and hence the achievement of more accuracy in depicting reality. The Romantic revisions not only made possible a more useful orientation to reality, but at the same time they exposed the fact that the Classical viewpoint oversimplified and staticized reality as a problem.

Nevertheless, no matter how useful the Romantic revolt against the Classical laws of art, eventually it swung to the opposite extreme—to the belief that no laws, only emotions were necessary; hence the Romantic attitude eventually degenerated into a lack of adequate, precise formulations. It was not realized that in denying the art laws of the past it was still necessary to retain the notion of law—to replace old with new laws. The Romantic attitude made further progress possible to a point; after that the Romans took over the task.

The Greeks, nevertheless, began the release of mankind from the supernaturalism of the Orient, as exemplified particularly in Egypt. They took the first major steps from religion to science. They were the first to begin the release of the individual from the dominance of dictatorial, omnipotent forms of government; the first to begin science in the more modern sense, contributing to astronomy, biology, mechanics, etc., achievements which were hardly improved upon until the 17th century. They were also the first to forge that supreme trait of man: the ability to create and consciously analyze systems of human reason. Finally their artists were the first to analyze consciously the visual depiction of reality and the human form in particular.

Our history has shown us how art operates as a documentary instrument. It serves as a record of how "visualization" and "thinking" have interdependently developed, with the cortex gaining increasing control over the thalamus of man's nervous system. Moreover, men have recorded in their art their beliefs about the world in which they live and what they believe will happen to them when they die. In short, "art" comprises the "visual" presentation of the general kind of orientation towards reality adopted by any culture. All this we shall find again reflected in the art of the Romans.

11. Names of Egyptian artists have come down to us; however, no records have been found indicating their specific works, only the school to which they belonged.

36. Left, Fresco from the Villa dei Misteri near Pompeii. Greco-Roman, 1st Century A. D. Alinari photo. Right, Mural, Villa of L. Herennius Florus at Boscoreale. Greco-Roman, 1st Century B. C. Courtesy of The Metropolitan Museum of Art.

The notion prevalent today is that the Romans were little interested in art and that what they did produce was not important. Such an evaluation stems from unconscious and so uninvestigated assumptions about art. The fact is that the prime achievement of the Romans was in realizing an extensive degree of realism in their sculpture; because such an objective is not considered important today, it is naively assumed that it never was considered important as art in the past, or that it never comprised an important aspect of the general evolution of art.

Realism, practicality were outstanding elements in the lives of the Romans. From earliest times, they had been a people primarily concerned with the development of politics, agriculture and war, all eventually reflected in what they depicted in their art with considerable accuracy—i.e., battles, sacred processions and the like. The records that we have of art theory at the height of the Roman period reflect the utilitarian attitude. (In many instances these attitudes are similar to certain present day notions.) Cicero considered the "beautiful" and the "useful" as one;[12] this is well illustrated in the following quotation from his writings: "In navigation, what is so necessary to a ship as bulwarks, keel, prow, stern, yards, sails, mast and yet combining so much beauty with their respective configurations, that they seem invented less for the purposes of utility than to charm the eye with their grace and symmetry. . . . In architecture, the columns give support to porticos and temples, and yet are not more useful than ornament. . . . It was

12. With the Greeks there was also a concern with the beautiful and the useful, but less in the utilitarian sense of the Romans and more in the sense of morality and religion.

132

not taste but necessity . . . . that suggested the roof of the Capitol, or the slanting roof of other buildings; for when the problem of throwing off the rain from both sides of the edifice was solved, the beauty was the consequence of its utility; so that if the Capitol had been built above the clouds, where rain could never fall, no other conformation would have been equally pleasing to the eye." [13]

The religion of the Romans was a reflection of their more practical attitude towards the problems of existence. They divested the gods of much of their past power and hence they could be depicted more realistically. The Idealist Greeks, as we noted earlier, made no effort to give their depictions of gods a distinct personality; often they were even of doubtful sex. As their art progressed, they made their gods more individualized. The Romans, however, gave their deities definite sex and complete individuality. In short, religion was brought down to daily living by the Romans. The Roman citizen was simply obliged to perform his religious observances in the prescribed manner and let it go at that. In the 1st century B.C., "A President of the College of Pontifs [state priesthood] himself declared that religion was composed of three kinds: (1) mythology, which consisted of the purely ornamental fictions of the poets; (2) philosophy; (3) the religious ceremonies of the State, which existed solely to provide the statesman with an instrument for managing the ignorant proletariat." [14]

Human culture had now become more complex. Consequently there was an increase in the number of individuals, rulers, officials, etc., who controlled the affairs of government. Accompanying the rise in the number of these individuals was a large demand for portraits. The artist's task was now to depict specific individuals—in other words, the particular individual form. In Greece one had to achieve heroization in order to have a statue made of him; in Rome one had to attain the rank of official in the government. Greek artists perfected the Egyptian idealization of the individual, while Roman artists were definitely bent on showing exactly what a particular man looked like (figure 34). The Romans, unlike their predecessors, considered their rulers as men like themselves and depicted them as such, and not until later times was the ideal resorted to for depicting rulers. Every wrinkle, every wart, etc., was indicated; the more realism the better. The particular had now become the "ideal"!

Thus the great conflict in Egyptian art between the real and the ideal was resolved in Greek art and concluded by the Romans. Egyptian art, frustrated by rigid, religious forces exhibited ambivalence between the extreme of idealism and almost literal portraiture, but in Greco-Roman art there was a more consistent development from idealism to more and more realism until literal portraiture was finally realized. Where the Greek Idealists used their consciousness of differentiation in order to achieve a similarity between the general form of art and the human form, the Romans used this consciousness to achieve in their art, similarities to the differences to be observed in each individual human form. While the Egyptians, Greeks and Romans all produced realistic human portraits, the Romans, with their unrestricted concentration on particulars, achieved the greatest degree of realism.

But in spite of their practicality and the contributions they made in the achievement of realism in three-dimensional depictions, the Romans eventually came to a point where they considered the idealistic art of Greece superior to their own. This is of particular interest as it introduces a problem which crops up throughout the whole subsequent history of art—the struggle between the world of reality and the fantasies of that reality. Although we shall pursue this problem in detail later, we may well examine here a few reasons why this occurred. As the Romans' practical realism reached its heights, they attempted to escape that reality in the idealizations of Greek art. There they found a perfect world depicted; all was serene, quiet, harmonious. The Romans had, in their accurate, sculptural recordings of the particulars, worked out the conclusions of a phase of art and culture in general, but they then failed to realize the next step forward, and so took futile refuge in the past. Thus once they had achieved a high degree of realism in art, we find them looking backwards at the old notion of an ideal. Their portraits began to resemble those of the Egyptians in the sense that they were idealizations of the individual. The return to the ideal, along with the mystical philosophies, was but a retreat from reality. With that the artists of Rome were finished, as far as any further developments were concerned.

13. Reprinted by permission of the publishers from Frank Chambers, *Cycles of Taste,* p. 68, Harvard University Press, Cambridge, 1928.
14. From *Wonders of the Past,* Vol. 2, "The Gods of Ancient Rome," p. 943, by W. R. Halliday. New York, 1937. Courtesy of G. P. Putnam's Sons.

We can see in the theories of Plotinos an indication that Rome was well on its way to the end. He remodelled Plato's absolute theory of "beauty" and created a world of escape from reality. Eventually the decay of Rome was such, according to Kallen, that it was expressed in two maxims: "Let us eat and drink and be merry for tomorrow we die"; and "Let us turn our backs on all worldly treasure in order to lay up treasure in heaven." [15] It was the latter attitude that eventually came to reign. If Plotinos was the transition from the "eating" to the "heaven" philosophy, then Augustine brought it to a head — escape from the here-world began with a vengeance. Thus when the Romans began to revive the old Greek ideal, they began the transition to the Christian manipulation of the ideal.

Now for a brief consideration of what the Greeks and Romans did with the two-dimensional painting medium. Practically no original examples of Greek painting, except on vases, have survived, although there are numerous anecdotes about Greek painters. It has been generally assumed that Roman painting as seen in Pompeii is a reflection of the Greek painting from which it is said to be copied.

In these paintings we can see the beginnings of much which emerged more clearly in later cultures. Still-life, landscape, etc. — all manner of subject-matter was tackled by the Greek and Roman painters, although the human form remained dominant throughout.

Following the example of the sculptors, the painters had already made a major step forward by breaking away from the limitations of a flat surface and achieving three-dimensional illusions of the human form for the first time. It is natural that sculpture, the first medium in which realistic results were secured, should influence the early painters in their attempts to depict form on a flat surface; hence most of these early paintings have the look of sculpture. The Pompeian painters had not yet achieved the ability of the sculptors contemporaneous with them to record details and individual characteristics, such as warts, wrinkles and facial expressions.

Apparently the primary problem which interested the painters of Greece and Rome was the depiction of three-dimensional illusions upon a linear surface. The Pompeians painted many kinds of Architectural effects both on the inside and the outside of their buildings, and even went so far as to paint illusions of windows upon their walls, through which illusions of buildings were seen (figure 36).

As in the sculptural reliefs, the paintings were generally incorrect in perspective. Lacking adequate knowledge of the laws of perspective, these artists resorted to a degree to the older method of depicting form on a flat surface; they drew what they *knew* about a particular aspect of an object, even though that aspect could not be seen from the artist's point of observation. They could not see from any one point of observation *all the planes* which they otherwise knew existed for a given object, e.g., a building. Being confused between what they could see and what they knew existed, they recorded as much as they could, both what could be seen from a fixed position and also aspects of the subject which could not be seen. In other words, the psycho-tactile factor was still dominant, although much less so than in previous linear art.

A square building, for example, was sometimes drawn with three sides, presumably from a fixed point of view, although a single point of observation permitted the artist to see only two sides. The artist was conscious that a building had four sides, but not knowing how to indicate four — which he would probably have done if he could — he did the next best thing, and made three. Something similar was done in the problem of high and low points of observation. If the roof could not be seen from the artist's position of observation, nevertheless he knew the building had one and so in some cases he simply put it on. Moreover, he could see that objects became smaller as they receded, but he did not adequately comprehend the laws for this. Thus it is apparent that these painters were able to observe certain details accurately, but were unable to coordinate them from the restricted single point of observation. If one examines the

15. Horace M. Kallen: *Art and Freedom*, Vol. 1, p. 81. Reprinted by permission of the publishers, Duell, Sloan and Pearce, Inc. Copyright 1942 by Horace M. Kallen.

Pompeian paintings of buildings, it will be seen that various parts of them are in correct perspective, but that all parts are not in correct perspective to each other. In short, Greek and Roman painters appear to have been unable to discover adequately enough the problem of visual order called perspective; there was still lacking a clear distinction between the object (and sculpture) and the image (and painting) of the object. But depictions of three-dimensional forms on a flat surface were considerably developed by their advances in modelling illusions of light and shade. Artists had now progressed to such an extent that the scientific laws of perspective seemed ready to be discovered momentarily. Thus the two-dimensional medium was set well on its way by the Greeks and Romans, but further development was delayed until the Renaissance.

To sum up: We have seen that the representation of the human form has progressed from generalized to particularized realistic depictions. The various reproductions in this book show how the depiction of the general human form in sculpture was gradually developed from crude beginnings in Pictographic times, through the Egyptian, Greek; and finally with Roman art we see the perfection of specific, particular, individual human forms. Here as far as the human *form* is concerned, the depictions of the artist have become very similar in structure to the structure of reality, since by depicting particulars accurately, it shows that no two individuals are ever the same. With the Romans, as later chapters will make more clear, sculpture as a recording medium had come almost to the end of its usefulness.

So we have witnessed the gradual evolution of man's ability to achieve ever greater accuracy in his seeing and recording of that seeing in art. There has not been a straight, unbroken evolution, but evolution nevertheless (figures 32 to 35).

Throughout the remainder of our history, we shall witness the continuation of the conflict between the "ideal" and the "real," between the artists' recordings of nature and the reality of nature as it actually appears; the lines of this argument were begun with the art of the Egyptians, but in logic they were first laid down by the Classical Greeks—nature on the one side, the ideal on the other. In the two periods of history subsequent to the Greek there appeared extreme examples of the two sides of this struggle—the real in the Roman culture and the ideal in the Christian.

In the next chapter we shall see mankind dip deeply into the well of primitive behavior, an event not to be matched until the nazi-fascism and/or communism of our own times. Art of course followed the tide. The tug of war between the religious and the scientific attitude which permeated all the philosophy of Greco-Roman times came to its first conclusion with the religious factor regaining its old dominance and holding it for a thousand years. Man fell back to the stage of Egyptian culture, and in many respects even much further back than that. What happened was that philosophy was captured as the tool of the religionists, just as a thousand years later it was to be recaptured by the scientists. Each group molded the discoveries of philosophy to opposite ends.

Thou shalt not make unto thee any graven image, or any likeness of any thing that is in heaven above, or that is in the
earth beneath, or that is in the water under the earth: thou
shalt not bow down thyself to them, nor serve them: for I
Jehovah thy God am a jealous God. . . .

2nd commandment

Christian doctrine . . . was at once a revival and
a modification of primitive ideas. 31
                                  Carl Becker

But assuredly, we are not to suppose that progress along the lines of advance implies that there is in detail no retrogression—no resolution of higher entities into others of a lower status—no degradation or descent within the pyramid. Disintegration or devolution, no less than integration with emergent evolution, has to be reckoned with in the history of natural systems. 234

C. Lloyd Morgan

During the Middle Ages the external world had had no conceptual hold upon the mind. Natural facts were insignificant compared with the divine order and intention which Christ and his Church had revealed: . . . . whatever significance the items of daily life had was as stage accessories and costumes and rehearsals for the drama of Man's pilgrimage through eternity. How far could the mind go in scientific mensuration and observation as long as the mystic numbers three and four and seven and nine and twelve filled every relation with an allegorical significance. 239

Lewis Mumford

Medieval people were naturally interested in food, clothing, shelter, and other needs of the flesh, but staring them ever in the face, following them like shadows, were their devil-fixation and hell-neurosis. The more they became absorbed in earthly problems, the more they betrayed the Christian theory of life, and heightened the possibility of being thrown, after death, into burning lava, or devoured by tailed drakes. Few had the temerity to face such dire consequences. 22

Harry Elmer Barnes

As the above quotations indicate, we are about to enter a world entirely different from the one we have just been observing. Up to this point we have noted man's gradual advance in understanding and controlling his environment, and the attendant increase in realism in his attitude towards the world and art. While the element of fantasy was inevitably present in the degree to which the various arts failed to portray nature-appearances accurately, nevertheless, the recording of nature in general gradually increased in accuracy; correspondingly the element of fantasy was reduced. In the Greco-Roman culture man finally came face to face with himself, believed in himself. He was ready to realize that the only reality a god or gods could have was in himself.[1] Hence the Greco-Roman conception and depiction of the gods had gradually become more realistic, more like actual men, less like gods.

But then the first severe trial came, the fall of the Roman Empire; the existing social order declined into impotence. The stability once supplied by the Empire was gone; men found themselves in a world of confusion. As in our own times, individualism of a sort had been carried to such extremes that

1. Xenophanes had understood this when he said that "if oxen and horses or lions had hands, and could paint with their hands, and produce works of art as men do, horses would paint the forms of gods like horses, and oxen like oxen, and make their bodies in the image of their several kinds . . . ." (As quoted by Bertrand Russell: *A History of Western Philosophy*, p. 40, Simon and Schuster, New York, 1945.)

the individual found himself alone and fearful in a world he could not understand. Old values no longer could supply adequate security and new ones were needed. When they failed to appear, men sought to submerge consciousness of self by escaping to older forms of interpreting reality. This escape resulted in the loss of faith in man and regression to the ancient faith in a superior power, culminating in Christianity, actually a composite of many old magic and religious forms.

The Christians were able to convince mankind that what they offered was superior to anything else as a solution of contemporaneous problems. They were able to do this, chiefly because they possessed a better organization than any of their competitors. Actually, however, the Christians had no more of a solution for the problems of the real world than did the confused rulers at the end of the Roman Empire. They, as much as those to whom they offered salvation, feared and refused—or failed—to face the confusion of the actual world. And so they led human beings to escape via the most tremendous fantasy which man's imagination had yet invented. Instead of proceeding from the axiom that the world could be made a better place in which to live, the Christians contended that the world had been the way it was since Adam and would continue so eternally. They sought only to make life's misery endurable through promises of paradise after death.

More severe distinction between earth-life and life-after-death was made in the Christian dogma than in any preceding religion. The Egyptian's religion, for example, simply promised him a continuance of earth-life; and thus through religious observances and funeral rites one sought to circumvent the termination of the earth-kind of life after death. As for the Greeks and Romans, to quote J. H. Robinson, they "thought of the next life, when they thought of it at all, as a very uninteresting existence compared with that on this earth. One who committed some signal crime might suffer for it after death with pains similar to those of the hell in which the Christians believed; but the great part of humanity were supposed to lead in the next world a shadow existence, neither sad nor glad. Religion, even to the devout pagan, was mainly an affair of this life: the gods were to be propitiated with a view to present happiness and success.

"Since no satisfaction could be expected in the next life, it was naturally deemed wise to make the most of this one. The possibility of pleasure ends—so the poet Horace urges—when we join the shades below, as we all must do soon. Let us therefore take advantage of every harmless pleasure and improve our brief opportunity to enjoy the good things of earth. We should, however, be reasonable and temperate, avoiding all excess, for that endangers happiness. Above all, we should not worry uselessly about the future, which is in the hands of the gods and beyond our control. Such were the convictions of the majority of thoughtful pagans." [2]

But for the Christians, as Robinson has pointed out, "Life here below was but a brief, if decisive, preliminary to the real life to come." [3] Hence the Church authorities utilized every means they could think of to relegate earthly "reality" into the background as a temptation of the Devil. As John the apostle put it: "Love not the world, neither the things that are in the world: if any man love the world, the love of the Father is not in him." And Robinson tells us: "Christianity . . . . laid persistent emphasis upon man's existence after death, which it declared infinitely more important than his brief sojourn in the body. Under the influence of the Church this conception of life had gradually supplanted the pagan one in the Roman world, and it was taught to the barbarians. The other worldliness became so intense that thousands gave up their ordinary occupations and pleasures altogether and devoted their entire attention to preparation for the next life. They shut themselves in lonely cells; and, not satisfied with giving up most of their natural pleasures, they inflicted bodily suffering upon themselves by hunger, cold, and stripes. They trusted that in this way they might avoid some of the sins into which they were prone to fall, and that, by self-inflicted punishment in this world, they might perchance escape some of that reserved for them in the next. As most of the writers and teachers of the Middle Ages belonged to this class of what may be called professional Christians (that is, the monks), it was natural that their kind of life should have been regarded, even by those who continued to live in the world, as the ideal one for the earnest Christian.

2. J. H. Robinson: *An Introduction to the History of Western Europe,* Vol. I, p. 57, Ginn and Co., Boston, 1924.

3. J. H. Robinson: *The Human Comedy,* p. 117, Harper and Brothers, New York, 1937.

"The barbarians were taught that their fate in the next world depended largely upon the Church. Its ministers never wearied of presenting the momentous alternative which faced every man so soon as this fleeting earthly existence should be over: the alternative between eternal bliss and perpetual, unspeakable physical torment." [4]

Man was offered an after-life superior to (or far worse than) anything in earth-life. All were promised paradise eternal, if their credentials, secured only from the Church, were in order. But for those who would not "believe," there were cruel, unbearable consequences, both *real* and unreal, both for the "flesh" and the "soul." Through the magic-religio-philosophy of the Church, misery was imposed on humans as a justifiable way of life. Real life became a matter of willingly accepting pain, even seeking it out in order to escape it in an after-life.

And as life became even more meagre and barren under the reign of Christianity, it was not to be wondered at that the masses hoped and came to believe that a better world than this one must surely exist. Without such a hope and belief their cruel existence would have been unbearable. It was this life which Jules Michelet, a 19th century French historian, described as follows: "This instability of condition and tenure, this horrid, shelving declivity, down which a man slips from free man to *vassal*,—from vassal to *servant*,—from servant to *serf*, is the great terror of the Middle Ages, the basis of its despair. There is no way of escape; one step, and the man is lost. He is an *alien*, a *waif and stray*, a head of *wild game*; serfdom or death, these are the only alternatives." [5]

"True, the virgin, the ideal woman, rose higher from century to century, but the woman of real life counted for mighty little in these rustic communities, these massed aggregates of men and cattle." [6]

And so rather than restoring man's faith in himself, the Christians carried him to the opposite extreme. They dug up from the past the old totalitarian symbol, a single, omnipotent authority, an absolute dictator. Man became an abject slave, worshipping a god who preached that misery on earth meant the greatest happiness for eternity. Religion became a force decreasing man's awareness of himself and the world in which he lived, and so obstructing progress.

Up to a point religion had served an evolutionary function in the development of man, since it made possible the transition from magic to philosophy. But once this momentous step in the development of man's abstracting ability was achieved, religion automatically began to operate as a regressive factor and hindered further development. That religion, revived by the Christians, was a regression is even further borne out by the fact that it offered no evolutionary developments from past religious beliefs, no creation of new notions, but was mainly a gathering up of past doctrines. (Totalitarian systems in our own times offer an analogous situation.) Revived out of their proper context, however, these doctrines became instruments of devastating regression. We can note here only the more important ones.

First of all the Church adopted and developed the administrative devices invented by the Romans. As J. H. Robinson wrote: "It was by no means merely a religious organization, as churches are now, but became a great international State, embracing all western Europe. It was the real successor of the Roman Empire." [7]

Closely related to this was the fact that the monotheistic system, perfected by the Hebrews, was elaborated by the Christians so as to produce the most effective results for the priestly rulers. Heretofore, numbers of gods were recognized and worshipped. Although the medievalists did not deny their existence, they contended that all of them, Venus, Bacchus, etc., were demons who peopled that realm invented by Augustine, the "City of the Devil." Statues of the pagan gods, Augustine said, were demons in stone. The Christians recognized only a single god, who demanded the obedience of all. In short, the change was from a comparatively democratic to a definitely totalitarian form of religion. As Barnes points out:

4. Robinson, *History of Western Europe*, Vol. 1, pp. 57-58.

5. Jules Michelet: *Satanism and Witchcraft*, p. 35, translated by A. R. Allinson, Walden Publications, Wehman Brothers, New York, 1939.

6. Ibid., p. 38.

7. Robinson, *History of Western Europe*, Vol. 1, p. 28.

37. Brassempouy head, detail of figure 24. Photo Archives Photographiques: Paris.

38. Figure of a bishop, detail of figure 41, center.

"It [Christianity] destroyed all conflicting cults with an incredible ferocity. Peasant and scientist, literate and illiterate, all had to share, willingly or not, the same basic beliefs. Nothing less than rigorous conformity was demanded." [8]

To reinforce their power, the priests renewed and stimulated the old forms of magic practice, animism, witchcraft and sorcery. For example, Robinson writes: "It will be noticed that the habits of the animals were supposed to have some spiritual meaning and carry with them a lesson for mankind. It may be added that this and similar stories were centuries old. . . . Even the most learned men of the time believed in astrology and in the miraculous virtues of herbs and gems. For instance, Albertus Magnus, one of the most distinguished scientists of the thirteenth century, agrees that a sapphire will drive away boils, and that a diamond can be softened in the blood of a stag, which will work best if the stag has been fed on wine and parsley." [9] And as in Primitive societies, empirical evidence was completely disregarded. This is well illustrated in the following example from Jules Michelet: "a Sorceress confesses [after being tortured] she had recently dug up a child's dead body from the churchyard, to use it in her magic compounds. Her husband says, 'Go to the churchyard and look: the child is there now.' The grave is opened, and the body found intact in its coffin. Yet the judge decides, against the testimony of his own eyes, that it is only an *appearance,* an illusion of Satan. He credits the woman's confession in preference to the actual fact,—and the poor creature is burned." [10]

Along with all this the medievalists juggled Greek logic to suit their wishes. The arbitrary manipulation of Greek logic was shackled with the Primitive's magic and Oriental religion. It was the strangest assortment of social utensils ever put together by man.

Finally *art* was used by the Christians as one of the principal means of "pushing its roots deep among the masses." At first Christian artists more or less took over the pagan style and thus the earliest Christian art was quite realistic (figure 42, left). However, as the Church became more organized and powerful, restrictions were increasingly imposed upon the degree of imitation permitted in art, and, in time, reality as it actually appeared to the eyes was no longer depicted.

8. H. E. Barnes: *An Intellectual and Cultural History of the Western World,* p. 307, Reynal and Hitchcock, Inc., New York, 1941.

9. Robinson, *History of Western Europe,* Vol. 1, p. 291.

10. Michelet, op. cit., p. 164.

39. Detail of African sculpture. Private collection.

Nearly all that mankind had previously gained in an increasingly useful, realistic view of the world was thrown to the winds; and where previous art-changes had in general resulted in lessening fantasy in art, now the effort was made to increase it. Instead of trying to make art correspond as much as possible to actual reality, the Christians, in their art, deliberately and *consciously,* made reality into what it was *NOT.* We are here confronted with the problem of a culture in which conscious, organized restriction was imposed upon the visual ability available to human beings at the time. This is not exactly new in the history of art, since such conscious control was exerted by the Egyptian priests. Moreover, there was the example of the Orientals contemporary with the Christians who were known to possess "fear of the excessive likeness" in art.[11] Indeed the Orientals taught theologians of the West much about the fantasy manipulation of reality. H. Frankfort writes: "it would be shortsighted to overlook the fact that the creatures of Oriental imagination were also appreciated in the Middle Ages for non-aesthetic reasons. The tortured consciousness of sin, the turbulent speculations on the powers of evil, found relief in the use of ready-made forms." [12] What was new about the Christian restrictions on reality, then, was the extent and efficiency of the Christian priests in this direction. They not only terminated realistic recording, but eventually, as we shall see, reduced art to the lowest level, to the level of primitivistic representations of nature's appearances (figures 37, 38, 39, 40, 41): art was made once again to function symbolically as picture-writing. Thus the historic trend of visualization was reversed.[13]

11. Joseph Pijoan: *An Outline History of Art,* Vol. II, p. 76, copyright by University of Knowledge, Inc., Consolidated Book Publishers, Inc., Chicago, 1938.

12. H. Frankfort: *Cylinder Seals,* p. 317, Macmillan and Co., Ltd., London, 1939.

13. Because of ignorance and vestiges of the old Paleolithic fear, the art and culture of Christianity has been commonly regarded as a strange and "beautiful" epoch. Writers seem never to tire of rhapsodizing about the spiritual uplift of the cathedrals, with their spires and lofty interiors, inspired by and inspiring profound devotion. The powerful tenacity of these symbols comes from the fact that they strike men at their weakest point—i.e., their ignorance of the "unknown," and not only of the unknown, but ignorance of the implications of notions dealing with the "unknown." In all the complexities of our civilization man still has to free his mind from the god-myth and its attendant primitive superstitions. Hence, instead of rhapsodizing about medieval cathedrals, we propose to examine what purpose was served by the return to a primitive level of recording enforced by the Church.

40. Vision of the Apocalypse, tympanum, Church of St. Pierre, Moissac, 12th Century. Photo, Giraudon, Paris.

It is to be expected that the Christian religion eventually produced a type of art best expressing the difference between earth-life and the more "important" life-after-death. In other words, art was used to represent another world and its supposed inhabitants, and the visual characteristics of that other-world could not resemble too much those to be observed in earth-life. Since no one had ever seen God, heaven, hell, etc., what better form of art could be devised than that which depicted the other world and its occupants in visual forms unlike anything on earth? Deliberate distortions of reality made the art forms appear to be other than that which we usually associate with the everyday, commonplace or recognizable forms of reality. The following by J. H. Robinson bears on this point: "One characteristic of the medieval imagination is its fondness for the grotesque. It loved queer beasts half eagle and half lion, hideous batlike creatures,—monsters like nothing on land or sea. They lurk among the foliage on choir screens, leer at you from wall or column. . . ." [14] These changes of the reality appearances of man, beast, etc., facilitated their identification with another world (figure 40, 41). In this manner art was used to achieve an effect of another "reality," a world not of this world.

Yet, at the same time, they were given forms suggestive of the familiar forms of earth-reality. For example, the human depictions did possess the *general* forms of real human beings. Thus even though the real world was denounced continually and in no uncertain terms, it was nevertheless by necessity exploited to the full in order to give reality to the other-world. Factors of the real world were used by their "transference" to the symbology of the other-world; the paternal and maternal relationships were, of course, extensively exploited. Therefore, although reality was changed to create another world, a certain amount of the reality of the real world was retained in order to give credibility to the fantasy. As Walter

14. Robinson, *History of Western Europe,* Vol. 1, pp. 298-299.

41. Left and right, details from figure 40. Photo Giraudon, Paris. Center, figure of a bishop, designed for trumeau of a cathedral, southern France, 11th Century. In the collection of the Minneapolis Institute of Arts.

Lippmann once wrote: "If it is true that man creates God in his own image, it is no less true that for religious devotion he must remain unconscious of that fact. Once he knows that he has created the image of God, the reality of it vanishes like last night's dream." [15]

By distorting reality, art served the important function of preventing the identification of art symbols with the actual world of reality. At the same time art gave a certain reality to this other-world by using forms from the real world. A clear instance of actuality's being used to give credence to the myth and yet keep the latter distinct from the former is found in the fact that most of the sculpture from the 7th to the 11th centuries was kept under life-size.[16]

An especial effort was made to dissociate the figure of Jesus from that of a real man. "Yea, though we have known Christ after the flesh, yet now henceforth know we Him no more." [17] Towards the attainment of such objectives there arose the problem of how Jesus could most effectively be depicted in art. Pijoan writes: "Some authorities like Tertullian believed that Christ should be pictured in an unattractive manner, that he should even inspire terror, that we might not fall into temptation through his physical beauty. Others agreed with the gentle St. John Chrysostomus that Jesus should be presented with a grace and charm that would supplement His divine precepts in drawing souls to His service." [18] Hence the Church imposed restrictions upon art so that it would serve the definite psycho-logical function of making *real* the doctrines of the new religion.

15. From Walter Lippmann: *A Preface to Morals*, pp. 35-36. New York, 1929. By permission of The Macmillan Company, publishers.

16. G. H. Chase and C. R. Post: *A History of Sculpture*, p. 182, Harper and Brothers, New York, 1924.

17. Paul, 2nd Corinthians 5:16.   18. Pijoan, op. cit., p. 36.

42. Left, The Good Shepherd, 3rd Century A. D. Lateran Museum, Rome. Photo, The Bettmann Archive. Center, Prophets, trumeau, Church of St. Pierre, Moissac, ca. 1135. Photo, Marburg. Right, statue of Mycerinus and Queen, Egyptian, Dyn. IV. Courtesy, Museum of Fine Arts, Boston.

Paramount in considering the importance of art in these times is the fact that the masses could not read; their reading ability was actually on the Primitive picture level. Under such conditions the "concrete" character of pictures and visual art in general rather than the "abstract" character of words was more effective in fabricating and propagating Church doctrines. To the illiterate, a visual picture of the tortures of the damned, for example, could be far more persuasive than words. Such depictions by means of the projection mechanism were identified by the masses as actual reality. Did they not actually *see* in the depictions what happened to the damned? As Michelet wrote: "This doctrine men saw inculcated in the *artless* sculptures carved around church doors, from which they learned the dreadful lesson how fiends experienced a wanton delight in causing pain." [19] Moreover, art as it was then known not only gave undisputed credibility to the other world, but was also instrumental in stimulating the imaginative activities in the production of "visions" and the like. Thus visual depictions were in a position of tremendous influence, and art was used as a primary source of power over the masses to canalize them "visually" and "mentally."

No wonder then that art was very carefully supervised. Artists themselves were regarded as no better than the most ordinary of workmen, and like the latter, possessed no position of value within the social system. They were labelled as "mechanic" artisans, a term derived from another term meaning adulterer. Personal initiative on the artist's part was taboo; he was subject to the severest dictates as to how he was to make his art. He was simply told that, "The composition of figures is not the invention of painters, but the law and tradition of the Catholic Church, and the ordination and dispensation of our

19. Michelet, op. cit., p. 63.

146

43. Left, French Romanesque Madonna, 12th Century. Courtesy of The Metropolitan Museum of Art. Center, detail, altar shrine, by Valentin Lendenstreich, German, 15th Century. In the collection of the Minneapolis Institute of Arts. Right, detail, figure of Moses from the Well of Moses, by Claes Sluter, ca. 1400. Dijon Museum, Photo, Giraudon, Paris.

fathers . . . ."[20] Breaking any rules, intentionally or otherwise, incurred penalties for the artist. The Church was his law and sole patron, circumstances, incidentally, comparable to those in all recent totalitarian countries. In short, the Church "commands" and the painters simply "execute."

That the Church leaders well recognized the power of art as an instrument of propaganda may be seen in the following statement of Gregory: "To adore a picture is one thing, but to learn through the story of a picture what is to be adored is another. For what writing is to them that can read, a picture is to them who cannot read, but only look, since in it even the ignorant can see what they should follow." [21] And John Damascene said that images, "were devised for greater knowledge and for the manifestation and popularization of secret things, as a pure help and benefit to salvation; so that by showing things and making them known, we may arrive at hidden truths, desire and emulate what is good, shun and hate what is evil." [22]

Notice that even language is manipulated to achieve results similar to those of fantasy in art. Thus the emphasis upon "greater knowledge," "secret things," "hidden truth"; in short, we are not only concerned with primitive practices in *art*, but also in the use of language, the magic-of-words. "There is a

20. Decrees of the Second Council of Nicaea, as quoted by Frank Chambers: *The History of Taste*, p. 16, Columbia University Press, New York, 1932.

21. From St. Gregory's Letters, as quoted by Chambers, *The History of Taste*, p. 7.

22. John Damascene, On Images, as quoted by Chambers, *History of Taste*, p. 5.

147

hidden and secret meaning in each individual word." So said Origen, in speaking about the allegorical method of scripture interpretation.[23] Just as it was assumed that the visual art represented real and actual things, so it was assumed that words did likewise; words were as potent as things. As H. E. Barnes has pointed out: "language had to be used in extraordinary ways. Simplicity and clarity were eschewed. The vaguer the statement, the more ingenious interpretations one could attach to it." [24]

Music, like the rest of the arts, was also carefully supervised: "The attractions of musical rhythms to the ear were so well known to the early Christian church fathers that rhythmic tunes came under a ban." [25] Thus we see that other symbols were manipulated similarly to art, each helping to substantiate the credibility of the other; over all that reached the senses of men—words, music, pictures, etc.— there existed the strictest surveillance.

In short, symbols, the most potent evolutionary invention of man, the means by which he can gain an ever increasing comprehension of reality, were converted by the Christians into a powerful, regressive force, and perhaps for the first time in human history, were consciously manipulated on a tremendously ambitious scale. All that humans thought, saw and felt in the real world was redirected into clothing a grandiose fantasy with reality.

In speaking of symbols, Reiser writes: "With the coming of human group life and a mechanism of social heredity, the *symbol* begins to function. The symbol is a substitute stimulus, and as a social product it becomes somewhat arbitrary, in the sense that if a person is educated in the proper way any sound or visual image (idol) can acquire the power to elicit those biological responses which are innate in all human organisms. The effectiveness of the religious symbol (idol) rests on its power to evoke a response which provides an outlet for those compulsory reactions of fear, reverence, subordination, etc., which, especially in primitive religion, dominate human nature." [26]

Serge Chakotin has pointed out the effectiveness of the symbolic propaganda of the Church. He writes: "Early Christian history is full of examples of propaganda; never since, indeed, has propaganda by means of symbols been carried on on such a scale until our own times. It might almost be said that it was then that what we call modern propaganda was most thoroughly exploited. Its extent and its efficacy depended largely on the fact that the symbol of this propaganda, the Cross, had all the elements of success: a strong appeal to the emotions, evoking the idea of sacrifice, and great ease of reproduction. It is the simplest of all known symbols, and could be spread abroad everywhere and act with the utmost ease as a conditional factor of the reflex of rallying. It is well known what importance this symbol had at the outset of the persecutions, in the catacombs. Other symbolic forms—magnificent liturgies, music—and also the rational organization, almost from the outset, of the diffusion of the Christian idea, by means of ecclesiastical institutions and propagandist missionaries, account for the power of the Church, especially the Catholic Church, in the Middle Ages and down to modern times." [27]

An interesting aspect of the Christian use of symbolism is to be seen in such devices as the dove, fish, anchor and olive branch, which stood for such notions as the soul, etc.[28] However, this was not

23. Quoted by Barnes, *History of the Western World*, p. 308.

24. Barnes, *History of the Western World*, p. 310.

25. N. B. Zane: "Appreciation of the Space Arts," p. 59, Part III, in *Studies in Appreciation of Art*, edited by R. W. Leighton, University of Oregon Publication, Vol. IV, No. 6, February, 1934.

26. From Oliver L. Reiser: *Philosophy and the Concepts of Modern Science*, p. 212. By permission of The Macmillan Company, publishers.

27. Serge Chakotin: *The Rape of the Masses*, p. 145, Alliance Book Corporation, New York, 1940. By permission of George Routledge and Sons, Ltd., London.

28. Such symbols as these are actually of the ideograph type. Birds, for example, early in the formation of written language, meant "destiny"; the bird form had many meanings in Primitive times due to the fact that the flight of birds was employed for divination purposes. (See W. A. Mason: *A History of the Art of Writing*, p. 254, The Macmillan Co., New York, 1920.) Hence the use of bird, fish, etc., forms by the Christians was in many cases a return to symbols which had been employed in the earliest times of human culture to express magical meanings.

a simple case of one object standing for another of quite different visual characteristics; that which was symbolized by the dove, fish, etc., actually took on certain traits of the doves and fishes. In this way certain characteristics of the reality symbol were projected upon the makeup of such non-visual factors as the "soul," thus giving them tangible, visual qualities. Besides projecting upon non-empirical factors the quality of empirical things, such symbols made possible a certain degree of freedom for each individual's imaginative potentialities. Thus a familiar object, like the dove, stimulated each person's particular imaginative comprehensions of the soul's characteristics. To a certain extent each individual could imagine the character of the soul in the best way possible for his own peculiar needs and ability to comprehend.

The potentialities of such symbols are related to one aspect of the problems involved in the Iconoclastic Controversy, as we shall attempt to demonstrate. While there were many authorities who would admit "beauty" in art if it were transformed into "righteousness" (thus, as Chambers points out, art served the function of sermons), nevertheless, various sects and Christian orders repeatedly warned against its use.

Thus too many colors (or too realistic a depiction, even if it be of Christ) were severely criticized by such as the Cistercians, for instance, who would have none of the color display such as is found in the Chartres windows. They preferred instead two colors, yellow and gray, with geometrical patterns in place of the customary figures.[29] Some indeed taught that art was synonymous with ungodliness: "St. Jerome, St. Ambrose, St. Bernard, St. Anthony, St. Francis, St. Thomas Aquinas, the Cistercians, the Cluniacs, and many other leaders of Christianity as well as the Christian orders and institutions, did not weary of protesting, warning, prohibiting any art or any element in it that was for sensuous enjoyment."[30] This situation came to the place where even the desirability of art in any form was questioned. Thus Gardner wrote: "There was always in the Church, especially among the severer religious orders, a strong vein of asceticism which objected to all religious representations, and considered them a concession to the spirit of the world and a danger to the spiritual life."[31]

The Iconoclasts and those with similar tendencies represent the ultimate extreme of this attitude towards art, and in various regions and times during the reign of Christianity the image was taboo. For some two centuries the Iconoclasts made it their concern to destroy all images used for purposes of worship; they even went so far as to make artists flee for their very lives. So while there was considerable dispute as to the manner in which art should preach its sermons, there was an even greater dispute as to whether or not art images should be permitted at all.

Apparently the Iconoclasts considered those images of God evoked by non-visual means to be far more persuasive in conjuring a reality of the other world than were those evoked by any direct visual means such as painting or sculpture. In brief, the Iconoclasts evidently advocated the arousal of images by non-visual means. Such images conceived by each individual's peculiar imagination, as stimulated by religious words and music, would seem to have great potentialities, greater perhaps than those resulting when each individual projected reality into a definite limited visual image as created by an artist. The latter type, since it fixed the image, would not allow for the wide range of variables in the various imaginative potentialities and peculiarity needs of each different human.

In general we could say that the dove, fish, anchor, etc. symbols were on a scale intermediate between the fixed art symbols of the Christian religion on the one hand, and on the other the Iconoclast's notion of eliminating all visual art symbols. But in still another respect, the proponents of imagery acquired some of the power of the Iconoclast's world of non-imagery by using images to arouse the more powerful "visions" inherent in each individual's imaginative capacity. This device of the priests consisted of directly teaching that the images depicting the other-world were deceptive, in the sense that the believer was required to worship the image with Oriental slavishness, but at the same time, because the image cannot be God but only a mere image, then the Christian, like the Oriental believer, must also deny the image. Only under these conditions were the images accepted as depictions of the actual other-world. In other words, the

29. See P. A. Sorokin, *Social and Cultural Dynamics,* Vol. 1, p. 313.

30. Ibid., Vol. 1, p. 313.

31. P. Gardner: *The Principles of Christian Art,* p. 185, John Murray, London, 1928. In fact (see quotation heading this chapter) the second commandment explicitly forbids the use of images for any purpose, religious or secular.

obedient believer must orient himself to the image (in the words of Coomaraswamy) by "on the one hand affirming things of God by way of praise, and on the other denying every one of these limiting descriptive affirmations, for though the worship is dispositive to immediate vision, God is not and never can be 'what men worship here.' "[32] This was indeed a clever deception, since it made the image more than the image. "Half revealed and half concealed," says Coomaraswamy. Thus the symbols, the distortions of reality, were properly loaded with the mystery of the other-world. For similar purposes, this very type of deception is contained in the theory inflicted upon mankind by the priests, that man is both animal and divine.

In the end, however, the image worshippers won the argument. It was decreed by the Second Council of Nicaea, which officially closed the Iconoclastic Controversy and which was agreed to by both Greek and Roman churches, that, "just as the figure of the precious and life-giving Cross, so also the venerable and holy images, as well as painting and mosaic as of other fit materials, should be set forth in the holy churches of God. . . . For by so much more frequently as they are seen represented, by so much more readily are men lifted up to the memory of their prototypes, and to a longing after them. For the honor which is paid to the image passes to that which the image represents, and he who reveres the image reveres in it the subject represented."[33]

It is interesting to speculate whether or not the images of visual art are more effective than those produced by non-visual means, such as words or music. One wonders how the course of civilization might have been changed had the Iconoclasts had their way. That it would have produced more than a minor change in the structure of the Western world is amply indicated by the tremendous effect of precisely such an event in the Moslem world where the Koran did not permit the production of human or animal images.

If one accepts the theologians' basic assumption that religion must compete with the appearance of the real world, then art is a powerful, indispensable tool to the formation of religion. Without it in some form the real world cannot be competed with successfully. But the basic assumption of the Iconoclasts was just the opposite. It is a question of which is more fundamentally effective in an effort to overcome the competition of the real world.

Regarding this problem, the position which music held in medieval times is important. Although carefully controlled, music became the most readily approved of all the arts, and it would seem that it occupied this esteemed position because it possessed that very power which we assume the Iconoclasts saw was lacking in the visual arts. That is, it was possible with music to arouse more potent images, because of the absence of limitations upon the individual imagination that existed in the products of the painter and the sculptor.

In any case, as we have already explained, the visual arts were used to give "reality" to the other-world; and yet, in order to do this the artist had to avoid using the forms of reality literally so that a sufficient distinction between this and the other-world could be maintained. But in this there was the difficulty of finding some standard visual formula which would capture the attention of each unique individual and satisfy him with an adequate illusion of the "reality" of the other-world, a problem, incidentally, that the Iconoclasts would have avoided. The Council of Nicaea gave much of its attention to the question of whether or not images should be used in worship, and if so, just what would be the best way to depict, for example, Jesus. In the case of music (and words) this conflict was easily eliminated, as this art medium acted merely as an excitatory agent to the image-making apparatus of the human nervous system. Instead of supplying some standard image, as in painting and sculpture, music aroused an image suitable to each person's individual and peculiar imaginative abilities and needs. It was considered a spiritual and divine method of communication which would insure the capitulation of the masses to their masters in this world as well as the next. In short, in the realm of fantasy, as far as religion is concerned, music has far more possibilities than painting or sculpture.

An interesting sidelight on this problem is the fact that reputedly the Iconoclasts at first opposed sculpture but approved of painting, and that eventually they were able to impose restrictions upon the

32. A. Coomaraswamy: "The Christian and Oriental or True Philosophy of Art," in *Why Exhibit Works of Art*, London, 1943, p. 52.

33. Decree of Second Council of Nicaea, as quoted by Chambers, *History of Taste*, pp. 5-6.

sculptural medium by means of specific laws as to its use. Apparently they decided to admit sculpture (since they could not enforce their will by completely eliminating worship-images) on the condition that the painting medium, which did not possess the major reality characteristic of the third dimension, be given precedence over it. In the painting medium they evidently felt that images were freed as much as possible from the here-reality.

Until the realism of late medieval times we find that sculpture was mainly confined to relief, i.e., it tended towards the character of linear art. In those cases where sculpture tended towards the round, or was completely in the round, distortion of the objects depicted kept the three-dimensional aspect from reflecting too much the forms of similar objects in actual reality. As a matter of fact, when sculpture was again used extensively in Romanesque times, the linear medium was dominant; consequently the distortive reality practices and formulae of the painters served as the model for the efforts of the sculptor, ruling out the possibilities of gaining the realism that had once been achieved in sculpture. This linear dominance was so thorough that at first in Romanesque times sculpture was comprised largely of low relief and incised lines. Only gradually did the round appear, and when it did, the old realism of sculpture had been completely replaced by the distortive practices of the linear arts.

It was during the height of the primitivistic epoch that the Christian religion achieved its greatest successes and power over the masses of humanity in the Western world. In time, the symbols "God," "Devil," "Hell," and "Heaven" became accepted realities, through the influence, among other things, of the other-worldliness suggested by the primitive-fantasy depictions of art. It would seem, now that the belief in the existence of the other-world had been created, that the Church could afford a change towards more realism; but as a matter of fact, this change was being forced upon the Church because man was once again becoming more realistic in his attitude towards the world about him.

Thus in Gothic times the distortions of reality were gradually lessened; a type of idealistic realism became the new objective of art. The Church symbols no longer frightened their victims with, for example, a cruel, threatening countenance of Christ; instead he was depicted as beaming with beckoning kindness and the like, and St. Mary as well as other female symbols were given physical attraction (figure 43). The clothing worn by the figures in Church symbols was similar to that of the contemporaries who produced the art. Seduction now replaced force!

In short, the here-world was becoming more alluring; the priests were forced to give to the propaganda symbols of the Church some of the characteristics of the new worldly attractions. Eventually the priests reversed almost everything once again by making the other-world take on more and more the reality appearances of the actual-world. In the Gothic period there was a return to Egyptian portraiture-idealism where individuality was retained but idealized.

Many medievalists saw the danger in changing to the literal trappings of the real world, and sought a solution in another direction for their weakening dominance over human life, namely, mysticism. In this way they sought to discard reality completely.

In conclusion: we have seen how the conflict between the real and the ideal in Egyptian art was gradually resolved by the consistent working out of these problems in a developmental manner during Greco-Roman times. But then the Romans regressed, leaving the achievements of their realistic direction and returning to the idealism of the past, the idealization of the particular individual—a return not to the idealism of the Greeks, but to the idealistic portraits of the Egyptians. The Christians continued the regression until very primitive forms of art were the visual mold for reality. Part animal and part human forms (the old Egyptian device) reappeared along with all kinds of fantastic animal forms. In examining the reproductions in this chapter we can see how closely the Christian arts resemble the efforts of earlier Primitive cultures. With the Christian arts, the development of accuracy in the depiction of reality was reversed; a regression occurred which in many aspects fell to the level of Paleolithic activities and beliefs. Finally when Gothic art replaced Romanesque, the direction was once more reversed: the ideal set the pattern once again.

We have seen man develop from the magic to the religious stage, from the religious to the philosophical, and then regress from philosophy to the primitive "philosophy" of religion. In this latter stage man made a God and a Devil in his own image, and these became recurrent nightmares, harassing his days and nights. As in the lives of individual humans, so in the greater historic organism, there are great periods of waste and regression. Such was the age of Christianity. But indulgence in fantasy resulted in reality's becoming more and more unbearable, until in the end it had to be faced once again. Meanwhile, human existence was, in the words of Jules Michelet, one "everlasting weary round regulated by the two bells, whereof the one says *Ever* and the other says *Never*."[34]

34. Michelet, op. cit., p. 127.

There is no more momentous revolution in the history of thought than this, in which the achievements of thinkers and workers, of artists, philosophers, poets, and statesmen, were given up for the revelation of prophets and a gospel of worldly renunciation . . . . The scientific output of the most luminous minds the world had known was classed with the legends that had grown up by the campfires of primitive barbarians. All was pagan; which meant that all was delusive and unreliable except where it could be tested in the light of the new religion or where it forced itself by the needs of life into the world of common experience . . . . It was, therefore, a calamity for historiography, that the new standards won the day. The authority of a revealed religion sanctioned but one scheme of history through the vast and intricate evolution of the antique world. A well-nigh insurmountable obstacle was erected to scientific inquiry, one which has at least taken almost nineteen centuries to surmount. 313

J. T. Shotwell

All history was henceforth essentially nothing but the
conflict between these two cities; two moralities,
one natural, the other supernatural; two philosophies, one rational the other revealed; two beauties,
one corporeal, the other spiritual; two glories, one
temporal, the other eternal; two institutions, one the
world, the other the Church. 309

George Santayana

Having sharp and strong wits, and abundance of leisure, and small variety of reading, but their wits being shut up in the cells of a few authors (chiefly Aristotle, their dictator), as their persons were shut up in the cells of monasteries and colleges, and knowing little history, either of nature or time, [they] did out of no great quantity of matter and infinite agitation of wit spin out unto us those laborious webs of learning which are extant in their books. 302
Francis Bacon

Every culture lives within its dream. That of Christianity was one in which a fabulous heavenly world, filled with gods, saints, devils, demons, angels, archangels, cherubim and seraphim and dominions and powers, shot its fantastically magnified shapes and images across the actual life of earth-born man. This dream pervades the life of a culture as the fantasies of night dominate the mind of a sleeper: it is reality—while the sleep lasts. But, like the sleeper, a culture lives within an objective world that goes on through its sleeping or waking, and sometimes breaks into the dream, like a noise, to modify it or to make further sleep impossible. 239
Lewis Mumford

In our charitable moments our enlightened futurists of culture will grant that the Middle Ages constituted but an intermission in the drama of cultural progress, a detour on the somewhat winding but ever ascending highway to the modern world. 285
Oliver L. Reiser

The direction into which human activity had been taken by the Christians could lead only to the ever-increasing regression of human culture, and as conditions for the welfare and even survival of the great mass of human beings became more and more inadequate with each century of Christian domination, a point was eventually reached where the undisputed power of the Church was challenged and denied.

It is true of course that all notions of "reality" are merely interpretations, whether they are what we call "fantasies" or "facts"; moreover, all "interpretations," including fantasy, are "realities" of some *kind*. This, however, is but one aspect of the problem. The more important fundamental consideration is whether or not our interpretation secures the most *useful* survival possible for human life. If useful survival is our objective, we must inquire how it can best be achieved, given the particular structural function of both the human nervous system and its world environment. The results of such an inquiry can give us a coherent method for securing useful evaluations about the problem of "fantasy" and "reality" in the function of art.

The world in us and about us *is not* something over which man has complete control; everyday experience teaches us that the manner in which man is able to manipulate the structure of the reality outside and inside him is in one sense very definitely limited. Man must conform to the structure and natural function of the organism and environment, the factors which constitute "reality," if he is to be able also to manipulate and exploit that reality for his own purposes; in fact, the extent of his ability to do so depends precisely upon his ability to conform to the structural function of the world process. This Francis Bacon recognized in the 16th century when he wrote: "In order to master Nature we must first obey her." To the extent, then, that man is able to comprehend and abide by the particular conditions of actual reality in and outside his skin, whether he be eating or thinking—to that extent he will be in the position of taking the fullest advantage of his potentialities for manipulating nature for his particular needs. Hence the possibilities of nature *expand* or *shrink* according to whether humans regard or disregard the structure of the world.

From such a point of view we can better evaluate the crucial difference between "reality" and "fantasy" trends in interpretation. In the latter tendency the responsibilities and consequences connected with the manipulative activity are ignored and the results are disastrous: the need for adequate realistic conformity to the Process Structure of nature is not realized. Although the medieval Christians were compelled to come to some kind of terms with the real world, they tried to make it come to terms with their *a priori* beliefs; they attempted to impose upon the facts of life a form of logic arrived at independently, for the most part, of the consideration of the real world. The inevitable result of such a one-sided tendency is an antagonism between man and his environment, with ensuing conflicts, maladjustments and non-useful, un-sane survival. In the more realistic trend, man strives ever to increase his knowledge of the laws of nature within which he must operate; this in turn makes it possible for him to employ usefully his ability to manipulate nature for his own particular needs. Thus an isomorphic relationship is established between man's activities and the Process Structure of nature, and harmony is attained between the "necessary conformity to nature" on the one hand and the "possible manipulation of nature" on the other. In this way man can produce useful survival and so human progress. This direction of an increasingly accurate understanding of nature has always produced more useful survival for human life. Therefore, it should be no surprise that this attitude is sought and recovered each time mankind wanders too far in the direction of fantasy, or harmful manipulations of nature.

Thus, although for centuries the fantastic Christian dream suppressed this realistic trend, as it has been suppressed at times before and since, in the end this dream-world was forced to give way to the here-world attitude of the Renaissance culture. Once again man returned to the direct investigation of reality.

Now there are some who point out that we cannot call the whole Christian period all bad any more than we can call any other culture all good. With this attitude we agree. The degrees, however, of positive or negative qualities in a given culture must be considered, and from this point of view the Christian period was predominantly regressive.

There are others who tell us that the late medieval churchmen finally saw the "bright light of civilization" and were actually responsible for the beginning of that great era of knowledge called "science." They take issue with those who regard the Renaissance as the crucial turning point from the ignorant domination of the Church in the affairs of mankind, and insist that the road to what we call "science" had its roots in the commerce, education, and so-called humanities of the 12th and 13th centuries. It was then, they claim, that the enlightenment began which came to its full development in the Renaissance. We would agree that this too is undeniably true, but only on a negative basis. It cannot be denied that during the late medieval period events took place which helped in the rebirth of science, but it should also be pointed out that the changes which took place were forced upon the Church. A return to a scientific attitude as well as a renewal of realism in art—both long suppressed by the ecclesiastical authorities—began again in late medieval times simply because the Church was compelled to come to terms with the new conditions demanding these changes.

These new conditions were of two general kinds. On the one hand, as we have just suggested, men had departed so far from actual reality with the doctrines of the Church that survival necessitated a reversal of these tendencies. On the other hand, the Church leaders, once power was indisputably theirs, exhibited more and more interest in secular attractions, such as commerce, banking, etc., until a point was reached where they no longer represented what they claimed to. One of the inevitable results was the search for more reliable orientations to actual reality; thus "science" of a sort—and more realistic, i.e., more scientific art—made their appearance.

Once it became apparent that the method of reasoning by the evidence of verifiable observation was potentially dangerous, the Church leaders realized the necessity of seizing this method and making it part of and subject to the dictation of ecclesiastical objectives. In this way they hoped to assimilate science and control it before it became so powerful as to displace the Church. Therefore, the Church maintained its power over the activities of scientists; scientists had to confine themselves to certain kinds of studies, those which it was hoped would maintain and even further substantiate ecclesiastical doctrines. This was inevitable under a totalitarian system in which the leaders claimed to possess the final, absolute answer to all problems. A dictator cannot tolerate any activity which questions his omniscience or, worse, sets down such claims as a simple case of fraud. There is no better proof of this than the totalitarian systems of our own times in which art and science, in their higher, more civilized sense, are thoroughly suppressed. Similarly the Christians confined artistic and scientific activity to those aspects which would strengthen the ideology enforced by the dictatorship.[1] Whitehead has pointed out that the Europeans in the year 1500 knew less than Archimedes, who died in 212 B.C.[2] In short, science, as we have come to understand it, could not begin until it was freed from the frozen doctrines of the Church.

Therefore, if it is contended that under the domination of the Church, with all its barbarities and primitive activities, there were, nevertheless, men who were preoccupied with logic and science, it must also be recognized that whatever was done in these fields, was done for the general purpose of strengthening the Christian faith. And this is precisely what we would have done, presuming that we had similar objectives; and precisely what we would not have done, were our objectives those of modern science. That science was considered at all was primarily because the Greeks had already inoculated the Western world with its necessity. So, outside of a few incidental achievements, the general result was the debasement and degradation of the very attitudes towards the objective world which were later to civilize humans a little more than they had been before.

The activities of Roger Bacon serve as an example of the type of scientific effort that went on in these late medieval times. Bacon, although a foremost expositor of the inductive method of reasoning, nevertheless tried to utilize his scientific activities to prove the Church's fantasy-theories of reality. Of course there was an eventual threat to the Church in this, just as there was in the activities of the scholastics. Thomas Aquinas, for example, in separating reason and faith as two distinct activities, inadvertently freed the former to more dangerous uses as far as faith was concerned.

Giotto occupied a position in the realm of art similar to that of Roger Bacon in science. While there was an increase in the realism of his art as compared to that of the Romanesque period, nevertheless he was weighed down and frustrated by the doctrines his art propagated and so his figures still seem to be occupants of another world.

It will be seen, then, that in this controversy over the antecedents of the Renaissance, we do not hold to either extreme: that the Renaissance was a new culture which suddenly burst into being in the 15th century; or that these new developments in science, art, logic, etc., had a *positive* beginning in the 12th and 13th centuries.

With the Renaissance, we find men again seeking a means for displacing the false interpretations of reality proferred by Church doctrines. An example of the inception of this new attitude may be seen in the fact that certain 15th century humanists read Aristotle in the original, and, as H. E. Barnes tells us, made every effort to unearth the actual Aristotle who existed before scholastic distortions were imposed upon his works. And, writes Barnes: "Their work represented the first contact of western Europe with the true Aristotle—Aristotle for his own sake and not as a buttress to Catholic Christianity. They took delight in showing how Aristotle had been misconstrued and hushed up by the scholastics." [3]

1. If one wishes to know what the attitude of the Church was toward science, he need but look around him today and see that Church leaders are still practicing the same old "scientific" attitude of medieval times—that is, trying to control the extent and area of scientific research so that the Christian myth will not be exposed as such.

2. A. N. Whitehead: *Science and the Modern World*, p. 8, The Macmillan Co., New York, 1931.

3. H. E. Barnes: *An Intellectual and Cultural History of the Western World*, p. 552.

The Renaissance scientists also (among whom there were many artists) were not only expositors of the scientific method, but men who refused to twist science into an apology for the doctrines of the Church. In short, the negative status of science in the 12th and 13th centuries, when the Church leaders made every effort to keep scientists in the service of the Church, was changed to a positive status, when the men of the Renaissance willingly took up science and used it to free men of ecclesiastical dogma. It is significant that these positive scientific achievements of the Renaissance resulted in a frantic effort on the part of Church leaders to bring all men back to the confines of ecclesiastical authority; renewed cruelty was unleashed on those who dared to question Christian dogma.

Thus it will be seen that the differences between negative "science" and that in the Renaissance are extremely crucial and have everything to do with whether or not we have any science worth being called science. It would seem necessary, therefore, to inquire for what purpose "scientific" investigations were made, because the fact that science exists is not so important as the *kind* of science we have; a problem modern totalitarian nations evoke today. It was of the positive, new science that Whitehead wrote: "The sixteenth century of our era saw the disruption of Western Christianity and the rise of modern science. It was an age of ferment. Nothing was settled, though much was opened—new worlds and new ideas. In science, Copernicus and Vesalius . . . . typify the new cosmology and the scientific emphasis on direct observation." [4]

As a matter of fact, before the Gothic period was over in northern Europe—the last unmolested period of Christian art—the Renaissance had begun on its way in Italy. It is significant that throughout the centuries of the flight from reason, Italy maintained some "tradition of pagan knowledge" and was "not the main scene of theological speculation, in spite of and perhaps even because of the fact that the papacy resided there." [5] It was in Italy that the great rebirth of knowledge occurred, releasing man from primitive bondage towards the attainment of the scientific attitude.

What we call Christianity was actually comprised of two opposing forces: one inherited from the Greeks and Classical times in general; the other from archaic, primitive times of magic, and the supernaturalism of Oriental religion. Each held back the other, until Renaissance artists and scientists broke the grip of the myth.

4. From A. N. Whitehead: *Science and the Modern World,* p. 1. By permission of The Macmillan Company, publishers.

5. Erich Kahler: *Man the Measure,* p. 260, Pantheon Books, Inc., New York, 1943.

IV IMAGES REPLACE OBJECTS

With the Renaissance, the actual was re-discovered: it became interesting on its own account, not as a mere instance of a general rule. 29

Bertrand Russell

Who would believe that so small a space [the eye] could contain the images of all the universe? O mighty process! What talent can avail to penetrate a nature such as these? What tongue will it be that can unfold so great a wonder? Verily, none! This it is that guides the human discourse to the considering of divine things.

Here the figures, here the colours, here all the images of every part of the universe are contracted to a point.

O what point is so marvellous! 212

Leonardo da Vinci

Those who are enamoured of practice without science are like a pilot who goes into a ship without
rudder or compass and never has any certainty
where he is going. 212   Leonardo da Vinci

The frog instantly dies when the spinal cord is
pierced; and previous to this it lived without head
without heart or any bowels or intestines or skin;
and here therefore it would seem lies the foundation
of movement and life. 212   Leonardo da Vinci

But since we see that the bird is equipped for many
obvious varieties of movements, we are able from
this experience to declare that the most rudimentary of these movements will be capable of being
comprehended by man's understanding; and that
he will to a great extent be able to provide against
the destruction of that instrument of which he has
himself become the living principle and the propel-
ler. 212   Leonardo da Vinci

The painter contends with and rivals nature . . . .
recalling to the painter by what rules and in what
way he ought by his art to imitate all things that are
the work of nature and the adornment of the world.
212   Leonardo da Vinci

Preamble to perspective—concerning the functions
of the eye:
Consider now, O Reader, what trust can we place in
the ancients who have set out to define the nature
of the soul and of life,—things incapable of proof,
—whilst those things which by experience may always be clearly known and proved have for so many
centuries either remained unknown or have been
wrongly interpreted.
The eye which thus clearly offers proof of its functions has even down to our own times been defined
by countless writers in one way, but I find by experience that it acts in another. 212
          Leonardo da Vinci

Perspective is a rational demonstration whereby experience confirms how all things transmit their
images to the eye by pyramidal lines. 212
          Leonardo da Vinci

In our investigations of the Renaissance, we shall confine ourselves to the important events of the times, particularly those characteristics of the period which show the significant advances made in the break with the
unrestricted authority of the Church. The present chapter will be concerned primarily with the Florentine
sculptors and painters.

Foremost among these advances were the renewed values put upon the individual; this was
especially noticeable in the case of artists. In Greco-Roman times artists were just beginning to be recognized
as individuals in their own right and of importance as such. The Christians, however, left the artist in a

situation far from respectable. He was returned to the position he had held in Egypt, i.e., he was merely another worker who carried out orders as directed; but the great difference was that the Egyptians respected their artists. With the Renaissance, however, the artist regained the social position that had begun to be his in Greco-Roman times, only now his status as an individual became more complete. Paralleling this event in art was the fact that after the beginning of the 15th century, biographies and autobiographies were common events. And artists began to claim the right as authorities in matters dealing with art.[1]

Along with the supreme importance of individualism and uniqueness in art, came accusations of plagiarism. In past times, when all artists worked more or less in a single style, "plagiarism" was by necessity the rule of the day. But now that this attitude was reversed, all artists signed their works. Some of them, such as Raphael, came to live like princes, surrounded by all the trappings and wealth which went with such a position. But this liberation of the artist did not mean that each could do just as he pleased— as do the artists today with their erroneous interpretation of individual freedom. Rather, as Alberti wrote: "Now, as to those several kinds of *Designers* which we have here before mentioned, though they go several ways to work, nevertheless they all direct their aims to this end, namely, that their labours may appear to him that shall well observe them, as Natural, and as like the life as may be; for the bringing of which to effect, it is most evident, that by how much the more exquisitely they follow some certain determined rule or method. . . . so much the fewer *defects* will they be guilty of, so much the fewer *errors* commit, and in all manner of accounts their Works will succeed and come off with the greater advantage. . . ."[2] This discipline was the result of taking up the old Greek ideal of art, not in the manner of the Gothic artists, but in that of the original Classicists. (The Gothic ideal, as noted earlier, tended to produce the Egyptian type of portrait idealism.) The intentions of the Renaissance artists were not primarily to beautify the myths of the priests, but to attain a comprehensive orientation to the study and recording of nature.

We find that in general artists of the Renaissance evinced a keen scientific interest in their effort to record nature accurately. The writings of Leonardo (see quotations at the head of this chapter) as well as many other Florentine artists and writers give ample evidence of this. Some of them (e.g., Leonardo and Pillacuolo) practiced animal and human dissections. Illustrative of this trend is the fact that art and science were interchangeable terms. Not only were artists interested in various sciences, but many were Architects and wrote poetry and music. The many-sided interests of these men made it possible for them both to contact and to help form the new attitudes characteristic of the times. They possessed that essential characteristic for those who begin new epochs in art: they were able to respond to the new conditions of their times and incorporate them in their works.

Nevertheless, in spite of this trend towards scientific observation, accuracy and realism in art, a conflict persisted in a greater or lesser degree throughout the Renaissance (particularly among the Florentines) between a desire for realism and a tendency towards idealism. In the light of the factors that preceded and brought about the new culture, this was inevitable. Since the Church had interrupted the evolution of art, it was necessary for Renaissance artists and scientists to establish a contact with the *useful* past from which it would be possible to step off once again towards further progress. Each culture which performs an advance must necessarily start at the point where past advances ceased. This the Renaissance artists could not do with their immediate past—the Christian period. It was necessary instead to start from the achievements of that culture which the Christians had denied, as this promised more desirable survival. And to recover that knowledge and experience which had lain buried for centuries, it was necessary to *re*discover and *re*live the Classical problems and achievements by actually working them out once more. In this way,

---

1. Because of the fact that the Renaissance ushered in a period when each artist created an individual type of work, historians have dwelt on the artists of this period as individuals to the exclusion of an even more important consideration—their collective significance as a particular cultural phenomenon within the continuation of history as a whole. Biological information can be useful, but in itself does not supply us with adequate understanding of what has transpired in the past in the sense of *how* things came about. In order to attain such an understanding we shall concentrate on the aggregate consequences of the lives and works of individual artists. Should the reader feel the need of more detailed information about individual Renaissance artists than he will find here, we refer him to almost any history of Renaissance art. There is an overabundant supply of these which are little more than biographies of artists.

2. Alberti: *Treatise of Statues,* p. 146, John Evelyn's translation, 1664.

Renaissance artists were able to move on to the next evolutionary step in art. Hence they began under the direct influence of Greek and Roman works and theories, which at first resulted in their largely embracing the idealistic theory of Greek art; art was again considered superior to nature. We must note, however, that while the men of the Renaissance revived the philosophy and art methods of Classical Greece, they did not repeat exactly the efforts of the Greeks. For the revival occurred during times when what had just preceded was being eliminated, while at the same time Renaissance artists were seeking an objective never sought by the Greeks of the 5th century B. C. The Classical philosophy, as subsequent events indicate, served more as a base from which to obtain new bearings in the effort to strike out towards new values more appropriate to actual conditions—values the development of which had been suppressed by the Christians for ten centuries. Unlike the artists of the Gothic period, for whom the ideal notion of art was (as for the Egyptians) merely an appropriate visual device for fostering religious doctrines, the Renaissance artists used it predominantly as the means of securing a more perfect recording of nature—much in the manner of the original Greek Idealists before it became a static notion of reality. This is why Renaissance artists were primarily interested in the idealism of the "ancients" and not of the Christian artists. Thus "Gothic" became a term of contempt in Renaissance Italy.

Renaissance artists soon began to notice vaguely a contradiction in their notions of the ideal and their desire to "imitate" nature. Eventually we find a clear and unequivocal statement by Leonardo that the particular or individual is the prime objective of art recording. Nevertheless, confusion over this problem persisted. An excellent instance of this is to be found in the way the Renaissance artists used mathematics in order to achieve scientific knowledge of the structure of things, a notion borrowed from the Greeks. It was to be expected in an age of science (science being a form of knowledge in which there is always an effort to measure the structural order of relations) that artists should have assumed that the human form has a mathematical foundation. However, their error was in using mathematics in a manner similar to the Greeks, as a means by which the general could be compiled into a set of static measurements. The Greek methods were devised for obtaining the depiction of the general, whereas Renaissance artists wished in the long run to obtain an ever more accurate recording not of the ideal but of particulars. What was actually needed was a general theory or method possessing variables to cover the diversified characteristics of reality where no two figures are ever the same. However, in time Renaissance artists learned to use the mathematical or ideal procedure simply as a method for studying the human form—as a sort of working model which could then be transposed into the depiction of the particular human forms recorded in their finished works.

As artists tended more and more towards the recording of the individual rather than the general, the mathematical procedure proportionately disappeared. The precision of mathematics was not to be recovered in the depiction of visual phenomena until the invention of the Camera, which works like a variable mathematical method of visual recording as suggested above. But theories of the ideal, during the Renaissance, were never entirely discarded. There existed a dichotomy between the ideal and the real throughout the theory and art-making of these times, and so there was bound to be confusion. We find writers contradicting themselves in an effort to reconcile the real and the ideal.[3] If some artists insisted upon the ideal, there were others who insisted that nature as it actually appeared was the ideal, so to speak. There are a number of aspects to this confusion between the real and the ideal which will be taken up in detail in the next chapter.

A similar dichotomy in religion is found during the Renaissance—a conflict between the here-world and the other-world. The here-world, however, was gradually triumphing over the other-world in man's philosophy of life as well as in his art; and, as Kallen shows, even though the artist continued the use of religious subjects, nevertheless, "in this theme his symbols and allegories stood less as presentations of the Unseen than as signs of the Seen. . . . Both patron and artist thus employed figures of a past tradition to signalize a present meaning."[4] Kallen gives examples such as Donatello's *David* being used to

3. See the quotations from contemporaries in Chambers' *History of Taste*, Chapter 3.

4. Horace M. Kallen: *Art and Freedom*, Vol. 1, p. 133. Reprinted by permission of the publishers, Duell, Sloan and Pearce, Inc., copyright 1942 by Horace M. Kallen.

symbolize the downfall of the "Goliath of tyranny" and Michelangelo's *David* representing Florence as she prepares "to meet her foes." [5] That is, the old symbols thus were freed from the rigid purposes of solely depicting a mythical world and converted to the symbolic representation of the real world of events. In a similar manner the old symbols served the artist directly. If he had to make Church pictures in order to live, still he utilized these subjects to exercise fully his increasing concern with perfecting his recording of reality.

Another instance of the growing importance of the here-world is the depiction of the donors within religious paintings. At first these donors were shown rather small and in some unobtrusive corner. But in the later works we find them depicted on the same level of importance as the religious figures. Finally they became even more important and eventually some even occupied the chief positions. Hence the donors' wives, children, dogs and later their mistresses appeared in religious paintings. In fact, the donors eventually were to demand special places for their portraits, and some did not even bother with having themselves depicted as participants in the religious subject of the Church painting.

Still a further indication of the increased importance of the here-world and the here-people is to be found in the invectives Savonarola levelled against art and artists. He said: "The figures that you cause to be painted in the churches are the portraits of your idols, and the young people say then at sight of this woman or that: behold, that is St. Magdalen, or, that is St. John, because you make your figures in the churches like to this man or that woman." [6] At another time he said: "Painters, you do ill, you bring vanity into the churches, you vest the Blessed Virgin as if she were a common woman." [7] Savonarola was thus aware that the other-world, which the art particularly of the Dark Ages had implanted into men's minds by means of its distortions of reality, was breaking down. [8] But in spite of pressure to return to past ways, artists in general continued to make the individuals of the other-world more and more like actual human beings. Where previously the Church art had shown the human form in the alleged shape of God, angels, etc., now these representations were very much in the actual shape of human beings.

Once the notions of the Christians were divested of absolute authority, a basis for progress was again possible. Thereafter it was necessary to pass beyond the ideal notions of the Classical Greeks. As actual earthly existence gradually crowded out and made less important the other-world of the preceding culture, the more realistic or scientific observation of nature made it possible for men of the Renaissance gradually to dispense with the methods and methodologies of an ideal—both that of the Greeks and the more severe kind of the Christians. Eventually we find criticisms levelled against those who took the "antique" rather than nature for their model. [9] And the evidence of the actual art shows us that the artists were increasingly concerned with recording nature more and more accurately. Accordingly, artists again tended to swerve sharply towards one of two polar objectives, either towards the real or the ideal.

It was the search for more and more realism which eventually brought about a most significant and basic change—a change that now occurred for the second time in the history of art: that is, the replacement of sculpture by painting as the *dominant* medium for recording nature. Let us see how this came about.

As we have noted in the previous chapter, Italy was the scene of the first resumption of the concerted quest for further accuracy in the recording of nature. This was first apparent in sculpture; hence we should first examine the part played by the sculptor's work as the vanguard of the new direction.

The point at which we look in on the Renaissance sculptors finds them beginning the revival of the Greek and Roman arts, and at first, as we have already suggested, seeking a perfectionistic depiction of

---

5. Ibid., p. 133.

6. As quoted by O. Hagen: *Art Epochs and Their Leaders*, p. 27, Charles Scribner's Sons, New York, 1927.

7. As quoted by Sheldon Cheney: *A World History of Art*, p. 524.

8. Botticelli and Michelangelo were both supposed to have taken Savonarola's criticisms seriously, and the former never afterwards would depict any of his contemporaries in his religious paintings.

9. Thus Raphael was accused of using the same model for all his pictures. The similarity of his figures was probably due more to his use of the old Greek method of compiling the best parts of many models into a single figure of perfection so that eventually he followed a formula for depicting the human form, just as had the Classical Greeks.

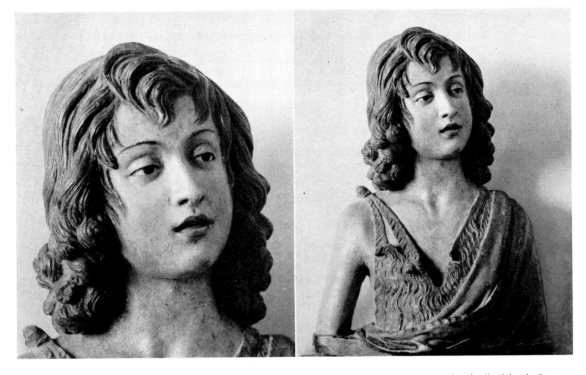

44. Benedetto da Maiano (Florentine, 15th Century) Saint John the Baptist, painted terracotta. Also detail of head. Courtesy of The Metropolitan Museum of Art.

the general human form as they *re*lived the Classical problems. Alberti wrote of the idealization factor which he found in these arts: "Among the ancients, we see statues of two or four horses and of their drivers, so exactly like to each other, that art in them may be said to have exceeded nature, in whose works we hardly ever see one feature so exactly like the other." [10] In other words, art was thought to supersede nature on its own grounds; art was the criterion of reality.

From emulation of the Classical, Renaissance sculptors passed to the Romantic and finally to the Realistic art of Rome, thus recapitulating those periods of art from 5th century B.C. idealism to Roman realism. Not only was more realism demanded by the patrons of art, but *realism became a unique problem for the artist.*

This was especially evident in the realistically painted sculpture.[11] Although sculptured works as far back as Paleolithic times were usually painted, realism in the use of colors and modelling of tones was not highly developed until the Renaissance. In general, sculptors of earlier times had used paint simply to achieve a general color for the forms. The Renaissance sculptors, however, had their sculpture painted with the intention of directly competing with the products of the painter.[12] In addition to more realistically

10. Alberti's Treatise on Painting, as quoted by Chambers, *History of Taste*, p. 65, Columbia University Press, New York, 1932.

11. Richter states that in Renaissance times wood and terracotta sculpture was painted but that marble and stone works were not because they were copies of Classical works which, because of centuries of weathering, had lost their color. (*The Sculpture and Sculptors of the Greeks*, p. 113.)

12. This practice (which so far as we know began with the Greeks) of a *painter* being employed to finish a sculptor's works, was continued in Renaissance times. Often a specific painter would be stipulated in the contract for the sculpture. It would be logical to assume that this practice was not necessary in earlier times when coloring was simplified; then the sculptor could easily have done it himself. But as the tendency towards realism increased, the assistance of a painter's special skills was needed.

painted statues, the sculptors of the Renaissance attained more dynamic and in general, more animated, depictions than had been done in the past; singing boys, wrestlers, horses and their riders depicted in movement, etc., were common. But in reaching this seemingly close approximation to nature (that is, in attaining more success with the difficult "living qualities" such as animation and color), it became apparent that the medium of sculpture had now arrived at the outmost limit of its potentialities to achieve further realism.

Heretofore there had always been greater degrees of realism which the sculptor could strive to achieve in his recordings; but Renaissance painted sculpture reached so close in some respects to reality that it was forced to stand in severe as-a-whole comparison with nature's forms. And when thus compared, it gave the appearance of something hovering between petrified life and death, a frozen *cut-out* from reality (figure 44). The animated, dynamic works were merely staticized motion, congealed life. In their final attempts to achieve more reality, sculptors were overstepping the potentialities of their medium. The petrified character of the results in color and motion made this apparent; the recording of reality could not be developed further in sculpture. The successful depiction of motion was not to come for several centuries, not until the invention of the moving-picture camera. The colored figures of the Renaissance needed a color-environment—sky, clouds, water, trees or interiors, etc.—to avoid the undesirable cut-out appearance of dead life. And these the sculptor could not successfully record. This was a serious defect which the intense realism of the sculpture only heightened.

In an attempt to go beyond the "cut-out" result the sculptor had recourse to relief carving. However, these reality recording developments now being attempted could be successfully realized only in another medium. As we shall see, the sculptors were actually trying to compete with the medium which was to become the dominant method of art-making for the next four centuries—namely, the linear medium and specifically oil painting. Berenson's remarks on this problem are excellent: "Donatello's bust of Niccolo d'Uzzano shows clearly, nevertheless, that the Renaissance could not long remain satisfied with the sculptured portrait. It is coloured like nature, and succeeds so well in producing for an instant the effect of actual life as to seem uncanny the next moment. Donatello's contemporaries must have had the same impression, for busts of this kind are but few. Yet these few prove that the element of colour had to be included before the satisfactory portrait was found: in other words, that painting and not sculpture was to be the portrait-art of the Renaissance."[13]

A further instance that the sculptors were engaged in problems which could be more effectively realized with the painting medium was their particular kind of preoccupation with relief, namely, perspective. Ghiberti, a sculptor, made the following statement: "Observing the laws of vision, I succeeded in giving them an appearance of such reality that if seen from a distance, the figures seemed to be in the full round. In the different planes, the nearer figures are the greater; those further away diminish in size just as occurs in nature."[14] In this statement we see a preoccupation with a method of depiction particularly adapted to the two-dimensional medium of painting. Obviously, in his own medium, sculpture, Ghiberti was already able automatically to produce the "full round" in "perspective." But the painter could not depict the actual round of things in space; he needed the laws of perspective in order to achieve linear recordings or *illusions* of the full round.

The unconscious error in Ghiberti's theory was the implication that real objects *actually* diminish instead of only *appearing* to diminish in size the further they are from the observer. He did not coherently realize that this phenomenon does not occur to the actual forms of objects but only to the light image that bounced off the forms of objects and impinged upon the eye-brain. That is, not the form but the image of the form diminished in size. To have been consistent with his theories, Ghiberti would have had to discard his medium of sculpture and take up a linear one. In fact, so much were his interests those of a painter, even to the point of coloring his sculpture, that the wonder is that he did not discard the chisel entirely for the brush. Ghiberti says that he strove to the utmost to imitate nature. But the "utmost imitation" of nature could *now* best be achieved by painting, as the following makes more clear.

13. Bernhard Berenson: *The Italian Painters of the Renaissance*, p. 26, The Clarendon Press, Oxford, Revised Edition, 1930.
14. As quoted by Pijoan: *An Outline History of Art*, Vol. III, p. 49.

The laws of perspective were formulated for making images, i.e., illusions of form, on a flat surface. These laws did not apply where carvings of form took place. Perspective was indispensable to painting —i.e., the *illusion* of form-space—but necessarily dispensable to the sculptural medium—i.e., the carving of *actual* forms in actual form-space. Since perspective in sculpture occurred automatically, the deliberate application of these laws only served to frustrate realization of the characteristics peculiar to sculptured recordings. After all, perspective did not exist in the actual forms of actual reality or sculpture, but only in the images of the forms produced by light. Therefore, to carve forms and to apply the laws of images (perspective) to carvings simply resulted in a compromise between the linear and sculpture mediums, that is, relief-carving. This was just what Ghiberti and other sculptors did.

If Ghiberti had tried to utilize the legitimate potentialities of the sculptural medium in securing the kind of perspective effect he sought, he would have had to employ the following possible, but impractical, solution: to make all his figures in their actual life size and then place the distant figures in the distance and the near figures near. Thus the nearer figures would *appear* larger than the distant, only this time they would actually appear, to use Ghiberti's words, "just as occurs in nature." As it was, however, Ghiberti reversed all the reality characteristics of his medium; he reduced the size of the figures that he wanted to appear in the distance and put them immediately behind the nearest figures. With this compromise between the potentialities peculiar to painting and sculpture, he failed to realize the full potentialities of either.

Reliefs, therefore, are an attempt either to give the linear medium the advantages of the three-dimensional one, or else to give sculpture the advantages of the linear medium, depending on the degree of roundness or flatness in the relief. From this point of view reliefs are a bastard art and must be regarded as "primitive" attempts to depict either in the round or the flat mediums—depending on the medium towards which the relief tends most strongly. Accordingly, if the relief is very flat it is but a frustrated attempt to paint; if very round, a frustrated attempt to sculpt. In denying the artist the full advantages of either painting or sculpture, the method of relief at the same time fails to compensate with any other advantages which might make it worth the sacrifice. The artist who employs relief gives up far more than he gains. Thus we can formulate a law: the lower the degree of relief the more the potential advantages of the linear arts are utilized; similarly the higher the degree of relief, the more the potential advantages of sculpture are utilized. But the more the advantages of one medium are employed, the more one loses those advantages possible in the other. In short, with the relief method one cannot attain or supersede the superior qualities potential to either sculpture or painting.[15]

Ghiberti's activities, and those of other sculptors who experimented with relief perspective, provide an excellent example of the overlapping of objectives in the transition from the three-dimensional and major medium of the past—sculpture—to the linear or two-dimensional medium of painting. Thus the value of Ghiberti's concern with perspective—a concern typical of Renaissance sculptors generally—was the assistance it gave to painters in solving problems peculiar to their medium. It is interesting to note that in many ways the painters found the sculptors important and vital teachers; many important painters emerged from sculptors' studios. In some cases, sculptors, sensing the inadequacy of their medium, occasionally resorted to the painter's tools. Such, for example, was Verrocchio, the teacher of Leonardo. Of considerable interest in this regard are the disputes, which we shall examine presently, between sculptors and painters, as to which medium was superior.

But we need to be clear on one point. The sculptor did not work on problems of perspective in his medium primarily for the purpose of assisting the painter with his problems. He did so mainly because he wanted for his own medium the more extensive depictional potentialities that lay in knowledge of perspective. Previously the sculptor was severely limited in his depiction of objects; with perspective this limitation seemed to be overcome. But, as already explained, for the sculptor the employment of perspective forced a compromise between the possibilities peculiar to his medium on the one hand, and the painting

15. In this respect it is interesting to recall that the Romans who desired a great deal of realism in their art, made such high reliefs that they were often on the verge of becoming complete sculpture. There have been cultures in which the relief seemed to be preferred to the round of sculpture; e.g., the Assyrians, with a culture war-like and largely primitive.

medium on the other. The potentialities of perspective were likewise compromised, since this required the complete use of illusionistic depictional methods. Therefore, the sculptor in attempting to capture perspective for his own medium—a method better suited to the painting medium—inadvertently assisted the painter in solving the latter's problems.

In Greek and Roman times, when sculpture was the more highly developed and the major art medium, it exerted a strong influence on painting. Many of these paintings, especially the earliest which have survived, appear like painted statues. The Renaissance sculptors influenced the painters in a somewhat different way, as we have noted. But the effect of painting on sculpture was not salutary. Although the sculptors tried to compete with the painters, first in the field of color and then in the realm of perspective, they eventually failed in both cases. Color and perspective became the prerogative of the painters and enabled them to envelop a wider range of subjects and characteristics than was ever possible with sculpture.

So long as art was restricted to problems primarily of developing the recording of *form,* particularly the human form, so long was sculpture able to continue as a useful, developmental medium. But once this problem reached the limit of its development, the problems which arose for further recording progress (e.g., modelling with color and perspective and so recording the environment) were such that the sculptors could no longer cope with them adequately. For now the advanced problems of art were not those of recording forms, i.e., *actual* forms, but of recording the light or images that bounced off the forms of reality. The contributions of Renaissance sculptors were not so much for the development of their own medium, but lay more in the fact that they inadvertently assisted painters. With the discovery of a coherent system of perspective, painters secured the necessary means for achieving more efficient illusions of three dimensions in space. Once this happened painters assumed the major role in subsequent art developments, and just as we observed a transition from sculptural to painting dominance in the Paleolithic period, when the animal subject predominated, so we shall see this occur again during the Renaissance, only now the human form predominated. Sculptors have of course continued to sculpt ever since the Renaissance. Old solutions persist long after newer and better ones have been devised to take their place, because the majority are conservative. But the three-dimensional medium will not appear again in any important art developments until the 20th century (and then tremendously changed), in spite of periodic attempts on the part of sculptors in the interim to restore their medium to the glory and renown it once possessed. And the concern evinced by artists of the early Renaissance with the art and notions of Classical times was never completely shed by subsequent sculptors until our own century. As later studies will reveal, this was not only because sculptors would not change, but because their medium could not be adapted to the full demands of the new conditions of art. Consequently what came to an end during the Renaissance was not the *use* of the sculptural medium, but rather its usefulness. Today the art of sculpture continues, becoming ever more mediocre, be it "Modern" or Academic.

We cannot emphasize too strongly that these medium transitions were not as sharp as may appear in our analysis. One medium was not completely dispensed with when the other became predominant; rather as one medium became more useful the other gradually receded into the background. We must recognize also that when we observe a medium returned to a major position in art making, it is used in a different way for different purposes than in the past. If these phenomena were properly understood, we could dispense with a lot of useless arguments concerning whether this or that medium was superior in this or that time. In an effort to avoid such futile arguments, we have tried always to context our statements about the termination or the resumption of one medium or the other in terms of *major* or *minor* mediums in the sense of their degrees of *usefulness* or *uselessness* to art progress at a particular time. With this in mind we are now in a position to observe the manner in which the two-dimensional medium was utilized in the effort to continue the progress of art beyond that point where the three-dimensional medium could no longer go.

It may be helpful first, however, to review briefly the rotation of the two principal mediums of art, the linear and the three-dimensional, as they evolved after the first or "Decorative" stage of art through periods of representing animals predominantly and then humans predominantly. The art of painting had been going on for many thousands of years prior to the Renaissance, side by side with the activities of sculptors. We have shown that the first medium to be developed to major status for representational purposes during Paleolithic times was the three-dimensional one, while the linear medium trailed behind, at first in the rudimentary stage of engraving or drawing, which later developed into painting or color-modelling. Both mediums were at first used primarily for depicting animals. In Paleolithic times when the sculptor reached the limit of his ability to depict animals, the painter took over the major art role, since he was able to record animal forms more accurately. So ended the first epoch of man as an artist.

There then followed a similar rotation of the two mediums, but this time it was for the purpose of recording the human form. In Egyptian art sculpture was predominant once more, although of course the painting art was also employed. But just as in Paleolithic times, the line engraving dominated at first and only later did modelling with paint begin. In the painting of Greece and Rome we saw the beginning of efforts to depict three dimensions on a flat surface, but during this time the dominant progress still continued in sculpture. It was with Greco-Roman times that painting again reached the stage of modelling that had first appeared in Magdalenian art. Only now the method of illusionary art was to reach a considerably higher stage of development, both in the subject recorded and the accuracy of this type of recording.

Thus from Paleolithic times up to the height of Greek culture, attempts at representing the FORM of the *human* figure were, with rare exceptions, confined to the medium of sculpture. The sculptor's medium supplied the artist with the means to produce actual forms and so the achievement of tactile correspondence to the actual forms of the human figure. This medium made the representation of form far less difficult to attain than in the medium of painting where perspective—and the visual consciousness it implied—was a necessary part of the artist's equipment and hence a far more difficult thing to achieve. In sculpture "perspective" was unconsciously and automatically secured, but in painting it had to be deliberately and consciously achieved. In short, man again in tackling a new subject, the human form, had to learn to record it by gradual stages, taking the easier, simpler, more direct paths first before passing on to more difficult methods. We have seen that three-dimensional depictions of the human form were carried to the point where that medium could not be exploited further to gain increasing recording accuracy.

Thus the linear depiction of the human form also had to progress from the simple to the complex. The Egyptian painter (painter-engraver, to be more accurate) first developed a particular formula for depicting the human form on a flat surface; he did this in such a way that the difficult problem of foreshortening was circumvented. Hence the head was side-view with front-view eyes; the torso front-view with side-view pelvic section and legs; one can see various other difficulties with details such as hands, drapery, etc. We also saw how this type of artist combined side- and top-views of, for example, bodies of water, where "tactile" rather than "visual" laws of perspective were employed in order to show things on and in the water. These devices were then made into religious law as the method for linear art. Consequently Egyptian painting and linear art in general were never free to reach the level of recording proficiency secured by Paleolithic artists as seen in their most developed paintings and drawings of the animal form. We have already noted how the religious elements in Egyptian culture operated regressively, deliberately suppressing the free use and full development of the degree of visual consciousness then potential. But it is necessary for us also to realize the particular kind of visual consciousness which motivated the linear artist. That is, the tactile objective dominated, since his visual consciousness was more that of a sculptor. The tactile stage of visual consciousness comprised the linear artist's first attempts at form-illusion. At first this limited him to the outline of the form; next he attempted to make the three-dimensional forms of the sculptor. Only after this latter stage of development did the linear artist evolve to the point where he could distinguish between the form (sculpture) and the image of the form (painting). There were a few attempts to depict three-dimensional phenomena in Egyptian painting in a three-dimensional manner, particularly in the XVIIIth and XIXth dynasties, but, as G. M. Richter has pointed out, these deviations from the accepted conventions were sporadic attempts without any further development.[16]

16. G. M. A. Richter: "Greek Painting," p. 2, fn., brochure published by The Metropolitan Museum of Art, New York, 1944.

As regards the function of the two-dimensional medium, the linear art of the Egyptians formed the highpoint of the transition from the ideographic into (1) what later became an alphabetical form of communication and (2) into an art form that became mainly devoted to descriptive visual representations of reality. The latter, as man evolved, no longer needed to be a deliberate twisting of the appearances of reality in order to convey non-visual meanings as well as visual ones. This was possible because the old communication-function of linear art had largely been taken over by the new, non-pictorial, descriptive art of writing, which gradually evolved and was brought to a high stage of development in the Greek and Roman cultures.

The Greek painters who produced the next major developments in linear art first passed through many of the Egyptian phases of early times before they struck ahead of the most developed accomplishments of the Egyptians. Hence they kept the figure in a single plane, then overlapped figures to show the position of one further back than another.[17] Finally, the Greek painter stepped off into the problem of the third dimension depicted on a flat surface.

Now there are some writers who, in their enthusiasm or because of the handicaps of over-specialization, inform us that the Greeks were the first to employ foreshortening and modelling. Actually such efforts were first made in upper Paleolithic times. But these efforts were more or less confined to the depiction of animal forms. Therefore, if such a claim is confined to the context of the human form, and not painting in general, then it is correct to credit the Greeks with the first extensive achievements in foreshortening and modelling.

In Greek vases we see some evidence of the artists' struggle with this problem, and for a long time we see them trying to twist the lines to make the forms and the foreshortenings that linear art demands. Only later were details like the correct rendering of the side-view eye with the side-view head achieved. And only later did the Greek artist succeed with the more difficult poses of the human figure. Finally the environment began to appear, i.e., landscape and Architecture in which the figures exist, and with these attempts began the struggle to cope with the problem of perspective. But perspective was never correctly solved. Numerous vanishing points were employed in each individual work, because of the operation of the psycho-tactile factor. Along with these efforts modelling began, not only with lines but with light and dark in colors. But even in this effort many sources of light were represented, an error similar to that of the many vanishing points for perspective. Nevertheless, in Greek and Roman painting the dominance of the psycho-tactile influence was largely being overcome.

But with the advent of the Christians the general mass of human beings were hurled back into the old, primitive Pictographic and Ideographic stage of communication. (See chapter 8.) With the opening of the Renaissance, we see that the transition in the function of two-dimensional art, begun by the Egyptians and carried further by the Greeks and Romans, was again set in motion. Once more the art of alphabetical writing symbols took over the old task of picture art. Once more descriptive art was largely freed from non-visual functions. This process was of course considerably accelerated by the invention of the printing press, which made available the means for the widespread dissemination of the new method of writing. Artists could again concentrate solely upon the task of capturing ever more accurate descriptions of the world as it actually appeared to their eye-brains.

The discovery of a successful method of perspective gave to Renaissance painters the principal tool with which to overcome the difficulties of recording the round of nature objects upon a flat canvas or wall surface. Previously, notions of perspective had been dominated by the *tactile visual factor*, but in the 15th century the *image* came to predominate in determining the laws of perspective. It was the painters, not the sculptors, who developed the useful application of these laws to the production of art, for the obvious reason that painting required perspective in order to gain the correct illusion of roundness in space.

But the Renaissance painters, as the sculptors, had to pass through many of the later stages of Greek painting in order to put their medium back on the road of development which the Christian regression had suppressed for so many centuries. If we choose an arbitrary point, say the work of Giotto, we can say that it took a good century longer before painters recovered not only the ability to draw the

17. See ibid. for the various stages in the development of Greek painting.

45. Left, Giotto, The Baptism of Jesus. Arena Chapel, Padua. Alinari photo. Right, Masaccio, The Expulsion from Paradise. Brancacci Chapel, Santa Maria del Carmine, Florence. Photo, The Bettmann Archive.

figure, but to replace the rigidity of Christianity and recover the life-like quality which had begun to enter painting 1000 years or more previously in the Greek and Roman linear arts (figure 45).

For the painters of the Renaissance, as well as for the sculptors, it was a natural course of events to begin with the emulation of the Classical attitude toward art. In this regard it is essential to note that very little if any ancient painting was discovered until comparatively recent times. Hence what influence the "ancients" had upon early Renaissance painters had to pass to it from the other two arts—sculpture and Architecture. Consequently the time necessary for the development of painting was increased, since painters had practically to go through the entire evolution which ancient painters had gone through. One has only to examine the fairly recently discovered paintings of Pompeii and to compare them with the 13th and 14th century Italian works, to realize how much early Renaissance painters could have profited by having the ancient paintings to guide them. Thus Vasari correctly wrote that the artists he placed in the first or early period of Italian painting "deserve all the praise and credit that can be awarded to their works, since it must not be forgotten that they had received no aid from those who preceded them, but had to find their way by their own efforts." [18] From this point of view Vasari was more or less correct when he wrote of Giotto as "the master by whom the true art of painting was recovered, after it had been lost during many years preceding his time. . . ." [19] And that "if his rude figures want the reality of life, let it be remembered that Giotto had never seen the works of any better master than he was himself." [20] What Vasari did not see was that painting would have to be freed from the necessity of making the doctrines of the Church the prime interest of the artist, before the recording direction of realism could be freed to further progress.

18. Giorgio Vasari: *Lives of Seventy of the Most Eminent Painters, Sculptors and Architects*, Vol. 4, p. 394, (Edited by E. H. and E. W. Blashfield and A. A. Hopkins), Charles Scribner's Sons, New York, 1926.

19. Ibid., Vol. 1, p. 78.   20. Ibid., Vol. 4, p. 395.

46. Left, Giotto, detail of figure 45, left. Alinari. Right, Masaccio, detail of figure 45, right. The Bettmann Archive.

Thus the earlier Italian paintings were in general influenced by sculpture, which helps to account for the fact that the human form was stiff and static in its posture and treatment. They look like paintings of sculpture; they have the rigidity of stone and lack the flexibility that is potential to the medium of painting. Moreover painters in the beginning of the Renaissance period not only followed the course taken by sculptors, but as we have already suggested, many of them emerged from the workshops of the latter, where they received their original training.[21] In short, sculptors, for apparent reasons, were the first to lead the way in the quest for realism. And, as Berenson wrote: "Thus, at a time when painters had not yet learned to distinguish between one face and another, Donatello was carving busts which remain unrivalled as studies of character. . . ."[22]

We see then in this new era of painting the general developmental characteristics found in each new art cycle, the transition from the simple to the complex, from the static to the dynamic, etc. This is the natural order of development. The artist must first concentrate on securing a solution to the new problems with the most simple, direct means available. Once these visual-thinking orientations are securely grounded, he can then tackle the more difficult, complex, dynamic factor.

21. According to Vasari (ibid., Vol. 1, p. 249) it was Masaccio's friend, Brunellesco, the sculptor, who taught him the science of perspective.
22. Berenson, *The Italian Painters of the Renaissance*, p. 26.

47. Left, Leonardo da Vinci, detail of figure 48. Alinari. Right, Pompeian nude, detail of figure 36. Alinari.

However, it should be pointed out that in the early and most primitive stages of the linear medium dynamic depictions are possible. But as this medium gets closer to an accurate recording of the human form, then in the same degree efforts at dynamic depictions vanish. The reason for this is the need for learning the anatomical structure in its easiest poses. Therefore, in this medium we have a situation something like this: the earliest and most primitive stage allowed for dynamic depictions of the human form because the artist was not yet frustrated by anatomical problems; in other words, the manner of drawing the human form in this stage was simple, and it was fairly easy to activate this simple form into a dynamic pose.[23] But once linear art reached the more difficult anatomical problems, these had to be mastered before the dynamic factor could again be utilized. With sculpture the problem was different; here where the artist was recording in the third dimension from the very beginning, he could not, except in a minor detailed way, depict dynamic poses; he was compelled to strive at once for the ever more accurate depiction of the anatomical character of the human form. Hence, the sculptor did not reach the stage of dynamic depictions in the primitive period of his medium, as did the linear artist, but only in the final developed stage.

23. The works of the Paleolithic artists in east Spain are an example of this stage of dynamic effort in linear art.

Therefore the manifestations of dynamic recordings in linear art in one case were not an indication of a highly developed art, and in another case they were. But in sculpture dynamic recordings occurred only in one stage, i.e., when that medium reached a high development.

Thus in the painting of the Renaissance in which artists were attempting to grasp anatomical structure, it was necessary first to depict figures statically before complex, dynamic poses could be attempted.

Another instance of the painters' progress from the simple to the complex is seen in the fact that at first they concentrated upon the depiction of the single human form to the exclusion of most other subjects or objects. In this way also the influence of sculpture was shown. Thus, according to Vasari, Squarcione criticized Mantegna, his pupil, because he "copied from antique marbles, from which no man can perfectly acquire the art of painting, seeing that stone must ever attain somewhat of the rigidity of its nature, and never displays that tender softness proper to flesh and natural forms, which are pliant and exhibit various movements. He added that Andrea would have done much better with those figures if he had given them the tint of marble and not all those colors: they would then have been nearer to perfection, since they had no resemblance to life, but were rather imitations of ancient statues in marble, and so forth." [24]

Many paintings have only single figures or very few, rather than groups. Gradually, more figures and other objects were depicted and finally the dynamic factor was attempted. The natural order of development is again seen in the fact that Renaissance painters began with the depiction of the side-view of the head and progressed to the three-quarters and front-views. Berenson informs us that the full face was seldom attempted until the beginning of the 16th century.[25] As regards the factor commonly known as "composition"—the structural arrangement of the art contents—here also development can be seen from the simple to the complex. Hence in the earlier pictures we see one or a few figures depicted statically and arranged simply in a simple environment. Later we see more complex and dynamic arrangements of the art contents. At first the figures are set inside a room or Architecture is indicated for background. Then there are combinations of the figure with the landscape and finally in much later works we find very complex arrangements of figures in dynamic activity, such as battle scenes and the like. With the introduction of landscape or environment in general, many objects and effects could be put into the contents of art which had been impossible when the limited medium of sculpture dominated the art scene. However, the human form remained the dominant subject of art throughout the Renaissance. Each new change just mentioned reveals an increase in the ability to record nature more accurately and completely.

We have already noted that among modern historians it has become the generally accepted attitude to discard the old notion of a Renaissance and to regard the Middle Ages beginning with the 12th century as the time of the actual Renaissance.[26] While it is true enough that after the Romanesque period we find more realistic knowledge and art, especially from the 13th century on, it is also true that not until the 15th century does the knowledge and art of Europe reach the stage of realistic recording development attained in Greco-Roman times, and only then does man begin to progress, after one thousand years of sky-gazing (figures 46, 47). It has become such a habit with writers to go through the motions of being awestruck with the art of Giotto, that it is customary to begin the discussion of Italian painting with an exaltation of his virtues. Today this is not necessary. We suggest that the more pertinent matter concerns the recovery by Italian painters of that which had been suppressed by the Christians—and it was Masaccio who began the recovery of what the Christians had suppressed. In contrast to each other we can realize how much Giotto is the theologian and Masaccio the scientific artist. It was Masaccio who made the first great effort in the direction of perspective. He discovered that the human form is not surrounded by a sharp, clear outline as in sculpture; that the factor of atmosphere affects color and intensity of vision in general. In short, it was with Masaccio that the great impetus towards nature as the criterion of reality was again recovered and again development was resumed. If we assume with Vasari that "the true art of painting was recovered" with Giotto, nevertheless, the more important fact, something Vasari and his

24. G. Vasari: *Lives of the Painters*, Vol. 2, p. 260, Charles Scribner's Sons, New York, 1926.

25. Berenson, op. cit., p. 27.

26. H. E. Barnes: *An Intellectual and Cultural History of the Western World*, p. 546ff.

48. Leonardo da Vinci, Leda and the Swan (one of many copies). Villa Borghese, Rome. Alinari photo.

contemporaries could not know, was that only with Masaccio did the art of painting begin to recover a stage of development attained over a thousand years before by the Greek and Roman painters. The works of this artist, who died in his 27th year, became the fountainhead for the great artists who followed in the evolution of art; Leonardo and his generation of artists continued what Masaccio had begun. Leonardo wrote that, "Masaccio, showed by the perfection of his work how those who took as their standard anything other than nature, the supreme guide of all the masters, were wearying themselves in vain." [27] Later Vasari, along a similar line, wrote of Masaccio that it was he who "first attained the clear

27. *The Notebooks of Leonardo da Vinci,* Vol. 2, p. 276, arranged and translated by Edward MacCurdy, Reynal and Hitchcock, New York.

perception that painting is no other than the close imitation, by drawing and coloring simply, of all the forms presented by nature, exhibiting them as they are produced by her, and that whosoever shall most perfectly effect this, may be said to have most nearly approached the summit of excellence." [28]

Thus with Masaccio as their guide, the painters during and after Leonardo's time completely eliminated the stifling Gothic ideal and turned with a new attitude towards the recording of reality. Leonardo most typified the new direction towards the recording of nature. He stated clearly that "That painting is most praiseworthy which has the greatest conformity to the thing imitated." [29] He voiced the belief that the Classical method was unsuitable for those who were more concerned with the phenomenon of the unique individuality of reality than with seeking perfections upon it as such. Thus he wrote: "If nature had only one fixed standard for the proportions of the various parts, then the faces of all men would resemble each other to such a degree that it would be impossible to distinguish one from another; but she has varied the five parts of the face in such a way that although she has made an almost universal standard as to their size, she has not observed it in the various conditions to such a degree as to prevent one from being clearly distinguished from another." [30] Moreover, he said: "The painter will produce pictures of little merit if he takes the works of others as his standard; but if he will apply himself to learn from the objects of nature he will produce good results." [31] How much concerned Leonardo was with the accurate recording of nature can be seen in the following quotation from his *Notebooks*. Here he is giving the rules for what was actually a primitive method of Photography:[32] "As a means of practicing this perspective of the variation and loss or diminution of the proper essence of colors, take, at a distance of a hundred braccia apart, objects standing in the landscape, such as trees, houses, men and places, and in front of the first tree fix a piece of glass so that it is quite steady, and then let your eye rest upon it and trace out a tree upon the glass above the outline of the tree; and afterwards remove the glass so far to one side that the actual tree seems almost to touch the one that you have drawn. Then color your drawing in such a way that the two are alike in color and form, and that if you close one eye both seem painted on the glass and the same distance away. Then proceed in the same way with a second and a third tree at distances of a hundred braccia from each other. And these will always serve as your standards and teachers when you are at work on pictures where they can be applied, and they will cause the work to be successful in its distance.

"But I find it is a rule that the second is reduced to four-fifths the size of the first when it is twenty braccia distant from it." [33] One has only to read in Leonardo's *Notebooks*, particularly his "Precepts of the Painters," [34] "Colour," [35] "Landscape," [36] etc., to see what painstaking observation he turned upon nature and nature's appearances for the purpose of recording it more accurately. Indeed, Leonardo not only pointed in the correct direction which art would take in the future, but as Barnes says of him: "the most encyclopedic scientist of the age, the amazing Leonardo da Vinci (1452-1519), perhaps the most versatile genius of whom we have any record—compared with whom Aristotle seems almost a 'single-track mind.' A great painter, architect, musician, and art critic, he was also an incredibly versatile scientist. As a mathematician he had few peers among contemporaries. In astronomy he anticipated Copernicus and Galileo by his views of the motion of the earth. His investigations of mechanics, hydrostatics, and the expansion of steam and gases were revolutionary. He helped to create the science of chemistry, and came close to the discovery of the chemical composition of water. He devised the best botanical classification before Linnaeus, he was an erudite geographer and geologist, questioned the deluge and fully understood

28. G. Vasari: *Lives of the Painters*, Vol. 1, p. 229, Charles Scribner's Sons, 1926.

29. As quoted by Chambers, *The History of Taste*, p. 60.

30. *The Notebooks of Leonardo*, op. cit., Vol. 2, p. 275. Note the precisely opposite view here expressed by Leonardo as compared to Alberti's theory on p. 165.

31. Ibid., p. 276.

32. See ibid., Vol. 1, pp. 242-243, and 248, where the principles of the Camera Obscura are demonstrated.

33. Ibid., Vol. 2, pp. 250-251.   34. Ibid., Vol. 2, pp. 235-292.   35. Ibid., Vol. 2, pp. 295-299.   36. Ibid., Vol. 2, pp. 303-320.

the general nature and implications of fossils, was easily the greatest anatomist before Vesalius, and made the best anatomical drawings of their kind, unsurpassed to this very day. Leonardo's suggested inventions were astonishingly varied and numerous, and included rifle cannon, machine guns, mortars, bombs and shrapnel, submarines, flying machines, the steamboat, a marble saw, and a ropemaking machine. As an engineer he made phenomenal plans for the construction of tunnels, fortifications, water works, and the like." [37]

Richtmyer in his *Introduction to Modern Physics* has pointed out that if Leonardo's successors could have known of his works, the growth of science would have received a great impetus.[38] While Alfred Whitehead writes: "Perhaps the man who most completely anticipated both Bacon and the whole modern point of view was the artist Leonardo da Vinci, who lived almost exactly a century before Bacon." [39] Further, Whitehead regards both these men as "illustrating the various strains which have combined to form the modern world, namely, legal mentality and the patient observational habits of the naturalistic artists." [40]

However Leonardo's fundamental importance in anticipating correctly the course of future art history has been less recognized than his anticipation of scientific developments, although both fields are interrelated.

True, the Academic mentalities have been throwing art wreaths at him for generations, not because they correctly understood his significance in setting the realistic direction in art on its historic course, as one might suppose, but because they have used his art to substantiate their own prejudices. If the Academicians could correctly comprehend the fundamental function of Leonardo's works they would scarcely use him as they do; they would move on to new developments, as he certainly did in his own times. As for the "Moderns," especially those represented by such infantile behavior as painting mustaches on a print of the Mona Lisa—their prejudices *against* the art of Leonardo are based on the Academicians' prejudices, that is, they see in him only a realistic artist. Of course for the "Modern" who revels in change, not change *for something,* but simply *change,* it is intriguing and *seemingly* daring to dismiss an artist of the calibre of Leonardo with the hasty decision, for example, that he belongs to an epoch which was a "degradation of pure visual art by extraneous aims and ideals." [41] But were they to examine the contradictions in their silent basic assumptions, they would be in a position to discover that Leonardo has just as important a place in the history of art as they now give to Cézanne. Furthermore, they would find that the places of both these artists in history are quite different from those which the Academicians award to Leonardo and the majority of "Moderns" give to Cézanne. For it was with Leonardo that painting finally came into its own, both in theory and practice; the vital significance of this will be apparent as our discussion develops.[42]

While Renaissance linear art was still in its first stages, following the example of the sculptors, all went well. But trouble set in once painters began to achieve good recordings of three-dimensional reality. Not since Paleolithic times had painting threatened sculpture's dominance. Painters were now treading

37. Barnes, *History of the Western World,* p. 573.

38. F. K. Richtmyer: *Introduction to Modern Physics,* p. 18, McGraw-Hill Book Co., Inc., New York, 1928.

39. From A. N. Whitehead: *Science and the Modern World,* p. 62. By permission of The Macmillan Company, publishers.

40. From A. N. Whitehead: *Science and the Modern World,* p. 63. By permission of The Macmillan Company, publishers.

41. Oliver Bloodstein: "General Semantics and Modern Art," *Etc.,* 1:13, August, 1943.

42. If the Academic mentality finds it difficult to accept anything that is different from the revered past, then the so-called "Modern art" mentality finds it difficult to accept anything in the past that is different from the revered present. To give only one example, the former adore the realistic and have contempt for Primitive arts, while the latter adore the Primitive and are contemptuous of the realistic arts. Thus the either-or stalemate which prevails today.

with a very deliberate step in territory which had been for many thousands of years the unquestioned possession and responsibility of the sculptors. Quite naturally arguments arose as to the relative merits of the one medium over the other. Although similar discussions had occurred in Greek times, it was not till the Renaissance that they came to a lively head.

Frank Chambers tells us that arguments over the merits of these two mediums began in the times of Petrarch, who pointed out that sculpture was not only more durable, but also more naturalistic, as well as being the medium adopted by the ancients.[43] Chambers further shows that criticism in the sense that we know it today was little practiced. Instead, *artists* discussed the relative superiority of painting or sculpture, Raphael or Michelangelo.[44] It was a vital question, as our history shows, and there were often violent arguments as to which medium was superior in its potentialities for recording nature most completely. Thus Vasari records the following: "It is related that Giorgione, being in conversation with certain sculptors, ... these artists maintained that, since Sculpture was capable of exhibiting various aspects in one sole figure, from the fact that the spectator can walk around it, so it must, on this account, be acknowledged to surpass painting, which could not do more than display a given figure in one particular aspect. Giorgione, on the contrary, was of opinion that in one picture the painter could display various aspects without the necessity of walking round his work, and could even display, at one glance, all the different aspects that could be presented by the figure of a man, even though the latter should assume several attitudes, a thing which could not be accomplished by sculpture without compelling the observer to change his place, so that the work is not presented at one view, but at different views. He declared, further, that he could execute a single figure in painting, in such a manner as to show the front, back, and profiles of both sides at one and the same time. This assertion astonished his hearers beyond all measure, but the manner in which Giorgione accomplished his purpose was as follows. He painted a nude figure, with its back turned to the spectator, and at the feet of the figure was a limpid stream, wherein the reflection of the front was painted with the utmost exactitude: on one side was a highly burnished corslet, of which the figure had divested itself, and wherein the left side was reflected perfectly, every part of the figure being clearly apparent: and on the other side was a mirror, in which the right profile of the nude form was also exhibited. By this beautiful and admirable fancy, Giorgione desired to prove that painting is, in effect, the superior art, requiring more talent and demanding higher effort: he also shows that it is capable of presenting more at one view than is practicable in sculpture." [45]

Two other famous participants in these arguments were Leonardo and Michelangelo. Leonardo, who had practiced extensively in both mediums, made the claim that painting was incomparably superior to sculpture, and his evaluations of the two mediums were based on a realistic analysis. He wrote in his *Notebooks:* "That sculpture is less intellectual than painting, and lacks many of its natural parts:

"As practising myself the art of sculpture no less than that of painting, and doing both the one and the other in the same degree, it seems to me that without suspicion of unfairness I may venture to give an opinion as to which of the two is the more intellectual, and of the greater difficulty and perfection." [46] A little further on: "The sculptor cannot render the difference in the varying natures of the colors of objects; painting does not fail to do so in any particular. . . . [the sculptors] can neither represent transparent bodies nor luminous bodies nor angles of reflection nor shining bodies such as mirrors and like things of glittering surface, nor mists, nor dull weather, nor an infinite number of things which I forbear to mention lest they should prove wearisome." [47] He then concluded: "In fact, painting is adorned with infinite possibilities of which sculpture can make no use." [48]

43. Chambers, *History of Taste,* p. 39.

44. Ibid., p. 39.

45. G. Vasari: *Lives of the Painters,* Vol. 3, pp. 8-9, Charles Scribner's Sons.

46. *The Notebooks of Leonardo,* op. cit., Vol. 2, p. 229.

47. Ibid., Vol. 2, p. 229.

48. Ibid., Vol. 2, p. 230. Today these evaluations by Leonardo represent views that have yet to reach artists of the present. The sculptors particularly are unaware that they are fiddling with a long defunct medium. This applies both to those artists striving to be "Modern" and to the Academicians.

Unlike Giorgione, Leonardo did not try to show how the painter could compete with the sculptor on the latter's own grounds; instead he pointed out exactly those potentialities which painting possesses and sculpture does not.

Michelangelo's reply to Leonardo's calm analysis was the emotional, angry outburst, "he who wrote that painting is higher than sculpture was ignorant as a maid servant" and "that oil painting was an employment only fit for women, or idlers of mean capacity." Michelangelo we must realize, was futilely straining to place sculpture back on its old pedestal of supremacy. His life of continuous struggle is revealed in his work, which became tortuously difficult. He finished few things that he began, as though in a hurry to do something else which would this time surely outdo painting. Thus he tried to drown out painting with tremendously large and ambitious sculptural projects never to be realized. Ironically enough, among all his most ambitious projects the only one he ever completed was in the medium of painting—the Sistine ceiling, which he stubbornly signed "Michelangelo sculptor." Thus, while it is true that he also employed the painting medium, his disparaging comments about it signify the insecurity of the sculptor in the face of changing conditions. In the huge array of paintings for the Sistine Chapel, he squeezed the medium into the confines of the sculptor's limitations; it was as though he wished this to prove that painting could do no more but rather less than sculpture. The painted *stone* figures—for that is what they are—are actually no more than studies for colored sculpture, like a project which was never carved. He was correct when he signed it "Michelangelo sculptor."

One feels that basically he was never quite sure whether or not Leonardo was correct about the relative worth of the two mediums. In a letter which he wrote to Varchi, replying to the latter's book on the relationship of sculpture and painting, we can see that he was at a total loss as to what to make of the whole problem; his words seem to be throwing a thick fog over the issues involved. Apparently under the influence of Varchi's theorizing about the problem, Michelangelo decided that painting and sculpture were the same thing, as though he wished to placate painting by settling for equality, since he could not obtain superiority for sculpture. But he was never to know what to make of this problem. At the end of his life, he correctly complained that both painting and sculpture "have been my ruin!" [49] The furious struggling restlessness, the nervous existence which characterized Michelangelo's life, were symbols of a dying epoch in art in which sculptors strove to keep their medium in the foreground of the art scene.

In the end, as we have seen, sculptors tried to utilize methods of depicting nature which were better suited to the medium of painting. Both Brunellesco and Donatello, for example, constructed an entire room in perspective, and the latter also made reliefs representing rooms and contents in perspective. We have already discussed Ghiberti's use of this same visual device, which actually belonged to the two-dimensional medium. Michelangelo likewise utilized relief methods.

Earlier we explained how relief-carving was a compromise between the two important mediums, although for the most part it was generally more linear than sculptural. Confusion on this very point was the basis for the following argument between Michelangelo and Leonardo regarding which medium was superior. Michelangelo wrote: "I do say that painting must be good when it goes toward relief, and relief must be considered bad when it goes toward painting. Therefore, sculpture is the guide of painting; the former is the sun and the latter is the moon." [50] Venturi informs us that Leonardo made the opposite claim, to the effect that painting is far superior to sculpture, and that a bronze relief with perspective had a far greater value than a statue of marble. To this Michelangelo replied, according to Venturi: "I consider the marble sculpture as the true sculpture, because the bronze relief is very similar to painting. And although both sculpture and painting derive from human intelligence, he who wrote that painting is higher than sculpture was ignorant as a maid servant." [51] In other words, Michelangelo contended that painting could rise in value to the extent that it would aspire to the character of relief, but in so doing could never become superior to marble sculpture in the round. (The assumption was that the best painters could do was to aspire as well as they could in the direction of sculpture.) Thus, the less painting was

49. Thomas Craven: *The Story of Painting,* p. 7, Simon and Schuster, New York, 1943.

50. As quoted by Lionello Venturi: *History of Art Criticism,* p. 96, E. P. Dutton and Co., New York, 1936.

51. Ibid., p. 96.

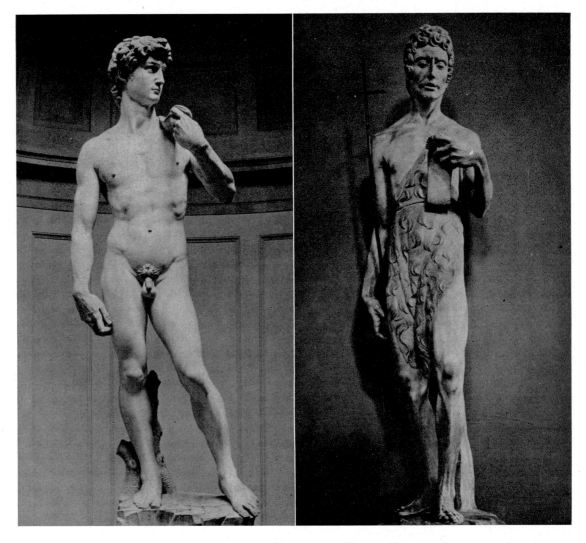

49. Left, Michelangelo, David, 16th Century. The Academy, Florence. Photo, The Bettmann Archive. Right, Donatello, John the Baptist, 15th Century. The Bargello, Florence. Photo, The Bettmann Archive.

like painting and the more like sculpture, the better it presumably became. (This was implicit, since relief-carvings were a compromise between sculpture and painting. In short, the tactile consciousness of the sculptor was dominating his evaluation of the art of images as distinct from the art of actual forms.) Leonardo insisted on the very opposite view, that sculpture could rise to higher levels to the extent that it acquired the character derived from perspective—the method for making paintings. For the sculptor this meant the use of relief-carvings, and thus sculpture might more nearly approach the superior domain in which the paintings existed. Here the assumption was the best the sculptor could do was to aspire in the direction of painting. In other words, the less sculpture was like sculpture and the more like painting it became, the better sculpture became. This was implicit, since relief-carving, the result of such a direction, was a compromise between sculpture and painting. Thus, in his turn Leonardo was insisting that the laws of illusionistic art should dominate the operation of that medium dealing with the recording of *actual* form. As a result, although Michelangelo and Leonardo each refused to compromise his own favorite medium, yet each insisted that the other do just that.

180

But Michelangelo correctly pointed out that relief was not "true sculpture," since it was very similar to painting. And on the other hand, Leonardo correctly pointed out that the relief done in perspective had greater value, implying that it was thus concerned with the then extant problems of art. However, what neither artist realized was that actually the relief medium was entirely superfluous, since it was a mere confusion of two mediums. Nevertheless each insisted in this argument that the other give up that very quality in his medium wherein lay its particular advantage over the other. Michelangelo's error was not in denying Leonardo's case for relief perspective and insisting upon the full round as the superior product of sculpture, but rather in insisting on being a sculptor when that art was as dead as the bloated muscles he sometimes carved on his figures. Neither was able to realize clearly that it was not a question of superiority of mediums as such, but rather one of function of mediums within a particular historical context.

We have quoted and analyzed this particular discussion to show how desperate the argument became over the matter of medium supremacy and the confusion that surrounded its discussion at the time. Nevertheless, in the long run, it was Leonardo who most correctly appraised the situation in regard to the execution of problems that faced artists in his times, since he realized the particular superior values of painting.

Vasari gives to Leonardo the credit for beginning the last and highest stage of Renaissance art, but to Michelangelo he gives the highest position of all the artists of this period. This evaluation has become the customary one by the majority of both Academic and Modernist observers ever since. This is because Aristotle's notion of the ideal has never been completely dispensed with. Nevertheless, one would be in error to regard the idealism of the Renaissance painters as literally the same kind practiced by the Greek sculptors. What similarity existed was greatest during the initial contacts with the Greek notion as it came to them through Roman art. Actually the revival of the Greek notion of idealism was an advance towards greater concern with actual reality for the painters of the Renaissance as well as for the sculptors, for with this notion artists were able to free themselves from the frigid grip of the Gothic or strictly Christian ideal. It was this change, therefore, that enabled the Florentines to resume the evolution of art, while artists in the rest of Europe still struggled to advance under the dominance of the Church. The Florentines became scientists in their art, investigating the structure of reality at a time when artists elsewhere remained more or less at the Giotto or Gothic level of art consciousness; that is, their task, as Giotto's had been, was largely to serve "visually" the theological interests of the Church.

In short, we must consider the ideal notion of the Greeks as the means by which the Italians freed themselves from the fetters of being *merely* Church artists, and so released themselves towards a renewed interest in the structure of actual reality. As a matter of fact, the subjects of Church art gradually became the occupants of the real world, so to speak, as we explained earlier (see page 164). Eventually Renaissance artists carried the Greek ideal towards ever greater degrees of realism as the post-5th century Greeks had also done, until artists appeared who sought for as literal a recording of reality *as they were able* to achieve. And even in those cases where artists insisted upon continuing the ideal objective—i.e., deliberately changing what they actually saw in reality—still their works showed a greater concern with actual reality than with idealism, because the predominant interest among Renaissance artists was in the structure of reality. The clearest manifestation of this was in their great concern with the problem of perspective—the structure of images. Therefore, we find that history—that is, the actual course of future art—confirms the correctness of Leonardo's views and practices as a scientific recorder of reality rather than those of Michelangelo, the Idealist-manipulator of nature. The death of Donatello actually marks

49a. Michelangelo, Day, detail from the tomb of Giuliano de' Medici, Florence. Alinari photo (from Sculpture Through the Ages, by Lincoln Rothschild).

the death of *useful sculpture;* in Michelangelo's works, we see the bloated muscles of a dead art form (figure 49a).

Arranged in the following are three principal differences between painting and sculpture in relation to each other as regards the problem of recording nature-appearances:

SCULPTURE:

Being three-dimensional this medium is similar in structure to the actual structure of nature forms. But it is extremely limited in depicting the number of different subjects and effects to be found in nature. It is practically impossible to depict the environment of an object except to a small degree which, however, entails compromising sculpture in the direction of painting; the result is relief or semi-sculptural method.

PAINTING:

Being two-dimensional this medium can only produce illusions of forms which, however, appear to be similar in structure to the three-dimensional structure of nature. But the number of subjects and effects which can be depicted in this medium is incomparably greater than in the case of sculpture; objects can be depicted with their environment.

SCULPTURE:

Recording of nature's color with this medium is extemely limited and inadequate.

PAINTING:

This medium is incomparably superior to sculpture in the recording of nature's color.

SCULPTURE:

Thus this medium is the most primitive method for recording the appearances of visual reality that man experiences by means of his eye-brain. The sculptor can record only actual forms and then only to a limited degree both qualitatively and quantitatively.

PAINTING:

This medium is the most highly developed method for recording the appearances of visual reality that man experiences by means of the images that form in the eye-brain.

50. Plaster casts of life masks of an Egyptian man and woman found in the studio of the sculptor Thutmose at El-Amarna, Dyn. XVIII. Berlin Museum.

The one point in which the painting medium is inferior to sculpture, the lack of an actual third dimension, is compensated for by its having a much wider range of possibilities for recording nature's visual phenomena in a far more complete manner. That is, if, on the one hand, painting is not a report of actual forms, as is sculpture, since actual form is lacking, yet on the other hand it supplies a very accurate report of the light-rays that bounce off the object and form its image in the eye-brain. This is important when we consider that what humans see *are not* the forms but the *images* of reality!

The resumption in Renaissance times of the linear medium as the major art method constitutes an historical transition of major importance from a medium which possesses a correspondence to the form characteristics of nature to one which possesses a correspondence to the color of the light-ray characteristics of nature. Such a change in medium remained unparalleled until our own times. It constituted actually a tremendous climax, a revolution in the evolution of man's visual consciousness.

In earlier chapters where we discussed the genesis of the linear medium of art, we found that it developed at a slower pace than sculpture, because the problems of visualization involved were considerably more difficult. We noted what a tremendous task it was for artists who were primarily tactile in their ability and orientation to learn to conceive of forms on a flat surface where no forms were actually achieved. We pointed out, however, that although the physical-tactile factor had been relatively eliminated in linear art, nevertheless, the psycho-tactile factor remained in operation for a long period, predominantly determining the basic laws governing the recording of visual phenomena. These laws were derived from what man "knew" about the actual structure of visible objects and not from how these structures appeared according to the laws of visual-images.[52]

These psycho-tactile reactions were the determinants of pictorial recording laws until the 15th century when *visual* perspective was discovered.[53] The laws of visual perspective determine the structure,

52. See William Ivins, Jr.: "On the Rationalization of Sight," *Papers,* No. 8, The Metropolitan Museum of Art, New York, 1938.

53. According to Ivins (see ibid.), Alberti was the first to discover the laws of perspective in 1435-36. Perhaps it would be more correct to state that the 15th century marked the discovery of the first coherent system of visual laws, since the quest for these laws had been going on for centuries, during which certain aspects of the problem had been discovered.

not of objects, but of the image of the objects which forms in our visual receptors. Men could now distinguish between the object and the image that light produced of the object in conjunction with the eye-brain operation of the artist. The great revolution in human vision lay in the fact that the visual-image reaction became the predominant criterion for the structural laws of pictorial recording, in contradistinction to the previous criterion—the laws of tactile experience, which were laws correctly applicable only to the production of three-dimensional or sculptured art. The transition from "tactile" to "visual" laws for linear recording was, however, a gradual one, passing with interruptions through many steps in the natural order of development of man's sensory orientation to the objective world of visual experience.

Thus it would follow *that the art history of the sculptural medium is the record of the development of tactile-consciousness, whereas, the linear medium is the record of the development of imagery-consciousness!* Of course both tactile- and imagery-consciousness are involved in some degree in both types of visual activity. However, we must distinguish between them in the following manner: tactile-consciousness is a form of primitive visualization in that the character of images as such is disregarded or remains unconscious in a greater or lesser degree. One is not aware of the *higher orders* of the abstracting process involved in visual activity. It is precisely this awareness which is not lacking in imagery-consciousness. In the one art the visual material of the eye-brain is employed as the means whereby one can interpret the *actual* character of the object's forms and then record them; in the other art this material is employed with the express purpose of recording the actual character of the light-rays that bounce off the object. As we said earlier, sculpture records the forms of the object that the light-rays indicate, while painting records the light-rays that were first stimulated by the forms of the object.

Since consciousness could most readily travel the easier path of tactile perception, and since this was the natural order of development of experience, then it was natural that tactile-visual-consciousness would reach a high degree of development first and also more rapidly than consciousness of the visual experience as images. Thus the tactile attitude dominated in the linear arts until such times as the laws dealing with tactile recording were developed to their useful limit and those dealing with the very different character of visual-imagery were gradually discovered,—the perspective of form, color and space.

Now we are in a position to make a more clear distinction between the recording behavior of the sculptor and that of the painter. The sculptor produces the forms of objects as he "knows" them to exist in space. In such cases the *forms* of the *art OBJECT* parallel the *form-structure* of the *nature OBJECT*. There thus exists a tactile correspondence to nature. The painter produces recordings of the objects in space which parallel not the object but the image of the object formed in the human eye-brain. In this case the art IMAGE of the object parallels the structure of the eye IMAGE. There is thus an imagery correspondence to nature. Accordingly, in sculpture, the art of the round, there were no problems of perspective; in the linear arts there were. For example, if the sculptor had to make parallel lines or planes he merely made them parallel and the natural operation of human vision put the lines and planes in their proper perspective. But in the linear arts, the artist had the problem of depicting an illusion not only of forms in space but put into perspective also. Hence, the sculptor *sees* lines that converge to a point, but he makes these lines parallel in his art; the painter sees lines also converging to a point but he records these just as he *sees* them. *And when the painter and the sculptor have finished, all parallel lines or planes in each of their works nevertheless APPEAR to converge towards a central point!* In other words, if the sculptor sculpted objects as he literally sees them, and the painter painted objects as he "knows" them to exist, then the results of both would not appear to correspond to the objects sculpted or painted. Therefore, if the sculptor did not do the opposite of what he "sees" and the painter did not do the opposite of what he "knows," then the art-results of both would not appear to correspond to the objects depicted. In short, the painter and the sculptor must paint and sculpt in such a way that the respective results of each, although arrived at in different ways with different mediums, in the end form similar types of images in the human visual receptors. Here we have an excellent example of how crucially important it is to note the differences in the similarities as well as the similarities in the differences. To the degree that we fail in such orientations, we incorrectly evaluate the structural function of the development of visualization.

Accordingly with the invention of visual perspective and the rise to dominance of the painting medium during the Renaissance, came the great turning point in the visual consciousness of man.[54] Men discovered the structure and function of the image of the human eye in contrast to the structure and function of the objective world of which the eye made images. If we do not realize the full importance of this we shall have difficulty appreciating the tremendous excitement for the Renaissance artists of problems of perspective and so will continue as so many "Moderns" do, to ridicule or abuse their preoccupations with this problem. Previous to the Renaissance, artists had tried to force the linear arts (i.e., the image) into the mold of the forms of nature in some degree, as they were otherwise correctly able to do with sculpture. But as the linear artist observed the uniqueness of his medium, he gradually tended towards another solution than the sculptural one. In the 15th century he discovered his error, which in turn led him to discovery of the structure of the images produced by the human eye. *Artists discovered that what we see is light, not forms or things!*

Above all we should realize that as a result of this discovery it became possible for man to observe and analyze his visual activity and to do so scientifically. Men could now begin consciously to see the difference between knowledge produced by sight as distinguished from that produced by other nerve receptors. It was the beginning of the modern science of vision! For apparent reasons this opportunity was of great value to many other fields, and so the discovery had repercussions far beyond the immediate field of art.[55]

Thus with the Renaissance we see the crystallization of notions which laid the foundation for the art of centuries to come. These were the times when the "art lover," the connoisseur, the art critic, again reappeared, when the artist became for the first time the undisputed authority in matters of art, for the time being at least. It is at this point in our studies that we can begin to see quite clearly that the evolution of visual knowledge has been a process of ever increasing consciousness of the image producing structure of the human eye—the image formed as a result of light-rays bouncing continuously back and forth between the world of things and the human eye-brain. *Man has thus made the first great discovery in vision, namely, that it is a joint phenomenon of the observer and the observed!*

Since we have noted that later Renaissance painters were largely characterized by a definite effort to achieve as much visual correspondence to the actual reality as was possible for them, we should here further clarify and emphasize this problem of relationships between reality and art, in the light of what has been accomplished by Renaissance artists.

Vasari made the claim in these times that "art has vanquished nature, or rather nature has confessed herself unable to do more than art can do." [56] From such statements we can see that the Classical notion—art can supersede nature—had now been replaced by the notion that nature was "unable to do more than art can do." If this notion still was false to a degree, it was less false and so more realistic than the Classical theory of art and nature. For now the artists were largely making a direct, coherent, conscious effort to achieve a correspondence to the actual appearances of nature, even though they deceived themselves concerning the degree of success they had. There was the painter Stefano, who, because of his skill in imitating nature, was called "Nature's Ape," while Vasari claimed that Bernazzone painted a strawberry bush with such realism that peacocks tried to peck the berries from the painted bush.[57] And in giving

54. The "avant-garde" of our times, however, see all this in a far different light. Regarding perspective one of their number claims that it "is a disease of the eyes." (Helion) (See *Art of This Century*, p. 95, edited by Peggy Guggenheim, Art Aid Corporation, New York, 1942.)

55. See e.g., Ivins, op. cit.

56. As quoted by Chambers, *History of Taste*, p. 61.

57. The truth of these stories is beside the point; their importance lies in indicating the objectives of these artists.

the reasons why he considered Raphael superior to all other painters, Vasari wrote: "It may indeed with truth be declared that the paintings of other masters are properly to be called paintings, but those of Raphael may well be designated the life itself, for the flesh trembles, the breathing is made obvious to sight, the pulses in his figures are beating, and life is in its utmost animation through all his works." [58]

In regard to these claims we must first of all keep in mind two interpretations of "reality": one in which art is considered superior to nature—the ideal; the other in which art is considered equal to nature—correspondence to reality. These two interpretations are played against each other and are often confused when an attempt is made to reconcile them. Result: a confusion which actually constitutes a third group of interpretations—various combinations of the two.

We must also recall that these various claims had already been voiced in the periods before the Renaissance. Just as the cave-man artist thought he had captured the actual reality; just as the Classical and post-Classical Greeks supposed they had achieved it in their "ideal," and the Romans in their portraits; so once again Renaissance artists supposed they had achieved a perfect recording of reality. Their concern, however, was *more* with what actually appeared to the eye-brain and not with what "ought to be," as in Greek Classical times.

Even of such "primitive" works as Giotto's, Boccacio had written: "he was of so excellent a wit that there was nothing in Nature, but that he could with his pen and pencil depict it, so that it seemed not to be a mere likeness but the very thing itself; and the visual sense of man was deceived, taking those things to be real which were only painted." [59] One recent critic tells us that when Dante saw one of Giotto's paintings, "he took the painted things for real persons, so truly did they represent nature." [60] The critic goes on to say, "the tale is hard to believe." Although there are many other similar remarks from Renaissance times, our critic, like many others, cannot believe it, because he reacts to the term "reality" as having one meaning, rather than a plurality of possible meanings. That is to say, he identifies with the term "reality" that which the term means in particular for him. He automatically assumes that "reality" meant the same thing for Dante as it does for himself. Of course this is not the case, nor could it be; the term is relative. As a matter of fact, the artists of each period, excepting the regressive ones, did depict nature more accurately than those in the preceding period, but in no case was a perfect recording of nature achieved.[61]

When we observe the art of Giotto, it is obvious that it was far from being as accurate a depiction of nature as that of Raphael. Yet Boccacio makes as great a claim for the former as Vasari does for the latter. Even though they appear to have similar meanings, these two statements take on different meanings if we evaluate them in the context of their times and the conditions of visual knowledge under which they were made. While both writers claimed that both painters accomplished the "thing itself" or "life itself," the actual works referred to tell us quite a different story. The works themselves inform us that the artists possessed different degrees of ability to record reality, but that neither painter achieved the "thing itself" or "life itself."

To comprehend correctly these quotations about realism, we must strictly avoid the identification of our visual knowledge with that of those who made the above remarks. Instead of projecting our times upon them, we should project ourselves into their times; we must, as far as possible, imagine that we are living in those times without any of the future knowledge or experience which has been discovered since. All the visual knowledge we would then possess in such a context would be what we had inherited from the past preceding the Renaissance and what we ourselves had been able to develop with that inheritance.

58. G. Vasari: *Lives of the Painters*, Vol. 3, p. 177, Charles Scribner's Sons. Chambers, in *The History of Taste*, pp. 58-63, gives numerous other interesting quotations along similar lines.

59. Boccacio, as quoted by Chambers, *History of Taste*, pp. 59-60.

60. *A Treasury of Art Masterpieces*, edited by Thomas Craven, p. 22, Simon and Schuster, New York, 1939.

61. Regarding the comprehension of this problem of consciousness of visual reality, the artist who has undergone a rigorous training in the attempt to record nature, has the advantage of actual experience, such as we discussed in chapter 3. He knows that his perception of visual reality is a changing affair; he may even recall times when he thought his drawing quite realistic until the instructor convinced him of his error with a few corrections with a piece of charcoal.

The belief of the artists of each period that they had achieved the ultimate in reality recording or had captured nature's reality, is accounted for in part by the finite character of their visual capabilities.[62] Their art demonstrated the full extent of their ability to see consciously the actual characteristics of nature's reality. In the case of the artists at the height of the Renaissance period, they assumed that they had fully captured in their art what they saw in nature. In this they were correct; what they did see in nature was secured in their art. But what was not to be found in their paintings they naturally did not see in nature either.

In short all that was coherently and consciously seen in the actual reality was put into the art; since they could not see any more in reality than they put into their art, they concluded that *all* that was in reality was *all* in their art. They erroneously assumed that all they saw was all there was to see! From this point of view it is possible to see how such extravagant claims as we have noted could have been made. Therefore, in realizing that vision was a process resulting from the relationship between the observer and the observed, they failed to realize that man's comprehension of that process of relationships was a finite, not a perfect or absolute one. If they had surmounted the delusional stage of perfecting nature in their recordings, they had yet to see the fallacy of assuming that their recordings were equal to nature's reality. Failing to see this point led Vasari to claim literally that the artists of his "third period" had attained the ultimate in the recording of nature. He writes that these artists: "have effected all that is permitted to the imitation of nature to perform, and to have reached such a point, that we have now more cause for apprehension lest they should again sink into depression, than ground for hope that they will ever attain to a higher degree of perfection." [63]

Nevertheless it should be remembered that the painters of the "third period" did produce works which constituted a tremendous recording advance over anything achieved in the past; until that time no man had ever seen such remarkable recordings of nature's forms and their colors, including those works where the artist has deliberately idealized nature. For even in the latter works the result was less ideal and more real than past idealistic art. The visual recordings achieved in these arts were something never before obtained; as such they practically overwhelmed the observer, swept him off his feet and so the impossible was claimed for these achievements, i.e., "pulse quivers," etc. Only by projecting, as we have been doing, does it become possible for us to realize the *experiential* effect such art produced upon those who made it and saw it for the first time. Above all we must realize that artists of the past measured the values of their achievements by the accomplishments of their past and not by a future that had yet to exist. To compare their works only with those of any point in the future after them is unfair if we wish to comprehend the values felt and achieved by past artists.

Still another factor is involved in these past over-evaluations of realism in art. That is, the fact that there are two general but interrelated levels in the experience and evaluation of the problem of reality and art: (1) The object of art as such; (2) the object of nature depicted by the art. In short, we are here concerned with the visual relationship between the object of art and the object of nature which it represents, i.e., the degree of recording accuracy. Vasari and his contemporaries were faced with the force contained in the art object—a force comprised, in some degree, of characteristics *not* to be found in actual reality. Primarily this factor is to be found in that degree that the art changes the reality, and so creates a fantasy of reality. That is, Renaissance art was still far from a correspondence with reality, and to that extent a non-realistic factor existed. Not being aware of man's finite comprehension of the relationships between the art- and the nature-object, observers like Vasari were captured by the power of art as such and thus attributed to the art more realism than it actually possessed. Hence a false degree of realism was accredited to the art because of an erroneous and unconscious identification of two general levels of experience—the art objects as such and the visual relationships between the object of art and the objects of nature it represents. It is immaterial to our present analysis whether the differences between

---

62. Here our discussion is only concerned with art in which the effort was to achieve correspondence to actual reality, and not with those instances in which the artist deliberately idealizes, i.e., deliberately changes the reality he sees. Yet in either case we are dealing with finite capacities in vision and knowledge of the visual process.

63. G. Vasari: *Lives of the Painters*, Vol. 4, p. 391, Charles Scribner's Sons.

the art and its correspondent forms in nature result from the degree in which the artist is lacking in ability to record nature accurately, or from such an inability along with a deliberate idealistic manipulation of nature. In either case the result can be employed to identify the art as the reality. We have seen this to be the case in all the past art so far studied, whether it was a Paleolithic work, an idealistic Greek sculpture, or even the distortions of primitive Christian arts. In each case, art always possesses a particular power of attraction by virtue of its differences from reality in contrast to the attraction of art which has a great similarity to reality. We cannot conclude our analysis of this problem until we come to the discussion of the errors and discoveries which occur in various aspects of so-called Modern art.

This sort of identification between the two general levels of art experience is by no means limited to the critics and artists of the Renaissance. Whether we know it or not, most of us are affected by both factors as though they were ONE! The differences in our *conscious* reactions to various arts are the result of over and/or under evaluating one or the other of the two levels of experience under discussion. Thus, some like Primitive or distortion arts in general, while others prefer only the more realistic kinds of art. But such either-or reactions lead only to blockages, since "art" is far too complex an affair for such simplified evaluations.

For example, those who today assume that Egyptian art is very "realistic" (an error often made by Egyptologists) do so because they are unaware of the various reactions which can be provoked by the two general levels of art experience. If on observing Egyptian sculpture one gets a feeling that it is a very "real" representation, it is because one fails to remember consciously that it is not an accurate depiction of the reality represented. In short we must become conscious of which of the two general aspects of art we are reacting to predominantly, i.e., to the "realism" of the sculpture as such, or to the realism of the sculpture in relation to nature. This confusion of the two art levels is particularly likely to happen in our times when we are much more accustomed to seeing various arts which distort reality; in the 19th century when realism was the order of the day, the degree of non-reality of Egyptian works was more clearly seen. An observer who feels that Egyptian art is a very real representation has been captivated by the indisputable force of the reality of the art forms as such. He then tends to regard the art as a separate entity unrelated to the actual object represented. Or else, he erroneously assumes that the relationship is actually an isomorphic one. The fact that no Egyptian ever looked like the sculpture does not enter to disturb his experience. In such cases the reaction is the reverse of the natural order of experience, in that the primary concern is with the forms of the sculpture as such and not with how these forms measure up isomorphically to the reality supposedly represented. The fact that no one today ever saw this particular race of Egyptians who made the art perhaps contributes to an unconscious assumption that they were radically different from ourselves in their physical appearances; that they actually looked like their sculpture. The overwhelming power of the sculpture assists considerably in producing this error. Actually it was what the Egyptians *wanted to look like* in the world of the dead! Yet, in figure 50 we can see how surprisingly like ourselves the Egyptians appeared. These are plaster casts taken from life and were found in the studio of an Egyptian artist.

All this is but to emphasize that we shall invariably fail in the task of adequate discrimination if we insist on a preponderantly "emotional" attitude towards the experience and comprehension of art. An adequate degree of cortical operation is necessary if we are successfully to experience and then evaluate the relationships between the two art levels being discussed, i.e., the art forms and their corresponding forms in reality. As we explained in chapter 7, the more "emotionally" and the less "cortically" the artist functions, the less his discriminatory capacity exists. Hence, if we are "emotional" enough, it is possible for us to have a feeling of actual reality in almost any kind of art; and the more "emotional" we are, the more primitive the art which can give us a feeling of "reality"; in other words, the nearer to the Primitive mentality one becomes in his art orientations.

We must keep in mind, therefore, that we are involved in *two* interrelated "reality" contexts in experiencing and evaluating any art; the *completeness* of the art reality as such, and the *incompleteness* of this same reality as a recording of nature's reality. If we do not possess this knowledge, or ignore it, we make inadequate "visual" discriminations between *degrees of reality* in art and the significance of these differences. To be sure the Egyptian possessed less visual consciousness of nature's reality than we do, but it was adequate survival for him *so long as he continued to progress*. In our times adequate visual survival in art can come about only if we also take full advantage of our visual *phylogenetic inheritance* from the past and *continue* its development. Only then will it become possible for us to produce the necessary and varied consciousness-of-visual-abstractions which are indispensable to the achievement of coherent understanding of the many kinds of art; only then does it become possible to evaluate discriminately the variety of reactions we have to art. When we possess such an up-to-date awareness, and we are observing, let us say, Egyptian sculpture, we begin by first experiencing the forms of the sculpture as such—the descriptive level. Then we observe the relationships between these art forms and their corresponding forms in nature, the degrees of correspondence and difference present—the inferential level. We can then decide what the significance is of this correspondence and difference.

We can now begin to see how important it is to be aware of the context in which works of art have been made and evaluations of them uttered. Today we can avoid the errors of the past because we know that we never know *all* about anything. Thus our visual capacity is also finite, as was that of those in the past, with this one difference, potentially our capacities are less finite. Through this attitude we acquire a flexibility of conscious response to the significant differences existing throughout history between art and nature. In other words, the act of "vision," the phenomena of "reality," the activity called "art"— all comprise a many-valued world of experience. Therefore, the terms "vision," "reality," and "art" etc., must also be considered as symbols for expressing multi-valued or multi-ordinal meanings, if we wish to have our words correspond to what we use them to talk about—the world of things.

In conclusion: we have witnessed the painting medium again resume the dominant position it once occupied in Magdalenian times. We are now able to comprehend even more clearly how sculpture comprises a lower order or more primitive method of recording reality than painting. From here on, specifically after Donatello, the sculptor is an artist piddling with a useless form of art. All he can do is repeat and *repeat* what has already been done better than he will ever be able to do it! For more than the next four hundred years the world of art belongs to the painter.

Ideal proportions and classical beauty be damned! 83
Francisco Goya

The principle of realism means denial of the ideal. 74
Gustave Courbet

At the beginning of the Renaissance, painting was almost wholly confined to the Church. From the Church it extended to the Council Hall and thence to the Schools. There it rapidly developed into an art which had no higher aim than painting the sumptuous life of the aristocracy. When it had reached this point, there was no reason whatever why it should not begin to grace the dwellings of all well-to-do people. 36

Bernhard Berenson

The Renaissance had resulted in the emancipation of the individual, in making him feel that the universe had no other purpose than his happiness. This brought an entirely new answer to the question, 'Why should I do this or that?' It used to be, 'Because self-instituted authority commands you.' The answer now was, 'Because it is good for men.' In this lies our greatest debt to the Renaissance, that it instituted the welfare of men as the end of all action. 36

Bernhard Berenson

In 15th century Europe a number of forces were molding the evolution of art. The ideal of the Classical Greeks had been reinstated in Italy, particularly in Florence, first in sculpture, then in painting, while the Gothic ideal persisted in the rest of Europe; but above all there was a widely prevalent force driving all European artists to seek ever greater realism in recording. These various forces of idealism and realism were seldom seen as sharply as the above might imply; one can only speak in general of the preponderance of one attitude or the other, and it should be kept in mind that various combinations can occur between the different kinds of idealism and the consequently different kinds of realistic trends, and that the functions of these forces change as they rise and fall or disappear in the evolution of subsequent recording art.

We have already discussed how the Italians freed themselves from the strait-jacket of the Gothic ideal and reinstated the pre-Christian ideal theory of the Classical Greco-Roman period. This theory with its mathematical rules for the depiction of the general formed a solid basis from which to proceed in the development of further comprehension of the structure of visual reality. From this *general* basis the Italians moved on to the study and depiction of the *particular* forms of reality, while the Classical theories remained as a controlled method of studying nature. Leonardo, for example, did indeed define the proportions of the human form as such according to some ideal mathematical order, yet we also find him experimenting with Photographic procedures as indicated on page 176, in which he was seeking the laws of the *actual* rather than the ideal. Thus in Italy the accomplishments of the Greco-Roman Classicists were recovered and the evolution of art was once again released towards further progress. Consequently the Italians, particularly the Florentines of the Renaissance, were the first to free art from the rigidity of the recording attitude inflicted by the Christians. At the same time they set the stage for the beginning of what was to become the final conflict between the real and the ideal in recording art.

Two other schools of painting developed more or less contemporaneously with the Florentines— the Venetian, and the Flemish or northern schools in general. The Venetians, who achieved their best work during and after the times of Leonardo, also threw off the Gothic ideal, but seem not to have been much concerned with the art of the Greeks. Michelangelo regretted the fact that these people did not have "the antique marbles before them day by day, as we [the Florentines] have!" [1] On the whole they did not paint in a sculpturesque manner, nor were they scientific as were the Florentines. Their particular contribution was an interest and concern with the problem of color. Thus Vasari wrote of the work of Titian (when the latter was about 30 years old): "he by no means neglected to draw from the life, or to copy nature with his colours as closely as he could, and in doing the latter he shaded with colder or warmer tints as the living object might demand, but without first making a drawing, since he held that, to paint with the colours only, without any drawing on paper, was the best mode of proceeding and most perfectly in accord with the true principles of design." [2] The Florentines considered color to be a mere appendage to the more important factor of form; for the Venetians it was the most important factor in painting. We can well imagine a typical Florentine painting repainted in other combinations of color and still retaining the essential interests of its artist, that is, the factors of form and the manner in which light and shade made them visible. But if we were to perform this experiment upon a typical Venetian work, the result would destroy the essentials of the painting, for here color is the key to the artist's essential preoccupation. For Venetian painters form was not the major problem. On this score they simply took what they needed from the Florentines; their primary interests and innovations were in the problems of color. It was possible for the Venetians to concentrate on problems of color not only because they could use the scientific laws of perspective and problems of form which had been worked out by the Florentines, but also because they could utilize the oil painting technic which had been developed by the Flemish.

Understandably the Florentines could not conceive of dipping directly into reality and recording it, as was commonly done among the Venetians. Thus Vasari wrote disapprovingly of Titian that, "he failed to perceive that he who would give order to his compositions, and arrange his conceptions intelligibly, must first group them in different ways on the paper, to ascertain how they may all go together; for the fancy cannot fully realize her own intentions unless these be to a certain extent submitted to the corporal eye, which then aids her to form a correct judgment. The nude form also demands much study before it can be well understood, nor can this ever be done without drawing the same on paper; . . . . nor does he who can draw, need to labour to hide his want of design beneath the attractions of colouring, as many of the Venetian painters, Giorgione, Il Palma, Il Pordenone and others, who never saw the treasures of art in Rome, or works of the highest perfection in any other place, have been compelled to do." [3]

So if we say that the Venetians were relatively more concerned with the direct act of recording reality, then we can say that the Florentines were more concerned with comprehending the structure of the act. If the Venetians did not become thorough scientists, they nevertheless possessed an essential freedom towards the effort to record reality. As a result, they were able to employ the factor of color in a more realistic manner than the Florentines. This freedom brought them a certain advantage over the Florentines, but the efforts of the latter to discover the visual structure of nature were essential to the task of more accurate recording. However, when the Venetians are compared to the foremost artists contemporary with them outside of Italy, it can be seen how much closer they were to the Florentines than to any other group of artists.

It is significant that with the Italian Renaissance the artist's knowledge of reality was first sought and obtained in the realm of form, for behind this factor is the knowledge built up by the works of thousands of years of sculpture. The Florentines were the first artists to break out of the Gothic cocoon of Christian idealism and it was they who made the first concerted effort to expand the knowledge of form, first in the sculpture, then in the painting medium, by picking up the ideal of the Greco-Roman period and going forward from there. It was the Florentines, we should recall, and not the Flemish or Venetians, who produced many painters who also sculpted and sculptors who also painted. Thus the knowledge amassed by the experience of sculptors was carried over into the particular demands of the painting medium. [4]

1. As quoted by Joseph Pijoan: *An Outline History of Art*, Vol. III, p. 135, The University of Knowledge, Chicago, 1938.

2. Giorgio Vasari: *Lives of the Painters*, Vol. 4, p. 259, Charles Scribner's Sons.

3. Ibid., Vol. 4, p. 259.

4. This task had already been carried considerably forward by the Greco-Roman painters, but the advantages of these achievements were not available to the Italians.

51.   Giorgione, Pastoral Symphony, Venetian, 15th-16th Centuries. Louvre. Archives Photographiques: Paris.

With the problem of form in painting worked out for them by the Florentines, it became possible for the Venetian artists to achieve the idealism peculiar to painting, i.e., *the ideal of color as distinct from the ideal of form.* For once these artists had achieved a great control over their efforts to record the color of reality (i.e., achieved the ability to record the *general* color of the objects of nature), then like the 5th century B.C. Greek sculptors in the case of actual form, they realized that man could make color effects and relations other than those in nature, and so the ideal of painting—color-idealism—was born. Thus began the conscious exploitation of the manipulative or idealistic possibilities of nature's color: and just as the Florentine artists tended to divide into those who directly sought ever greater realism of form and those who largely wished to retain the ideal notion of form, so the Venetians tended to divide on the issue of color. But in both groups those who sought to copy nature literally were the exceptions rather than the rule. These were times in which the ideal in form or color still held a dominant place.

As in the history of sculpture, so in the history of painting, it will take a long period (though a much shorter one than for sculpture) before the idealism peculiar to painting—color-idealism—is replaced by color-realism. Only after the epoch of painting dominance has run its full course of development into the 19th century will the knowledge of color pass from the ideal to the real.

Using as a guide the kind of art that preponderates, we find that the art of the Venetians lay approximately midway between that of the scientific Florentines and that of the northern artists who were concerned with the automatic or direct, sensory excitation of seeing. But in respect to the problem of

52. Lucas Cranach, the Elder, detail, Eve with the Serpent, German, ca. 1530. Courtesy of the Art Institute of Chicago.

53. Leonardo da Vinci, detail, figure 48. Florentine. (Alinari Photo.)

54. Giorgione, detail, figure 51. Venetian. Photo, Archives Photographiques: Paris.

color- and form-idealism, it was the northern artists who occupied a middle position, in that they did not overemphasize either color- or form-idealism, as did the two Italian schools. What idealism there was in regard to these two factors in their works was *merged,* neither being distinct nor predominating, as among the Italians. Their use of color was symbolical, whereas the Venetians used color to record idealized color experiences with reality. And where the northern artists used objects symbolically, the Florentines used objects as an incitement towards the investigation of form-structure in reality.

For in northern Europe (the Netherlands and Germany) in the 15th century, there was as yet no pre-Christian Classical influence. The realism that we see in these arts has a certain brittle quality, a lack of freedom and sensuousness, which can be attributed directly to the religious strait-jacket of Gothic idealism. Nowhere can this be better seen than by comparing the way in which the Italians and non-Italians

196

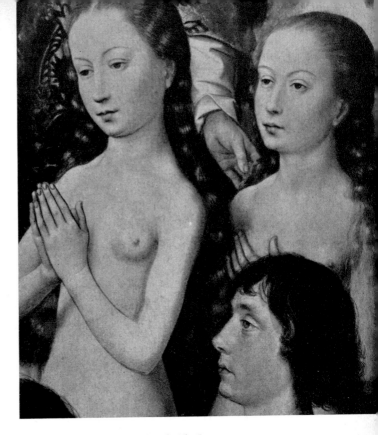

55. Hans Memlinc, detail, Triptych, The Last Judgment. Flemish, 15th Century.

painted a nude human form. The former monumentalized, the latter demoralized the appearance of the human form (figures 52, 53, 54, 55).

In the north the priest and the business man reigned supreme. They were the patrons of art; they dictated its contents. There was, as Lübke pointed out, "a general lack . . . . of that culture which regarded art as the highest adornment of life." [5] In Italy the artist occupied a high position, and even if he made a painting for the Church he saw to it, just as did the patron who ordered the picture, that it served other purposes than merely a strait-laced rendition of religious symbols. The men of power and wealth who patronized the Italian artists recognized the great importance of the artist and his art. Therefore, the artists here could become members of the elite, both in position and wealth, and, more important, could develop their interests in art towards increasing scientific realism, since they were not completely dominated by their patrons. On the other hand, as Lübke points out, "The mercantile and mechanical way of life of the North, with its narrowness, fettered the artist, and made free progress almost impossible even to the boldest spirits." [6] Thus with the exception of a few like Dürer they made no great effort at scientific investigations into the structure of reality; they lacked the influence of the Classical *attitude* to guide them into a search for the scientific laws of vision. The principal concern, particularly of the Flemish artists in the 15th century, would seem to have been natural phenomena as they actually appeared to their unscientific eyes. They were over-empirical, they lacked the deductive attitude stimulated in the Florentines by the old Classical theories of art. [7] But with this excessive empiricism there was mixed

5. Reprinted by permission of DODD, MEAD AND CO., INC. From *Outlines of the History of Art*, by Wilhelm Lübke, edited, revised and largely rewritten by Russell Sturgis, Copyright 1877, 1904 by Dodd, Mead and Co., new edition, June, 1937. See Vol. 2, p. 247.

6. Ibid., p. 247.

7. Something of the difference between these two attitudes is to be discerned in the following remarks by the Dutchman, Carel van Mander, writing in 1604. He was the Vasari of the north, recording the life and works of the artists past and

the religiosity of the Gothic ideal, leading to "realistic" fantasy. Or to put it in another way, the Gothic type of idealism was simply accepted without question. Hence, for the Flemish particularly, reality supplied objects to be used to stimulate the "reality" of another-world, a world depicted as "real" as the "real world." Consequently these artists were only continuing what we saw was the last great change in Christian art—namely, to depict the other-world with as much "realism" as possible.[8]

Italian artists were largely showing what they had discovered in the reality of the here-world, in form and in color, whereas the non-Italian artists were still to a large extent the servile tools of the Church; their art was strictly supervised by guilds, priests, etc. Thus for the Italians the other-world supplied subjects which were largely used to display their interest in recording reality, while for the non-Italians it served only to give reality to their belief in the other-world. They depicted everything, whether of this world or the other-world, whether an actual or an imaginary landscape or object or human, with this realistic idealism. Reality served primarily as the means for making as realistic as possible a highly developed Pictographic presentation of the ideal other-world.

One might say that the recording approach of the northern artists was preponderantly an automatic kind of visual activity; they functioned somewhat like a human Camera. This servility to the dictates of their eyes made it possible for them to record factors which may have been frustrated or suppressed if the inflexibility that is ever present in man's laws had guided their seeing. This is not to say that their procedure was superior to that of the Florentines; but it is true that when laws are adhered to rigidly, which are inadequately or dogmatically formulated, false vision or the retardation of its development may result. Actually there is danger in both views; for if the Flemish possessed a certain freedom to record reality, unrestricted by the static laws of the Greek ideal, yet without these laws they were unable to begin the evolution of their knowledge of recording reality in an orderly, coherent manner. Furthermore, since they lacked an adequate consciousness of the problem of the real and ideal, they were prevented from facing the fact that the Gothic ideal frustrated efforts at realism. Thus the lack of an adequate, scientifically controlled method of analysis of their efforts at recording, along with that degree of the Gothic ideal attitude that pervaded their art, in certain respects led to false vision.

This may be seen, for instance, in their over-concentration on minutiae; each detail was treated as though it were just as important as any other, as though light could be seen as falling with equal intensity everywhere. Their pictures are often so cluttered with objects that one has the impression of being in an antique shop. Nevertheless, even though each part is minutely painted, their works show disproportionate relationships between various parts. That is, there are deficiencies in structure—the as-a-whole order is wanting in coherence. Particularly is this to be seen in the handling of the nude form by both the Flemish and German artists: there is a lack in the proper proportions and relations of the various parts to one another, in contrast to the nudes of the Florentines, who made extensive studies on this score. An adequate knowledge of the structural relationships of forms and their colors in space was needed. We do not wish to imply that the northern artists had no "knowledge" of what they were doing; their works are obviously the products of knowledge. The lack was in *adequate* knowledge, the kind that the directly scientific attitude would have made possible. In short the over-empirical attitude needed to be supplanted by a conscious, inductive-deductive orientation, if the artist was to be able to comprehend coherently the reality before him and what he was doing or was not doing to it in his art. This lack of a scientific attitude accounts for the fact that the northern artists could not coherently develop their realistic drive.

present in his part of Europe. He wrote: "One might say that in the past the art of painting in the Netherlands has been practised with skill and not with science as it was by the Italians, who had the best of all methods—those based on the study of antique sculpture. Nevertheless, one is astonished by the fact, that at an early period, the artists of the Netherlands had a natural understanding of the human figure and, moreover, they had a beautiful and efficient technique for rendering it." (Carel van Mander: *Dutch and Flemish Painters,* p. 43, translated from the "Schilderboeck," and an introduction by Constant van de Wall. McFarlane, Warde, McFarlane, New York, 1936.)

8. A similar direction has taken place in every dictatorship of the 20th century, namely, to present as realistically as possible what in actuality does not exist.

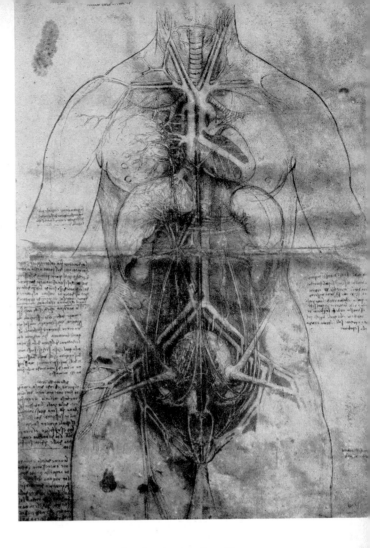

56. Leonardo da Vinci, Front of female figure, showing principal organs. Royal Library at Windsor. By gracious permission of H. M. King George VI of England.

Nevertheless the automatic submergence of the artist's senses to nature's visual stimuli will gain in significance as our history develops. Once the basic laws of visual recording had been worked out by the scientific Florentines, subsequent artists needed merely to learn these laws; then they could in a sense proceed automatically to record nature. Equipped with a knowledge of these laws, later artists could, like a good Camera which had been properly constructed, function correctly in their recording of reality, and so to a degree could submerge their senses to the visual phenomena at hand. Such a procedure was to become very useful in much later times when a more literal copying of nature was sought and achieved.

But an artist who assumed that this automatic activity was the entire process involved was mistaken. This is one of the many reasons why it was absurd for later artists to claim that "emotions" were superior to and in no need of "intellect." For without the "intellect" of the Florentines they could never have attempted to submerge themselves to what they imagined were merely the dictates of their "feelings" or senses. As students they learned the laws of perspective and anatomy as they had been basically worked out by the Florentines. Later generations only refined these laws, the knowledge of which made it possible for artists to record reality properly. Therefore subsequent artists gradually adopted a method which combined (1) the science of the Florentines and their emphasis on the structure of form; (2) the direct act of vision of the Flemish and other artists of the north; and (3) the color achievements of the Venetians. For each of these schools had achieved something that the others needed in order to gain still further accuracy in the depiction of nature's reality. Therefore we can say that it was the Italians who supplied the greatest fund of *knowledge,* knowledge of form from the Florentines, knowledge of color from the Venetians—while it was the Flemish and non-Italians generally who supplied the *attitude* towards art and reality which eventually became the dominant trend in later evolution of secular painting— that is, the effort towards ever more accurate recordings of actual reality.

199

57. Rembrandt van Rijn, Portrait of the Artist. Dutch, 17th Century. Courtesy of The Metropolitan Museum of Art.

58. Frans Hals, Portrait of an Officer. Dutch, 17th Century. National Gallery of Art, Washington, D. C. (Mellon Collection).

60. Peter Rubens, Portrait of Old Parr. Flemish, 17th Century. Collection, William Rockhill Nelson Gallery of Art, Kansas City.

59. Diego Velásquez, Portrait of a Man. Spanish, 17th Century. Collection of The Detroit Institute of Arts.

In the quotations following we can see how the artists of the times made distinctions between these three attitudes. Vasari reported that Michelangelo, after viewing some works by Titian, "declared that the manner and colouring of that artist pleased him greatly, but that it was a pity the Venetians did not study drawing more, 'for if this artist,' said he, 'had been aided by Art and knowledge of design, as he is by nature, he would have produced works which none could surpass, more especially in imitating life, seeing that he has a fine genius, and a graceful animated manner.' " [9] But artists of the north had a different criticism to make of Titian: "Certain German travellers being allowed to visit Titian's studio, were asked their impression of the works they saw. The Germans remarked that they only knew of one master capable of giving a minute finish, the artist being Dürer. Titian reasoned with them, and said that he would paint a picture which should have minute finish without sacrifice of breadth; the Tribute Money is the result of this assertion." [10] Dürer, on the other hand, wrote in a letter in 1506 that certain Italians "abuse my style, saying that it is not antique art, and therefore it is not good." [11] Michelangelo despised the Flemish art and described it thus: "In Flanders, too, they paint to deceive the external eye. They delight in showing actual stuffs: bricks and ruins and rags, and grasses, and the shadowed fields with trees, rivers and bridges—these they call landscapes—with a great many figures here and there . . . . two eyes alone are necessary." [12]

A combination of all three attitudes would have resulted in recordings superior in accuracy to that achieved by any one of these schools alone. Eventually these methods were merged to produce the most "realistic" art of all periods. But the knowledge of artists in the 15th and 16th centuries had not yet advanced to the place where such a combination was possible.

If we were to choose the artist who possessed the best qualities of all of these schools, it would probably be Leonardo. He was interested in anatomy and perspective, in form as well as color. For him there were three kinds of perspective, one of which he called the "perspective of color." [13] From the standpoint of the degree of contribution which an artist has made in the search for accurate methods of recording reality, Leonardo of all his contemporaries must be rated the highest both in his method of work and in his theories. For in Leonardo we see the adoption of the genuinely scientific attitude that was so necessary for the development of post-Christian art. In him we see that rare balance between the inductive and deductive attitude. But no men of his scientific stature have appeared in art again; artists after him overemphasized either the empirical or the theoretical. [14]

We have seen that in the 15th and 16th centuries several kinds of realism and several kinds of idealism were in operation throughout Europe. There was the idealism of form, peculiar to sculpture, but carried over into and transformed by painting; and there was the idealism peculiar to painting, which had its source in the manipulative possibilities of color. Thus the term can be employed to refer to the sculptural (or form) ideal, the painting (or color) ideal, or to combinations of both. And it can be used to indicate Gothic idealism in contrast to that of the Classical cultures. Hence our use of the term

9. Vasari, *Lives of the Painters,* Vol. 4, p. 286, Charles Scribner's Sons.

10. Ibid., editor's footnote #30, Vol. 4, p. 268.

11. Ibid., editor's footnote #36, Vol. 2, p. 162.

12. As quoted by Cheney, *A World History of Art,* p. 623.

13. Leonardo listed the three as follows: linear perspective, perspective of color, vanishing perspective. (See *Notebooks of Leonardo,* op. cit., Vol. 2, p. 241.)

14. Only in the 20th century do artists appear again who tend towards the balanced scientific attitude of Leonardo.

61. Peter Rubens, The Judgment of Paris. Flemish, 17th Century. National Gallery, London.
Photo, The Bettmann Archive.

62. Nicolas Poussin, The Triumph of Neptune and Amphitrite. French, 17th Century.
Courtesy of the Philadelphia Museum of Art, Philadelphia.

"ideal" throughout our history will extend beyond the old meanings and in general will cover any manipulation in art where artists past or present have *deliberately* changed nature, regardless of their reasons for doing so. In contrast to this "idealistic" trend, there was another in which the artists made a deliberate effort to record the appearance of actual reality. But the term "reality" is also, as we have repeatedly pointed out, a multi-valued term; its meanings are determined by the particular context in which it is allocated. Consider, for example, the "automatic" realism of the northern artists and the "scientific" realism of such an artist as Leonardo.

63. Poussin, detail, figure 62.   64. Rubens, detail, figure 61.

We have already noted that the Italians set the stage for what was to become the final conflict between the real and the ideal in recording art. This conflict was conscious with the Italians of the 15th and 16th centuries. We have seen even among the 15th century Italian artists a division into two camps—those who favored the "ideal" and those who contributed to the trend towards increasing realism. That is to say, artists began to lean consciously in the realistic or idealistic direction. For once the ideal of form or the ideal of color was thoroughly grasped theoretically, the conflict began between those who sought to manipulate nature-appearances towards an allegedly superior ideal (perfection of nature) and those who sought to perfect art by striving for a correspondence to nature. In the one view nature presumably attained its perfection in art; in the other, artists sought to attain the perfection of nature in their art.

Art in the rest of Europe at this time, however, consisted of an indistinguishable merging of the old Gothic idealism and the general trend towards realism that existed everywhere. By "indistinguishable," we mean that outside of Italy the conflict between the ideal and real was not a conscious one—there seemed to be no awareness of it as a problem. Artists simply carried on remnants of the old Christian ideal and merged it with their largely automatic efforts towards realism; under these circumstances the conflict between the ideal and the real could not be thrashed out. In Italy there was more consciousness of this conflict among the artists, and hence there we find successful attempts made in the direction of resolving this problem. It was there, particularly among the Florentines, that artists gained ground in the scientific comprehension of the structure of actual reality.

Therefore, where idealism was a consciously applied effort (i.e., regarded as a *problem*, either in form or color, as it was by the artists of the Italian Renaissance), we find artists freed of the *complete* dominance of the Church. But where idealism was largely unconscious, and of Gothic origin, as it was among contemporaneous non-Italian artists, the artist was largely under the domination of the Church. Here we have further evidence of the positive function of the *Classical attitude* operating to free art from the frustrating dominance of the Church.[15]

15. It was precisely because these artists were unconscious of or ignored this problem of the real and the ideal that their efforts towards realism regressed into the primitive and fantasy levels of earlier periods of painting, such as are seen in the caricatures of Bosch and Breughel. Not only the art but the religious system that fostered it regressed. And so Bosch pictured not only the corruption of men in these times, but also of the medieval system by which that corruption was realized. After Bosch, one has the impression of Breughel hurrying on the scene with a Rousseau-like, call-to-nature solution.

Not until the 17th century did the work of the Italians begin to have a marked influence upon artists in the rest of Europe. In the north we see it with the appearance of such men as Rembrandt, Rubens and Hals; in Spain, in such as Velásquez (figures 57, 58, 59, 60); in France, in the work of Poussin. But of all the places in Europe where the Italian Renaissance heritage began to exert its influence, it was only in France that it had a lasting effect. Elsewhere outstanding artists cropped up here and there in a sporadic manner, but in France we again witness a continuous flow of great artists such as had occurred in the Italian Renaissance.

In this respect it is important to note that it was only in France that a concern with the ideal notion of art gained a definite foothold, that the issues between idealism and realism were sharply seen and so consciously considered, as had been the case with the earlier Italians.

For the French continued that which had been begun by the Italians—a more clear-cut (we speak in comparative terms) separation of the ideal and the real into opposing camps, in the sense that there were artists who definitely took up one point of view and opposed the other. (England went through a similar but far less decisive process about one hundred years after France.) These attempts at the separation of the two incompatible trends in art made it possible for artists to begin working towards a resolution of them. The French artists drew the distinction between these two factors more and more sharply, more and more precisely until a definite, coherent decision was reached in the 19th century.

In the rest of Europe idealism appeared more or less in the attempts at realistic art: there seemed to be little consciousness of idealism as a problem to be resolved—no clear-cut desire or effort to confront the issues of the ideal and the real. Although much progress was made towards securing ever greater degrees of recording accuracy, nevertheless the failure to distinguish adequately between the real and the ideal prevented artists from realizing that they were involved in a continuous conflict between opposing factors. Therefore, if realism increased, it was always held within the old, silent, frustrating embrace of an idealism that had permeated the art of non-Italian Europe from the 15th century into recent times. It was only the French who eventually completely freed the real from the ideal.

Thus while Rubens, Rembrandt, and Van Dyck were painting in the Netherlands, we find in France a severely Classical type of painting (figures 61, 62, 63, 64) being produced by such painters as Poussin and Lorrain. And at the same time pictures of family life, peasants, "genre" type in general, in a realistic style reminiscent of the Dutch, were being painted by the Lenain brothers. In short, there was a very distinct demarcation between the two general trends—definite realism on the one side opposed by definite idealism on the other.

Such an artist as Poussin was influenced by that aspect of Italian Renaissance thought which emphasized the ideal in form. But the sense in which Leonardo, for example, had used the ideal had very little influence upon these early French Classicists, who accepted it as a final, static theory of art.[16] Poussin, the artist of this period who was most admired and emulated, went to live in Italy so as to be within the environment and attitude of what was then considered to be Classical culture. In his paintings he utilized Classical mythology extensively. As Reynolds put it: "Poussin lived and conversed with the ancient statues so long, that he may be said to have been better acquainted with them than with the people who were about him."[17]

Poussin became the prototype of the French Academy. It was Poussin's work, and that of the "ancients," which was displayed to artists as a perfect symbol of what the Academy expected from them— or else!

With the appearance of the French Academy, there arose for the first time a specific art organization fostered by and in direct collaboration with those who ruled the State. Art became just one more of the means used by political figures to secure the power of France in the world of nations. Colbert considered

16. Had the theoretical writings of Leonardo become public property, rather than remaining unknown to all but a few for several centuries, then it is quite possible that the entire course of subsequent art history would have been different; his knowledge and attitude towards the acquisition of knowledge about art would have had a great influence. Leonardo's potentially great effect upon the development of the scientific attitude was lost for similar reasons.

17. Joshua Reynolds: *Discourses,* p. 85, James Carpenter, London, 1842.

the function of art to be solely for the glorification of France and its king—something similar to what we find in totalitarian countries today. The static notion of an ideal art was appropriated, exploited towards political-cultural objectives. The French Academy was, in fact, the model for all subsequent reactionary institutions of art. Like most of its imitators to the very present, it served the purpose of stabilizing and keeping entrenched Aristotelian notions of the ideal in art. Through it the art philosophy of classicism was interpreted to suit the ambitions of those who were determined to dominate world culture.

Colbert appointed Charles Le Brun as director of the Academy, a man who was, as Wilenski has pointed out, "the artist whom Louis XIV and Colbert required at a particular juncture; he served their purpose and he saw to it that they also served his." "He had," as Wilenski writes, "great facility in painting, and as a decorator he had organizing abilities that approached genius. He was also an arrivist of the very first order." [18] Once Colbert had made him dictator over all art, Le Brun wasted little time before taking advantage of his power. He set up an art school within the Academy and then had laws passed forbidding anyone else to do likewise unless they wished to be fined or imprisoned. By another law he demanded that all those who had not joined the Academy must do so or face prosecution.[19] With such an official status, and with dictatorial powers behind it, the Academy was able to enforce upon artists its notions of what comprised art; those who failed to fall in line found it extremely difficult to make a living.[20] In fact, as Chambers points out, this institution marked the first organized persecution of artists by artists, setting up as it did, "a court of discipline and correctness, against whose decisions there was no appeal . . . [those who objected were] suppressed, boycotted or compelled to retire abroad."[21]

The rulers of the Academy regarded art as strictly an "intellectual" affair. The words of Poussin, "reason judges alone," expressed their creed. Logic was thought to reign supreme; "sentiments" and "feelings" were allegedly taboo. Following the example of the Classical Greeks, these artists intended to correct nature to secure an "ideal beauty," and in order to achieve this objective, mathematical formulae were employed and rules laid down for everything. Having come to the unique conclusion that *all* problems of art had been completely solved, the Academy elected one of its members to compile a chart depicting the "Rules for Great Art." Le Brun wrote a discourse on physiognomy in which he illustrated such facial expressions as anger, fear, and the like; this he claimed would assist the students *without the disturbance of consulting nature.* In another "discourse" of rules, he illustrated the similarity in the physiognomy of men and animals. In the order of their importance the Academy listed the following elements which made up art: drawing, proportion, expression, clair-obscur, ordinance, and last, color.[22] Drawing was of first importance, while color was considered merely an appendage to it. Recall that the Florentines had also rated drawing and color similarly. Chambers has pointed out that one of the great controversies over idealism and realism has centered around this very problem of drawing versus color.[23] It was the "ideal forms" that were striven for with drawing; the "real forms" were sought with color. This argument was based upon the historical achievements of the two mediums of sculpture and painting. It was with sculpture that ideal forms had been most successfully created. In such cases "drawing" was naturally paramount in the effort to achieve the form. On the other hand, color was the paramount realistic device in the art of painting; and the most accurate recordings of reality were developed in the color medium of painting. Those who insisted that form and not color was paramount, were attempting to impose upon painting the tactile limitations of sculpture. This insistence upon seeing painting in terms of sculpture was part of the effort to stave off the dissolution of the old Classical *form-ideal*.

18. R. H. Wilenski: *French Painting*, p. 78, Ralph T. Hale and Co., Boston, 1936.

19. See Wilenski's interesting discussion of Le Brun and the Academy, ibid., pp. 78-88.

20. The same sort of thing happens today when an artist refuses to bow to the dictates of the institutions that represent the power of the *status quo*. Many of these present day institutions, just as in the past, are significantly enough housed in pseudo-Classical Architecture and filled with innumerable originals and casts of the "ancients."

21. Chambers, *History of Taste*, p. 99.

22. Ibid., p. 99.

23. Ibid., p. 115.

But as we have noted above, just as in the sculptural forms or linear drawings, the artist can deliberately seek a correspondence with nature, or deliberately strive for that which nature is not, so in painting with color, the artist can deliberately seek correspondence to or differences from nature. Of course all recording art changes nature, since no artist can achieve a perfect recording of all nature's characteristics. Therefore, we can only speak of the intention, attitude or objective of the artist as distinct from the degree to which he attains whatever that objective may be. This is why we speak of the artist *deliberately* striving in this or that direction. In short, our problem deals with relative phenomena, not with absolutes.

Nevertheless with the revival of the Florentine emphasis upon form and the relegation of color to the background, there began from the very first years of the Academy heated controversies between the advocates of "form" and "color." There were soon artists who arose and stated flatly that color was the essential medium of painting; such views were vigorously opposed by the representatives of the Academy. On the whole the argument within the Academy was actually between those who wished to idealize the forms and those who preferred to idealize the colors of reality.

The revival of Classical art in France served a social as well as political function. The mythological and historical paintings with which the "elite" surrounded themselves, secured for them a world apart, far superior to that of the common man. The world of the latter was pictured only by "outlaw" artists outside of the Academy. A little later in both France and England the portrait became another means of visual differentiation between the ruling classes and the ruled. The former, in their portraits, were clothed in the trappings of the ancients, by which they thought to secure for themselves a world of perfection.[24]

The psychological results of these devices were not unlike those which the Church achieved when distortions of nature were used to indoctrinate a belief in another world. These Classical revivalists also tried to make two worlds (although both were more or less "here-worlds")—one for the rulers and another for the ruled. The manner in which this was accomplished is clearly demonstrated in the work and writings of Joshua Reynolds. More than a century after the founding of the French Academy, an institution of a similar nature and with a somewhat similar history was created in England. Reynolds played the part of Le Brun. He was thoroughly committed in theory at least to the old Classical ideal—an ideal inherent in but never realized by nature. Towards this objective he, like the French Idealists, recommended "a careful study of the works of the ancient sculptors. . . ." Only the artist could realize the ideal; only the artist could make nature perfect. Thus Reynolds wrote: "For the works of Nature are full of disproportion, and fall very short of the true standard of beauty."[25] And in another place: "And as there is one general form, which, as I have said, belongs to the human kind at large, so in each of these classes there is one common idea and central form, which is the abstract of the various individual forms belonging to that class."[26] Fortified with this Aristotelian theory, Reynolds was in an admirable position to paint portraits of the privileged classes. For he could refute the necessity of achieving a literal correspondence to reality and could rationalize his practice of bathing his sitters in an aura of fantasy. And so both the English and French Classical schools of portrait painters—big business, to say the least—developed the gentle art of seducing their client's ego, employing every possible device for placing the subjects of the portraits above the ordinary run of things. Reynolds wrote specifically that: "He, therefore, who in his practice of portrait-painting, wishes to dignify his subject, which we will suppose to be a lady, will not paint her in the modern dress, the familiarity of which alone is sufficient to destroy all dignity . . . and therefore dresses his figure something with the general air of the antique for the sake of dignity, and preserves something of the modern for the sake of likeness."[27] A perfect recipe even today for the artist who wishes to be a "successful" portrait painter! The actuality with a pinch of fantasy, and the sitter was surprisingly pleased with his appearance, especially since he appeared better than his fellows. Here were the same old Classical theories of the Greeks —art is superior to nature—used in this case for far different purposes. Reynolds put it this way: "His eye

24. In many other ways outside the field of art the "ancients" were used as an authoritative precedent to justify the dictatorial actions of those who ruled.

25. Reynolds, op. cit., p. 38.

26. Ibid., p. 43.

27. Ibid., p. 138.

[the artist's] being enabled to distinguish the accidental deficiencies, excrescences, and deformities of things, from their general figures, he makes out an abstract idea of their forms more perfect than any one original. . . ." [28] And so he made innumerable depictions of "originals" (that is, portraits) doing his best meanwhile to make each sitter appear "more perfect" than in reality, more perfect than the "original." In Reynolds' art we see a change from the old Greek ideal, yet his practice was as old as the early Egyptian dynasties. Such Idealists as Poussin had believed only in a *general* perfection of the human form; but Reynolds idealized the *particular* human form. That is, he generalized the individual—a more limited form of generalization.

In spite of or perhaps because of the rigid classicism of the French Academy, evidence of revolt against its authority began to appear soon after it was founded. In the writings of Roger de Piles we have evidence that a transition from the Classical theories of the Academy to a more realistic attitude was already under way. Chambers tells us that de Piles was a firm believer in the notion that "there existed one true idea of painting and one ideally perfect painter, . . . [and that he] wished that the moderns might learn to correct the imperfections of nature with the same success as had the ancients." [29] However, he was aware that even the sacred Poussin had failed to realize fully the potentialities of the painting medium in his erroneous effort to copy the "ancients" who were sculptors in their principal works. He wrote of Poussin: "By this means the naked of his figures, in most parts of his pictures, had something in it, resembling painted stone, and it is rather like the hardness of marble, than the delicacy of flesh, full of blood and life." [30] De Piles' theories were neither purely those of a Classicist nor purely those of a Realist, but a combination of both. It was as though he wished to resolve the differences between the two without giving up either. That he was aware at least to a certain extent of the differences beween the two main views of art is seen in the following passages: "If we compare the art of Painting, which has been form'd out of nature in general, with anyone of her particular productions, we shall find it comes short of her, and perceive it to be true, that Art is above Nature; but if we compare it with nature herself, who is the model of art, this proposition will presently be found to be false. Indeed, to consider things aright, whatever care the Painters have taken to imitate this mistress of their art, they have not hitherto been able to reach her; she has an inexhaustible store of beauties, and for this reason 'tis said, that in the arts we are always learning: By experience and reflection we are continually discovering something new in the effects of nature, which are without number, and always different one from the other." [31]

If anything, de Piles leaned towards a realistic attitude, as can be seen in another criticism he made of Poussin: "His chief aim was to please the eyes of the understanding, though without dispute, everything that is instructive in painting, ought to communicate itself to the understanding only, by the satisfaction of the eyes, by a perfect imitation of nature; and this is the only duty, and ought to be the whole aim of painting." [32] Moreover, he contended that we "ought to regard the Antique, as a book which is to be translated into another language, wherein 'tis sufficient he keeps to the sense and meaning of the author, without tying himself servilely to his words." And he was able to recognize that the notion of a general form was not to be found in actual reality where the "effects" of nature are "always different one from the other." Also he took the side of those who insisted that color was the essential problem of painting. But in his effort to combine opposing notions, de Piles was often confused and ambivalent, now giving more importance to the Classicist's, now to the Realist's notions of reality.

28. Ibid., p. 41.   29. Chambers, *History of Taste,* p. 108.

30. *The Art of Painting,* with the lives and characters of above 300 of the most eminent painters, p. 310, translated from the French of Monsieur de Piles, 3rd edition, London, printed for T. Payne, 1754.

31. Ibid., p. 15.   32. Ibid., p. 312.

65. William Hogarth, Portrait of Simon Frazer, Lord Lovat. English, 18th Century. National Portrait Gallery, London. Photo, The Bettmann Archive.

66. Hogarth, detail of figure 65. Photo, The Bettmann Archive.

At about this same time the realistic trends in art gained fresh impetus, as Chambers points out, in the new discoveries about nature by Leibnitz, a scientist and logician, who was not content merely to appeal to the Greeks and their logic, but rather sought directly to understand the world of reality outside of man's brain. After a lecture in which Leibnitz discussed the non-sameness of all objects in nature, it is said that he asked his audience to walk out to the lawn and examine the blades of grass. Everyone was astonished to find that no blade of grass was exactly like any other.[33]

It was through such an attitude and the ever present influence of the artists of the north, that a new incentive was aroused towards the portrayal of nature, not as it appeared in the art of the Greeks and Romans, but as it appeared to the artist's eyes. Artists were learning with renewed interest what Leonardo had maintained 200 years previously, that nature was the criterion of reality for art. Such an attitude of course threatened the dominance and authority of the Academy.

A little later Hogarth in England heaped rebukes upon those who were importing "shiploads of dead Christs, Holy Families and Madonnas,"[34] and declared further that he was not disposed to turn his studio into a portrait factory. In the effort to refute the theories of Classicist artists, whom he correctly ridiculed as "nature-menders," he wrote: "I have heard a blacksmith harangue like an anatomist, or sculptor, on the beauty of a boxer's figure, tho' not perhaps in the same terms; and firmly I believe, that one of our common proficients in the athletic art, would be able to instruct and direct the best sculptor living . . .

33. Chambers, *History of Taste,* p. 112.   34. As quoted by Pijoan, *An Outline History of Art,* Vol. III, p. 309.

210

67. Joshua Reynolds, Portrait of Sir William Hamilton. English, 18th Century. Gift of Edward Drummond Libbey. The Toledo Museum of Art, Toledo, Ohio.

in what would give the statue of an English boxer, a much better proportion, as a character, than is seen, even in the group of antique boxers . . . so much admired to this day.

"Water-men too, are of a distinct caste, or character whose legs are no less remarkable for their smallness. . . . There is scarcely a waterman that rows upon the Thames, whose figure doth not confirm this observation. Therefore were I to paint the character of Charon, I would thus distinguish his make from that of a common man's; and, in spite of the word low, venture to give him a broad pair of shoulders, and spindle shanks, whether I had the authority of an antique statue, or basso-relievo, for it or not." [35] Hogarth was emphatically for recording reality as he saw it, not as the "ancients" might have wished to see it (figure 65). This can be further seen in the following quotation in which he reversed the Classical theory. One can imagine that he had Reynolds in mind when he said: "Who but a bigot, even to the antiques, will say that he has not seen faces and necks, hands and arms in living women, that even the Grecian Venus does but coarsely imitate?

"And what sufficient reason can be given why the same may not be said of the rest of the body?" [36] Hogarth, like all those who strove in a decidedly realistic direction, was more scientific than the Classicists, in the sense that he appealed to observation for his criterion of art in the depiction of reality. Hence these changes in art parallel those occurring between the scientist and the philosopher; the latter found the highest reality through deduction; the former through observation of the reality about him.

35. William Hogarth: *The Analysis of Beauty,* J. Reeves, London, 1753.　　　　　　　36. Ibid.

68. Francois Boucher, Madame Bergeret. French, 18th Century. National Gallery of Art, Washington, D. C. (Kress Collection).

Artists were further stimulated to achieve more realistic depictions by the fact that the bourgeoisie rose to power in France during the 18th century, and the demand for realistic portraiture increased accordingly. Simultaneously there arose the public patron, and along with him the amateur artist.[37]

As a theorist, Diderot completed the transition inadvertently begun by de Piles towards more realistic art. In an effort to rid the artists of "mathematical proportions," notions of the ideal, he cited the fact that "Never have two singers sung the same air in the same way." [38] He accused the Classicists of turning out "copies of a copy"; he was not speaking Platonically here, but was referring to their copies of Greek art. He contended that the observation of nature disclosed that one never sees two objects alike and that each object is a process of ever changing experiences. If Reynolds contended that nature was never correct, Diderot maintained that "Nature is never incorrect." The manner in which he expected the artist to record reality can be seen in his reactions to a still-life by Chardin: "We have but to take these biscuits and eat them, this orange, open and squeeze it, this glass of wine and drink it." [39] Elsewhere he gave this advice: "Go to the wine-shop and you will see the true gestures of an angry man. Frequent public places, observe what passes in the streets, in gardens, in markets, in houses, and you will thus learn what are the real gestures of men in real life. . . . And then you will be ashamed of your insipid professor's teaching and you will be ashamed of imitating your insipid model." [40]

37. This had a harmful consequence in that almost every man came to consider himself a capable authority in matters of art. This developed to such a point that artists again came to be considered poor judges of their own or anyone else's art. In later chapters we shall see the reasons for this and why we are living in times which will bring about changes in this state of affairs.

38. As quoted by Chambers, *History of Taste*, p. 145.

39. How similar indeed is this remark to the one Vasari made about the art of Raphael, yet how different the degree of realism in both painters!

40. As quoted by Chambers, *History of Taste*, p. 145, from Diderot, *Essai sur la Peinture*, I.

69. Jacques David, Mlle. Charlotte du Val D'Ognes. French, 18th-19th Centuries. Courtesy of The Metropolitan Museum of Art.

All such arguments—those of de Piles, Leibnitz and Diderot—served to put flexibility into the otherwise rigid theories of the Classicists. This compelled the latter to become less dogmatic and more realistic in an effort to keep their theories of art in the dominant position; increasingly they had to accept, at least in their art, the trend towards increasing realism. Nevertheless they made every effort to refute the arguments of the Realists. Reynolds' reactions to the Leibnitz type of observation that no two things in nature are ever alike is worth noting: "Thus amongst the blades of grass or leaves of the same tree, though no two can be found exactly alike, the general form is invariable: A Naturalist, before he chooses one as a sample, would examine many; since if he took the first that occurred, it might have, by accident or otherwise, such a form as that it would scarce be known to belong to that species; he selects as the Painter does, the most beautiful, that is, the most general form of nature."[41] In this way Reynolds hoped to refute the conclusions of the Realists in their observations of nature. There are, however, important inconsistencies in his logic. For instance, it is true that all leaves of a particular tree tend towards a common or general form. But Reynolds proceeded to contradict that statement by saying that if we pick up the first leaf at hand its species might not be recognized through "accident or otherwise," which of course implies that this leaf might not possess that "general form [which] is invariable." His error was in not recognizing that the general form in reality is decidedly a variable. Of course, an artist can make an invariable general form of nature, but outside of his depiction of it, it is non-existent. It cannot be found in nature. Nature is a collection of unique individuals. That is why the "naturalist," after choosing the most "beautiful . . . general form," would still have in his possession a unique individual form. The "invariable general form" does not exist in reality; it is only an abstraction of convenience.

41. Joshua Reynolds: *The Works of Sir Joshua Reynolds,* His Discourses, Idlers, A Journey to Flanders and Holland, etc., Vol. 2, p. 237, London, 1801.

70. David, detail, figure 69.

In the long run, the Idealists of all times, like the Realists, have been selecting from among the varieties of nature for their alleged ideal. Had it been otherwise, the Idealists would have eventually arrived at some single monotonous rendition of the ideal form. But at the same time their "idealism" prevented them from fully utilizing, as did the Realists, the greater variety and interest to be found in reality.

Although widely divergent variations of the ideal occurred in the actual art produced by the Idealists,[42] the *theory* of the ideal remained fundamentally unchanged. And it is important to note the fact that idealism in any form brought to the painting phase of post-Christian times the very difficulties, attractions and errors that we have already observed resulting from the ideal theory in the Classical Greek period. That is, artists in discovering that it was possible to manipulate the appearances of reality, e.g., to make the human form allegedly "more beautiful" in color and/or form, etc., thus fell, willingly or not, into the old Aristotelian error of presuming that recording art could be something superior to nature. We cannot, however, dismiss this sort of attraction too lightly. And we will not if we realize that when an artist assumed this liberty with reality he was thus permitted to become, to a degree at least, a "creator" too, not merely the recorder of "nature's creations." He could, in this "creative" direction, take fuller advantage of the possibilities of paint pigments, possibilities denied him when he forced his paints to *record* reality. For in the latter case the seeking of an approximation to the original restricted the possibilities potential to his medium, while in the former case he was able to free the operation particularly of the color aspect of his medium to a tremendous extent. We should point out, however, that the major objection to the Realists' attitude was not on the grounds that one could after all achieve only a partial approximation of reality. What was objected to by those who preferred to manipulate reality deliberately was that the greater freedom to exploit the potentialities of the artist's medium was restricted by an effort at literal realism.

42. For instance, the change from the idealization of humans in general, to the idealization of unique or individual humans.

214

71. Jean Chardin, Portrait of an Old Woman. French, 18th Century. National Gallery of Art, Washington, D. C. (Kress Collection).

72. Francois Boucher, Madame Bergeret, French, 18th Century. National Gallery of Art, Washington, D. C. (Kress Collection). Detail of figure 68.

Thus the conflict was between the desire of the Idealists to participate as creators of the content of art, and the desire of the scientifically inclined Realists to restrict the role of *creator* to the discovery of ever more accurate methods of seeing and recording the seeing of reality. This dichotomy of viewpoints will not be resolved completely until the 20th century.

It is important to remember, however, that after the idealistic art of Greece, the Classical point of view never again appears clear-cut in the actual art; subsequent Classicists were increasingly compelled by the pressure of the general development of art history to follow from afar the tendency of the innovators towards more and more realism. The strictest adherence to the ideal theory after Greek times appeared among the 17th century French Classicists—Lorrain, Poussin and Le Brun. Beginning with the next century, the art even of those who continued to adhere theoretically to the old idealism, was becoming ever more realistic. The type of idealism that took precedence in the 18th century appears in those works where the color of reality was manipulated into results peculiar to the colors of paints. In short, the dominance of the Florentine mentality was replaced by the attitude of the Venetians. Hence, if in the 17th century we find such idealism as that of Poussin and Le Brun and such realism as that of the Lenains, then in the 18th century these divergent types were replaced by such as Boucher, Fragonard, Watteau, Chardin, La Tour and Greuze. In the work of such artists as Boucher and Watteau the major form that idealism took was in the realm of color and fantasy subject-matter (as had been the case among the Venetians), in contrast to such artists as Chardin, who, like their contemporaries among the Flemish and the Dutch, preferred the subjects of the real world. But the major problem was no longer between the recording of Greek statues and the recording of subjects from reality. For now the idealism of color was employed to depict the real world. Great advances in portraiture were realized by Boucher, Fragonard and La Tour, but their figures were clothed in a world of color that never existed. Their subjects were largely portraits of the upper classes or scenes of fantasy. But the subjects of the Chardin type of artist were taken from the real world and "the people" who were not of the "elite."

It was in portraiture that the new differences in art appeared at their clearest. For whether it be a Chardin, La Tour, Boucher (figures 68, 71, 72), great advances in the realism of depicting form had been made; it was in color that there was still an extreme idealism. It was the ideal peculiar to painting, not the one peculiar to sculpture that now dominated! In other words, painters had largely passed beyond the stages in which the form or tactile influence of sculpture dominated their efforts; for they had become conscious that the task proper to their medium was the realistic recording of the image. After this the predominant idealism that remained in painting was in the realm of color, but here too we witness a striving for ever greater correspondence to nature's color.

To be sure, with the discovery of many new works of Greco-Roman art in the latter half of the 18th century, a vociferous resurgence of the old Classical theory ensued. But the results of this were not the Classical art of old. Its most famous representative, David, was an artist who wavered from idealism to realism, and if he had been a lesser artist like Le Brun, writers would have spoken more of his opportunist ambivalence. He certainly painted as well for emperors as for "the people." In any case, this last splurge at direct idealism was more a preparation for the Romantic movement that was to follow.

That the Idealists became more and more realistic in their art is well seen when we realize that the last major Idealist, Ingres, was noted for his accurate portrait paintings, an occupation obviously far removed from the original notion of "idealism." Compare his works with those of Poussin, and this difference is clearly demonstrated. Such a comparison shows how little of the old sculpture-idealism was left among the Idealists of the 19th century. In fact, Ingres became a great Realist and was always a mediocre Idealist, as his paintings of Classical subjects make clear. If Poussin continues to be remembered for idealistic art, Ingres is remembered for his achievement in realism. However, in the degree that there was a residue of classicism in an artist's work, it did tend to have a certain stone-like quality. The difference between the Idealist's realism and the Realist's realism was well demonstrated when Manet exhibited his nude, *Olympia;* it had to be protected from the crowds by guards, because people were so horrified at what seemed like a realistic rendition of a nude woman rather than, to use the words of Pijoan, the "idealized symbol of classical virtue."[43]

But if artists were gradually freed from the rigidity of the old ideal notion, then later the attitudes of the Idealists were beneficial, in that they acted as a restraint upon those who would go "all out" for the so-called "emotional" point of view. The gradual trend away from the notion of the ideal and the particular rules identified with the "intellect," came to a head in the writings of Diderot, who advocated not only realism and observation of nature, but also the freedom of the artist from the restraint of any rules. Rules, said Diderot, seem to have been created for the "suffocation of genius"; he contended further that "geniuses are above rules and criticisms." With this he hoped to free artists from all "intellectual" restraint, and to him this meant classicism.

Thus Diderot cleared the ground for the Romanticists and Realists, who opposed the excessive and rigid intellectualism of the Classicists. The Romanticists hailed "feeling" as the major impulse of living and painting. Great art was identified with "feeling" and "emotion" and "sentiment"; the "intellect" was subordinated. As Goethe wrote, "Poets produce their best works, as women do pretty children, without thinking about it, or knowing how it is done."[44]

But however much the Romanticists may have thought they were against the old rules, they did not break completely with all the Classical attitudes. Romanticism is actually a combination of and a conflict between the notion of the ideal and the real. Thus if the Classicists talked about the intellect and the soul, the Romanticists talked about the passions and the soul. Both groups, due to their idealism, were agreed that the artist was, in the words of Delacroix, "above a mere photography." [45] And like their Classical

43. Pijoan, op. cit., Vol. III, p. 343.

44. As quoted by Chambers, *History of Taste,* p. 175. See also pp. 163-180 for an excellent discussion of the philosophical development that underlay the emergence of romanticism.

45. Ibid., p. 194.

73. Théodore Géricault, The Raft of the Medusa. French, 19th Century. Louvre. Photo, Giraudon, Paris.

opponents, the Romanticists were bent on escaping reality, if perhaps to a lesser degree. While they no longer depicted gods and goddesses, or made real people into divinity, they had a tendency to look for something almost equally unusual. Their interests were in the "dramatic," the "exciting," the "colorful," and the like. This may be seen in their depictions of lion hunts, murder, shipwrecks, massacres, harems and other Oriental subjects.

But where the Idealist had referred to the *universal soul,* the Romanticist referred to the artist's soul; the individual and his personal reactions were once more of importance. In this we are confronted with a transition similar to that which occurred in Greece, not only from the general to the depiction of more particulars, but also from a collective attitude to one of individual originality; in short, from collective idealism to individual idealism. The Romanticist, by a personal selection of particulars in reality, made his own personal ideal out of reality. Thus the great problem was no longer "what are fit subjects for art." Any subject was considered suitable; the important thing was what you did with it, whether you turned it into the romantic formula of excitement, strangeness, horror and the like. As Victor Hugo wrote: "There are, in poetry, neither good nor bad subjects, but only good and bad poets. Everything is a subject, amenable to art; everything has the right to be cited in poetry. Let us inquire into your motive for taking a subject, whether it be sad or glad, horrible or pleasant, sombre or bright, strange or simple. Let us examine how you have worked, rather than on what you have worked and why."[46]

46. Victor Hugo, from *Orientales* Preface, as quoted by Chambers, *History of Taste,* p. 150.

74. John Constable, Stoke-by-Nayland. English, 19th Century. Courtesy of the Art Institute of Chicago.

Nevertheless, the Romanticists furthered the cause of more accurate depictions of reality. They broke out of the narrow, Idealist visual-cage of preceding times and extended the whole visual panorama of reality for the artist to see and record. Thus, just as the sculpture of the Greco-Roman period had to pass through the stages of idealism and romanticism to realize the full potentialities of realism in that medium, so painting in the post-Christian period had to go through similar stages to achieve its full potentialities in this respect. The revolt of the Romanticists from the rigidity of classicism made it possible for artists to look afresh at nature and thus eventually arrive at a more realistic recording of it.

Typical of this increased realism achieved by the Romanticists is Gericault's *The Raft of the Medusa* (figure 73), representing a shipwreck which had actually occurred. It produced indignant reactions and was considered too exciting and horrible a theme for art.

The activities of the Romanticist, Delacroix, led him to a considerable interest in the problems of color, which affected his manner of manipulating drawing, that sacred element of the Classicists. Taking up the cudgels for the opposite side, Ingres reprimanded Delacroix to his face with the remark, "Drawing, sir, is the probity of art." [47] The renewal of this argument had a similar source as the earlier one, but now the

47. As quoted by Chambers, *History of Taste*, p. 197.

opponents were not as far apart as they once were, at least as far as the actual art was concerned. Ingres and Delacroix were the last important artists to argue this problem. With them we are approaching the end of the conflict-between the Florentine point of view and the Venetian, or the idealism of form and the idealism of color. When the Realists entered the picture these two impulses were submerged beneath the preponderant drives of securing an accurate recording of reality.

Nevertheless the reaction of the Romanticists from the rigidity of classicism eventually swung to the anarchy of laissez-fairism. To use the words of Whitehead, "reactions run to extremes." [48] Eventually all the stops were let out on the notion which Diderot had voiced, that "geniuses were above rules and criticisms." Hence Victor Hugo claimed that: "The poet may go whither he will, and do as pleases him; such is his law. He may believe in one God, or in many gods, or in none; . . . he may write in prose or verse, carve in marble, cast in bronze, set foot in this century or that land; he may be of the north or south, east or west, ancient or modern, his muse the Muse or his muse a fairy; he may wear toga or tunic, as he will. C'est à merveille. The poet is free."[49] In attempting to free themselves from the undeniably static laws of Classical theory these artists fell into the restrictions of the opposite extreme. Each now sought his own personal rules, as though each were free to act independently of the other. Thus in bringing forth needed freedom from old static notions, the Romanticist also brought the attitude of utterly unrestricted freedom which would eventually end in new difficulties and delusions. His denial of reason, which should have been confined to the Classical *kind* of reasoning that brought on the revolt, knew no bounds and turned out to be a revolt against any form of reason which placed any restrictions upon the artist.

We have already observed on numerous occasions that attitudes of "feeling" and "emotion" alone, or "intellect" and "reason" alone are based on false knowledge. The assumption that the artist could achieve complete control over his art by suppressing "feeling" and relying entirely upon the "intellect" was based on the fallacious supposition that something called "intellect" could be exercised independently of something called "feeling." (Such a supposition was possible because of the Aristotelian practice of splitting things verbally which in actuality cannot be split.) Actually, however, the Classicists experienced and utilized feelings just as we all are compelled to do. Their *feelings,* for example, attracted them to the Classical mode of art, but they recognized neither the presence nor the function of those "feelings" which played such a distinct part in the particular activity of their "intellect." It thus came about that this was the one vital aspect of their behavior which they did not reason about with their intellect! If they had, the whole structure of their art formulations would have appeared to be full of unaccounted-for gaps; because their philosophy also was based in some degree on precisely the factor which they so stringently denied—"feelings." Something similar happens in the case of those who emphasize the "feelings" in preference to the use of "intellect," but who *reason* just as much as their "intellect" opponents do. Moreover, this reasoning plays its part in the activities of their feelings.

Both the above extreme methods mentioned—the overemphasis upon the intellect or the emotions—are characterized by a concentration on one factor at the expense of the other, as though the emotions and the intellect could operate independently of each other—a neurological impossibility. Those who emphasized the intellect were unaware that they utilized feelings and those who emphasized feelings were unaware that they utilized intellect. Since both factors operate in all our activities, and since the artist, the philosopher, or the scientist is compelled to feel and reason, regardless of what they may "think" happens, both schools possess an indispensable part of the truth. But it was not until the 20th century that some artists again began to recognize clearly that "feelings" and "intellect" are interdependent, that both factors are always present in *all* our activities, regardless of what we may think "ought to be" the case.

Gradually, however, the metaphysical realm of the Classicists and the dream-world of the Romanticists were left behind in the quest for the eye-world of actual reality. The old Classical attitude, which was epitomized by the French Academy, actually ended in its last great artist, David (figures 69, 70). During the days of Napoleon, David made a final struggling attempt to reinstate what was left of the Classical method. He eventually failed. By now the bourgeoisie had come into their own; they could not

48. Whitehead, *Science and the Modern World,* p. 14.

49. Victor Hugo, from *Orientales* Preface, as quoted by Chambers, *History of Taste,* p. 200.

75. Jean Ingres, Portrait of Madame Leblanc. French, 19th Century. Courtesy of The Metropolitan Museum of Art.

symbolize their ego with the old classicism as had the rulers of the palace. The eroticism of the court was being displaced by the world of "the people" which Chardin and his like had looked at earlier. In time, as we have already suggested, the Realist's attitude dominated to such an extent that Ingres and other Classicists adopted a very realistic approach in their art. Especially in his portraits, an artist like Ingres was more of a Realist than a Classicist (figure 75). Ingres' work, with exceptions, appears to be vying with the Camera more than with a Greek statue. Moreover, Ingres urged the artist to "Contemplate beauty on your knees . . . . draw, paint, but above all copy with absolute fidelity, though it be but a still-life." This is a far cry from such Classicists as Poussin and Le Brun, who directed the artist's vision toward Greek statues and away from nature. There was no longer a wide gap between the two general kinds of art which we have found since the Renaissance.

Romanticism ended in its last great artist, Delacroix; nevertheless he was the forerunner of much that followed; his manner of applying paint and his interests in color foreshadowed the concerns of the Impressionists and the Post-Impressionists. What remained of romanticism and classicism after Delacroix and David was submerged by the rise of realism.

As a matter of fact, while the Romantic movement was still in full swing varying kinds of new Realists began to appear, who revolted against the Classical method even more than had the Romanticists. As the realism of the Romans followed after the romanticism of the Greeks, so in the 19th century Realists gradually took over the scene from the Romanticists. They strove to look at the world of nature unhampered by the fantasy methods of the Classicists or the Romanticists. But they did not oppose the Romanticists as much as they did the Classicists, partly because the former had helped to free artists from the fetters of the ideal, but also because these Realists were not entirely devoid of romanticism themselves, as we shall presently see.

76. Gustave Courbet, Mere Gregoire (Mme) Andler. French, 19th Century. Courtesy of the Art Institute of Chicago.

It was now that the term "realism" became a part of the vocabulary of such artists as Courbet, Millet, Th. Rousseau and the Barbizon school of landscapists. The latter group was following the example of the earlier English landscapist, John Constable, in painting nature directly out of doors (figure 74). To do this, and moreover to paint nature as one saw it, amounted in these times to as much of a revolution as anything that has ever happened. Previously landscape painting had been judged not by its correspondence to nature, but by comparing it to the works of Claude Lorrain, and the like. In fact, it is said that Constable had to place a violin against a tree in order to prove to his fellow artists that trees were green, not brown.[50] This artist was not at all impressed with the philosophical formulations of the Classicists. The visual evidence of nature was his criterion for reality and so for art. Thus he wrote: "It appears to me that pictures have been over-valued; held up by a blind admiration as ideal things, and almost as standards by which nature is to be judged rather than the reverse; and this false estimate has been sanctioned by the extravagant epithets that have been applied to painters, as 'the divine,' 'the inspired,' and so forth."[51] Therefore, he said: "When I sit down to make a sketch from nature, the first thing I try to do is to forget that I have ever seen a picture."[52] And along this line of thought, Courbet later advocated that, "The museums should be closed for twenty years, so that today's painters may begin to see the world with their own eyes." [53] At another time Courbet said: "My triumph is not only over the moderns but over

50. Cheney, *A World History of Art*, p. 812.

51. From a lecture at the Royal Institution of Great Britain, June 16, 1836, published by C. R. Leslie, in *Memoirs of the Life of John Constable,* Esq., R. A., pp. 354-355, 2nd edition, Longman, Brown, Green, and Longmans, London, 1845.

52. As quoted by Cheney, *The Story of Modern Art*, p. 89, The Viking Press, New York, 1941.

53. Ibid., p. 130.

77. Jean Millet, The Quarriers. French, 19th Century. Gift of Arthur J.
Secor, Collection of The Toledo Museum of Art, Toledo.

the ancients as well." [54] Such artists wanted to forget how their predecessors had made nature appear; they preferred instead to try to see nature as it actually appeared and use that for their guide. A sharp discrimination was made between the recording ability of artists in the past and the possibilities for accurate recording in the present. In other words, the new attitude was not to make nature more like pictures (idealism), but to make pictures more like nature (science), figures 76, 77, 78.

But as Courbet remarked, "In painting what I saw, I raised what they called the social question." He and Millet particularly were concerned with ordinary men and events; they painted peasants at their work, at their weddings and funerals. Millet, who believed that, "Art declined from the moment that the artist ceased to lean on nature . . . ." [55] also wrote, "I want the people I represent to look as if they really belonged to their station, so that imagination cannot conceive of their ever being anything else." [56]

Naturally such attitudes as those of Courbet and Millet disturbed the very roots of the *status quo,* not only in art but in the general social scene as well. Thus Meissonier (also a Realist, but one whose sympathies were with the rulers rather than the ruled), raged before one of Courbet's paintings, "Gentlemen, let us forget that he exists!" [57] And Baudelaire complained of Millet's figures, "They seem to say

54. As quoted by Pijoan, op. cit., Vol. III, p. 334.

55. As quoted by Chambers, *History of Taste,* p. 203.

56. As quoted by Pijoan, op. cit., Vol. III, p. 337.

57. Ibid., p. 334.

to us, 'we are the disinherited and the only ones who produce anything by our toil.' " [58] Daumier was jailed for his cartoon criticisms of the existing political regime, and Courbet was given a prison sentence and fined for his revolutionary activities.

Perhaps for the first time in history the artist, on his own initiative was using art as a social weapon. In the past he had been forced to make his art function as a social instrument according to the dictates of those who ruled the culture. The new trend had already begun in the latter part of the 18th century, but with the 19th century artists appeared who fully exploited their freedom to be the judges of the social motives of their art.

This period marks one culminating point of that long journey which began with the depiction of the human form by Pictographic man many thousands of years previously. Throughout that journey artists had gradually acquired the ability to record the animal and human form, and later their man-made and natural environments (e.g., Flemish, Dutch, and Barbizon schools). Throughout these times we have seen how priests of one sort or another maintained power over humans with various kinds of magic and religion; we have seen kings wresting the power from the priests; and now in the times under discussion, the ruled were again wresting power from the rulers. Amid the turmoils and revolutions of the times when a shift of political power from one class to another was in process, a new direction in art was thriving. In keeping with the tempo of their times artists became intensely interested in sociopolitical problems and some of them harbored notions then considered revolutionary as to what constituted the proper organization of human society. As Theodore Rousseau said, "For a new society a new art."

In the following from one of his manifestos, Courbet clearly expounded the new attitude: "The most precious of all things for the artist is his originality, his independence. Schools have no right to existence; there should be only painters. Without being of any school or party I have studied the art of the ancients and of the moderns. I have no more wish to imitate the one than to copy the other . . . . By gaining knowledge I wanted only to perfect my own individual power—power to transcribe the manners, ideas, and look of our time according to my own understanding: in a word, to produce living art, not only as a painter but as a man. I am not only a socialist but a democrat and a republican, a supporter of every revolution. Moreover, I am a sheer realist, that is, I adhere loyally to actual verity.

"The principle of realism means denial of the ideal. In line with the negation of the ideal, I arrive at the emancipation of the individual, and at democracy. Realism in its essence is democratic art. It exists by representation of things the artist can see and handle." [59]

"Painting is an entirely physical language, and anything that is abstract, invisible, does not come within its province. The painters of today (the Romantics) are entirely disassociated from the social conditions that surround us, and their works with their heroic or religious subjects are entirely out of harmony with the spirit of the age. It is nonsensical for painters to dish up themes in which they have no belief. Better paint railway stations, engines, houses, mines, and factories; for these are the saints and miracles of the nineteenth century." [60] And in speaking so Courbet hit the nail squarely on the head. For what was the essential basis of the progress of realism, but the ever increasing democratic attitude inherent in the notion of scientific recording? Now the artist was freed of having his art dictated to him; he looked upon the world as a free man; he reported the world back to his fellows as a free world, at least one potentially capable of being so. Therefore, if certain previous artists had considered accurate portrayal of reality as a disfigurement of art, then men like Courbet now remarked in the opposite vein: "Why should I try to see in the world what is not there, and to disfigure what is there by efforts of the imagination?"

We must realize that art was here at a parallel with the scientific attitude of the times, when men were bending every effort to investigate the phenomena of the empirical world. Modern industry and science were starting on their way. Similarly artists were taking a long look into the empirical reality and realizing more than ever before that reality is an ever-changing phenomenon. The artists of the "ideal" had been striving futilely to staticize life into a true-for-all-times absolute, and such an absolute always

58. Ibid., p. 337.

59. As quoted by Cheney, *The Story of Modern Art*, p. 131.

60. As quoted by Pijoan, op. cit., p. 334.

78. Gustave Courbet, Coast Scene. French, 19th Century. Smith College Museum of Art.

turned out to be a fiction in need of rejuvenation at the very moment the ideal seemed to have been attained. All this was the old dispute between the *art of man* and the *art of nature,* between those who strove to force the art of nature into an art of man and those who worked to make man's efforts at art correspond to the art of nature.

But the Realists, such as Courbet and Millet, who spoke for the common man, could not resist, at least to a degree, exploiting the device that men have always employed in art—they idealized, romanticized the depicted objects of their admiration. Who, for instance, ever saw a farm or peasants as they appear in the magic world of Millet? Until Photography dominated, art remained to some extent a form of Pictographic writing. Artists throughout history in some degree changed nature either to tell a message or as a departure for "creating" a visual experience. Only with the Camera could man fully release the urge to record nature as literally as possible, for with it so much realism was captured that men were irresistibly attracted to its achievements.

Thus all that the Realists were striving for in their art, eventually became the undisputed task of the Photographer with his Camera. In the works of the Camera artists we see completed the cycle of realism in the illusionistic arts comparable to the Roman portrait heads which completed a similar cycle of realism in sculpture. After the invention of the Camera in 1839, artists could just as well have left the job of recording nature with increasing accuracy to this far more efficient *method*. However, Photographers seem to have been more concerned with solving the problems of operating a Camera than with arguing over what were then considered the problems of art. They worked to perfect the results of their instrument and let the painters *talk* of how much more perfect *their* works were.

But even though Courbet and his type of artist were now being displaced, nevertheless they did serve certain important functions which account for the continued appearance of great recording artists even after the Camera entered the scene of art. On the technical side, for example, Photographs could not be made as large as paintings; they were limited to certain subjects, and the painter was for some time in sole possession of that powerful factor of color. Only in the realm of literal form-reporting did the Camera possess an important advantage, since it was accurate far beyond the ability of the painter's primitive medium. On the psychological side, Realist painters served to give prestige to the notion of accuracy in visual reporting. Hence, just as the sculptors of the Renaissance inadvertently assisted the painters to take over the major role in art, so the painters of the post-Camera period who sought literal realism have inadvertently assisted the Camera artists to take over the task of accuracy in visual reporting with the more modern tool of the Camera-Machine. And just as we saw in the Renaissance transition from the dominance of one medium to the dominance of another, many artists who both sculpted and painted, so in this period we find many artists who photographed and painted. Eventually the Camera was developed to the point where it stripped the painting artists of almost everything they had left.[61]

In the light of our present analysis, certain artists who worked just preceding the Camera's invention now assume far more importance than they have ever been given. These artists, still considered insignificant, were primarily interested in recording as literally as possible what they actually saw with their eyes. Like the early Flemish and Dutch whom we have noted, they strove to be literal in their behavior towards the spectacle of nature; but artists now possessed a more highly developed ability to visualize than had any of their predecessors. These Realists were the real forerunners of the Camera—the logical tool for obtaining the results they were seeking. They strove to submerge their visual organs to that which struck their eyes, to let the light-wave-reports of nature dictate to them. They were the obedient servants of the visual phenomena of nature. This almost robot-like activity, this direct approach to the act of vision, was necessary if one was to be a human Camera. And it was only natural that preceding and about the time of the Camera's invention such artists should appear, whose sole concern was to record—to record as faithfully as possible; to preserve that which was seen and as it was seen with the human eye. Thus they performed a useful service by bringing the whole problem of realism to a head, although they probably did not know at first that they were making a good case for Photographs and not for painting.

Those who consider themselves as "Moderns," and even those who do not, generally look with contempt upon these copyists of nature, especially those who immediately preceded or were contemporaneous with the Camera invention. In the nebulous compartments into which they generally chop up history, the Realists are not accredited a respectable place; they are completely eliminated from the category of the "great." To make things worse, the "Moderns" do not even explain this discrimination beyond a few contemptuous, unsubstantiated negations, which merely indicate that they possess an abundance of prejudices, but are lacking in coherent knowledge about the object of those prejudices. The Realists have become scapegoats for the Moderns' ignorance; they speak of them as "those mediocre artists who copied nature" and call them "uncreative." They are unconsciously demanding that the Realists be "creative" in the same way that they are, without realizing that the creation to which the Realists' works led—the creation of the Camera—ranks among the major "creations" of all man's art history.[62] Such artists pushed the problem of visual recording to the point where the Camera inevitably had to be invented to make possible further developments in that direction. In short, the work of these pre-Camera artists cleared the ground for the invention of the Camera. The subsequent developments stemming from the Camera extend far beyond the realm of art, and have become an indispensable part of our lives and our culture.

In the work of these literal copyists we have a good example of how artists can *appear* to be pursuing some aimless or useless direction, while the very opposite eventually turns out to be the actual case. In order to comprehend and appreciate more clearly their achievements, which are still unrecognized, let us try to project ourselves into the psycho-logical milieu in which they lived and worked and were stimulated.

In the early 19th century the Camera, Impressionism, and none of our so-called "Modern art" had yet been invented. In order to project ourselves adequately into these times, we must put aside contemporary prejudices against the direct and literal copying of nature and realize that it was a stimulating and useful objective in those times. We must remember that there was once a time when such realistic art did not exist and that this form of art, like the Modern schools, had to be created to exist at all.

[handwritten margin note: justification of literal copying in art]

61. This has since then deterred the outstanding non-Camera artists from wasting their talents upon this kind of art, but not the mediocre fellows, since they have no talent to waste.

62. Incidentally, a similar attitude is taken toward the Photograph in regard to its status as "art." We still argue the stupid question "Is Photography art?"

225

To realize how potently attractive realism is, we need only recall what pleasures we ourselves get out of Photographs when they give a clear report of the subject, and then remember that the artists we are considering had never seen a Photograph. Their art was the Photography of their times. It was they who were perfecting the accurate recording of nature. And to see how well they succeeded, we have only to compare their work with Photographs. To see a work of art which appeared to look exactly like nature was a tremendous and legitimate experience for the artists of these times. And to strive to invent and finally be among the first humans of all times to see a Photograph was an even more tremendous experience. We have all had this experience of seeing a Photograph for the first time, but few of us have had it when we were mature enough to comprehend our initial reactions to it and so we have lost or are unconscious of the experience. For us today a Photograph is a common but indispensable part of living. We forget that only a little more than a century ago no one had ever seen a Photograph and the nearest thing to it was the work of those artists who copied nature accurately, especially those who had, more or less, no other objective than that.

If those copying artists and their work had not existed, we today would have to achieve this kind of art ourselves. It was necessary, for historical, practical reasons, that this form of art be invented to meet the developmental demands through which man was passing in his visual art and general evolution. There is no greater mark of art ignorance today than to maintain that the Camera artist produces a "low form" of art. Such an attitude is the result of insecurity before genuine artists of nature. Such people get very excited, however, over a cartoon entitled "Guernica."

In any case the climactic effort to achieve as much realism as possible occurred with such artists as Louis Daguerre. An excellent example of the attitude of those who were engaged in this task is to be found in a letter by Joseph-Nicephore Niépce, a man who actually produced the first of the more modern kinds of Photographs, which were, however, not only crude but deficient as far as permanence was concerned. He wrote thus of the Diorama work of Daguerre: "But nothing is superior to the two views painted by M. Daguerre; one of Edinburgh, taken by moonlight during a fire; the other of a Swiss village, looking down a wide street, facing a mountain of tremendous height, covered with eternal snow. Those representations are so real, even in their smallest detail, that one believes that he actually sees rural and primeval nature, with all the fascination which the charm of colours and the magic of light and shade endow it. The illusion is even so great that one attempts to leave his box, in order to wander out into the open and climb to the summit of the mountain. I assure you there is not the least exaggeration on my part, the objects in addition are, or seem to be, of natural grandeur." [63]

The perfected Camera was finally invented by this same Daguerre, one of those artists who strove directly to look at visual nature as it actually appeared to the human eye-brain without allowing diverting and distortive influences of classicism, romanticism, or social interest to dominate their objective. The Classicists had directed their eyes towards a fantasy largely based upon the deductive procedure and art of the Greeks. The Romanticists had directed their eyes upon the unusual, the horrible, etc., which for them served also as a fantasy escape. The Socio-Realists put art to the services of the social turmoil of their times and thereby attempted to mold public opinion, but even this art still altered reality, if to a much lesser degree. But the literal copyists were concerned with the problems of recording and preserving what they had seen, of finding methods for recording reality as such ever more accurately, and it was towards this end that they directed all their researches. They were of course affected by the life around them, but made no direct attempts to do more than record the visual evidence of nature as such. And it was one of this group of artists who made the first successful Camera.

Now there may be those who will claim that even before these pre-Camera Realists came along, the Classicists and Romanticists could have recorded nature just as realistically had they wanted to. And this is true, IF they had wanted to! Unless we see the implications of that "if," we have missed the basic point which our history has endeavored to put across. In the evidence of the art itself we see the true situation. If there is some one lesson to be gained from our history, it is this: *what we think,* and what

63. Joseph-Nicephore Niépce as quoted by Victor Fouque: *The Truth Concerning the Invention of Photography,* p. 75, translated by Edward Epstean, New York, Tennant and Ward, 1935 (original edition, 1867).

we consequently see, are both bound together as ONE and INDIVISIBLE. What we think plays a part in what we are bound to see, as what we see plays a part in determining what we will think. In other words, if one trains himself to record what he actually sees, he develops an ability quite different from one who trains himself to record reality as he does *not* actually see it. It is not only a question of what an artist could do, but rather of what an artist trains himself to do. In the same way, a man may have the genius of an Einstein, but if he spends it on such profound medieval problems as how many angels can stand on the head of a pin, he will hardly become an Einstein. The situation is comparable in art: the artist's type of orientation to reality determines what he does with that reality.

Perhaps of all the organs of perception, none is more abused and misunderstood than the organ of vision. Where the eye-brain is concerned we simply take too much for granted. We assume that since we see, that's all there is to seeing. However, " 'I see,' said the blind man" is more often the case. Our history has shown how our "visual" functioning is intricately interrelated to the experience of the human organism as-a-whole-in-a-particular-environment. Moreover, the organism is affected by the entire past of man. Hence we cannot, on psycho-physiological, on historiographical, on scientific grounds in general, separate what we think about what we see from that which we will see when we perform the act of seeing. The processes of vision are an eye-brain complex and not pure-seeing or pure-thinking actions isolated from everything else, as so many often unconsciously or otherwise assume. A telling illustration of the interconnectedness of the organism's function as-a-whole can be found in the study of the "mentally ill" *who see things* because they "think" they see them. We are, of course, referring to the mechanism of hallucinations.[64]

Thus the Classicists who are primarily concerned with changing reality in some degree into that which it *is not,* are prevented from developing their *potential* visual capacities to the extent obtained by those who directly strive to copy nature accurately. In other words, the manner in which the artist develops his depictions of reality is determined by the visual-mold into which he squeezes his observations of nature.

Although the Classicists in general operated as a deterrent to the development of recording nature accurately, one aspect of their *attitude* played a great part in the progress even of Realistic art— that is, they stimulated man's "thinking" about what he "sees." Recall that from the Renaissance two general streams of art spread over Europe and that in France these divergent views parried each other sharply just as they had in Renaissance Italy, and became a stimulus to the thinking out of the problem of art in relation to nature. The main reason progress was produced where these divergent views more directly coped with each other was this: man could not learn to record nature accurately merely by trying to be a human Camera. (Recall, for example, the early Flemish.) The structure of nature had first to be understood and this knowledge could only be gained by increasing consciousness of the problem.

In short, the Classical attitude stimulated a theoretical consideration of art and reality. And so it was the Italians of the Renaissance who worked out the theories of visual structure and the French who then proceeded to refine these problems and work out the sociological problems of art and reality. Where this stimulus toward theory was slight—in Flanders, Germany, Holland, Spain, England—there we have only temporary eruptions of theoretical interests and temporary eruptions of great artists, and so no sustained evolution of theory and actual art. How much the Realists needed the foil of the Idealists is seen in the tendency of the Realist to become over-empirical and to produce a glassy, wooden or metallic reality. Similarly the Idealist tends to become over-deductive without the foil of the Realists.

64. An example from the author's experience further illustrates this point. Soon after having discontinued the painting of nature's objects, I had occasion to drive through a countryside which I had visited on a number of previous occasions and so was quite familiar with the landscape. During this drive I was looking at the landscape and began having strange but pleasant reactions to it. These were so different from any previously experienced, that I felt it was imperative to find out the source of the reactions. I then came to realize that I was seeing nature more directly than ever before, without the interference of my previous practice of always seeing nature reorganized in terms of a painting. Being no longer concerned with changing nature into a painting, I was thus enabled to visualize more objectively and so receive a more accurate report of the actuality—a new experience of reality. Nature not art was once more the criterion of nature-appearances. Hence the new source of pleasure was due to experiencing more of nature as such, not as a potential painting.

79. Still Life by Daguerre, 1837—earliest daguerreotype in existence. Photo, Dumas-Satigny, Paris, of original in collection of Societe Francaise de Photographie, Paris. Courtesy of the Museum of Modern Art, New York.

Thus throughout the pre-Camera period the Classicists served a positive purpose in forcing and stimulating deductive activities into the empirical consideration of recording art. In France where this situation appeared most strongly after the Italian Renaissance we find the most steady development. It was there that the most thorough analysis of art occurred during post-Renaissance times, and so it was there eventually that an artist, a literal Realist, successfully invented a mechanical eye to record nature-appearances more perfectly than it was ever possible to do with the old primitive tools and copying methods.

Man's ability to visualize had developed to such a degree of intensity that his recordings of nature were very close to what the eye-brain was able to see. To obtain even more accurate recordings of the world of vision than were possible with the old tools, a recording machine was needed. Daguerre, the copying artist, successfully invented one! Thus the human organism, as happened in so many fields in the 19th century, gave way to the greater accuracy and efficiency of a Machine which man had created. As man had made mechanical hands, now he made a mechanical eye; an extra-neural device to extend the potentialities of the human organism.

Looking back at the history of French painting from Poussin to Courbet we find three important stages: first a Classical or Florentine attitude; then an erotic or Venetian, and finally a realistic or Flemish. In this way French artists passed through in successive development, and then resolved, the main efforts that had been made by artists during the Italian Renaissance. Indeed, they perfected the last stage, the realistic stage, beyond any previous attempt, by perfecting a mechanical eye—the Camera.

With the Camera the artist realized a recording method that could automatically adjust its operations to the varying characteristics of reality phenomena. In short, the mathematical invariant method of the Greeks, by which they produced their "ideal" in art, now became the variable mathematical method of the mechanical Camera and its lens. The swing from the General to the Particular in recording art was now relatively speaking complete.

That which artists had always been seeking in one degree or another, often in spite of themselves, was now reduced to its most direct terms. The basic objective motivating the evolution of art ever since the first artist scratched one stone against another, or drew a stick across the ground, leaving a line behind him—the achievement of an accurate recording of the visual phenomena which surrounded man—had now been reached. Particularly since the Greeks this goal had been repeatedly voiced by artists and theorists. Many of them even thought the goal of perfect recordings of nature had finally been achieved. Thus Aristotle wrote that: "Dionysios drew them true to life." Pliny reported the stories of Parrhasios and Zeuxis; the former painted grapes which were so real that birds, it is alleged, came to peck at them, while the latter artist painted a curtain that appeared actually to cover a painting beneath it.[65] Bocaccio wrote of Giotto: "he was of so excellent a wit that there was nothing in nature but that he could with his pen and pencil depict it, so that it seemed not to be a mere likeness but the very thing itself; and the visual sense of man was deceived, taking those things to be real which were only painted." Vasari said that, "the paintings of other masters are properly to be called paintings, but those of Raphael may well be designated the life itself, for the flesh trembles, and life is in its utmost animation through all his works." Leonardo insisted that, "That painting is the most praiseworthy which has the greatest conformity to the thing imitated." Michelangelo decried the fact that, "In Flanders . . . . they paint to deceive the external eye." De Piles said that, "A perfect imitation of nature . . . . is the only duty and ought to be the whole aim of painting." Diderot exclaimed of Chardin's paintings, "We have but to take these biscuits and eat them, this orange, open and squeeze it, this glass of wine and drink it." Hogarth bluntly asked: "Who but a bigot . . . . will say that he has not seen faces, and necks, hands and arms in living women, that even the Grecian Venus does but coarsely imitate?" Ingres urged the artist to, "Copy with absolute fidelity." Courbet proclaimed, "I am a sheer realist." Just before these remarks by Ingres and Courbet, the perfected Camera appeared, invented by an artist-scientist, Daguerre!

And so ended one momentous epoch in the art history of man. Here also ended the usefulness of painting as a medium for recording the actual appearances of reality—the Camera artist replaces the painting artist!

65. Chambers, *Cycles of Taste*, p. 14.

Justification and admiration of realism as the aim of art.

When we consider that the art of painting and drawing has been cultivated ever since the earliest times of the world, it is indeed wonderful that it should have been reserved for our age to discover that all kinds of objects can be made to draw their own pictures, and that with skilful management, nature will do the work that has cost man so many weary hours; and will do it much more accurately and infinitely quicker than he can. 340

Fox Talbot, 1844

Photography is an art, and more than an art. It is
a miracle, achieved by the sun in collaboration with
the artist. 228
                          Alphonse Lamartine

What would not be the value for our English nobility of such a record of their ancestors who lived a century ago? On how small a portion of their family picture galleries can they really rely with confidence? 228

Fox Talbot

The beautiful execution of the photographic picture is an achievement surpassing any other kind of presentation; the correctness of the lines, the precision of forms, has been carried to the highest point in the daguerreotype pictures. 327

Paul Delaroche

What we see here [daguerreotype] is miraculous indeed! 228

Sir John Herschel

. . . . the daguerreotype is able to represent lifeless nature in such an accomplished way as only nature itself can do, and as would never be achievable by painting or drawing. 228

Gay Lussac

Throughout the period we have studied in the preceding chapter, *painters* ruled the world of art without question. There had been a formidable series of great recording-painters all the way from the 15th to the 19th centuries. There were sculptors, of course, during these times, but their works invariably fell far short of any of the great accomplishments in the sculptural medium up to Donatello. After the times of Donatello and Masaccio all the useful innovators employed the medium of painting. In those cases where highly gifted men such as Michelangelo and Rodin made the error of using sculpture, their works were actually those of frustrated painters, not true sculptors.

In short, the illusion of reality, the color-image of light, gave the greatest correspondence to the vision of reality seen with the human eye. The sculptor records the forms of reality, but we have seen how very limited this method of recording is. *The painter records light, he records the images that humans see and not the forms from which the images spring.* Thus, strange as it may seem, men have been able to produce a more accurate and more complete report of reality with *illusions* of reality than was ever possible by what seemed at first the more realistic method of recording—the recording of the forms of reality. With the invention of the Camera the superiority of light-recording over that of form-recording became an unquestionable fact as far as the depiction of nature-appearances is concerned.

Up to now, however, the relationships between the older forms of art and Photography have not been adequately worked out. Indeed, few have even considered the matter important enough for analytical inquiry. The dilemma over the relationships between the Camera and painting can be coherently resolved if we realize that up to the advent of the Camera, art had been evolving in its *major aspect* along the direction of securing ever more perfect recordings of the visible world. We have seen how the art of the past developed to a point where it became necessary to invent a Camera in order that accurate recording could be further developed. The hands of man, in conjunction with the old tools and mediums, i.e., handicraft, had reached the end of their potentialities in this regard; thus a mechanical instrument was devised in order to continue a development which had been begun by the handicraft-Photographers.

233

Prior to the appearance of the Camera all Mimetic artists, especially the literal Realists, were already "Photo-graphers" in the sense that the term means graphs or pictures of light-rays; this is exactly what these artists had been doing—recording, so graphing, light-rays. Thus the history of Photography is not something that began in 1839 or some independent development having no connection with "art," as is popularly assumed, but rather a natural, continued development of the major trend in the evolution of art which had preceded Daguerre's invention. As Erich Stenger wrote: "Are we to consider it an accident that the man who perfected the first photographic process was the 'artist-painter, Daguerre?'"[1] The principal and important difference between the "Photographers" before 1839 and those after that date who employed a Camera was that the former *copied* light-rays with a very *primitive mechanical method* invented in Paleolithic times, whereas the latter captured records of light-rays themselves with a *modern, highly developed mechanical method* invented in 1839. With the invention of the Camera, the direction towards realistic recording was completed as far as the old primitive hand or handicraft methods were concerned.

Hence an examination of *Photo*-GRAPHY will be of vital importance, not only that we may adequately understand what happened to the realistic trend after 1839, but also that we may be able to resolve coherently the present day dilemma over the copying or non-copying of nature as a contents of art. In short, if we are aware of the "from where" and "to where" function of the Camera, this should help us considerably in clarifying one major aspect of the present chaotic controversy over the "problem of reality," and whether it should be depicted by paint or modern Photography.

It should be mentioned, although it is not necessary for our purpose to go into detail, that prior to the invention of the first practical Camera, there had been many attempts at and methods for mechanically recording visual phenomena.[2] Aristotle seems to have been the first to have made, or at least to have left a report of the observation that light entering through a small hole into a darkened room would produce upon the opposite wall an inverted light-record of the scene outside the hole. This is the principle of the Camera-Obscura, which is a small box instead of a room. As we noted in chapter 10, Leonardo da Vinci is known to have been familiar with this latter device and to have used it in his work as an artist and a scientist. In the 16th century Danielo Barbaro, an artist, invented the notion of a lens for the Camera-Obscura room, which thus produced a brighter image upon the wall. In the 18th century the Camera-Obscura and similar devices became a regular part of the artist's equipment; and in the 19th century an artist, Louis Daguerre, invented the first practical process for making mechanical Photographs. Two years later, in 1841, Fox Talbot, an English scientist, perfected the first method for securing more than one reproduction by inventing the negative process.

The perfected Camera was the result of the combined interests of artists, opticians, chemists, physicists, etc., in creating mechanically accurate reproductions of the visible world. Of the men responsible for Photography, Beaumont Newhall writes: "Photography was brought into being by a desire to make pictures. Without exception, those men who were instrumental in making it practical were impelled by an artistic urge. Wedgwood was the son of the great potter; Niépce had been experimenting with lithography; Daguerre painted scenery and illusionistic panoramas; Fox Talbot wished to sketch but could not."[3] In other words, the artists and scientists responsible for the invention and development of the Camera were men with overlapping interests. Thus Lemaître, a lithographer, wrote of his contemporary, Daguerre, who was typical of the artists under discussion, that, "Daguerre, as a painter, has a fine talent for imitation and an exquisite taste for preparing his tableaux. I believe he has a rare intelligence for the things which deal with machines and lighting effects; the amateur visitor of his establishment is easily convinced; I know he has occupied himself for a long time with perfecting the camera obscura. . . ."[4]

1. Erich Stenger: *The History of Photography*, p. 72, translated and published by Edward Epstean, New York, 1939.

2. For an account of this aspect of the subject we suggest: Beaumont Newhall: *Photography, 1839-1937*, Introduction to Museum of Modern Art Catalogue, New York, 1937; Stenger, op. cit.; Lucia Moholy: *One Hundred Years of Photography*, Penguin Books, Ltd., Middlesex, England, 1939. For an excellent, detailed account read J. M. Eder: *History of Photography*, translated by Edward Epstean, Columbia University Press, New York, 1945.

3. Newhall, op. cit., p. 40.

4. As quoted by Victor Fouque: *The Truth Concerning the Invention of Photography*, p. 68.

234

Fox Talbot may be regarded as an "artistic-scientist" as Daguerre was a "scientific-artist." Talbot, in telling of how he first got the notion of the negative process, wrote that in 1833 he was attempting to take sketches with "Wollaston's Camera Lucida," "but with the smallest possible amount of success," so that he "came to the conclusion that its use required a previous knowledge of drawing which unfortunately I did not possess." Next he tried throwing the image of an object on a piece of paper in the focus of a Camera Obscura, making "fairy pictures, creations of a moment, and destined as rapidly to fade away." "It was during these thoughts that the idea occurred to me," he wrote, "how charming it would be if it were possible to cause these natural images to imprint themselves durably, and remain fixed upon the paper!" [5] Talbot recognized not only the scientific changes to be brought about by the new recording instrument, but also something of the changes it would bring into art. Thus he significantly titled his books, *The Pencil of Nature* and *On Photogenic Drawing*. His understanding of the changes brought about in art has yet to be grasped by many today.

Shortly after the appearance of Daguerre's invention, confusion descended upon the scene of art. Some artists rebelled against it, while others dropped their paint brushes to take up the more accurate tool, and still others kept both, just in case! Stenger tells us: "Among the fifty-nine daguerreotypists in Berlin and Hamburg before 1850 whose former professions could be ascertained, there were twenty-nine portrait and other painters, a master printer in lithography, one copper engraver and seven opticians. David O. Hill was also a painter." [6]

For a time the Photo-graphing artists employing the new Machine method tried to imitate certain time-honored effects obtained by the Photo-graphing artists who employed the old primitive handicraft tools. But it was not long before some painters, such as Carrier, were adopting the photo-grays and browns, as they were called, and so like the Camera ignoring color in nature.[7] It was unnecessary, however, and even harmful for the Cameramen to influence the painters or the painters the Cameramen. When the Photographer allowed himself to be influenced by the painting medium he was subjecting his art to a more primitive method of production with deleterious results. When the painter permitted his medium to be influenced by Photography he was competing hopelessly with a method far superior to his own.

Some men at the time of the Camera's invention realized the superiority of the new method. Jules Janin (1804-1874), a Parisian author, wrote at the time the first Photo-graphs were appearing: "Never has the drawing of the greatest masters produced anything like it. Consider that it is the sun itself, which here, introduced as the almighty impulse of an entirely new art, produces these incredible works. Here is no longer the trembling hand of man, which on moving paper copies the ever-changing scenes of nature. The miracle happens instantaneously, quick as thought, rapid as the ray of the sun." [8] In 1839 Paul Delaroche, the painter, said when he saw the first daguerreotypes: "The beautiful execution of the photographic picture is an achievement surpassing any other kind of presentation; the correctness of the lines, the precision of forms, has been carried to the highest point in the daguerreotype pictures." [9] In 1840 J. Weil wrote: "A light image—what a glorious conception. God spoke: 'Let there be light, and there was light.' Man spoke: 'Serve me, oh light,' and light served him." [10] An anonymous author made the following observation in 1864: "We command the sun—and he paints! And how he paints! He does not flatter like court painters, who adorn their sitters with eternal youth, unfading beauty and spirit, laughing at them behind their backs: whomsoever the rays of his eyes meet, he delineates with all their advantages and their defects. It is only since the invention of photography that physiognomy became a science. What no artist may accomplish, the sun brings out in open day." [11] The inventor of the card-photograph, a Photographer by the name of Disdéri, wrote: "Photography is an art: It uses its own means; it has its own original standard of the esthetic. The source from which it draws its creative power

5. William H. Fox Talbot: *The Pencil of Nature*, Longman, Brown, Green and Longmans, London, 1844.

6. Stenger, op. cit., p. 72.

7. There continues to be a good deal of this practiced today by both Camera artists and painting artists who are still attempting to solve the problems raised by the invention of the Camera by ignoring the differences between the two mediums.

8. As quoted by Stenger, op. cit., p. 181.

9. Ibid., p. 182.   10. Ibid., p. 183.   11. Ibid., p. 185.

is nature. The outward appearance of things are, as it were, the elements, the words of the language, which the photographer expresses in his work." [12] Paolo Mantegazza, the Italian anthropologist, declared: "The poet writes with the pen, the painter with the brush, the sculptor with the chisel; photography writes with light, the most divine of all of God's creations." [13]

These men realized the paramount advantage of the new tool of art-recording over the primitive hand tools—that it permitted the actual light-rays to record their own images upon the "canvas." It was now possible to engage the light-rays to register themselves and so to participate directly in producing the actual recording. No longer did the artist need to imitate light-rays emanating from the object being recorded, as was done in the primitive method of painting.

In this regard it should not be forgotten that what we see with our eye-brain is no more the object itself than the hammer striking the anvil is the sound we hear. What we actually "see" are electromagnetic light-rays, which our eyes "digest." Light-rays strike an object and are then reflected into our visual system. There they are edited, to borrow Max Born's expression, and the result of this editing is a *symbol*-image, having certain differences from as well as similarity references to the object from which they emanated. What we see, then, is light, not the forms of reality; what we see is an illusion of reality in the sense that *it is not* reality, but a visual language by which we comprehend actual reality.

With the invention of the Camera, artists possessed a highly accurate tool for recording the light that bounces off objects and forms the image of the world which human beings experience with vision. The process is somewhat similar to the functioning of the human eye-brain, but in some respects is less limited and in others more limited than the potentialities of the organic mechanism. The Camera can detect and capture visual phenomena which the eye cannot; for example, the recording of a perfect image of an object in very rapid motion. Moreover the eye cannot produce, as can the Camera, a permanent visual record which can be kept on file.[14]

In addition to these advantages, the Camera can make more neutral observations than are possible with the human eye. A Camera can be made to Photograph "cabbages and kings" with equal consideration. As Mumford has pointed out: "The photograph . . . . served as an independent objective check upon observation. The value of a scientific experiment lies partly in the fact that it is repeatable and thus verifiable by independent observers: but in the case of astronomical observations, for example, the slowness and fallibility of the eye can be supplemented by the camera, and the photograph gives the effect of repetition to what was, perhaps, a unique event, never to be observed again. In the same fashion, the camera gives an almost instantaneous cross-section of history—arresting images in their flight through time." [15]

On the other hand, the Camera, temporarily at least, lacks the color accuracy of the human eye, as well as its ability to register form-space. This lack of color accuracy has encouraged the primitive or handicraft Realist to delude himself about the Camera's productions. For a time painting artists could record this factor in a fuller sense than the Camera artists. However, in recent years the color Camera has been perfected to such a degree that Photographers are now on the way to securing complete dominance in the field of recording visual phenomena.

At present, however, the ordinary mirror is still the most accurate form of reproduction available. Most of us are no longer aware of its amazing accuracy. We have become so habituated to mirror-seeing that we have lost the astonishment of earlier men who saw their reflected images for the first time. This reflected image is so accurate that we are seldom conscious that it is a mere reflection! The drawback of the mirror, of course, lies in the fact that it is even less possible with it than with the eye to produce permanent records. Yet within the principle of the mirror may lie the secret to more accurate Photography.

12. Ibid., p. 185.

13. Ibid., p. 185.

14. There is one exception, however—the case of eidetic images. This form of imagery is largely confined to children and Primitive peoples. Among adults in "civilized" cultures it usually occurs only in geniuses and arrested development cases.

15. Lewis Mumford: *Technics and Civilization*, p. 242, Harcourt, Brace and Co., Inc., New York, 1936.

236

Leonardo recognized the mirror's accuracy and saw the value that the painter might gain from it. He wrote: "Painters oftentimes despair of their power to imitate nature, on perceiving how their pictures are lacking in the power of relief and vividness which objects possess when seen in a mirror. . . ." [16] Therefore, he advised: "When you wish to see whether the general effect of your picture corresponds with that of the object represented after nature, take a mirror and set it so that it reflects the actual thing, and then compare the reflection with your picture, and consider carefully whether the subject of the two images is in conformity with both, studying especially the mirror. The mirror ought to be taken as a guide—that is, the flat mirror—for within its surface substances have many points of resemblance to a picture; namely, that you see the picture made upon one plane showing things which appear in relief, and the mirror upon one plane does the same. The picture is one single surface, and the mirror is the same." [17]

Eventually, the Camera will be perfected to the accuracy of the ordinary mirror. When that happens, let us hope that at last the primitive hand-painting method of recording nature will be seen by all as the useless method it already is. And then it will finally be abandoned, because we will be able to recognize the superior value of accurate rather than fantasy recordings of reality!

Even with its present handicaps the Camera is incomparably superior to the primitive handicraft methods of recording. In the case of painting, the image has first to pass into the prejudiced eyes of the artist, who lacks the objectivity possible with the Camera (see diagram, p. 241); then with primitive tools the artist makes marks on a canvas and keeps adjusting them until these marks seem to correspond to the light-ray records in his eyes. He has no method for measuring the light-rays with any degree of accuracy; he must depend largely on his unaided eyes. The image in the artist's eyes supersedes the image which the Camera could make; but the image of the Camera is more closely related to the image in the artist's eyes than is the image on the canvas. In short, the original light-rays do not, as in Photographs, pass directly upon the canvas and participate in the recording. What the artist does is to imitate or copy light-rays with a very primitive *"mechanical* method." In Photography, a modern, incomparably superior mechanical method, the actual light-rays which bounce off an object and make it visible, register themselves directly on the Camera negative. That is why we speak of *taking* a Photograph and of *making* a painting! We never speak of *taking* a portrait with painting. Thus we recognize the differences in these two methods of recording in the very terminology we unconsciously use when speaking about them!

Later we shall see many reasons why those Photographers who realize and utilize the very qualities which make their medium superior to that of painting, are the only legitimate realistic artists of our times, as regards depictions of the appearances of nature. As a matter of fact, if you search throughout the recent history of art, you will not find one painting artist who has attained as high a degree of realistic perfection in his art as that which was realized by those artists working in a similar direction around the period when the Camera was invented. Only the Camera artists have attained and superseded considerably the achievements of the Realists preceding and contemporary with the Camera's invention and development. [18]

It is no accident that no great realistic artist has appeared since soon after the Camera was invented and developed into a practical tool. The necessary impetus which makes for success in this respect has been lacking, for this form of realistic recording had been developed to its last possible pitch of perfection with the old primitive hand methods. To continue in this direction it was necessary to grasp the Camera and use it properly.

Many artists soon after the appearance of the Camera saw their position threatened by the

16. *The Notebooks of Leonardo da Vinci,* Vol. 2, p. 237. Edited and with an introduction by Edward MacCurdy. Reynal and Hitchcock, New York.

17. Ibid., Vol. 2, pp. 254-55.

18. Of course mediocre artists have continued to be attracted, for any one of a number of reasons, to the *business* of making "realistic" art for a mediocre market. And in some countries, particularly in the totalitarian states, one has to be a mediocre artist to exist at all. It is indeed significant that the ranks of these primitive handicraft photo-graphers have been increased by the demands of dictatorial governments.

undeniable superiority of this new recording method. Consciously or unconsciously they could see that it was an extremely undesirable rival which could soon displace their medium as the major method for recording reality. As Lucia Moholy wrote: "The painters, as might have been expected, were among the first to discuss the new art. Some among them feared it might threaten their interests, artistic or professional, and they denounced the newcomer. It did not occur to them that—by allowing themselves to feel threatened —they, if unconsciously, attributed certain artistic values to the 'rival.' But they emphatically denied these values, thus making void the danger—if danger there was." [19]

Every effort was employed to discredit and displace Photography, to give it a disreputable name, and, moreover, as one observer remarked, to "keep camera men from having a taste" of the "grand society" of the painters, who were exceedingly "proud of their old aristocratic caste." [20] Thus the Daguerreotype was called "French humbug" and a "grandiose plaything" by German newspapers soon after its appearance. The poet, Alexander von Sternberg, wrote in 1846 to a chemist friend: "How far are you going to drive us with your desperate and devilish chemistry? You remind me that lately you had your followers and pupils invent the daguerreotype. It is true, but this invention is in my opinion no more valuable than railroads. You have castigated the beam of light, the most independent son of the heavens, so long with your chemical scourge, that he has learned drawing. But how does he draw? What does he do to the eyes, ears, nose and hands of our relatives and beloved ones? You have made the sun a portrait artist! That was an unfortunate idea. And what does he paint now? He can be an excellent sun and still be a charmingly rotten portrait painter!" [21] Jokes, such as the following from *Punch* (vol. 12, 1847) were common: "One of the advantages or disadvantages, as the case may be, of many photographic portraits, is, that they fade away by degrees, and thus keep pace with those fleeting impressions or feelings under which it is sometimes usual for one to ask another for his or her miniature. It may be a strong recommendation of cheap photography, that its pictures will last as long as the ordinary run of small affections, and, indeed, a superior specimen of the art may be warranted to retain its outline throughout a flirtation of an entire month's durability." [22]

There were lamentations and protests that this despicable Machine lacked a "soul," etc. The following are typical: C. Pestalozzi, a Swiss poet, wrote: "Art and the Daguerreotype: If you wish to behold merely the earthly beauty of your beloved in picture, Choose the daguerreotype, take what technique has to offer. But if you seek, when viewing it, her very soul and spirit, Hasten to the Artist, for only: The living Spirit can give you her Soul!" [23] In the same vein, Edward Schreiner of Munich, a painter and lithographer, declared that, "Photography exposes to view only the animal part of the human being." [24] Charles Baudelaire, the French poet, wrote: "In these sad days a new industry has made its appearance, which has contributed considerably to strengthen vulgar stupidity in its belief . . . that art is nothing, nor can ever be anything, but the exact reproduction of nature in all its detail . . . . And so it follows that an industry, which would give us a result identical with nature, is Art Absolute. A vindictive God heard the voices of this multitude. Daguerre was his Messiah . . . and the multitude perforce arrived at the definition: Art is Photography. From that moment, the whole filthy mob came rushing along, as one single Narcissus, to gloat over their trivial images in the mirror. A mad prank, it is an extraordinary fanaticism which has taken possession of all these new sun-worshippers." [25] An author,

19. Moholy, op. cit., p. 37.

20. As quoted by Stenger, op. cit., p. 185.

21. Ibid., p. 183. This was written just one hundred years ago, yet one runs across these very evaluations constantly in the art books of the present.

22. Moholy, op. cit., p. 51.

23. Stenger, op. cit., p. 183. The Idealists of course had an especially tough time of it when Photography broke into their world of perfection.

24. Ibid., p. 185.

25. Ibid., p. 184. Apparently by this time (1850's), the Camera had been accepted by the majority. Only the more "artistic" souls held out, as many are still doing today.

Francis Wey, asked: "Who, in the minds of painters and critics, is the first, the real, the great culprit? Who is the revolutionary, the pitiless imitator of modern art? It is photography." [26] Another author, Paul de St. Victor, declared: "Photography ruins art, it prostitutes taste and vision; it discourages the engraver, whose slow and careful tool cannot fight against its dexterity and its legerdemain contrivances." [27] Charles Blanc, an art critic, wrote in the 1860's: "Photography apes everything and expresses nothing of itself. It is blind in the world of thought." [28]

To realize adequately why objections to Photography took such vehement turns we must understand that the mechanical process of the Photographic method did much to strip the art of linear visual recording of its old world of fantasy. Recall those two general levels in the experiencing of a work of art, that is, the "reality" of the art object as such and the relationship between the art object and the nature object it depicts. Now in a Photograph of a person, for instance, the image was considerably like the sitter—the reality of the nature object—while the remarkable individual idealistically depicted in a painted portrait—the art "reality"—disappeared to a radical degree. In other words the Camera considerably closed the gap between the reality of art (the recording) and the reality of nature; and the Idealists of one sort or another along with their literary Romantic friends tearfully regretted the loss of the old fantasy (or "reality" of art), and could not see the importance of the great gain in correspondence between the reality of nature and the art of man's visual recordings.

Today after more than 100 years of the most astounding progress in the field of Photography, one can still find plenty of individuals uttering the same old prejudices voiced when the Camera first appeared. Many still insist that Photography is not "art," [29] that it is some despicable thing called "mechanical," that it lacks the "soul" of reality, and such like non-sense.

Although at this late date there are still many who will not grant that Photography has completely displaced the realistic artists who attempt to copy nature or imitate it in *any* manner, nevertheless the facts are that since the Camera's potentialities for accurate recordings are so much greater than those of the *primitive* method of painting, Photography has inevitably continued to be developed and today reigns supreme in the field of art and science where recordings of the visible world are desired for their accuracy and not their fantasy. Imagine for one moment what a tremendously informative experience it would be if we possessed a Photograph of Socrates, or Aristotle, or of an Egyptian king, or of Leonardo da Vinci, or Newton, and you begin to get the "feel" of the differences between painting and Photography.

Refusal or failure to recognize such a supremacy of Photography in these times is as anachronistic as it would be to refuse to travel by any other means than horse and buggy, no matter how imperative speed might be. Almost everyone today realizes that automobiles, trains, and airplanes have replaced the horse and buggy as a more efficient method of travelling, but very few recognize that artists who still copy nature with the tools of the cave-man are in this respect simply horse-and-buggy mentalities. In a similar manner the majority in the art world have gone their own way as though the invention of the Camera had nothing at all to do with the future course of painting. (Later we shall see that this includes most so-called "Modern" painters along with the Academicians.) Here is a choice example of a critic who is hardly aware of the function of the Camera and little suspects what has actually happened in the medium of painting. She looks upon Photography as something incidental to painting and considers the latter medium superior to the former, if only artists will make it so. "The beauty of the magazine ads and some of the fashion plates in color *photography is simply breathtaking.* They make one sick to think that the *painters are passing all this up*—this sophisticated beauty of modern life—to follow in the lead of Picasso silliness and Dali delusions of irrationality. When one observes what a man with some sense of good pictorial material, composition and light and shade can do with a mere machine, it seems a tragedy that he did not learn to paint instead—or that painters should be trying to forget the importance

26. Ibid., p. 184.

27. Ibid., p. 184.

28. Ibid., p. 184.

29. This opinion was given the dubious dignity of a judicial sentence in a Brussels court in 1893: "Art ceases where photography begins." Ibid., p. 186.

of subject matter, composition, light and shade, to waste fine painting technique on the ill-chosen, ill-conceived, ill-arranged, ugly and meaningless.

"Wake up, Knights of the Brush! Reclaim your ancient heritage of the visual loveliness of the natural universe. Stop sulking in your tents over camera competition and show the world that you can do all and more than color photographers can—and do it better, enriched with the lusciousness of deep pigment and the brilliant play of fine brush work. Leave to posterity a permanent record in a worthwhile medium of what the photographer can only give a temporary flash in the weak washes of colored inks. Don't let the fear of being 'photographic' addle your brains. Be modern in the logical manner by painting today as it appears." (emphasis ours)[30]

This is another facet of the contention popular today that when you Photograph a person you capture a record only of that aspect of the individual which existed during that fraction of time it takes the shutters of the Camera to snap. In the words of our critic, "the photographer can only give a temporary flash in the weak washes of colored inks." And it is further contended that the painter is able to capture much more of a record than this ("all and more"). Thus the painter will tell you that he makes a thorough study of the individual, regards him from all points of view, talks to him, etc. He then proceeds to paint, incorporating within the portrait all the various characteristics he has observed and experienced. Hence it is claimed that the record produced by the painter is a more complete one, one which is not confined to a single phase or instant of "mechanical" observation and recording, as is the Photograph. In all, so the story goes, the painter is "selective," the poor Photographer is merely "mechanical."

Let us see if an analysis of the facts verifies or disproves the above contentions. Continuing with the portrait example, let us try to learn who makes the most *useful* recording, the realistic painter or the Photographer. To begin with we point out that it is impossible to paint the type of portrait implied above, because in painting one can record only visible phenomena and then only statically. In other words, the most accurately painted portrait that was ever made does not record *more* visual data than any good Photograph. But, say the advocates of realistic painting, our method records all kinds of characteristics which cannot be observed and recorded by the Camera operating in such a short space of time. We grant that the painter can observe more characteristics than are evidenced in any single Photograph, but we would like to inquire what would be the result *if* he could incorporate all these observations in his recording.

The answer to this problem involves us in time-space considerations. Let us suppose, for the sake of argument, that the painter could achieve a recording that was not limited to a single point in time-space as is the still Camera. To make such a record would involve his being able to depict many dynamic time-space points within a static or single time-space context. Such a portrait, however, would be unrecognizable as the individual who sat for it, for the obvious reason that it is impossible for anyone to assume all these characteristics at any one given time. The painting, a static not a dynamic record, is suited only for representing a single point in time-space! To the degree that it includes more than a single time-space point, then to that very degree the result would be an inaccurate record and increasingly unrecognizable as the number of these points was increased. So it is just as impossible to make such a portrait as it would be for an individual to possess at the same time all the various characteristics he had at the ages of 10, 23, and 39.

Yet the Realists of today claim that they accomplish such impossibilities and that this accomplishment makes their medium superior to that of the Photographers. The fact is, that they are forced to confine themselves to the Photographer's limitations—a single time-space context, only their results are greatly inferior. In other words, whether they know it or not, and they generally do not, the painters are competing with the Camera artists and not vice versa as is popularly contended. And to the degree that the painters do other than the Camera artists, they simply achieve that much less realism or accuracy. As we have explained, the method and medium of the painters are very primitive; the best they can do is to copy light-rays with crude methods and tools. But the Photographers capture imprints registered by actual light on a far superior, *scientifically constructed "canvas."* The painting method we have been analyzing achieves a fantasy-reality; the assumption that some unique series of the subject's

30. Evelyn Marie Stuart: *The Art Digest,* 18:13, November 15, 1943.

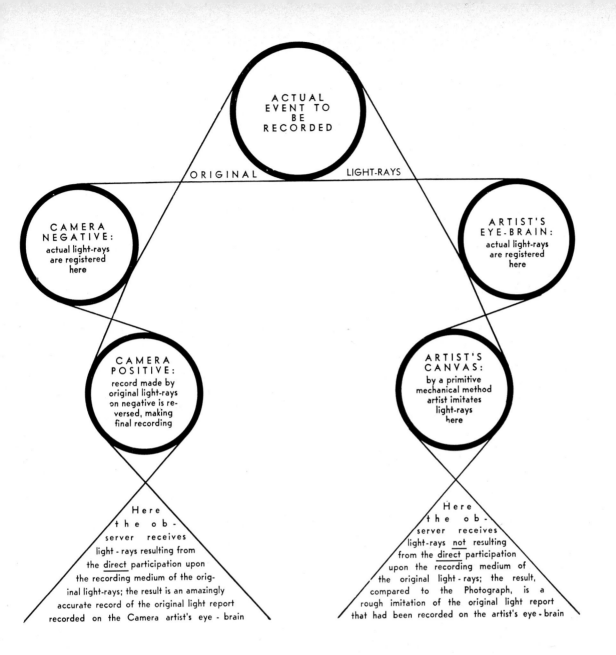

reality characteristics can thus be captured in the painting medium is simply a delusion. One important observation reveals how the mechanical snap of the Camera's shutter secures for us records which the old primitive methods cannot. Consider how many rapid facial and bodily movements occur in a human being, of which the human eye is able to catch only a blurred report. But a whole new world of vision is opened to us, since with the Camera, man is able to stop at any point he wishes all kinds of rapid actions—a smile, a gesture—and thus observe visual material never before seen by humans. It is obvious that all this is impossible for the artists employing the old primitive materials.

Therefore, we find that the painter is not only as limited as the Photographer in his recording, but actually is considerably more limited, because of his very primitive method for securing his recordings of nature.

Here are a few experiments which will throw more light on this problem. Take the works of *any* single portrait artist, dead or alive, that you care to choose. On one side of a room imagine that we stand ten of this artist's portraits, on the other side the ten individuals who sat for them. By comparing the two groups, *or any such two groups,* you will notice at once a very outstanding phenomenon. On the one hand, the differences between the actual individuals are extremely obvious; on the other, the portraits or visual records of these individuals, relatively speaking, show a pronounced resemblance. In the painted portraits there is a *reversal* of the outstanding characteristics of reality, namely, the unique differences between each individual are considerably minimized. This experiment will hold with all realistic artists in varying degrees.

Suppose, however, that five of the most realistic portrait painters be assigned to make portraits of one particular model, and that all conditions—pose, light, etc.—are as similar as possible for each artist. In each result, we shall see what we are in the habit of calling a "good likeness." Next we repeat the experiment with similar conditions, only this time we have five competent Photographers make a "portrait" of the very same model. The differences between the five Photographs will be considerably less than the differences between the five paintings. Furthermore, the degree of similarity between the model and the portraits is considerably greater in the case of the Photographs. It is true, of course, that just as great differences could be obtained between five Photographs. Therefore, let us phrase the problem this way: the reverse cannot be accomplished—no painter can produce works that can exceed the Photograph in similarity to the model. Because the Camera, when handled competently, will always exceed the painter with his primitive handicraft tools in producing more objective and so more scientifically accurate recordings.

Of course it can be claimed, correctly enough, that the Camera can also be used to produce fantasies. The Camera, after all, is not an infallible instrument: much depends, as with so many human inventions, upon the discrimination and competence of the humans who use it. Nevertheless, when used properly, the Camera's record of light is incomparably more objective and so more reliable in its reports than any other recording method.

Finally: compare a group of portraits by any painting artist to a group by any other painting artist. You will find between these two groups the unique differences that one would expect to find between individuals. However, this is not due solely to the differences between the various subjects of both groups of paintings but largely to the personality differences between the artists concerned. This is the very factor which can operate more freely when primitive tools are used and which prevents the artist from securing the efficiency of the Camera. Such experiments illustrate the fact that painted portraits are partly a recording of the characteristics of the subject, partly a recording of the artist's individuality! These factors vary to that degree that the painting artist is or is not interested in recording the subject as he actually appears. But strive as he may, the artist cannot exercise the *degree* of neutrality which is possible and to a great extent unavoidable when a mechanical instrument like the Camera is employed. Inevitably he puts his personality into the recording of nature by projecting himself into the makeup of nature. Hence the battle cry of the "Knights of the Brush" as they rush out of their tents—that they are "human" recorders, and that the Photographer with his Camera is a "mere machine"—is actually the confession of a handicap on their part. And so here again we have another reversal of popular notions on the subject.

But artists, critics, etc. generally assume that this projection of the artist's personality into his works is but another manifestation of the alleged extraordinary power and visual acuity, etc., which only the artist is able to exercise. Through this power the artist is presumably enabled to see things in "reality" which we ordinary mortals cannot. While artists usually have a better trained visual ability than most, this is no license for accrediting existence to visual phenomena which even the artist has never seen before, at least in the manner in which they appear on his canvas.

This is particularly applicable to those present day portrait painters who are mainly concerned with making money, for such artists make short work of what is and is not seen; they simply make sure to see what their subjects want them to see. Result: the client is afterwards able to discover a most remarkable personality in the painting, one he may or may not have suspected he possessed. However, when in doubt, the ordinary mirror is suggested as an excellent check for rectifying any illusions which may arise in such titilating situations.[31]

---

31. Humorously enough, the Academic type "beautifies" his subject, whereas the "Modern" prefers to distort in the very opposite direction. We shall, in the proper place, pursue the peculiar "soul-state" of these latter kinds of portraits. Here we are only concerned with the rumor that a "soul-state" exists in Academic portraits.

In short, the painter can only try to do what the Photographer does, without hope of ever approaching the accuracy and efficiency of the results obtained with the Camera. *Whatever the painter tries to do that is unobtainable with the Camera, then to that very extent his paintings fail to correspond to the reality being recorded.* Therefore, the contention is false that the painter can secure a more complete record of reality than is possible for the Photographer. Such art is now a closed chapter in art history, and to continue it can only further propagate harmful fantasy. On this latter problem we shall have more to say elsewhere.

Before Daguerre's invention, the realistic quest by means of the old handicraft method produced useful survival in the evolution of art. Soon after this, however, the results produced became obsolete and today are incomparably inferior to Photographs. The appearance of the Camera marked the first major change in art mediums since the dawn of art history. It has altered the course of the old quest for realistic recordings into undreamed of achievements.

It should be made clear that in the present discussion we are concerned only with those handicraft arts which are competing with the function of the Camera. What we have said about realistic painting should not be taken in any sense as an evaluation of such art in the past, since the past was without a Camera. We are considering only those artists who, when perfected Cameras are available, continue to make more or less literal recordings of nature.

All other types of art, mainly those which distort nature in one way or another, will be considered later in relation to this problem. The great painting artists saw, either consciously or otherwise, that painting had reached the pinnacle of its achievement and had come to the end of its potentialities to record nature accurately. They understood that men cannot simply repeat that which has already been accomplished and still produce useful developing work. Therefore, they sought for another direction in which the art of painting could develop. This direction, as we shall soon see, was Impressionism, with its inevitable subsequent developments.

The problems of depicting the appearances of nature were not to be solved with the old primitive copying method of handicraft, but with the modern up-to-date method of recording or registering light with a Machine. Thus the problem of the Camera artists was to seek ever more accurate Machines for permitting the capture—the direct *recording* of light.

Painting had once extended the recording scope possible with sculpture; now the Camera had extended once more man's ability to record ever more accurate and ever more extensive aspects of visual reality. In the development of Photography, as in that of previous art mediums, there was progress from static to dynamic recordings—that is, from "stills" to motion-pictures.

A Frenchman, Lumière, made the first "moving" Photographs, one of which recorded a locomotive speeding directly toward the Camera. The first audience to view this Film is said to have rushed for the doors as the train approached. One of the first strips of moving-Film made in this country recorded a somewhat similar phenomenon—cavalry charging in the direction of the Camera.

Soon, however, the story-telling Film made its appearance. It conveyed its message solely by means of the visual actions depicted, and in order to do this adequately, the action was considerably forced and exaggerated. The direct consequence of this attempt to convey non-visual material by visual means alone was a distortion of actual reality. Because the entire communication load had to be carried by the visual level without the assistance of sound, silent pictures were largely incapable of direct, natural action. In the beginning this could not be avoided.

Sound pictures were first attempted two years after the appearance of Daguerre's invention, and there were many subsequent efforts to solve the problem by men who felt the need for capturing more accurate records of reality. But for many years inventors occupied with sound-picturization in Films were considered as fools seeking the impossible or the useless, and all their efforts were discouraged by the business interests involved. (Though man throughout his history has been doing the "impossible," few believe in its achievement, even when finally achieved.) Moreover, the "knowing" ones predicted that such an invention, if it were possible, would not be wanted by "the people." As a result of all this, the slow development of sound-picturization delayed the evolution of the moving-picture. Slowly and cautiously, in the good old conservative manner, a longer and more devious route was taken in order to increase realism. In those places where the visual level failed to make clear the intended meanings, written titles were scattered throughout the Film; in other words, literature came into the Film as a substitute for science! [32]

Eventually, however, sound for Films was perfected enough to be presented to the public, and thus another step was taken towards more realistic recordings. At first the limiting effect of the sound equipment then available considerably staticized the action of the pictures; progress was again delayed until this problem was faced and solved. In the silent pictures the visual-level had been over-emphasized out of all proportion to reality. Now in the new sound-pictures the sound-level was over-emphasized and our ears were pounded into deafness by the naive attempt to make the auditory-level carry the major load and compensate for the temporarily limited operation imposed upon the visual-level by the inflexibility of the sound equipment. After a long and unnecessarily wasteful period the two levels were synchronized properly and good sound-Films, at least technically, were achieved. Today they are practically the only type being made; *dynamic, visual-sound* recordings are an accepted fact.

And thus the Camera has been developed to the point that it can produce exactly the kind of record which the painter claims, but actually cannot produce—the depiction of many points in time-space. Through the use of the *moving*-Film, a record can be made which reports many aspects of any subject. And if we employ a sound-Camera we are able to create a life-like visual-sound record of the dynamic character of actual reality. In this manner it becomes possible to collect dynamic visual-sound histories which can project the past into the present and future far better than any other recording method that man has produced in all his history. With the Camera it became possible to achieve what the painter is only under the delusion of producing—records of numerous time-space aspects of the individual or event; and these are not achieved, as the painter attempts to do, by pushing these various aspects into an unreal mold of a single time-space static context. The moving-Film can record the many time-space points into a continuous series of pictures that correspond to a startling degree to the dynamic structure of the visual phenomena recorded.

The most recent development which has emerged from Photography, and the developments in auditory communication, is Television, which promises to produce the most remarkably realistic records that man has ever dreamed of. Television is the present day high point in the development of Photography in the wider historic sense, and of the Camera in the recent specific sense.

These recording devices—the Camera, static and dynamic, and Television—like most of man's inventions within the last two centuries, have potentialities for increasing or decreasing the sanity of mankind. But whether a Machine produces madness or sanity, the blame cannot be put upon the Machine, but upon the men who use it and upon all of us who permit them so to use it.

So far the sanest use of the static and dynamic Camera has been in the field of science. Scientists have far surpassed artists in grasping and using the tremendous constructive potentialities of Photography. The Camera is used in criminology, in all kinds of industries, in aerial and submarine Photography. Without it all branches of medicine would be disastrously curtailed, for medical workers are coming to rely less and less upon unaided vision and more and more upon extra-neural seeing—X-ray Photography, micro-Photography, etc. Many crucial experiments going on today would literally come to a standstill without the

32. Nevertheless it was in this period that this country produced its first great artists: the two Architects, Louis Sullivan and Frank Lloyd Wright; and the Film director, D. W. Griffith. All were artists of the Machine mediums. The significance of this will be considered in later chapters.

80. Shot from film, Intolerance, 1916, by D. W. Griffith. Museum of Modern Art Film Library, New York.

assistance of various kinds of Photography. Paleontology, entomology, botany, mineralogy, geology, geography, geodesy, ethnography, anthropology, archeology, meteorology, zoology, astronomy, are only a few of the fields which rely heavily on Photography of one sort or another.

It would seem that the artist would also do well to adopt a scientific attitude towards the use of the Camera's potentialities. Unfortunately, the few artists who now realize the potentialities peculiar to Photography and motion-pictures as distinct from the other arts must be satisfied with only occasional opportunities to give full expression to their knowledge. For in the fields of "art," where the Camera is not enmeshed in the money fixation of Film producers, it is held back by those "artistic" individuals who think in terms of the Camera's primitive progenitor—painting.

It is these "artistic" ones, for instance, who rhapsodize about the silence of the early Films as an "artistic" asset, and applaud that phase in which written titles supplemented the visual level. They do this because they are continuing to *identify* the moving-Film with the older, more primitive recording device of painting. Instead of looking ahead at what realistic recording could become, they prefer to look back at what it once was. If they recognized the *functional* differences between the new art medium—the Films— and the art produced by the old medium—painting—they might discover the necessity for a scientific attitude to achieve future progress. But these "artistic" souls are like those conservatives who in 1839 hailed painting as perfection enough and insisted that the Camera was a degradation of "art." The main impetus behind such evaluations, conscious in some cases, unconscious in most, has been a drive, not toward the creation of more perfection in *realism,* but toward more "perfection" in *fantasy creations.* The fact is that the old silent pictures were attractive to the majority precisely to that degree of fantasy, and so escape, which they were able to fabricate. Those Films which strove to face reality, to depict it as accurately as that was possible on the visual level alone, were, with few exceptions, the least popular. And this is still true. For in the fantasy world of escape, events and human actions were shown, the like of which had never been and could never be seen in actual reality.

The tremendous attraction of fantasy was demonstrated by the first reactions of the general public when sound-Films were introduced. As some had predicted, the audiences, conditioned to experiencing that particular kind and degree of fantasy inevitable in silent pictures, were, temporarily at least, very annoyed. There were reports of angered patrons who left their seats and demanded the return of their money; they were angered because their idols spoke with a human voice as they themselves did.

Here again there was a difficulty over the two levels of reality, just as in any art form: (1) The realistic aspect, i.e., the correspondence of the recorded object with that which was recorded. The fact that actual human and other forms were recorded in actual motion comprised the realistic aspect of the silent Films; it was a great advance in realism over the still Photographs, lending so much realism that even the unnatural actions of the actors were accepted as reality. Thus during the early days when movies were shown in western towns, it was not unusual for cowboys to pull out their guns and help shoot the "villain," so completely were they captured by the particular "reality" of the Film records. (2) But there still remained the level of the "reality" of the art object as such, regardless of its relationship to the reality it represented. The unnatural, ideographic mold into which the action of the Film's contents was forced in order to compensate for the absence of the audible spoken word, produced a great degree of a particular type of fantasy. The vast majority of the Film spectators unconsciously felt this. Francis X. Bushman, one of the "stars" of silent Film days, has related an incident which well illustrates this aspect. He told a newspaper reporter that, "somebody got the idea of booking me into the so-called theaters along with one of my pictures. After the show I'd come out on the stage and say a few words. I remember how ignorant the people were in the small Pennsylvania towns. When I stepped in front of the screen they were scared of me—a puppet come to life. If I touched a child they'd grab it away for fear it would be cursed." [33] The Film had made an unreal object out of the actor; hence the fear of the latter when seen in person. Hence also the original resentment of sound-Films. The addition of sound further closed the gap between the reality of the object represented and the art object, thus further decreasing the old fantasy experiences.

On close examination it will be found that in every case of a change from one medium to

33. Excerpt from *PM,* September 24, 1944; copyrighted by The Newspaper PM, Inc., New York.

another—from Sculpture to Painting, from Painting to Photography, from Still to Motion-Pictures, from Silent to Sound-Films—the majority have wanted to hold on to the unrevised old ways and damn the new, because the appearance of the latter in each case cut away some portion of fantasy-reality from their lives.

But the motion-pictures, in spite of technical advances, still tend for the most part—just as does present day painting—toward fantasy. Since the majority of Films are primarily concerned with depicting events which never have happened and never can happen in actual reality, outside of a Film set, they act as an opiate to release one from actual reality—a reality which is difficult for many who can think on high levels and even more difficult for the many who must spend their whole lives scrambling for a monotonously bare existence. Through the opiate of the Films these people are wafted into a world where all ends in an erotic, artificial, if temporary happiness. It is a vicious pathological circle in which one escapes for two or three hours a world to which he must then return; this cycle is repeated and repeated and nothing is resolved. The Film makers do almost nothing to help us face or try to solve the problems of or enjoy the benefits of actual reality and thus to create a better world in which to enjoy living.

For a certain sum of money they peddle Film-drug fantasies to every part of the world, under the guise of "entertainment." These productions called "entertainment," however, have turned out to be the initial and formative stage of political propaganda Films—or perhaps we might say that the fantasy direction in the entertainment Films has materialized into what is commonly called propaganda and the picture makers of Hollywood are largely responsible for showing the way towards this bastard utilization of the Films. For they did what almost every propaganda Film maker strives to do—to make the world appear to be a better or a different place than it actually is. The world of reality is changed into a "beautiful" world of fantasy, catering to all the frustrated ambitions of people the world over. Thus the strictly "entertainment" Films actually do formulate public opinion, even though some advocates of "entertainment," through ignorance or hypocrisy, maintain that Films should not do so.

Many examples may be found of the influence which movies exert upon the lives of those who attend them, from their smoking habits to the furnishing of their homes, etc. Film manufacturers are well aware of this and exploit their product by selling under-cover advertising space in them. Thus in 1942 it was reported that: "Western Union, Remington Rand, Lipton's Tea, the makers of Ritz crackers and of Bromo-Seltzer—pay high fees to three successful promoters in the movie capital who have a virtual monopoly on getting plugs for manufacturers into the pictures." [34]

If there are any doubts as to the results the Films have upon audiences, read the following from the article just quoted: "When Charles Boyer, in *Love Affair,* throatily ordered pink champagne for Irene Dunne, he started a minor revolution in the wine industry. Immediately restaurants all over the country were amazed by the demand for this exotic beverage. Thus, from Nome to Jacksonville, Hollywood stars lay down the law on fashions, manners, speech and behavior." [35]

"The experts find that the average spectator believes that the scenes and characters he sees in a movie are *authentic or typical* [emphasis ours]. Ninety percent of a large cross-section of moviegoers thought that *Mr. Smith Goes To Washington,* melodramatic fiction, gave an accurate picture of the United State Senate. So profound was the effect of this picture—which showed a gallant scoutmaster elected to the Senate and there battling corrupt politics—that in a Texas congressional district the Boy Scouts were able to campaign *their* scoutmaster, 31-year-old Gene Worley, into the House of Representatives. In a similar investigation, 65 percent believed that *Down Argentine Way*—a product of Hollywood's wildest imagination and bad taste—showed Argentines as they really were." [36]

Therefore, it was but a short step to convert the fantasy method of Film making deliberately into propaganda or political fantasy; a development which has reached its zenith in totalitarian states. The leaders of the latter nations also wished to depict "realities" which did not exist in order to pacify, delude

34. Frederic Sondern, Jr., with C. Nelson Schrader: "Hollywood Handles Dynamite," *Reader's Digest,* January, 1942, pp. 95-96; reprinted from *The Commonweal,* December 12, 1941.

35. Ibid., p. 95.

36. Ibid., p. 96.

and exploit the masses, thus keeping them under control. They quickly converted the basic Hollywood formula to serve the purpose of direct political action. Their Films also showed the "people" that the world was a beautiful place in which to live, but instead of the world of Hollywood or America, it was that particular corner of the world in which each totalitarian slave lived. In this sense, the people of Hollywood, inadvertently or otherwise, became the progenitors of still another and even more barbaric use of the Films.

It is of interest, therefore, that in totalitarian countries the number of "entertainment" Films from Hollywood has been definitely limited by import regulations in order to remove a strong competitor to the local propaganda-escape Films. For Hollywood showed a world of "rugged individualism" where all were free to become rich, independent, powerful, loved by fabulously beautiful women and the like. The anarchy of the individual is a far more attractive theme than the autocracy of the state; consequently the dictators have to control carefully the number and kind of American Films permitted in their countries.

On the other hand, the leaders of the Russian government have been aware perhaps more than any other government of the force and punch which "actual reality" can convey.[37] They were little concerned with "entertainment" such as other nations indulged in. Hence they very pointedly utilized the political effectiveness of the "feeling" of reality by clever manipulations of it. For instance, they stressed with tremendous exaggeration that part of "reality" with which they were particularly concerned, but depicted it in the way they wished others to see it. This was done by eliminating all other *relevant* factors. That which was detrimental to the message being conveyed was either avoided entirely or distorted to suit the prejudices motivating the Film's making. It mattered little how important these factors might have been. Reality was cut or tailored to order! All this was done in the name of something called "dialectical materialism" or "the end justifies the means" and many other such word-noises. But let us call it propaganda, by which we understand the art of making things appear to be what in actuality they are *not;* a form of fantasy which manipulates reality to exploit the naivete of the masses. Because certain factors which are otherwise actually to be found in reality are exaggerated and manipulated, the submissive observer is given such an effect of "reality" in such a strong dose that in the resultant emotional splurge he is rendered incapable of realizing that factors have been left out or distorted to suit the intentions of the Film makers. Thus his thinking direction is hypnotized and its eventual course determined. Such propaganda has produced political priests and missionaries whose degree of fanaticism and barbarism has been equalled only in the Dark Ages.

Recall the analysis of the cowboys shooting at the Film villain and the Film audience's fear of the actual person of the actor; here we have examples of just how these "realistic" Russian Films are constructed to function, for it is these two levels which are *consciously* manipulated. Moreover, the bulk of their Films up to just before the last World-Civil-War, have remained silent. This was doubtless largely intentional and not due merely to lack of equipment, as some have assumed. Thus, although on first observation Russian movies appeared to be very realistic, actually the reality was changed into something it was not. A similar sort of behavior is to be found in the Russian use of so-called realistic painting which is employed solely for propaganda purposes. The masses are depicted as healthy, well-fed individuals, admiring their saviors, the heroic leaders—and the depictions give at first glance the feeling of being very realistic. But the leaders and the types of individuals or automatons that the leaders demand are actually depicted according to the old ideal formula—the leader is made to appear extremely handsome, kindly, god-like, and the people happy, "super" men and women. Thus although presented in a "realistic" fashion, the depictions are distortions or fantasies of the actual reality.

The movies, both the Russian and the Hollywood type, serve a similar purpose and function as did the art of the medieval Church; they subject the masses to the control of "priests" and their cohorts. The Christians of medieval times deliberately used forms unlike those of reality in order to convince people of the existence of another world; today the movie makers can use the most realistic representation of the forms of actual reality in order to convince us that what does not exist does exist. In both cases an art con-

37. Just before World-Civil-War II, however, the Russian rulers began to employ the opiate attraction of the Hollywood formula, in the sense of the "boy-meets-girl" sort of thing, but still directed to their previous political ends.

tents is used which is derivative from actual forms with which everyone is familiar—forms of the real world. But the Christians presented these forms as being distinct from the original, that is, as representative not of this world, but of another. The movie makers today also present deliberately manipulated forms from the real world, but do not, like the Christians, present them as representative of another world; they are presented as being of this world, yet actually they are (although in a lesser degree than in the Christian art) a false report of reality. The Christians elementalized the situation; they got their fantasy over by distorting real forms. The movie makers get their fantasy over by a seeming reality, and have far outstripped the Church in the realm of fantasy.[38]

The medium of motion-pictures still has, however, certain technical shortcomings which permit regressive manipulations of reality for propaganda and fantasy purposes. The reality imperfections of the medium are well utilized by those who pervert it for various types of fantasy, be they political, religious, or ambiguously called "entertainment." We have already mentioned some of the factors involved in this problem. One of these is the matter of color. The black and white of the Films is extremely unreal and so far there has been a persistent tendency, where color has been used, toward color-fantasy rather than color-realism. There seems to be a deliberate attempt to secure certain color effects found in particular types of past painting. To be sure the Camera method has grown out of the painting arts, but the new art still has a hangover from the past methods. If we could only realize that the Camera has grown *out of* the art of painting, then we could better realize that the task of Films is not to imitate it but to continue to develop from, not back towards painting.

But realism continues to step in brusquely and break up the dreams, the fantasies of another world. First, the still-Photograph broke in upon the fantasy of painting; then the moving-Photograph upon the fantasy of the stills; then sound-Photographs upon the silent pictures. Each step wiped a bit of fantasy from men's minds. Color, the next step, is yet to be released from the Midas grip of fantasy. The fact that color has been the last factor to be developed in Photography is significant, for thus the developments through which Photography has passed are similar to those we have witnessed in the other mediums: first form, then movement, then color.

If we look back at each step of advance in the Films, we recognize a phenomenon already observed in the history of art. Each bit of progress achieved more correspondence to the structure of actual reality. Were this fact recognized, Film progress would suddenly be accelerated beyond our expectations. It would then be seen that color-Films *must* be achieved as such, and not as imitations of the primitive medium of painting.

Both color and form-space experiments were already making much progress before the recent World-Civil-War. However, we shall probably have to wait until the form-space factors have been perfected as far as that is possible in black and white Films before the cautious ones realize that to bring this to proper perfection, literal color-realism is necessary. In time someone in the Film business will "discover" that *accurate* color-realism is the objective to achieve. At first it will be howled down just as sound-Films were; then finally accepted by "the people" and the new type of Film will probably be glorified into some form of abuse, until new changes arrive once more to alleviate the abuse and contribute new developments. When that time comes, color-Films will have achieved the perfection of the ordinary mirror, which so far remains the most accurate nature-recording method in the possession of man. When color-realism has been perfected, this will automatically produce more perfection in the form-space characteristics of the recordings.

It will also be found that the square edge of the projection screen needs to be changed to a shape which better corresponds to the *function* of human vision. For example, when we use our eyes, the area visualized is never framed in a definite, sharp, or even square border; our peripheral vision blends the edges. Were we to put this effect into the Films, realism would be considerably increased.

The question of course arises as to just what effect these achievements will have upon the use of the Film. It should make possible the elimination of many prevalent regressive manipulations of reality,

38. In one small town where the author lived the movie houses were closed on certain evenings when important church affairs occurred.

in the sense that every advance in accuracy of recording has resulted eventually in decreasing the fantasy that has arisen in the particular medium, be it language, Films, or what not. And following such developments a general revival of interest in the problems of reality should result; a renewed wave of enthusiasm will appear for making the moving-pictures more similar in structure to the structure of reality. This isomorphic advance will naturally call for an entirely different use of Films.

No doubt with the new advances, new types of fantasy will slip in, but it is within the realm of possibility to prevent it. When we anticipate any advances, we need also to anticipate abuses that can arise; i.e., acquire predictability. Since more development is always possible, we need to recognize coherently and emphasize the means by which it is obtained; in this case the structure of the Films must always be made more similar to the structure of that which is being depicted, and the means by which it is assimilated —that is, the structure and function of the observer—must be considered. Thus it will be possible to realize sane predictability in our attempts to modify progressively anything which is useful.

It is possible that most of the needed improvements we have suggested for the Films can be better achieved with Television. There is a definite possibility for this where the mechanical processes are concerned, and, as regards the social function of this medium, it would seem that the opportunities for advance are even more considerable with Television than with the moving-pictures. For Television does not have the developmental limitations of the Films and eventually it could displace motion-pictures. Television, in fact, is the logical outcome of Photography, as the latter is the outcome of painting. With it man will be able to produce the most perfected types of reality recordings, along with many new potentialities not to be found in past methods.

One of the great advantages of Television is that it can be used in each individual home. This automatically eliminates certain disadvantages connected with the necessity of exhibiting recordings to large motion-picture audiences seated over a large area. In other words, the observer can easily adjust his position to the projection screen, thus making it possible to televize objects large enough so that the human form can be shown *life-size*. The relationships between the position of the observer and the observed (Television screen) can be such that the recordings will convey the life-size effects one would normally see if at the scene of the actual event. The projection screen would need to be as large as the entire visual area of the human eye, with a blended *peripheral* border to conform with the function of the eye. Such a screen would permit the depiction of the largest and smallest objects just as they would normally *appear* to the eyes if the observer were at the actual scene itself. In other words, the size of the screen, i.e., the area of vision, would be large enough so that the effect of natural vision would be obtained. Such changes would naturally increase tremendously the realism of recordings of visible phenomena and, just as in previous communicational developments, human life and relations would consequently be altered.

Such an arrangement is impossible where large audiences are involved. The objective of visual recordings is to convey an equally perfect record for each individual observing them, but this is impossible with any mass audience—in a movie or at the actual scene of the original recorded event. Television is a remarkably perfect answer to this situation, in that each one of us can have the very best "ring-side seat" at the scene of any event transmitted from anywhere in the world or universe.

There is an unfortunate probability, however, that the life-size Television screen will become the monopoly of business groups—those who run the movie and radio industries. The case of the development of motion-pictures has well demonstrated that in our present culture the money-desires of business groups are far more important than the usefully creative achievements of human beings. They probably will see to it that the individual home, where the Televizing instrument belongs, will be fitted with only a small screen, just large enough to be more or less bearable for the undiscriminating majority, but not large enough to compete with the movie screen in theaters. Along with such a cramped visual record, one that will aggravate rather than satisfy, the attempt will probably again be made, as in the development of Films, to have sound carry the major load. But as in the case of the Films, so in Television the sound and vision must finally be oriented to correspond as much as possible to actual reality.

Pure rationalism

Half-way measures will continue, however, as long as consumers are willing or able to tolerate hackneyed solutions of Television for the home. It may finally become intolerable for the simple reason that sound for Television will be "life-size," so to speak, while the vision will not. It is to be hoped that the resulting crucial discrepancy between the sound and visual experiences of Television will eventually aggravate the user to the point where business mentalities will be compelled to do what they should have done in the first place, namely, produce as much correspondence as possible between sound and vision. In sound as well as in vision an improvement over that in the Films can also be obtained; there will only be the need to orient the sound to its natural volume, since the observers who listen will not be spread over the large area of a movie theater. This correspondence to reality must also be sought where the time element is concerned, so that it will be possible to see-hear events when they occur.

For this is another important advantage of Television, that with it events may be recorded realistically, not only in their visual-sound characteristics, but also with a far more realistic time-space element. That is, the difference in time between the actual event and the televized recording result involves fractions of a second, just as with radio. Indeed with Television the art of recording reality has become a most highly developed form of communication.

How far man has developed in regard to visual communication can be realized by recalling primitive man's rough, hand-made pictures sent by foot-runner to their destination. Compare this to Television, where a communication is established by means of the transmission of *actual light-rays* as well as *actual sound-waves* within a fraction of a second after they have occurred. In the past, human contact was localized: one could speak only to a limited number of people at a given time or in a life-time. In writing about the phenomenon of Television, Mumford says: "Plato defined the limits of the size of a city as the number of people who could hear the voice of a single orator: today those limits do not define a city, but a civilization." [39] And in the future any one man, potentially, can speak to all men on the earth and be seen and heard at the same time. Thus by extra-neural devices, the former direct contact of person to person, between speaker and audience, may be recovered, only this time it can be on an international scale. [40] As Mumford has pointed out: "As a result, communication is now on the point of returning, with the aid of mechanical devices, to that instantaneous reaction of person to person with which it began; but the possibilities of this immediate meeting, instead of being limited by space and time, will be limited only by the amount of energy available and the mechanical perfection and accessibility of the apparatus." [41]

Educationally the potentialities of Television are stupendous; the possible consequences are at present almost inconceivable. For example, a Russell or an Einstein could lecture to the students of all universities in the world at the same time. The student body would be a world student body. Our best educators could teach in all the universities to all students within the space of a single life-time. Moreover, these lectures could be "canned" and re-broadcast throughout the future of man, for further study and analysis. [42] Einstein's now famous initial lecture on the theory of relativity would not have disappeared into the air, remaining only in the less effective form of printed words, but could have been *delivered* again at any time in the future.

Childish Rote impression of Learning

In regard to the further educational potentialities beyond Television, it might be of interest to consider a probable development. Imagine that one of the greatest surgeons in the world is performing

39. Lewis Mumford: *Technics and Civilization*, p. 241.

40. In fact, it is imaginable that a device could be invented which would automatically transform the language of the speaker being televised into any other language desired.

41. Mumford, op. cit., p. 239.

42. This could, of course, have been achieved by the motion-pictures, but Hollywood "stars" are more important than Einsteins, Russells, etc. Something considerably worse can happen to Television if dictators confiscate it.

the most recent, extraordinary operation upon the human brain. While he and his assistants are working, the entire procedure is recorded by a new device, capable of depicting the operation afterwards in its three-dimensional, life-size, color-sound characteristics. This is done simply by means of light, which is not thrown upon a screen, but projected into actual space in a room. Copies of this record can be sent to all the medical schools and institutions the world over, just as medical papers and moving-pictures are now sent. Here the students expose the record and this is what they see and hear:

The operating table, the patient, the nurses and doctors appear in life-size form-space, and life-like color-sound, as though the original operation were occurring once more in the very room in which the record is being exposed. The doctors and nurses are seen each performing their respective tasks and every instruction and comment of the head surgeon can be heard as he performs this latest advance in brain surgery.

As for the students who are studying the scene before them, instead of merely sitting in rows of chairs watching, they move all around the scene before them, even into the very scene itself! The student has even more freedom to observe than would be possible at the original operation, for he can step right into the body-image of the surgeon, putting his eyes into a position over the surgeon's hands and watching what he does as well as if his eyes were those of the surgeon.

In any case, Television will tremendously extend the *personal* influence of single individuals, and this influence of course could be for better or worse—depending! Mumford has written in regard to the use of such mechanical apparatus, that: "in the long run, they promise not to displace the human being but to re-focus him and enlarge his capacities. But there is a proviso attached to this promise: namely, that the culture of the personality shall parallel in refinement the mechanical development of the machine." [43] In short, all the technical realism of the Films and/or Television will not protect us from those who wish to use these inventions to broadcast lies. It should not be forgotten that the most powerful form of fantasy in the motion-pictures has been obtained by a particular use of "realism"—see any totalitarian Film. Therefore, we must not lose sight of the fact that the Film and Television can be made to present disastrous fantasies.

We have seen throughout history that the abilities of artists do not exist in a vacuum, that art is a participant in the rest of culture. No matter what artists can do or are potentially capable of doing, there must always be a corresponding change on the general cultural level if any marked advance in art is to be achieved. Therefore, it is useless to expect much rapidity of advance, even if the technical means are at hand, unless the general social-behavior of both the consumer and producer of art is also advanced. So long as life is so miserable for the majority (and we are not here referring only to mere physical sustenance), so long will there be a demand for fantasy-escapes from a miserable world.

Obviously Films and Television can have a tremendously educative power and could be one of our most effective instruments for encouraging a "world view" attitude on the part of humans toward each other. But the function and development of art are determined, as we have already emphasized, by man's interpretation of reality about and within him. The function and development of art were first determined by a magic interpretation of reality; next by a religious interpretation and then by a philosophical one. The arts of Photography and Television have been developed by a scientific interpretation, and if they are to continue a sane development, there must continue to be a scientific interpretation of reality underlying their use.

All this has finally brought us to the close of the first great epoch of man's art, from PICTO-*graphs* to PHOTO-*graphs*—the epoch in which man has striven to record the "art of nature."

We have now traced the development of Painting, and of Painting into Photography, of Pho-

43. Mumford, op. cit., p. 241.

81. Harold Edgerton, Multiple-flash photo

tography into moving-Films, of Films into Television, and have seen how the first "scratches" of the earliest members of the human race developed into countless remarkable methods for recording various aspects and levels of nature's reality, not only macroscopic and telescopic, but microscopic as well. We have seen that the writing-recording method of Paleolithic man—Pictographs—developed into the art of writing and in recent times reached a high state of perfection in the Photograph. Again, as in Pictographic times, man can write his history with pictures, but now with the superior moving-pictures, with moving-light-sound-pictures.

The first phase in man's efforts to record the "art of nature" was concluded when the 5th century B.C. Greeks perfected the sculptured depiction of the human form in general; later Greeks depicted various classes of humans and finally the Romans achieved accurate portraits of specific individuals in stone. Subsequently there occurred similar transitions in painting—the Classical, the Romantic, and the Realistic periods. Whereas the sculptural cycle concluded with the accurate portrayal of the individual in stone, the painting cycle concluded with the highly accurate recording of the individual object in the Photograph. It is a long step from the time when days, weeks, months, or years were spent on some single recording of nature, to the present when a single recording can be made in one hundred-millionth of a second.

*To what purpose?
mechanical image?*

*Fact of mechanism,
nothing accepted!*

Thus the first major epoch of art culminated in an accomplishment which had been one of the paramount concerns of Leonardo; he had correctly predicted the future of art when he wrote: "The mind of the painter should be like a mirror which always takes the color of the thing that it reflects, and which is filled by as many images as there are things placed before it." [44] For with the Camera the recording artist now has a "canvas" that captures (like the mirror) but makes permanent records of the light-rays which objects reflect into the human world of vision. With this accomplishment a whole new aspect of vision is flung wide open for investigation. Man's consciousness of vision is now greatly altered and considerably enlarged. With the assistance of the scientifically constructed mechanical eye man can now see an image which the human eye could not heretofore capture and retain long enough to hold in visual consciousness—not to mention the tremendous amount of visual phenomena that was never before visible to human sight.

Actually the Camera and Television represent the perfection of various factors we have watched develop in the art of sculpture and painting. In the Photograph we see: (1) the perfection of the forms of reality; (2) the development of movement and sound. In the future we should see: (1) the realization of natural size in vision and volume of sound, as well as time correspondence; and (2) the replacing of idealistic color of present day Films with natural color as much as possible. When this has been done we will have seen the problems of form and color, as they have evolved first in sculpture and then into painting, finally reach their greatest developments in the various types of present day Photography, but especially in future Television. Then it should be possible for even the "artistic souls" to realize that literal recording is the height of achievement in that form of art where the depiction of nature's appearances is the objective sought. Then we shall realize that idealism, in form or color, was only a step towards literal realism, not a goal or final objective.

It should no longer be necessary to ask the all too frequent but inane question, "Of what use is art?" We have seen the very crucial, varied roles which art has played in previous cultures. But there is another aspect to consider—the totality of all past effort in art; if we were deprived of this, there would be havoc in our present mode of life, if not the destruction of man's present civilization! If there had not been an activity such as art, man, even with his science, would not have produced a Camera, for without the activity of art to influence his vision, he would have learned to look at the world in a far different manner. Men had to be interested in the direct act of observation peculiar to art before they could think of recording their observations with scientific methods. Artists were the first to invoke the scientific attitude in the field of vision.

Through the efforts primarily of artists, men now possess an extra-neural eye that captures and then files for future use accurate records of a great variety of light reports. Today the light-sound events of time-space can be recorded in life-size, light-sound terms. In the past the best that men could do was to copy light with the crude paint-method and copy sound with the non-sound medium of writing. Today the work of the painter and the scribe is done with a single, highly developed Machine that does not employ the old primitive method of copying but a method by which it is possible to register the imprint made by actual light-sound events that occur in the universe.

In spite of all abuses Photography and Television are playing a major, crucially indispensable part in building a new civilization. Of this Oliver Reiser has written: "Here and there we see evidence of a breaking with the old forms and techniques. But as we rise above the past, we experience its power to drag us back. None the less—and in spite of setbacks—we do glimpse the form of a new world order emerging: a world-state guided by a world sensorium and animated by a social consciousness born of science. Through radio, telegraph, rapid transit, and newspapers, a consciousness-of-the-world is being transformed into a world-consciousness. The new organ of integration is gradually crystallizing its own skeleton. Eventually the political, economic, and religious motives will again unite, producing a philosophical synthesis quite radical and startling in character.

"Let us see how this will come about.

"On the physical side, the world is growing into a new unity through manifold processes of integration. When the problem of wireless communication was solved, the range of man's auditory environ-

44. *Notebooks of Leonardo,* Vol. 2, p. 235.

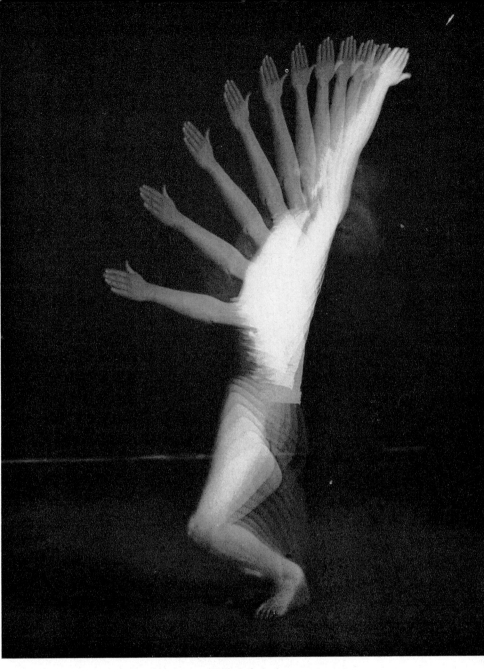

82. Harold Edgerton, Multiple-flash photo.

ment was enlarged to the point where we can now hear sounds at practically the same moment that they are produced in any other part of the world. The radio has thrown around the world a girdle that greatly extends man's environment. In a similar way the moving picture has projected man's visual world beyond the ordinary limitations of time. Events that happened in distant places and at former times can now be reproduced at will. Thus the instruments which enable us to transcend the normal restrictions of time and space not only are changing the content of our thought, but also are *intensifying our awareness*. The instruments of publicity—radio, newspaper, television, etc.—are now accepted institutions of society, and these are making us more aware of each other and of ourselves. By enlarging the sensory environment we are changing the inner life of the organism." [45]

In short, as the Films in their turn approach their limitations for further development, another medium is arising, gradually forming to carry still further the evolution of recording art—the Machine medium of Television. Today we live in a world of Machine-art!

45. Oliver L. Reiser: *The Promise of Scientific Humanism,* pp. 278-279, Oskar Piest, New York, 1940. Permission of Creative Age Press.

255

CAMERA TO CUBISM

. . . . try to forget what objects you have before you, a
tree, a house, a field or whatever. 264

Claude Monet

If in London we are reproached for showing unfinished work—here [Paris] we are accused of having sick eyes, "the sickness of painters who see blue."
271   Camille Pissarro

13 TOWARDS A NEW CONTENT

But surely it is clear that we could not pursue our studies of light with much assurance if we did not have as a guide the discoveries of Chevreul and other scientists. I would not have distinguished between local color and light if science had not given us the hint; the same holds true for complementary colors, contrasting colors, etc. 271

Camille Pissarro

With the invention of the Camera we have witnessed the conclusion of one epoch of painting-history—that epoch predominantly characterized by the attempt to copy and create a permanent record of nature's appearances. In this epoch, as we saw, there were the successive stages of recording animals, humans, interiors, exteriors, etc., in fact the recording of nearly all the general macroscopic visual manifestations of the outside world. After taking over this recording function of past artists, the Photographers penetrated even further into the visual phenomena of nature, e.g., microscopic and telescopic Photography. Hence from this point on the painting artists in the old sense had finished their recording task.

But soon after the Camera was invented, a new phase of painting art appeared which was to develop into the realization of a heretofore minor, unconscious aspect of pre-Camera art. While this direction was new and different, it was nevertheless very related to the past. The rest of our history will be primarily concerned with this largely unconscious aspect of past arts as it gradually enters the consciousness of artists in modern times.

In all cultures the element of the subconscious plays a vital role. The past is related to the present and the present to the future, but so far few in any culture have been able consciously to predict the larger consequences which their art formulations would have upon future cultures. Yet within each culture there are subconscious factors which not only are affecting that culture, but are precisely those factors which the following generation perceives and consciously utilizes or rejects in the formation of the new culture. It is to our advantage to ferret out these unconscious elements and utilize them consciously in the observation and examination of art as it moves from one phase to the next. This is exactly what we have tried to do so far. In the new epoch we are now approaching, the character of the unconscious material has undergone considerable change; in the past it largely consisted of a striving to secure an ever more accurate recording of nature's art; after the Camera it consisted of the attempt to find a new contents for art.[1]

In short, "art" is a dynamic, ever-changing process. Every new art casts a new light upon the past and the future. But too few understand this properly and so we continue to impair our art experiences with true-for-all-time-definition-reactions. Even though our actual art experiences have changed, we can continue to react by verbal definition because of the arbitrary possibilities of language. On the verbal level, we can continue to abide by old or manufacture new absolute definitions, even though they may have *no basis in fact*. Under these circumstances, since our formulations do not correspond to the facts of experience, we inevitably impose static definitions upon a dynamic world of events. Because the world reality is a dynamic affair, each new generation is forced to revise the absolute formulations of its predecessors. But then each new generation repeats the mistake of the last one by trying to impose the new absolutes which they have fabricated upon those who come after them. So it will continue until we recognize that the behavior and experience of humans are not static, but part of the dynamic, asymmetrical

---

1. Here we are speaking of the consciousness of a culture as-a-whole, as distinct from the consciousness of individuals. In other words, the various periods of culture have exhibited a conflict between the real and the ideal; only individuals have taken a definite stand as regards the development of culture or art. But in the period we are now studying even the innovators are as yet largely unconscious of the new direction in which they are involved.

83. Edouard Manet, The Outlet of the Boulogne Harbor. Courtesy of the Art Institute of Chicago.

process of reality. Moreover, as Korzybski well shows, our language must also be changed in order that the symbols we use for communicational purposes *correspond* to changes we have made or are being forced to make by the demands of the ever-evolving new conditions. *Words are never things,* and to have any useful application at all, must correspond to something on the objective level. If these facts were realized, we could achieve better predictability.

We cannot repeat too often that the word "art" is not art! Nor is the term "art" a *label* for some one-valued constant, as it is commonly employed. It is a label for a *process* which is infinite-valued, dynamic and asymmetrical. What has been can never be again! We can see from our history so far that the label "art" is applied to a constantly changing affair in a constantly changing context. The term "art" is a many-valued variable and so it is ambiguous unless placed in a definite context indicating what aspect of the variable one is referring to when using the term. Or to use Korzybski's terminology, art is a "multi-ordinal" label!

Some readers may protest that so far in this history, art has been treated as a constant, since we claim that all art which *achieved progress* up to the Camera was an attempt to record reality accurately. To this we would reply that our alleged constant of realism was presented as in a continuum of *constant change*. At each stage of development a more or less common objective was being sought, but at the same time differing degrees of realistic recording were produced, determined by the increasing ability of man to visualize. The variables within the constant of "realism" would have been missed entirely, if, as is generally the case, we had regarded all this art within the confines of some static definition of "reality." Our use of the term was flexible and we recognized that its meanings varied (*as did the art*) with the times; and so it has been possible to present art history in a manner which coherently covers the actual

262

facts of art. To put it another way: our use of language was such that it was similar in structure to the structure of the facts which we symbolized with it. The flexible potentialities of our language must be utilized so that it will correspond to the modifications we are always compelled to make in the world of things symbolized with language.

With this in mind we are now ready to consider a new direction in art, which was another climactic repercussion of the Camera's invention upon the course of the hand-art of painting. It is significant that two major events in the art world occurred within the space of a year. One was the invention of a successful Camera in 1839; and the other was the publication by the scientist, Chevreul, the year before, of his "scientific theory of coloring." The first event clearly meant that the painting artist need no longer consider the recording of nature as his task, while the second event gave the artist coherent knowledge as to how to proceed in what was now to become the new task of painting.

The new direction in painting was initiated by a small group of artists working towards new values and goals which even today are understood very inaccurately, or at best inadequately. In our own times when we are in the midst of a climactic revision of the methods by which man has for so long oriented himself to the world about him and within him, it is rarely recognized that in the field of art these changes began with the invention of the Camera and Impressionism.

It was with the art of Impressionism that this other repercussion from the Camera, this other change from the past, definitely began. (It hardly seems an accident, therefore, that it was in the gallery of a Photographer—that of the famous Nadar—that the Impressionists were able to hold their first great exhibition in 1874.)

Before we examine Impressionism it will be necessary to note briefly what immediately preceded it. For a time most artists were influenced by the Camera product and utilized it in the attempt to increase realism in their own works. But though following the lead of the Camera, these artists were never able even to begin to approach its accuracy. Hence they turned to the one factor as yet untouched by the Camera, the factor of color. Leaning on this, they tried to compete with and outdo the Photograph. In short, the Camera artists, by invading and taking over the domain of recording the *forms* of nature, thus forced painting artists to transfer their interests and efforts, for a time at least, to the factor of color, a domain at first untouched by the Camera. As a result, a new kind of color-realism appeared, the forerunner of Impressionism. Realism was sought principally by means of local color, that is, the recording of the general color tone of the subject being depicted. Such painters did not try to record the precision of detail as is seen in the Photograph, for this they knew was futile. The results depended mainly upon the color-value effect. Hence freer painting methods were employed and the third dimension was no longer emphasized as it had been. In these particular works such a method resulted in a "blurred" painting technique, which on close examination, gave the effect of the subject's being "out of focus." But if one got far enough away from the painting, there even appeared to be precise detail, and it gave quite a realistic effect. The painter, using to the full the one advantage left to his medium, tried to compensate for and compete with the many advantages of the Photograph. With color carrying the main burden, such artists made an illusion, as it were, of an illusion.

The transition from these local colorists to the Impressionists is seen in the works of Edouard Manet. We find Manet slashing his paint across the canvas (figure 83), without the subtlety of those referred to above, and showing a definite concern and emphasis upon the problem of color-*light*. Manet, in fact, insists that, "The principal person in a picture is the light." [2] Moreover, to Manet it mattered little whether the subject was a "pineapple or a nude." We shall find his attitude to be very close to Claude Monet's. Manet was not only a friend of the Impressionists, but he left a decided imprint on their initial efforts toward Impressionism. The two principal factors in his work, the slashing paint stroke and the factor of light, are found in the developments of the Impressionists. In short, Impressionism did not burst upon the art scene; it developed gradually from the efforts of the artists who had preceded it.

In recent years it has become popular to credit Joseph Turner with being a forerunner of Impressionism. In fact a group of Impressionists sent him a letter acknowledging this to be the case.

2. As quoted by Camille Mauclair: *The French Impressionists,* p. 42, Duckworth and Co., London, E. P. Dutton and Co., New York, 1903.

84. J. M. W. Turner, The Slave Ship. Courtesy, Museum of Fine Arts, Boston.

But there were critical differences, in that the Impressionists were more scientific and Turner was more of a Romanticist (figure 84). Where the Impressionists were concerned with the understanding of nature's color-structure, Turner was more concerned with nature's light and color as a stimulant to intense flights of color-fantasy. Nevertheless, even though he was not concerned with the particular interests of the Impressionists, his work was valuable to those interests insofar as it played a part in encouraging and releasing them. He gave to color an importance never before accorded it.

The principal concerns of the Impressionists were with colors and their shapes. Monet, in giving some advice to a friend, had this revealing statement to make: "When you go out to paint, try to forget what objects you have before you, a tree, a house, a field or whatever. Merely think, here is a little square of blue, here an oblong of pink, here a streak of yellow, and paint it just as it looks to you, the exact color and shape, until it gives you your own naive impression of the scene before you."[3] He contended that nature's forms being those of trees, fields, etc., were an impediment to the attainment of his objective. Thus he is said to have expressed the wish to have been born blind and then suddenly to have acquired sight. Under such conditions he felt that it would be possible "to forget what objects you have before you."

However, Monet's wishes and evaluations to the contrary, the Impressionists did not actually strive to free themselves completely from the model. They got around the difficulty in the problem of nature's forms as much as possible by being very particular to choose subjects—usually landscapes—which allowed more freedom with nature forms than other subjects. And in that choice these artists had changed the traditional place and function of nature's subject-matter. In the past the artist's medium and

3. As quoted by Lilla Cabot Perry: "Reminiscences of Claude Monet," *The American Magazine of Art*, XVIII:120, March, 1927.

85. Claude Monet, Rouen Cathedral. Courtesy of The Metropolitan Museum of Art.

method had been revised with the primary object of conforming to the demands of recording more accurately the particular objects of nature to be depicted. But with Impressionism, as will gradually become more clear, this procedure was reversed; the artist subjugates the nature objects to the demands of the particular goal which he is seeking, regardless of the factor of realism as such. These new artists selected the subjects which most permitted them to exercise their particular interests, first in color and second in shapes. In short, *previously the object had stated the goal of the artist; with Impressionism the artist states the goal of the object. This is the crux and prime revolutionary import of Impressionism.* The significance of this change will become more clear as we realize the implications involved.

Putting this change in terms of the medium we find this: up to the advent of the Camera, artists (including the Idealists to a degree) had restricted the potentialities of their medium to the demands of the nature object, the demands of recording accurately. With Impressionism the nature object was subjected to the potentialities of the medium beyond those of accurate recordings. This opened up new possibilities. It is the failure to see exactly this point which has led to so much misunderstanding by those who pass Impressionism off as merely another phase of realism in art.

In any case, the new direction inaugurated by Impressionism finds the appearances of nature's objects in a secondary role. It was because of this change that Impressionism became the first major effort toward achieving a *man*-art goal in contrast to the former *nature*-art goal. Towards this then unachieved goal we shall find that the Impressionists' contribution consisted of preparing the factor of color for that objective, and not, as is commonly supposed, of understanding color simply in order to copy nature more accurately. If they had intended merely to achieve realism, they certainly would have been and could have been far more realistic than they were. Their most realistic work was done in their early formative years when they were painting in the "local color" manner. As they developed, it became apparent that realism was contrary to the objectives of these artists. As a matter of fact, the less realistic they were, the more satisfactory their color-results.

This becomes apparent if one observes Impressionistic paintings closely. Let us consider some specific works.

Most of us are familiar with the many church paintings which Monet made. Consider for a moment the one, now at the Metropolitan Museum, of the Rouen Cathedral (figure 85). This subject-matter, as compared to the customarily chosen sunlit landscape, would seem to be divested of the very quality of color which so interested the Impressionists. The answer to this seemingly paradoxical choice of subject can be found by recalling Monet's *attitude* expressed in a previously quoted statement (see page 264). The forms, or, as Monet saw them, the "shapes" of the church presented the artist with geometric shapes in which *there was more freedom to paint a "square of blue" or "an oblong of pink,"* etc. The *Architectural* shapes of a church provided him with an ideal opportunity to insert freely colors of his own choosing. Thus in the painting of the Rouen Cathedral a great deal of white paint was used, although the material of the church is "French limestone" and is darkened with age. In painting such a subject the artist freely exercised his particular color interests in terms of *paint*-color, in terms of the artist's desire *to invent new color experiences,* rather than merely to create a substitute for the actual reality by copying it as well as he could.

In the case of the human form as subject-matter, however, Monet was not able to accomplish this severance from the model as easily, because the subject made it almost impossible for him to "forget what objects you have before you." The subject of a landscape supplied him with forms and shapes which could be handled more arbitrarily and which imposed less of a hindrance upon him as regards the form. Arbitrariness in the handling of form was severely limited when the human being was his subject-matter.[4] This can be clearly seen in the studies of the human form which Monet made; he is less at ease and more bound to the color and shape of his subject. Consequently most of his paintings of the human form are, in comparison to his other works, in a lower color key. This was not because his subject was in a lower key, but because he could not free the usual intensity of his color with such a subject. In other subjects, which are actually in a low key with dark, even muddy colors, like the buildings, churches and streets of Paris or fog scenes in London, he was able to send the pitch of his colors up to the point of a sunlit landscape.

This characteristic can also be seen in the works of Camille Pissarro. For example, he called one of his paintings of the Place du Theatre Francais "The Effect of Snow," yet the "effect" produced by the color is definitely one of early morning with the sun rising through a slight rain. In such an example we are again confronted with a subject which is hardly the kind we would associate with the brilliance of Impressionistic painting. Those who are acquainted with this section of Paris where the buildings are a dark dirt-gray, as in most of that city, could hardly imagine it during a snow fall looking anything like Pissarro's painting of it. The cold white, blues and grays that dominate are in sharp contrast to the yellow-orange colors that dominate Pissarro's painting.

But Pissarro, unlike Monet, liked to paint the human form and was concerned with indicating its third dimension, to a certain degree at least (figure 86). Monet, like most Impressionists, seemed little interested in the *form which could be secured with color*. At times he emphasized form, while in other works he ignored it; but whichever he did it was because of the color interests that operated in the particular work and not because of any prime interest in form as such. In the main he was interested in the *shapes* of color—a linear interest. In this sense, then, Pissarro was not a "pure" Impressionist. In comparison to Monet, he was an Impressionist who was able to move ahead into regions which were to occupy the efforts of those who took up the next developments. His efforts constituted more of a transition

4. Only those who went further, the Post-Impressionists, etc., were able to free themselves from these restrictions as regards the human form, for reasons to be explained in the next chapter.

86. Camille Pissarro, The Cafe au Lait. Courtesy of the Art Institute of Chicago.

from Impressionism to Post-Impressionism which was to follow. This accounts for the high esteem in which he was held by his successors, especially by Paul Cézanne.[5]

Another factor of interest is this: the light effects in Impressionistic paintings usually are reminiscent either of a sunrise or a sunset, regardless of the light or weather conditions that might have prevailed in the subject. Even in the fog paintings of Monet, one has the impression of a sunset. Surely no fog was ever filled to the brim, so to speak, with such an abundant, brilliant display of color. This tendency to give the impression of one or the other extremes of sunlight was to be expected, for in these two phenomena the artist had the most brilliant color demonstration of which nature was capable. And this was what the Impressionists were seeking—the fullest brilliance of color possible with their pigments.

Contrary to the impression created by the artists themselves, they were not so much interested in recording all the variations of color which are to be found throughout the day, but rather in using these various light conditions as stimuli for achieving the *color-results peculiar to paint-pigment*. From this point of view we can see why their works give the effect of extremes of sunrise or sunset; not only because they studied these phenomena in nature, but also because they utilized the most brilliant and intense potentialities of their paint-pigments. Their results therefore were achieved not through the copying of nature's appearances, but through the *creative* utilization of nature's *color-building-method*. Metaphorically speaking, the sun shone always at its brightest in the paintings of the Impressionists. If the sun was not shining, they made it shine; if subjects like city scenes were not brimming with color, the Impressionists invariably saw to it that they did in their paintings.

Thus, if we are to comprehend Impressionism correctly, we must realize the changes which the artist made when depicting nature. As we have explained before, in the previous epoch of art history artists tried to record reality so that it corresponded as nearly as possible to the actual appearances of macroscopic nature. But with Impressionism, this direction was reversed and we find the *nature object being formed to fit the art* rather than the *art being formed to fit the nature object*. The nature object, as such, now plays a minor role.[6]

The Impressionists were the first artists to concern themselves *extensively* with *color in terms of paint-pigment* and with painting as a medium with color potentialities peculiar to it beyond the mere imitation of nature. At first these artists were striving principally to capture the powerful color effects of sunlight. But this was only a phase, leading to a goal of a different kind. Their study of the structure of color and its operation in nature was also instrumental in their gaining a better understanding of *their own means* of producing color-results. It was thus that they discovered a new range, intensity and arrangement of color peculiar to paint-pigments as differentiated from nature-color. It is for this reason that eventually these artists modified the color of "reality" to suit the particular possibilities of their pigments. Thus paint-pigments were no longer used to compete with nature. The artist's interest in paint was now as a means of producing color-inventions in contrast to the old concern with paint as a means of imitating nature-color. So Pissarro painted a subject of dark streets and buildings during a snow fall with light yellow-orange colors, and the result looks more like a landscape in early morning sunlight during a light rain. The subject and especially the color were changed considerably from the way they appeared in reality.

The fact that the Impressionists made an intensive study of Japanese prints throws additional evidence in the direction of the above discussion. Thus the Impressionist was as much as saying that he, like the Japanese artist, was not at all interested in literally copying nature's shapes or colors, that he wanted to give free reign to color in a high key irrespective of the subject's color, and in general to treat the contents of his work very simply.

---

5. Another example demonstrating that he was not only an Impressionist, as was Monet, but that he was directly attracted to the artists who developed Impressionism further is the fact that he was influenced by Seurat. One has to admire the old painter's courage.

6. This becomes more apparent with the Post-Impressionists. Cézanne put it this way in 1904: "One is neither too scrupulous nor too sincere nor too submissive to nature; but one is more or less master of one's model, and above all, of the means of expression." (Paul Cézanne *Letters,* edited by John Rewald, translated by Marguerite Kay, p. 237, Bruno Cassirer, London, 1941.)

All this recalls again Monet's advice to "forget what objects you have before you"; he could just as well have said the same about the color factor. In this respect it is interesting to know that during the last 34 years of his life Monet finished all his paintings in his studio. Here he was better able to go further in eliminating the dominance of nature's objects, thus facilitating his dominance over the objects and their colors.

In short, these artists were trying to achieve the brilliance of color to be observed in nature, as such, but were hindered in such an achievement if they attempted to copy nature with paint. It is, in fact, impossible to do so with paint. In order to achieve their objective the artists could not permit nature to dictate, as in the past; instead they studied the *structure* of nature's color demonstrations and by using the *method* rather than the *results* of nature they were able to utilize full *paint-pigment brilliance*. Hence the artist achieved brilliant displays of color, as does nature, but color peculiarly possible to the potentialities of paint. The interest of the Impressionists in the color-operations of nature was like that of a student who wanted to learn the building method from the master, *not for purposes of copying his works but for purposes of creating something new with the method*. They had a desire to learn from nature and then convert this knowledge to objectives desired by man.

But the Impressionists, of course, were never fully aware of all this except in a highly intuitive sense, and of this we shall have more to say presently. Consequently they never realized the tremendous changes which they were inaugurating in the field of art—that they had begun the Inventive attitude towards the utilization of the visual world, the form-colors of reality. (This attitude of course appeared much more strongly in the Post-Impressionists who followed virtually on their heels.) But a lack of sufficient coherence on the points which were motivating them subconsciously for the most part, accounts for the ambivalence in their works: at times there is apparently more of an attempt to copy than at other times, when the subject is deliberately disregarded. Such confusion often accompanies change until the problems involved are cleared up by adequate conscious examination. But we must be clear on this point: the Impressionists were intent on learning the building method of nature-color in order to use it for purposes peculiar to man and not in order to duplicate the appearances of nature as was the case with copying artists.

Certain negative factors, however, unavoidably resulted from the attempt to change to a new direction. Because of their color-form manipulations of nature, these artists *automatically produced fantasies of nature's actual appearances*. Nature was changed into that which it obviously *is not*. It was precisely this characteristic which unconsciously attracted the majority of those who became Impressionist enthusiasts, albeit under the false guise of "realism," as we shall show.

In viewing Impressionist landscapes, the like of which had never been and could never be seen in actual reality, and which possessed those other-world characteristics found in Japanese prints, the spectator (and often the artist as well) was transported to an ideal world. Consider, for example, a typical Monet landscape, with water, trees, houses, sky, etc. The water will be represented with all kinds of very light, intense blues, greens, pinks, etc.—a body of water such as one would never see in nature. Much liberty will be taken with the forms of various objects as well as with their colors. What Monet achieved is not a copy of nature, but a *man-made* fantasy of it. From his paintings one gets the impression of something dream-like, certainly not life-like. Who indeed could look at such paintings and believe that nature ever looked like that? But there are those who do.

Hence the majority of the observers were attracted to the element of fantasy rather than to structural factors. While the genuine Impressionist was attracted somewhat by the fantasy, still by comparison the structural color factor exerted the predominating attraction.

The acceptance of the new art as "realistic" did not happen all at once. Previous to their exposure to this art, contemporaries of the Impressionists had been conditioned not only to highly realistic forms of painting but also to Photography. It is not surprising that they revolted at first against the new art; it seemed to be entirely opposed to the most recent achievements in visual recordings. It was, moreover, contrary to all that was then considered the great art of the past and hence the conclusion was that only madmen could hope to be taken seriously, painting in such an "awkward, childish manner." These paintings were not literally realistic and it was thought that there could be no other legitimate criterion for their justification.

The intensity of the initial opposition against the Impressionists is shown in the invectives that were hurled at them. In one letter Pissarro says, "Gérôme regards us as pimps!" [7] When the Caillebotte collection was given to the state, the fact that Impressionist works were to enter a national museum aroused violent opposition. For example, "In April, 1894, the review *L'Artiste,* attempting by means of a questionnaire to determine the general view, found that the Caillebotte donation was considered 'a heap of excrement whose exhibition in a national museum publicly dishonors French art.' " [8]

Specifically they were accused of not being able to draw correctly. In 1877 one French critic (Roger Bellue) said of an exhibition of both the Impressionists and the Post-Impressionists: "They display the profoundest ignorance of drawing, composition, and of colour." [9] Gérôme, the Academician, said, while looking at a Monet, that it was "A blank canvas, bought from the dealer and put in a frame—nothing more! Absolutely nothing! One looks at it, one sees nothing—and you know that sells very dear. It is too grotesque!" [10]

Nevertheless the new art was exhibited at quite frequent intervals and as people began to experience it in more and more exhibitions, something happened to the spectators, something similar to what had happened to some of the Impressionists themselves some time before; the art began to appear "realistic." The art public gradually became attracted to what appeared to be the color effects of the sun in the new paintings, just as the painters themselves had been some time before. Few stopped to inquire how this reversed position came about. The indoctrination was now established that the color in these paintings was a scientifically accurate reproduction of nature-color, but this was a false indoctrination, as we shall presently show.

Let us see what brought about this change of attitude. Obviously the Impressionists were primarily interested in the color effects stimulated by an object, rather than its forms or details. The artist painted in a highly simplified manner; we do not see the shingles on the roof or the cobblestones on the street. Everything was loosely painted with slashes of color next to each other and at the same time liberties were taken with the actual appearances of nature. Nevertheless the appearances of nature objects were treated in such a way that they were certainly recognizable as such, and so could be utilized *as adequate stimuli* for projecting previous experience with these subjects in actual reality upon the objects indicated in the painting, thus giving the latter a cloak of reality. The observer was now willing to accept the trees, water, houses and all the objects indicated in the painting, as such, since the color "realism" had unconsciously become the main point of interest in realistic experience. The observer was no longer interested in the specific realism of forms, but only in what he thought was the specific "realism" of color. Thus, with the assistance of the projection mechanism, it was possible to ignore what were actually the unrealistic color-forms in the paintings, and to regard Impressionism as simply a new method for achieving "realistic" recordings of nature. To see that this was an error, you have only to look at any Impressionistic painting and imagine if you possibly could ever see anything like it in actual reality. Or place such paintings next to those of Theodore Rousseau, early Corot, Daubigny, Courbet, and many others, which were obviously more in correspondence with nature's reality appearances, and *see the differences.* Neither the color nor the treatment of nature's appearances in general was ever "seen" to exist in that manner in which the Impressionists depicted it. But, as we have said, it was precisely this character—the fact that the painting was not like nature—that actually attracted the observer. Little did the admirers of the new painting suspect that the new "realism" they had discovered was not nature's realism; that this form of painting served them simply as a point of departure, *as a stimulus by which they could indulge in fantasies of reality.* The conscious attraction was based on the assumption that Impressionism was "realistic"; but the basic unconscious attraction was exactly that element of unreality in these paintings which made them fantasies of actual reality. Consequently, it was also missed that these works were not

7. Camille Pissarro: *Letters to His Son Lucien,* edited by John Rewald, assisted by Lucien Pissarro, translated by Lionel Abel, p. 239, Pantheon Books Inc., New York, 1943.

8. Ibid., p. 239, ed. fn.

9. As quoted by Margaret Bulley: *Art and Counterfeit,* p. 68, Methuen and Co., Ltd., London, 1925.

10. As quoted by Sheldon Cheney: *The Story of Modern Art,* pp. 185-186.

87. Claude Monet, Parliament of Westminster. Courtesy of the Art Institute of Chicago.

scientifically accurate color reproductions of reality; instead scientific knowledge of the color-structure of reality was employed by these artists in order to exploit particular color potentialities of their paint-pigments! The failure to understand this accounts for the fact that there are still writers arguing about whether or not the Impressionists were "scientific." Actually we are again faced with the very error we saw made so often in the past due to the identification of the two general levels of art experience—the art object as such, and the relationships between the art object and the nature object it represents.

Consequently the unconscious attraction to the element of fantasy in Impressionism, erroneously justified on the basis of its being realistic, prevented the observation of another and more useful aspect of this art—that it was the start towards achieving a new contents for art. Man had begun on the road to inventing art experiences which were no longer subservient to the forms of nature as they appeared, but the weight of tradition persisted, and so it was assumed that because all good art of the past had been "realistic," all art of the future must also be proved "realistic." In this way the observer verbalized his experience before the new art with old formulations no longer applicable, while at the same time he was actually attracted by fantasies of reality and missed the new positive factors.

271

So strong is this canalization to "realism" that many of the innovations since the invention of the Camera which are definitely not realistic, arts which actually distort nature, have come to be accepted as realistic; works of Manet, Dégas, Monet, Pissarro, etc.[11] Hence if previously the spectators had denounced Impressionism because it broke with "tradition," then in later times we find the notion that Impressionism is "realistic." The conservative spectator and artist have reversed their evaluations and they now accept this art as a continuation of the realistic "tradition," although, as we have seen, this certainly was not the actual experience they were having with Impressionism.

One historian insists: "today the very word Impressionism evokes a judgment without appeal."[12] More recently this has been carried further by the "Moderns," who regard Impressionism as contemptibly "realistic." Numerous examples could be cited from prominent critics of today, but a few will suffice.

Cheney contends that Impressionism, "was really one more bypath in the territory staked out by the Renaissance realists of the fifteenth century. It led its doctrinaire devotees directly away from the paths that were to converge in post-realistic modernism. It became one more phase of scientifically true, nature-bound art."[13] In addition to this, according to Cheney (in an earlier book), "Impressionism . . . hastened recognition of the shallow character of all Realistic art."[14] In the same book he quotes Pfister as follows: "impressionism appears as a mere surface-art, and therefore a superficial art, a mechanical craft and no art at all."[15] The critic, James Sweeney, writes: "In its attempt at a conscientious snapshot-transcription, it had subordinated emotional, selective *looking* to a scientific, non-selective *seeing*."[16] And Walter Pach has declared that, "the Impressionists furnish the last chapter of the scientific and realistic effort of modern times, while the two painters [Cézanne and Redon] . . . initiated the departure from it."[17] It is as simple as that! It is no doubt convenient to dismiss these artists as Realists, claiming, of all things, that they were scientifically realistic. (This last evaluation is derived from a false interpretation of the Impressionists' "scientific" interest in color, as that has been explained.) If they were so realistic as these critics claim, why should a violent controversy ever have occurred over this very factor in their work?

In the quotation above from Pach we find another error prevalent among Modern art critics in their evaluation of Impressionism, and from this we get another clue to understanding why they have failed to evaluate Impressionism correctly. They fail to realize that the great turning point began with the Impressionists, Monet and Pissarro. And that this change was *not* initiated, but merely carried further by Cézanne, Seurat, van Gogh and Gauguin. The probable reason for their erroneous evaluation is something like this: the all-important "sensibilities" of the "Moderns" are like those of the man who cannot drink wine any more, but must have straight rum to feel anything. That is, the "Moderns" have become so habituated to having their distortions of reality in art in such strong doses that they have lost their capacity to discern the finer degrees of this phenomenon. They are so habituated to the strong shots of Picasso, Dali and the rest, who literally tear pell-mell into the effort of bending reality every which way, that they can no longer see distortions in their lesser, more subtle manifestations as in Monet and Pissarro. They fail to recall that when Impressionist paintings were first seen by artists, critics and laymen, all of whom had been accustomed to literal realism in painting as well as in Photography, the new paintings seemed to (and actually did) distort nature *considerably*. It was no accident that the majority of contemporaneous critics and laymen accused the Impressionists of abusing the appearances of nature. If there was one thing these old Academi-

11. The psychologist should find this phenomenon a wonderful subject for investigation. Today we find even van Gogh in YMCA's, doctor's offices, shop windows, pool rooms, bowling alleys, etc., while not so many years before, this artist's brother, a picture dealer, had to find room for these works under his own bed.

12. Pijoan, *An Outline History of Art,* Vol. III, p. 346.

13. Cheney, *The Story of Modern Art,* p. 188.

14. From EXPRESSIONISM IN ART, p. 31, by Sheldon Cheney, published by LIVERIGHT PUBLISHING CORPORATION, New York, 1939.

15. Ibid., p. 77, as quoted from Dr. Oskar Pfister, *Expressionism in Art*: Its Psychological and Biological Basis, p. 189, E. P. Dutton and Co., New York, 1923.

16. J. J. Sweeney: *Plastic Redirections in Twentieth Century Painting,* p. 7, University of Chicago Press, Chicago, 1934.

17. Walter Pach: *The Masters of Modern Art,* p. 38, The Viking Press, New York, 3rd Printing, 1929, copyrighted by B. W. Huebsch, Inc., 1924.

cians were able to judge, it was whether a painting was primarily realistic or not! Since they claimed that the Impressionists were not realistic, one should pause and check (at least twice) before assuming that they were wrong about everything.

At first Impressionism was rejected, by the old Academicians of the 19th century, because it was not "realistic." Later it was accepted precisely because it was not realistic, as that was explained, under the guise that it was, of all things, realistic. Now today the "Moderns," those who insist that art must be non-realistic, refuse to accept precisely such art in Impressionism because they insist it is "pure realism." So they throw Impressionism back into the Realists' camp, although it had been thrown out and correctly so by the Realists earlier. This insensitivity to the finer shades of the problem is also the reason that the majority of the "Moderns" find no difficulty in calling the whole period of art from the Renaissance through Impressionism "realistic" without any discrimination about degrees or the significance of "realism" as a problem of "art." At the same time all art before the 5th century B. C., and after Impressionism is considered as pursuing a similar objective in different ways, just because nature is distorted in all of it. And here again there is no discrimination about the significance of degrees or kinds of distortion involved.

It is this prejudice-guided orientation to the history of art which prevents both the Realists and the Moderns from being sensitive to the more subtle manifestations of the very notions for which each claims to stand. Thus the Academic mentality is inadequately, if at all, aware of the great evolutionary role of arts prior to the 5th century B.C., while the "Modern" mentality is inadequately, if at all, aware of the great revolutionary arts since the 5th century B.C. They have chosen to forget, because it is convenient, that the goal of "realism" was the *goal of revolutionary minorities* during the pre-Camera period.

It must be emphasized that we are here dealing with a most important and crucial phenomenon. If we can comprehend it coherently, we shall have removed from our path one of the major difficulties to the correct evaluation not only of the revolution in art during the last one hundred years, but also, by implication, of the rest of art history. In this history we shall place Impressionism in that heretofore no-man's land between the private histories of the Academicians and the Modernists. For in Impressionism we have witnessed the first major revision in the visualization of reality, in that the *structure of nature* is now beginning to replace the *macroscopic level* as the FIRST ORDER EXPERIENCE. As a result man was now able to begin molding nature to suit his creative desires in place of copying nature as in the past. The Impressionists took the first great step towards the emancipation of the artist from the now useless painting task of being a mirror of nature's macroscopic reality. They tackled the examination of one of the elements of visual reality—color—which, as we shall see, was subsequently employed for the building of a new content. This was the tremendous contribution of the Impressionists to the evolution of man's art. All this, we shall find, will eventually evolve to a point where artists will discover an entirely new orientation towards nature and its use in the making of art. When our studies reach this point we shall see how very different our conclusions about Impressionism will be from the prevalent contention that the Impressionists sought only to record the seen color of nature.

We have already noted that the Impressionists themselves probably were not conscious of having reversed the position of the nature object in relation to the artist's medium. However, the objective they were seeking entailed this revision whether they were conscious of it or not. But many things the artist evokes by speech or painting entail factors of which he is not and cannot be aware. Acting upon the artist in a multitude of ways is the history or heritage of art, and to this the great artist is sensitive in more ways than he knows. It is this sensitivity which enables him to throw off *habit* for *useful adventure*. It is the operation of this element which enables the trail-blazers to reach useful objectives.

Apropos of this is the following statement by John Dewey: " 'Intuition' is that meeting of the old and new in which the readjustment involved in every form of consciousness is effected suddenly by means of a quick and unexpected harmony which in its bright abruptness is like a flash of revelation; although in fact it is prepared for by long and slow incubation. Oftentimes the union of old and new, of foreground and background, is accomplished only by effort, prolonged perhaps to the point of pain. In any case, the background of organized meanings can alone convert the new situation from the obscure into the clear and luminous. When old and new jump together, like sparks when the poles are adjusted, there is intuition." [18]

18. From *Art as Experience,* by John Dewey, p. 266, New York, 1934. Courtesy of G. P. PUTNAM'S SONS.

88. Camille Pissarro, The Train to Dieppe. Courtesy, Durand-Ruel.

This "slow incubation" is a never-ending process within the "organism" of art history, this process extends through all the activities of past artists; the living useful artist enters this continuum and sets free his intuitive faculty which permits him to adjust to and hence become a constructive, living part of the historical organism. This aspect of human experience was so strong with the Impressionists, for reasons to be given later, that they attempted to resolve the dilemma between their "feeling" and "thinking" by falsely supposing that there existed an incompatibility between the "intellectual faculty" and the "artistic sense." Such a conclusion did not prove, as some critics assume, that the intellect was harmful to artists, but rather indicated the *state* or the *kind* of intellectual activity in which they were involved.

274

Nevertheless, under such circumstances, theirs was a difficult and often thankless task which few cared to risk. Something of this struggle is to be found in the following remark by Monet: "It is not agreeable to talk of one's self; and then upon certain points my memory fails. What I *do* know is, that life with me has been a hard struggle, not for myself alone, but for my friends as well. And the longer I live the more I realize how difficult a thing painting is, and in one's defeat he must patiently strive on." [19] From this one gets a distinct reaction that Monet knows that he "feels" much more about art than he is able to realize consciously, that he feels there is something missing and searches almost desperately to find it — "and in one's defeat he must patiently strive on." We find a similar sort of expression by Paul Cézanne; time and again he says "I have not realized." It is no accident that this struggle is a unique characteristic of all those who inaugurated the new trend in art. Presently we shall need to consider the reasons for the preponderance of the particular kind of difficulties these artists experienced; the conflicts and pressures set up between what one consciously *knows* and what one can only consciously *feel*. From Impressionism to Cubism all artists with but few exceptions, relied to a considerable degree upon the intuitive factor and had great difficulty formulating non-intuitive evaluations.

Often we miss the significance of statements made by artists, especially from Impressionism on, because we do not understand or take into consideration the psychological background of these statements, or because we disregard the historical time-context in which they were made. There is always involved in them the artist's conscious knowledge on the one hand, and on the other those intuitive actions which he does not consciously comprehend. In other words, an artist's remarks, like his works, are always incomplete and for that reason always subject to revision. There is usually a great deal to be found in them which a cursory observation will not reveal. Always we are confronted with what the artist "knows" or thinks he knows, as well as what he does not know, and often cannot be in a position to know. Yet the latter factor is frequently to be found churning, attempting to come to consciousness, in the intuitive aspect of the artist's verbal utterances and his behavior on canvas.

These matters receive too little of our attention. Once an artist is recognized as outstanding, we are inclined to react to his words and works as though he were an omniscient oracle of perfection; but previous to his "recognition" he is likely to have been subjected to just the opposite treatment. However, it is largely because we ignore the particular nature and function of the intuitive level that we fall into the error of regarding whatever an artist says as some final edict or pronouncement from which it can be clearly deduced that he is either a charlatan or a perfect genius. These either-or-attitudes of *allness* lead to false evaluations and prevent a recognition of the fundamental significance of what the artist is saying or trying to say. So when we study the Impressionists and their works we must recognize the fact that every evaluation they made is in some way related to what they accomplished in their work, and that both desirable and undesirable factors are present.

In many ways we are in an advantageous position for discovering certain notions in the utterances and in the works of past artists which were not and could not be apparent to those who originally made them. This is so because we can evaluate what artists in the past said and did in the light of what happened in subsequent developments. Thus, for example, we can see what happened to Impressionism in the various schools that followed. We can observe how the intuitive factors among the Impressionists came to consciousness in the efforts of those who followed their direction, how what was only vaguely felt at first became conscious in later times. As Alfred Whitehead puts it: "Each generation criticizes the unconscious assumptions made by its parents. It may assent to them, but it brings them out in the open." [20] Some make conscious what has been silently operating in the past and rest content upon it; a very few utilize this consciousness to build further.

As our studies progress we shall find how great an error it is to accept the prevailing assumption that free reign can be given to the intuitive factor and that cerebral activity can be regarded only as something to be avoided. The fact that artists of recent times depended heavily upon the intuitive factor is certainly a suspicious reason for concluding that this is necessarily the criterion for behavior under present

19. Quoted by W. H. Fuller, *Claude Monet and His Paintings,* p. 36, J. J. Little and Co., New York, 1899.

20. From A. N. Whitehead: *Science and the Modern World,* p. 36. By permission of The Macmillan Company, publishers.

conditions. As we proceed we shall find that just as it was unavoidable for the Impressionists to rely so greatly upon intuition, so, in our times, it will become unavoidable not to do so if we wish to secure useful art survival. In other words, present day conditions are entirely different from those in the very recent past. As a matter of fact, with Monet and with the Post-Impressionists, over-dependence upon the intuitive element prevented them from realizing further objectives in the direction they had chosen. They were thus unable to release the full potentialities of their cerebral activity which would have permitted them to develop further, in fact, to carry their intuition further. This accounts for the fact that Monet lived through Impressionism, Post-Impressionism, Cubism, etc., and yet up to the time of his death in 1926 he remained unaffected, to any noticeable degree, by all that had followed Impressionism.

Nevertheless, the Impressionists made *possible* a great change in the attitude of artists towards their work. This was implicit in the significance of the very term "Impressionism," and it should be illuminating to regard briefly the controversy which has existed over this label. It seems that it began when Monet once gave a title to a painting which contained the term "impression." A hostile critic immediately seized upon it as a label of ridicule. In this way the school got its name. Since it was acquired by accident, many have tended to assume that the label was not applicable, meanwhile ignoring the fact that Monet did use it in the first place. Moreover, if we investigate the term, we find it has its value, however it may have arisen. We accept it in the general meaning it has in art—that of the artist's recording the effect nature has upon *his* sensory receptors of eye-brain activity. In this sense the term could have been much more illuminating than it has been taken to be. It correlates with the highly intuitive character of Impressionist activity, that which Monet called painting "just as it looks to you . . . until it gives you your own naive impression of the scene before you." And this attitude for the first time brought to light that aspect of any artist's activity of which we have just been speaking—that there were components of his behavior, his reaction to reality over which he had no conscious control, yet which played their part in determining the eventual character of his work. Furthermore, the nature of the "impression" was determined by the particular personality structure of the individual who produced the art. For example, if an imbecile makes a drawing he is bound to produce not great art (as some think) but an imbecilic impression of the world about him. Hence it would probably be more correct to say that "Impressionism" came into use as a result of Monet's discovering a characteristic not only of his own work, but of all art which had ever been produced—namely, unconscious factors. This was an opportunity for artists to become conscious of the fact that *all* of an artist's activity is not the result of conscious intentions, that many experiences are motivating the artist which are beyond his conscious control. This is a lesson that many artists still have to learn: that we never know all about art, *so we never know all about what we do as artists*. Today a few artists have realized this and are ridding themselves of the false practice of attributing some extra-human power to themselves, both in their ability and knowledge about art. It is no longer necessary to "know" all about art and moreover it is impossible. Thus the artist is absolved of the necessity for creating harmful theological absolutes in order to maintain a position of omniscience.

The upshot of this situation has since been that some artists have chosen to sink ever further into the irresponsibility of the unconscious, while others, the genuine innovators, have chosen the responsibility of increasing their consciousness of what they are doing.

Intuitively Monet had labelled one of his paintings with a term which gave the clue to a new and more realistic attitude toward the artist's activity and productions—an attitude which has yet to sink in. There was now an opportunity to replace the metaphysics of the past with a theory of the unconscious. It was the opportunity for artists to begin a trend in cerebralization comparable to that of the scientist, to seek verifiable knowledge rather than impressive logic. All this has more significance when we consider that in these times the field of psychology and psychiatry was having a rebirth, a scientific one. Freud and others were at work.

So Impressionism brought the opportunity for a turning point in the attitude of the artist away from that of the philosopher and theologian, closer to that of the scientist. The artists and scientists of these times, just as they had both worked on the problem of Photography, were analyzing the structure of nature's color, but in relation to their special as well as overlapping interests. The full significance of their overlapping paths will become apparent as their affinity to each other increases from Impressionism on.

276

89. Claude Monet, Etretat. Courtesy of The Metropolitan Museum of Art.

Art is a harmony parallel with the harmony of nature. 52
Paul Cezanne

If the idealist assert that color lives only at top, in the mind, irrespective of physical correlates in the organism; or if the realist assert that it lives only at bottom, in the thing, irrespective of psychical correlates in the organism; I respectfully submit that each goes beyond the evidence. 234

C. Lloyd Morgan

14 THE QUEST FOR STRUCTURE

We know and we do not know.   127
Paul Gauguin

It is better not to know than to know wrong.
Paul Gauguin

It is a long way from convention, from mere intuition, to real understanding.   127   Paul Gauguin

Where do we come from—What are we—Where are we going?
Paul Gauguin

. . . . yes, untruth if you like, but more true than literal truth.   253   Vincent van Gogh

I believe in the absolute necessity for a new art of color, of design, and—of the artistic life.   133
Vincent van Gogh

. . . . I do not want to be in the right theoretically, but in the presence of nature.   215
Paul Cezanne

Time and reflection . . . . modify little by little our vision, and at last comprehension comes to us.   66
Paul Cezanne

. . . . you must see in nature the cylinder, the sphere, the cone, all put into perspective 215
Paul Cezanne

There is a general tendency today to regard the Impressionists and the Post-Impressionists as isolated cases, in the sense that they supposedly represent fundamentally opposing attitudes. Impressionism was allegedly something "tainted" with "realism" and so had to be "reformed" by the Post-Impressionists. Consequently, Monet was considered insignificant compared to Cézanne. But "to be is to be related"—not separated. We shall find it more profitable to search for the significance between these two general groups of artists in terms of the relationships that exist between them. Analysis shows that the Post-Impressionists developed further the color theories and *general direction* begun by their immediate predecessors. Most important, what was largely unconscious with the Impressionists was precisely that which became increasingly conscious with the Post-Impressionists.

We have seen how the Impressionists worked on the problem of color, not as is generally supposed, simply in order to copy nature-appearances, but for the possibilities it offered the Inventive ability of man. It was with this end in view that these artists studied not only nature but also the analytical works of scientists regarding the structure of nature's color spectrum. The next steps in the study of visual structure were taken by artists like Vincent van Gogh and Paul Gauguin. They made discoveries regarding other characteristics of visual structure besides the element of color upon which the Impressionists had largely concentrated.

It is of interest to see how the Post-Impressionists carried further the manipulation of color begun by the Impressionists. We noted how great a liberty the Impressionists took with nature's color and light, as exemplified in fog paintings, gray buildings, etc. But they did not go so far as to try to paint night scenes. Monet is said to have tried and given up. The Impressionists were still bound sufficiently by nature's subject-matter that they were limited in the liberties they could take with the manipula-

90. Vincent van Gogh, Landscape—Street at Auvers. John T. Spaulding Collection, Boston (Fogg Museum of Art).

tion of light. Van Gogh, however, was able to go further in this respect, and did a number of night scenes (both interiors and exteriors) in brilliant color.

Gauguin, van Gogh (figures 90, 91) and others were now greatly changing the colors and *forms* of reality into other colors and shapes. Such artists deliberately avoided making a literal copy of nature and deliberately changed it into what we can easily see it IS NOT. They emphasized not only the factor of color—their inheritance from the Impressionists—but also the factor of color-organization in definite shapes. In Monet *color dominated the consciousness* of the artist's activity. Van Gogh took Monet's color achievements one step further by making *more conscious the linear contour organization* of color-shapes on a flat surface. Monet, for example, was predominantly interested in the color of a tree, but van Gogh was also interested in its contour; thus he wrote, "one should say if the shape is round or square." [1]

1. *Further Letters of Vincent van Gogh to His Brother*, 1886-1889, p. 393, Constable and Co., Ltd., London. Houghton Mifflin Co., Boston and New York, 1929.

Gauguin in turn was *more conscious of the space divisions of his color-shape organizations*. Whereas van Gogh emphasized the separation between color-areas by stressing contours and breaking up the areas between them with a feverish, swirling use of elongated Impressionistic brush strokes, the separation between the shapes in Gauguin's work was secured by clearly distinguishing each space-area of color. Of all the Post-Impressionists he came the closest to the Oriental type of linear art. He did not break up his shapes with feverish, but with calmly placed, unobtrusive brush strokes. He treated his shapes as solid semi-linear areas, emphasizing the space element in two-dimensional terms. In brief, the elements of Monet's art, developed by van Gogh's innovations, were carried still further by Gauguin, who emphasized in a more direct and controlled manner the factors that interested van Gogh, as well as the structural factor of space.

But with both van Gogh and Gauguin, the major emphasis was a linear one; more so with the former, as the latter was interested in space, if only from a two-dimensional point of view. Gauguin's concern with form was not sufficient to overcome this linearity, but compared to van Gogh, his work was more on the order of relief-sculpture. Hence it is no surprise to find that Gauguin worked in the sculpture medium and made reliefs.

On the basis of the fact that both van Gogh and Gauguin studied the works of Oriental artists (and in Gauguin's case the works of Primitive peoples as well) it has been generally assumed that they were reviving certain factors in more primitive arts and injecting them into the stream of Western art. Such an assumption, however, is not *fundamentally* correct, as we shall show.

It is true that both van Gogh and Gauguin presented these arts as the authority and justification for the distortions they practiced upon the appearances of nature. Van Gogh wrote: "All my work is *in a way* founded on Japanese art." (emphasis ours)[2] Notice the significant reservation of the phrase "in a way"—by which he disclosed that he felt other factors of a basic nature were involved, factors which we shall presently see were more difficult to comprehend. In still another place he says that Japanese art is like the Primitives.[3] While Gauguin wrote: "I have gone far back, farther back than the horses of the Parthenon . . . as far back as the Dada of my babyhood, the good rocking-horse."[4] And also: "Have before you always the Persians, the Cambodians, and a little of the Egyptian. The great error is the Greek, however beautiful it may be . . . ."[5] Moreover he said: "You will always find nourishing milk in the primitive arts, but I doubt if you will find it in the arts of ripe civilizations . . . ."[6] We believe, however, that even if these artists had never seen the works of Oriental and Primitive peoples, the Post-Impressionistic type of art would have evolved anyhow. For the factors fundamental to its evolution were already inherent in the developments which Western art was undergoing. Historically it was "in the cards." But the artists who performed these developments were far from being historians. They had to reason out their action somehow and this they did along lines which, as we shall see, were based on observations of symptoms rather than fundamentals. (For that matter, who doesn't remember that Whistler, certainly a very different type of artist from those we are studying, also justified his art with the practices of the Orientals, yet vehemently abhorred the works of Gauguin, van Gogh and Cézanne?)

Nevertheless, given the fact that art was now developing further and further from the accurate recording of nature, it is easy to see how certain works of the past, especially those that were most removed from literal copies of nature, would naturally attract artists like van Gogh and Gauguin. We must remember that there was no contemporary art which distorted nature to the extent that the new artists were resolved upon. Comparable distortions could be seen only by looking to the arts of the past ("farther back than the horses of the Parthenon"), or of living Primitive cultures, or of the Orient. This art then was used not only to justify the new direction, but it also served as the only available stimulus to the seemingly comparable trends of van Gogh and Gauguin, even though their work was developing towards a very different objective than these arts which they used to justify their liberties with nature's appearances. It was easy to make the erroneous assumption that they and the Primitive artists were seeking similar objec-

2. Ibid., p. 114.
3. Ibid., p. 117.
4. As quoted by R. J. Goldwater: *Primitivism in Modern Painting*, p. 61, Harper and Brothers, New York, 1938.
5. Ibid., p. 59.
6. Ibid., p. 59.

91. Paul Gauguin, Why Are You Angry? Courtesy of the Art Institute of Chicago.

tives because none of them copied nature literally. Although not playing a fundamental role, these older arts superficially accelerated a direction already basically determined by the previous course of Western art —which had, after all, produced van Gogh and Gauguin.

But when Gauguin praised the Persians, the Cambodians, the Egyptians and the Primitive arts, and condemned the Greeks as a "great error," he was stating a theory of art history still in force today: that the only "worthwhile" art is to be found in the works of the Orientals, the Christians, the living Primitives and the art before that of the Greeks. Heretofore, the Classical arts of Greece and Rome had been held up high as the guide and goal of all art; with the Impressionists and even more so with the Post-Impressionists, the Primitive cultures and the semi-primitive ones of the Orient were elevated to the pedestal once occupied by the stone gods of Greece. There they remain undisputed even today, as can be seen from this recent statement: "Gauguin and the Symbolists had brought recognition of the fact that there was valuable precedent for the Western world's movement toward a new art in the art expressions of the antique world and the Orient."[7] It is easy to assume, if one so desires, that "Modernists" and Primitives were all travelling along a somewhat similar road to "great" art.[8] But long ago Pissarro voiced a considerably more intelligent view of these matters, which many today would do well to stop and con-

7. Martha Candler Cheney: *Modern Art in America,* p. 29, Whittlesey House, McGraw-Hill Book Co., Inc., New York, London, 1939.
8. For example, see Goldwater, op. cit.

sider. In a letter to his son he wrote: "I saw Gauguin; he told me his theories about art and assured me that the young would find salvation by replenishing themselves at remote and savage sources. I told him that this art did not belong to him, that he was a civilized man and hence it was his function to show us harmonious things." [9] But in van Gogh and Gauguin we see more sharply than in Pissarro the struggle between the reality of nature and its distortions (fantasy) and between observing the appearances of nature and studying its Structural Process. And because of this Pissarro was better able to avoid a false evaluation of Primitive art.

In the work of the Post-Impressionists there appeared more sharply than ever before the age-old schism between the art of nature and man's unconscious wish to create and not merely copy. Unknowingly these artists were helping to clear the ground of one kind of content to make way for another. But they had to undergo a struggle, since they were not conscious of the fundamental objective involved. They were able to feel many things intuitively, and made an agonizing effort to drive these intuitions into consciousness in the attempt to grasp what was occurring. This can be seen in what they wrote in their letters and journals about their art.

In speaking of the distortions in his work, van Gogh wrote: "my great longing is to make those very incorrectnesses, those deviations, remodellings, *changes of reality,* in order that they may become, yes, *untruth* if you like, but *more true* than literal truth." (emphasis ours)[10] And he spoke of the "necessity for a new art of color, of design, and—of the artistic life." [11] He also declared of one of his paintings: "But there is *a certain life* in it, perhaps more than in some pictures that are absolutely faultless." (emphasis ours)[12] Again he wrote to his brother of lines, shapes and colors in a group of his paintings: "Altogether I think nothing in it *at all* good except the 'Field of Corn,' the 'Mountain,' the 'Orchard,' the 'Olives' with the blue hills and the portrait and the 'Entrance to the Quarry,' and the rest tells me *nothing,* because it lacks individual intention, and feeling in the lines. Where these lines are close and deliberate it begins to be a picture, even if it is exaggerated. That is rather what Gauguin and Bernard feel, they do not ask at all the correct shape of a tree, but they do insist that one should say if the shape is round or square— and honestly, they are right, exasperated by the photographic and empty perfection of certain people. They will not ask the correct tone of the mountains, but they will say: By God, the mountains were blue, were they, then chuck on some blue and do not go and tell me that it was a blue rather like this or that, it was blue, wasn't it? Good—make them blue and it's enough!" [13]

Gauguin referred to the structural factors when he said: "The artist . . . . (if he wishes really to make a divine creative work), must not copy Nature, but use the elements of Nature to create a new element." [14] While Gauguin was only partially conscious that he was seeking a new contents for art, nevertheless, he was implicitly advising the artist not to copy nature, but to use the *method of nature* in order to achieve an art peculiar to man.

Van Gogh, in insisting that his work was "more true" as a result of his non-conformity to nature ("untruth"), was actually expressing two opposing intentions: if he wished to record reality as it appears, he had to copy it; if he copied it, then he could not deliberately change it, but changing the reality produced that "certain life" which he so much wanted to achieve. This same conflict and confusion was involved in the arts which he admired and regarded as equal to his highly esteemed Japanese prints. He wrote in a letter: "Japanese art is a thing like the Primitives, like the Greeks, like our old Dutchmen, Rembrandt, Potter, Hals, Van der Meer, Ostade, Ruysdael." [15] And Gauguin reported of van Gogh in his

9. *Camille Pissarro's Letters to His Son Lucien,* p. 221. Edited by John Rewald, assisted by Lucien Pissarro. Translated by Walter Abel, Pantheon Books, New York, 1943.

10. As quoted by Walter Pach: *Vincent van Gogh,* p. 38, Artbook Museum, New York, 1936.

11. *Further Letters of Vincent van Gogh,* p. 19.

12. As quoted by Pach, *Vincent van Gogh,* p. 38.

13. *Further Letters of Vincent van Gogh,* p. 393.

14. From PAUL GAUGUIN, by Beril Becker, p. 221, published by LIVERIGHT PUBLISHING CORPORATION, New York, 1935.

15. *Further Letters of Vincent van Gogh,* p. 117.

journal: "In spite of all my efforts to disentangle from this disordered brain a reasoned logic in his critical opinions, I could not explain to myself the utter contradiction between his paintings and his opinions. Thus, for example, he had an unlimited admiration for Meissonier and a profound hatred for Ingres. Dégas was his despair, and Cézanne nothing but a faker. When he thought of Monticelli he wept." [16] Nevertheless a similar conflict is to be seen in Gauguin also—in his admiration for the "nourishing milk in the primitive arts" on the one hand and on the other for the work of Ingres, certainly an art of a "ripe civilization."

It might be helpful to our understanding of these artists and their milieu to compare Gauguin's art evaluations with those of, say, Leonardo. We cannot take the evaluations of the former as literally as we can those of the latter. Compare the conflicts of Gauguin between "realism" and "primitivism" with those of Leonardo between "realism" and "idealism." In Leonardo's day the problems of art were more clear-cut; the new values were conscious, comparatively speaking, and being gradually achieved. The central problem was not simply one of realism, but rather how much of it could or should be attained. Leonardo wrote of art and many other subjects in a clear and verifiable manner. We can understand him without difficulty. Although a transition was in progress from one medium to another in his time, compared with the late 19th century the basic objective of art remained unchanged. Gauguin, however, lived in a period of man's evolution when the unconscious was creating a more terrific effect upon man's behavior than had been the case in the past. Human culture was already involved in that rapid shift of events in the thick of which we are today. Old values were crashing; the freedom of the individual had now become a great problem. "Where do we come from—What are we—Where are we going?" is the title of one of Gauguin's paintings. *The subconsciousness of man was becoming a more direct, uncontrolled participant in men's lives than when it had been diverted and controlled by magic and religion.* (Significantly, in these times the birth of psychoanalysis was in process!) Stability, relatively speaking, was not to be secured until new values were discovered and achieved.

What Gauguin wrote reached deep into the world of the subconscious. His problems cannot be so clearly seen or grasped as those of Leonardo. Gauguin was involved not only in a tremendous change in human behavior (which had yet to reach the consciousness of men adequately) but also in the break-up of an art content, which had been employed for thousands of years, and which was to lead to changes so momentous in character that it is overwhelming to surmise their implications. If we understand this, it will help us to account for the often contradictory behavior and statements of Gauguin and his contemporaries, and thus should help in clearing away certain prevalent misunderstandings about both the work and words of the Post-Impressionists.

Thus van Gogh never gave a very coherent answer as to why his distortions of nature were "more true," because he never knew precisely why. His reasons for making such statements were based on intuitive experiences and, like Gauguin, he could bring forth only the symptomatic justifications for his art attitude. Gauguin, in the first four quotations at the head of this chapter, was trying to express how he and his contemporaries arrived at their decisions in art. William James put it this way: "A man's conscious wit and will are aiming at something only dimly and inaccurately imagined. Yet all the while the forces of mere organic ripening within him are going on to their own prefigured result, *and his conscious strainings are letting loose subconscious allies behind the scenes* which in their way work toward rearrangement, and the rearrangement toward which all these deeper forces tend is pretty surely definite, *and definitely different from what he consciously conceives and determines.*" (emphasis ours)[17]

In spite of the complex of various forces acting upon the Post-Impressionists, these artists were able to push forward, dared to take risks and remained flexible in their reactions to nature and art. In short, they allowed themselves to respond to their intuitive faculties, even though their conscious intentions may have often contradicted them.

Van Gogh, for example, was able to speak usefully about art in many ways because he formulated his notions directly from experience. *Experience* was paramount with him and so he was prevented

16. *The Intimate Journals of Paul Gauguin,* translated by Van Wyck Brooks, preface by Emile Gauguin, pp. 13-14, William Heineman, Ltd., London, 1931.
17. As quoted in *Art as Experience,* p. 72, by John Dewey. Courtesy of G. P. PUTNAM'S SONS.

92. Vincent van Gogh, La Berceuse, Mme. Roulin. John T. Spaulding Collection, Boston (Fogg Museum of Art).

from being tied dogmatically to his errors; he was thus more free to pursue those evaluations which were correct. Moreover he made no pretence of knowing more than he did; he understood that he was participating in the beginning of a new direction in art, not the discovery of final truth. Thus he wrote to his brother: "one feels instinctively that many things are changing and that everything will change. We are living in the last quarter of a century which will end again in an enormous revolution.

"But suppose both of us at the end of our lives see its beginning. We shall certainly not live to see the better times of pure air and the refreshing of the whole society after those big storms.

"But it is already something not to be the dupe of the falseness of one's time, and to scent the unhealthy closeness and oppressiveness of the hours that precede the thunderstorm.

". . . . the following generation will be able to breathe more freely." [18]

But to rely on the intuitive factor to the extent that van Gogh did also had dangers. These Post-Impressionists were flexible, they were open to experience, but they were not yet conscious enough of what they were seeking. There were two general aspects to their art: the positive side, the concern with structure, and the negative or fantasy aspect, resulting from the distortions and changes of reality. Together

18. *The Letters of Vincent van Gogh to His Brother,* 1872-1886, Vol. II, p. 619, Constable and Co., Ltd., London. Houghton Mifflin Co., Boston and New York, 1927.

these two factors produced a dichotomy. Hence the contradictory words of van Gogh, "untruth" and "more true." *This was not a resolution of a problem, as is generally assumed, but rather the posing of a problem that awaited resolution.*

Up to the invention of the Camera there had evolved different kinds of fantasy arts: the first resulted from various degrees of inability to record nature accurately; nature was changed into what it IS NOT by the particular degree of recording deficiency (and restrictions of magic or religious forces) in the particular culture. In general, the degree of this type of fantasy increases the further back one goes in history. The Greeks began the second kind of fantasy. The Classical view, still extant today, was that the productions of the artist were superior to those of nature. But to the degree that artists strove to produce works superior to nature, they produced fantasies.

With Impressionism began still another stage of fantasy, which was in some respects similar to the earliest kind. That is, the art gave the appearance of the artist's being unable to depict nature accurately, just as do the more primitive arts. But critics of the 20th century have unconsciously rationalized it with Greek theories. (We shall give some examples of this presently.) In the earliest type of fantasy, however, artists produced less and less fantasy in direct ratio to their ever increasing ability to achieve their objective of recording nature accurately, until finally the Camera was produced. Whereas the fantasy from Impressionism on resulted from a desire *not* to copy macroscopic nature accurately and later developed into the discovery that man could make an entirely new art contents without copying nature's appearances. But until that objective was adequately comprehended, the artist produced more and more fantasy in his art content in direct ratio to his increasing refusal to copy the actual appearances of nature. Thus, the further the Post-Impressionists carried the search into the structural building method of nature, that is into the Structural Process of nature, the more the fantasy aspect inevitably increased.

True, both the fantasy and the structural factors are interdependent in the particular art under discussion, but the predominance of the one factor over the other establishes the *focal* point of our experience with the art. Our experiences are centered primarily either upon the structural factor or upon the fantasy factor; the former allows for further progress, but the latter, as we shall show, results in regression. But just as with Impressionism, so also with Post-Impressionism (and other "distorted" arts found in history) the principal attraction for most of us has been the fantasy aspect, although, in the majority of instances this attraction is not coherently conscious. This can be seen very clearly in the evaluations of present day critics, who justify the fantasy in Post-Impressionist works with various elaborate verbalisms, which are actually nothing more than disguised Aristotelian theories of the ideal.

We have already noted that since the art of the Greeks, when recording of the general human form was brought to its greatest perfection, most art formulations have continued to be based, implicitly or explicitly, on the Aristotelian notion that depictions of art are superior to nature, that art presents a "superior reality." But the invention of the Camera rudely interrupted for a period the validity of these formulations. However, when the distortion of reality appeared in art again, especially when it became very obvious with the Post-Impressionists, the old notion was taken up and again art was considered superior to the reality. The old Greek fiction was dusted off and put back to work, but this time to rationalize an art considerably different from those arts for which it had been formerly employed. Once more non-artist critic-philosophers saw their opportunity in the field of art, and so began the most fantastic verbal nonsense ever to occur in the history of art.

One of the popular fabrications intended to justify distortions of nature-appearances, runs something like this: the distortions are not intended to facilitate the recognition of the objects depicted, but rather to "draw out," as one writer puts it, the reaction which the artist experiences before nature. In this way the artist allegedly secures the "essentials" of nature in his painting. The English critic, Herbert Read, says: "The actual appearance of the visible world is no longer of primary importance. The artist seeks something underneath appearances, some plastic symbol which shall be more significant of reality than any exact reproduction can be." [19] This statement has certain points of similarity with what van Gogh said many years previously (see p. 285), but what a difference. The painter was searching, he was expressing

19. Herbert Read: *Art Now,* p. 67, Faber and Faber, Ltd., London, 1933.

93. Vincent van Gogh, Sunflowers. Neue Staatsgalerie, Munich. Photo, The Bettmann Archive.

his thalamic ("emotional") reactions to the products of his search, but for the critic the search has ended and he freezes the efforts of genuine artists in a disguised theory of the Aristotelian ideal.

Others have talked of the art as presenting a more "authentic and permanent reality," again the ideal notion in disguise. Still others have attempted to dispense with the fact that the Post-Impressionist kind of art, as well as other types of distortion art, IS NOT what the artist sees, by claiming that "the act of vision is now of minor importance," and referring us to an "inner vision." We are told that only the artists of the past, especially the "realistic" ones, needed to give importance to the act of vision. Or they appeal to the art of Primitives and children, talk of "pre-logical vision" and "the innocent eye," [20] or "the uninstructed eye." [21]

20. Ibid., p. 80.

21. Ibid., p. 98. In the field of criticism these days one frequently finds that the visual behavior of children and Primitives (and even of the insane) is put forth as a criterion or justification for adult behavior.

94. Claude Monet, Morning on the Seine, Giverny. In the Collection of the Minneapolis Institute of Arts.

95. Vincent van Gogh, The Starry Night. Collection The Museum of Modern Art, New York.

96. Paul Gauguin, Day of the God. Courtesy of the Art Institute of Chicago.

97. Paul Cézanne, Still Life. John T. Spaulding Collection, Boston (Fogg Museum of Art).

If these terms have any meanings, we can find them by examining the examples of art which the critic admires when writing in this manner. Then we find that the "something" which is supposed to be "drawn out," which is "underneath appearances" and is a "new reality," "more significant of reality than any exact reproduction can be," and which is seen with an "innocent," "uninstructed eye," with "pre-logical" or "inner vision," is simply a distortion of nature's appearances which results in fantasy! For if this "something" exists at all, it exists only on the artist's canvas, not underneath nature's appearances.

But these distortions of nature which appear in the new art do of course have some kind of a "reality." This may appear to be a contradiction of what has already been said—let us see. When we observe any one of van Gogh's well-known sunflower paintings, we are at once struck by a certain kind of "reality," which seems to emanate from them (figure 93). This reality, however, is not the reality of nature's flowers but of painted nature flowers. In other words, the reality-reaction we experience from the painted-flowers stems from the painting's fantasy depiction of nature's actual appearances. No one has seen or will ever "see" such sunflowers in nature. But man is able to paint such "flowers," to which we can react, and hence they are obviously a particular kind of reality. From this basis we should be able to discuss more profitably and efficiently the "problem of reality" by distinguishing between different *kinds* and *degrees* of reality. The fantasy is a reality insofar as it exists in some perceptible form to be experienced. However, it is exactly this kind of a "reality" experience which *today* results in maladjustment in art as well as in anything else. This will become increasingly apparent the further we pursue the course of the general body of so-called Modern art. (Of course one can insist that there exists a degree of this fantasy in the most realistic painting of flowers. This is true, but to an insignificant degree compared to the predominance of this factor in the flowers painted by van Gogh. The Realist deliberately strives to eliminate this difference between nature and his painting of it; van Gogh strove to accentuate this difference. And that is the important difference in the similarity, as far as objectives and consequences are concerned.)

In short, here again we find the two kinds of reality experiences, that of the visible reality of the world as such, and the "reality" of the painted fantasy of any part of that world. In this fantasy art we are attracted to the unexpected, the uncommon, the unfamiliar and above all, the unreal appearances of sunflowers. It is these characteristics that present day critics talk about, oblivious of the psychological significance of their experience with the painted flowers of van Gogh. Thus one critic writes: "And the sunflowers have a dynamic and mobile life which thrusts them forward with an impact upon the consciousness of the beholder more forceful than that made by any field-grown flowers." [22] Such experiences are analogous to the attraction of fairy-tales where natural laws are defied and overcome at every turn of the page. Hence one of the factors that could be this "something" that critics are always talking about is certainly not "underneath appearances," but obviously right on top of the canvas surface—a fantasy of reality.

If critics had understood this point, they might have suspected that the "reality" being searched for in the new art certainly was of some other kind than that which could result from *any* rendition of nature's appearances. But even though these distortive arts did not conform to the copying tendencies of past arts, critics have interpreted them as being fundamentally directed towards some kind of a representation of nature's macro-reality. Since artists had apparently always recorded the macroscopic "reality" of nature, it was difficult to assume that they could ever do otherwise and still be legitimate artists. In this way critics have concluded that the Post-Impressionists, and such artists, were still primarily concerned with painting what they saw in nature, but were now able to see things the old Realist recording artists could not. The new arts were thought to represent reality also, only "better" than the old arts. And by insisting (like the Aristotelians they were) that the distortions were "more significant of reality than any exact reproduction can be," they automatically achieved a justification for distorting reality. In short, the canalization of traditional thinking is not only "safe," but it also saves one from doing any *new* thinking. As a result it was not realized that the new direction was breaking up the macroscopic appearance of nature in the effort to achieve an entirely new kind of reality for art. Until this was adequately realized, the process of breaking up nature's appearances offered two roads for artists to take. One was the search for and the examination of the Structural Process of reality; the other took the artist in the direction of

22. M. C. Cheney, op. cit., p. 24.

fantasy. And since artists had not yet recognized adequately enough the distinction between the structural and the fantasy factors, the latter consequently provided the main attraction in their art—it was less difficult to reach this experience than the other.

We have now considered three general factors involved in the art transitions under discussion: (1) the macro-reality of nature; (2) the fantasy of that level of nature produced by art; (3) a new level of nature's reality towards which artists are orienting themselves to a large extent unconsciously—the Structural Process level of nature which will eventually be used to achieve a new direction for art.

Any *useful* artist achieves certain advances in spite of certain inevitable handicaps, due to the imperfections inherent in the particular stage of art development in which he is involved. These imperfections are apt to confuse us, as they are a distinct aspect of the artist's achievements. Indeed, it is precisely these imperfections that the useful artists of the next generation seek to overcome, a task they approach by beginning with the advances that are a part of the imperfections. *The great danger is to reverse the procedure and mistake the imperfections for the advances.* This results only in regressions, regressions which will become apparent when we analyze in later chapters the works of those who made the error of developing the defect of Post-Impressionism (fantasy) rather than its assets (structural pursuits).

But notice that both van Gogh and Gauguin were ever striving to bring to fuller consciousness their involvement on the one hand in the distortion of reality and their concern on the other with problems of structural organization irrespective of actual reality appearances. They did not think that they had arrived at some new and final truth; they knew that they were in the process of reaching for something not yet achieved.

You must see in nature the cylinder, the sphere, the cone.

Paul Cézanne succeeded in bringing to fuller consciousness that for which his generation—the Impressionists and other Post-Impressionists—had striven. Significantly enough he was born in the year 1839, the year the Camera was invented—significant, because of all his contemporaries he achieved the most in directing the evolution of *non*-Camera art towards the new direction, and away from the direction now the sole task of the Photographer. He, incomparably more than van Gogh or Gauguin, made very definite the changes of which Impressionism was the great beginning.

Take a typical Monet, a van Gogh, a Gauguin, and a Cézanne and arrange them side by side in the order given; then one begins to see the development from one to the other (figures 94, 95, 96, 97). In Monet one sees the consciousness of and emphasis upon color; in van Gogh the consciousness of and emphasis upon linear organizations of color-contour-shapes; in Gauguin the consciousness of and emphasis upon the organizations of color-shapes in two-dimensional space. Finally in Cézanne, we find the consciousness of and emphasis upon all the above factors along with a direct concern with the factor of three dimensions—the turning into form of van Gogh's linear shape with the space of Gauguin, so to speak, all put into organizations. Each thus showed a development *from* the other. This explains van Gogh's predominant admiration for Gauguin, and Gauguin's for Cézanne. On the other hand the latter, according to Vollard, accused Gauguin of stealing his thunder. And Bernard reports that Cézanne accused van Gogh of painting like a madman.

In Cézanne we find the apex of his generation's discoveries. He completed the achievements of his times when he took the shapes and turned them into forms, into the third dimension. But notice that these forms are not complete; he did not try to paint the entire round; he did not paint the forms as though they had a back to them. They turn only as far as a hemisphere and stop abruptly at that point where they reach beyond the visual range of the observer. They are painted as though a plane, parallel with the face of the canvas, cut them all in half. Most of the sharp emphasis in Cézanne's painting occurs exactly at that point where Renoir, for example, would blend his contours in order to give the complete illusion of form. Cézanne worked as if in relief rather than in the sculpturesque manner of Renoir. This explains why the latter painter was able to turn to sculpture (and not only because the condition of his eyesight forced him to), but Cézanne — never! Renoir was simply concerned with the round of natural phenomena; his problems of seeing and painting were of a simpler kind, uninvolved in any extensive questions of art or reality. Renoir, in fact, was more of a Realist in the older sense, for he was more interested in the roundness of the reality as such and with subject-matter as such than with the then important problem of structural relationships between the reality and the canvas. The structural problem of representing forms on a flat surface did not perturb him. Cézanne, on the other hand, although concerned with the problem of roundness was also preoccupied with the conflict of that factor in relation to the linearity of the canvas. In this connection he was led to make the statement that it had taken him forty years to realize that painting was not sculpture. This indicates that he had undergone a great deal of perplexity regarding the opposing nature of his three-dimensional interest on the one hand, as observed from the study of nature, and the linearity of his medium on the other, where the structural phenomenon of form had to be resolved somehow. In this respect it is of interest to note that among the many Louvre copies that fill Cézanne's sketch-books, few are of paintings; most are of sculpture.[23] For him sculpture, as distinct from painting, presented a problem, not a solution as in the case of Renoir, who faced no such problem, whether painting or sculpting.

A great deal of false evaluation has been made about the two- and three-dimensional aspects of Cézanne's works. Many theorists make *a priori* assumptions to the effect that Cézanne perfected a resolution of these factors, when actually he was in a state of conflict over these two aspects of dimensions throughout all his works. He tended to emphasize now the two-dimensional and at other times the three-dimensional factor, as though trying to find out which to subdue and how. On the other hand, he sometimes deliberately employed a mixture of both two- and three-dimensional emphasis for organizational purposes. The very great importance of Cézanne's interests in the problem of three-dimensional reality and the two-dimensional canvas will become more apparent as we observe this conflict run its course through the Cubist period. For this problem of painting and dimensions was not solved, as later studies will explain, until Cubism had been completed, properly evaluated and digested.

In Gerstle Mack's book on Cézanne we find the following points of interest which bear on the problem of the round in Cézanne's work: "Cézanne's passion for breaking up his planes and surfaces into a complex but always harmoniously graded patchwork of color led him, somewhat arbitrarily, to deny all virtue to any painting in which large areas of the canvas were covered by flat unbroken colors. Gauguin in particular was his *bête noire*. Bernard tells us that Cézanne 'spoke very harshly about Gauguin, whose influence he considered disastrous.' When Bernard protested mildly that 'Gauguin admired your painting very much and imitated you a good deal,' Cézanne replied furiously: 'Well, he never understood me; I have never desired and I shall never accept the absence of modelling or of gradation; it's nonsense. Gauguin was not a painter, he only made Chinese images.' "[24] Cézanne thus emphatically denied the validity of Chinese art and by implication all such art in the Orient or elsewhere. For such art ignored his dictum of the "cylinder, cone and sphere, all put into perspective." The problem he had set for himself was the rendering of three-dimensional structure upon a two-dimensional plane. He refused to dispense with one or the other as van Gogh and Gauguin did by eliminating the three-dimensional factor in preference to the two-dimensional character of the canvas surface. And this very decision made Cézanne advance beyond his contemporaries and prevented him from coming under the hindering symptomatic influence of Oriental

23. See John Rewald: "Proof of Cézanne's Pygmalion Pencil," *Art News*, XLIII:17, October 1-14, 1944.
24. Gerstle Mack: *Paul Cézanne*, pp. 307-308, Alfred A. Knopf, Inc., New York, 1942. Copyrighted by Gerstle Mack, 1935.

98. Paul Cézanne, The Basket of Apples. Courtesy of the Art Institute of Chicago.

art. From this point of view, Mack does not comprehend Cézanne's aversion to flat painting correctly when he says, continuing the above quotation: "Monsieur Bernard might have retorted that Chinese images were by no means the lowest form of art, though it is not recorded that he did so. Undoubtedly Cézanne's judgment on this point was a narrow one, but tolerance and genius do not always go hand in hand. His indifference to Byzantine art and the work of the great Italian primitives can be ascribed largely to this same abhorrence of flat painting in any form." [25] Our evaluations made from an analysis of Cézanne's work indicate that these remarks were anything but "narrow ones," unless we are to deny that very quality which made Cézanne's contributions to art so superior to those of either van Gogh or Gauguin; the latter two artists not only tolerated but preferred flat painting, and in this respect they were disastrous influences, just as Cézanne insisted they were. This was not simply a case of "tolerance and genius"; these evaluations about flat painting were as much a part of Cézanne's paintings as the brush marks he left on them.

As a matter of fact, Gerstle Mack and those who evaluate this problem similarly are the ones mistaken about Cézanne's views on flat painting. If the latter failed to comprehend why the Byzantine and Italian primitives' works were painted as they were, at least he saw quite clearly that his interests in art were different from theirs. If one must accuse Cézanne of error, then it is because he did not

25. Ibid., p. 308.

comprehend the function of this flat painting within the historical process. (But here he certainly was not alone in his times or even at this late date.) At least his intolerance was based on what flat painting did *not* possess, which is far more desirable than tolerating them for what they do not have, as so many do today.

However, it is interesting to speculate whether a device to be found in Cézanne's paintings, and even more so in his water colors, was not borrowed from Oriental arts. This device is particularly prominent in the works of such Japanese artists as Hiroshige. We know that Monet, van Gogh, Gauguin and others of this group were influenced by the study of Japanese prints. But Cézanne evidently was not. If we can say that he "took" anything from the Orientals, however, it might have been that one device in particular by which they seek to indicate *space*. From the top or from the bottom, or from both the top and the bottom of the border of the painting, the Japanese artist will blend a dark color gradually into the sky or the ground or both. This gives a very decided effect of relief; it sets the frame of the picture forward from its contents, giving a decided two-dimensional illusion of space to the landscape behind the picture edge. It is a device which is also used behind hills, at the water's edge, etc. Something very similar is to be found in the works of Cézanne and is particularly prominent in his water colors (the medium, incidentally, of the linear artists of the Orient). In Hiroshige this device was used, with rare exceptions, only horizontally not vertically. Although the Chinese held to this rule more or less, they were not so rigid about it and employed it in a more subtle and extensive manner than the Japanese. On the other hand, Cézanne used this device in all kinds of more complex ways and places in his paintings, wherever he might need it. He used light strips as well as dark blends to separate one object or plane from another (figure 99). Beyond this, however, he could find no need for the Oriental arts, and did not fall under the otherwise retarding influence which at best could have only a superficial relation to the basic problem of the new art of the West.

Whatever similarities can be found between the art of the Orientals and Cézanne were not necessary to the latter; what he strove for was bound to occur in the course which Occidental art had taken. Hence it is quite possible that he discovered this device without reference to Oriental art. Certainly his fundamental objective and those of Oriental artists were extremely different.

We have already stressed the confusion over the problem of fantasy and structure which exists in the works and words of Post-Impressionists. In their art and in what they said about it, there were negative and positive qualities, but in general critics have failed to discriminate between the various factors involved. Consequently there has continued to be confusion between the old and the new factors. Good examples of this may be found in the misevaluations most critics have made of that now famous remark by Cézanne that he wanted to make of Impressionism something solid and durable, like the old masters. From the evidence of Cézanne's work as well as other remarks he made about art, we explain this in the following manner: the old masters did not attain as strict a copying of nature as those Realists who worked around the time of the Camera's invention. But even though these old masters did not record with Photographic accuracy, they accomplished a creditable recording. How was this done? The artist made his recording under the assumption that he was putting down with paint what he saw. This was correct as far as it went. But, as we pointed out in earlier studies, what the artist saw was incomplete; in short, he did not see enough to make a completely accurate recording. Hence, subconsciously, the inherent ability of man to invent, to make arrangements with forms and colors, supplied the deficiency in his ability to visualize. This can be seen very sharply in the work of the Italian primitives, where a recording of a head, for example, is far from "reality," yet the artist was able to devise a collection of forms definitely indicating a human head.[26] In other words, the artist devised color-form organizations quite different from those of nature, or from those recordings by later artists who could record more accurately. For the more primitive the seeing involved in an artist's activity, the more he must rely on his ability to invent color-form organizations in order to achieve his purpose. The degree to which he must rely on invention is in direct ratio to the lack in his ability to record accurately (or to his conscious desire to change reality). On the other hand, the more accurately the artist is able to depict nature, the less he needs to rely on the Inventive faculty and the more he does rely, or can rely, on nature. This

26. We use the example of Italian primitive painting because it makes our point more clear, but we do not forget that Cézanne abhorred this type of painting because it was flat.

99. Paul Cézanne, The Pistachio Tree at the Chateau Noir, water color. Courtesy of the Art Institute of Chicago.

can be seen by comparing an Italian primitive with, for instance, a Courbet. Similarly the Inventive or "designing" activity which the artist uses to substitute for his particular degree of recording inability is far more in evidence, for example, in the old masters than in the much later artists like Courbet, who were able to visualize and so record nature much more accurately. These later artists relied almost completely upon nature's invention and design for their art recordings and comparatively little upon man's invention and design, which, so long as the contents of art were the objects of nature, led to fantasies of reality. (See page 288.) They did not need to "organize" nature's forms, because they were able to rely more explicitly, relatively speaking, upon the actual organizations of nature forms. In short, the 19th century Realists to a considerable degree depicted the art of nature, whereas the older artists to a considerable degree imposed the "art" of man upon nature in the effort to compensate for their inability to copy nature accurately. Still another level is involved when we are dealing with those artists who were not striving for literal recordings, but deliberately changed some aspect of the reality — that is, the Idealists of form or color or both. Yet to a certain degree they too made a deliberate effort to record what was seen so that their problem was somewhat similar to that of those who strove for literal realism. In both cases a limited comprehension of actual reality existed, but the Idealists also attempted deliberately to change reality in some degree. Therefore, to that degree that an artist does not achieve an accurate recording, he imposes his own invented organizations upon the actual appearance of nature's form-organizations. This imposition upon nature can be due either to an inability to record realistically (here distortion of nature is not deliberate) or to an idealistic objective (here distortion is, at least *to a certain degree, deliberate*).

It was this *Inventive aspect* in the work of the old masters which attracted Cézanne. It supplied him with that which he was *deliberately* seeking. Thus he wrote in 1904: "what you must strive to attain is a good method of *construction*. Drawing is merely the outline of what you see." Thus: "Michelangelo is a constructor, and Raphael an *artist* who, great as he is, is always limited by the model." [27] Cézanne was here attempting to show the distinction under discussion by comparison of two artists, one of whom employed more idealism (and so more distortion) than the other. Michelangelo more deliberately changed actual reality and so employed more "invention" than did Raphael. Yet the most deliberate realism that either of these artists ever achieved, involved considerably more invention or manipulation of reality than is to be found in works by later artists.

The interest of Cézanne in Poussin is in a way a special case. Here we are confronted by an interest in a Classicist whose models were those of Greece and Rome. Of what interest could he be to Cézanne? Unlike the Realists among the old masters who unconsciously (or otherwise) altered reality, Poussin deliberately and consciously (as did Cézanne) exercised his Inventive capacity with the organization of forms and colors. But he did so in order to attain the "ideal" which could not be secured merely by trying to copy nature literally. In other words, the *method* to be found in Poussin's art was the important point of interest to Cézanne, not the idealism which resulted. It was in this sense of the Inventive organization of nature's color-forms that Cézanne expressed the desire to "do over Poussin from nature."

Therefore, being absorbed in the creative possibilities of organized color-form, Cézanne looked to that part of the past which appeared to give him something of what he himself was seeking — that part of Western, three-dimensional painting produced by artists still far enough away from the achievement of accurate recording that they had to rely heavily on invention. This he found in the old masters and the Idealists.

There are disputes as to whether Cézanne composed as did the old masters. In some ways we find that he did, but in a most important aspect he did not. That is, since he was not bound to the effort of trying to record nature accurately, as were the old masters, he had more freedom to subject nature forms to particular organizations. (Even the Idealists were bound to actual reality, as regards the freedom needed by Cézanne to attain his objective.) For example, he could bend contours to certain desired lines or planes that he wanted, regardless of the infractions consequently imposed upon the actual forms of nature. *His objective was not to idealize nature, but to use nature forms as the means for achieving*

27. Paul Cézanne *Letters*, p. 242, translated by Marguerite Kay, edited by John Rewald, Bruno Cassirer, London, 1941.

100. Gustave Courbet, An Alpine Scene. Courtesy of the Art Institute of Chicago.

101. Claude Lorrain, Landscape with a Piping Shepherd. Collection of William Rockhill Nelson Gallery of Art, Kansas City.

a "good method of construction" in the creation of art. Thus he was in a position to do more inventing in the composing of a picture than past artists since Renaissance times, because their method tended to put them predominantly in the position of striving to copy the forms and organizations of nature. Cézanne's freedom in composing from nature was not possible for the old masters, nor did they desire it. On the contrary they had to make their composing bend as much as they could to the contours of nature as

299

they actually appeared to their eyes. Hence, if the compositions and forms of the old masters were relatively possible in reality, those of Cézanne were definitely not. The wholeness, the compactness, the unity of Cézanne's work as compared to that of previous painters, was possible because he used nature as a subject for organization, to be deliberately remolded to fit the organization of form preferred by himself; while past painters copied nature and so had to submit as much as possible to the organizations found in nature. Cézanne deliberately engaged the Inventive factor as the predominating determinant of his contents, whereas the old masters deliberately tried to capture reality as it appeared to their eye-brain. Compared to Cézanne's freedom, even the Idealists were largely bound to actual appearances. Previously the appearance of nature was accepted as the "master" of man's art, but Cézanne was striving to become the master of the appearances of a man-created art. Thus in 1904 he wrote to Bernard: "One is neither too scrupulous nor too sincere nor too submissive to nature; but one is more or less master of one's model, and above all, of the means of expression."[28] Note that Cézanne does not here make the Aristotelian error of claiming that his distortions are superior to nature; nor does he do so in anything he has written. He had the great respect for nature that all great artists possessed. He claimed only to have made better paintings from nature than any of his contemporaries; today many realize that he was not merely boasting.

But one might well say, granted that what we have called the Inventive aspect and its particular function in pre-Camera art increase as one goes further and further back into history, why did Cézanne stop his admiration with Signorelli and the Venetians in general? Gauguin did go all the way back, "farther back than the horses of the Parthenon," while van Gogh admired the semi-primitive arts of the Orient. But Cézanne would go no farther back than the Renaissance artists. The reason for this was that where the painting arts were concerned Cézanne was interested only in those non-accurate recordings of the past which contained a concern either with form, as in Signorelli, or color, as in the Venetians, and the organization of both these factors, as seen in both. Van Gogh and Gauguin, with their predominantly linear interests, could easily apply themselves to Oriental prints and to the arts of even more primitive cultures, as well as to the Italian primitives, Giotto, etc. They were interested in the flat painting of the past, while Cézanne, for reasons already given, was interested primarily in that type of painting which dealt with the problem of the round being depicted on a flat surface.

Cézanne acknowledged, in one way or another, his interests in artists who were noted for achievements in one or more of five factors—color, form, space, organization and accurate realism. On his walls, according to Ambroise Vollard, were the following "engravings and photographs": *The Shepherds of Arcadia* by Poussin, *The Living Bearing the Dead* by Signorelli, *The Burial at Ornans* by Courbet, *The Assumption* by Rubens, *Love* by Puget, *Psyche* by Prud'homme, *Roman Orgy* by Couture, and some Delacroix and Forains.[29] Gerstle Mack wonders why the works were "mostly bad." Certainly the evidence of Cézanne's own work, which is now hailed to the skies, should stimulate a further inquiry as to why he hung upon his walls these works, some of which the "Moderns" call "bad." Cézanne unquestionably was a man too much withdrawn from any extensive human contact. As a result, he was maladjusted in certain aspects of his behavior. But it is a great error to think him intolerant and "narrow" in the one passion, the one very rigorous discipline of his life—art! We have explained the presence of some of these works in his studio by pointing out his need for certain structural factors to be found in past arts. On the other hand certain things, such as the *Roman Orgy* by Couture, had little if any of this to offer; yet they had two other functions:

> (1) The nudes in the realistic arts served as a means of studying the human form (but for his own purposes), for he had no nude models and so he studied them second-hand from the works of Realists and Idealists. Moreover, he directly used figures that he found in the works of other artists, often the most obscure and ordinary Realists.
>
> (2) He was never able to feel consistently secure that his way and not the Realists' was the correct direction, and no doubt there were moments when he admired their accurate recordings. We must realize that the direction in which art was evolving had not progressed far enough in Cézanne's work that he could clearly see where it was headed.

28. Ibid., p. 237.

29. Ambroise Vollard: *Paul Cézanne His Life and Art*, p. 99, translated by H. L. Van Doren, Frank-Maurice, Inc., New York, 1926.

102. Paul Cézanne, L'Estaque. Courtesy of The Metropolitan Museum of Art.

The conflict between nature-appearances and his search into the Structural Process of nature (the ultimate purpose of which Cézanne was in no position to be adequately conscious of) naturally aroused pressures and frustrations in the face of "realistic" art, with its centuries of authoritative tradition. The "tradition" of which Cézanne was a part was merely a few years old. He was interested in comprehending the structure of nature in order to use this knowledge as the means by which to construct a work of art. But this effort was not fully resolved in his times and partly explains why he said: "Nature presents the greatest difficulties to me . . . ." [30] and why repeatedly he spoke of his efforts to reconcile his "sensations" in the presence of nature.

Cézanne did not feel the need to delude himself, as most critics do, by ignoring the difficulty and doubt which he experienced between his "sensations" and the appearances of "nature"; neither did he rationalize the problem as some new "reality" discovered by presumably lifting the cover of nature and peering "underneath appearances." His statement, "I have not tried to reproduce nature: I have represented it," [31] is of great interest, since it exactly indicates the kind and degree of consciousness he had of his work.

30. As quoted by Gerstle Mack: *Paul Cézanne*, p. 311.

31. As quoted by Herbert Read: *Art Now*, p. 67, Faber and Faber, Ltd., London. 1933.

To a considerable extent, however, both Gauguin and van Gogh allowed their art to run into literary channels, with the structural factor playing a lesser role; while Cézanne stressed structure far more and the realistic and literary aspect of the subject far less. In a letter to Bernard he advised him to "avoid the literary spirit, which so often leads the painter astray . . . ."[32] Thus the confusion of the three greatest Post-Impressionists was different in each case, in that each admired some painters that the other did not; but on the whole their difficulties were similar.

They were all outcasts in a culture in which the significance for art of the Camera's invention had not yet been realized. Their works and their personal lives were objects for ridicule and abuse of the lowest sort. Van Gogh, in one of his letters, wrote: "Taking if you like the time in which we live as a great and true renaissance of art, the worm-eaten official tradition still alive but really impotent and inactive, the new painters alone, poor, treated like madmen and because of this treatment actually becoming so at least as far as their social life is concerned."[33]

It was van Gogh who supposed the world could be saved with Christianity; it was Gauguin who became disgusted with "civilization" and left to live with a Primitive people. On the social level Cézanne found it just as difficult to fit into his culture as did his two famous contemporaries. Fortunately, however, he had enough money to give him at least *that* kind of security in his environment. But Cézanne, least of the three, expressed his social difficulties in his art. He accepted society as it was, even though he found his place in it not at all to his liking.[34]

How little understood and how difficult life was made for the innovators of these times can be seen by a glance at some of the defamatory remarks made by critics between the years 1874 and 1934, about both Impressionists and Post-Impressionists.

Louis Leroy—1874: (In *The Charivari*)
"This painting, at once vague and brutal, appears to us to be at the same time the affirmation of ignorance and the negation of the beautiful as well as of the true. We are tormented sufficiently as it is by affected eccentricities, and it is only too easy to attract attention *by painting worse than anyone has hitherto dared to paint.*"[35]

Albert Wolff—1876: (*Le Figaro*)
"Following upon the burning of the opera-house, a new disaster has fallen on the quarter . . . . an exhibition which is said to be painting. The innocent passer-by enters and a cruel spectacle meets his terrified gaze. Here five or six lunatics . . . . have chosen to exhibit their works. "There are people who burst into laughter . . . ."[36]

Roger Bellue—1877: (*Le Chronique des Arts et de la Curiosité*)
"(The pictures) provoke laughter and yet they are lamentable. They display the profoundest ignorance of drawing, of composition, and of colour. When children amuse themselves with a box of colours and a piece of paper they do better."[37]

Jean Gérôme—1894: (*Journal des Artistes*)
"I repeat, only great moral depravity could bring the State to accept such rubbish—they must

32. Ibid., p. 378.

33. *Further Letters of Vincent van Gogh to His Brother, 1886-1889*, p. 123.

34. This latter is illustrated in the following incident: When Gasquet's son was introduced to Cézanne and expressed his admiration for two of Cézanne's works he had seen, Cezanne immediately burst out, "Don't you make fun of me, young man!" When his anger had subsided, he tried to explain himself: "You are young—you don't understand. I don't want to paint anymore. I've given up everything—listen to me, I am an unhappy man—you must not hold it against me—how can I believe that you can see something in my painting, in the two pictures you have seen, when all these fools who write nonsense about me have never been able to perceive anything? What a lot of harm they have done me!" (Mack, op. cit., pp. 351-352).

35. As quoted by Sheldon Cheney, *The Story of Modern Art*, p. 182. Leroy is the critic who daubed these artists Impressionists in the attempt to ridicule them. Thereafter the label became official.

36. As quoted by Bulley, op. cit., pp. 68-69.   37. Ibid., p. 68.

have foolishness at any price; some paint like this, others like that, in little dots, in triangles—how should I know? I tell you they're all anarchists—and madmen!" [38]

Robert Ross—1910: (*The Morning Post*)
"A date more favorable than the fifth of November for revealing the existence of a widespread plot to destroy the whole fabric of European painting, could hardly have been chosen . . . . There is no doubt whatever that the vast majority of the pictures . . . . will be greeted by the public with a . . . . damning and . . . . permanent ridicule . . . . If the movement is spreading . . . . it should be treated like the rat plague in Suffolk. The source of the infection (*e.g.* the pictures) ought to be destroyed." [39]

W. B. Richmond—1910: (*The Morning Post*)
"(The works) showed intellectual, emotional, and technical degeneracy; wilful anarchy and notoriety-hunting, which, were it not transparent, might be compared with criminality . . . . Cézanne might well be the father of the Post-Impressionists . . . . He should have been a butcher . . . . For a moment there came even a fierce feeling of terror lest the youth of England, young promising fellows, might be contaminated here . . . ." [40]

Albert Sterner—1934:
"Nevertheless, in all the history of painting and craftsmanship, its inevitable coexistent, a greater bungler cannot be found than Cézanne." [41]

In the year 1902, Octave Mirbeau approached the then Director of the Beaux-Arts, M. Roujon, his object being to secure official recognition for Cézanne in the form of the Legion of Honour. Vollard describes this meeting: "Mirbeau had no sooner said that he was pleading the cause of a certain painter for the cross than the superintendent, presuming that his visitor had the judgment not to demand the impossible, reached for the drawer which contained the ribbons committed to his keeping. But the name of Cézanne made him jump. 'Ah! Monsieur Mirbeau, while I am director of the Beaux-Arts I must follow the taste of the public and not try to anticipate it! Monet if you wish. Monet doesn't want it? Let us say Sisely, then. What! he's dead? How about Pissarro?' Then, misinterpreting Monsieur Mirbeau's silence: 'Is he dead too? Well then, choose whomever you wish. I don't care who it is, as long as you do me the favor of not talking about Cézanne again!' " [42]

But in spite of all this, art was pushed through the first climax of the transition and came to a second climax in the works of Paul Cézanne (figure 103). He in turn became the focal point of the future, the Cubists, in whose works a third climax was achieved. It was Cézanne who spoke directly the language of those who followed him: "you must see in nature the cylinder, the sphere, the cone . . . ." This was his advice to those who followed him and developed what he had begun. There has of course been much discussion as to what Cézanne meant by this statement. In full it reads: "you must see in nature the cylinder, the sphere, the cone, all put into perspective, so that every side of an object, of a plane, recedes to a central point." [43] Now the first part is quite clear, if we match what he said with what he did in his work. Obviously, he meant that all forms of nature could be reduced to these three basic shapes, the cylinder, sphere, cone. And, as he said, if one could paint these three basic shapes properly, then one should know how to paint. The remainder of the statement is more obscure. Some say he was voicing ordinary perspective theory. But this is not true because he did not say every side of *all* objects, of *all* planes. He said "*an* object," "*a* plane." This would seem to be a reference to individual central points for each object and

38. As quoted by Mack, op. cit., p. 332. We include this remark by an artist who continued realism to the bitter end, because he best represents the type of artist the critics of his time preferred. This remark was stimulated by Caillebotte's bequest of paintings to the Luxembourg.

39. Reprinted by courtesy of *The Daily Telegraph and Morning Post,* London. (As quoted by Bulley, op. cit., p. 68.)

40. Reprinted by courtesy of *The Daily Telegraph and Morning Post,* London. (As quoted by Bulley, op. cit., p. 68.)

41. Albert Sterner: "The Cézanne Myth," *Harper's Magazine,* May, 1934, p. 673. Of course prejudices in the opposite direction have led to similar non-sense.

42. Vollard, *Paul Cézanne His Life and Art, pp.* 175-176, translated by H. L. Van Doren.

43. As quoted by Mack, op. cit., pp. 377-378.

each plane (*a device later used by the Cubists*), and would be consistent with his painting. If Cézanne were painting a group of square houses, he did not keep them all square or all in the same perspective, should his composing needs demand otherwise. Instead he altered the perspective, regardless of the scientific central point of vision for all parallel planes; he modified nature forms, or, to put it more accurately, he modified the perspective image so that it conformed to the structural demands of his painting's organization. He did so even if this meant that a number of "central points" of vision were thus established in a single picture. In other words, the use of many vanishing points in each painting was one of the structural potentialities which Cézanne gained from the general liberty he took with nature's forms for organization purposes. Perspective was regarded as a variable like the forms and colors of nature objects, that could be adjusted to whatever demands were made by the painting's organization.

Therefore, the facts—the paintings—are the answers to the arguments about Cézanne's perspective. Cézanne did with this problem what he did generally with most previous laws of art recording—he made his own "perspective laws." If he had not, he would have been forced to copy nature. And with this liberty he gained a greater release for his organizational activities. Accordingly, it is erroneous to assume that this theory given above was an exposition of conventional perspective theory. His paintings obviously do not bear out its application. We can account for the ambiguous language of his remarks on perspective by realizing that his objective compelled him to revise the Realists' theory of perspective. Such efforts are no longer necessary since later artists have discovered the fundamental objectives toward which Cézanne strove.

There has also been much ado about Cézanne's water colors, as to whether they were finished or unfinished, whether they were studies for his paintings or independent of them, etc. But certainly Cézanne did not devote a great deal of time and effort and accomplish such magnificent results just to produce a lot of "unfinished experiences." The great majority of his water colors were often more definitely in the direction towards which he was working in his paintings, and in fact, his paintings are considerably influenced by his experiences in water color. That is how the blank unpainted surfaces came to appear in his paintings. He did something similar when he let the initial washes of color remain uncovered by overpainting. It was in his water colors, which he never exhibited and seldom showed to anyone, that *he felt more free to plunge in the direction which he felt a fundamental need to pursue.* Thus in them, more frequently than in his paintings, he was able to exercise a greater freedom from the dictates of nature's appearances and so proportionately give that much greater concentration to the organization of color-shapes. In short, in water color he had less fear of what others would think, since they remained more or less a private matter. Moreover, working with a medium in which he could let the flat paper show through the marks made upon it and even leave great areas of it untouched, Cézanne was able to accomplish more satisfactory regulations of his eternal conflict between a round world and the flat surface upon which he worked. If in his paintings he was able to leave a patch of bare canvas here and there, in his water colors he could often leave major portions of his working surface bare of even a single touch. It was in these efforts that we find some of his most successful water colors; it was these results he tried to obtain in his paintings, even to the bare patches of canvas and the use of washes of oil paint.

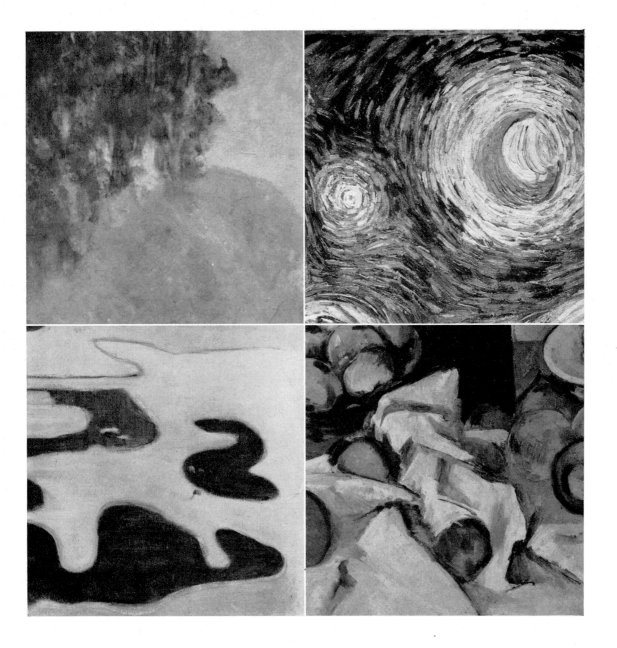

103. Above left, Monet, detail of figure 94; above right, van Gogh, detail of figure 95; below left, Gauguin, detail of figure 96; below right, Cézanne, detail of figure 98.

In his most ambitious paintings, the huge pictures of women bathers, Cézanne's well-known incapacity to work without models compelled him to reach further along the road he was travelling, perhaps in spite of himself. These bather projects, almost an obsession with him, have also been greatly misunderstood. In them, along with his last landscapes, he reached far into the approaching future, and hence they are among the most important of his works. In them we find the kind of painting that the next generation started off with. It is no accident that Picasso, just before he entered the Cubist period, painted a large canvas of nude women (*Les Demoiselles d'Avignon*, 1906-07), reminiscent both in size and subject of Cézanne's ambitious bather pictures.

In his writings as well as in his works we see that Cézanne's interest in nature was directly and unequivocably in the observation of the Structural Process of nature as it applies to art, in the organization of color-forms-in-space. Thus he wrote: "Design and color are not distinct; in the degree in which there is color, there is design; the more colors harmonize with one another, the more defined is design. When color is at its richest, form is most complete. Contrasts and relations of tones—there is the secret of design and pattern." [44] He was the first artist of more recent times to speak directly and emphatically of the eye-brain in relation to art: "In the painter there are two things, the eye and the brain: each should help the other . . . . The eye should concentrate, devour; the brain formulate . . . ." [45] And: "an optical sensation is produced in our visual organ which causes us to grade the planes represented by sensations of color into full light, half-tones and quarter-tones (light does not exist for the painter). [46] Necessarily, while we are proceeding from black to white, the first of these abstractions being a sort of point of departure for the eye as well as for the brain . . . ." [47] Elsewhere he wrote: "Everything, particularly *in art,* is theory developed and applied in contact with nature." [48] And "I believe in the logical development of everything we see and feel through the study of nature . . . ." [49] And finally we see Cézanne as an historian: "The Louvre is the book in which we learn to read. But we must not be content to memorize the beautiful formulas of our illustrious predecessors. Let us get out and study beautiful nature, let us try to discover her spirit, let us express ourselves according to our own temperaments. Time and meditation tend to modify our vision little by little and finally comprehension comes to us." [50] Here he is saying, "Study the past, but do not mock it. Study nature, learn the method by which nature's art is constructed" —this was what he meant when he said "discover her spirit," so that we can "express ourselves"—by this he meant that with this knowledge of nature's structure man can learn to create art instead of merely imitating nature's art.

The correctness of what we have attributed to Cézanne's remarks is borne out by the subsequent meanings his art had in further developments, which we shall study presently. Above all he was conscious, as he put it, that *"a new era of modern art is on the way."* (emphasis ours) [51]

In this respect it is interesting to compare him with Seurat (figure 104), an artist who did more or less what Cézanne did and progressed along similar lines. Seurat had something to offer simply because he moved on from what had been done and produced developments; moreover he was an artist

44. From Emile Bernard: *Souvenirs sur Paul Cézanne*, p. 37, Chez Michel, Paris, 1925.

45. As quoted by Margaret Bulley in *Art and Counterfeit*, p. 6, Methuen and Co., London.

46. He was here distinguishing between painting and sculpture, in the sense that in the latter medium actual light participated in the lighting up of the forms.

47. As quoted by Mack, op. cit., p. 381.

48. Ibid., p. 364.

49. Paul Cézanne *Letters,* edited by John Rewald, p. 266.

50. As quoted by Mack, op. cit., p. 382.

51. Ibid., p. 363.

104. Georges Seurat, Port of Gravelines, Petitfort Philippe. John Herron Art Institute, Indianapolis.

105. Paul Cézanne, Mont Sainte Victoire. Courtesy of the Philadelphia Museum of Art, Philadelphia.

who wholly and deliberately adopted the scientific attitude that has characterized the work of the important artists who came after him. Had he lived longer—he was only 31 when he died—his achievements might have outstripped those of Cézanne. On the other hand, Cézanne saw that his own work was not a final solution, and was therefore able to make important advances which Seurat could not reach, since in the latter's work everything seemed settled. It was as though Seurat were striving to make a final, complete statement about art, as though what he did were a finished problem. Thus there was a danger for others in Seurat's work of accepting this finality, consciously or otherwise.

One worthwhile result, however, emerged from this very finality: Seurat was able to make something monumental of the art development of his times. That which was a monument of finality for Seurat was for Cézanne only a step along the way to even greater achievements in art. (This is why Seurat was primarily *admired* and Cézanne was primarily *used* by the innovators of the next generation.) Seurat is frozen reality made into Architecture; *Cézanne is the progressive architectural dissection of reality.*

We can find these two types, or variations and combinations of them, throughout the history of art. The one type—Gauguin and Renoir belong here, as well as Seurat—goes so far and no farther, but clearly and sharply emphasizes an aspect of what has been done in his times. The other type consciously strives to "realize," to reach past his own achievements, and his art is never ready to produce a monument, although he may occasionally try it. He emphasizes the discoveries of his times in their implications for the future.

The great importance of Cézanne's work is not that it is a recipe for people who don't know what to do, four decades after his death; the significance of his work to the development of art lies in the fact that he made a definite, clear swing from the old to the new epoch of art history. As for those who would like to continue conveniently to do as Cézanne did, they should remember that this is precisely what Cézanne never did! He would have abhorred the absolutes and many false evaluations that have been made of his work. His work teaches us not to repeat what has already been done, but to move on to doing what remains to be done. As he said, "we must not be content to memorize the beautiful formulas of our illustrious predecessors." We stress this because the great majority of artists today are wasting their time being Post-Impressionists under one guise or another.

And today there is no longer any reason for any kind of Post-Impressionistic art, since the purpose for which it was originally invented has been accomplished and its positive function completed by those who invented it. To persist in this direction, as so many artists are doing today, only leads to an inferior grade of Post-Impressionism, not only useless but detrimental to the further evolution of art. But this sort of activity will undoubtedly continue until we learn that art is not some hunt for a final absolute, but an ever changing affair of asymmetrical development or regression. We cannot even begin to comprehend the basic significance of Cézanne (or any other painter or artist) if we regard him as seeking or having achieved some kind of perfection for which all great painters have allegedly striven.

Notice that the men who make progress (the men from whose art the absolutes are fabricated!) do not foster absolutes in their own work. That is why they can move from what has been, instead of merely repeating with elaborations what has already been concluded. Cézanne clearly stated in a letter written during the year preceding his death: "To my mind one should not substitute oneself for the past, one has merely to add a new link." [52] And this is precisely what he did! For in him the efforts of his generation were more complete and he therefore became the principal focal point for those who came after him and pushed the evolution of art further along. Just as what was unconscious in the "struggle" of Monet, became fully conscious in Cézanne, so we shall find that what was unconscious in Cézanne came to greater consciousness with the Cubists.

A year before his death he wrote these prophetic words: "I am too old; I have not realized; and now I shall not realize. I remain the primitive of the way which I have discovered." [53] This was Cézanne's advice to those coming in the future: *"I am the primitive of the way!"*

52. Paul Cézanne *Letters*, op. cit., p. 248.

53. Quoted by Elie Faure, *Cézanne*, p. 63, translated by Walter Pach, published by the Association of American Painters and Sculptors, Inc., copyrighted 1913.

To be is to be related. 174

Cassius J. Keyser

. . . . you must see in nature the cylinder, the sphere, the cone 215

Paul Cezanne

15 THE GREAT DECISION

The Cubistic school was the summit of a revolutionary process in Art which was already started by the Impressionists at the end of the last century. 124
                                    Naum Gabo

Although the Cubists still regarded the external world as the point of departure for their Art they did not see and did not want to see any difference between, say, a violin, a tree, a human body, etc. All those objects were for them only one extended matter with a unique structure and only this structure was of importance for their analytic task . . . . When we look through a Cubistic painting to its concept of the world the same thing happens . . . . which occurred in the world of physics when the new Relativity Theory destroyed the border lines between Matter and Energy, between Space and Time, between the mystery of the world in the atom and the consistent miracle of our galaxy. 124
                                    Naum Gabo

The role of cubism has been precisely that of a poser of problems, with reference to the future mode of artistic creation, diametrically opposed to all traditionalism and all naturalistic imitation, and as such its business is to raise all sorts of new questions (like those of elementary architecture, photography, the films, etc.). 99   Theo van Doesburg

Thus cubism has never been a recipe for making descriptive pictures or a mechanical method for multiplying picture motifs. 99
                                    Theo van Doesburg

Our history has shown that the evolution of man is an asymmetrical order of relationships. In a sense we can regard history as analogous to a chess game in which each new move changes the entire character of the game from what it has been. At the same time each new move determines what will be or can be the next move. And as in chess it is not permissible to play over a move already made.

We have briefly stressed this point here because we are now approaching a unique climax in the art history of man—the appearance of Cubism. With the entrance of this art into the historic scene, the radical change from one system of art to another becomes more clearly apparent. Hence it becomes necessary to keep in mind the as-a-whole character of the historical milieu into which the Cubists are about to enter.

Let us review briefly what has transpired during the period from just before the Camera up to

Cézanne by listening to each of the artists as he speaks of the ever changing visualization of nature's reality.

Ingres:

". . . . above all copy with absolute fidelity, though it be but a still-life."

Courbet:

"If you want me to paint an angel, show me one!"

"Realism in its essence is democratic art."

Manet:

"The principal person in a painting is the light."

Monet:

". . . . try to forget what objects you have before you . . . Merely think, there is a little square of blue, here an oblong of pink . . . ."

van Gogh:

". . . . yes, untruth if you like, but more true than literal truth."

Gauguin:

"The artist . . . . (if he wishes really to make a divine creative work), must not copy Nature, but use the elements of Nature to create a new element."

Cézanne:

"One is neither too scrupulous nor too sincere nor too submissive to nature; but one is more or less master of one's model, and above all, of the means of expression."

". . . . you must see in nature the cylinder, the sphere, the cone . . . ."

With Cézanne, the old objective, characterized principally by an effort to record as literally as possible what is seen in nature's appearances, was definitely replaced by another, characterized by a study of the various *structural aspects* of visual phenomena. Although all the outstanding artists from Monet on had talked about structural factors and the changes of reality, their consciousness of the basic significance of either of these factors was so inadequate that they were torn between the conflicting elements of fantasy on the one hand and the quest for structure on the other. Evolution had not yet gone far enough from the old kind of art to bring the new objective into sharp focus, and so neither the fantasy aspect nor the structural one could be clearly distinguished.

The task of the new generation was to bring to a conclusion the particular researches of Cézanne. But it was not until after his death in 1906 that his work exerted any great influence. Therefore during the first few years of the 20th century it was the negative, the symptomatic aspects of Post-Impressionism that held the attention of the majority of artists, and various Primitive and Oriental arts exerted a predominant influence.

Let us examine first one of these groups of artists—the so-called Fauvists. It seemed that in the beginning they were going to tackle the basic problems then evolving. In 1908, Henri Matisse said that there should be nothing in a picture that could be described with words. He claimed that when he saw a picture he forgot what it represented, that all that is "important is line, form and color . . . ." [1] Here we see that Matisse claimed to do what Monet more vaguely expressed the desire to be able to do. It has been reported that Matisse never rejected the values of Cubism, that he believed it to be a "step in the right direction." But actually Matisse only flirted with Cubism and then from a very safe distance. The Fauvists, of whom Matisse was the leader, studied Cézanne only superficially. Matisse is a sophisticated combination of Gauguin and van Gogh (see figure 149); a little like the latter in his method of applying paint and a little like the former in his attitude towards the depiction of reality. With this there is an insignificant dash of Cézanne. None of the Fauvists was at first aware of the full significance of Cézanne's three-dimensional discoveries and hence none of them utilized that characteristic which made his work distinct from and an advance over that of his other contemporaries. The Fauvists' interest in his work was largely confined, on a superficial level, to the color and linear aspects of Cézanne's organizations. On page 287 we spoke of the two aspects of the work of the Post-Impressionists, their "achievements" and their "imperfections." The Fauvists misevaluated the imperfections as the achievements of their predecessors. Consequently they accomplished little more than a further distortion and simplification of nature's appearances into two-dimensional

1. Henri Matisse: "Notes d'un Peintre," *La Grande Revue,* Paris, December 25, 1908.

color-areas. They simply polished up the discoveries of their predecessors, van Gogh and Gauguin, and in the end had nothing new to offer.

Lemaitre, in his evaluation of Fauvism, was therefore in error when he wrote: "A picture was not simply a more or less faithful, more or less original copy of a 'model.' A picture was henceforth considered as a complete creation, a self-contained, absolute entity."[2] The Fauvists may have originally intended to achieve a "complete creation" in place of copying nature, but actually, so long as their art merely consisted of distortive copying of nature-appearances, they created only a substitute for such an objective. While they were copying nature less than artists in the immediate past, they were still copying nature. Actually such art was neither a literal copy of nature nor a literal "creation" of man, but a compromise between the two.

In the end the Fauvists not only failed to progress beyond the achievements of the Post-Impressionists, but their works are incomparably inferior, since they stressed mainly the superficial, the negative aspect—fantasy—until it became the principal objective of art. Meanwhile the important, the positive factor—the element of structure—became a mere appendage to the fantasy in their works. This direction, as we shall see, became a dead-end, an attempt to escape from the pressing and vital problems facing artists at the time, a futile attempt to escape to the world of the Primitive, Oriental and child artist. Matisse and the Fauvists, in general, failed to see the error of van Gogh's and Gauguin's attraction to the Oriental arts. As Cézanne had indicated in his criticism of Gauguin, such influences only hindered and were contrary to the development of Western art. But Matisse was tied to the Oriental formula to an even greater extent than his predecessors had been; if Gauguin had to escape to a Primitive society to find his world of fantasy, then Matisse escaped by changing his culture into another-world, even painting Oriental subjects without giving up his own culture to live among the Orientals. The one extroverted himself to another culture, the other introverted himself in this culture. Put a Matisse next to a Gauguin (or a van Gogh) and see the differences. In the work of the two latter artists we see the struggle of men for a knowledge of art; while in the work of Matisse we see a sophisticated, talented performer. Gauguin once wrote in his journal: "I am not learned, but I believe there are people who are learned. I also believe that some day some learned man will discover the exact difference in weight between genius and talent."[3]

Like many an artist since, Matisse lacked the sustained courage to push on after stepping off in the new direction. He had achieved more consciousness of that for which his predecessors were striving, but the theory of art he voiced in 1908 (see page 314) always remained far in advance of his actual works. He lacked an adequate consciousness of the implications of his theory. Hence he was able to assume that he had finally found a complete recipe for painting and so in the long run was limited to futile attempts to outdo his predecessors by elaborating upon the fantasy aspect of their accomplishments. The activities of the fantasy factor did much, as we shall see in various examples, to keep artists from piercing the intuitive level and securing an adequate consciousness of where art was being taken. That is, the possibilities of achieving consciousness were made still more remote and difficult because these fantasies of nature's appearances produced temporary satisfactions.

In 1908, Matisse had also expressed a theory (the negative aspect of his views) which came to dominate the future character of his work. He wrote that what he dreamed of was an art balanced, "pure and calm," devoid of disturbance in its content, an art for the intellectual worker, the writer or the business man, that would be "something like a comfortable armchair in which one can rest from physical fatigue."[4] This is exactly what he has been attempting to do ever since. In fact, he reiterated in 1928 what he had said in 1908, that a picture must appear quiet. The spectator must not be disturbed, or feel the need of "contradicting himself, of coming out of himself."[5] Quite unintentionally perhaps

[handwritten margin note: Fetish of change]

2. Reprinted by permission of the publishers from Georges Lemaitre, *From Cubism to Surrealism in French Literature*, p. 68. Harvard University Press, Cambridge, Mass., 1941.

3. *The Intimate Journals of Paul Gauguin*, p. 206, translated by Van Wyck Brooks.

4. Matisse, "Notes d'un Peintre."

5. Florent Fels: *Henri-Matisse*, Editions des "Chroniques du Jour," Paris, 1929.

Matisse is here telling us that art served the same purpose for himself as he wanted it to serve for the on-looker: a refuge from the disturbing, confusing problem of reality. In these notions we can see that Matisse has done what so many others have throughout this century—he has attempted to justify his fantasy art with some sort of "social" objective. And so he has become the "great" artist in the collection of the "serious" amateurs who want to escape reality in a dignified fashion, as contrasted to those who desire the more violent irresponsible escape supplied by Dali and his kind.

During the period when the Oriental type of Fauvists were producing an art of escape, other artists began to study and utilize certain characteristics of Primitive arts, particularly those of Africa. These arts had been lying around in natural history museums for some time, but had been regarded more as curiosities than as significant art phenomena. But European art had now arrived at a stage where certain similarities to these Primitive arts were apparent. They served a function similar to that which the Oriental prints, etc., had for the previous generation, and since they were even more primitive than the Oriental arts, the distortive *stimulus* was increased. But just as with the Oriental arts previously, the function and influence of Primitive art for Europeans was over-evaluated. The basic motivations of Western art still remained buried in the subconscious and so there was still a failure to realize that Primitive art had merely a superficial similarity at best to the direction which Western art had already taken. Cézanne's work had been in several exhibitions and his influence was beginning to be felt; but it seemed that what he stood for remained in the background until this new primitive spree was over.

The harm to Western art of these primitive influences has far outweighed whatever benefits they have had. There is no question that we can learn from early forms of human behavior and perhaps recover some of the desirable attitudes which have been neglected or even lost in the ever-increasing complexity of present day culture. But this does not mean that we can merely hi-jack the past and use "as is," any more than we can recover the vitality and intense curiosity of an infant to the life around it by merely becoming infantile. It is certainly a sad commentary upon our reasoning attitudes to find that so many have not learned anything from the Primitives except, of all things, to try ludicrously to imitate them. This produces as destructive results for us as for the Primitive when he tries to imitate us.

Since the Primitive or African influence was greatest in the work of Picasso, he will serve as a good example of what was happening.[6] In the beginning phase of his "Negroid" period, Picasso's work was composed of a direct, simple emphasis upon the three-dimensional factor of form. Roundness was emphasized even more than in Cézanne. A maximum of simplification and exaggeration of the main aspects of the subject-matter (just as is practiced in Primitive arts) resulted in a further sacrifice of nature's actual appearances. Details were omitted, forms thickened and enlarged for the sake of increasing the emphasis upon the three-dimensional character and organization of form. It is this phenomenon which blazed forth from the African sculptures into the eyes of artists, suggesting one method for securing organizations of color-form to be imposed upon the actual appearances of nature forms.

However, Cézanne had played long and hard on this theme and it was plain enough in his works. Thus the question arises why artists like Picasso failed at first to base their work directly upon Cézanne's, but attempted to use mainly Primitive art to help them in this direction. We have already explained that artists during these transitional times were abjectly dependent upon intuition and hence were influenced first by factors which would most easily and directly reach the intuitive faculties. Form, as such, was practically shouting, primitively, blatantly, from the sculpture of the Africans, while in Cézanne's work more subtle problems of form were being worked out. Because of an excessive reliance upon the intuitive factor, such artists as Picasso saw superficially in the art of the Africans that which was more completely and fundamentally indicated in the subtler works of Cézanne.

During the period from 1906-07 Picasso's work moved from the very round to the flat. It became African Fauvism, in contrast to the Oriental Fauvism of Matisse. But by 1908 Picasso was again painting in the round. Here we see his ambivalence between the flat and round influences of his times, the Fauvist and Oriental influences on the one hand and the form-structure influence of Cézanne and Primitive sculp-

---

6. Picasso in fact went in the African direction with as much gusto as Matisse went in the Oriental. It is no accident that these two artists, who stressed the symptomatic influences of the Primitive and semi-primitive arts to the fullest in the major portion of their life works, have become the most popular of those among so-called Modern artists.

tures, on the other. But when he decided, for the time being at least, to work in the three-dimensional manner, he was influenced by African art more than by Cézanne and his general concern for form and structure was swathed in the fantasy cloak of Primitive art. Temporarily he went all the way in his use of the Primitives and mistook the art of Africa as a ready-made formula for European art.

Other contemporaries of Picasso, such as Fernand Léger, for example, who were not subservient to the African influence, managed anyway to arrive at three-dimensional concerns with structure. Léger took a more discriminatory attitude towards the art of Africa and did not find it necessary for his art to take on a primitive appearance. It was he, therefore, more than any other outstanding artist of the pre-Cubist period, who took Cézanne's dictum literally, and his work became an emphatic affirmation of Cézanne's notion that nature must be "interpreted," as he put it, in terms of the cylinder, sphere and cone. In these efforts of Léger we see the beginning of Cézanne's dominant influence in the determination of Western painting.

Léger's work of this period exposes as an error the popular assumption that the more spectacular Picasso produced the most important art of these times. It was Léger and Braque and others like them who went directly to the core of the extant problems by recognizing the significance of Cézanne's work in regard to the transitions to be made. This can be seen by comparing their works of this period.

But Picasso managed to overcome his attraction to primitivism, at least long enough to participate usefully in the Cubist movement. One kind of development in Cubism is very clear-cut in Picasso's work and so through it we shall first analyze this movement. By implication we shall be studying the works of Georges Braque also throughout our analysis of Picasso-Cubism, since the works of these artists were quite similar during this period.

We have already pointed out that in 1906 and into 1907 Picasso in his "Negroid period" returned to flat renditions, but that by 1908 he was painting in the round once more. But it should be stressed that Cubism was not derivative from African art any more than Impressionism and Post-Impressionism were derived from Japanese or Oriental art. The direction of Cubism was inherent in the character of the developmental process of Western art. In short, if there had been no African sculpture, there still would have been Cubism of some kind. Naum Gabo is correct when he insists that: "Many falsely assume that the birth of Cubistic ideology was caused by the fashion for negro art which was prevalent at that time; but in reality Cubism was a purely European phenomenon and its substance has nothing in common with the demonism of primitive tribes. The Cubistic ideology has a highly differentiated character and its manifestation could only be possible in the atmosphere of a refined culture."[7]

In the 1908 work of Picasso, Léger and Braque, we see Cézanne made more conscious, as it were, done in the simplest manner possible. There now appeared the first clear-cut manifestations of Cubism, that is, a greater concentration than ever before upon the analysis of the three-dimensional structure of visual phenomena as such. Cézanne was now playing the major role in the determination of Western painting.

The principal stimulus motivating the Cubists as they began their work was the concern with the structural factors of visual phenomena. Unlike the Fauvists, they were not content simply to manipulate to a certain degree the color-areas of nature. They realized that all that could be done here had already been done by the Post-Impressionists, particularly van Gogh and Gauguin. Thus they looked to Cézanne, who pointed in a direction which permitted the further evolution of art. In the effort to "realize" the implications of Cézanne's researches, their subsequent work was characterized by an ever increasing manipulation and simplification of reality. While the Cubists were never entirely free from the influence of nature objects as such, they were *predominantly* concerned with the form-structure which resulted from the ever increasing elimination of nature's forms. By contrast with the Fauvists, the Cubists' interest in subject-matter was secondary, and it diminished in importance as Cubism developed.

In correlating our theory of the development of Cubism with the actual paintings, two factors must be kept in mind: (1) dates attributed to the paintings are not always reliable; (2) the artists did not achieve an unbroken development; they wavered back and forth, now going forward, now going back to what had already been done.

7. Naum Gabo: "The Constructive Idea in Art," p. 3, *Circle*, International Survey of Constructive Art, edited by J. L. Martin, Ben Nicholson, Naum Gabo: E. Weyhe, New York.

106. Pablo Picasso, Fernande, 1908. On extended loan from Henry Church
to the Museum of Modern Art, New York.

During 1908-09 the trend towards the analysis of three-dimensional structure rapidly evolved
into the more precise geometry of Cubism. Picasso was now sharply defining the forms or structure of
nature in terms of angular demarcations which emphasize the planes as they go in and out of the third
dimension (figure 106). Cézanne's dictum was beginning to stand out in sharp relief, as Picasso blocked
out the forms of nature into their simplest, exaggerated geometric components. But notice that the general
form of nature was still retained; the artist was concerned only with angularizing nature's forms without
disturbing too much their original relations and shapes.

In the first stage, then, the Cubists "geometrized" and "angularized" the forms of nature into
planes, but retained in general the arrangement and closed character of these forms as seen in the original.
Next the forms began to OPEN, and become planes which slip and slide into each other. The beginning
of this transition can be seen in figure 107, but even more clearly in the head of figure 108. (Examples
that better illustrate the point here being made could not be obtained. See *Picasso: Forty Years of His Art,*
page 70, figure 90, *Woman in a Landscape,* 1909.) Figure 109 is a good example of this transition in its
further development. In this second stage the continued manipulation of nature resulted in breaking up
and opening the forms and hence releasing them towards their particular potentialities as planes suitable
for distribution over the linear canvas. In this stage we see the beginning of the resolution of that problem
which had so perplexed Cézanne—his concern with the three-dimensional reality being "represented" upon

107. Pablo Picasso, Head, 1909. Collection The Museum of Modern Art, New York. Photo, Peter A. Juley and Son.

a two-dimensional medium. Recall that he had once remarked that it had taken him forty years to realize that painting was not sculpture. Cézanne was never able to solve this problem to his own satisfaction and complained bitterly and repeatedly that he was never able to "realize." This was because he was never willing to give up either the *plane* of his medium or the *forms* of his subject-matter. He tried to compromise these oppositions. We can now better understand why he emphasized the planes parallel to the canvas surface, and why his forms were cut in half by a plane running parallel to the canvas plane. (Notice the presence of the hemisphere effects of Cézanne's forms, discussed in the previous chapter, in these early stages of Cubism.) This was the linear character of the canvas exerting its influence upon the three-dimensional reality being "represented." It was this influence also which led Cézanne to leave unpainted surfaces in his canvas (a device used so often in the course of Cubist development), for in this way the stark, untouched, two-dimensional plane of the canvas could play its part directly in the work. This was carried even further in Cézanne's water colors, where only a series of planes were usually indicated, a part here and there of a form, while the major portion of the paper was left untouched. In such activities Cézanne was endeavoring to realize a satisfactory harmony of the *forms* of reality upon the *plane* of his linear medium.

This sort of treatment of the problem of the forms of reality and the flat surface of the canvas began with the work of Cézanne and included most Cubist works. It is comparable to the efforts of the

319

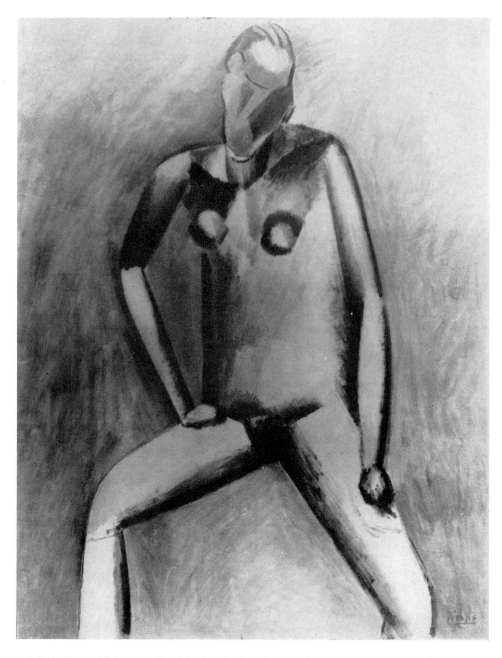

108. Pablo Picasso, Nude, 1910 (?). Collection of Mr. and Mrs. Walter C. Arensberg.

Renaissance sculptors who used reliefs and color in the attempt to solve new problems that actually were the prime concern of the painter with his linear medium. Similarly the problem of Cézanne and the Cubists could have been better realized in a three-dimensional medium. In this respect their works also take on the character of a kind of relief, in that there was an attempt to preserve the flat character of the painting medium and at the same time a concern with the problem of form-structure.

Nevertheless Cézanne's statements about this problem and his work in general began to be clarified by the activities of the Cubists, and the problem was temporarily resolved in the Cubism of Picasso and Braque, who did give up one of these factors for the other. Thus in figure 109 planes in

109. Pablo Picasso, Woman with Mandolin, 1910. Collection of Roland Penrose, London. Photo, Museum of Modern Art.

preference to forms are beginning to dominate, while a more decided manipulation of nature's forms and the increasing presence of the Inventive factor are evident in the ever increasing geometrical delineation of the planes and forms.

Notice also in figure 109 that the background is already being treated as a distribution of planes across a plane parallel with that of the canvas. The subject-matter of the background lent itself to this more easily than does the human form. But in the next step (figure 110) this treatment was successfully extended to the figure, that is the figure and background were now treated as a unit.

Throughout the development of the second stage of Cubism, from 1910 to 1912 (figures 109,

110. Pablo Picasso, Portrait of Kahnweiler, 1910. Collection of Mrs. Charles B. Goodspeed, Chicago.

110, 111), the planes were cut loose from the closed forms and were gradually transformed more and more to the disposition of the linear surface of the canvas. This is especially clear in figure 111, where the hemispheres of Cézanne have now almost disappeared. Observe further how the artist has changed the very character of the geometry employed during these transitions, in order finally to produce planes which would be two-dimensional. For example, in figure 109, the diagonal character seen in figure 106 is still retained. But observe the background of figure 109; the right-angle is beginning to predominate. The planes used to depict the figure shoot in and out of the third dimension, as in previous Cubism (figure 106), but in the background, particularly on the left side, there appear a series of planes parallel to and

111. Pablo Picasso, Portrait with the words "J'aime Eva," 1912. Collection, Ferdinand Howald, The Columbus Gallery of Fine Arts.

repeating the square plane of the canvas. As a matter of fact, it appears, significantly enough, that the objects represented are actually the square planes of the *back* sides of numerous canvases. Further development appears in figure 110, as the flat, square, open construction of the figure breaks its boundaries and becomes one with the background. The method for treating the background of figure 109 becomes in figure 110 the means for treating the painting as a whole. The diagonals going in and out of the third dimension are still somewhat in evidence, but they have greatly flattened out; form as such has almost disappeared; the problem for the most part is one of LINEAR space and shape. Nature's objects are obviously being manipulated with considerable freedom, becoming more of a spring-board from which the

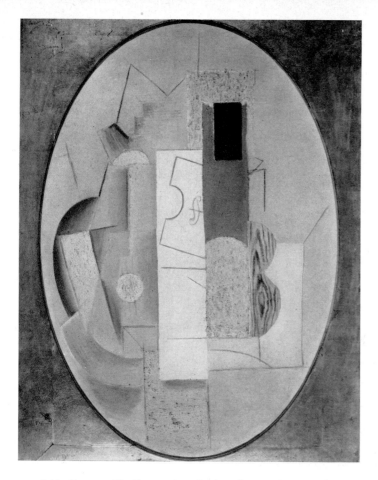

112. Pablo Picasso, Still Life, 1913?. Collection of Mr. and Mrs. Walter C. Arensberg.

artist releases his Inventive ability. This second stage is concluded in such works as figure 111. Here the figure and the background have been consciously worked out with the objective of making a complete linear unit. The right-angle now dominates the diagonal, the reverse of the early stages, and the flat character of all the planes is deliberately placed parallel to the canvas plane. Form is indicated only in minor notes; the main emphasis is upon parallel linear planes and spaces. The round aspect of forms also has become circles, planes and lines parallel to the canvas plane.

As Cubism definitely enters the linear phase, *papier-colles* make an appearance. In these works the flat or unpainted paper or canvas is retained and frequently comprises the major area of the works. (Figures 117, 118.) This device first appeared in the works of Cézanne.

In the second or middle stage of Cubism there was a higher degree of abstracting from nature's reality than had appeared in the preceding stage, in the sense that the Cubists were now abstracting more from the Structural Process of nature and less from the nature forms resulting from that process. The objective here was not only to explore the possibilities of form manipulation of nature-appearances, but more important, to release further the Inventive factor, to create and arrange shapes so as to exploit further the particular potentialities of the two-dimensional canvas surface as such. This stage, as we shall later explain, is the high point of Cubist development. In the works of this period we find that the final developments of art in the 19th century, where the Inventive factor was at a minimum and nature-appearances at a maximum (relatively speaking), had now been reversed by the Cubists, the content of whose art was at this stage to a large degree invented; only vestiges of nature's appearances remained. In short, the change is from the RECORDED forms of nature to the now largely CREATED shapes of man.

In the third and last stage of Cubism, 1912-1914 (see particularly figures 112, 113, 117, 118), we find in most of the works flat, overlapping planes. Without equivocation the various shapes, with definite,

113. Pablo Picasso, *Still Life with Guitar*, 1913. Collection of Sidney Janis. Photo, Museum of Modern Art.

closed boundaries, are placed deliberately along the two-dimensional plane of the canvas. These closed shapes, the dominant and often the only kind of shape used in these works, present us with an interesting phenomenon. Look back at figure 106; here the artist also used closed areas, but these, relatively speaking, had more of the character of the actual three-dimensional closed *forms* of nature. After these works the attempt was made to solve the old Cézanne dilemma by "representing" the three-dimensional structure of reality upon a two-dimensional plane. The Cubists' solution—that is Picasso's and Braque's—was to eliminate the three-dimensional characteristics of reality and reduce structure into two-dimensional terms.

Now we can understand why these artists opened the forms of nature; principally because by so doing they freed themselves from nature's three-dimensional context. This made possible such extensive manipulations of nature that the macro-reality appearances were almost entirely removed. And in direct ratio to this increasing removal of nature's appearances the Inventive activity of the artist increasingly operated to replace the former. This continued until the forms became shapes, slipping and sliding into the linear plane of the canvas. In other words, the forms of nature were opened and then flattened onto the flat canvas surface. Thus the artist released them from their original context, so that he could transform them into a more or less invented structure corresponding to the structure of the canvas. In so doing he was unconsciously striving to achieve a correspondence to the actual canvas surface.

In retrospect we can see how much of a Cubist Cézanne was himself. In fact Cézanne was the first Cubist. It was he who first performed the daring innovation of breaking open the closed forms of nature to pick out, study, rearrange and reform its planes. It was he who first spoke of "planes overlapping and straight lines falling." Even his painting technique was used by the Cubists, Braque and Picasso, as well as his freedom to ignore one-point perspective. In fact it was precisely this freeing of the artist from the dictates of the laws of perspective which pointed out to the Cubists the manner in which the further

114. Georges Braque, The Waltz, 1912. Courtesy, The Art of This Century.

dissolution and dissection of the old reality could be accomplished and thus make way for a new reality content for art. In the long run, therefore, what the Cubists accomplished was but the continuation to its inevitable conclusion of what Cézanne had already done to a considerable extent in his late works.[8] Unfortunately the majority of artists assumed that the purpose of this freedom from the laws of perspective was a license for recording the macroscopic level of nature in any manner they pleased. They did not realize that its prime value lay in its being one of the major steps which freed the non-Camera artist from the necessity of using nature objects at all! Nor did they realize that what the Cubists had done was to change from three-dimensional perspective laws to two-dimensional ones. The significance of this modification will become apparent when we discuss the "Two-Dimensional" schools of post-Cubist painting.

Although the Cubists had achieved considerable correspondence between the structure of their content and the medium of their art, it can be seen that in certain crucial respects there was still a lack

8. There is a popular attitude that Cubism was the beginning of the break-up of nature's macroscopic level of reality. Actually this process *began* with Impressionism in a subtle manner which *increased* in tempo through Post-Impressionism and mounted to a *climax* with Cubism. The Cubists simply finished the breaking up of nature's macroscopic reality with which artists of the entire Transitional-Period had been engrossed. The Impressionist painters had broken and dissected the *color* of nature into spots of paint in order to study and exploit its color-structure; the Cubists broke and dissected the *forms* of nature into "cubes" in order to study and exploit its form-structure.

326

of correspondence between the structure of the art content and the characteristics of visual structure in actual reality. That is to say, the one is linear and the other three-dimensional. Hence in "solving" Cézanne's problem a new one had arisen which was to make a great deal of trouble for artists. We shall consider some aspects of this here.

It is of considerable interest to observe how the problems of dimensions swayed and pushed the various Cubists in the attempt to solve it. We have already seen that Picasso and Braque sacrificed the third dimension for the two-dimensional linear "reality" of the canvas. But between 1912 and 1913, when the work of Picasso was generally becoming more and more linear, we find that he was also making several attempts to return the third dimension in his work. See, for instance, *Picasso: Forty Years of His Art*,[9] where twelve drawings from this period are reproduced, all of which emphasize the third dimension. Here we have evidence of the pull of three-dimensional reality as opposed to the two-dimensional character of the medium. On the same page there is also reproduced an attempt made in 1913 at three-dimensional constructions in which actual materials, such as wood, cardboard, etc., were employed for the forms and the flat medium was dispensed with altogether. It was in this period also that Picasso depicted not one but several views of the human figure with one view overlapping the other.[10] In each of these three examples there was an attempt by the artist to reinstate the missing third dimension.

In the works of Juan Gris in the same period, 1912-1914 (figures 115, 119), we see the persistence throughout of both two- and three-dimensional shapes and forms treated with precise geometric technique. He compromised, as Cézanne did, and tried to keep both factors. Léger's preferences at this time tended more definitely towards the third dimension than any of the other Cubists. His works were bulging, practically bursting with cylindrical forms as well as cones, spheres, squares (figure 116). In short, we see two opposing extremes: Picasso and Braque (figure 114) are flat; Léger is round. Gris is a compromise, with his angularized depth on the order of a *bas-relief*. These comprise the three general approaches to the problems posed by Cubism.

We can now begin to see more clearly than before the basic conflict between the three-dimensional world on the one hand, which forced itself upon the sense of the artist, and his two-dimensional medium, fundamentally opposed to it. It is a conflict, largely unconscious, plaguing artists to this very day.

In addition to the various solutions which the four leading Cubists had tried to make of the problem of the three-dimensional environment and the two-dimensional art medium, there are several other very interesting conflicts in their works, all of which were a part of a fundamental ambivalence. Braque and Picasso eliminated nature objects to a considerably greater extent than did Gris or Léger, but in the matter of painting technique Braque and Picasso are the romantic Cubists; they retained the *free* brush technique originating with the Romantic art of the past. It is also the painting method, significantly enough, which was employed by previous Realists to imitate in a suggestive manner nature's textures and forms—trees, clouds, sky, water, etc.—which the artist could never copy very well with a precise painting technique. In this way the romantic Braque and Picasso unconsciously sought to retain one more figment of the old realism of art.

Gris and Léger were able, to a considerably greater extent, to throw off the technique of the past methods of painting and art realism. They were concerned with painting techniques which would emphasize the geometrical character of their contents. Particularly was this true of Gris, who produced his shapes and forms in a rigorous geometric manner. For the most part he cleaned away the brush strokes in his work and thereby obtained a greater emphasis upon the forms of his shapes rather than upon their textures. In this way Gris went one step further than all the other Cubists by indicating more directly the fundamental implication of the new art, namely, that the quest for structure was the important aspect of the new direction.

Léger began his Cubist phase with a relatively tight technique from which he relaxed as this period of art developed. In regard to the degree of tightness or looseness in technique, Léger may be placed midway on a scale between Braque and Picasso, on the one hand, Gris on the other. (After Cubism,

9. *Picasso: Forty Years of His Art,* p. 84, edited by Alfred H. Barr, Jr., Museum of Modern Art Catalogue, New York, 1939.
10. Ibid., p. 77.

115. Juan Gris, The Violin, 1913. Courtesy of the Philadelphia Museum of Art, Philadelphia. Gallatin Collection.

116. Fernand Léger, Contraste de Formes, 1914. Collection of Mr. and Mrs. Walter C. Arensberg.

however, Léger adopted a much more rigorous, disciplined type of technique, similar to that employed by Gris. He also adopted the latter's juxtaposition of round forms and flat shapes.)

The contrast between the romantic and more disciplined Cubists is further borne out in what they wrote. We find Braque and Picasso talking like romantic mystics (comparable to van Gogh's mentality); Léger like a materialistic philosopher (comparable to Gauguin); while Gris was the scientist of the group (comparable to Seurat and Cézanne).

It was Gris, incidentally, who made an impressive monument of Cubism, as Seurat did of Post-Impressionism, and in this respect it is interesting to note that Lipchitz quotes him as having said: "In many ways I feel at one with Seurat."[11] (Seurat in turn felt a close kinship with another monumentalist, the Realist, Ingres.)

The main effort in the Cubist researches of Picasso and Braque, as we have pointed out, was away from the three-dimensional forms of nature's macro-reality towards two-dimensional shapes to fit the reality characteristic of the linear canvas. One result of this was that the forms of nature were almost completely transformed into the invented shapes of man. But just as nature forms were almost displaced by invented shapes and these were about to be closed, these artists began to bring nature shapes back in two dimensions.

For when nature's macroscopic reality was about to be completely eliminated from the contents of their art, the Cubists failed to realize the fundamental significance of this situation, that the ultimate goal for which they had been unconsciously striving was the complete elimination from art of all distortion, of any kind of imitation, of nature-appearances. Judging by their subsequent actions, however, they were not at all pleased to find that the macro-reality had practically disappeared from their work. As a matter of fact, once nature's appearances were about to disappear completely from the canvas, the Cubists quickly dropped their discovery and began to return to the old reality, under the guise of new kinds of *recognizable* objects. This regression occurred clearly in what we have designated as the third stage of Cubism.

The decision of the Cubists determined *their* evaluations of Cubism's worth and *their* future post-Cubist course. We emphasize "their future," because we shall find other artists who formulated entirely different evaluations of Cubism's worth and strove to realize a different direction for art. It remained for these others to go on from where the Cubists had left off.

We can better understand why the Cubists reacted as they did if we project ourselves into their situation and environment. When they began their work, the works of the Post-Impressionists, the Fauvists and those influenced by African art were furthest removed from the appearance of reality. They had never seen Cubism until they *invented* it! So powerful was the impact of this experience of seeing nature for the first time so highly abstracted, that their reaction to the new forms being evolved predominated over or was more conscious than their reaction to these forms as originally those of nature objects. This is borne out by the ensuing development of Cubism, in which the steadily increasing elimination of nature forms was proportionately replaced by forms invented by the artist. In other words, the character of Cubist development makes apparent the character of the artists' preoccupation with art.

From this it has been argued that nature's appearances do not have to be eliminated; that one need merely abstain from being conscious of the nature object as such in the art contents in order to procure (as it is often called) a "pure form" experience. Such an argument is motivated by the wish to stop art at a particular stage of development in order to keep from losing altogether the old contents— nature's appearances. This position is impossible to maintain, for if one does not move forward, he will certainly move backward. Hence if this attitude is put into effect, the fantasy factor, resulting from the changes of reality, takes command and the structural concerns then progressively degenerate. This was exactly what happened in post-Cubist art, as we shall see.

We have seen that the Cubists *had* been moving towards an objective that called for the increasing elimination of nature's macroscopic level. They *had* been actually pushing their art towards a new kind of reality. But they mistakenly expected to find reality-reactions similar to those experiences in previous arts; they attempted to *identify* the new content with that in the old art reality. Inevitably,

11. As quoted by Jacques Lipchitz in Buchholz Gallery Catalogue for Juan Gris Exhibition, March 28 to April 22, 1944.

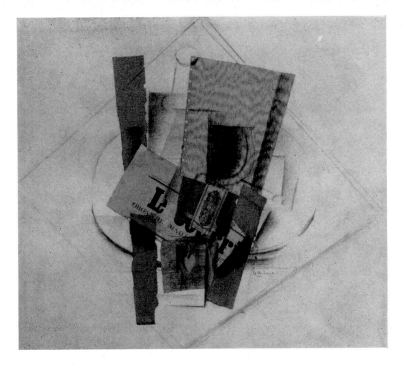

117. Georges Braque, Le Courier, 1913. Courtesy of the Philadelphia Museum of Art, Philadelphia. Gallatin Collection.

118. Pablo Picasso, Still Life with a Calling Card, 1914. Collection of Mrs. Charles B. Goodspeed, Chicago.

then, they found the new lacking in "reality"; unconsciously they had assumed that "reality" in art could only be achieved by some manifestation of the appearances of nature forms. It was the old schismatic situation of attempting to *create by copying* to some degree the forms of reality.

This assumed lack of reality (lack of the old reality, to be more exact) compelled them to seek some kind of a *recognizable* reality. Hence after 1910 the Cubists began to employ various types of recognizable material, and during the next two years various reality devices gradually made their entrance more and more into Cubism. There was a direct reinstatement of the old contents in the form of Photographs, prints of realistic paintings, imitative textures; along with the usual material of trees, human figures, fruit, etc. And there were also used man-invented objects such as painted letters, newspaper print,

331

calling cards, and ingredients mixed into their paints which produced raised, textured surfaces; along with the usual material of bottles, musical instruments, pipes, glasses, etc. (figures 112 to 114, and 117 to 119).

It was this device of depicting already invented objects of which the Purists erroneously made so much.[12] They did not realize that the new art direction was never meant merely to serve the purpose of manipulating the visual characteristics of inventions from other fields. It was, as others correctly realized, necessary to invent a contents *peculiar to art!* These devices were only a substitute for and so an inadequate realization of man-invented art forms.

But the Cubists who used these devices hoped, probably unconsciously, to kill three birds with one stone, so to speak. First, since these subjects were inventions of man, they did have characteristics similar to the objective sought in Cubism. At the same time, since they were recognizable objects, they produced a substitute for the loss of the old recognizable objects of nature. Moreover these objects, as in past art subjects, permitted fantasy in that they could also be manipulated. That is, pitchers, glasses, musical instruments, and the like, could be distorted into many fantasy shapes and still retain recognizable characteristics of the original objects.[13]

Therefore in these emergency reality devices of the Cubists, as well as in their experiments with the third dimension, we are confronted with the two general factors of which we have been tracing the course throughout the transition from Impressionism to the end of useful Cubism, the elements of fantasy and of structure.

In such works as the three-dimensional drawings and especially the three-dimensional constructions of Picasso, in the raised surfaces used by Cubists, in the cylinders of Léger and the *bas-reliefs* of Gris we see further attempts to secure structural factors in the art contents.

In all these ambivalences—between nature objects and invented objects, between three dimensions and two dimensions, and between free and tight techniques—which characterize the entire life work of all the Cubists, especially after 1914, we see the conflict, the dichotomy generated by the fact that the evolution of art had come to a point where the old and the new must part. Eventually each Cubist tried to solve this conflict by not giving up either the fantasy or structural factors. Thus they retained rather than resolved the dichotomy. It is interesting to note in Léger's art nearly all the dichotomies which appear in the various efforts made in his generation: he imitated and invented, he varied from a more free to a more precise technique; he used both two- and three-dimensional illusions; he used both natural and man-made mechanical forms or their equivalents. Although in his Cubist period proper he did not employ man-invented objects to replace nature objects to the extent the others did, in the post-Cubist period he came to use such material even to the extent of painting Machine-like assemblages of objects—bottles and glasses, pieces of Architecture, musical instruments, tiled floors, etc.—along with nature objects such as leaves, tree-trunks, flowers and women.

The question we must now try to answer is why the Cubists solved the "problem of reality" in the way they did. First of all, we must recognize that, like all the transitional artists from Impressionism on, they were definitely unconscious of the fundamental nature of their researches. They relied very heavily upon the intuitive factor. Besides the evidence of their work we have their writings, and that

12. The Purists were artists who tried to invent a contents for painting from objects that were invented for a contents other than painting. (They used mostly glassware and crockeryware for their subjects.) It was this same type of attempt to compose the contents with man-invented forms that led Léger to employ Machine forms, i.e., man-invented forms as distinct from nature forms. However, the Purists went little further than making a precise geometric elaboration of such paintings as figure 113 of Picasso.

13. "Modern" critics have made 1912 Cubism the dividing line and are fond of labelling the stages subsequent to that date "synthetic" and "subjective" as opposed to works previous to it which they call "analytic" and "objective." "Analytic" Cubism, we are told, simply breaks up nature's reality (but what kind of an analysis is made and for what purposes remain obscure), while "synthetic" Cubism retains some aspects of the natural forms in conjunction with invented forms. But every Cubist painting is in some degree synthetic as far as nature's reality is concerned, and every Cubist painting is also analytical of the phenomena of visual reality. In short, ALL Cubist painting is both "analytical" and "synthetic," both "subjective" and "objective." Furthermore, this is true of all art, be it good or bad, old or new, Primitive or "Modern" or what not. These terms then, not only split what cannot be split in reality, but actually cover all art, although explaining no one kind of art specifically in contrast to another. As Cubism evolved through the second stage, artists decreased the macro-reality of nature and increased the Inventive aspect of their works. This direction was reversed in the last or third stage of Cubism.

119. Juan Gris, Abstraction, 1915. Smith College Museum of Art.

of their apologists, which bear out this point. As Picasso put it: "When we invented cubism we had no intention whatever of inventing cubism. . . ." [14] "No one of us drew up a plan of campaign. . . ." [15] "Young painters to-day often draw up a programme to follow, and apply themselves like diligent students to performing their tasks." [16] Not only did the Cubists lack a conscious program, but apparently some of them disliked anyone else's having one.

But the fact that the Cubists did not know what they were doing, which we will not dispute where fundamentals are concerned, does not indicate that such behavior establishes a justifiable precedent. In fact, as our analysis will show, the Cubists were offering the young painters the very weakness in their own behavior which actually resulted in defeat for themselves after they had achieved the principal values of Cubism.

For once nature-appearances had all but disappeared from art, the intuitive faculty, dependence upon which had worked fairly well in the past, was no longer adequate to cope with future problems. When the content of art was being transformed from the old to the new, none of the transitional artists could see where they were headed until they had gone so far that the goal came in sight. These conditions naturally required men who had the courage to depend heavily upon the intuitive factor and dared to grope their way into the new road toward which they were drawn. But once this objective came into

14. Christian Zervos: "Conversation with Picasso," *Cahiers d'Art,* p. 176, Nos. 7-10, 1935. All quotations from this article are based upon a translation by Myfanwy Evans, in *The Painter's Object,* by permission of John Lane The Bodley Head, Ltd., London.

15. Ibid., p. 176.   16. Ibid., p. 176.

view, as it did in the Cubist works by 1910, a crucial situation arose: *a decision had to be made*. Nature's appearances had now been practically eliminated; if artists were to continue in this direction, it was plain that they would either have to give up the old art content for good or else deny the value of so doing. The decision now to be made was whether to accept this new situation or reject it! The Transition-Period—for that is what we shall hereafter call the period from the Camera and Impressionism to Cubism and Constructionism—had now arrived at its inevitable goal; thus there was no longer any necessity for over-reliance upon intuition. In fact, to face the demands of the new conditions it was imperative that artists abandon their past overdependence upon intuition and produce non-intuitive conclusions regarding the new conditions.

In the face of this epoch-making situation, the Cubists dogmatically decided on continuing in the old manner rather than facing the facts and realizing that now they must construct non-intuitive formulations about their previous intuitive behavior. (As late as 1935 Braque still continued to call for an art "born of intuition.") This decision *after* Cubism led them into the blind alley of escape. Had they not insisted on retaining their complete, abject faith in intuition, which had meanwhile reached the zenith of its usefulness, they might have been able to comprehend the new art reality emerging in their works. As it was, however, the Cubists definitely ended their participation in the solution of these problems in the year 1914; in that same year regressions took a strong upper hand in their works. At first there was an ambivalence between the old art and the new; they were unwilling to give up either. Actually they wished to halt the advance which they now feared almost as much as their detractors. But they did not have the courage to admit that they lacked the courage to go further; so they decided to make the retreat appear like a great advance along the traditional direction all great artists had allegedly taken.

To maintain their position with some semblance of still being "radicals," they have been compelled to deny that there is any fundamental difference between one art or another, past or present, and to maintain that all strive basically for the same thing. As Picasso has said: "Cubism is no different from any other school of painting." [17] Indeed!

It goes without saying that what this alleged basic striving is supposed to be is kept in a carefully obscured condition. They have kept on reiterating that we must permit the "passions," the "emotions," the "instincts," etc. rather than the "intellect" to guide the artist. After 1914 the Cubists (particularly Braque and Picasso) developed a mounting hostility to disciplined and rigorous methods of reasoning. Obviously, reason might lead them to the opposite of their own "emotional" decisions and they might have to admit the fact that they had finally reached a complete impasse in 1914 which they did not dare to surmount. [18]

Nevertheless, the Cubists up to 1912 had achieved tremendously important and courageous works; they had done much to clear the air. Each in his own way—Léger, Gris, Picasso, Braque—contributed much which pushed the essential problem closer to a solution. They have left us Cubist paintings which will be among those masterpieces of the past to be retained within the permanent collection of the art of mankind.

It was during the times of the "great decision" that obvious changes and breakdowns appeared in our civilization, all of which had been developing for some time. The first World-Civil-War was being fought; psychoanalysis was reaching into the subconsciousness of men through the medium of Freud; Pavlov was busy investigating the structure of the nervous system in dogs; Einstein and others were changing our entire notion of what constitutes "reality"; already the Cubists had unwittingly established some conclusions on this problem. At about the time that the Cubists were wrestling with the problem

17. "Picasso Speaks," *The Arts*, 3:315-326, May, 1923.

18. A more thorough study of this change of stomach on the part of Braque and Picasso is reserved for a later chapter.

334

of the three-dimensional world and the two-dimensional medium of the painter, two great scientists solved a problem of dimensions by inserting a hyphen between two terms in place of the word "and"; the result was time-space.

Cubism showed the new road along which art of the future must travel; it was not a break with the past, since it was actually but a further step along the evolutionary path that past artists had been taking. Thus certain scientists and artists, men of courage, daring and adventure, were radically altering former notions of "reality."

During the period which falls between the two World-Civil-Wars, scientists have by necessity been working out the development of a language ever further removed from that in common use. This happened by necessity because they were in the process of symbolizing the new view of the world reality rapidly being discovered, for which the old symbology was inadequate. Thus the scientist's language symbols changed in order to correspond to the new notions of reality, while the everyday language continued to symbolize the old, now useless notions of reality. As a result, says Alfred Korzybski: "The chasm between human affairs and science became wider and wider." [19]

Similarly artists created a visual language incomprehensible to the layman. Innovators among the artists as well as the scientists were definitely breaking with the old Aristotelian theories of world reality, but the vast population of the world refused to admit that the old ways had collapsed. The majority of these artists and scientists failed in turn to realize their responsibilities as social beings—that it was their responsibility to make clear to the general population what they were doing.

In short, throughout this century the artists and scientists have been constructing new criteria for human behavior in a world where the vast majority refuse, in theory at least, to change. And today this gap between these two fields and humans in general has come to its saturation point. Increasingly more and more individuals are endeavoring to establish the consciousness of the relatedness between art and science and the relation of both to society at large. The advanced members of these fields are trying to convey to us that the more than 2,000-year-old reign of Aristotelianism has now come to a close. Its system of logic is no longer adequate to cover the new conditions; by necessity revision is in order if we wish to recover adequate sanity in our culture.

19. Alfred Korzybski: *Science and Sanity: An Introduction to Non-Aristotelian Systems and General Semantics*, p. 197.

IMITATION TO INVENTION

The process of abstracting in different orders being inherent in the human nervous system, it can neither be stopped
nor abolished; but it can be deviated, vitiated, and forced
into harmful channels contrary to the survival trend. . . . 179

Alfred Korzybski

. . . to be an abstraction does not mean that an entity is nothing. It merely means that its existence is only one factor of a more concrete element of nature. 355

A. N. Whitehead

The number of orders of abstractions an 'animal' can produce is limited. The number of orders of abstractions a 'man' can produce is, in principle, unlimited. 179

Alfred Korzybski

Does Fido 'know', or can he 'know', that he abstracts? It seems undeniable that Fido does not 'know' and cannot 'know' that he abstracts, because it takes science to 'know' that we abstract, and Fido has no science. 179

Alfred Korzybski

All human experience, scientific or otherwise, shows that we still copy animals in our nervous reactions, trying to adjust ourselves to a world of fictitious, simple animal structure, while actually we live in a world of very complex human structure which is quite different. 179

Alfred Korzybski

So we see clearly that outside of our skins there is something going on, which we call the world, or a pencil, or anything, which is independent of our words and which is not words. 179

Alfred Korzybski

Before we can approach any extensive analysis of the arts following Cubism, we must first examine a term new to the vocabulary of artists. This is the term "abstract." It came into extensive use because it was assumed that it clarified the fundamental characteristics of certain arts which followed on the heels of Cubism. We propose to show in this chapter that the word "abstract," when properly used is today indeed crucially indispensable, not only for the analysis of "Abstract" art, but also for the analysis of *any kind of art of any time*. Certain preliminary clarifications, however, must be attempted by considering some of the characteristic confusions in the use of the term.

There is a common practice of vaguely labelling all art "abstract" except those types which *literally* copy nature-appearances. But it is incorrect simply to say that this or that art is abstract, or that only this art is abstract and others are not. ALL art entails abstracting of some kind. If, however, we agree that all art is an abstracting affair and say no more, we say little, because we stress similarities and neglect the more important differences. This results in the prevalent confusion of different *orders* and *kinds* of abstracting and so false knowledge ensues. "Abstraction" must be regarded as a multi-valued term which must be put into a specific context in order to make clear the specific *kind* of abstracting to which we are referring. All art is involved in abstracting in some degree, from some level of nature's reality. In brief, each kind of "art" "abstracts" differently.

The history of art abstracting falls into three general interrelated sections: the art which abstracts from the macroscopic level of reality—this is the older level from Pictographic times to the invention of the Camera; the newer level abstracts from the *Structural Process of reality;* the Transitional-Period lies between the above old and new forms of abstracting. Both the old and the new levels of abstracting are used in the art which began with Impressionism and ended with Cubism. The new level of abstracting begins to appear clearly in certain arts which follow the conclusion of useful Cubism, arts we have yet to

341

study. The majority of "Moderns" and others, however, are still haggling on the old reality level of abstracting.

John Dewey, in his *Art as Experience,* has made a more concerted effort than the author has been able to find in any other book to explain the function of the abstracting process in art. Dewey is not as obscure as most writers on art, but in his discussion of the abstracting process certain implications and contradictions appear. An examination of Dewey's discussion of this subject, however, may help us to gain a better understanding of the abstracting process in art. Naturally we cannot stop to analyze his entire book, but the ensuing passage contains the core of his theory on "abstracting." "Every work of art 'abstracts' in some degree from the particular traits of objects expressed. Otherwise, it would only, by means of exact imitation, create an illusion of the presence of the things themselves. The ultimate subject matter of still life painting is highly 'realistic'—napery, pans, apples, bowls. But a still life by Chardin or Cézanne presents these materials in terms of relations of lines, planes and colors inherently enjoyed in perception. This re-ordering could not occur without some measure of 'abstraction' from physical existence. Indeed, the very attempt to present three-dimensional objects on a two-dimensional plane demands abstraction from the usual conditions in which they exist. There is no *a priori* rule to decide how far abstraction may be carried. In a work of art the proof of the pudding is decidedly in the eating. There are still-lifes of Cézanne in which one of the objects is actually levitated. Yet the expressiveness of the whole to an observer with esthetic vision is enhanced not lowered. . . ." [1]

"It is everywhere accepted that art involves selection. Lack of selection or undirected attention results in unorganized miscellany. The directive source of selection is interest; an unconscious but organic bias toward certain aspects and values of the complex and variegated universe in which we live. In no case can a work of art rival the infinite concreteness of nature. . . . The one limit that must not be overpassed is that some reference to the qualities and structure of things in environment remain. Otherwise, the artist works in a purely private frame of reference and the outcome is without sense, even if vivid colors or loud sounds are present." [2]

Let us begin with the first two sentences: "Every work of art 'abstracts' in some degree from the particular traits of objects expressed. Otherwise, it would only, by means of exact imitation, create an illusion of the presence of the things themselves." But even if an artist could succeed in making an "illusion of the presence of the things themselves," he would still be involved in an abstracting process from nature, for the simple reason that his result is *not* made of flesh, bones, etc., but of paint and canvas. In other words, it would *not* be *the* "object expressed" and therefore would have to be an abstraction from it. In fact, the artist could not avoid abstracting, even if he could make a duplication, exact in every respect (not merely an illusion) of the very thing itself; i.e., even if his resultant art INCLUDED (abstracted) ALL the characteristics of the object depicted. But this latter is impossible! And to avoid abstraction is also impossible! Therefore, ALL artists who depict nature must abstract in *some degree,* the degree depending upon the extent to which the artist chooses (or is able) to disregard or to regard the actual appearances of nature.

Similarly the artist who does not depict the appearances of nature also abstracts, but on a *different level.* If such an artist did not abstract from nature, then his art would have to EXCLUDE ALL the characteristics and qualities which are to be found in nature. This would entail the production of an art which would have no resemblance or correspondence whatsoever to any quality or what not to be found in the reality about us. But this is impossible for the obvious reason that all such art has the qualities of form, color, etc., which are qualities to be found in nature. No art can avoid these qualities on one level or another, for we live in a world of such phenomena and the world affects us in some way in everything we do. To deny that such art abstracts from reality, one would also have to prove that the artist came upon the notion of form, color and the like, without previous recourse to nature. So it becomes just as impossible to *exclude all* the characteristics and qualities of nature as it is to *include all* of them in a work of art! Art and nature are always related in some way in every form of art, regardless of what the artist is doing or imagines he is doing.

1. From *Art as Experience,* by John Dewey, p. 94. Courtesy of G. P. PUTNAM'S SONS, New York, 1934.
2. Ibid., p. 95.

342

Before the Camera, as we have seen, the artist had been concerned with abstracting from the appearances of nature. All copying and distortive-imitation artists more or less abstract from this level. But Inventive artists today, like the scientists, are concerned with the *newer level,* the Structural Process of nature rather than the gross macroscopic level of reality. However, as we have implied, the artist who abstracts from the first or older level is involved in the second or newer level of abstraction to that degree that he exercises his Inventive activity deliberately or unconsciously to alter the actual appearances of nature.[3] But for the time being it is important that we have the two distinct levels clear in our mind; later we shall go into an extensive analysis of the manner and various complex conditions under which these levels tend to overlap and the significance of this overlapping.

The important difference between artists who do depict nature's appearances and those who do not is this: the former abstract in a greater or lesser degree from the macroscopic level, while the latter abstract directly from the STRUCTURAL PROCESS LEVEL of reality. In short, the problem of abstraction is a matter of abstracting from *different levels* of nature's reality. So we find that in *all art* the artist is involved in some kind of an abstracting activity (that is, "selecting, picking out, separating, summarizing, deducting, removing, omitting, disengaging, taking away, stripping," etc.[4]) from nature, whether the art *depicts* nature's appearances in any way or does not depict nature's macro-reality forms in any way. The main difference between one kind of art and any other is a matter of levels of reality and degrees of abstracting from the level (or levels) of reality involved.

Dewey's formulations lack this more comprehensive, more complete understanding of the abstracting process. This is why he employs the limiting term "object," or an ambiguous term like "physical," to denote what the artist abstracts from. True, Dewey has said that "Every work of art 'abstracts' in some degree," but he is seemingly unaware that one can *also* abstract from the Structural Process level of nature.

It might be possible to assume that Dewey did not limit his abstraction to "objects" when he wrote that the "re-ordering [of lines, planes and colors] could not occur without some measure of 'abstraction' from physical existence," if we give the implication of his term "physical existence" a good stretch. But we find him talking in terms of the object: "The ultimate subject matter of still life painting is highly 'realistic'—napery, pans, apples, bowls. But a still life by Chardin or Cézanne presents these materials in terms of relations of lines, planes and colors inherently enjoyed in perception." Thus the same confusion continues here. In fact Dewey's failure to realize the Structural Process level from which one can abstract accounts for many of the nebulosities in his analysis of art.

For example, in what Dewey says about the work of Chardin and Cézanne we find him unaware of the important fact that these two men actually abstracted from nature in extremely different ways. The former abstracted primarily from the level of nature's appearances, while Cézanne was considerably involved in the newer level of abstracting. Specifically Cézanne was one of the Transition-Period artists making the changes from the old macro-level to the new structural level of abstracting from nature; while Chardin was one of those artists who worked toward the result that was eventually perfected in the Camera. Moreover, what Dewey says about Chardin and Cézanne is extremely ambiguous, since it is actually applicable to *all* artists who use nature objects; it is impossible for artists to depict nature without presenting "these materials in terms of relations of lines, planes and colors inherently enjoyed in perception." Consequently Dewey not only fails to distinguish between Chardin and Cézanne, but also between those artists who use nature-appearances in a variety of ways. He makes these erroneous generalizations because he *identifies* different arts, which actually abstract from nature in different degrees, on different levels. In short, when Dewey applies his theory, that all art abstracts in some degree, he fails to recognize adequately the degrees of abstracting involved on the old level, not to mention the abstracting problems involved in the Transitional-Period. Consequently, it follows that he is entirely unaware of the newer level of abstracting.

Incidentally, Dewey's non-recognition of this newer level is reflected in the fact that Cubism,

3. See p. 298 ff. where this was explained as it appears in Cézanne's work.

4. Standard dictionary meanings.

among other arts, is not even mentioned in the index of his book; apparently he is little interested in it.[5] It is precisely because he has failed to realize the significance of Cubism that he is prevented from realizing the fundamental nature of the distortions or abstracting process which preceded it and out of which Cubism grew.

Thus he writes: "There are still-lifes of Cézanne in which one of the objects is actually levitated. Yet the expressiveness of the whole to an observer with esthetic vision is enhanced not lowered." Obviously he is unaware that Cézanne's "levitation" of objects was one indication of his *unconscious* effort to abstract from the Structural Process level of reality; that it was a part of his striving, not simply to achieve what he did, but to secure that which seemed to be just out of reach, that which he strove all his life to "realize," of which he was the "primitive of the way." He strove to free the use of nature forms from their limited context in order to release further the Inventive potential inherent in the artist. In short, the levitation of the object, and other similar devices of Cézanne, only indicated a striving towards an objective, not its attainment.[6]

We would agree with Dewey if we were to take out of context this sentence: "There is no *a priori* rule to decide how far abstraction may be carried." On this basis it might again be argued that he did have an understanding of the Structural Process level. But when Dewey applies his theory, we find he does not mean what he says. If there is no *a priori* rule, why stop one's interest in the development of the abstracting process at some one (19th century) stage? What about all the other 20th century artists who carry abstraction further—Cubists, De Stijlists, Suprematists, Constructionists? They are never brought up for consideration anywhere in Dewey's book.

We also disagree with Dewey that "the proof of the pudding is decidedly in the eating," since even a cursory glance at the contemporary field of art reveals that today so-called art lovers are willing to eat anything.

We find a further clue to the type of art Dewey is attempting to justify with his theories in the words "the infinite concreteness of nature." In other words, the macroscopics of nature are presumably infinite, but then abstraction is supposed to be limited to this level of concreteness; and so, although Dewey stresses that he objects to the narrowing of the field of art experiences to some one kind, nevertheless his whole book is fundamentally devoted to eulogizing one particular variety of art abstracting—old and new or pseudo-Post-Impressionist types.

So that while Dewey has said on the one hand, "There is no *a priori* rule to decide how far abstraction may be carried," on the other hand he says, "The one limit that must not be overpassed is that some reference to the qualities and structure of things in environment remain."

But, as we have already implied, there is no need to fear that any artist will ever be able to "overpass" the "one limit" of having "some reference to the qualities and structure of things in environment"—it is impossible to do so! An artist would have to be born in a vacuum in order to produce an art which would not have some reference to the environment with which we are acquainted, that is, if he could succeed in inventing art in the first place. Since, however, there exists no such vacuum, there exists no such opportunity for artists to overpass the "one limit" Dewey states.

Actually he is referring to the appearances of things, not to the *Process Structure*. So what he is trying to say is, that if the artist does not abstract from the appearances of nature, he is going beyond any reference to the environment around him; and this, as we pointed out several times, is an impossibility, *no matter what the art content happens to be*. His difficulties, therefore, stem from considering abstraction as dealing only with the macroscopic level. Hence it inevitably follows that he does not recognize the new *20th* century manifestations of non-Camera art which correlate with modern scientific attitudes in general and which no longer use the objects of nature for a content.

Thus if we read the first two and the last two sentences of the entire quotation we are here analyzing, we find an interesting phenomenon that bears out our general criticism of Dewey's notions about art. "Every work of art 'abstracts' in some degree from the particular traits of objects expressed. Otherwise,

5. Of further interest are the works which he reproduces in his book. Outside of Matisse, the most recent artists are Renoir and Cézanne!

6. See the analysis of this and similar phenomena, particularly in chapters 14 and 20.

it would only, by means of exact imitation, create an illusion of the presence of the things themselves." And "The one limit that must not be overpassed is that some reference to the qualities and structure of things in environment remain. Otherwise, the artist works in a purely private frame of reference and the outcome is without sense, even if vivid colors or loud sounds are present." In the first quotation he is telling us that *unless* we literally copy nature we are compelled to abstract from nature. In this way a distinction is made between literal and non-literal recording art, particularly the Post-Impressionist type. The implication, explicit elsewhere in his book[7] is that literal copying is empty of purpose, but that non-literal copying is not, because there abstraction and so selection occurs. But in the second quotation it is implied that unless the artist retains some reference to the appearances of nature he is completely cut off from reality. Thus for Dewey the danger of the "realistic" method is that it can end in mere "illustration," and the danger of the "abstract" is that it can end in "scientific exercise."[8] The implication is that the literal copyists and those who do not copy nature-appearances at all are both producing non-art and do not abstract from reality. But abstraction from reality, and so some relation with reality, exists in *all* art, because it is impossible that it be otherwise.

If Dewey does not see the evolutionary process of art, then what is he attracted to in such artists as Cézanne, Matisse, Renoir? It is the fantasy aspect of reality to which he is primarily drawn, an attraction that has been explained in the discussion of Post-Impressionism. It is critically important to emphasize, and the point will become increasingly clear as our history progresses, that a contemporary of Cézanne could be attracted predominantly to the structural factor in Cézanne's work, as was the artist himself. But in our generation this experience is inadequately achieved *unless one also understands works subsequent to Cézanne which have further developed this factor of structure*. Otherwise, one is predominantly attracted to and captured by the fantasy aspect of Cézanne and the like.

Thus when Dewey speaks of what his preferences in art express to him, it is only to be expected that he should make such remarks as "Art is the extension of the power of rites and ceremonies. . . ."[9] and "what the work expresses is as if it were something one had oneself been longing to express."[10] If this is true, we can only conclude that his "longing" has largely been for an art of fantasy and that is why he confines his art experiences to a position which lies between the two opposite forms of contemporary abstracting—at one pole that which is largely (literally) abstracted from the macroscopic level and at the other pole that which is not abstracted at all from that level of reality.

But Dewey is not aware of the fantasy factor; he mistakes it for some unique reality that the artist discovers in actual reality. If it is a "reality," it is the reality only of a fantasy of nature to which he reacts; the structural aspect of this art has only a secondary interest for him, despite his emphasis upon the latter.

When he writes that, "the very attempt to present three-dimensional objects on a two-dimensional plane demands abstraction from the usual conditions in which they exist," he is referring, it would appear, not only to the abstracting process from nature, but also to the effect upon that abstracting process arising from the fact that the artist must abstract from three-dimensional phenomena onto a two-dimensional surface. So far so good. But we find that this phenomenon of dimensions appears to have been brought up mainly as another attempt to justify the distortion of nature and thus nullify the Realist's insistence upon the more accurate copying of reality. In doing so Dewey appears to have forgotten, for the moment, that many other artists (i.e., Ingres, Courbet, etc.) who abstracted from three-dimensional objects on a two-dimensional plane, found that these conditions made no "demands" which compelled "abstraction from the usual conditions," at least to that extent found in the artists' work (Matisse, Renoir, etc.) which he is attempting to justify with his statement. After all, if the conditions involved not only do not compel such artists as Ingres or Courbet to distort to the extent that Cézanne and others did, but even allow them to approximate to a considerable extent the "usual conditions in which [objects] exist," then these conditions certainly cannot be the reasons why such artists as Cézanne distorted nature, at least as the problem is rationalized by Dewey.

In another effort to justify distortions of nature, Dewey says, "It is everywhere accepted that art involves selection. Lack of selection or undirected attention results in unorganized miscellany. The

7. See Dewey, op. cit., p. 287, for example.   8. Ibid., p. 313.   9. Ibid., p. 271.   10. Ibid., p. 105.

directive source of selection is interest; an unconscious but organic bias toward certain aspects and values of the complex and variegated universe in which we live." The statement implies that nature is "unorganized miscellany," since this is allegedly what results if the artist literally records rather than deliberately employs selection when depicting nature. (Actually every artist, good, bad or otherwise is compelled to exercise a certain degree of "selection" and "bias" in his abstractions from reality. It is inevitable! To avoid it, an artist would have to *include* all the characteristics of that which is being abstracted—an impossibility.)

But Dewey can observe a Matisse, for example, and speak of it as a *distortion of reality* and then claim for it a reality which would normally be denied because of those distortions. In such a case the art-distortions are projected upon actual reality—art becomes again a criterion of reality (idealism).

In short, Dewey's is the Aristotelian view of reality, both in his notion of limiting the artist's abstracting to the appearances of nature and in his making art the criterion of reality. He is, however, apparently not conscious of this; for he states (quite correctly) that the older theory of art was centered in Aristotle as the authority.[11] And he also says that Aristotle meant by "imitation" something entirely different than has been assumed. Since we discuss Aristotle's theories in another chapter, we shall here briefly comment upon this apparent contradiction: the reason past artists were able to appeal to Aristotle for their "realism," whether of the literal or ideal type, is also the reason Dewey can appeal to him by swinging Aristotle's theory in the direction that he, Dewey, is prone to follow; in short, Aristotle's notions can be made to cover almost anything. Especially is this the case when we find that Aristotle wrote not only about literal "imitation," but also about changing reality (distortion) in his theories of the "ideal." Within this wide range one can cram any art which retains nature-appearances in any way. In fact, most "Modern" art is but the last feeble dribbling of the old Aristotelian theory of art—art is "better than the real"; hence great art does not literally copy the real. Thus Dewey finds no difficulty in justifying his prejudices for a Post-Impressionist variety of art with Aristotelian formulations.

Confined as he is in his art experiences to the Transitional-Period, unable to account coherently either for what preceded it or what followed it, Dewey is also unable to understand correctly the period to which he is partial, namely, the art lying in between the old and the new. The majority of would-be Modernists who are in a quandary trying to comprehend what is meant by abstracting in art, are in general partial, as Dewey is, to that art in which nature is not literally copied, but from the contents of which nature objects have not been literally eliminated.

But Dewey made an effort to explain what he meant by the term "abstract," while most critics and artists, being unable to handle the term coherently, have tried either to deprecate its possible significance or further obscure its meaning. Their efforts have been made in the hope of absolving those artists labelled "Abstract"—by choice or otherwise—of the necessity of accounting for the function of the term in art criticism. Thus Hans Arp's "clever" but meaningless remark, "But then nothing is less abstract than Abstract art." [12]

What may well become the classic example of confusion over the nature of the abstracting process is the following by Picasso. He claims: "There is no abstract art. You must always begin with something. Afterwards you can remove all traces of reality . . . ." [13] From this one extracts the following series of remarkable implications: (1) Abstract art is non-existent, (2) apparently because one must always start from something, (but this would imply that all art is abstract since abstraction implies beginning "with something"); (3) finally one removes all traces of reality, which is tantamount to removing all traces of abstraction; (and this would seem to take us right back to a state of non-existent "abstract art").

Artists and critics have in general attributed their difficulties to the term itself rather than to the actual difficulty—the manner in which they manipulated it. And since they claimed that the fault lay with the term, the next obvious step, and a convenient one, was to attempt to dispense with its use altogether, or to replace it with terms that continue to be equally confusing. In any case, the effort was to evade the

---

11. Ibid., p. 283.

12. From "Abstract Art" in *Art of This Century,* p. 29, by permission of Peggy Guggenheim, editor.

13. Christian Zervos: "Conversation with Picasso," *Cahiers d' Art,* p. 174, Nos. 7-10, 1935; translation by Myfanwy Evans.

inescapable, fundamental issues involved, not only in the terminology in question, but in the actual problems of art.[14]

In short, the "problems of reality," in the sense of nature's appearances, and the problem of Cubism—the elimination of those appearances—plague the "Modernists" today. And so we see many desperate efforts to get around the troublesome lack of correspondence between art and nature. Although no substantiations are supplied, it is claimed that art has its own independent reality, that art distorts rather than copies nature in order to attain its alleged reality status.

This is what Alfred Barr is saying in the following: " 'Abstract' is the term most frequently used to describe the more extreme effects of this impulse away from 'nature.' It is customary to apologize for the word 'abstract,' but words to describe art movements or works of art are often inexact . . . .

". . . . the adjective 'abstract' is confusing and even paradoxical. For an 'abstract' painting is really a most positively concrete painting since it confines the attention to its immediate, sensuous, physical surface far more than does the canvas of a sunset or a portrait. The adjective is confusing, too, because it has the implications of both a verb and a noun. The verb *to abstract* means to *draw out of* or *away from*. But the noun *abstraction* is something already drawn out of or away from—so much so that like a geometrical figure or an amorphous silhouette it may have no apparent relation to concrete reality. 'Abstract' is therefore an adjective which may be applied to works of art with a certain latitude, and, since no better or more generally used word presents itself, it shall be used from now on in this essay without quotation marks." [15]

Now "abstract" is undeniably used to label those works presumably tending away from, or, as some would erroneously have it, divorced from nature. But we deny that *any* art tends away from or is divorced from nature; art can only tend "away from" certain aspects or characteristics of nature, and not nature as such. True it often happens that the dictionary and rules of grammar leave us in a confused state. The confusion of those who do not make art, but only write about it, results from too great a concern with what words presumably mean, independent of the reality. But of what use is it to consider such matters as absolutes that can never be altered, especially when such rules obviously lead to confusion? Why not look at the facts and then make our terms correlate with rather than dictate to them? In other words, use what Korzybski calls the *natural order of evaluation*. In this way we find that an "abstract" *painting* is actually no more "concrete" than a "canvas of a sunset or a portrait," because whatever the contents of the former, say simply a painting of a *square form,* it is *as much an illusion of what it represents as is that art which depicts a sunset.* The difference is that one is an illusion of a geometric form and the other an illusion of a sunset. The one is no more concrete than the other! To consider Barr's other point, we find that even if the art content is only a square form, still the relationship "to concrete reality" is, on the contrary, very apparent, for the simple reason that the artist abstracted from nature the notion of form-color organizations, as such. Those who write, as Barr does, of "no apparent relation to concrete reality" do so because they are conscious of only one level of reality. The problem at hand is one of the degree or kind of *relationship* which the art (any art for that matter) possesses to *"concrete" reality.* And to ascertain these relationships requires a consideration of the kind of abstracting involved.

Kandinsky, the artist and theosophist, was one of those who used the term "concrete." He claimed that if you see an apple in a painting, you cannot eat it; therefore, it is a concrete thing in itself, whatever that may be. In this way the problem is avoided rather than solved, for thus we ignore the fact that our

14. One writer, for example, has the temerity to blame the "public" for the inevitable confusion that resulted from its use: "The word 'abstract' has from the beginning proved a source of confusion. It continues to be employed despite efforts at substitution (non-representational, concretionists, non-objective) merely because the public has come to associate the term with pictures that do not represent nature." (G. L. K. Morris: "On the Mechanics of Abstract Painting," *Partisan Review,* Vol. 3, p. 405fn., September-October, 1941.) The "public"—composed largely of innocent bystanders, trying to understand these experts—is blamed, although the writer must know that even among the Abstract artists there is utter confusion over the employment of the term "abstract"—which is just as true of the use of the substitutions offered. Why not admit that the term originated with the artists in the first place, and that the artists themselves have been confused ever since over its use?

15. From the catalogue for the exhibition, "Cubism and Abstract Art," with preface and text by Alfred H. Barr, Jr., p. 11, The Museum of Modern Art, New York, 1936.

notion of the painted apple nevertheless originated with what Kandinsky called the "eating apple." In other words, even though the one is not the other, still the visual similarities between them indicate that their relationships must be explained in terms of *functional* relations rather than the falseness of isolation.

Here is another classic example of the general way in which the discrediting of the term "abstract" is rationalized. Le Corbusier, the French Architect and painter, writes: "Today it is suggested that we repudiate this event [Cubism], that we abandon the grandeur of this conquest! This art, which has been called abstract through a disquieting misunderstanding of vocabulary; (whenever there is a question of an artistic baptism, idiotic terms are dug up, for it is always the enemies who do the baptizing), this art is concrete, not abstract." [16]

And in a similar vein Lipchitz has said: "As for 'abstract art,' I was never an abstractionist, though I may have given the appearance of being one. As a matter of fact, I do not believe you can put the two words together. If you say art, you mean something concrete. You may have an abstract idea. But art is creation, not analysis; science is analytic, but art is of its essence synthetic. Art for me is not a fragment, it is a totality." [17]

Why this hostility, shared by all these "masters of modern art," to the term "abstract"? Why this proposed substitution of the term "concrete"? It is first of all an attempt to reconcile with actual reality the distortions of it in "modern painting," in the sense that the term "concrete" implies the opposite of the term "abstract." [18]

In all these nebulous uses of the term "concrete" one basic motive is to be seen—the attempt to make art as real as (or more real than) reality in order to justify the contrary appearances of all this "Modern" art, i.e., its distortions of reality. By labelling this art, in which the appearances of nature are distorted, with such a term as "concrete," it is hoped that the art will gain equal if not superior *reality status* to nature. For this reason Barr, Kandinsky, Lipchitz, Le Corbusier and numerous others invariably use the term as though it had only one meaning. For example, Barr speaks of "concrete painting" as well as of "concrete reality" without any distinction between degrees or kinds of "concreteness." Without this distinction one implies that the art in question (for our purpose it matters not what kind) would have to be "a totality" (Lipchitz), i.e., the result of the artist's abstracting *ALL* the characteristics from reality. Only if this were possible, and it certainly is not, could one speak of art and reality as simply "concrete" without distinction.

If, however, we insist on speaking of art as "concrete," then we must practice the differentiational attitude, i.e., distinguish degrees and kinds of concreteness, thus avoiding the identification of art and reality, with consequent false knowledge (see Whitehead quotation at beginning of chapter).

One other critic who also proposes the term "concrete" or "something in itself" to cover the meanings of so-called "abstract" art, objects to "abstract" because its meanings, as he claims, are generally associated with mathematics and "logic." And for some unexplained reason this is not supposed to be good. This amounts to an attempt to divorce art analysis from a consciousness of the fundamental mechanism which characterizes *all* human cerebration, whether one is an artist, a mathematician or a gangster, since everyone "abstracts" in one way or another.

But those who reason in this way need have no fear that any mathematician will accuse them of infringing on the mathematical type of reasoning. And just because the mathematician has already given the term "abstract" certain functions does not automatically rule out its possible beneficial use in art analysis. It would seem reasonable to assume that the connotations of this term as generally used in mathematics and science bode no evil for artists; on the contrary, familiarity with these subjects should alleviate the extensive confusion to be found in art discussion, writing, etc.

For science creates extensions of nature. Similarly, in the new art of our own times there is no

16. Le Corbusier: "Painting and Reality: A Discussion," *Transition*, p. 113, No. 25, Fall, 1936.

17. As quoted by J. J. Sweeney: "Art Chronicle: An Interview with Jacques Lipchitz," *Partisan Review*, XII:88, Winter, 1945.

18. We assume this to be the "meaning" intended, since it is generally used in opposition to the term "abstract." We point this out because the term "concrete" is used in as vague and careless a manner as the term "abstract"; any direct, precise context for the term is avoided. For this reason, no matter which term is used, semantic non-sense continues to prevail.

longer the problem of merely manipulating the macro-reality, but rather of extending the potentialities suggested by nature's Structural Process. Thus both art and science function as related, participating determinants of the view we humans have of reality; both give immediate experience as well as forming our experience in general. Art and science are not separate worlds of abstracting experience but parts of all abstracting experience, parts of the totality of human cognition and living. It is about time that we free the field of art from the false ethereal reputation it acquired in its long contact with the magic and religious history of mankind. We have seen how art has played a major role in molding the magic and religious beliefs of mankind. But although art is no longer tied to such functions, there is still a hangover from primitive times in that even today art is considered comparable to magic and religious experience. Only now it has become the private escape for the artist, his hangers-on and the patrons who are his masters. The activities of the scientist have been already freed to a considerable degree from the dominance of magic and religion.

The process of abstracting is in general similar for the scientist and the artist. The difference is not in method of abstracting, but in the fact that they abstract different things from the world about us. But all these abstractions performed by artists and scientists have a greater common purpose, namely, to produce the totality of the given culture in which they are activated. The greatest purpose of the scientist and the artist is similar; each contributes to the totality of the cultural make-up and each can contribute from his field to that of the other. The more the scientist experiences art and the artist science, the better scientists and artists they will become, because they will be more familiar and integrated with the milieu in which they live and work and build. In fact, at crucial moments of change in the orientations of men, scientists and artists are to be found working along a similar path towards the future.

Of course the prevalent fear among artists is that increased cerebral activity will wreak havoc with their treasured "sensibilities"; but these primitive beliefs will not alter the responsibilities which the course of history has thrown into their laps. In any case, these are rationalizations stemming from fear generated by ignorance. *And if any of the responsibilities now facing the artist seem akin to those we generally associate with the field of science, it is because we live in an era of science, not theology.* It is not because a group of artists arbitrarily decided to make art into a science in the effort to secure a new direction for art, but because certain artists recognized that conditions being what they are in the present state of the historical process, certain demands were consequently made upon them; it is these conditions which require artists to cultivate the rigorous attitude of science. The development of art through the Transitional-Period correlates, as we have noted, in many ways with the changes and discoveries occurring in various branches of science. And as in science, so in art the discovery of the abstracting process was *not* an accident; it was discovered because that *kind* of consciousness was needed. From Cubism on, the demands upon the artist's responsibilities include first of all his acquisition of a coherent "consciousness of abstracting." So long as artists could abstract from an object they could see in nature, so that they needed merely to repeat more (Realists) or less (Idealists) what they saw, so long were the demands of "consciousness" less stringent than today.[19] But once the objective of that transition had come into sight, a high degree of consciousness was necessary. Most artists refused to make the effort to acquire this, but preferred to follow, from 1914 on, the Pied Pipers of intuition, the former Cubists. The result was that the previous step-by-step flow of evolution from Impressionism to Cubism suddenly terminated and chaos took its place. In short, the chaos of "Modern art" is not an accident.

Today in the new problems of art, one does not see a content ready-made in nature; as a result artists are now more dependent than in the past upon their ability to think, to analyze, to reason, and to do so as consciously as possible. Only thus can they recognize the factors which play across their nervous systems, determining their art-results, and only thus can they consciously acquire some measure of necessary useful control over their activities. Without such an awareness the artist cannot discover the otherwise *silent* abstracting process with which he intuitively struggles to realize his work. Uncovering these unconscious

---

19. This is true, however, only from one point of view, since our history has shown the long, elaborate evolution through which pre-Camera artists had to pass in order to achieve an adequate consciousness of their ability to visualize and then record the world revealed by light.

factors allows him to achieve a fundamental insight into the structure of man's evolution as an artist, and the possibility of "realizing" his function in the present state of evolution.

Korzybski writes on the subject of the abstracting process: " 'Thought' represents a reaction of the organism-as-a-whole, produced by the working of the whole, and influencing the whole. From our daily experience, we are familiar with what we usually denote as being 'conscious'; in other words, we are aware of something, be it an object, a process, an action, a 'feeling', or an 'idea'. A reaction that is very habitual and semi-automatic is not necessarily 'conscious'. The term 'consciousness', taken separately, is not a complete symbol; it lacks content, and one of the characteristics of 'consciousness' is to have some content. Usually, the term 'consciousness' is taken as undefined and *undefinable,* because of its immediate character for everyone of us. Such a situation is not desirable, as it is always semantically useful to try to define a complex term by simpler terms. We may limit the general and undefined term 'consciousness' and make it a definite symbol by the deliberate ascribing of some content to this term. For this 'consciousness of something' I take 'consciousness of abstracting' as fundamental. Perhaps the only type of meanings the term 'consciousness' has is covered by the functional term 'consciousness of abstracting', which represents a general process going on in our nervous system. Even if this is not the only type of meanings, the term 'consciousness of abstracting' appears to be of such crucial semantic importance that its introduction is necessary." [20] How crucial this information can be for the artist is now apparent. True, we abstract whether we are conscious of it or not. But only if we become "conscious of abstracting" can we see the degrees and levels on which we abstract, both with words and art. If we do this, we will not identify through confusion of various degrees and levels of abstracting. In short, today the problems of abstracting are such that a disciplined "consciousness of abstracting" is necessary if the present chaos is to be checked and further progress is to be adequately released and achieved.

The world of art today is regarded, for "psycho-logical" reasons, as a world of unlimited freedom; unconsciously or otherwise the implications of the term abstract are felt—and correctly so!—as a threat to that freedom of irresponsibility. Involved throughout this discussion of the term "abstract" we have seen that the general tendency among artists today has been to circumvent the responsibilities of their times by concocting emergency rationalizations of unrestricted freedom. Not knowing precisely what to do, they would like to believe that one can do whatever he pleases. We are beginning to see, however, that artists are not as free as they imagine and that notions of unlimited freedom are fictions which men are able to manufacture only because with reason one can reason anything. But this irresponsible form of reason only leads to disaster, because man is unable to change anything simply because he chooses to reason it this way or that. That which will make the artist free is not, as so many assume, freedom from discipline, but rather the achievement of a rigorous "consciousness of abstracting." Without a scientific awareness of the abstracting process, we shall not be able to see "where we are going or what the good of going there may be." All artists of all times of all kinds abstract, and whether that abstracting is harmful or beneficial can be ascertained only by a consciousness of the *kind* of abstracting involved!

20. Korzybski, *Science and Sanity,* p. 413.

We are the painters who dare to think, and to measure. 372
Theo van Doesburg

It is the task of art to express a clear vision of
reality. 232
                                        Piet Mondrian

The evolution of painting is only the intellectual
search for truth by the cultivation of the eye. 372
                                        Theo van Doesburg

11/30/57

Cubism did not accept the logical consequences
of its own discoveries. 232   Piet Mondrian

Yet all the world knows that even a single line can
arouse emotion. 232   Piet Mondrian

One can rightly speak of an evolution in plastic art.
It is of the greatest importance to note this fact, for
it reveals the true way of art; the only path along
which we can advance. 232   Piet Mondrian

Structure in harmony with the picture's own plane
or in harmony with the space created by the colors
can be controlled by the eye. Structure is completely different from arrangement (decoration) and
composition according to taste. Most painters work
in the manner of pastry cooks and milliners. On the
contrary, we work with the principles of mathematics (euclidean and non-euclidean) and of science,
in other words with intellectual means. 372
                                Theo van Doesburg

We are seeking neither the "Luna-Park" emotions
nor the sexual and sadistic attractions which tempt
a snobbish and blase bourgeoisie. The pictures
which consume the spectator—we have enough of
that. All these beautiful things we leave to those
who have need of them. 371   Theo van Doesburg

We can now examine a type of art which stemmed directly from Cubism; a school of painting which is also popularly included under the loosely used term "Abstract art." It was the artists of this school who erased the objects of nature from their canvases with less qualms than had been the case with the Cubists, and the majority of the artists who followed. We are referring to the two-dimensional schools of painting, the De Stijl and Suprematist schools especially.

To appreciate the significance of these artists, let us return to the consideration of a very import-ant problem which produced the greatest difficulties in all forms of art no longer employing nature-appear-ances for the contents. Once the artist's canvas contained only invented contents, a crisis arose which, for the most part unconsciously, has been the basic factor discouraging the majority of artists who left the tradi-tional practice of using nature forms for their contents. The problem was this: artists found that their invented content had a "lifeless" quality, that it lacked a satisfactory feeling of "reality," a reality which past forms of art possessed.

Let us see how this happened: when the artist eliminated the appearances of nature entirely, a particular reality mechanism of paramount importance could no longer operate. This was the identification-mechanism. In other words, it was no longer possible to project the familiar macro-reality forms upon art as everyone had been in the *habit* of doing. One could no longer "identify" the visual phenomena of the natural world with the visual phenomena presented by the canvas! Therefore, in eliminating nature objects, artists lost *that particular reality* which those objects had previously produced for art. And thus it came about that artists continued to look, unconsciously or otherwise, for the old reality-reaction after it had been removed from their work, rather than becoming conscious of the new art reality which now began to emerge.

120. Below, Piet Mondrian, Composition, 1913. Above,
Piet Mondrian, Composition, 1913. Both works are
from the Rijks Museum, Kröller-Müller, Otterloo, The
Netherlands.

120 (a). Piet Mondrian, Composition, 1917. Rijks Museum, Kröller-Müller, Otterloo, The Netherlands.

So far we are regarding this problem only in relation to those arts from which nature objects have been completely eliminated. However, these difficulties with the "reality problem" occurred even in arts which retained some degree of the macro-reality; for the identificational difficulty is actually a matter of *degrees*, varying with the degree of the old abstracting that remains in the art. (Some individuals have difficulty even with a Cézanne.) That is why the "Moderns" vary so much in the amount of abstracting they do from the old level and the new. Their dependence upon the old is determined by the degree of courage they have to grasp the new.

120 (b). Above, Piet Mondrian, Composition, 1915. Rijks Museum, Kröller-Müller, Otterloo, The Netherlands. Below, Piet Mondrian, Pier and Ocean, 1914. Collection The Museum of Modern Art, New York.

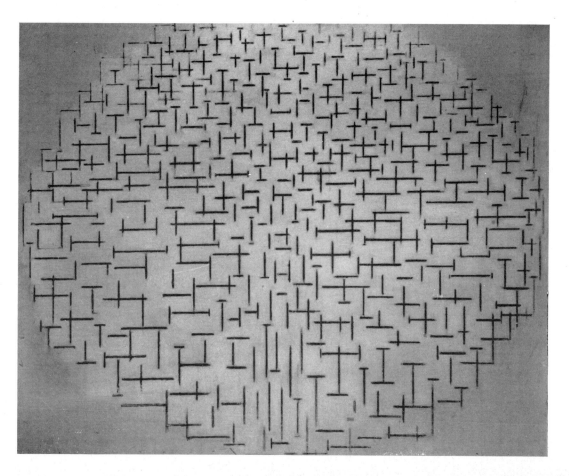

It is apparent how the mechanism of identification played a major role in all past art. Up to the end of Cubism the spectator was always presented with some recognizable aspects of the natural world around him. But in certain arts, especially after Cubism, the spectator, as well as the artist, was confronted with particular forms which had never been seen until the artist invented them! In the Post-Impressionist type of art the artist *deliberately* had shown nature forms as they had never been seen before the artist painted them—still they were recognizable as nature forms. But in the art we are now considering the spectator is confronted with forms that had never been seen in any way previous to their *invention* by the artist—they were not nature forms. They could not be identified with any other previously seen forms. Thus the content of the new kind of art was not a *representation* of forms from the familiar recognizable world of vision, but rather, a *presentation* of new forms *created* by the artist. For this reason identification of nature and art was completely frustrated and failed to function as in the past. This led observers of the new art to complain repeatedly, "But that doesn't look like anything I have ever seen before!" In this the observers were quite correct; however, what they did not realize was that this did not necessarily condemn its possible significance.

Meanwhile a new problem of "reality" had arisen, the problem of how to make the artist's inventions have the quality of reality which one experiences before the old arts and in actual reality. Like most of the spectators, most of the artists were thrown into a quandary. For they also felt a decided lack of "reality" in their works, once the appearances of the natural world had disappeared. At this juncture they were faced with two general choices if they were to continue making art: they could either return to the old practice of using nature objects in one way or another, or they could find some way of securing a satisfactory reality for their invented forms which would dispense with the necessity of *identification* with nature-appearances. After Cubism the general trend of artists (led by, of all people, the former Cubists themselves) was to return and so regress to the practice of manipulating nature's objects.

A few painters, such as the De Stijlists and Suprematists, detected the futility of this regressive decision and so searched elsewhere for a solution. The Suprematist school was founded by the Russian, Kasimir Malevitch, in Moscow in 1913; De Stijl was founded by the Hollanders, Piet Mondrian and Théo van Doesburg in 1917. Although the latter school was formed quite late, the members of it, along with the Suprematists, had come upon the art scene immediately after the Cubist experiments had indicated the new direction. Thus before the Cubists had finished with Cubism those who were to carry on their work had already appeared. In fact, men like Doesburg, Mondrian and Malevitch had taken up the problem of Cubism even before the formation of the above mentioned two-dimensional schools. They had closely observed the Cubist development and some of them had participated in it, although in a very different manner from that of its originators (figure 120). The first step they took was to go further with the method of abstracting already adopted by the Cubists. In short, they abstracted to the very limits of the macro-level of "reality" (figures 120a and 120b). Another good example of this is a work of Doesburg (figure 121).

In these examples, supplied by Doesburg, we see the different stages of abstracting by which the final painting result was achieved—a process of abstracting less and less from the macroscopic level of nature.[1] Most interestingly, these four stages of the Doesburg example roughly provide illuminating illustrations of the history of art up to and just beyond Cubism. The objective of the first stage was to secure an accurate recording of nature's appearances, and this is represented by the Photograph—the culmination and final achievement of this objective which predominated in the efforts of past artists. If, for the sake of illustration, we next consider the Photograph as representing the actual reality of nature from which the artist was abstracting—as Doesburg undoubtedly intended—we can symbolize the rest of art history with the three other paintings; they can represent the transition from the old level of abstracting to a stage very close to the new structural level of abstracting from nature. In the final stage we see that the artist has been seeking to abstract less and less from the *macro*-reality level until he achieved an organization of related two-dimensional planes in two-dimensional space which seemingly do not retain the appearances of nature. By 1919, however, Doesburg significantly enough abandoned this method of abstracting. (In later works he was to employ mathematical relations as a more fitting method for determining the structure of his work: e.g.,

---

1. In later discussions it will be seen that this was a process of abstracting in higher and higher orders from the macroscopic level of reality.

Dessin Arithmetique, the title of a 1930 work.) He had probably recognized, in one way or another, that actually his method achieved only a higher degree of abstracting from the old reality level than had been secured by previous artists of the past. This was not his objective. He wanted to invent his art contents, a contents which would be independent of the necessity of being bound by the macroscopic form of nature in any way. He may have observed that so long as he used the macro-level of nature as the starting point of his art, so long would his final result be determined and limited by these same forms. This would naturally be the result so long as the artist did abstract from that level of reality. This can easily be seen in the Doesburg examples by comparing the Photograph—the source of abstraction—with the last painting stage —the result of abstraction. Notice that the general anatomy of the cow remains indicated in the final painting: i.e., the backbone, hip-bone and hind leg, shoulder and front leg, the stomach and teats, the neck and head; the legs of the human figure and the board are indicated in shapes at the bottom. This is an excellent example of how the artist's desire to invent is *limited* to the framework of the object or objects from which he abstracts. In other words, the artist (inadvertently) is still painting a cow, a nature form, though abstracting to a lesser degree from the macro-level as compared to previous art. The artist is painting a cow as other artists have done; the difference is in the *degree* and *kind* of abstracting from the macro-level of reality. In short, it was simply the old method of abstracting carried almost to the limit of its possibilities in a particular direction. We say "almost," because the old level could be abstracted even further. But there is a limit, and beyond this the artist must abstract directly from the Structural Process level of nature to abstract in any further higher orders. In short, (1) if the abstracting process is continued until all remnants of nature objects have been eradicated, then the result is such that (2) what follows is no longer determined by the limiting forms of nature. However, in that case the artist could just as well have dispensed with the first step and begun directly with the second for all the difference step one would make in the final result.

There will be those who will claim, for the sake of argument rather than knowledge, that one can abstract from a cow in such a manner that no one could ever realize the source of abstraction. This is true; but so long as the artist is abstracting from the form of a cow or what not, so long will he in some degree be bound to the dictates of the subject's forms and so remain bound to the old limited manner of art abstracting. The artist's abstracting would not be limited by the subject's forms, only if he did *not* abstract from them. Therefore, the important thing is not whether such form sources of a painting can be detected, but the consequences of nature forms' being the source of abstraction. If we wish to set free the potentialities of the new direction, it is imperative that we eliminate the limiting and so frustrating operation of abstractions derived from the imitation in any degree of nature-appearances.

At any rate this form of art arose as the one major attempt in the medium of painting after Cubism to overcome, consciously or otherwise, the difficulties which appeared with the loss of the old reality identification mechanism. The first step taken by these artists was to eliminate three-dimensional illusions in favor of two-dimensional ones, just as had been done in the evolution of Cubism. The change was from the laws of three-dimensional "perspective" to those of two-dimensional elevation "perspective." They no longer depicted the round of visual phenomena but only the surfaces or planes of forms. Only the following characteristics of visual reality remained indicated in the art: namely, the before and behind—two-dimensional space—and the up and down—two-dimensional surfaces; i.e., form and space were reduced to two-dimensional phenomena.

For simplicity of presentation we shall refer to both the Russian and the Dutch schools as the Two-Dimensionalists of post-Cubist painting.[2] They differed from the Cubists in that they employed a higher degree of abstracting from the nature object and eventually completely eliminated the latter. From their studies of the Cubists (who themselves failed to attain sufficient consciousness of their own researches) the De Stijlists and Suprematists made more conscious the character of the new direction. They eventually eliminated the objects of nature rather than compromise as the Cubists had done, and thus they made a courageous effort to solve the problems relating to the achievement of a new art contents. They were considerably convinced that man could invent his own contents rather than rely upon the manipulation of macro-reality. Unquestionably, the Two-Dimensionalists surpassed all other forms of painting since Cubism:

2. Those who paint three-dimensional forms will simply be called Three-Dimensionalists.

121. Théo van Doesburg, The Cow, 1915. Reproduced by permission of The Museum of Modern Art from *Cubism and Abstract Art* by Alfred H. Barr, Jr., New York, 1936.

of all their contemporaries in the paint medium they came the nearest to pointing out the new direction of the future.

But it would appear from the writings and art of Mondrian as well as the other Two-Dimensionalists that none of them was adequately aware of the problems of art and reality as we have discussed them. The fundamental problem involved in all the activities of these artists was (in varying degrees) one of insufficient "consciousness of abstracting." For example, the Two-Dimensionalists hoped that by eliminating the third dimension they could also eliminate the illusionistic character of forms and thus attain a greater reality for their man-made shapes. We shall see that although this step did in a sense achieve a greater reality—by producing a correspondence to the linear reality character of the canvas surface—still that very objective was limited by the *reality* confines of the linearity of the canvas. It is true that the Two-Dimensionalists' work seemed at first to achieve a greater semblance of "reality" than appeared in those paintings which were inventions along the three-dimensional order.[3] Of course the Three-Dimensionalist painter could invent his own art contents without imitating in any way the three-dimensional appearances of nature. Psychologically, however, when three-dimensional forms were used, the medium of paint and canvas generally offered the majority of artists no other alternative than to imitate, for those who retained three-dimensional forms on their canvas almost invariably produced, or in time returned to the production of, forms having some degree of dependence upon the appearances of nature objects. For illusions of forms forced the artist to revert to recognizable forms in order to give the illusions some semblance of valid reality.

The realism gained by the linear solution of the Two-Dimensionalists, however, *was only in relation to the linear reality of the canvas, not in relation to the still greater potentialities open to the artist*

3. We emphasize again that we are dealing only with paintings, since the problem will be very different when we deal with those arts which employ forms made out of actual materials.

122. Théo van Doesburg, Composition, 1915. Courtesy, Mme. Théo van Doesburg.

if he achieved an adequate appraisal of the reality structure of the actual world of visual phenomena. In other words, such art results correspond to the limiting dimensional character of the canvas surface and not to the dimensional characteristics of nature. Consequently, in such art one of the main characteristics of the reality was lacking—the structural element of *actual* three dimensions.

In eliminating the third dimension these artists mostly *avoided rather than solved* the problem confronting them. For although the *illusion* of the third dimension was removed they *still retained the illusion of two dimensions.* The Two-Dimensionalists were *confusing* the linear reality character of the canvas surface with the three-dimensional reality character of the actual world of visual phenomena from which they were consciously or unconsciously abstracting. *They were assuming, unconsciously or otherwise, that the criterion of reality was the canvas surface, rather than the reality of the actual world.* In short, these artists were abstracting from three-dimensional phenomena and trying to confine these abstractions to the limitations of the linear character of their medium. Thus they were working in exactly the reverse of the direction they should have adopted. They were not adequately aware of the nature of the abstracting process in which they were involved nor of the limiting character of both their medium and their criterion of reality. Hence they were involved in difficulties, maneuvers and confusions similar to those which had occupied Cézanne and later had stumped and defeated the Cubists.

Now we have noted that the majority of "Abstract" artists made their crucial mistake in identifying the "reality" peculiar to arts which abstracted from nature's macroscopic level with that reality sought for and expected in invented forms; they did not recognize, because they were psycho-logically unprepared to, that Inventive forms could only be adequately realized by abstracting from the Structural Process level of nature's reality. This explains why the majority of so called Abstract artists avoided the consistent and complete invention of their art contents. Not seeing this problem clearly, they were compelled to retain some of the old reality level in their art. As a result of this confusion and identification of different levels of abstracting, the "Abstract" artists continued this confusion in their actual art, now abstracting from one level, now from another, or more often than not from both at the same time. *They were attempting the futile, wasteful task of securing a reality for the results of abstraction from the Structural Process level by imposing upon it in some degree the results of abstraction from the macro-level.* There were two general possibilities, as we have already suggested: the artist could eliminate the macro-reality altogether, or put more of it back into his art contents. The latter led to chaos—a chaos which generally goes by the name of "Modern art"; the former led to more problems, to be sure, but they were useful problems which could be solved. Although the Two-Dimensional artists correctly chose the course of eliminating the macro-level, their error lay in regarding the reality character of the canvas surface, rather than the three-dimensional reality of the world, as the criterion of reality.

Hence both groups of painters, the Three-Dimensionalists and the Two-Dimensionalists, had an inadequate consciousness of the crucial fact that it was from the Structural Process level of reality that they were essentially attempting to abstract, and that *neither the MACRO-REALITY APPEARANCES, nor the CANVAS LINEAR REALITY, nor THREE-DIMENSIONAL ILLUSIONS could be the criterion of reality in the new direction which art was taking!* In short, in order to gain the proper and adequate kind of reality for the new kind of art contents the artist had to secure a *correspondence in structure to the STRUCTURAL PROCESS LEVEL OF REALITY.*

Up to this point two general kinds of identification have been analyzed. In one the forms of nature's macro-reality level are imposed in some degree upon the reality of man-made forms, and in the other the structural limitations of the artist's medium are imposed upon the invented contents.[4] Hence in the first case it is predominantly the *old content* which frustrates the intention of the artist towards the new direction; in the second case it is predominantly the *old medium* belonging to the *old content* which frustrates the artist. Remove these identifications and in great measure the extant confusion in art today is removed.

Perhaps it was in great part the pressures and frustrations resulting from this confusion, confusing the reality of the medium with that of nature, which led Mondrian to speak in the following manner: "Cubist plastic, pushed to its limit, that is how neoplastic finds itself 'on the edge of the abyss' . . ."[5] He was correct; an "abyss" had been reached, just as in Cubism, but with this difference: the Two-Dimensionalists had gone further in other respects with the problems posed by Cubism. For they had done what the Cubists failed to do; they had succeeded in producing works whose contents were completely invented. However, the limitations of the linearity, i.e., the reality confines of the medium, can be seen in the limited variety of invention that has been produced by the artists working in this direction.

So far we have seen that the Two-Dimensionalists recognized the non-reality, or the inadequate reality of three-dimensional *illusions.* In this they were correct. Their error lay in assuming that this could be remedied by removing the third dimension, not recognizing that they were now even more limited in another way by the reality confines of the canvas surface. Moreover, they had not eliminated illusions; they had, at a price, simply reduced the quantity of illusion, because the illusion of space still remained. How to eliminate this lack of reality was the next task that some artists tackled.

One way in which the elimination of such illusions was attempted was in such works as *Black on Black* (1918), Rodchenko, and *White on White* (figure 130), Malevitch. But these steps rather than achieving greater "reality" for the contents of the new art, only took the artist even closer to the limitations

4. Of course when the Three-Dimensionalist does abstract from the third dimension without employing the appearance of nature's objects, there still remains the problem of an illusion of the third dimension. This problem will be considered again in the next chapter.

5. "De l'Art Abstrait"; "Réponse de Piet Mondrian," in *Cahiers d'Art,* p. 42, No. 1, 1931, translation by Harry Holtzman and Martin James. All quotations from Mondrian by the kind permission of Harry Holtzman.

123. Théo van Doesburg, Composition, 1918. Courtesy of The Art of This Century.

of the canvas. In these examples, however, it would appear that the artists were actually attempting to remove even the illusion of two dimensions. But this could best be achieved and a more genuine reality produced by painting one color across the entire surface of the canvas. In this way the artist would not be fabricating *illusions* of nature objects, or of three-dimensional or two-dimensional inventions. *By this action the artist would simply be giving a color to the actual reality surface of the canvas.* This would seem to be exactly the reason which must have led one of the Two-Dimensionalists to do this very thing. Thus Rodchenko took three canvases; one he painted all blue, another all yellow, and another all red.[6] With that he announced the "death of art," and that he had now done his last painting.[7] It was the year 1922. And in this action, under the circumstances, he was consistent. However he realized it, he did comprehend that this was the last action left for canvas or *linear* artists.

6. It was a surprise to the author to discover that this had been done, as he had originally come to this conclusion without imagining that anyone had actually done as Rodchenko had.

7. See *Cubism and Abstract Art,* p. 126, The Museum of Modern Art, 1936.

124. Piet Mondrian, Composition, 1925. Collection The Museum of Modern Art, New York.

Incidental to this event, it is of interest to notice two artists who made strikingly parallel remarks when painters were faced with a momentous change. Paul Delaroche, when he saw the Daguerreotype in the same year it was invented, exclaimed: "Painting is dead from today on!" [8] He well recognized that the copying of nature with the old primitive medium of painting was now no longer useful. He did not recognize, however, that other avenues of enterprise were still open in the old medium.[9] More than three-quarters of a century later Rodchenko, faced with the end of the painting medium's *usefulness* in the new direction which Delaroche had failed to recognize, made an even more encompassing announcement; he spoke of the "death of art." He would have been more correct if instead he had repeated Delaroche's statement, for it was now quite accurate. Both these statements are instances where the particular artists were able to see the

8. As quoted by Erich Stenger, *The History of Photography*, p. 182.
9. It is true that later Delaroche revised his reaction and came to contend that Photography could be of great service to the painter. But here he erred again, for all subsequent great painters went away from rather than towards the objective of the Camera.

125. Kasimir Malevitch, Suprematist Composition: Red Square and Black Square, 1914-16. Collection The Museum of Modern Art, New York.

termination of the old, but in the first case the new direction was not seen and in the second there was inadequate confidence in the new.

However, there remained still one more step for the canvas artists: that of stretching up a piece of canvas, leaving the surface bare and undisguised with color. (Perhaps this also has been done by someone.) This would be the final and most complete reality a canvas could possess, the reality of the canvas *as such, not* as a representation of anything else. Thus, in the end the most complete reality a canvas could secure, and all it now had to offer in the new direction was the empty face of a bare canvas! Once this had been done, other artists, like Rodchenko, might realize the bitter truth, that they had come to the end of the painting medium's usefulness.

THE EMPTY CANVAS SYMBOLIZES THE FACT THAT THIS MEDIUM CAN HAVE NO MORE TO OFFER IN OUR TIMES! And so in the hands of the Two-Dimensionalists, *useful* painting came to its end. The word "useful" has been utilized for the benefit of those who continue to paint, and to avoid confusion over the fact that the majority of artists will for some time in the future blissfully continue to paint. Therefore, we do not claim that the *use* of painting is ended, but rather that its *usefulness* has. Whatever continues to be done in this medium can only be a feeble reminiscence (or corruption) of what has already been done incomparably better in the past.

Not only Rodchenko but also Doesburg correctly recognized the end of painting. In 1924 the latter warned that "Modern painting approaches its end." [10]

The work of the Two-Dimensionalists was shouting something at them, something which they could not quite comprehend: it was an ordeal for them which one cannot fully appreciate unless he has experienced the pressures involved in such a predicament.

10. As quoted by R. J. Goldwater; *Primitivism in Modern Painting*, p. 132.

364

126. Théo van Doesburg, Composition, 1920. Courtesy, Mme. Théo van
Doesburg.

In the meantime there are many who have, for some years now, been pointing to the Two-Dimensionalists, particularly to Mondrian, informing us that here is plain evidence that the non-imitative arts have finally come to a dead-end. To be sure, these learned judgments have come from most of the so-called Modernists and their apologists (a judgment which greatly pleased the Academicians), who have committed themselves to a continued manipulation of the appearance of nature's objects. They are the ones who have felt that the macro-forms of nature should be returned in one degree or another, a solution the opposite of that taken by the Two-Dimensionalists. In the works of Mondrian especially they have hoped to prove, once and for all, that they have chosen the correct direction and that the "pure ones" will have to adopt this decision too, if they wish to find anything further to put on their canvases. The few straight lines which remain in Mondrian's work prove, so they claim, that this art has reached a point beyond which there remains nothing else to do.[11] It is all as obvious as that—after all, what can an artist do after he has reduced art to three or five lines? Thus the learned critics, and the majority of artists (Academicians and "Modernists" alike) have happily concluded that there is no alternative for such artists but to do as they have safely done all along, i.e., manipulate the objects of nature for the production of their art contents.

11. The year 1936 saw one of the finest exhibitions that the Museum of Modern Art has ever put on—"Cubism and Abstract Art." It was then that we heard so often that in Mondrian one could see that the end had been reached in "Abstract" or "non-figurative" art. Since this book was written, "Abstract" art has become quite a popular affair—"everybody's doing it." But almost all of these artists, even though many of them may blandly praise Mondrian, are agreed, consciously or otherwise, that beyond Mondrian's lines one cannot go. This is proven by the fact that they fill their art contents with the old subject-matter ("expressing themselves," they call it) rather than attempting to go beyond the "few lines" of Mondrian.

127. Kasimir Malevitch, Suprematist Composition, c. 1915. Collection Art of
This Century.

These observations and evaluations produced such obvious and convenient conclusions that it
was hard to resist them. The problem of eliminating nature objects from the art contents had indeed caused
a great deal of frustrating confusion. But now at long last the whole thing seemed about to clear up: the
non-imitative artists had seemingly been stopped by a few straight lines of Mondrian! They did not see
that the error of this painter was not in the kind of art but in the kind of medium he employed for
making such art; that the use of this medium resulted in the error of making the canvas surface rather than
nature the criterion of art reality.

Little did the detractors of the new direction realize how far-reaching the actual implications
were: that *all* painting, even the painting of those who had seen the end of the new art direction in
Mondrian's works, was terminating its useful existence; that the works of Mondrian signalled, not the
end of the art direction indicated in his works, but rather the termination of the medium he was using,
the primitive tools of canvas and paints!!

Of all the innovators of the Two-Dimensionalist schools Mondrian and Doesburg stand alone.
Of all their *painting* contemporaries they were the most clearly cognizant of the essential problems facing
the artists of this century.[12] They continued while all around them other painters deserted the problems
of art for the more convenient forms of the old art contents, because they had an excellent insight into what
was to come. This will be seen in the quotations we shall give from their writings.

Doesburg and Mondrian are among the very few artists of this century who have produced
works and theories which will remain respected in the art history of human beings. They were the last

12. It is essential that the reader keep in mind that we are confining our analysis here only to the medium of the painters and
are not considering the sculptors' and the Constructionists' mediums.

366

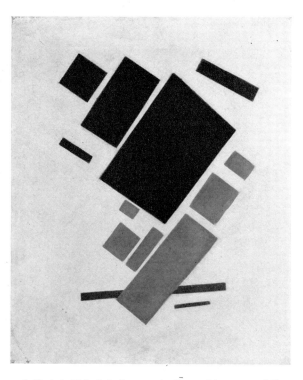

128. Kasimir Malevitch, Suprematist Composition, 1914. Collection The Museum of Modern Art, New York.

great artists to use the medium of paint, and their works have much to teach us, although most artists are oblivious of this.[13] Perhaps this has been due to the fact that their works appear too obvious to intrigue any interest. But many who have tried to produce this kind of art have had cause to alter that opinion soon after their initial efforts.[14] Instead of studying painters like Doesburg and Mondrian, most artists prefer instead to become hypnotized by the Pied Pipers from Spain—Picasso, Dali and Miro. One day we shall recognize the full stature of the Hollanders, and when we do we shall act as though they had just been discovered.

anti-Picasso

During the major portion of their post-Cubist life, Mondrian and Doesburg insisted that the artist unreservedly eliminate macro-reality and invent his own contents. Once they reached this point in their development, the titles of their works were simply *Composition,* or *Composition in White, Black and Red* and the like. They neither employed verbal labels which would arouse recognizable nature phenomena in the observers of their art, nor did they depict the macro-level of nature's reality. Both in their works and theories, the implications of the new direction were faced.

13. To be sure, Picasso beat loudly on his drum; nothing else could be heard. Then there were such hastily made criticisms as this by Ozenfant, who spoke about the works of Doesburg and the like as a "squaring-up; which instead of being forms of pure construction . . . . [are] a very exact and innocent imitation of tiled surfaces and other building materials (the Neo-plasticists: Mondrian, van Doesburg, etc.)." (Amédée Ozenfant: *Foundations of Modern Art,* p. 77, translated by John Rodker, Brewer, Warren and Putnam, Inc., New York, 1931, by permission of Harcourt, Brace and Co.) If anyone was "innocent," it was the author of such statements!
14. Indeed, if the art of Doesburg and Mondrian were "easy," most so-called Modern painters would be working in this manner. However, the significance of this art lies not so much in the difficulty of mere execution as in the courage and conviction which were demanded in order to dare to do it, and do it properly.

> It is not enough to explain the value of a work of art in itself; it is above all necessary to show the place which a work occupies on the scale of the evolution of plastic art. Thus in speaking of art, it is not permissible to say "this is how I see it" or "this is my idea." True art like true life takes a single road. 232   Piet Mondrian

As can be seen in the above quotation, Mondrian readily recognized the erroneous and harmful tendency of his contemporaries in their over-emphasis upon the subjective factor, and the greater need for emphasis upon and cognizance of the evolutionary character of art developments. He insisted that the artist should be the vehicle of art, and not the opposite; that the art, not the artist, was the important factor. In other words the significance of art is not a matter of personal desires or prejudices, as he pointed out, but one of a relation of the work to the historic evolution of man's art. Perhaps he was not always correct or clear on the subject, and some notions of his later writings contradict some expressed in his earlier ones. (This is also true of his art.) But in principle he had the proper attitude toward these problems, an attitude which few artists today, including most of his "admirers," even realize exists, let alone understand. In fact, Mondrian's insight into contemporary problems, as is the case with every great artist, far exceeded his actual achievements. He was one of those rare individuals who look ahead of what they have achieved because they know that the development of art has not begun with them and will not end with them.

When one recalls all the egotistical, operatic mumblings of Picasso, Miro, Dali, etc., in their efforts to escape from a world undergoing changes which they cannot comprehend, and then compares their utterances with the writings of Mondrian, one begins to see the significant differences. In 1931 Mondrian wrote: "There is therefore no occasion today 'to rest awhile or to pause'. And if some are tired, let others replace them. . . . just as in life. 'To advance without interruption, eyes fixed upon a distant goal', that is exactly what we have to do. Because this goal is not 'chimerical', and one does not thus 'isolate oneself' from life, from its contributions, its direction, its warmth. On the contrary, this distant goal is in direct relation with life today; it is not only clearly traced in our mind but is even already realized as art. Neoplastic work is deduced from life, of which it is at the same time the product, from continuous life, which is 'culture', evolution." [15] Mondrian was aware that the new direction in art was involved in achieving a *new* contact with the world of reality *of which it was "the product,"* and that it was not, as was popularly thought, a denial of that reality. This distinction is made even more clear in the next quotation, where he is talking about what we have been calling the two general levels of reality abstracting. He writes: "The laws which in the culture of art have become more and more determinate are *the great hidden laws of nature which art established in its own fashion*. It is necessary to stress the fact that these laws are more or less hidden behind the superficial aspect of nature. Abstract art is therefore opposed to a natural representation of things. But it *is not opposed to nature* as is generally thought." [16]

We must understand that here Mondrian was referring to the fact that art has become a problem of more and more concern not with the copying of nature-appearances—what he calls "the superficial aspect of nature"—but with the Structural Process of reality which he calls "the great hidden laws of nature." Hence the new attitude in art is opposed to the copying of nature-appearances "but is not opposed to nature," because the new artist, to put it in more conscious language, still abstracts from the structural level of reality *upon which he depends for his method of making art*. Mondrian's inadequacy as regards the latter factor was his failure to recognize the more comprehensive structural demands and potentialities of the "laws of nature." If he had, as we shall explain presently, he would have discarded the limiting medium of paint.

15. Piet Mondrian: "De l'Art Abstrait"; "Réponse de Piet Mondrian," *Cahiers d'Art*, p. 42, No. 1, 1931.

16. Piet Mondrian: "Plastic Art and Pure Plastic Art," *Plastic Art and Pure Plastic Art*, 1937, and other essays, 1941-1943, p. 54. (The Documents of Modern Art: general editor, Robert Motherwell), Wittenborn and Co., New York, 1945, by permission of Harry Holtzman.

129. Théo van Doesburg, Rhythms of a Russian Dance, 1918. Collection The Museum of Modern Art, New York.

But he also wrote: "It is a happy fact that our generation is not only considerably preoccupied but also 'effectively occupied' with plastic art. Thus, it has created a pure plastic art, that is to say, a plastic art without sentimental, literary or descriptive notions. Form and color have attained their proper use: henceforth they are only means of plastic expression and no more dominate the work as was the case in the past.

"It is thus that they are really integrated, that is to say that they enter more and more into equivalent contrast with the foundation which will produce a more real equilibrium.

"All this is not according to precedent but under the influence of the progress of science and all of life." [17] Here he points out the fact that by eliminating the macro-character of reality and all that it once implied, the artist has been freed to release his ability to invent his own content which thus corresponds more to the Structural Process of visual reality. That is, "form and color" of nature objects

17. Piet Mondrian: reply to a questionnaire directed by Christian Zervos to a number of artists, *Cahiers d'Art,* p. 31, Nos. 1-4, 1935, translation by Harry Holtzman and Martin James.

130. Kasimir Malevitch, Suprematist Composition: White on White, 1918. Collection The
Museum of Modern Art, New York.

no longer dominate the production of the art contents, but rather, the *notion* of "form and color" supplies the means by which the artist creates his own content. And finally Mondrian emphasized what needs to be emphasized time and again in these days, that the new direction is "not according to any precedent," as is generally assumed, but according to the "influence of the progress of science and all of life"—according to the direction in which it is now possible for human development in art and science to tend.

Fundamentally he was trying to say that today it is not the appearances, but the laws of nature's process which are the guide for the creation of the new art. Therefore, the new artist is not opposed to nature, but rather has revised the past orientation to nature as regards the genesis of an object of non-Camera art. This change was due to the new view of "reality."

Hence it is an error to accuse the new artist of indifference to "nature"; it is more correct to see the new orientations being made to these problems by the new artist. Mondrian correctly insisted that: "It is, however, wrong to think that the non-figurative artist finds impressions and emotions received from the outside useless, and regards it even as necessary to fight against them. On the contrary, all that the non-figurative artist received from the outside is not only useful but indispensable, because it arouses in him the desire to create that which he only vaguely feels and which he could *never represent in a true manner without the contact with visible reality and with the life which surrounds him*. It is precisely from this visible reality that he draws the objectivity which he needs in opposition to his personal subjectivity. It is precisely from this visible reality that he draws his means of expression: and, as regards the surrounding life, it is precisely this which has made his art non-figurative." [18] In other words it would be more correct to state that the past "objective" of the artist's activity has simply been revised, not eliminated. Thus Mondrian considered as fallacious that all too popular theory in the art world to the effect that those who

18. Mondrian, "Plastic Art and Pure Plastic Art," *Plastic Art and Pure Plastic Art,* p. 62, Wittenborn and Co., New York, 1945.

370

do not depict nature, who do not abstract from the macro-reality, are not only opposed to nature, but are therefore cut off from it. Acceptance of the simple fact that it is impossible for an artist to be cut off from nature might have saved us from many useless arguments. The great obstacle was that most of us saw the problem of nature's reality as a matter of one level only, the macro-level. But we repeat, if it were possible for an artist to divorce himself from reality, it would be impossible for him to produce art.

It was because Mondrian understood these facts that he recognized the essential values of Cubism; in fact he was one of the very few men of his generation who faced the future properly by facing the implications of Cubism, while the former Cubists continued in their false role of "radicals." If he had done nothing else, he would have done much. Thus he was able to appraise correctly the events of 1914: "Intuition enlightens and so links up with pure thought. They together become an intelligence which is not simply of the brain, which does not calculate, but which feels and thinks. Which is creative both in art and in life. From this intelligence there must arise non-figurative art in which instinct no longer plays a dominating part. Those who do not understand this intelligence regard non-figurative art as a purely intellectual product." [19]

In regard to this last sentence, we have frequently emphasized that no one's art can be "purely intellectual" (or purely "feeling") no matter how hard one might try. That men can talk of being purely intellectual or purely emotional is only proof that men can talk anything with words—not that men can do anything in reality. Mondrian is telling us that the old attitude of *over*-dependence upon "intuition" is now over, as we have repeatedly pointed out; not only is it no longer necessary, but it is decidedly harmful and in the new direction of art we must develop *non*-intuitive formulations of our intuitive activity. If we do not, if we continue to depend too much upon intuition, we shall have failed to realize the crucial fact that "instinct no longer plays a dominating part" in the task ahead for the artist. Not comprehending this, artists will not correctly comprehend the future.

In the works of Mondrian we see one of the greatest *painters* of the 20th century, and the last great painter in the primitive medium of painting. He is one of the very few men of our century who helped to form the new direction of art. He saw that one epoch of man had closed and that another was open; that the art of nature is being replaced with the art of man. Therefore: "Non-figurative art brings to an end the ancient culture of art; at present therefore, one can review and judge more surely *the whole culture of art*. We are not at the turning-point of this culture; *the culture of particular form is approaching its end. The culture of determined relations has begun.*" [20]

In certain very surprising respects, the termination of the painting medium in the straight lines of Mondrian discloses a striking parallel with the very first efforts of artists at the beginning of human art. We are referring to the first experimental efforts by which lines were made with the finger in clay, or drawing one stone across another, and the like, as explained in chapter 5 (page 62). We can say of these first attempts to scratch lines and then use them as symbols, what Korzybski said about the beginning of oral communication: "we never realize, even now, that these historically first grunts were the most complex and difficult of them all." [21] After these lines had been developed into a non-imitative symbology, we saw a development arise in which man began to record, with arrangements of these lines, the visual world about him. Eventually he achieved a very accurate recording of the macro-reality, although the steady development was interrupted here and there by a few outstanding regressions. The natural consequence, the final evolution of this art direction, culminated in the invention of the Camera. Thus the first era of man's art history began with straight lines and ended with Photographs!

19. Ibid., p. 54.   20. Ibid., p. 54.   21. Korzybski, *Science and Sanity,* p. 438.

131. Piet Mondrian, Composition with Blue, 1926. Courtesy of The Philadelphia Museum of Art, Philadelphia. Gallatin Collection.

Next came the Transitional-Period which superficially seemed to have all the characteristics of a return to ever older forms of art, and appeared to put the whole preceding era of history into reverse. That is to say, the Impressionists imitated nature less than their predecessors, the Post-Impressionists less than the Impressionists, until artists were finally influenced by Primitive arts. But the process did not stop here; artists continued to imitate less and less until the macro-reality disappeared almost entirely in the works of the Cubists. The Two-Dimensionalists took the last step when they stopped abstracting altogether from the old level of reality; nothing remained on the canvas but a few straight lines in the works of Mondrian. To be precise, eventually nothing was left but the bare canvas, as far as the painting medium was concerned.

Thus the era begun by the first human artists with their lines had now terminated its long anthropomorphic journey, and a new era, a non-anthropomorphic era had begun, also signalled into being once more with straight lines, the straight lines of Mondrian. It is interesting also to notice that the beginning and development of the first great era of art history was found in France and Spain, and that it has now concluded with the Cubists in France, of which the foremost artists were both French and Spanish.[22]

In a sense we can say that the entire history of man was unwound to reach the straight lines again in order to begin, as the Pictographic artists had done, a new era of art, and thus to achieve a new visualization of the world reality. This leads us to another interesting comparison: if we compare the first lines of the first artists with the lines of the high point of Mondrian's art, we find that *both are INVENTED and not copies of nature-appearances*. In brief, in each of the two great eras of man's art, the beginnings had to be invented. In the first instance, the invention of lines was actually the invention of the *materials*

22. We have also stated that Mondrian did the last useful work in the painting medium, thus seemingly positing two different conclusions. However, we shall later make clear these two different conclusions of painting, which occupy two different contexts.

372

132. Théo van Doesburg, Composition, 1929. Courtesy of The Philadelphia Museum of Art. Gallatin Collection. Photo, Courtesy of Mme. Théo van Doesburg.

and means by which it later became possible to record macro-reality. In the second instance, the invention of lines led to the invention of a *method* by which a new insight into nature's reality structure would be achieved for the making of art. Each invention led to the discovery and examination of one of the two general levels of nature's reality; each was converted to the useful needs of man.

Therefore, art, but only in one sense, has been returned to its beginning, to its original manifestations! This event is being discovered in various fields of human research. Those who have studied the Primitive properly have discovered certain desirable and *natural* forms of orientations to the environment which were lost in the epoch of dichotomies, the Aristotelian period, and which *must* now be recovered and used in a higher form of human behavior.[23]

But the return is not a literal return, and this is where the error can be and is usually made. This error is a prevailing one in this century and occurs because we are attracted to the *manifest* rather than to the *latent* level of the new direction. As we pointed out in our analysis of the Transitional-Period, the similarities with preceding forms of art were only symptomatic, not basic; the Transitional-Period consisted of the effort not to repeat the past, but to reach the Structural Process level of abstracting in order to begin the next evolutionary cycle of art. It was only after the Transition-Period had been concluded that such an art direction became regressive, for after Cubism most artists attempted to return to the old content and to retreat from the new once reached by the Cubists.

23. On this point Reiser wrote (p. 15, *The Promise of Scientific Humanism*): ". . . . this third type of semantics [non-Aristotelian] seems to resemble in some respects a return to the first type of orientation, [primitive 'mystical participation'] in that this new level of orientation will be associated with its own unity of man and nature. I mean by this that after the present stage of specialization in science has passed, or has been supplemented by an era of co-ordination and synthesis of knowledge, we may again attain an understanding of the interconnectedness of things (events) which resembles primitive man's sense of 'participation,' at least to the extent that here, on a higher level, we again realize the limitations of the classical Aristotelian 'laws' of thought."

133. Théo van Doesburg, Composition Simultanée, 1929. Collection, Professor O. Müller, Basel. Photo, Courtesy of Mme. Théo van Doesburg.

134. Piet Mondrian, Composition with Red, 1936. Courtesy of the Philadelphia Museum of Art, Gallatin Collection.

Malevitch recognized something of this problem when he remarked: "The square of the suprematists and the forms arising from this square are to be compared to the primitive lines (marks) of primitive men, which in their ensemble do not portray an ornament but the impression of rhythm."[24]

It is of interest also to consider the well-known fact of Mondrian's attraction to the "primitive quality" of music, such as boogie woogie and the like: "What neoplasticism understands by this free rhythm which is opposed to natural rhythm, can be comprehended a little by listening to 'american jazz', where it is so closely approximated but not realized—melody, that is to say, limited form, not being entirely destroyed."[25]

We have made the analogy that as man steps off into the new era of art, the artists of the Two-Dimensionalist schools have produced the straight line which parallels the very beginnings of art made by the very first artists of man. Both outstanding artists of the Two-Dimensionalist schools, Mondrian and Malevitch, noticed similarities in their art to that of the Primitives—Malevitch in drawing attention to the "primitive lines," Mondrian in his attraction to primitive-like music.[26] It would seem that they both made the error of *identifying* the simple beginnings of the new era of art with the efforts of Primitives. They gave incorrect importance to the similarities and failed to see adequately the even more important difference: namely, that each kind of art was headed in a different direction. They were not able to see that they, like the first artists of mankind, had discovered the material which could be employed, by developing the elementary character of the lines into the means with which to begin a new era of art.

In this sense then this event was a case of phylogeny being recapitulated in a reverse manner, as though man had to return all the way to his original ability to invent in order to rediscover and so become conscious of potentialities which he inherently possessed and was now in a position to use once more in a different way for a different objective. The first invented lines of the first artists led to the abstracting from the macroscopic level of reality, while the invented lines of Mondrian led to the abstracting from the Structural Process level of nature's reality. In short, it is possible to say that *man started out on each of the two eras of his art history by abstracting from the Structural Process level of nature, which in each case consisted of the preliminary elementary abstraction of invented lines. The first eventually led to the accurate recording of nature's art-results, the second to the invention of art-results peculiar to man.*

There are thus actually two such Transitional-Periods in art history, each the reverse of the other. When the first artists discovered and invented the first lines they automatically began the first Transitional-Period. This period consisted of developing the use of the lines until they became recording devices. In this way was born the beginning of the first great era of man's effort in the field of art, the era of recording nature's macro-reality, *the recording of nature's art.*

The reverse of this process began after the Camera and especially with the Impressionists. From then on the macro-reality of nature was eliminated more and more from Monet to Mondrian, until the artist had returned to the original invention of man, the line. Specifically, this latter Transition-Period ends with Cubism; Mondrian not only participates in this period but overlaps into the period following—the second great era of man's art history, the era of man's inventing his own art contents by employing nature's method.

As we have repeatedly stressed, the eventual objective of past as well as present art has been to too large a degree an unconscious affair. It is in our times, however, that the development of art has reached far enough that it has now become not only possible but crucially necessary to see clearly what has happened along the road of man's art development, if one is to realize what is happening today. It is possible for our generation to see that man is passing by necessity from the reign of Aristotelianism, which

24. As quoted by Goldwater, op. cit., p. 134.

25. Mondrian, "De l'Art Abstrait"; "Réponse de Piet Mondrian," *Cahiers d'Art,* p. 43, No. 1, 1931.

26. Mondrian's attraction to primitive-like music is, however, also symptomatic of that inadequate clarity of understanding which we noted. For "boogie woogie," etc. is a form of music which has captured the senses of so many who, like the Primitives, must raise a lot of noise in the dark. The mad dances (jazz) came with the last war and have continued ever since. Yet Mondrian unequivocably stated that, "Primitive expression lacks consciousness, the product of centuries of human culture." (*Plastic Art and Pure Plastic Art,* p. 18, Wittenborn and Co.) In short, he was torn between the extremes of "Modern art"—its symptomatic and fundamental levels.

for some time now has been an impossible system for coping with the new conditions. Today new systems of human orientation are being formulated along non-Aristotelian directions. But even many of those in "art" and "science" who are contributing to the formation of the new attitude are not aware that they are doing so. It is, however, in art and science that these new changes are most in evidence, not only because the times are opportune for a non-Aristotelian attitude, but because we must make these revisions or sink along the direction which the totalitarian mentalities everywhere are advocating. Thus today, on all sides, by both destructive and constructive forces, we see pressing demands for revisions of things so many of us thought would last forever.

In the meantime an overwhelming majority of artists, so overwhelming one would imagine no artist does otherwise, continue to struggle with the primitive attitudes, methods, materials, and tools of paints and canvas. In the next chapter we shall further see why not only the old contents but the old medium must be discarded in non-Camera art. It parallels so many other events of our times which force us to replace old tools and old methods with new ones which more adequately meet the demands of present day conditions.

The fundamental foundations of art should rest upon firm ground: real life. As a matter of fact, space and time are the two exclusive elements which fill real life (reality).

Therefore if art wishes to comprehend real life it must base itself equally on these two fundamental elements.

. . . . To realize that we live in forms of time and space, this is the unique aim of our creative art. We grasp our reins in our hands, our eyes looking straight ahead, our spirit taut like a bow and we shape our work as the world shapes its own creation, the engineer a bridge, the mathematician the graph of a plane's path. 139

N. Gabo and A. Pevsner, 1920

The immediate source from which the Constructive idea
derives is Cubism. . . . 124   Naum Gabo

18 NON-ARISTOTELIAN ART

The specific triumph of the technical imagination rested on the ability to dissociate lifting power from the arm and create a crane: to dissociate work from the action of men and animals and create the water-mill: to dissociate light from the combustion of wood and oil and create the electric lamp. For thousands of years animism had stood in the way of this development; for it had concealed the entire face of nature behind a scrawl of human forms: even the stars were grouped together in the living figures of Castor and Pollux or the Bull on the faintest points of resemblance. 239

Lewis Mumford

We see this adversary to the Old Order, the Machine, as—at last—a sword to cut old bonds and provide escape to Freedom; we see it as the servant and saviour of the New Order—if only it be creatively used by man! 364   Frank Lloyd Wright

We can find efficient support for our optimism in those two domains of our culture where the revolution has been the most thorough, namely, in Science and in Art. 124

Naum Gabo

While various Painting attempts followed in the wake of Cubism, some of which we have already examined, a group of artists in Russia were working more directly on the correct interpretation of certain problems confronting contemporary art, particularly on problems of the medium. In their works we shall find that they proceeded with the realization of an art content which was the result of direct abstraction from the Structural Process level of reality. *The very first thing these artists did was exactly the opposite of the solution advanced by the Two-Dimensionalist schools, that is, they put back into art the ACTUAL third dimension!* How did they accomplish this? *Principally by discarding the primitive mechanical tools of paints and brushes and canvas and chisels, and in their place employing the three-dimensional materials of industry as well as the more modern fabricating tools like Machines!*

In 1913, before the end of Cubism, the new art made its appearance in Moscow in the works of Vladimir Tatlin. From that point on a group of artists in Russia formed the beginnings of an art which was distinct from all other contemporary manifestations. With these men a new type of artist emerged, far different from the traditional notions; they possessed a wider consciousness of the world around them than was the case with most members of the other schools of art. They adopted both a sociological and scientific attitude. They sensed that a new civilization was in the process of being born. The first World-Civil-War was in progress, which ended for Russia in a revolution. A new Russia was in the making—the Soviet Union. Its leaders proclaimed a new and better order of society, a "collective" society. It was in this revolutionary environment that those who were later called Constructionists made their first great effort. Here where a new form of society, a new civilization was being born, the Constructionists felt that they and their new art belonged.

They soon became the principal artists of Russia. They executed commissions for the government and were in charge of the schools for art instruction. There was no compulsion from the Communist Party. In short, these artists were freely permitted to put their notions of art into the life blood of this new social organism. In 1920 a great Constructionist exhibition was held in Moscow. But in this same year unfortunate events began to divide these artists. The pressure of political conditions was beginning to affect them; one faction, of which Tatlin and Rodchenko were adherents, wished to place their art at the service of the "revolution"; others, like Antoine Pevsner and Naum Gabo refused, and consequently found their studios closed. The former group became the equivalent of what we call commercial artists; they dutifully made art fit into the dictates of the *status-quo* masters, the politico-soldier mentality. In any case, the new art could not survive in Russia. Those who placed Constructionist art at the service of the "revolution" found that this meant the complete elimination of Constructionist art; those who failed to comply, found their studios locked, and shortly afterwards they left Russia.

About five years after the revolution, Constructionist art was forced from the country. The official purging of the Constructionist movement was announced with the terse statement that such art comprises "aspects of free original thought incomprehensible to the masses." [1] The politicians had generously given them five full years to get their work across to "the masses"; five years in which to get across to a people just emerging from a feudal society, the results of thousands of years of art evolution; five years in which to convey the highest form of art abstraction ever produced by man, to a people most of whom had yet to learn to read and write. But the leaders treated themselves much more leniently, and gave themselves *unlimited time* in which to reach the promised political utopia—a utopia that has turned out to be the most deadly exploitation of the "worker" yet conceived in our times.

Explaining this right-about-face, Horace Kallen wrote: "For the revolutionaries desirous of overturning the world's old political economy and the innovators passionate to set up unprecedented seeings and doings were brought together by the common emotion of their different challenges to the *status quo*. And thus, until the politicians were able to possess themselves of the instruments of power, they were everywhere disposed to assimilate innovation in the arts to revolution in society. Bolsheviks and Fascists, being foes of the existing order, affected to be friends of Futurism, Expressionism and the like; as soon however as they had made themselves masters of the existing order, they turned against the esthetic creeds they had espoused—the Bolsheviks within less than a decade, the Fascists in half that time, the Nazis as a step toward power. The betrayals were a foregone conclusion. To the politician, liberty was merely an instrument of revolution, a means to power; to the artist it was the be-all end-all of his enterprise, at once its end and means both. Like the liberty of science, the liberty of art and the authority of dictatorship cannot live in the same world together." [2]

The "ignorance of the masses" now became the weapon by which the politicians disposed of anything with which their own ignorance could not cope. At first the Communist Party had claimed that their objective was to *elevate* the masses to the higher levels of prevalent culture, but now, suddenly the leaders decided (in this they were emulated by the fascists and nazis a little later) that it was much simpler to pull the culture down to the level of the masses themselves. The revolution was now in reverse! Today their great claim is to have turned Russia into something of a Pittsburgh. Thus, like other leading nations, Russia has turned to cultivating a predominantly materialistic, militaristic philosophy of government. Men are compelled to think and live in a culture made for robots.

The most important characteristics of recent human development, i.e., freedom in thinking and art, were suppressed. Dictatorship was to solve everything. (But dictatorship, as Karl Mannheim well pointed out, is "like the physician who believes he is curing a sick child by forbidding it to cry." [3]) Kallen tells us that: "it wasn't long before an inquisition into relativity, psychoanalysis, and diversities in ethnography, geology and astronomy condemned them as heresies in conflict with dialectical materialism. . . . No discipline escapes the heresy hunt, the censorship, the purge. . . .

1. These politicians of the Russian revolution, who so pride themselves in being "realistic," failed to be aware even of the simple fact that the most developed orders of art and reason had always been "incomprehensible to the masses," because rulers preferred to keep the masses conveniently down rather than push them up, just as these Russians were now doing by suppressing the development of advanced art and reason.

2. Horace M. Kallen: *Art and Freedom,* Vol. 2, pp. 851-852. Reprinted by permission of the publishers, Duell, Sloan and Pearce, Inc. Copyright 1942 by Horace M. Kallen.

3. Karl Mannheim: *Man and Society in an Age of Reconstruction,* p. 109, Harcourt, Brace and Co., Inc., New York, 1940.

"A conformation to the official doctrine as rigid as any as was ever required of Bruno, Galileo or Kepler is demanded of all workers in the sciences, from agronomy to astronomy."[4] And so modern composers in Russia were ordered to make music that could be whistled; Cubism was decried as but an expression of decaying capitalism. In the fields of art and music it would seem that the "dictatorship of the proletariat" was actually allowed to exert its influence. But this "dictatorship" existed only where it happened to fit in with the "plans" of the leaders, whose art desires and ignorance paralleled those of the masses.

The "new" art was described as the "picturization of the Soviet Regime." Like it or not, this was the artist's job. Thus the Russians traded a 20th century internationalist art for a 19th century nationalist variety, which was steeped in, of all things, bourgeoise tradition and a Christian-like deception of Utopia! (It is not an accident that the art of the Soviets reflects the period in which the notions of Marx originated.) Thus art was pushed all the way from the latest innovations in our times, back to the practices of that confused period between the invention of the Camera and the first Impressionism.

Apparently the Camera alone was not good enough to do the "picturization," a task for which it had been especially invented. For the Camera had the mechanical impudence to record things very much as they *were,* regardless of the specific commands of the Soviet leaders. Artists can be made to picturize anything. They could be easily molded to answer the demands of the leaders, just as artists in the Dark Ages were molded and shackled by the priests. In Russia art was used in a similar way and for a similar purpose as it had been in the Christian era.

Of this political barbarism Mumford wrote: "Obedient corpses, galvanically summoned to action by their superiors, are not effective or desirable substitutes for living men. Nor is *rigor mortis* an equivalent for unity of spirit."[5] But, as we have noted, two Constructionists, Pevsner and his brother Gabo, refused to be "obedient corpses" and promptly left Russia.

One aftermath of the very brief existence of "revolutionary" art in Russia has had a most ridiculous aspect. Henceforth, when it was convenient, any kind of "radical" art was labelled "Communistic," "Red," "Bolshevistic," etc., in all countries except Russia, where all such art is forbidden![6] In the meantime, of course, the Soviets were building up the same *kind* of art which was encouraged by the *status quo* in all the "capitalistic" countries. Thus the Soviets, contrary to their labels, were actually producing "capitalistic" art, in the sense that they were advocating, just as were the governments in capitalistic countries, the old, dead 19th century nationalistic "realism" method of art. Two great private collections of "Modern art" which had been confiscated by the Soviets were presented to the masses as examples of "capitalistic art," although the *status quo* among the capitalist nations regarded this very same art, at least until recently, as "Bolshevistic." The truth of the matter is that neither form of government was directly responsible for the new arts, that it came about in spite of either of them, and today the *best* of it continues in the same manner. We specify "best" because just as the worst of the old reactionaries, the old time Academician, furnished the subsequent and venerated art tools for the totalitarian countries, likewise the worst of so-called Modern art later furnished the decadent members of the so-called "capitalist" class with their peculiar desires for an art-escape. (In recent years it would appear that the "Realists" of "Modern art" are looking to the new "capitalism"—Stalinism—e.g., Picasso.) Nevertheless, the fate of the Constructionists and many other kinds of artists, in the Russia of the 1920's, is one that today faces artists everywhere in every nation that is not yet totalitarian.

4. Kallen, op. cit., Vol. 2, p. 857. See especially Chapter XXIV, Vol. 2 of Kallen's book. It is well documented.

5. Lewis Mumford: *The Condition of Man,* p. 230, Harcourt, Brace and Co., Inc., New York, 1944.

6. In Paris as late as 1937 the author found that this name-calling was still being practiced among artists, even though the Soviets forbid the artists to depart from art canalizations prevalent in most reactionary art schools in the so-called bourgeoise world. With this name-calling the all-out reactionaries have clothed the Russian dictatorship with the false mantle of radical progressivism, and today, when we are confronted with the fascist threat of the Russian leaders, the naive sections of the progressively minded public refuse to believe that such a threat exists.

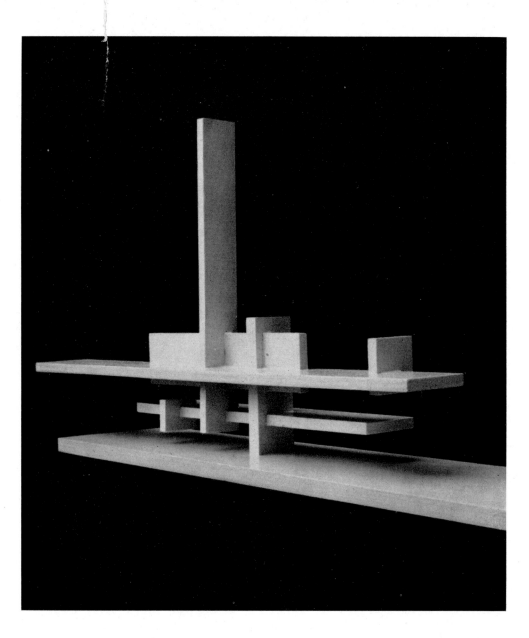

135. Jean Gorin, Relation of Volumes in Space, 1930.

Let us return now to a discussion of the significance of what may appear to have been a comparatively simple move on the part of the Constructionists—that is, putting the actual third dimension back into art by employing the three-dimensional materials of industry, etc. We shall show that in our times, men have discovered through Constructionist art something that they have unconsciously been searching for throughout their history and especially during the last 2,000 years of art; namely, the invention by the artist of his art content.

Ever since the Greeks invented the supposed superiority of man-art over nature-art, a unique difficulty has pervaded the efforts and researches of artists up to the very present. The difficulty was how to reconcile the art of man with the art of nature! Once the Greeks attained the "perfect" recording of the human form in general, there automatically came into existence two distinct objectives in man's art. On the one hand the objective was to record macro-reality ever more accurately. There was, as we have seen, a gradual development in this direction—an evolution in which more and more particulars were included, until, just over a century ago the Photographic method was perfected for recording the uniquely particular or individual characteristics of the objective world. The other objective of man's art, which was especially evident after the notion of the general or the "ideal" was *invented*, has been the effort to achieve something more than merely the literal imitation of nature. Stimulated by an inherent urge, man has tried to exert his ability to invent, i.e., to create, rather than use nature as it actually appears. In other words, although man used nature-art for his art content, some artists, rather than striving only for literal recording, wished to participate "creatively" in the final form of the result. It is no accident that the term "invention" is profusely employed in the art literature dealing with theories about the "ideal." What is this but an expression of the desire not simply to imitate, but to create, to invent? However, the 5th century Greeks, and the artists of the Renaissance, and all those who afterwards sought the "ideal," were thwarted in their effort to release the Inventive potential in man because they sought their objective by remaking nature's own forms, just as the majority are still doing in our own times. This not only confined and restricted the Inventive activity of the artist to the limiting forms of nature-art, but also set him in direct competition with nature, *on its own grounds,* so to speak. This was a competition in which the cards were stacked against man!

Today the impediment to this objective to create, to invent, has been removed by the Constructionist decision; man no longer needs to copy or manipulate the art of nature. When artists of the 20th century finally realized that a mechanical recording instrument had been invented that was incomparably superior to the old primitive recording tools, it then became possible for the advanced artists to leave the recording task to the Camera artists entirely and to concentrate on the Inventive factor which had previously been frustrated by the Mimetic task demanded of art.

In our analysis of the Transitional-Period we pointed out how the dictation of the objects of nature began to lessen. Previously artists had made their medium increasingly answer to the dictates of the object, but especially with the Impressionists they began to explore the creative potentialities of their medium, particularly in the realm of paint-colors. Then we saw van Gogh do likewise with the *line* potentialities of man's medium; Gauguin with the *area* and *space* factors; Cézanne with the *three-dimensional* problem. Finally the Cubists made the great change, and with colors, lines, forms and space began to release the Inventive factor ever more until the contents of art had become almost completely invented by man and not copied from nature.

We have shown also how with the appearance of the Impressionists—significantly the period that marks the beginning of the elimination of nature copying—artists began to become conscious of the differences between the linearity of the canvas and three-dimensional reality. There was Paul Cézanne's remark that it took him forty years to realize that painting was not sculpture. And Juan Gris, who said, "For a painter . . . . I insist on *flat* forms, because to consider these forms in a spatial world would be an affair for a sculptor." [7] It is interesting to note, however, that ever since the Transitional-Period more and more Painters did Sculpture as well, e.g., Gauguin, Renoir, Gris, Braque, Picasso, Matisse, etc., while Mondrian and Léger and others were always talking about the "plastic." Few, however, have been

7. Juan Gris: "A Lecture by Juan Gris," *Cahiers d'Art,* p. 13, Nos. 5-6, 1933.

136. Charles Biederman, Construction, 5/40 (6). Painted glass and wood. 25″x25″x3¾″.

fully aware of the problem. Cézanne and many of the later Painters "solved" the apparent contradiction in the dimensions of reality and their medium, mainly by unconsciously assuming in such problems that the canvas, the sculptured object and nature were all individual realities, legitimate independent realities in their own right: one reality for Painting, one for Sculpture, and one for nature. Certain crucial relations between them and their significance were missed. The Painters did not see the contradiction in the fact that their interests in form-structure omitted its essential characteristic of being actually three-dimensional. We have noticed evidences of these conflicts ever since the Camera; for example, Cézanne and the Cubists destroyed the static, perspective point of view; the latter showed more than one view of the object or a separate viewpoint for each individual part of the Painting and even resorted to actual three-dimensional materials to make art. And, as we have just noted, many Painters from Post-Impressionism on dabbled in the medium of Sculpture. In short, the preoccupation of many artists was tending towards what was called a "spatial world."

In other words, as the Transitional-Period was characterized by an ever decreasing importance of the nature object and the ever increasing but largely unconscious interest in the Structural Process as the *source of abstraction,* the Painters had a tendency now and then to supplant their Painting with Sculpture. This was because, as abstraction from the macro-level decreased and abstraction from the structural-level increased, the need was unconsciously felt for realizing a proper reality for the results of these activities with the structural-level. This was a need for an actual three-dimensional factor and not an illusion of it. Consequently Sculpture, so to speak, seemed to pull every now and then at the sleeves of the Painter.

When artists removed the macroscopic level of nature from their art, it should naturally have occurred to them at the same time that the medium which belonged with the past art was just as obsolete. But outside of a few who have made the change in the medium (some of whom do not adequately recognize the significance of the change), most artists have attempted to continue in the old medium methods. There are many reasons why this is the case, but mainly it is because the medium of paint had been a traditionally dominant one for over five centuries, ever since the Renaissance. As a matter of fact, men had been painting for many thousands of years and under these circumstances few dared to assume that Painting would ever come to an end. Artists had become so conditioned or canalized to the notion of painting illusions that when the necessity for making such illusions no longer existed, they utterly failed to recognize the fact. Consequently it never occurred to Painters to ask themselves why they painted, or why paint and canvas came into use in the first place. To be sure, many "Modern" artists frankly admitted that they painted illusions but it never seemed to occur to them to ask *why.* They simply accepted it as a matter of course. Conservatism stifles curiosity!

Since it is not understood fully enough why artists began to make illusions in the first place, non-Camera artists do not realize that there is no longer any need for making them today. Recall that during the Renaissance illusionary methods again took the *dominant role* in the evolution of art, for the good reason that this was the *best* means of continuing further the progress in the accurate recording of nature-appearances which the Sculptors had begun. Man has produced *useful* illusions of reality only where it was impossible to do otherwise or to do better with some other method, and also only where it was possible to make illusions that would satisfactorily function as such. It is apparent why humans, trees, etc., could not be depicted in the Sculptor's materials beyond a certain point. These materials were extremely limited in their possibilities for depicting nature; Painting, on the other hand, was considerably more flexible and offered the only other possibility until the incomparable method of the Camera was invented. Then just as Painting had taken over from Sculpture, the Camera took over from Painting. Each medium was an improvement over the others in the effort to reach a similar general objective. Until the invention of the Camera the artist was compelled to resort to primitive illusionistic methods, since it was the only useful way in which the realistic objective could be secured.

But today there are very decided reasons why we should not make illusions if our objective is to produce invented forms. The three-dimensional illusions of the older arts functioned satisfactorily to give a feeling of "reality," because of the mechanisms of *projection, recognition* and *identification.* We have already noted that these mechanisms could not function as satisfactorily in illusions of invented forms as was possible with the old content, since the recognition of these forms as reality could not be based on their being form-illusions of familiar things of the world of vision. These forms had never been seen until the artist invented them! Moreover in this task the artist was *not* compelled to employ illusions of the third dimension, because it was now *not* the most efficient way in which to do the job at hand. To achieve the highest degree of "reality" possible for the new art contents it was necessary that it be as similar in structure as possible to the structure of nature's reality process.[8] In other words, *in the new kind of art, it was not only possible to return the third dimension, but it was just as crucially necessary that it be done as it once was necessary to eliminate it during the Renaissance.*

But notions of tradition and precedent are factors which exert a strong pull even on those who do break with the old, especially when we are not conscious of the fact; and more than 2,000 years of painting three-dimensional illusions is, for most artists, quite a thing to part with. It was a conservative attitude similar to this which led the Academicians to believe that man would forever *paint* nature-appearances just as he had apparently always done. Consequently, we find today that all the old types of artists and most of the "Modern" artists refuse to give up either the old content or the old medium*s*. Here we have the two kinds of conservatives again—those who would keep the old contents and those who would retain the mediums of the old contents. This is, of course, just one more aspect of the general confusion in the field of art. As Korzybski has pointed out: "The main semantic difficulty, for those accustomed to the old, consists in breaking the old structural linguistic habits, in becoming once more flexible and receptive in feelings, and in acquiring new *semantic reactions*."[9]

Thus while some succeeded in becoming aware of the uselessness of the old contents, even here, as we have seen, their awareness was far from adequate. Indeed, how could they see the latter adequately when they were conscious of only half the problem and saw nothing amiss with the function of the old primitive mediums? Even if Painters got so far as to be no longer concerned with producing an illusion of nature's form appearances, they were, unconsciously, now involved in producing two- or three-dimensional illusions of the form appearances of their inventions. And each of these Painters who did not change his medium was eventually compelled to return to the old content, in one way or another, in order to give these illusions an adequate sense of "reality." For in that way they again put into operation the old projection mechanism, i.e., the reality of the forms of nature-appearances was projected upon the art content as had been done in the past. In brief, failing to achieve adequate reality for the new content, each was eventually compelled to return to the old reality content—a retreat, not a solution.

Thus although the Two-Dimensionalists, for example, set out in the correct direction, those who continued to use the wrong medium inevitably regressed. They performed, however, two major services for art: (1) they proved, unintentionally, of course, that Painting had come to its end; (2) likewise they offered worthwhile knowledge to the Constructionists who were going in the right direction with the right medium for the attainment of the new art. Just as Renaissance Sculptors like Ghiberti were working out problems like perspective, a problem which required the two-dimensional medium for its adequate realization; so in our times certain Painters have worked directly on problems of invented art which require three-dimensional solutions for their full realization.

So we can put it this way: some Sculptors of the Renaissance and some Painters of the 20th century were occupied with the correct direction but were frustrated because they refused to revise their medium. In fact, all *new progressive objectives* which the Painters of our times have evolved can only find their adequate realization in the Constructionist method. The Constructionists do not paint nature-appearances; they do not make illusions either of nature or man-art! They are the artists who have succeeded in achieving the new orientation to art that is now in order.

From Impressionism on there were indications that not only the content was changing but that there was also an attempt to change the medium; but it was the Constructionists who took the final decisive step of subjecting the reality of nature to the potentialities of man's ability to create art with the materials he has invented. At last that which Monet and his friends had initiated was completed. The "oblong of

---

8. Speaking more correctly, we should rather refer to the structure of reality as a four-dimensional manifold. However, we have chosen to speak only in terms of three dimensions for simplicity of presentation.

9. Korzybski, *Science and Sanity,* p. 379.

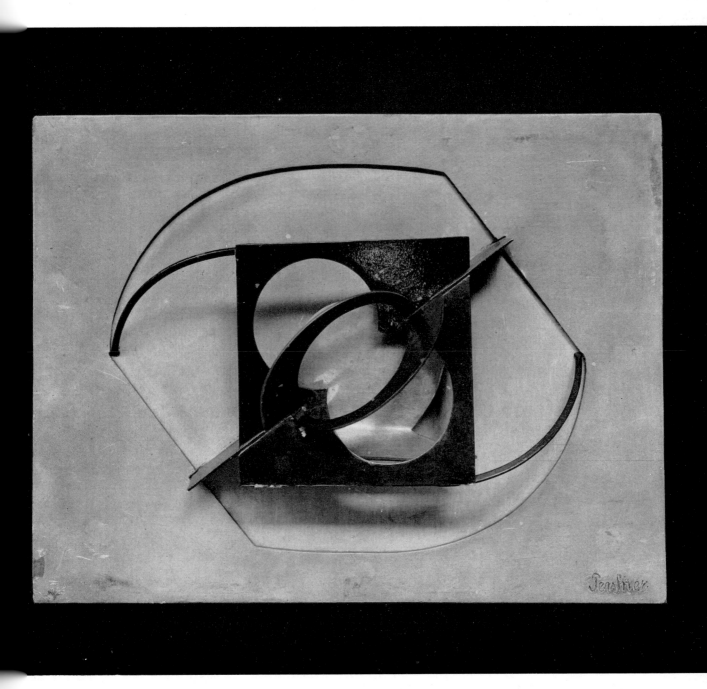

137. Antoine Pevsner, Abstract Construction, 1923. Courtesy, Wadsworth Atheneum, Hartford.

pink," the "square of blue," the "streak of yellow," had been fully realized. Man was now truly a "creative" artist!

We can today see more clearly what a momentous event Impressionism was. It was the Impressionists in particular who decisively began the transition away from dependence upon the forms and colors of nature, who began also the investigation of nature's structure. Therefore we have the highest respect for a movement in art which has been popularly regarded with contempt by the insecure "Moderns." True, the Impressionists themselves were little aware of much which they began, but at least they had the courage to walk forward while the majority stayed behind crying "verboten" to every forward step. Today we can fully realize how erroneous it is to whittle the Impressionists down to mere nature-gapers. You "Modern" critics who feel so superior to the Impressionists' understanding of art—they began something you never understood! Before they did their work, nature's objects had stated the goal of art; after them, man stated the goal of his own non-Camera art!

Less than three-quarters of a century after the appearance of the first successful Photograph, artists discovered how to invent their own art contents, independent of copying in any degree the macroscopic forms of nature. After 2,000 years of direct effort to do so, man is now able to use "invention" in his art, no longer frustrated by the Mimetic factor. *He no longer competes with nature at all,* but as we shall see, he *continues to employ nature,* in a more effective manner, to gain his desired objective of "invention."

In an early chapter where we discussed the early stages of the development of Sculpture, we remarked that the Inventive and Mimetic factors are never found isolated from each other throughout man's entire history of art; the problem always was a matter of *degrees* and *kinds* of Mimetic and Inventive behavior. This is still true as regards Constructionist art; the Constructionist, to mention only this one aspect, does not invent the notion of three-dimensional colored forms; he finds the source of this notion in the phenomena of nature. What he does invent is the *particular organization* of three-dimensional color-forms! In the past the artist "imitated" the *results* of nature-art; today the new artist only "imitates" the *method* of nature-art! This is the crux of the matter. As we have made clear in the chapter on the term "abstract," an artist, in order to avoid the Mimetic factor in any degree would have to exclude *all* the characteristics found in nature—an impossibility (see page 342).

Therefore, the prevalent notion is false that the Constructionist is concerned with the denial of nature: the Constructionist is striving to do what all the great innovators in art have always done, *to continue the evolution of the artist's ability to abstract from the objective world around him for purposes of achieving a legitimate contemporary art.*

We have noted that the new reality level from which the artist can now abstract is the Structural Process level, the *building method of nature,* and no longer the macro-level, the form-results of nature. We have also noted that many of the Painting artists were unconsciously struggling under various handicaps to abstract from the Structural Process level rather than from the results of that level.

Naturally the first move in the direction of abstracting from the Structural Process level would be to acquire the *reality characteristics* of this level. *To accomplish this objective it was necessary to employ a medium or mediums whose structure CORRESPONDED to the structure of reality.* Here lies the solution of one of the main difficulties which faced the Two-Dimensionalists and others—"the problem of reality." By making this change in medium the new art direction of invention acquired one of the characteristics of *reality* which was lacking in the linear medium, i.e., *actual* three-dimensionality in *actual* space. Thus a correction was made from the dead-end medium of the Two-Dimensionalists to the actual space-form art of the Constructionists. It was in that change that the Constructionists achieved an adequate reality for the new art. Now a man-invented form, for example, a man-made sphere, an actual three-dimensional sphere, was just as real as an apple, but there was no need for it to be the form of an apple; and since no Painting of a sphere was made, no illusion of it was made. Here was the solution for those who *painted* two- and three-dimensional illusions of invented forms. By giving the invented contents actual three dimensions in space, the Constructionists achieved a *structure for their new art contents which was SIMILAR (NON-IDENTITY) IN STRUCTURE TO THE STRUCTURE OF ACTUAL REALITY.* As in nature—the criterion of reality—the *art of man* now possesses the three-dimensional characteristics of REALITY.

138. Naum Gabo, Construction in Space, 1928. Rhonoid. Courtesy of The Philadelphia Museum of Art. Gallatin Collection.

Thus, reality recognition is dependent no longer on the identification of nature objects as depicted in the old contents; in the new contents the reality factor is achieved by the direct method; there is a similarity to the reality characteristics of nature's Structural Process.[10] This is possible because *the particular form-RESULTS in the new art do not duplicate, in any degree, the form-RESULTS in nature*. The new art seeks only a *correspondence to the Structural Process, not to the results of that structure in nature*.

Since man is no longer compelled to imitate the forms of nature, he is thus no longer compelled to retain the limitations and restrictions of the old mediums. The old materials and tools are severely limited to doing only the job for which they were originally devised. Now that man can invent his own art, he can use the most modern materials and Machine methods of industry; with them he is free to achieve the greatest of the possibilities open to the Inventive ability of man as an artist. In brief, man can change from the old primitive Mimetic methods and materials and tools to ones that are particularly suited to the new demands of art. The building method is similar in both nature's and man's art, only now the form objectives are very different and so the materials and tools are changed—the old primitive mediums are discarded.

At this point in our discussion, some readers may be confused over the "reality" characteristics attributed to the new art, because they would appear to be the very characteristics obviously possessed by the old medium of Sculpture. Although the preceding discussions have actually already answered such questions as might arise over this problem, it is necessary to go into more detail, for even some "Constructionists" are not clear or are in error about it.

We can begin with some preliminary distinctions between the art of Sculpture and that of Constructions. In the former, as we shall explain, the concern is with abstracting from the *results* of nature's Structural Process, whereas, in the latter the artist abstracts directly from the Structural *Process* level in order to *invent* his own art contents; he avoids manipulating nature's object-results for this purpose. This difference in abstracting, with its resultant differences in content is the basis for the distinctions between the two arts that Naum Gabo, one of the original Constructionists, makes in the following: "Up to now, the sculptors have preferred the mass and neglected or paid very little attention to such an important component of mass as space. Space interested them only in so far as it was a spot in which volumes could be placed or projected. It had to surround masses. We consider space from an entirely different point of view. We consider it as an absolute sculptural element, released from any closed volume, and we represent it from inside with its own specific properties."[11]

Of course the reason the old Sculptors were restricted to the solid mass is that they were restricted to abstracting from objects of nature which were also of this mass character. As explained elsewhere, the limitations of the medium restricted the artist more or less only to those objects in nature which permitted abstractions of solid mass.[12]

---

10. Incidentally, it is of interest to note that when we talk about the contents of a Painting we usually say "*in* a painting" and "*on* a canvas," although it is the latter statement which is more correct. Even the terminology we use, unconscious of its implications, discloses our desire for real forms in real space in our two-dimensional art ("*in* a painting") which is actually only an illusion ("*on* a canvas").

11. Naum Gabo: "Sculpture: Carving and Construction in Space," in *Circle*, pp. 106-107. For Gabo the term "sculpture" is a label that includes Constructionist art.

12. It was these very restrictions, the reader will recall, which partly accounted for the transition from the Sculptural to the Painting medium in the Renaissance. However, in our times the transition is from a two-dimensional medium of illusions to one of actual three-dimensional reality.

However, Gabo also says: "I do not intend to deny the other sculptural elements; . . . by saying, 'We cannot measure or define space with solid masses, we can only define space by space', I did not mean to say that massive volumes do not define anything at all, and are therefore useless for sculpture. On the contrary, I have left volume its own property to measure and define—masses. Thus volume still remains one of the fundamental attributes of sculpture, and we still use it in our sculptures as often as the theme demands an expression of solidity." [13] But no genuine Constructionist—and this is true with one exception, as far as we know, of Gabo's own work—ever handles the *entire* object of art as a mass or single chunk of form dropped into space, as do others, often erroneously listed as Constructionists, e.g., Brancusi, Giacomette, Moore and Hepworth. These latter artists have remained tied to the old Sculptural method, mediums and content.

It should be pointed out, however, that now and then some of the early and even later Constructionists lapsed into an occasional return (in some cases permanent) to the old contents of art. Such and similar errors simply indicated that the problem of Constructionist art had not yet been formulated clearly and definitely enough to promote a definite, clear impetus in the Constructionist direction. As a matter of fact, Gabo's distinction between the old and new "Sculpture"—that the old is tied to the limited notion of mass—is a criticism applicable to the works of the majority of "Sculpture" often labelled "Constructionist" art.

An analysis of Gabo's theories in *Circle* shows, however, that he does not make specific distinctions between the three mediums of Painting, Sculpture, and that employed by Constructionists. Thus he writes: "I leave it to my friends the painters to explain the principles of a constructive and absolute painting and will only try to clarify the problems in my own domain of sculpture." [14] As our history indicates, it is crucially necessary to make a distinction between the two general levels of abstracting and to comprehend the relations of the two general mediums to these abstracting levels.

One of the very important differences between Sculpture and Constructionist art is in the different materials and tools that are employed. It is no accident that the new art has introduced new materials and the Machine tool. Gabo writes regarding materials: "There is no limit to the variety of materials suitable for sculpture. If a sculptor sometimes prefers one material to another he does it only for the sake of its superior tractability. Our century has been enriched by the invention of many new materials. Technical knowledge has elaborated methods of working with many of the older ones which could never before be used without difficulty." [15] Our analysis will show that the old mediums tied to the *primitive* methods are largely no longer useful if one's intentions are to take full advantage of the new direction in present day art as exemplified by the works of genuine Constructionists. The methods and materials and tools of the old Sculptor's profession are obsolete; they were invented for the precise purpose of *recording the forms of nature*. These materials and tools were so well suited to the job that there has been no fundamental change in them since the days of the Paleolithic Sculptor. It is necessary to realize that the old Sculpture materials, except those that can be freed directly and not partially into the Constructionist direction by new methods of working them, are as limited as the old contents that went with the old mediums. This is to be expected, since the old mediums were devised for their suitability to the old contents of art. Both the contents and most of the mediums of the past are limited to old notions and inevitably frustrate attempts in the new direction indicated by Constructionist art. It is precisely for this reason that, when the old content was on the verge of disappearing in Cubism, these artists made various attempts to alter and extend their old medium with the introduction of many kinds of materials, such as sand for example. (We do not insist that this was conscious with the Cubists.) Today it is quite useless to paint illusions of forms; and the materials of the old Sculptural method can be freed from the old art forms only in a very limited manner as compared to the possibilities of the new Machine-made materials.

It would be more correct, therefore, to point out that the Constructionist direction is peculiarly suited to and demands the employment of the newer materials of industry and the latest types of Machines. If we restrict ourselves to the limited possibilities offered by the old Sculpture materials, which were confined to the depiction of a limited number of natural phenomena, we cannot fully exercise the *unique* poten-

13. See *Circle*, pp. 107-108.   14. Ibid., p. 104.   15. Ibid., p. 105.

139. Jean Gorin, Construction in painted wood (emanating from an equilateral triangle), 1945. Photo, Yves Hervochon, Paris.

tialities offered by the Constructionist method of art. We shall go further and say that the old materials and methods would prevent one from becoming a genuine Constructionist. That is why those who attempt to use these old materials and old tools and old methods of making art, in the Constructionist direction, produce works which have more affinity to the old Sculpture (e.g. Brancusi, Moore and the like) than to authentic Constructions such as those of Pevsner and Gabo.

The majority of so-called Constructionist Sculptors work in wood, plaster, marble and stone, *all the old primitive materials of the Sculptor's profession;* and we might add, the artists free the old materials with new methods of working them only to an insignificant degree. And, as is to be expected, the artists who use these old Sculptural materials especially along with the old hand methods of fabricating them are thus greatly limited to the old results of Sculpture. That is, the results are more or less the same old chunks of block Sculpture, and whatever characteristics of the new direction there are, are decidedly in a minority both in quality and quantity. Just as the Sculptor's materials are decidedly form-limiting in the old function of art, so they are even more limiting for the new task of art. Therefore, it is no surprise to find that in the results of those artists who try to invent with the old methods and hand tools there is a close resemblance to the results obtained in the older arts. Hence their results resemble the types of nature objects to which the old Sculptor was limited. (See figures 142-143.) Such artists go only so far and then hurry back to the delusional comforts of the old content.[16]

The same holds true for the Painting medium. Although it is not as limited as the Sculptor's medium, attempts to paint three-dimensional illusions of an invented content inevitably tend towards anthropomorphism, as is seen in Sculpture "inventions." The three-dimensional Painter was forced in some degree to return to nature forms because, as we explained elsewhere, he made illusions of forms rather than using actual forms.

In "Modern" Sculpture we see another aspect of this problem. Here the forms are actual forms; however, when the artist limits himself only to blocks or chunks of form, he is, unconsciously or otherwise, abstracting from the limited form appearances of nature objects. As a result such forms are forced in some degree into the old organic Mimetic direction, as in past Sculpture, in order to gain "reality." This is so much the case that every now and then this type of Sculptor will produce a very realistic work; eventually he regresses to the extent of making only such art.

It has often been contended that there is nothing against a Constructionist's using any kind of material, so long as his work fits the properties of the materials employed. There may not be restrictions as such concerning materials, but nevertheless, they do automatically arise, since it makes all the difference what materials are used to attain a particular objective. We contend that it is just as incongruous to expect Michelangelo to make his kind of art with the forms and materials of a Constructionist as it would be for the Constructionist to make his kind of art with the forms and materials of Michelangelo. The content and the medium for the content form a unity; each is chosen because it offers the best means for attaining a particular objective. As we stated above, the materials, by virtue of their limitations or possibilities, determine the extent to which a content-objective can be realized. Compare plastics with marble and the like: the differences in possibilities are at once very obvious. The objective of producing a Construction is not merely to adapt it to the properties of the material selected. This art is made not only to exploit materials. *The problem is one of selecting those mediums which are in accord with the objectives, not merely of some arbitrarily chosen medium, but of Constructionist art.* True, when we use glass, for example, we must use it as glass and not as steel, but we choose glass and not marble because our intentions are those of a Constructionist and not a Sculptor in the old sense. And unless we select mediums which are in accord with the particular, the unique objectives of the Constructionist direction, then the objectives of the new art cannot be adequately secured. There is no better verification of this point than the fact that all Painters and Sculptors working towards the non-recording direction, who insist on retaining the now antiquated handicraft mediums, eventually return in some degree to the old contents—if one can say that they ever left it in the first place.

Quoting Gabo further on this problem of the new forms created by the new art, we find him

16. That this type of art closely approximates Paleolithic and predynastic Egyptian Sculpture art is of significance in ascertaining the level and kind of abstracting involved (figure 187).

140. César Domela, Composition, 1936.

writing: "The constructive mind which animates our creative impulses enables us to draw on this inexhaustible source of expression and to dedicate it to the service of sculpture, at the moment when sculpture was in a state of complete exhaustion. I dare to state, with complete confidence in the truth of my assertion, that only through the efforts of the Constructive Idea to make sculpture absolute did sculpture recover and acquire the new force necessary for it to undertake the task which the new epoch is going to impose on it.

"The critical condition in which sculpture found itself at the end of the last century is obvious from the fact that even the rise of naturalism through the growth of the impressionist movement was not able to awaken sculpture from its lethargy. [17] The death of sculpture seemed to everybody inevitable. It is not so anymore. Sculpture is entering on a period of renaissance. It again assumes the role which it formerly played in the family of the arts and in the culture of peoples. Let us not forget that all the great epochs at the moment of their spiritual apogee manifested their spiritual tension in sculpture. In all great epochs when a creative idea became dominant and inspired the masses it was sculpture which embodied the spirit of the idea." [18] Constructionist art is not only a regeneration of the old medium of Sculpture, as Gabo says; it is a re-emergence of it but in a very much transformed, *developed* form. Whatever "recovering" the old medium may have had at the hands of the Constructionist method, may have improved the products of the older method, but such works, as we have pointed out, fall far short of the new Constructionist direction because of the inherent limitations of the old materials. We must emphasize that the "renaissance" of "Sculpture" has been accomplished by *altering the medium* considerably so that the new artist can meet "the task which the new epoch is going to impose." So vast have these alterations been that Sculpture as we have known it in the past is no longer practiced, but *eliminated* by the demands of Constructionist art. *In fact, the revision of the Sculptural medium by the Constructionists has been as crucial and extensive as has been the revision of the Painting medium by the invention of the Camera!*

When Gabo contends that Sculpture was always the art to appear at the high points of art history, he over-evaluates the function that this medium has played in art development. In so doing he achieves importance for the latest manifestations of that medium method in the art of Constructions. But we believe the importance of such art in the present can be shown in a more valid manner. As our history has disclosed, Sculpture was developed as the first major medium for recording nature, particularly animals, but before the close of the Paleolithic period Painting had become the major medium. However, in the Egyptian, Greek and Roman cultures Sculpture was again dominant, this time for recording humans. The Greeks and Romans in their respective accomplishments were the last great Sculptors of history. The Sculptural medium as we have known it in the past came to an end in the beginning of the Renaissance period when the Painters took over. In another sense, however, the medium of Sculpture has now been transformed into the particular form of Constructionist art. It has been transformed both in function and appearance: now the new Machine materials and Machines of industry are to form the new medium and tools of art. Today artists are beginning to use three-dimensional materials for the third time in history; not clay or marble but metals and plastics. The three-dimensional non-illusion art, therefore, appeared in the dominant role at the beginning of each new epoch, and continued to dominate until its limitations were reached, at which point the illusionistic arts entered the scene to carry further the evolutionary task begun by the non-illusionistic medium. It is a similar kind of medium transition which is now happening in the 20th century! With Cubism and the art of the Two-Dimensionalists the new direction of evolution has been exhausted as regards the Painting medium. To go further, actual three-dimensional materials must be used; otherwise regression sets in. Thus the great epochs of art have never been confined only to Sculpture or Painting, but to their successive rotation and transformation as art was developed throughout the evolutionary process. What dominated above all was the main direction of art evolution, and each medium occupied a superior position over the others whenever it served that evolution better.

17. In previous analyses we have already explained why the direction of naturalism, when it reached a certain stage of development, automatically eliminated Sculpture as a method of further art development. A rise in naturalism, as that has been explained, did not occur through Impressionism.

18. See *Circle*, p. 110.

141. Charles Biederman, Construction, 2/47 (1). Plexiglas, painted wood and metal, $48\frac{11}{16}''$x$41\frac{1}{2}''$x$7\frac{3}{16}''$.

Obviously we need to make more rigorous distinctions and differentiations between Sculpture and Constructionist art, because the latter is certainly not Sculpture as we have known it in the past. Semantic considerations point the way to settling the discussion. It all depends on what we mean by the term "Sculpture." If we mean it strictly in the old sense of the old art, it is undeniable that Constructions are not Sculpture. On the other hand, if we wish to make the term more general, i.e., covering all objects of art that employ actual three-dimensional forms, then "Constructions" are undeniably "Sculpture." But it would be much more useful to all concerned to realize a more *extensional* attitude as regards this otherwise "time-honored" term. To begin with, we have already stated that Constructionist art is historically the re-emergence of the Sculptural medium, but radically transformed so as to be able to function in conditions far different from those in the past. Therefore, if we speak of "Sculpture" in terms of its larger significance, i.e., the historical-process transformation of the medium, then Constructions are Sculpture, but a particular *kind* of Sculpture, very *different* from all past Sculpture. Psychologically, therefore, it would be advantageous not to apply the label "Sculpture" to Constructions, but simply to maintain that the latter are an extension of the old medium. There is no great need to call the new art "Sculpture," and perhaps if we did not, this would help to keep the air clear of much confusion. Since the transformation of the Sculpture medium in Constructions is as radical as the transformation in the content, to label them "Sculpture" is actually as erroneous as it would be to insist on calling Photographs Paintings!

The fact that there is some confusion of the old and new mediums and contents in our times even among Constructionists, shows that we must distinguish between two phases of Constructionist art. The first phase began just before the close of Cubism during the last war; the second is occurring with a new generation making a more precise distinction between Painting, Sculpture and Constructionist art. (Here again is a situation similar to that in the Renaissance, where we must distinguish between Painting of the 15th century when Sculpture and Painting were still intermingling, and the Painting which came later, especially in the following century, when the observation of nature far outweighed the diminishing influence of Sculpture. Constructionist art is going through a similar transition in which we distinguish between early and later stages.)

We must clearly realize that the non-Camera artist today can no longer depend upon nature's objects nor the art-*results* that occur in nature, nor upon the old methods and materials, but upon knowledge of nature's Structural Process, the building method which occurs in nature, and upon the new Machine-made materials and methods of industry. It will be these methods which the artists of the future will use to build their own art content. The new content cannot be found ready-made in nature; only the method for building it can be found there. This distinction is of vital importance and the realization of it would eliminate the popular tendency to identify the new art as derivative from the objects of nature, as was possible in past art. In the latter the content was the result of models seen in nature, while in the new art the content can never be seen in nature. The old art depended upon *imitating* or copying in some degree the *structural RESULTS* of nature, while the new depends on the utilization of the Structural Process by which it is possible for man to achieve his own art-results.

This new way of looking at the world is not, however, to be mistaken as something peculiar to art; far from it. All modern advances in science today are delving ever deeper into the submicroscopic level of nature; just as in the field of psychology men are penetrating beneath the level of consciousness. Similarly the new trend in art is already creating an entirely new type of seeing activity. All this should make clear how much more it is necessary today to be aware of the abstracting process than it was in the past when seeing for the artist was a much simpler affair than it is today.

In the period from Paleolithic times to 5th century B.C. Greek times man was relatively unconscious of the basic factors operating in his art. But from the 5th century B.C. to the invention of the Camera, excluding the Christian period, man experienced an increasing consciousness of his problems of art. From the Camera to Constructions, the first period above is seemingly repeated, and again artists are unconscious, relatively speaking, of the basic motivations operating in their art.

The Transitional-Period artists (particularly the first major ones, the Impressionists) were the least able to explain their art; this was quite natural. But this inability diminished, relatively speaking, as this period of history unfolded to its final conclusion. But once the latter occurred, the old inability returned,

399

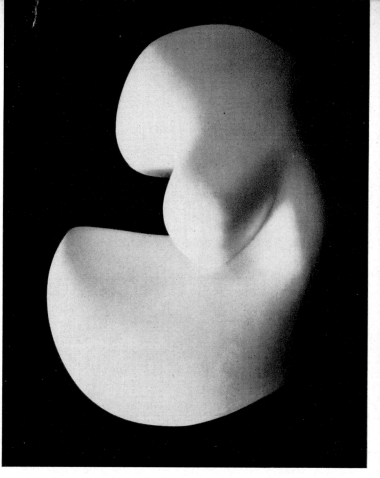

142. Constantin Brancusi, Maiastra, 1912. Courtesy of The Art of This Century.

143. Hans Arp, Human Concretion, 1935. Collection The Museum of Modern Art, New York.

since only a few were able or willing to continue to face and grasp the opportunity for attaining adequate consciousness. The majority made a dash to an intra-uterine security where "emotions" ruled supreme. In short, the majority did precisely the opposite of what needed to be done.

But with the 20th century Constructionist mentality there begins, as with the 5th century B.C. Greeks and the artists of the Renaissance, a renewed developing consciousness of the problems of art, a consciousness of a new era.

It is interesting to notice how this need for consciousness gradually became manifest. From Impressionism all the way through Cubism, artists were passing through experiences and discoveries which correlated with those in the world of science. The Impressionists unwittingly discovered a characteristic of all art—the subjective aspect of the artist's behavior; hence the fitting label "Impressionists." But once this was discovered, the majority of artists misunderstood and presumed that this was a license to be "purely subjective" and nothing else. They failed to understand that the reaction stimulated by the outside world was *colored* by the artist's own organism and thus that the artist plays a part in determining what the world looks like to him. In other words, they did not recognize the *part* man plays in making things appear as they appear and become what they become to him. We have already examined the part this subjective activity has played in art. We have seen how it operated until the end of the Transitional-Period when artists vaguely hit upon the next great discovery, i.e., abstracting—more specifically, the abstracting mechanism of the nervous system by which the "impression" is achieved. At that moment artists were in the position of going further and realizing the subjective-objective character of their reactions to the world of reality. But this is a point that most artists have yet to comprehend. Just as it was no accident or whim that the "impressionist" reactions of artists were discovered (a discovery comparable to and contemporaneous with Freud's recognition of the unconscious level), so also the abstracting process was discovered because that knowledge was crucially needed for the tasks confronting man. Indeed, discovery implies "consciousness" and in that sense each artist must discover the knowledge of his times for himself. If this knowledge does not have the character of a discovery, it will be of no avail to the artist.

400

In later chapters we shall find that the important matter before artists today is not their popular fear that increased cerebral activity will harm their treasured "sensibilities." The important matter is rather the necessity for a rigorous examination of the implications of each new development and how the process of this development plays its part in determining our actions, whether we like it or not. This change towards a more scientific attitude has not come about simply because this or that artist thought it would be a rather interesting thing to try, but because some artists have discovered that there is no choice in the matter, given the fact that particular objectives are potential to present day art. If our goal is to experience art in a satisfactory, useful-survival manner, certain responsibilities peculiar to our times must be met. History being what it is, art having evolved as it has, certain demands are made upon each of us. Fundamental among these demands today is the necessity of developing an adequate consciousness of abstracting!

For the entrance into the art scene of a man-invented art content was a tremendous historical decision, bringing in its wake a host of unheard of implications which crucially revised notions that had been cherished for thousands of years as the rule for all time eternal.

We have called this chapter "Non-Aristotelian Art." The reasons for it should now begin to be apparent. The formulations of Aristotle—which were the result of all previous art history reaching a climax in Greek times—have exerted a consistent influence in different degrees and kinds of consciousness or unconsciousness over the art and theory of the past 2,000 years. It is beside the point that the interpretations of Aristotle have been many and varied; this will be discussed in a separate chapter. What is important for the present discussion is that Aristotle and Aristotelian theory have tied art to the manipulation of the macroscopics or appearances of nature. That is, all such theory has been confined to problems dealing with the macroscopic aspects of reality, no matter how the theories differ in other respects. In contradistinction, the new era of art, as begun by the Constructionists, deals with an entirely different attitude towards reality as regards the production of an art of man. This change in the abstracting process of course changes the whole theoretical basis of art; artists can no longer abide by the Aristotelian notions of the relationships between art and nature or the "imitation" of "things as they are or ought to be." Hence in order to distinguish properly between the art of the preceding epoch, the Aristotelian period, and the new epoch, the new direction must be recognized as a non-Aristotelian one, since this is precisely its general character. This new kind of art has already begun the non-Aristotelian epoch which will characterize the future.

We have seen that after the first or "Decorative" stage of art, the succeeding arts until recent times have been predominantly anthropomorphic. But since 1839, when the Camera was perfected, up to the opening of the current century, a unique historical event has been taking place, the like of which has never occurred before. This period of transition can be designated as the change from anthropomorphism to non-anthropomorphism, a change which is of greater proportions than that from animism to anthropomorphism. Today we are at the beginning of an entirely different era of man's evolution; in art this is seen in the fact that three-dimensional mediums are being used to build an art contents neither animistic nor anthropomorphic in character, but a contents invented by man, a non-anthropomorphic contents.

The future world of art will no longer reflect or interpret the phenomena of world reality in the image of animal or man, but will reflect the fact that man is a part of a world reality which is interpreted with the attitude cultivated by advanced scientists. In art and science a few pioneers are making it possible to fit man into a more useful and more civilized formulation of the world in which we live and the organism with which we must live in it. Man has enough knowledge today that he need no longer invent myths to dispel the fears aroused by his ignorance. It is now possible for future man to acquire what Oliver Reiser has fittingly called a *"world sensorium."*

401

Once more art and science are ready to join hands as has occurred many times before in the history of human beings. In considering "art" as a "science" today we shall not be setting a precedent; actually we shall be but continuing the past scientific pursuit of art, the art attitude that had the greatest survival value in pre-Camera times because it most usefully continued the evolution of art by achieving ever more accurate recordings of nature's macro-reality.

There are many who will fail or refuse to understand and realize the significance of the transformations which are today occurring in art and science. In the field of art there is still much work to be done, the road is difficult and today so many are tired. Too many would rather remain with their unhappiness, masochistically speaking, than awaken and live a full life again; they are the ones who resent the temerity of those who say that the solution of our problems requires particular change, not just any change, and not a return to the past. But perhaps when there are a few more who see the new directions in art and science, it will become possible to arouse the rest out of their restless and nervous slumber.

Therefore, those who will make an effort to understand what awaits us in the future must expect no easy road. Because in the world today we are canalized with methods (usually called "education") whose rationalizations have been perfected and enforced for over 2,000 years. These old Aristotelian formulations of human behavior are no longer capable of meeting the new conditions in which we now live; they must be largely revised and replaced by non-Aristotelian psycho-logics. In certain quarters ART and SCIENCE have already begun the march towards this objective!

But many will say, if Constructionist art points out the one healthy non-Camera direction to take, why have some given it up sooner or later? This is an important question, because many young artists will one day become Constructionists and will experience the difficulties which have discouraged so many others. In order to understand these difficulties better, let's go back to the very first artists of mankind. They had a similar problem, in that they were beginning not only the first great epoch of art, but "art" itself. Like us, they had made a discovery that it was possible to invent man-made lines; in addition to this they had the colossal task of inventing the notion of art in the first place and eventually of discovering and learning how lines could be converted to the depiction of nature's appearances. First they learned how to abstract a few characteristics and then gradually more and more from the reality. In short, their abstractions were very limited in the beginning. This trend developed until man had reached the limits of his ability to abstract from reality with his old hand tools and so the Camera was invented to replace the latter and continue the further development of this form of "art." Consequently, all further abstractions of a *developmental* character along this line were accomplished by means of a mechanical instrument, which has in turn been developed to the abstracting performances of Television. *Thus we saw how one aspect of man's attempts at art had passed through an evolution that began with simple invented lines and developed to the present complexity of the Television instrument.*

Now in our times, the beginning of the second great epoch of art history, we are up against similar difficulties in our efforts to develop abstracting from the newly discovered level of reality. And this is where the trouble comes in that has discouraged those who once were Constructionists or only gave lip-service to it. Like the very first artists of mankind, we Constructionists are compelled to begin with relatively little knowledge and ability in our efforts to produce the first simple abstractions from the new or structural level of reality. Through the works of Mondrian in particular art had been brought back to the straight line, the beginning of *art-invention!* And like those who began the first epoch, by gradually abstracting from these lines into depictions of nature, so we Constructionists today must gradually learn to abstract from the new level by abstracting these lines into a new kind of art content. *In short, we must learn to abstract more and more characteristics from the Structural Process level, as the early Paleolithic artist once did from the macro-level of reality.*

Yet when we regard the task which faced the first human artists, our task is not as difficult. They had to discover the notion of art. We need but continue to build on what has already been done. From this point of view Constructionist art is not merely a beginning. Actually when we consider the new art from the broader general view of history, we discover that *Constructions represent the highest developed order of abstraction from nature so far produced by mankind in the field of art.* In other words, man as an artist has had to evolve through many thousands of years to discover adequately that he can abstract directly from the Structural Process level of nature and thereby be able to invent his own art content. *Nature's art and man's art are now distinct from each other; man RECORDS the first and INVENTS the second!*

It is not to be expected that the new artists should have a complete program of art when it is but a little more than three decades old, suppressed and ignored so completely that only a handful of competent men have ever dared to work in that direction and then under severe handicaps. It would be just as foolish to expect the first artists who made the first lines to have known also that they would eventually use these lines to depict nature or that later it would lead to the invention of the Camera.

We are in the very beginning of a new epoch of man's art; this is its joy, its adventure and its great difficulty. From this point of view, we understand some of the important reasons why many lost their courage to continue as Constructionists *without compromise*. We are in the process of learning the A, B, C's of the new era of art—gradually we shall discover a more complete program. We are entering virgin territory where only those with sufficient courage dare tread. As pioneers we must build roads where there never have been any. And we have to risk defeat. But in avoiding that defeat we would actually be risking everything in order not to take any risks at all.

Nevertheless, the Constructionist can no longer be so effectively opposed with the old Aristotelian formulations of art, which have been perfected for more than 2,000 years and until now have never been adequately or fundamentally challenged. With the present history it is now possible for the Constructionist to cope with this situation and put the past where it belongs, in the past.[19]

In the meantime we should not feel insecure because we cannot give an "absolute" answer to any and *all* questions about the new direction in art. Our security must be based not only on what knowledge we possess but also in realizing where our ignorance begins. Therefore, we do not find it necessary to claim dogmatically, at whatever the price, that the ultimate, the final objective is this or that; rather we try to present our data as the most adequate now known for the realization and the function of the new art. These possibilities must be pursued wherever they may lead, just as any scientist pursues his problem with the experimental attitude. In a later chapter we shall discuss some of these possibilities— some that have been achieved and some that show promise for the future.

In the Constructionist direction, therefore, we find at last the answer to and the means of fulfilling the demands for an art reality in our times. These artists, like many of their contemporaries, sought the answer to the problems of the 20th century; but the Constructionists and the Two-Dimensionalists alone made the most courageous and daring effort of all and between them found the art which answers the historical demands of the present.

Thus we have observed and analyzed the evolution of visual knowledge as it has appeared to us from the very beginning to the very present moment in art. If in the past there existed two different mediums (Sculpture and Painting) dealing both with the same problem (depiction of nature-appearances), then since 1913 we have two different mediums, each dealing with a distinctly different problem— Photography to *record* nature's art, Constructions to *create* man's art.

Our history has thus far shown how man probably invented or discovered the notion of art and how he invented Sculpture and Painting in order to copy the art of nature. And now, finally in the 20th century we have seen how man discovered that he could INVENT, that he could CREATE his own art!

19. Unless otherwise indicated, the author assumes sole responsibility for the theoretical exposition here given of Constructionist art. In no way are the various artists who are used to illustrate Constructionist art to be held responsible for the author's views. Only three articles by one Constructionist (Naum Gabo) were available to the author during the writing of this book. Numerous attempts were made to secure writings by various Constructionists, just before and immediately after the recent war, but only one short article by Naum Gabo and several articles by Jean Gorin were obtained, and these arrived too late to be incorporated in the text.

VII THE CHAOS OF TODAY'S ART

Thus cubism has never been a recipe for making descriptive pictures or a mechanical method for multiplying picture motifs. 99

Theo van Doesburg

We continue to think of new things in old ways. 301
James Harvey Robinson

. . . . Cubism was a revolution. It was directed against the fundamental basis of Art. All that was before holy and intangible for an artistic mind, namely, the formal unity of the external world, was suddenly laid down on their canvases, torn in pieces and dissected as if it were a mere anatomical specimen. 124

Naum Gabo

Plastic expression depends upon the epoch, it is its product. The mentality of each epoch therefore requires a particular plastic. Which does not necessarily mean that the value of each work of art is lost: otherwise museums would be ridiculous. But it is very evident that we desire, in our closest environment, works which correspond to our mentality. However, the diverse mentalities, even of the same epoch, are of very different character. Happily we have no need to grope in obscurity: if we observe the different plastic expressions, they show us the mentalities which correspond to them. The greater the number of those who create or seek a certain plastic, the more uniform will be the corresponding mentality. 230

Piet Mondrian

Outside of that which is created by thought, there is only the baroque of fauvism, animalism, sensualism, sentimentalism, and that hyperbaroque admission of weakness: fantasy. 372

Theo van Doesburg

The great contemporary changes in art which we have just examined, were, as we have seen, actually set in motion the day Daguerre made his first successful Photograph a little over a hundred years ago. The significance of this art-event is understood today little better than it was in 1839. At that time similar radical changes were also occurring in science. Since then, in art and science, there has been a gradual transformation from an Aristotelian to a non-Aristotelian attitude, as we shall explain more fully in later discussions.

This transformation became very apparent in the works of the Cubists. They progressively discarded the old Aristotelian view of the world, the concern with some kind of an "imitation" of nature's appearances. The very nature of the Cubists' development, at least up to 1910, reveals that their *prime interest*, consciously or unconsciously, was not with "imitation" but with form-inventions. Their efforts progressed more or less consistently towards the elimination of the old contents and in a few works they succeeded almost completely in replacing the appearances of nature with what were largely inventions of man.

Why, then, did the Cubists shatter nature's appearances, and subsequently return to the very practices they had once denied, return to play with the broken parts of nature's appearances?

To understand adequately the nature of their post-Cubist regressions, we must be aware of the psychological pressures in which these artists were involved. The impact of the transition from the old to the new method of abstracting, implicitly indicated by Cubism, was so great that the controversy over it has not yet subsided after almost four decades. One of the major difficulties in achieving orientation to the new changes was the terrific tempo of the transitions from Impressionism to Cubism. In a short space of time the whole past was threatened with very fundamental revisions. Such a tremendous, rapid reorientation was involved for the Cubists that when they arrived at the inevitable result of Cubism, they apparently found themselves in possession of far more than they had bargained for. The implications of their discovery shattered the old Aristotelian foundation of art, wherein the artist "imitated" nature's appearances. Cubism announced the end of nature-imitation (as far as non-Camera art was concerned)—the end of the limited Aristotelian view of art and reality! In short, the decision that faced artists as a result of the implications of Cubism was so momentous that the Cubists themselves led the flight from it. It was a retreat from which none of them ever recovered.

In the face of undeniable difficulties and pressures the Cubists made two very serious errors. First of all, instead of evolving Cubism to a three-dimensional solution, achieving a correspondence to the structure of reality—the solution of the Constructionists—they reduced their work to the limiting two-dimensional reality structure of the canvas. In other words, they confused the linear character of the canvas with the three-dimensional one of reality. Failure to change to a medium that would permit of adequate reality for the invented forms of man, left the artists with a "feeling" that these forms lacked adequate reality. In this latter they were correct. But instead of realizing that the fault lay with their no longer useful medium, they made another error and concluded that the elimination of the old macro-reality content was responsible for the lack of adequate reality. Thinking to correct this, the Cubists began to replace the invented shapes with the old recognizable content and so with the old reality, but now largely a fantasy of that reality. In this way a false sense of "reality" was achieved.

Once the Cubists decided that the lack of reality in their work was due to the removal of the macro-level appearances of nature, they were defeated; from then on as ex-Cubists [1] they regressed to stages of art which they had previously left behind and which could only be continued by elaborating them more and more. Each step took them further from objective reality until, as we shall explain later, they fell in one degree or another into the abyss of Surrealism.

Since then artists and critics alike have attempted to claim that the desertion of Cubism was the only possible course. Their basic assumption is the false one that the only reality is the macro-reality level. In the following, for example, Georges Braque implies that the artist cannot continue his development if he eliminates this level: "Reduced to discoveries of form and to the art of painting, the artist will remain riveted to one spot. Escape is no longer possible. In which Vlaminck is correct to write that cubism was the negation of the *art of painting*. Perhaps he thought to confuse us. For my part, I rejoice never to have indulged in the 'art of painting', for it would have been sad to reduce art to the victory of the brush over mystery." [2]

And Amédée Ozenfant, misunderstanding the significance of the elimination of the macro-reality level, says that the Cubists eliminated nature. He puts it this way: "It was only after Cézanne's death that the Cubists, with no uncertain finger, pointed nature to the door." [3] And: "Cubism is painting conceived as related forms which are not determined by any reality external to those related forms." [4] Of course it is impossible that nature be shown "to the door." Nature continues to play *some kind* of a part in determining the contents of *any* kind of art, with or without the permission of artists. It is impossible to create *anything* in art which is not related in some way to nature's reality.

This kind of theorizing on the part of artists who had been involved in Cubism has encouraged similar views among the critics. Sheldon Cheney asserts that: "Their [the Cubists'] own work became a little bloodless, thin, because they were preoccupied with the geometry that is, after all, the grammar and

---

1. Since this is a more correct label, we shall use it when referring to the post-Cubist careers of these artists.

2. Georges Braque: reply to a questionnaire directed by Christian Zervos, *Cahiers d'Art*, p. 24, Nos. 1-4, 1935. All translations from this article are by Harry Holtzman and Martin James.

3. Amédée Ozenfant: *Foundations of Modern Art*, p. 64. Brewer, Warren and Putnam, Inc., New York, 1931.

4. Ibid., p. 76.

not the essence of the painting. Their very excitement led them into being cerebral in their approach; but as theorists they served the whole world of art." [5] Cheney says "bloodless, thin" where others say "cold and intellectual." The "grammar" vs. the "essence" theory is simply another version of the false assumption that the only reality level from which the artist can abstract is the macro-level. Curt Ducasse also was reasoning along these lines when he maintained that "To praise a picture for its composition is thus the same as to praise a book for its grammar or its arrangement." [6]

A similar assumption occurs in the next three quotations. Howard Hannay insists that in Cubism "you have, not sentiment, but pure theory, and all that can be analysed is the theory." [7] And Lionello Venturi contends that "A cubist painting, because it is concerned with theory, is a piece of criticism, good or bad as the case may be." [8] How this assumption—that Cubism is *only* theory—is reached becomes more clear when we read such statements as the following by Venturi, which is subsequent to his remark that the content of painting has always been concerned with the "visual effect of nature": "Cubism not only opposed the expression of this content, but denied all content." [9] At least on the verbal level such critics are consistent, for if Cubism is "pure theory," then it certainly can have no content. (As a matter of fact, the above quotations are excellent examples of pure theory!) But in so saying, one denies that the demarcation of colored areas upon the canvas surface is "content" at all; one is actually saying that there is nothing, where obviously we do find something on the objective, i.e., the non-theoretical level. A canvas with colored shapes painted upon it is a manifestation of facts, facts about which we may theorize. Actually every work of art "is concerned with theory," because whatever art we make implies some kind of a theory about the world in which we live, regardless of whether or not the artist is conscious of it. Our discussions of the various artists and their orientations to the problems of reality have amply shown this to be the case.

But the critics assume that if nature's appearances are absent, then a content is absent. Even if one of the Cubists had nailed a thousand three-inch balls on a large surface of wood, such critics would presumably still fail to see any "content," since they are trying to define as nonentity something which actually exists. Actually, arts which do not picture apples or flowers are *as real* as arts which do. By ignoring these facts critics hope to avoid the new problems of art and "reality." For if a wooden ball is as "real" as an apple (or a painted ball is at least as real as a painted apple), then we are confronted with *different kinds* of reality (or illusions of reality), which must be accounted for *as such*.

But in order to comprehend these fundamental points, it was necessary to make the activities of art a conscious discipline; and such an attitude was opposed by the Cubists. As Cubists they had been well able to "feel" their way to the objective towards which the intuitive efforts of the Transitional-Period artists had been directed. This predominantly intuitive approach had been valuable, but now, if adequate consciousness of the new direction was to be achieved, there was a need for artists who would *also* operate non-intuitively. But just when precise formulations of what had occurred in the Transitional-Period were possible and imperative, the ex-Cubists chose to make their "feelings," without the interference of reason, the final criteria for future behavior.

In the end the romantic attitude, which had made it possible for the Cubists to achieve Cubism, turned out to be the very factor which prevented them from continuing further in the new direction. Cubism was the last fruitful activity resulting from the "freedom" fostered by the romantic attitude. Thereafter the Romanticist has been a lost individual and the final gestures of this attitude are to be seen

5. Sheldon Cheney: *The Story of Modern Art,* p. 460. The Viking Press, Inc., New York, 1941.

6. Reprinted from THE PHILOSOPHY OF ART by Curt John Ducasse, by permission of The Dial Press, Inc., Copyright 1929 by The Dial Press, Inc., p. 218.

7. Quoted by Venturi in *Art Criticism Now,* p. 27, The Johns Hopkins Press, Baltimore, 1941, from *Roger Fry and other Essays,* by Howard Hannay, p. 89, G. Allen and Unwin, Ltd., London, 1937.

8. Lionello Venturi: *Art Criticism Now,* p. 28.

9. Ibid., p. 34.

in the "chaos" of "Modern" art (the latter term is defined in the following footnote).[10] All new developments, as we have already seen, were secured by individuals working with a consciously directed discipline.

To protect their evasion of the implications of Cubism, the ex-Cubists usually speak of their ignorance of what they did as Cubists as though it were an asset. The implication seems to be that their ignorance constitutes some omnipotent insight, and that hence their results are far superior to those secured by consciously formulated assumptions. To justify their retreat from the achievements of Cubism, they are compelled to discredit reason. Thus Braque wrote: "Reason, being reasonable, has never led to creation. To write a poem, to paint a picture, to carve a stone are unreasonable acts."[11] Furthermore, Braque protests that "our" purpose was not to try to solve problems, for "it is enough to have the skill of finding them." Similarly Picasso complains that "Everyone wants to understand art." He is annoyed that everyone should be concerned with art and "demand its credentials."[12] But what else could they say if they were to defend their position? They could not defend themselves in the light of reason, so they denied it. Hence Braque writes: "All recourse to logic presumes a deficiency of the instinctive faculties, an incapacity to act."[13]

But in the end what is Braque's statement but an "appeal to logic"? Therefore, the fundamental issue seems to be whether we will appeal to *responsible* or irresponsible logic, to verifiable or theological methods of behavior. Braque, like so many of his contemporaries, erroneously concluded, because his Cubist successes were achieved with a highly intuitive approach, that this was an adequate standard for all future behavior. In the end he must cry out in desperation: "It is therefore necessary to shake all reasonable truths and to rid man of his logical reactions against magic."[14] We must understand that the ex-Cubists, having avoided the decision of Cubism, are determined to justify their escape from reality into a world of paint-fantasy.

Many wonder why the principals in the formation of Cubism—Braque and Picasso—have remained on the whole so silent about it, as though it were some secret they would not reveal. It would appear, however, that if they have any secret it is that they simply have nothing more to say. Thus while they maintain repeatedly, as if it were a commendable achievement, that they were not aware of what they were evolving when they produced Cubism, the price they have paid for not recognizing the basic values in their own great achievements has been to end in the rut of confusion and defeat. They were defeated by the very factor of past art they had once unwittingly done so much to break with—the macro-reality, which they now were making into a world of make-believe. As Naum Gabo has so well put it, "their desire to destroy the old prevailed over their desire to create the new, and on the other hand in attempting to create the new they could not free themselves from the external forms of Nature."[15] Elsewhere he has written: "many Cubists themselves have tried to find a way out, but the lack of consequence has merely made them afraid and has driven them back to Ingres (Picasso, 1919-23) and to the Gobelins

10. In order to simplify and clarify our terminology, we shall limit our use of the term "Modern" or "Modernist" in the rest of this history. Since almost all so-called Modern art is largely negative, regressive, we shall, unless otherwise indicated, apply this label only to the regressive "art" which has occurred since 1910. When we refer to the positive, progressive aspects of contemporary art—genuine Camera artists, genuine Two-Dimensionalists and genuine Constructionists, if the names of schools or artists are not directly employed, we shall refer to them with such labels as "innovators," "advanced artists," and the like. In no case will these artists be referred to as "Moderns."

11. Braque, op. cit., p. 21.

12. "Conversation with Picasso" as recorded by Christian Zervos, *Cahiers d'Art*, pp. 173-178, Nos. 7-10, 1935. Translation by Myfanwy Evans in *The Painter's Object*, with the permission of John Lane The Bodley Head, London.

13. Braque, op. cit., p. 21. Braque is perfectly correct, granted that one is struggling to preserve such a method of behavior: an "appeal to logic" might reveal a deficiency in one's attitude towards the use of "instinct" and might raise the question of the useful or non-useful value of one's actions. In fact, one is liable to discover that one's "incapacity to act" consciously guided by the "appeal to logic," compels one to seek refuge in so-called "instinctive faculties" in order to act at all!

14. Ibid., p. 22.

15. Naum Gabo: "Constructive Art," *The Listener*, Nov. 4, 1936, published by the British Broadcasting Corporation, Vol. XVI, No. 408, p. 846.

of the sixteenth century (Braque, etc.). This was not an outlet but a retreat." [16] This was the price of over-emphasis on "feelings" and "intuition." This was what led Mondrian to ask: "How many errors have been and are being committed through vague and confused intuition?" [17]

We have noted that even before the Cubist movement proper was finished, the artists who failed to recognize the new level of reality were attempting to reinstate the old reality by employing textures, pasted newspapers, etc. According to Raynal: "In the opinion of certain Cubists, it was not illogical to imitate Nature in some of its aspects, even to the point of incorporating in the picture the object itself, if the work was to maintain some correspondence with reality." [18] The raised paint surfaces, the use of wood, cardboard, metal and the like, and invented shapes *expressed the unconscious effort to abstract from the Structural Process level of nature* and so a striving in the new direction. But the employment of Photographs, prints of objects and the like were *expressions of the effort to revert to and reinstate the old macro-reality once more.* The use of still a third group of elements, like playing cards, newspaper print, various kinds of labels, matchbox and tobacco covers, represented the attempt in the direction of both the new structural and the old macroscopic levels. For these objects were invented by man on the one hand and at the same time they were "recognizable" objects. But even these devices failed to sustain them in their strong attachment to the past. As ex-Cubists they made the grand compromise; since neither the old nor the new alone was tolerable, then both were combined, and it has been this method which they have since employed.

After 1914 we find them desperately trying to abstract from two different levels of reality at the same time, unable to comprehend either the distinction between them or the resultant schism in their work.

The Cubists were unable to approach "reality" on a cooperative basis. Thus even though they came to feel that reality in art had been lost because the nature object had been removed, nature as it appeared to their eye-brains was not a satisfactory reality either. Their conscious or unconscious conviction that their art was the criterion of reality operated in their works in a mounting crescendo after their desertion of Cubism; witness the increasingly subjective attitude towards reality which they cultivated after 1910 and especially after 1914. The visual world became subject to the dictates of the artists, as though they were "free" agents who could do as they pleased, independently of the world reality. The "problem of reality" had been a frustrating experience for them until they presumptiously "solved" it by making themselves "masters" of reality. Not only did they make the two-dimensional laws or limitations of the canvas the criterion of reality whenever the fancy struck, but also they made the objects of reality assume whatever color-form fantasy their canvases might permit. In short, as far as a content was concerned, such artists were neither satisfied with nature as it appeared, nor with their art when the macro-level of nature forms disappeared altogether. Their inevitable solution was to dive into a world of fantasy.

It is true that in the art of the Transitional-Period the element of fantasy was always present, but from Impressionism to 1910 Cubism the structural factor had also been gradually increasing. After 1914, however, fantasy became the chief objective of the majority of those who presumed to be following the new direction. Things eventually came to such a pass that the new art of fantasy was justified by pointing to similar works produced by children, Primitives and psychotics. The parallel is ironically justifiable. For like psychotics, such artists imagined they had private telephonic communication with an omnipotent force which absolved them of such mundane necessities as being responsible for their behavior.

16. Naum Gabo: "The Constructive Idea in Art," *Circle,* p. 6.

17. Piet Mondrian: "Plastic Art and Pure Plastic Art," *Plastic Art and Pure Plastic Art,* p. 54. (The Documents of Modern Art, general editor, Robert Motherwell) Wittenborn and Co., New York, 1945.

18. Maurice Raynal: *Modern French Painters,* p. 20, translated by Ralph Roeder, Brentano's, New York, 1928. Alfred Barr, Jr., on the other hand, considered it paradoxical that the Cubists should resort to literary devices. He writes in the Museum of Modern Art Catalogue, *Picasso: Forty Years of His Art* (p. 85): "Anti-'literary' in their art, the cubists paradoxically painted letters. Sometimes the letters seem chosen at random but often, as has been mentioned, they refer to drinks or newspapers, and sometimes to people, almost in the manner of literary dedications . . ." These "literary" devices were simply a substitute for the loss of the old reality contents.

Thus instead of developing Cubism to its further potentialities, they merely retraced and elaborated upon former kinds of abstracting. All this had been *fundamentally* arrived at, but for a useful purpose, in the arts from Impressionism to 1910 Cubism. It is true that they did not produce exactly the same kind of distortions, but it was precisely these differences which were in the direction of regression. They did not supersede what had already been done; they corrupted it! They have become what might best be labelled "Inbetweeners." Their Cubist experience was too potent to be entirely disregarded, yet they never dared to see it through. They were trapped, as Gabo says, between what they had destroyed and what they had created.

Alfred Korzybski, speaking about similar problems in science, explains the reasons for this confusion between the old and the new. What he writes is directly applicable to the situation we are discussing in the field of art: "When new non-euclidean or non-newtonian systems were produced, many of the older scientists could 'understand' them, could even master the new symbolic technique; yet their 'feelings' etc. were seldom affected. They 'thought' in the new way, but they continued to 'feel' in the old; their *semantic reactions* did not follow fully the transformation of their 'ideas', and this produced a split personality." [19]

However, since these artists were unable to make a decision between the old and the new, it was inevitable that, as the years went by, the macro-reality became more and more dominant in their works, while structural interests regressed proportionately, to become a mere appendage to the other.

In the work of Léger we see a particular type of conflict between the old and the new. Léger, more than all the ex-Cubists, had made an attempt to reach the new. It was he who had been attracted to the most pronounced example of man's Inventive activity, the modern Machine. But, like the others, he soon "found himself," and after 1918 he began in earnest to oscillate between the old and the new, but in a unique manner—that is, from one level of abstracting to another within the confines of each individual canvas. On the one hand, the "hemisphere" character of Cézanne's work is very evident; every form appears as though it has a flat back to it. But in each canvas Léger also uses flat shapes, which are comparable to the unpainted parts of Cézanne's canvases. Here we see a continuation of Cézanne's conflict between the round world of reality and the flat world of the canvas. Certain factors which are present in nearly every one of Léger's works show the kind and the manner of oscillations in which he is involved. These are: (1) Two-dimensional illusions of (a) invented and (b) nature forms; (2) three-dimensional illusions of (a) invented and (b) nature forms. He does not treat these factors as problems, however, but as *devices*. He merely uses all aspects of these factors in various combinations. His color is that of the Impressionists, treated as "local color"; his treatment of nature objects is that of Henri Rousseau, the Italian primitives and the like; Cubist and De Stijl devices are employed in various ways. When he says, "Our tastes, our traditions, go back to the primitive and popular artists, preceding the Renaissance," [20] we agree insofar as he has thus correctly explained his own "taste" and that of some others, but as an historical statement it is a false interpretation; it is an interpretation of history which partly explains his art, but not the history of man's art.

It is Picasso, however, who leads all other Modernists in the more popular type of oscillation between copying and non-copying art. His acclaim as the foremost contemporary artist is to be expected in a world where escape from reality is so frantically sought that men can and do make a career of producing escape-art. Picasso does not disappoint his public. He strives regularly and frequently to present some "new" diversion. Unlike Léger, Picasso's individual works generally remain on some consistent level and kind of abstracting; his oscillation appears as he passes from one work to the next.

Since he is such an extreme example of what the majority of artists did after Cubism, let us briefly review his history here. Before the end of 1914 Picasso had begun to play with Cubist devices, to make them merely a means for prettily ornamenting the surface of the canvas. By this act he completely concluded his participation in the further progress of art, that he might devote himself to the task of being

19. Korzybski, *Science and Sanity*, p. 27.

20. "Painting and Reality: A Discussion," by Fernand Léger. Le Corbusier, Louis Aragon, *Transition*, p. 105, No. 25, Fall, 1936.

144. Pablo Picasso, The Three Dancers, 1925. Collection of the artist. Courtesy of the Museum of Modern Art, New York.

Picasso, the performer of surprises. In 1915, in addition to doing works like those just mentioned, he began to make realistic drawings; he went all the way back to Ingres and tried to improve on him by imitation.[21] For some ten years afterwards he alternated between idealistic realism and ornamental elaborations upon Cubism on his separate canvases. That is, he attempted to keep in more or less separate courses the old and the newer levels of abstracting. It was in this period that he made his *Woman in White* (1923), which has been widely reproduced, and hailed, not for contributing to progress in art, but, allegedly, for being able to breathe new life and "charm" into a style of art that has admittedly been "exhausted by overuse."[22]

From the mid-twenties to the early thirties the Cubist devices, which had previously been largely confined to still-life subjects, bottles, tables, etc., began to be combined with his renditions of human and other natural forms. Pseudo-Cubism and "realistic" works continued, but the number of Cubist-like still-lifes diminished. He seemed to be trying now to combine in one canvas the two previously separate forms of his art: that is, his previous "Classical" figure depictions were now rendered in primitive terms (see figure 144); the human form was reduced to a formula, which permitted it to be broken up with the remnants of Cubist devices or "recipes." In this manner what had formerly been more or less a strict division of realistic human forms and Cubistic-like still-lifes were combined to make a primitive-like distortion of the human figure. The original Cubist impulse was transformed to take on the forms of nature reality, *the reverse of its original objective*. By joining together Cubism and nature-appearances in a primitive-like embrace, Picasso made another attempt to resolve the conflict between the old and the new abstracting. The conflict, however, was ceaseless between all the old arts, particularly Primitive and Classical art, and the new direction he and other Cubists had discovered in their youth.

21. It was in 1915 that he made a "Cubist" drawing of a seated man: underneath this we see lightly drawn a more realistic version of the same subject. It was a drawing of his own conflict between the old and the new. (See p. 94, *Picasso: Fifty Years of His Art*, by Alfred H. Barr, Jr., Museum of Modern Art, 1946.)

22. Alfred Barr, Jr.: *Picasso: Forty Years of His Art*, p. 115, Museum of Modern Art Catalogue, New York, 1939. In sale of prints this work has been a staunch competitor to Whistler's painting of his mother.

During the thirties Fauvist devices and technics, which had begun to appear in the primitive aspects of the preceding period, are employed extensively. Many of the works remind one of Matisse, done in an even more primitive manner. All the conflicting factors of dimensions and subjects continue. He goes from flat to round, from realism to highly abstracted works, from a little pseudo-Cubism to a denial of Cubism; nothing has been resolved. It is as if he were now trying with a Fauvist technic to draw together the irreconcilable elements, the new and the old, the Cubist and the "Realist."[23]

By now Cubist activity had completely degenerated; its feeble function was merely that of distorting nature and achieving primitive-like, low-order abstractions from reality. In early post-Cubist works the artist was still interested, to a degree at least, in the transformation of the object into structural arrangements of lines, shapes, and colors achieved with what remained of his Cubist ability. But in later works he is concerned directly with creating recognizable fantasies of nature (often painting vermilion lips, pink cheeks, shiny black hair, etc.), and with retaining the organic character of nature objects. His Cubist experiences have now regressed into the direction which characterizes Surrealism. From having served a structural, organizational purpose in man's effort to invent his art, Cubist devices became almost nothing but distortion devices.

The Studio, by Picasso (figure 145), supplies a clear example of how former Cubist devices are converted for purposes of manipulating nature-appearances. Here Cubism is used for "making descriptive pictures" and "multiplying picture motifs." Depicted is a room with a door, framed picture and a mirror (?); at the left, the standing figure seems to be the artist painting on the canvas in front of him; there is a table with a tablecloth on which rests a bowl of fruit; on the right, resting upon a small table, there appears to be what one writer claims is a plaster bust, which the artist is painting. As in the art of children and Primitives, these objects are depicted in elevation, a sort of flat schematic symbolization of reality. In short, there is a *low or primitive order of abstraction* from reality.

When observing *The Studio,* with its primitive-like *recordings,* one obviously carries to it experiences which have made him familiar with similar objects in reality; otherwise recognition would not take place. But it is our attitude towards these experiences which determines the manner in which we shall react to and absorb such (or any) recordings of reality. In other words, what we "see," in nature or art, is determined by what we "think" about what we see. Thus, those who insist on literal recordings, or those who believe the non-Camera artist should invent his own contents without imitating nature-appearances, will reject *The Studio* type of art, because recording and Inventive interests are being manipulated merely for the purpose of producing primitive-like depictions of the macro-reality. Such art is both a false recording of reality and a substitute for genuine invention. If, however, we desire an art which takes us to another world, as it were, we shall accept *The Studio* and gladly.

Those who adopt this latter attitude are able to project upon the canvas, just as is done in realistic art, their experiences with similar phenomena in actual reality. These projections of objective experiences are then intertwined with and consequently transformed by the visual material presented by the painting.[24] The result of this intermingling becomes a substitute for the experience of objective reality. The painting supplies the visual mold into which the objects of reality are compressed. In our painting example we do not actually *see* an artist in his studio, but "feel" that it is an artist, because of certain remote resemblances between the visual mold and the actual reality. But it is a metamorphosis, a change of form "as if by magic."

---

23. This has continued to the very present. His works since 1939 appear to be largely a continuation of decadent Cubism. But instead of the predominance of curved lines of the thirties, there has been a predominance of straight, angular lines, which has been considered by his admirers to be some kind of a remarkable reappearance of Cubism! The realistic portraits, in paintings and sculpture, have continued to make regular appearances, done in the style of certain contemporary painters and sculptors or of his own pre-Cubist portraits.

24. The process just discussed, that of association, projection and identification, is similar to the function of the comic strips. Incidentally, it is of interest to know that Picasso is reported to have said that comic-strip art was the most important art of America. Such an evaluation would not be surprising, since the method of caricature is characteristic of "Modern" art.

145. Pablo Picasso, The Studio, 1927-8. Collection The Museum of Modern Art, New York.

Many of those who prefer *The Studio* type of art are amazed at being able to obtain such strong "reality" feelings from it. These experiences are not surprising, though certainly alarming, if it be considered that some individuals are able to see "real" things without the apparent aid of any outside stimulus at all, i.e., psychotics with their illusions, delusions, and hallucinations. Such art experiences are very "real" indeed—but they are the reality-of-fantasy.

The desire to produce fantasies of reality motivates the major portion of post-Cubist art, although it is often falsely rationalized as some new aspect of reality or as "reality in itself," independent of the world outside. This erroneous evaluation has led many to assume that some mysterious aspect of reality lurks around us, which only the artist, with his omniscience, is able to discover.

Actually, the spectators as well as the makers of this kind of art are involved in a "primitive" level of "visual" experience, which produces a false report of objective reality. Contemporary primitive-*like* art is simply a maladjusted projection by the artist upon reality: the observer must project in a similar manner if he is to produce the type of experience the artist intended. The actual experiential result of such art as *The Studio* occurs inside us, manufactured by our nervous system; this result is not to be found only on the canvas or only in the reality; it is a combination of both. Since the painted material arouses the projection mechanism, the final experience is a combination of nervous-system activity and the painting. All art experiences involve us in circular relations: i.e., our experiences in the real world are taken to "art," there affected in one way or another; with these we return to the real world, for better or worse. In other words, no art is independent of reality; it is always related in some way. "To be is to be related."

Such art as *The Studio* reverses the whole visual evolution of man, for it goes all the way back to the early recording examples of the caveman's art, back to art as a magic function. Of course there is a great difference between this kind of art and that made by Primitive artists. In the latter, the artist consciously sees no more of the reality than he depicts in his art-magic, whereas *The Studio* type of artist

146. Pablo Picasso, Woman in an Armchair, 1929. Collection of the artist. Courtesy of the Museum of Modern Art, New York.

deliberately avoids seeing the world reality correctly in order to cultivate an art-magic. Primitive art is the result of a low order of visual ability, an incapacity to pass beyond a certain degree of abstraction from reality. In the case of *The Studio* type of artist, the capacity for a considerable degree of abstraction from reality is present, but is deliberately suppressed to achieve a low level of abstracting behavior. The Primitive artist is unable to achieve a high degree of abstraction from the macro-level of reality; the Picassoites and similar types of artists are unable (psychologically) to cope *properly* with abstraction from the Structural Process level of reality.

In order to make this point more clear, observe two works by Picasso (figures 146, 147). One, a Cubist painting, illustrates the trend towards the higher orders of creative abstracting from the Structural Process level; the other, entitled *Woman in an Armchair,* is an example of the trend towards lower or "primitive" orders of abstracting from the macro-level of nature. The subject of the latter is a woman sitting in an upholstered chair within a room. The original objects have acted as a point of departure, as a stimulus to change the forms of nature into a world of fantasy. Now, although the type of fantasy here being considered indicates a definite effort to retain recognizability of the subject as such, we must emphasize that it is not the higher order of recording abstracting from reality of an Ingres or a Courbet, but *low-order* abstracting, something *like* that found on certain levels of Primitive or child-art. Manipulations resulting from primitive-like seeing are imposed on the high-order visualization of which we are capable.

416

147. Pablo Picasso, Seated Figure of a Woman, 1910?, 1911?. Collection of Mr. and Mrs. Walter C. Arensberg.

In contrast, observe the reproduction of the Cubist work. Here too the subject—also a seated female figure—serves merely as a point of departure, but now as a stimulus to the artist's desire to create his art content. Here, contrary to the example of the *Woman in an Armchair,* there is no effort to retain or salvage the recognizability of the subject as such. Recognizability is, on the contrary, sacrificed in the effort to create the content. The artist is striving towards a *higher order* of abstracting from reality.

In both the low- and high-order abstracting examples the Inventive ability of the artist is exercised. But there are extremely important differences: the Inventive ability in the former kind of art is deliberately utilized to achieve a fantasy substitute for the macro-reality, whereas in the latter kind it is deliberately utilized towards achieving an invented art content.

The functional purpose of all man's art may be divided into two very general types: those arts which foster harmful experiences in reality; those arts which enhance, increase the horizon of useful experience in actual reality. In varying degrees the major portion of present day non-Camera art—be it the work of a Marin or a Benton or a Picasso or a Vlaminck—transforms the reality with which we are familiar into a substitute world of false visual experience. Such artists, especially the Picasso and Dali type, do not achieve for us what all past worthwhile artists have—they do not increase the scope of useful experience with actual reality. On the contrary, they render us incapable of adequate orientations to it, because the world of fantasy they depict encourages one to assume falsely that one can do as one pleases

417

in the world of reality. Through fantasy art the artist and spectator are trying to escape to an unattainable world. This leads to a schizoid existence, because the experiences in art and in reality are opposed to one another.

In studying anything that man makes, does or thinks, it is well to realize that of all the various forms of living organisms, man has the greatest potentialities to make reality appear what it *is not*. This is apparent in language and art, both of which reflect our notion of and attitude towards reality. With art or with words man can picture or speak any distortion of reality which enters his head. The animal, on the other hand, never has a "problem of reality"; that is, it is not able to become conscious of and then modify its environment as man can. The animal cannot interfere with the natural process; man can and certainly does. This human ability to modify the environment has both beneficial and harmful implications. On the one hand, man is able to realize and extend inherent potentialities of nature, but on the other, if he disregards the natural laws which govern the structure of reality, he will attempt to "extend" nature in ways which are pathological.

Of course, those who like to speculate with words may ask, "Who is to say what constitutes reality? Does not the scientist tell us that all we ever know is hypothetical and not the actual reality?" But we do not make hypotheses merely for the sake of making them. *We make hypotheses in order to improve our ability to survive in a useful manner.* A study of history reveals that man has advanced from the cave days by always modifying his hypotheses to correspond to new, more accurate information as it becomes available. Recognition that knowledge is always hypothetical and tentative allows man to revise his hypotheses constantly; by so doing he achieves an increase (*not* perfection) in the correspondence between his knowledge and his experience in reality. In short, hypotheses are revised in order to gain the maximum of useful survival.

The terms "reality" and "experience" are *not things*; both must be regarded as symbols which can communicate useful or harmful interpretations of the objective world. From this point of view, as regards the art under discussion, the deliberate changing of reality into that which it *is not* is hardly conducive to adjusted survival.

Thus we have seen the Cubists advance and then retreat—create Cubism and then along with the reactionaries seek to escape its full implications as regards further evolution of the abstracting process in art. Because they could not go further, they had to stop making Cubist pictures; if they had continued in that direction, the best they could have managed (as Picasso admits) would have been merely to make more Cubist pictures. They lacked the courage to pursue the direction set by Cubism and naturally were bored with the thought of just making more and more Cubist pictures. This is why Picasso thinks that Cubism could only lead to "another form of Cubism." (He should have looked at Mondrian, Doesburg, Pevsner!) It is actually his own experience which he is projecting upon everyone else's experience with Cubism. Otherwise he is perfectly correct in that it certainly applies to artists like himself.

But Cubism continues to irritate many kinds of painters and critics because of certain basic conflicts and difficulties. From this point of view the actual attitude of the "Modernists" is exposed in a remark by André Derain. Of the Cubists he wrote: "They can't bulldoze me: I know all about it." [25]

25. As quoted in *Modern French Painters,* M. Raynal, p. 68.

Cubism stands like the conscience of ex-Cubists and others, ever reminding them that they have avoided what they should have faced.[26]

On the whole these artists and their followers and apologists have been striving to describe their desertion of Cubism as being just the opposite. The ex-Cubists, relying on the laurels and notoriety of their Cubist reputations, proceeded to give the impression of continuing radical developments by restoring in non-Camera art that which they had so daringly striven to eliminate with Cubism. Today they would have us believe that Cubism was a mere step toward the "victories" they achieved in later years. But their behavior is more aptly summed up in the following: "You painters who were the persecuted of the pre-war [1914] period—you fauves and cubists whose execrated pictures were the distress of mothers and the dream of boys, you who at that time re-created the world—have passed thirty years curled up comfortably on your treasure, on your discoveries. . . . What danger do you run and where is your importance?"[27]

To be sure they have continued to be "radical," but in the sense that reaction can be radical. Our century has seen the rise of a unique phenomenon in the shape of "radical" behavior which is not always what seems to meet the eye. It is an age in which many revolutionists in various fields turn in their tracks and differ from the usual reactionaries only in *kind*. Changes in human behavior are so far-reaching in our times that not only the usual reactionaries, but even one-time radicals are opposed to change. This situation is unique and important for a clear understanding of contemporary problems.

The great error has been to allow the ex-Cubists to continue in the disguise of revolutionaries. The Cubists, known only in a vague way to themselves, had revolted against a dying age of art, and in so doing had revolted against the conservatives in order to continue progress. After Cubism they revolted against the progress which they themselves had played the foremost role in making possible. As ex-Cubists they became the vanguard of those revolting for the sake of revolting. They revolted against their own revolution because it was the only revolt left for them—a useless, empty end. Naum Gabo, one of the original Constructionists, sums up these problems when he writes: "The logic of life does not tolerate permanent revolutions. They are possible on paper but in real life a revolution is only a means, a tool but never an aim. It allows the destruction of obstacles which hinder a new construction, but destruction for destruction's sake is contrary to life. Every analysis is useful and even necessary, but when this analysis does not care about the results, when it excludes the task of finding a synthesis, it turns to its opposite, and instead of clarifying a problem it only renders it more obscure. Life permits to our desire for knowledge and exploration the most daring and courageous excursions, but only to the explorers who, enticed

26. It would make an interesting book to compile case histories of all those who reacted against Cubism from the point of view that we are here discussing. Consider, for example, a few excerpts from an interview with Chagall. They are typical of the kind of linguistic speculations employed in the effort to give the impression that he has risen above the accomplishments of Cubism, an art which he claims to admire.
". . . . my first aim is to construct my picture architecturally . . . . Impressionism and cubism were relatively easy to understand. . . . I am not a reactionary from cubism. I have admired the great cubists and have profited from cubism. . . . I felt painting needed a greater freedom than cubism permitted. . . . A cow and woman to me are the same—in a picture both are merely elements of a composition. In painting, the images of a woman or of a cow have different values of plasticity,—but not different poetic values. As far as literature goes, I feel myself more 'abstract' than Mondrian or Kandinsky in my use of pictorial elements. 'Abstract' not in the sense that my painting does not recall reality. Such abstract painting in my opinion is more ornamental and decorative, and always restricted in its range." (Quoted in "An Interview with Marc Chagall," by J. J. Sweeney, in *Partisan Review*, XI:88, Winter, 1944.)
Actually Chagall's work indicates that he is thoroughly opposed to Cubism, but has never been able to shake off its irritating effects. He is merely trying to justify himself for doing that which Cubism obviously repudiates. In a similar vein is the following by Lipchitz:
"Cubism was essentially a search for a new syntax. Once this was arrived at there was no reason for not employing it in the expression of a full message. This is what I feel I have done and what I am still trying to do. This is why I say I am still a cubist, but expressing myself freely with all the means at my disposal from the cubist point of view, not merely limiting myself to cubism's syntax." (Quoted in "An Interview with Jacques Lipchitz," by J. J. Sweeney, *Partisan Review*, XII:88, Winter 1945.) Instead of calling Cubism "theory" or "grammar," as do the critics quoted earlier, Lipchitz says "syntax"—and for much the same false reasons. What he is claiming for Cubism is that it is merely a "method for multiplying picture motifs," which Doesburg correctly contended it was not.

27. Louis Aragon in "Painting and Reality: A Discussion," *Transition*, p. 120, No. 25, Fall, 1936.

far away into unknown territories, have not forgotten to notice the way by which they came and the aim for which they started. In Art more than anywhere else in the creative discipline, daring expeditions are allowed. The most dizzying experiments are permissible, but even in Art the logic of life arrests the experiments as soon as they have reached the point when the death of the experimental objects becomes imminent. There were moments in the history of Cubism when the artists were pushed to these bursting points; sufficient to recall the sermons of Picabia, 1914-16, predicting the wreck of Art, and the manifestos of the Dadaists who already celebrated the funeral of Art with chorus and demonstrations. Realizing how near to complete annihilation the Cubist experiments had brought Art, many Cubists themselves have tried to find a way out, but the lack of consequence has merely made them afraid and has driven them back to Ingres (Picasso, 1919-23) and to the Gobelins of the sixteenth century (Braque, etc.). This was not an outlet but a retreat." [28]

The date of Picabia's "sermons"—1914—is significant, the year the Cubists, after four years of ambivalence, deserted Cubism completely and then, as ex-Cubists, led the flight of the "Modernists" from the "great decision."

Thus after participating in a movement which shook the world of art to its very foundations with one of the most daring and courageous experiments in all history, Braque is reduced to this evaluation of his and Picasso's achievements as Cubists: "How many times didn't Picasso and I discuss suppression of the subject! Here on the wall is a proof of these old preoccupations. But we quickly deduced that total indifference to subject would have immediately led us to an incomplete form of art. We loved painting too much to come to that." [29] But what has been the history of the "suppression of the subject"? Braque and those who think like him, have chosen to forget that ever since Impressionism, on through Cézanne and to the Cubists, those who have been shown *repeatedly* to be in error were those who always wanted *more* importance for the nature subject in non-Camera art. The new direction of non-Camera art continues in spite of the ex-Cubists and to their continued irritation, just as they once made Cubism grow to the irritation of reactionaries. As ex-Cubists they lead the reaction against their own creation, and against subsequent genuine innovators. These latter have taken over the task of consolidating the gains of the Transitional-Period as they had finally appeared in Cubism. It is a task of exploiting the results of previous revolutions —not creating new ones. This task is a responsibility which few artists have cared to accept. It seems more alluring to fabricate arbitrary "revolutions." Therefore, the majority decided to keep on turning the world of reality upside down, then rightside up, sideways up, anyway up—what did it matter, so long as one was "Modern"! Since these "Modernists" were unable to face the co-operative tasks and responsibilities confronting them, and since they wanted to be "revolutionary," the only recourse remaining by which they could avoid the one and secure the other appeared to be to "express oneself"; to ignore history if it would not allow for any more "revolution." Thus was the anarchy of the lost individual opposed to the co-operative responsibilities arising out of the conditions of our times.

28. Naum Gabo: *Circle*, pp. 5-6.   29. Braque, op. cit., p. 24.

We do not believe in miracles, we are realists. There is more "miracle" in the tension of some basic colors or in the balance of some lines, than in all the unhealthy exaltations that are presented to us today as modern painting. Enough of painting on the basis of sickness. 371

Theo van Doesburg

How many errors have been and are being committed through vague and confused intuition?   232

Piet Mondrian

What we call progress consists in coordinating ideas with realities. 178

Alfred Korzybski

A civilization which cannot burst through its current abstractions is doomed to sterility after a very limited period of progress. 357

Alfred N. Whitehead

It is true that I have a strong impression of an external world apart from any communication with other conscious beings. But apart from such communication I should have no reason to trust the impression. 102

A. S. Eddington

We are more likely to see what we expect to see or are more used to seeing. 208

Matthew Luckiesh and F. K. Moss

When we identify. . . . we disregard the inherent differences, and so proper evaluation and full adjustment become impossible. 179

Alfred Korzybski

Our analysis has found first Photography, then Impressionism to be the turning points in the transition from one epoch of man's art to another. The latter definitely ushered in a new non-Camera art which was to appear in the future. From Impressionism on the innovators changed nature's appearance in order to free themselves from its limiting forms, thus gradually releasing the Inventive potential inherent in man. Although these artists up to and including Cubism deliberately distorted nature's appearance, they were largely unconscious of the distinction between the basic function of the Inventive factor in their work and in past art. For example, the Cubists would turn a painting upside down in order to destroy the recognizability of the nature objects in their work. They did this in an effort to release their Inventive ability further by freeing themselves from the *limiting forms* of nature. By employing this naive method they forced the circumstances by which they unconsciously strove to reach the newer level of abstracting. They resorted to this roundabout method because they were not conscious of the advisability of inventing directly. Finally the very character of the evolution of Cubism compelled them to face this inevitable prospect and it was then that they completely deserted the fundamental implications of Cubism.

The majority of artists since then have not understood that the Cubists deserted Cubism, since later artists have feared its implications as much as the Cubists themselves. Failing to perceive clearly the important discoveries of their predecessors, they were also prevented from seeing clearly the very errors which prevented the Cubists from adequately understanding their own creation. Hence, while the younger generation inherited the revolutionary fervor of their predecessors, few profited from the lessons that Cubism offered.

The results of Cubism had indicated that the old method of abstracting from the macro-level could now be replaced by abstracting from the Structural Process level of reality, but the majority of artists have been only vaguely aware, if at all, of the very important differences in the abstracting methods of the past and the present. Instead of this understanding there appeared a general reluctance to risk giving up the old level of abstracting altogether. The majority lacked the courage to acknowledge and face the very problem which defeated the ex-Cubists. Problems, however, are not eliminated simply by refusing to acknowledge their existence. This has been repeatedly tried since 1910 but the chaos of art has only been increased rather than remedied.

423

148. Thomas H. Benton, detail of The Arts of Life in America. Collection of The Whitney Museum of American Art.

Today it is critically necessary for artists, if they are to comprehend adequately the new relationships between reality and art, to acquire a "consciousness of abstracting." It is precisely because artists and critics generally are unaware of the Structural Process level as distinct from the macro-level of reality, that they are involved in the current dilemma between the old and new methods of abstracting. Whether they know it or not, they want to keep "art" at some stage of the Transitional-Period, i.e., some one of the many stages between the old and the new. They are the Inbetweeners, the "middlemen" of art. One of Pissarro's remarks about such artists in his own times may be aptly applied to them: "they are all the same, they want to run with the hare and hunt with the hounds." [1] They compulsively oppose not only the art from which the Transitional-Period departed—realistic art—but also that which finally emerged from the conclusions of the Transitional-Period—the non-copying in any degree of the particular form-color organizations of nature's appearances.

These Inbetweeners of today's art, both artists and critics, take many forms. But all of them, in one degree or another, are interested primarily in the fantasy manipulations of nature's appearances. Nature's macroscopics must be present in some way and to some degree in order to give these individuals what they imagine constitutes a satisfactory experience in non-Camera art. They cannot fully break the hold of the past nor fully realize the potentialities of the present, principally because they assume that there is only one level of reality—the macroscopic level—from which the artist can abstract.

When we realize how momentous is the change in which our times involve us, we can better understand the varying degrees of reluctance among the vast majority of non-Camera artists to dispense with the old abstracting level and to accept the new one. After all, for the artist to invent his own content without resorting to the substitute of manipulating nature's appearances, is not only a very difficult task, but also requires what is for most non-Camera artists the alarming psycho-logical decision of severing oneself from the "traditional" content, not to mention the traditional art mediums.

To judge the degree to which the old and/or new level is motivating any particular artist, one needs only observe which type of abstracting has the ascendancy in his works. It should be helpful to consider each general type according to the degree to which recognizable nature forms are present in the works which they have made, or, in the case of the critic, for which they apologize.

At one extreme are the present day "Realists," who are clearly reactionary. They are represented by the nationalistic artists, including the artists of Russia and all totalitarian nations, and in this country by such as George Biddle or Thomas Benton (figure 148). The "social-scene" art of the latter has been periodically hailed as an American Renaissance. Actually their art is the incongruous result of mixing 19th century nationalism in art with a little 19th century Post-Impressionist distortion. They have dressed up the Post-Impressionist method of art in one of Billy Sunday's old suits and called it "social art," etc.

1. Pissarro, *Letters to His Son Lucien*, edited by John Rewald, p. 44.

Although their capacity to profit from the Post-Impressionists has been very meager, to say the least, it is interesting to notice that few indeed of these "Americans" have cared to acknowledge any indebtedness to "foreigners."

In any case, whether they merely paint descriptively or have a "social message," they create fantasies of life around them. No person or thing ever looked the way they paint them! But these fantasies are offered to us as the voice of today's reality, and it is claimed that, "This trend is toward the social integration of art in the lives of the people of the nation." [2] Meanwhile, they cannot explain, without resorting to verbal obscurities and contradictions, why they must change nature's appearances into what they obviously ARE NOT.

If these artists genuinely wished to report the social happenings on the macro-level of visual experience, they should employ the Film medium. But we must understand them as *frustrated Realists,* frustrated by the products of the Photographer, who is the legitimate recording Realist today. Hence they are compelled to distort, if they are to do something the Camera cannot do. At the same time their distortive activities are rationalized as proof that they are "Modern" too.

Those who directly imitate or admire the Post-Impressionistic method of art today constitute the next group of Inbetweeners. Many of these artists, such as Derain, Roualt, Bonnard, Matisse (figure 149), etc., once claimed to be largely concerned with "pure design," and disclaimed the importance of subject-matter. Their apologists also have insisted on the importance of pure design, but all the artists they admire are largely concerned with manipulating the "design" of nature's appearances. Albert Barnes, a collector of Post-Impressionist works, including the 20th century variety, has the following to say: "The chief point of difference between the old and the new may be said to be that the moderns exhibit greater interest in relatively pure design.

"In order to show the development of this interest, it will be necessary to trace the evolution of plastic design as something in itself, apart from the question of subject-matter." [3] This proposal to study the present day interest in design as "something in itself, apart from the question of subject-matter" is often made.

Clive Bell was one of the first to claim a split between subject-matter as such, and subject-matter as "pure form." He wrote in 1913: "Who has not, once at least in his life, had a sudden vision of landscape as pure form? For once, instead of seeing it as fields and cottages, he has felt it as lines and colours." [4] Bell implies that subject-matter can be split into what is and what is not subject-matter, but Alfred Barr says explicitly, "take away the subject matter of most realists and you have comparatively little left. But the colors, shapes and lines of the expressionists have a life of their own which can survive without any subject at all." [5]

2. George Biddle: "The Victory and Defeat of Modernism," *Harper's Magazine,* 187:35, June, 1943.

3. Albert C. Barnes: "The Transition to Modern Painting," p. 128, *Art and Education,* by John Dewey, Albert C. Barnes, and others, Barnes Foundation Press, Merion, Pa., 1929.

4. Clive Bell: *Art,* p. 53, Frederick A. Stokes Co., New York, 1913.

5. Alfred Barr, Jr.: *What Is Modern Painting?* p. 22, Museum of Modern Art, New York, 1943. It seems that Barr is one with Whistler, who wrote many years ago that, "As music is the poetry of sound, so is painting the poetry of sight, and the subject-matter has nothing to do with the harmony of sound or of colour." (p. 34, *Mr. Whistler's Ten O'Clock,* Thomas Bird Mosher, Portland, Maine, 1925.)

149. Henri Matisse, Odalisque with Raised Arms, 1923. Courtesy of The Art Institute of Chicago.

In other words, it is contended, to quote Barr again, that *"how* they paint can be separated from *what* they paint."[6] But it is impossible to separate lines, etc., (the supposed "how") from subject (the "what"), since the subject of nature comprises the lines, etc. Consequently you have not a little, but *nothing* left if you take away the subject of "realists" *or* "expressionists" or the work of any artist whose content is made up in any degree of the appearance of nature forms. Barr categorizes the following as "expressionists": van Gogh, Gauguin, Marin, Roualt, Beckman, Orozco, Matisse. As far as the works of these artists are concerned, we think it remarkable indeed if one could separate the subject-matter from the lines, colors, etc., and not have, just as in the case of the Realists, "comparatively little left." In fact, nothing would be left! Take for example *The Starry Night,* by van Gogh (figure 150), which Barr reproduces in the work quoted from. It consists of depictions of trees, houses, hills and sky. Now "take away the subject matter," i.e., trees, houses, hills and sky, and see what is left! Obviously the artistic surgery which Barr claims to perform, remarkable as it is, is only a verbal feat.

Here is another example of the same sort of verbalisms by Barr. He wrote in reference to Picasso's *Les Demoiselles d'Avignon* (figure 151): "If these were real women with faces like that. . . . no one could stand looking at them. But they are not real faces: they are areas on a painted canvas. . . ."[7] It is true that these are not "real women," but they are also not merely "areas on a painted canvas." These "areas on a painted canvas" are actually primitive-like or *low-order* abstractions from "real women." We are not confronted with a problem of whether or not "real faces" are presented, since it is evident enough that "real faces" cannot be paintings or vice versa. But *depictions of* "real women" are presented. In all arts which employ nature forms, the forms are those of nature, however distorted, and *are not* just some-

6. Ibid., p. 22. 7. Ibid., p. 26.

426

thing called "plastic design" or "areas on a painted canvas." Such contradictions are a result of a general tendency to categorize and then to discuss certain aspects of a problem as though they were in isolation. Discussing them in this way relieves the theorist of confronting problems which inevitably appear false when one recognizes that everything is related.

Whatever one calls these forms, they cannot be split up into two different kinds of forms which have an independent existence. As a matter of fact, those arts which each of the above critics admires above all others are those where nature objects are of extreme concern to the artist. But our critics put the problem of subject-matter to one side, when it is convenient, so that they can talk unmolestedly about alleged "plastic design," "pure form," etc.

This does not prevent them, however, in other places from putting "pure form," "plastic design," etc. to one side, when it is convenient, in order to show how superior on a "realistic" basis this art is compared to that which literally copies reality. Barr, for example, writes about a painting of a village by Stuart Davis: "But with all these omissions and simplifications and rearrangements Davis has given a clearer and more complete idea of the village than does the snapshot." [8] In this case it would appear that the "what" that is painted is important and superior to the art of the "Realists" (implied by Barr's reference to the snapshot). Therefore, we are left with the following contradiction: on the one hand such art is superior to the Realist's, because it produces "a clearer and more complete idea" of nature forms; on the other hand it is superior because nature forms are not important anyway, since the Modernist's work "can survive without any subject at all." [9]

Albert Barnes says further regarding the above problem: "Cézanne's forms are essentially abstract, but they are achieved through the medium of subject-matter that has sufficient point of contact with the real world to establish relation with our funded experience of real things. For example, the hands in the 'Portrait of Madame Cézanne' are obviously distorted and unnatural, but they recall human hands, in their essential and abstract quality, with a forceful, moving reality greater than any photographic imitation of hands could produce." [10] Barnes correctly states that Cézanne's portrayal of hands is "distorted and unnatural," but then he states that these same depictions of hands are a "moving reality greater than any photographic imitation." To be sure, the hands in the Cézanne painting do "recall human hands," but so does the drawing of a four-year-old when the same object is indicated with six straight lines. Certainly the mere fact that Cézanne's painting recalls human hands does not automatically establish it as a criterion for the proper depiction of reality, since a fantasy depiction of the same subject also depends precisely on this mechanism of recall. Thus the "greater moving reality" which Barnes refers to in the Cézanne can only be the greater moving "reality" of a fantasy and not that of a correspondence with nature's actual appearances. As a matter of fact the attraction of fantasy reaches its highest peak when it offers an experience clothed in the reality of recognizable forms and yet is an experience impossible to realize in actual reality. This is exactly the kind of experience that is of paramount importance to the apologists for any of the varieties of "Modern" art. [11]

8. Ibid., p. 4.

9. As a matter of fact, with "snapshots" one could give an incomparably better "idea of the village" than with any painting. Painters like Davis actually give us *their* fantastic idea of a village, a false "idea of the village." Davis admits that subject-matter is merely an excuse for the exudation of the artist's personality when he writes: "Art is not in the subject-matter but in the artist, and communicates his personal realization directly through its form." ("What about Modern Art and Democracy?", *Harper's Magazine,* 188:17, December, 1943.)

10. Barnes, "Renoir and Cézanne," p. 148, *Art and Education.*

11. This is precisely why almost all artists prefer to depict fantasies of recognizable objects, rather than fantasies of invented objects. This is also why most of our Post-Impressionism enthusiasts prefer a Renoir to a Cézanne; the former was far more interested in the objects of nature as such. Hence when Renoir depicted a nude woman, he kept it looking much like a nude: Cézanne tried to make a nude part of the architecture of a landscape he was painting. In short, such admirers of the Post-Impressionists have a greater preference for those works where the structural factor does not become dominant, since this tends to cut down the force and prominence of the fantasy of nature reality. For this reason Renoir is more desirable than Cézanne; and Matisse is preferred by such individuals among contemporary artists rather than, let us say, Mondrian.

150. Vincent van Gogh, The Starry Night. Collection The Museum of Modern Art, New York.

Consider for example the remarks of a painter who worked in Cézanne's country and lived in that artist's studio: "Cézanne's landscapes are, in my estimation, among the first ever produced that *recreate* and express nature in its *true* atmosphere." (emphasis ours)[12] This writer too would have us believe that Cézanne in some mysterious manner combined *actual* reality with the extensive *changes* he made in that reality, all to get a "true" reality. The above author himself reproduces Photographs of the "scenes" that Cézanne painted, to show how the actual subject appears and differs from the Cézanne paintings.

Venturi has another version of the same general theme: "We feel the representation of the country in the distance, as if it were near, without ever losing awareness that it is far; and that is one of the miracles of art."[13] This is just as non-sensical as if we were to say, "We feel that Cézanne is not realistic without ever losing awareness that he is realistic." As a matter of fact, Barnes does say something like this when he refers to "unreal reality,"[14] and for apparently the same reasons as Venturi; namely, to give to fantasy a justifiable basis of realism. This is put still another way in the following: "Cézanne's uniqueness and perhaps his historical greatness is found in his power to synthesize abstraction and reality."[15] This statement is as good an example as one could desire for illustrating the philosophy of the Inbetweener, the one who tries to sit on the fence between the new and the old. For his purpose he must avoid recognizing the distinction between the old and the new. (Of course an artist cannot "synthesize abstraction and reality," for the simple reason that he can only abstract from reality.)

It is to be expected that the art which actually does not have "any subject at all," which is

12. Erle Loran: *Cézanne's Composition*, p. 28, University of California Press, Berkeley, 1943.

13. Quoted by Loran, ibid., p. 32, from *Cézanne*, by Lionello Venturi, p. 56, P. Rosenberg, Paris, 1936.

14. See "Ancient Chinese and Modern European Paintings," by Albert C. Barnes and Violette de Mazia, Catalogue of Bignou Gallery, May-June, 1943.

15. Loran, op. cit., p. 63.

428

151. Pablo Picasso, Les Demoiselles d'Avignon, 1906-07. Collection The Museum of Modern Art, New York.

comprised of invented forms, calls forth vehement protest from the Inbetweeners. For example Barr writes: "But in his art the abstract artist prefers impoverishment to adulteration." [16] In other words, although the lines and forms of "Modern" art are so important that one can supposedly take away the subject-matter that comprises the forms and still have a great deal left, nevertheless if an "Abstract" artist actually replaces subject-matter with invented lines, etc., he has apparently impoverished art.

Related to our problem here, Barnes writes: "The idea of abstract form divorced from a clue, however vague, of its representative equivalent in the real world is sheer nonsense. In Cubist paintings that move us aesthetically there are always sufficient representative indications, as well as reliance upon other and traditional resources of painting, to stir up something familiar in our mass of funded experience." [17]

"The very great majority of cubist paintings have no more aesthetic significance than the pleasing pattern in an Oriental rug." [18]

"We maintain that such form [non-representative] can be no more than decoration, that plastic form at its best does seek to give an equivalent of something real—of fundamental aspects, of essences, though not of insignificant detail. In fact, at all stages in the history of painting, from Masaccio to Manet and Matisse, the departures from literalism by which a more satisfactory design is secured, accomplish *also* a better effect of realism. We have not gotten farther away from realities, but nearer to them." [19]

We have repeatedly emphasized the impossibility of an artist's divorcing himself from the "real world," regardless of the kind of art he makes. In art there can *never* be a problem of whether or

16. Alfred Barr, Jr.: *Cubism and Abstract Art,* p. 13, Museum of Modern Art, New York, 1936.

17. Barnes, "The Evolution of Contemporary Painting," p. 157, *Art and Education.*

18. Ibid., p. 157.

19. Barnes, "The Transition to Modern Painting," p. 131, *Art and Education.*

152. Jacques Lipchitz, Seated Pierrot, 1921. Courtesy of The Art
of This Century.

153. Henri Laurens, Man with Clarinet, 1919. Courtesy of The
Art of This Century.

not an artist chooses to produce a "clue" to reality in his work; there is rather *always a problem of what the artist has done with reality*. But Barnes erroneously assumes that a work of art is divorced from reality simply because the macro-level is not present. If Barnes cannot see in art comprised only of invented forms, any relation to what he calls "mass of funded experience," then it is only because his conscious experience is largely limited to the Aristotelian view of reality. We repeat, no artist can *include* or *exclude all* the characteristics of reality.

Of course, if "departures from literalism" secure "a more satisfactory design," would it not be even more satisfactory to depart still further and eliminate nature objects altogether? This would release to a greater extent the very factor (inventiveness) by which the artist secures a "more satisfactory design." In other words, if a departure from "reality" secures more success in the objective at hand, then why stop *half-way* at the Post-Impressionist stage? Barnes would appear to contend that an "equivalent of something real" must be retained. In other words, the significance of the particular "design" Barnes is referring to depends for him upon the possession of a certain degree of resemblance to nature's form-appearances. The kind of design he is primarily interested in is the manipulation of nature's design, not the direct creation of man's "design," nor the direct recording of nature's "design." Obviously, however, the most satisfactory depiction of nature's design would be secured by obtaining as much correspondence as possible to that of nature. Otherwise, if we stop the abstracting process anywhere between the two polar levels of abstracting—the macro and the structural—then we are, to use Barnes' words, getting "further away from realities, not nearer to them," because our results are fantasies of reality. But few seem to realize that the greatest degree of an "equivalent of something real" is to be found in completely invented forms or in accurate recordings of nature forms. Hence the Inbetweeners, when pressed too far from the old contents by arts that eliminate nature-appearances, reverse the consideration of the problem, and the art that a while

430

ago was solely or largely concerned with "plastic values" is suddenly greatly concerned with the reality of nature, even more "real" than a "photographic imitation."

But today most artists and critics, fettered as they are to some erroneous play upon the Post-Impressionist theme, are essentially preoccupied with the defects—the fantasy aspect—of Post-Impressionism, and miss entirely its positive contributions towards the new direction of future art. In previous chapters we showed why fantasy appeared and was unavoidable in the otherwise progressive phases of the Transitional-Period. We explained that this factor was its defect, and not its asset, and that the historical greatness of Cézanne, for instance, did not lie in fantasies of reality, but rather in the research he accomplished as he tried to discover a new "reality" context for man's art. Thus in regard to Venturi's discussion of Cézanne's "distances," the fundamental reason Cézanne pulled the distant parts so close to the foreground in his works was that he *preferred* the sort of organization achieved by this distortion. The important factor was not the new way in which reality was depicted (which only produced the fantasy of reality to which the majority are attracted), but the fundamental structural concern of the artist in his abstractions from nature. For that matter, the great problem for Cézanne in his art was the fact that his abstractions were contrary to what he saw in nature. The majority of artists and critics, however, have chosen to regard this characteristic of Cézanne's work as some mysteriously realistic result, since it offers them a very convenient method of making or rationalizing art and at the same time appears to avoid all the difficulties that perturbed Cézanne.[20]

It certainly is no accident, then, that the majority of those who claim experiences of "pure form," "pure design," etc., are able to exercise it only in those arts of the past and present which retain in one degree or another forms which resemble the objects of nature. But since they do not see the predominance of fantasy as their principal attraction in art, they are incapable of properly comprehending even the very arts they idolize—Post-Impressionist arts.

The artists in the next group to be considered, abstract less from nature's appearances than do the pseudo-Post-Impressionists. Typical of artists in this group are Braque (figure 154), Lipchitz (figure 152), Léger, Laurens (figure 153), Masson, etc. Here we find many ex-Cubists who refuse to be considered as "Abstract" artists because they erroneously identify the term with any art which abstracts to a higher degree than they customarily do. Georges Braque, for example, opposes all arts striving in the actual direction set by Cubism and indiscriminately lumps them together under the ambiguous label "abstract." Thus: "Abstract art, anxious to avoid all compromise with things, has rejected them from its paintings. It has not yielded to the evidence that, by the simple fact of their presence, things provoke new states in the artist. The importance of subject is so considerable that the different schools of painting are best distinguished by the vocabulary of subjects they have invented." [21] Braque chooses to forget that even though

20. Efforts to make it appear that Cézanne and similar artists reproduced some profound quality of nature-reality remind us that the same non-sense was tried with the Impressionists. In both Impressionism and Post-Impressionism the first reactions of the opponents of the art were to the effect that such works distorted reality. (And these reactions were and remain correct.) In order to get around this embarrassing situation the apologists of "Modern" art tried to reverse the actual situation and claim "mysterious" reality qualities for such art. This verbal subterfuge worked so well in the case of the Impressionists that the common opinion today is that they were mere "Realists." If it works as well in the case of Post-Impressionism, as it seems to be in the process of doing—what with Pepsi-Cola calendars carrying the naive imitations of such art—then it will be popularly assumed that these artists too were mere harmless Realists in the great tradition of the past.

21. Georges Braque: reply to a questionnaire directed by Christian Zervos, *Cahiers d'Art,* p. 24 Nos. 1-4, 1935. We must emphasize again that Braque's use of the term "invented" refers only to manipulation of the appearances of nature. "Invention" in this sense implies a certain degree of copying of nature's appearances and therefore is not invention in the Constructionist sense of the word. By comparison it is pseudo-invention.

154. Georges Braque, The Table, 1928. Collection The Museum of Modern Art, New York.

the majority feel the need to manipulate nature's appearances, this does not automatically establish a valid precedent. We would rather emphasize that the important matter is the attitude of the artist toward "things," for this provokes the particular reaction he exposes in his work regarding the interpretation of reality. Braque implies that the invented content does not provoke what he calls "new states in the artist," presumably because the artist has nothing to react to if he does not react to the macro-level. However, the remarks of Braque about such art are, humorously enough, a good example of at least one kind of reaction and experience which the allegedly "cold," "empty," "cerebral," and non-existent content can provoke in certain types of personalities. We must admit that he has a very decided reaction to it, in spite of his insistence that "A white square is a mute square." [22] The question, then, has never been whether one content can produce experiences and another not, but rather, which type of art experience is the most appropriate for our times. For some purposes, Braque's contention is correct that one can "best distinguish" *most* schools of art, one from the other, by their particular manipulation of nature's appearances, but the *most distinguishing, marked differences* to be found are between *all those schools that do not* and *all those that do eliminate macro-reality.*

22. Ibid., p. 24.

Joan Miro (figure 163) also objects vehemently to "Abstract" art. As he put it, "Have you ever heard of greater nonsense than the aims of the abstractionist group?"[23] Miro too had started out painting in the Post-Impressionist manner, and gradually developed towards Cubism, only to retreat once this stage had been experienced. Then, like the ex-Cubists and particularly like Picasso, he decided to keep a little of his Cubist training and combine it with Surrealism, increasing the latter as time went on, until he decided, just as Picasso did, that he could practically get along without Cubism. In 1936 he remarked: "As a matter of fact, I am attaching more and more importance to the subject matter of my work."[24] This was, in fact, inevitable as soon as he deserted the positive direction of Cubism. James J. Sweeney, writing on Miro, rationalizes the problem as follows: "The need of Miro's generation was a recall of the imagination to painting. In combating the abuses which had derived from an exaggerated interest in the descriptive possibilities of painting, Miro's immediate seniors, the cubists and others, had gone dangerously far in the direction of denying those features any value whatsoever. The young men of the early 1920's recognized the importance of a renewed stress on spiritual values in painting.

"This new romantic spirit, however, demanded a fresh field. Psychoanalytic research and the unfamiliar words of free, irrational association which it revealed, offered a suggestion. It was eagerly accepted. But in reacting against the cubists' exaggerated emphasis on formal fundamentals, many of the most talented surrealist painters forgot the lessons that the previous generation had learned. Miro, however, was an exception. Thanks to his almost all-exclusive interest in painting, he has been able to keep his finger on the benefits that the severe disciplines of the earlier generation had won, and at the same time meet the problem of his own generation with an equal or even greater effectiveness than any of his contemporaries."[25]

In these explanations of Miro's behavior we again find very apparent an insecurity before both the genuine old and the genuine new. Actually what Miro has done in his alleged insight into the positive and negative qualities of Cubism and Surrealism consists of making Cubism a "recipe for making descriptive pictures or a mechanical method for multiplying picture motifs. . . ." In other words, Cubism for him simply consisted of a method for manipulating forms of reality, while the Surrealistic attitude served to prop up the waning interest in the description of macro-reality. The past stimulus for describing macro-reality with non-Camera mediums is now defunct, and has been replaced by the pathology of Surrealism. This is the excuse for continuing the old reality content with the old primitive mediums.[26]

In any case, in Miro's and Sweeney's remarks we see further variations on the theoretical theme of the Inbetweener. The principal difference between the artists and critics of this group and of the preceding one is that the former prefer to stop the Transitional-Period a little further on, i.e., in an early stage of Cubism, where distortion is more extensive, and hence where a greater degree of fantasy is obtained.

There are certain groups of contemporary painters, however, who consider themselves the rightful heirs of that which the Cubists inaugurated. Many of these artists have come to call themselves "Abstract." In general it is impossible to apply specific labels for the various groups of "Abstract" artists. They are such an unstable lot that what they stand for one year they are against another. At one time or another, however, some of them have claimed to be primarily interested in producing a "pure form" content. With the term "pure form" they imply that they do not *in any way* derive their art results from the world reality outside; some actually state that the forms "come from nothing." Maurice Raynal frames the theory in this subtle fashion: "lines and colors have their own language. . . . they are quite capable of their own autonomy and can create a work of art independent of all actual associations."[27]

23. Quoted by J. J. Sweeney: *Joan Miro,* p. 13, Museum of Modern Art, New York, 1941.
24. Ibid., p. 13.
25. Ibid., p. 13.
26. Surrealism will be considered in a later chapter.   27. Maurice Raynal: *Modern French Painters,* p. 19.

An examination of the art of the Abstract artists with whom we are concerned here, however, shows that they abstract from nature only in a slightly higher degree than their ex-Cubist predecessors. And like the ex-Cubists they are also interested in fantasy manipulations of nature's appearances. The principal difference is that the ex-Cubists consciously discarded the inevitable outcome of Cubism and stated that they were again interested in some form of the old nature-appearance content; whereas certain Abstract artists denied any such interest. This has not prevented some of them from insisting on nature forms as the "starting point" for their alleged "pure forms." This paradoxical situation promotes a maladjusted type of visualization. That is, such an artist will observe some painted or actual object of nature, say a human figure, and claim that while observing it he saw no figure, only "pure forms."

Recall Clive Bell's claim that he could look at "fields and cottages" and see "pure form." Bell used this claim to rationalize his preference for an art in which "fields and cottages" were clearly presented. Nevertheless, the fallacy is apparent, whether it is an "Abstract" artist or a Clive Bell who claims to see recognizable phenomena as "pure form."

J. W. Dunne supplies us with an excellent parallel to this sort of visual activity in art, which can be used to demonstrate the fallacy of the "pure form" rationalization: "You are now reading this book, and your field of presentation contains the visual phenomena connected with the printed letters of the word you are regarding. It contains also, at the same instant, the visual phenomenon pertaining to the little numeral at the bottom of the page. This you 'failed to notice'; but the numeral in question was, clearly, inside the area covered by your vision—it was affecting your brain *via* the eye, its psychical 'correlate' was being offered to your attention. And that statement holds good for a host of other visual phenomena . . .

"It would be unsafe to say that these comparatively unnoticed phenomena were not being consciously observed. When you are watching a fall of snow, observation may be concentrated upon a single floating flake; but that does not mean that you failed to perceive the remainder. Were these to vanish, leaving the single flake in the air, their disappearance would instantly distract your startled attention from the object of your previous occupation." [28]

Of course we never "see" *all* there is to see; whatever we "see" varies in degrees all the way from consciousness to unconsciousness. Furthermore, what we eventually see is determined not only by what there is to be seen but by what we expect to see. *The danger in this latter factor is that we will see what we do because we expected to see it, although the facts may be quite different.* False notions, attitudes and indoctrinations can accomplish the illusion of seeing what does not exist, as well as not seeing what does exist.

How is such visualization accomplished? Imagine that we are standing before an actual landscape and like Clive Bell or certain "Abstract" artists, we claim to see "pure form" instead of the "fields and cottages" at which we otherwise admit we are looking. For the sake of argument, let us further assume that it is possible to divide nature into the two separate visual contexts implied above, namely, "lines and colors," which are "fields and cottages," and "lines and colors" which are *not* "fields and cottages," but "pure forms." Now recalling Dunne's examples, we find that the eye-brain records the visual scene as-a-whole, in that the light-rays have no concern with whether or not we wish to receive them, or how we want them to appear. It matters little whether the eye-brain in question be that of a Sargent or a Braque. But if we were a Clive Bell, i.e., a Post-Impressionist mentality, or an "Abstract" artist of the type under discussion, we would "fail to notice" "fields and cottages," because we did not want to see them, and instead would see only what *"appeared"* to be simply "lines and colors." Those who claim this remarkable visual feat consequently claim that they are reacting only to "lines and colors." But if we are observing "fields and cottages" we are compelled to react to them in some manner (whether we want to or not), for the apparent reason that we are experiencing "fields and cottages," if not consciously, then unconsciously. To use the words of Dunne, the "psychical correlate" is being "offered to our attention" as-a-whole, regardless, we might add, of the manner in which it is desired or digested. Hence the experience claimed is actually one of reacting to lines and colors which *are fields and cottages* and not fields and

28. J. W. Dunne: *An Experiment with Time,* pp. 15-16, A. and C. Black, Ltd., London, 1927, by permission of J. W. Dunne and The Macmillan Company, New York.

cottages which are lines and colors called "pure forms." It makes no difference whether or not one knows this or desires that such an experience take place. From this it follows that these alleged "pure form" experiences are actually a particular kind of interpretative response to visual phenomena that is false to facts. As our analysis now indicates, there exists no such division as we assumed for the sake of argument, because whatever lines or colors we see are the lines and colors of fields and cottages, etc. The assumption that there existed such possibilities of visualizing reality resulted only in the suppression of the actual appearance of facts and the lack of any adequate conscious control of the experience, thus leaving the unfettered unconsciousness to determine the results of one's reactions to whatever the visual stimulus was.

Artists who visualize in this unique manner—seeing recognizable phenomena as "pure form"—have obviously trained themselves to ignore and suppress reality as such.[29] In doing so they reverse the natural order of visualization, because normally one tries to see things as they appear, not as what they obviously *are not*. This reversal of the natural order of visualization can result in severe and harmful delusions. For one intentionally trains himself not to see the actual reality characteristics of nature, and consequently he cannot see these characteristics in his art either, for here it is difficult to comprehend except where the forms of nature are deliberately retained in an obvious manner. Because such an artist comprehends reality only as a matter of one level, the macro-level, he is thus compelled in a negative direction towards his objective. That is, he must concentrate upon suppressing (perhaps it would be more correct to call this activity *re*pressing) that level, rather than realizing that he can eliminate it consciously by abstracting directly from the Process Structure level of reality. It is easy to form this habit of repression, because the macro-reality characteristics of the objects in the art being discussed—the unconscious material— are disguised in the attempt to pass the censorship of consciousness. Instead of trying to increase his *consciousness of natural forms* in a highly abstracted work, this type of "Abstract" artist actually attempts to make himself *UNconscious of natural forms* while observing reality or art. *But ignoring the reality characteristics of nature does not prevent one from being affected by the fact that what one is looking at is an apple or a landscape and not a screw driver—or a "pure form,"* for that matter. Such artists are being affected *un*consciously by that which they choose to repress consciously. Their conscious activity is determined largely by their experience on the unconscious level, where it is impossible to ignore the fact that confronting one is an apple or a landscape, not a pure form. Hence nature forms do appear in the works of these "pure-formists," but in a disguised manner, so as to evade the censorship of the conscious. The degree of disguise is determined by the intensity of the censorship, and its kind by the psycho-logical structure of the artist's personality.

It is not surprising, therefore, to find very often in the works of these "pure form" artists consistent and particular selections of nature forms or subjects. If, as they claim, these subjects were not of interest to them, then their works would not disclose such a consistent selection of particular kinds of nature objects. For example, an artist would be compelled to abstract differently from a nude than from a truck. Obviously the source of abstraction plays its part in determining the *limitations* or *possibilities* of the art-results, which will vary according to whether we are abstracting from the old or new or both levels combined.

To attain the greatest approximation to "pure form," the artist must eliminate abstractions from the macro-level of reality and proceed to abstract from the Structural Process level. As it is, those who seek "pure form" are practically claiming that the forms of nature become "pure" the moment the artists produce, so to speak, impure renditions of nature's forms; i.e., deliberately change nature's forms into what are actually pseudo-invented forms. Such a solution amounts merely to suppressing the old content on the conscious level so that the manipulation of nature may result in something erroneously called "pure form." And as Mondrian pertinently remarked: "But if the purpose was nothing but plastic expression, why then use figurative representation? Clearly, there must have been the intention to express something outside the realm of pure plastics. This of course is often the case even in abstract art." [30]

29. Actually this kind of visual behavior is on the general level of the infant, who sees the world for the first time and apparently sees only "lines and colors" that have as yet no conscious, recognizable significance to him.

30. Mondrian, "Plastic Art and Pure Plastic Art," *Plastic Art and Pure Plastic Art,* p. 59, Wittenborn and Co., New York, 1945.

There are of course instances where nature is so thoroughly disguised that it takes time even for the experienced to discern it. On a number of occasions the author has pointed out to various artists some obviously recognizable objects in their work, sometimes objects very familiar to the artists, yet they would deny vigorously that such was the case. These denials were "sincere" in intention because they literally were not prepared to see such material. The author himself experienced this stage of inadequate consciousness; only later was he able to see many recognizable objects in his own works. The more intensely the artist strives to eliminate macro-reality, the more difficult it becomes for him to recognize these forms. The old content cannot be eliminated merely by the negative action of repression. Only by sufficient "consciousness of abstracting" can this conflict be cleared up.

From our discussion we can see the importance of such attitudes as those expressed by R. W. Pickford: "Psycho-analysis has shown that it is very important to distinguish between different conscious and unconscious levels of meaning of paintings and other works of art. When a painter is working on a picture, or thinking it out, or when a beholder is liking or disliking it, or thinking about it, he seems to be motivated at the same time upon many different levels. These levels range from the deepest unconscious impulses to the most fully rational and precisely formulated ideas and intentions. Such levels of meaning and motivation are not separate, but are actively related to each other in complex ways. The conscious attitude of a given person to a certain painting will depend on its relation to the motivations by which he in particular is influenced at different levels; on the peculiar ways in which his motivations at these levels are interrelated; and on the degree of insight he has into the parts played by disguises and transformations of the lower levels of meaning in building up the higher levels. . . .

". . . . Much of the satisfaction given by the painting, however, may be derived from unwitting response to the unconscious meanings, and it is a fair assumption that both conscious and unconscious meanings are present in all works of art and deeply affect our appreciation of them."[31] Further on we read: "Paintings, like dreams, differ widely in the clarity with which they display the latent content, in the coherence and meaningfulness of the manifest content for conscious and for unconscious apprehension, and in the degree of polish applied."[32]

The artist must be aware not only of the fact that he is abstracting, but also of the *kind* of abstracting in which he is involved; otherwise nature's appearances inevitably creep back into his art contents via his subconscious activity. And the greater the effort to eliminate nature, the greater will be the disguise. We repeat, only adequate consciousness of abstracting will alter or resolve this process. Then it becomes possible for the artist to comprehend properly why he seeks to invent his art contents, if this is what he wants to do, rather than copy or manipulate in any way the macro-reality of nature, which most artists generally do in some degree. He must be fully aware of what he wants his art to be, as well as what he does not want it to be. Both are interrelated problems! To leave them on the unfettered subconscious level results invariably in the artist's being tied to the old level of abstracting in some degree and in increasing degrees as time passes. So long as "Abstract" artists resist cultivating adequate "consciousness of abstracting," so long will they fail to release their art activities from the grip of past, outmoded and harmful methods of abstracting from reality. To the degree that the old remains in their art, to that degree will "Abstract" artists be prevented from fully reaching the new. This means they will remain in conflict with both the old and the new!

Our contention that most "Abstract" artists are more concerned with abstracting from the old level than from the new is decisively substantiated by the reactions most of them have to *genuine* Constructionist art which presents them with exactly the kind of experiences they allegedly seek. In Constructionist art there are no "fields and cottages" or any other resemblances to nature forms. Yet when most "Abstract" artists are confronted with it, they react in much the same fashion as the observer concentrating on the single snow flake, who is startled from his "previous occupation" by the disappearance of all the other snow flakes. That is, once the form influence of "fields and cottages" or nudes and apples, etc., is completely

31. R. W. Pickford: "Some Interpretations of a Painting called 'Abstraction'," *The British Journal of Medical Psychology,* XVIII:219, 1939–1941, The University Press, Cambridge.
32. Ibid., p. 221.

removed from the art content, the "pure form" enthusiasts are immediately at a loss as to what to make of it. In short, they are *not* having the kind of experience either in nature or art which they claim, since they find inadequate the very kind of art which most achieves what they themselves claim to seek. At best some of them claim that Constructionist art has taught them "emphasis upon exactness in the absorption of form by color, contour, and tone." [33] Such artists have come as close as one can to learning nothing from Constructionist art.

Some "Abstract" artists will deny that they are opposed to Constructionist art and do so in all sincerity. However, their insistence upon the use of the primitive medium of paint sets them in opposition, whether they wish to be or not. So they remain in the old conflict between the past and the newer levels of abstracting. Like their ex-Cubist predecessors, they do not know what to do, even though they are further from the older degree of abstracting from nature's appearances than their forerunners. Confused as they are between the old and new poles of abstracting, the "Abstract" artists, like all the Inbetweeners, reject the Constructionist as well as the old realistic arts. Yet significantly enough they insist on having present in their own art, elements found in the contents of both the old Realists and the Constructionists. Confined as they are between the old and the new, it is not surprising that most of them who once saw the necessity to eliminate the old content have eventually returned to it in later years and deserted the new for good.

One of the first to do this, and a very typical case, is Jean Helion. This artist has followed the same course we have seen taken so often before, that which the ex-Cubists were the first to follow—that is, deserted the fundamental direction indicated by Cubism. In an interview Helion was quoted as follows: "I have not changed my direction, only my level. Abstraction is a state of high concentration and beyond a certain point it becomes sterile. Abstraction was once a liberation from the mania of over-representation in painting. Now it is time to free abstraction from the mania of non-representation. It becomes a fear of life from which it must be freed. I did not escape from one prison to get back into another, no matter how beautiful." [34] Here obviously we see another variation of the same old rationalizations employed by all those who would desert the Inventive direction for a direct return to the manipulation of the old art contents. Helion cannot admit unequivocally that he has adopted the reverse of his former direction. He would rather have us believe that "abstraction" was solely for the purpose of liberating us "from the mania of over-representation," and that once this objective was attained, as he claims it has been, "abstraction" becomes "sterile" and so it appears that we must be "liberated" again, this time "from the mania of non-representation." What a theory of history—for this is what it is! Imagine artists spending their lives avoiding now this "mania," now that. It will be interesting to know when the next liberation will be in order, this time presumably again from copying.

Soon after his recent about-face Helion was claiming that a painting "must investigate the mysterious side of man with Surrealism." [35] And Surrealism, as a subsequent chapter will make clear, is the epitome of the retreat from Cubism.

Today "Abstract" art is practiced by a great number of artists. But it has little if any relation to the genuine direction once called "abstract," which sought to continue the direction of Cubism. Those who practice it today are simply using the efforts of earlier Abstract artists as a new way to liven up the expressionist method of art. (It follows, and quite consistently, that almost all so-called Abstract art has become largely a matter of automatic "writing," a glorified doodling. By trying to return to the free-associational and free-actional world of the child, these artists attempt to escape the crisis of the adult world of art.) In short, they are doing to Abstract art precisely what the ex-Cubists and their followers did to Cubism—making out of it a new but futile way to "liven" up the old subject-matter.

33. G. L. K. Morris: "American Abstract Artists," 1939 catalogue.

34. "Effect of Prison on Abstract Artist," The Newspaper *PM,* April 30, 1944.

35. Jean Helion: "How War Has Made Me Paint," *Art News,* XLIII:17, March 15, 1944. Compare Helion's theory with Sweeney's (see p. 433). They present similar views about Cubism (or Abstract art) and Surrealism.

And so humorously enough, we witness the preceding generation, the ex-Cubists, forever apologizing for Cubist art and disowning and denouncing "Abstract" art. While the present generation of "avante-guard," the "Abstract" artists, are now in their turn apologizing for the "pure form" variety of "Abstract" art, but not for Cubism. Thus progress comes, but with a heavy, cautious footstep. . . .[36]

Our analysis of the various groups of Inbetweeners has indicated that the differences between them are of no great significance. Of particular importance is their basic similarity to each other. In general the artists in each group are abstracting from the macro-level of reality, some distorting it to a greater, others to a lesser degree. These distortions are rationalized by artists and critics of each group as a better, or more moving reality; in other words, the Aristotelian theory of the ideal, of superiority to nature. (This will be the subject of discussion in the next chapter.) Moreover, the artists and critics of each group have assumed a basically similar position towards historical analysis. A direct consideration of the "Moderns'" general attitude towards history will give us a clearer understanding of the abstracting dilemma in which they are all involved.

Once the Transitional-Period of art was well on its way, the theorists of the new art encountered difficulty in making it compete with the old Academicians' interpretation of history. The latter could show an almost uninterrupted trend towards ever more accurate recording. They could show that the more advanced culture became, the more realistic art became; and that the more primitive the culture, the more distorted nature appeared in art. In short, they could present an "evolution" theory of art, something the Modernists were unable to do. The first reaction of the latter to this position, especially after 1910 (the beginning of the crisis of Modern art), seems to have been to belittle the value of history. Since the past would not fit neatly into the present, they tried to ignore it. Thus Clive Bell wrote in 1913: "To bother much about anything but the present is, we all agree, beneath the dignity of a healthy human animal." [37] And because he was unable to demonstrate that Modernism was the result of an orderly growth from the past, he vehemently denounced history and evolution, as the following clearly shows: "No one can have less right than I, or indeed, less inclination to assume the proud title of 'scientific historian': no one can care less about historical small-talk or be more at a loss to understand what precisely is meant by 'historical science.'" [38]

"... for assuredly, to understand art we need know nothing whatever about history." [39]

"To appreciate fully a work of art we require nothing but sensibility. To those that can hear Art speaks for itself: facts and dates do not. . . ." [40]

"... I can say whether this picture is better than that without the help of history. . . ." [41]

"I care very little when things were made, or why they were made; I care about their emotional significance to us." [42]

"... and whether history be true or false matters very little, since my hypothesis is not based

36. This chapter reached its present form some years ago. Since then "Abstract art" has become the rage. There now exist galleries which deal exclusively in this type of art, and recently the Chicago Art Institute put on a large exhibition of Abstract *and* Surrealist art: the two are appropriate companions, as will be seen more clearly in chapter 23. For in all this so-called Abstract art the significant characteristic to note, the one we have repeatedly emphasized, is the general dependence upon the forms of nature as a *crutch* to *stimulate a vague effort* to invent. In this situation Surrealistic devices serve to stimulate "interest" in the continued use of the old subject-matter. In this chapter we have given much discussion to the "pure formists" among Abstract artists, but since this was written the vast majority of such artists have discovered that they were attracted all along to the old art content, and so they are now doing consciously what before they did unconsciously. We have, however, decided to retain the emphasis upon the analysis of the pure-formists, since it clearly explains why the majority of "Abstract" artists were compelled to desert the Inventive direction for the useless manipulation of the objective world with the pathological vision of Surrealism.

37. Bell, *Art*, p. 251.   38. Ibid., p. 97.   39. Ibid., p. 98.   40. Ibid., p. 98.   41. Ibid., p. 99.   42. Ibid., p. 99.

on history but on personal experience, not on facts but on feelings. Historical fact and falsehood are of no consequence to people who try to deal with realities. They need not ask, 'Did this happen?'; they need ask only, 'Do I feel this?' " [43]

"To criticise a work of art historically is to play the science-besotted fool. No more disastrous theory ever issued from the brain of a charlatan than that of evolution in art. Giotto did not creep, a grub, that Titian might flaunt, a butterfly. To think of a man's art as leading on to the art of someone else is to misunderstand it." [44]

In spite of all Bell says to the contrary, what he is here giving us is *his* theory of art "history." He is simply telling us that he chooses to evaluate the art products of history without any responsibilities or criteria except his own feelings. This is but another way of saying that the historian is perfectly free to behave as he likes. Such an attitude persists to the present among the "Moderns," although it is not often so bluntly put. But contrary to Bell and the Modernists in general, we are all historians whether or not we like it or know it. Our only choice is whether we are to be responsible or irresponsible historians! Hence the desire expressed for unrestricted historical freedom is instructive.

In any case the "Moderns" rejected the Academicians' evolutional theory and replaced it with a *theory of history* that forced them unconsciously to assume that art reached its highest developments in the least developed cultures, and reached its greatest decadence the more the *general* culture of man progressed. For, after casting about a bit, the "Moderns" saw that in the art before that of the 5th century B.C. Greeks, in the art of the Primitives and Orientals and the medieval Christians, nature's appearances were also distorted. They then arrived at one of their basic but uninvestigated assumptions that Modern art is simply a "regeneration" of what all "great" art has always done. For them all "great" art is the same. Hence Clive Bell contends that, "essentially, all good art is of the same movement: there are only two kinds of art, good and bad." [45]

Thus he can also maintain that: "There is no mystery about Post-Impressionism; a good Post-Impressionist picture is good for precisely the same reasons that any other picture is good. The essential quality in art is permanent. Post-Impressionism, therefore, implies no violent break with the past." [46] And another writer can insist that Cézanne is a "classicist" and a "rediscoverer" who "has appeared in the role of a revolutionary because so vast a heritage of misconceptions and bad taste about painting had to be overcome." [47]

The theory implicit here is that art cannot evolve toward an ever greater future but only return toward a great past. Hence extreme measures are necessary at times in order to put art back on the road along which all great art always has travelled. It was this regenerative function which Cubism was conveniently discovered to have served. Thus, Picasso especially, in order to justify his subsequent position, has tried to put across the view that all art strives to do much the same thing when it is great. Accordingly, Picasso has written: "Cubism is no different from any other school of painting. The same principles and the same elements are common to all." [48] And: "Drawing, design and color are understood and practiced in cubism in the same spirit and manner that they are understood and practiced in all other schools." [49]

Cubism, which practically turned the world of art upside down, is thus regarded as directed along the same lines as all past art. There are undeniable similarities between Cubism and all past art, but the differences are more important, and that is exactly what Picasso and others have done their best to obscure. As previous studies have fully demonstrated, the differences between Cubism and past art were precisely what caused the furious controversies.

Thus we can understand Picasso's insistence that "Arts of transition do not exist. In the chronological history of art there are periods which are more positive, more complete than others. This means that there are periods in which there are better artists than in others." [50] Evolution, asymmetrical order,

43. Ibid., p. 100.
44. Ibid., p. 102.
45. Ibid., p. 42.
46. Ibid., p. 41.
47. Loran, *Cézanne's Composition*, p. 131.
48. Pablo Picasso: "Picasso Speaks," *The Arts*, 3:315–326, May, 1923.
49. Ibid.   50. Ibid.

155. Left, Cézanne, detail of figure 105; right, Picasso, detail of figure 110.

differences—all these are implicitly denied; art is always the same. But there is one difference, and a very simple one—there are bad and good artists, bad and good art. If all good art strives for the same objective, then a *particular* type of art, different from the past, cannot be implicit in Cubism.

Le Corbusier puts it this way: "Cubism had opened the door toward the universality of the great periods in art." [51]

The non-artist critics have come to much the same type of evaluations regarding Cubism. For instance Maurice Raynal writes: "In reality, however, let me say once for all that there is not and never has been any such thing as Cubism. I have accepted the term, the slur which Matisse flung at the movement, only as a generally intelligible description of the question under discussion. There has been merely a new orientation, a rejuvenation of the good painting of all time, practised by the best artists of to-day." [52] Still another non-artist critic, Maud Dale, contends: "Cubism was for the public a painful but very necessary operation, from which it is being permitted today to recover, in the hope that it is cured." [53]

It is almost beyond belief that Cubism, an art that created such a terrific upheaval, should at last turn out to be no different from what has always been great art in the past, to be, in fact, the most conservative of lessons in art. But this of course simplified everything for everybody, especially for the ex-Cubists in their desertion of Cubism. It is to Georges Braque's credit that he was not a party to this subterfuge. He wrote: "The art of our generation has suffered a great deal from the habits of comfort. To 'put our work over' subterfuge was used. The collector was made confident by having him believe that our paintings were in the direct line of the old masters. They should, on the contrary, have been presented under their true light, shown in their aggressiveness with all the ruptures they involve, and to have them accepted for what they are. By masquerading their dynamism, the collector was not placed in a heroic position, but was maintained in a state of torpor. The collector should, however, have been made aware that the importance of a work of art is measured by the conflicts it provokes, by the passion it raises, by its contribution of new elements, by its power to destroy accepted truths, by its role as leaven for the generation at work, as well as for the one that will succeed it." [54]

51. "Painting and Reality: A Discussion," in *Transition*, p. 117, No. 25, Fall, 1936.

52. Raynal, *Modern French Painters*, p. 22.

53. *Before Manet to Modigliani*, edited with a preface by Maud Dale, p. 7, Alfred A. Knopf, Inc., New York, 1929.

54. Braque, *Cahiers d'Art*, p. 21, Nos. 1–4, 1935.

156. Picasso, detail of figure 111; right, Mondrian, detail of figure 120(b) above.

The vast majority of the "Abstract" artists too have adopted the theory of "regeneration." Thus one of the most frequent spokesmen for "Abstract" artists wrote in 1939 that a "comprehensive survey of Abstract art throughout history" would include: "the Stone Age, and various phases of abstract art through Egypt, Greece, China, the Arab Periods (when all art was required to be non-representational), through Cubism, into the contemporary European and American movements." [55] The following by the same writer shows to what lengths one can carry vague generalizations about something referred to as "abstract": "The opposition which abstract art has encountered during its attempts at becoming established in America gives particular cause for surprise in that from earliest times the native American art was very abstract in feeling. The solemn colonial portraits (frequently the work of unsophisticated sign-painters), the carved figures on New England ship-prows, the recently discovered rural 'primitives,' not to mention countless utilitarian objects impeccable in taste, show that Americans were once a people for whom plastic and architectural sensibility was natural and inborn." [56]

These Modern artists and critics who claim to be concerned only with "pure form," maintain that all past great art was "great" because of the alleged "pure form" qualities it possessed, and they even maintain that the "pure form" can be seen quite apart from the subject-matter. Thus Venturi has written of Giorgione's art (figure 51): "Men, women, and trees were only an excuse to show his love of nature, light and color. . . . Giorgione excluded subject-matter and discovered the value of motif in painting." [57]

They have explained that past great artists were primarily concerned with "pure form," but that the surrounding culture imposed upon them the necessity for depicting the objects of the recognizable world. This rationalization has been used by all the various kinds of "Moderns." The difference lies only in the degree to which the particular type of Modernist insists upon the distortion of the old content. Each "Modern" criticizes those past or present arts in which the old content is recorded to a greater or lesser degree of accuracy than he himself contends is proper. In any case, however, the argument is that literal recording was imposed upon the past artists' "plastic" interests.

55. G. L. K. Morris: "American Abstract Artists" catalog, 1939.
56. Ibid. Several years later (see *Partisan Review*, VIII:403, September-October, 1941, "On the Mechanics of Abstract Painting") Morris changed his mind about past art being "abstract." Then during the late war he seems to have changed it once more, since he returned to the old content and painted "war scenes."
57. Lionello Venturi: *Art Criticism Now*, p. 9.

Albert Barnes, for example, who is particularly disposed to Post-Impressionist types of art, argues in favor of the early Italian painters in this manner: "A variety of circumstances prevented the early Italian painters from making a sharp distinction between their interest in design and their interest in illustrating a religious or historical narrative. The spirit and state of culture of the early Renaissance required that painting fulfill definite public functions. It was necessary that church frescoes should illustrate religious motives, that portraits should reproduce their originals, that pictures ordered by states or guilds should portray specific occurrences of interest to their purchasers. The general conditions were such that books were accessible only to the few, and their function was largely taken over by painting. All these circumstances made it impossible that properly plastic or pictorial motives should operate without constraint. The history of the transition to modern painting consists of an account of the removal of all such irrelevant compulsions, and of how the employment of the various plastic means came to be more and more directed to the realization of pure design." [58] Our analysis in earlier chapters has clearly demonstrated the fact that the recording of particular events by these early painters was certainly not the result of "irrelevant compulsions" arising from the general lack of adequate reading matter. This should be obvious if for no other reason than that such interests did not in the least diminish, but continued to increase, even after books became generally available. The presence of Photography in recent years only points up the fact that the recording interest is today prevalent to a most intense degree.

Therefore, we disagree that "what makes the art of Giotto great is not the religious subject-matter, but the plastic form, the design, by which deep human values are conveyed." [59] Obviously, the principal values conveyed by Giotto's art (figure 45) are precisely those which Barnes denies such a status; namely, the religious subject-matter. One can only arrive at this contention by identifying symptomatic characteristics as fundamental ones. That is, the Giotto type of art is restricted in its degree of recording accuracy, thus *appearing* comparable to what *appears to be* (but is not) the fundamental objective of Post-Impressionist works. Accordingly Barnes can write: "Giotto is, in his way, as far from literalism as Renoir." [60] And, "In this sense Giotto seems far more modern than such painters as Van Dyck, Reynolds, or David, in whom the rôle of painting is instrumental to such cheap human activities as personal flattery or surface imitation." [61] In comparing Giotto and Renoir only certain apparent similarities are considered. But if we consider why each type of artist was non-literal in his recording, then we are led to the more important matter of *differences*. It is no accident that we hear nothing about "pure design" in Giotto's times, but a great deal about how "real" was the painter's recording of reality. Recall Bocaccio's remarks about Giotto quoted in an earlier chapter. (See p. 186.) That which Barnes labels "plastic form" in Giotto's art is largely the result of primitive-like recordings, which were nevertheless as accurate as the painter was able to make them.

Recall what has been said previously about the function of the Inventive factor. The latter was used unconsciously by Giotto in order to compensate for the degree of inability he possessed to record accurately. This is more evident in Giotto than in any later, more realistic artists who were able to record considerably more of the particular arrangements of nature objects. In the most primitive of Primitive arts, the so-called design factor (the operation of the "Inventive" factor) is even more easily seen acting as a *substitute* for the artist's inability to record nature accurately. But the Inventive factor was in any case part of the general attempt to record, whereas in more recent arts this factor is part of a deliberate attempt to do just the opposite, i.e., nature's appearances are consciously distorted in the attempt to dispense with the recording objective and release the creative one. This has been most clearly shown in our analysis of the Transitional-Period arts. Therefore, the fundamental issue to recognize is that the Inventive factor operates in all art, in differing degrees, for differing, sometimes opposite purposes.

These differences may be sharply seen if we compare works of Giotto (figure 45), Ingres (figure 75) and Cézanne (figure 105). In Giotto we see that the organization of the content is the result of a naive effort to record reality. Such organizations are even more evident in the arts of children and Primitives. Little if any consciously directed knowledge is used to realize the particular color-form organizations of reality found in Primitive or primitive-like art. Such organizations are largely the result of the

58. Barnes, "The Transition to Modern Painting," p. 129, *Art and Education*.
59. Ibid., p. 129.   60. Ibid., p. 129.   61. Ibid., p. 130.

natural, "instinctive" operation of the organism. In the most primitive of Primitive arts the organization of the content is largely determined by the unconscious operation of the Inventive factor.[62] But the innovators of past art history were involved in constantly decreasing the Inventive factor in the content in order to increase their ability to record the specific form organizations as seen in the reality.

Hence in the work of Ingres there exists a high degree of consciously directed behavior. Here we see that the forms and their organization correspond to a considerable degree to the reality. The so-called "design" or organization of the color-form contents is largely determined by nature's appearances. The Inventive activity of man is reduced to a minimum as regards the content appearances.[63]

With Cézanne the situation is radically altered. We have seen that from Impressionism on the non-Camera innovators increasingly suppressed the recording factor in order increasingly to release their desire to create. Cézanne's organization of the content resulted from the deliberate conscious alterations of what he actually saw. Thus we can see how erroneous is the generally held notion that the intentions of such artists as Giotto were the same as Cézanne's or any of the Post-Impressionists.[64] For Giotto strove to record what he saw as accurately as he was able, while Cézanne's objective was research into the structure of nature.

But instead of differentiating between the Mimetic and Inventive factors, the general practice is to identify them. The result is the "chaos of Modern art." The important differences, say between a Giotto, a Cubist, or between both of these and a Mondrian, are ignored. The convenience of mere rejection is preferred to the usefulness of adequate, verifiable analysis of the great, crucial differences not only between past and present but also within the various contemporary arts.

As our historical analysis continually demonstrates, basic to the coherent comprehension of "art" is the realization that we are dealing always with a "problem of reality," a problem of abstracting, and not only with fantasy, as the Moderns would like to believe. Man's understanding of "reality" has changed with the times, and with it has changed the art corresponding to each time.

We must comprehend the past notions of reality and be conscious of those we ourselves abide by, if we are to understand properly the past and/or present. Then we can discern that the whole history of art is fundamentally characterized by man's increasingly or decreasingly accurate interpretations of the objective reality and so more useful, or more harmful, utilization of reality.

"Art," like "science," is the history of man's evolving penetration into the structure and potentialities of "reality." And, as scientists today are aware of more than the macro-level (they now are concerned with the sub-microscopic level), so today some artists are concerned with the Process Structure of reality. The present preoccupation with the Structural Process level emerged as a result of the asymmetrical evolution from earlier concerns with the macro-level. As new factors are discovered they invariably alter our previous notions and evaluations of past art and reality.

Each kind of art is a unique time-space event! To achieve greater synchronization between our observations and theories necessitates non-identification of the various *kinds* and *degrees* of abstracting that occur in art history. This would correct the current confusion over the different levels of the abstracting process evident in Modern art.

The essential points to note are the differences in the similarities as well as the similarities in the differences. The usual procedure in the evaluation of history has been to concentrate too exclusively upon similarities to the neglect of differences. An example is Barnes' continuity theory of art history. He contends "that painters who have been dead a thousand years looked upon the same world that we see, were moved by it in the same ways and sought to do the same things with it that we do. . . ."[65] This

62. Recall the Decorative period which we posited as the first stage of man's art; here we have the extreme example, since in the beginning, art was entirely "Inventive."

63. The highest development in this direction occurs in the medium of Photography where there exists the least amount of "invention" in forming the image of reality. Yet there exists a high degree of invention here as regards the *method* used to capture the image.

64. Of significance here is Cézanne's "indifference" to Byzantine art and the Italian primitives. See p. 308 in Gerstle Mack's *Paul Cézanne*. Gasquet informs us that Cézanne regarded Cimabue clumsy and Fra Angelico naive. See p. 168, Gasquet's *Paul Cézanne*, Editions Bernheim-Jeune, Paris, 1926.

65. Barnes and de Mazia, "Ancient Chinese and Modern European Paintings," Bignou Catalogue, May-June, 1943.

could well be called an identification theory of history: similarities are identified with each other by disregarding important differences involved in the similarities. Result: false knowledge.

Basic to the erroneous knowledge of present and past art is the attempt to answer the question "What IS art?" The implication of the question is that there can exist only one kind of "art," but the facts are blatant evidence of the existence of many arts—a plurality, not singularity! To ignore this is to invite difficulties at the start of any inquiry. Is it any surprise then that we are prevented from realizing the important differences between all arts and their asymmetrical relationships which constitute the process character of art history?

But, as we have seen, the Moderns' desire to achieve historical support for their own art, motivated them to identify the past and present. Although their desire for historical support was justified, the means for attaining it were not. For this was done by largely ignoring the critical differences between Modern and past arts. If the old Realists had claimed that *all* great art was "realistic," the Moderns claimed that *all* great art was not. Both tried to solve the irritating differences between themselves and those between the past and present with the futility of an either-or position.

In more recent years this either-or position has undergone an interesting change which indicates the essential conservatism of the new *status quo*—the Modernists. As we know, in the early part of the century it was considered revolutionary to go further and further away from the old type of art and its contents. This continued until the old contents had been practically dispensed with. Then, especially after 1914, it became "revolutionary" to do exactly the opposite! Providing an artist had once been so revolutionary as to eliminate "subject-matter," it became possible to be revolutionary by claiming that subject-matter was now, as Miro put it, of "increasing importance." Eventually, the ex-Cubists, and others such as Miro, were vociferously informing us that they were not "Abstract" artists. Now it would ordinarily be amusing to see erstwhile revolutionists hurry for shelter under the cover of tradition, if such nonsense were not so widely accepted as a revolutionary change of events. But obviously few knew what was happening. Few realized the tragic joke, that all these artists were supposedly being "radical" by returning to what they had once denied.

In the 20's and early 30's it was the fashion to point out that the "great Modern masters" could whip up a good Academic piece of realism; but now it has become the fashion to point out that the new editions of "Modern masters" have at one time or another done some "remarkable" work in Cubism, Abstract or Constructionist art. (The old Academician has frequently accused the Modern artist of merely following what is fashionable, and it would appear there is ample ground for his contention.) In these unique times, the old kind of conservative is no longer the potent force he was at the beginning of the Transitional-Period. He sits on the sidelines, waiting for the major contestants to conclude their conflict. The most destructive force today is exerted by the vast majority who present themselves as revolutionary, working out a new "wave of the future" and the like. Not only are they the most powerful today, but they have done immeasurable harm by greatly discrediting the genuine forces of progress. Because they, the rebels, are passing themselves off as revolutionists, while the genuine revolutionists are labelled rebels.

Today, then, the Modernists have actually come to the conclusion of their old opponents that nature's appearances must be retained in a non-Camera art content. The only reservation is that nature's appearances must be deliberately distorted rather than literally recorded to attain an alleged "better reality." And with this the present day successors of the old Realists agree. (The non-Camera literal recorder has almost completely disappeared from the scene.) The principal difference regarding distortion between contemporary "Realists" and "Moderns" is that the latter allow for unlimited distortion. Both are in complete agreement, however, in their rejection of that art which completely eliminates the old for the new created content. Both wish to abstract in the old *and* the new way; hence both produce pseudo-recording-pseudo-creative art—a compromise between the old and new. Both are even agreed that non-Camera art can usefully carry a "social content" (more correctly, a political propaganda content; because all art has some kind of a social content). This was an unheard of practice for the Modernists until the most popular member of this latter group called the tune with a cartoonist painting labelled *Guernica*.

Today, therefore, we are faced with two kinds of conservatives—the false successors to the old Realists and the false successors to the Transitional-Period artists. So the present situation is complicated by the fact that we have not only the usual conservative with us, but also a conservative in the false disguise of Modernism. Neither has learned that "what has gone, has gone forever." As a justification for his own point of view, each type of conservative has been reduced largely to violent attacks upon that part of history his opponent reveres. Each chooses to ignore the fact that the genuine innovators of the new direction have evolved something very different from the entire past history of man's art.[66] Each tries to escape the historical problems facing all of them, which arise from a period of profound crisis. Both types of conservatives try to escape into a static theory of art true for all times. To do so one must ignore the precedent of change for the fiction of some "permanent," unchanging quality in art. Yet this fiction would deny a legitimate existence to the very arts which all the conservatives revere, because the history of art is the history of change, and, every so often, as in our own times, of fundamental change. The *static, fictional* view of the historical process is based largely on similarities; the *dynamic, realistic view is based not only upon the similarities in the differences but also the differences in the similarities.*

The static attitude leaves us with a theory that says *all* "great" art *is* this, and only this, never anything else. It forces us to impose the demands of the arbitrary operation of language upon facts to which the language does not correspond in structure. Thus arises false knowledge: thus the chaos of Modern art, in which artists are floundering in confusion between the old and new methods of abstracting from reality.

The dynamic attitude leads to a mode of orientation that discloses "all great art" to be of many different kinds depending upon its historical context. Thus we are able to adopt methods of thinking, and so language, which permit us to adjust the *focus of our inquiries* according to the unique problem at hand. Then we discover that the process of history is comprised of asymmetrical order which calls for the elimination of the identification mechanism.

James Harvey Robinson frequently pointed out that the conservatives have continually invoked history to substantiate their claims, but that the innovators, not understanding how valuable to themselves a proper comprehension of the past can be, have neglected history as the weapon of their opponents. But, concludes Robinson, the innovator must realize that history is his weapon by right, and that he must wrest it from the destructive mentality of the conservative. After all, *the genuine innovator wants to see history objectively, and so truthfully because his position depends upon it! The conservative's position, however, compels him to falsify history because his position depends upon it!*

In a previous chapter we discussed the courageous effort which the Two-Dimensionalists made to comprehend consciously what was happening in the evolution of art and the positive contributions which they made towards achieving the new goals. We have shown that, unlike the Cubists, they did not lose their convictions as to the lasting value of Cubism, and that they understood its significance far more than the Cubists themselves. Thus Mondrian wrote of Cubism (as if in answer to Picasso's claim that "If cubism is an art of transition I am sure that the only thing that will come out of it is another form of cubism." [67]): "It is quite true that the 'work' of the cubists has not the faculty of being continued, of being developed: that it is perfect in itself. But it is not right to say that cubism, insofar as it is *plastic expression,* cannot be perfected or continued. On the contrary, the history of art clearly demonstrates to us that plastic is a continuous evolution." [68] And, to repeat an earlier quotation from Doesburg: "The rôle

66. It is not an accident that Picasso, Benton, Barnes, Biddle, Sweeney, Miro, Cheney, Dali, Venturi, Barr, Helion, Chagall, Braque, Lipchitz, etc.—all superficially at least representative of different positions, are fundamentally in agreement on one thing —that Cubism went too far from what they imagine art should be today.

67. Pablo Picasso: "Picasso Speaks," *The Arts,* 3:315-326, May, 1923.

68. "De l'Art Abstrait"; "Réponse de Piet Mondrian," *Cahiers d' Art,* p. 41, No. 1, 1931.

of cubism has been precisely that of a poser of problems, with reference to the future mode of artistic creation, diametrically opposed to all traditionalism and all naturalistic imitation, and as such its business is to raise all sorts of new questions. . . ." Mondrian also wrote: "One can never appreciate sufficiently the splendid effort of cubism, which broke with the natural appearance of things and, partially, with limited form. Its determination of space by the exact construction of volumes is prodigious. Thus the foundation was laid upon which a plastic of pure relationships, of free rhythm, which until now was the prisoner of limited form, could arise.

"If there had been enough consciousness to understand in what measure limited form is hostile to true plastic and in what measure it is individual and tragic, there would have been less risk of falling back into romanticism or into classicism, as happens to modern movements in general." [69] And: "Evidently, cubist work, perfect in itself, could not be further perfected after its apogee. There remained two solutions for it: either to retreat on the natural side, or else to continue its plastic toward the abstract, that is to say, to become neoplastic.

"Logically, the cubist artists themselves could not make this last step: they would have denied their own nature. Just as they succeeded Cézanne, others had to continue cubist plastic. And that has been done." [70] He could well say "And that has been done," for he was one of the few who genuinely continued the direction implicit in Cubism. He was, in fact, in his Cubist works, the greatest Cubist of them all. [71]

But in setting forth Mondrian as one of the great painters of his generation, and, indeed, the last great *painter* of history, we must point out his errors as well. We must recognize that the works and theories of *any* artist are never perfect. But where the great innovators are concerned, it is almost a rule in recent history that their conservative contemporaries pronounce them *all* bad, while the conservatives of the following generation pronounce them *all* good. The consideration of Mondrian's imperfections, as well as his achievements, is especially crucial now that he has died, and thus is in a proper state for receiving a fate opposite to that which he received in life, i.e., being clothed with the infallibility of omniscience.

Our criticisms of certain aspects of Mondrian's activities do not detract in the slightest from the extremely important, desirable values which this artist has produced for the evolution of man's art. We can no more do this to Mondrian's work than we can detract from the value of Picasso's contributions to the development of Cubism. It is especially necessary to point out the regressive aspects of Mondrian's last works and theories for the very important reason that younger artists, who are about to arrive on the scene and eventually take over the task of art, need to discriminate between the developmental and the negative aspects of Mondrian's *or any other artist's work and theories.* This is imperative if they are to successfully grasp the opportunities which await them and were made possible by such men as Mondrian. It is with this attitude that we propose to examine wherein Mondrian too was involved in the dilemma of contemporary abstracting.

We have already commented on the Cubists' *opening* up of the forms of nature in order to reach the artist-inventor stage of human behavior; and have spoken of the fact that when these forms were finally opened enough so that the Inventive effort was about to be freed, the Cubists, frightened away, closed the forms of their art *again* around the forms of nature—i.e., they returned to the old content. But by their previous dissection of the nature object the Cubists had penetrated beyond the old content. In this process of dissection planes emerged, largely invented, which revealed to artists like Mondrian the possibility of inventively organizing space as part of the interior as well as the exterior structure of the art object, rather than considering space as merely a medium into which were dropped blocks or chunks of forms, forms in some degree imitative of nature. Thus Mondrian opened the forms of nature until he reached the Inventive content, but he never went on to close them completely. He then evolved an art

69. Ibid., p. 42.

70. Ibid., pp. 42–43.

71. It is interesting to note that Mondrian (like Monet and other Impressionists) turned in his Cubist period to subjects like buildings, trees, and the sea—subjects where one could achieve greater freedom with the nature objects than was possible with human and even still-life forms. The latter subjects were the chief forms employed by the original Cubists.

157. Georges Vantongerloo, Volume Construction, 1918. Courtesy of The Art of This Century.

which was to characterize the remainder of his life work. Mondrian painted the whole of his canvas surface white with space. Across this space he stretched black lines firmly, tightly and cleanly, thus making the space visible and inventively organized. Into certain of these areas he would slide red, blue, and yellow planes to shut out the white space, thus obtaining an organizational balance against the rest of his canvas, through which the illusion of space literally poured. To further the effect of the lines in space, Mondrian made the frames of his paintings recede in two or three steps, as though to push forward the lines. Incidentally, the Two-Dimensionalists worked in the proper medium only when they made the frames for their paintings. These frames play an important role *in* the work. So long as we reproduce Two-Dimensional art without the frames, we are reproducing only a part of the work.[72] Inside some of Mondrian's paintings,

72. The author regrets that he was unable to obtain any photographs of Two-Dimensional art which included the frames, except in two cases, and one of these frames was such a careless affair, both in workmanship and organization, that it was necessary to delete it from the reproduction, for it certainly did not appear to be the work of the artist.

we find him using thick paint to make raised surfaces for certain areas, as though he wished to make the space and lines real and not mere linear illusions.[73]

But in all this effort to make the linear medium do what only a three-dimensional medium could properly do, the painter was led to the frustration and compromise that had similarly occurred among the sculptors of the Renaissance, who tried to do what only painters could properly do. Many of the actions of the Two-Dimensionalists reveal that they felt the lack of the third dimension.

For instance, beginning in 1915 the Two-Dimensionalist, Malevitch, was making a series of perspective recordings of three-dimensional problems;[74] while Lissitzky considered that he was evolving a transition between painting and Architecture.[75] All this is evidence of the disturbance of the three-dimensional factor in the works of the Two-Dimensionalists.

Finally among the De Stijlists are to be found actual Constructionists like Georges Vantongerloo (figure 157) and later César Domela (figure 140). Others such as Doesburg were Architects.

In any case, the Two-Dimensionalists went steadily further away from the old macro-level of abstracting, away from what Mondrian called the "limiting form" of nature, until eventually they were abstracting on the new reality level. They pushed the old medium as far as it could be taken in the new direction. They made clear to a considerable degree the new method of abstracting a "created" contents for man's art, even though they failed to achieve the more complete reality for that contents. Just as important, the results of their efforts had shown that painting as a medium was no longer useful.

Although the change to two-dimensionality did help to get away from the old content, this was, as we have already pointed out, an inadequate solution; the consequences were that certain dimensional characteristics of the reality process were lost, thus creating a crucial defect in the art product and leading to a dead end in the painting medium. Mondrian, as we have already noted, was unable to take the final step that would have freed him entirely from the old content and the old primitive medium that went with it. To the degree that one is confined to the old medium or content, to *that degree* one is limited in reaching the new. And, as we shall make clear, for Mondrian the linear medium appeared not only legitimate but even superior to all others for the fullest achievement of the new art. This was his fundamental error in judging the *new relations* between the *artist,* his *medium* and *nature.*

The question arises of why an artist should choose a medium that compelled him to work in a two-dimensional context. First of all, we must understand that Mondrian applied the term "limiting form" not only to natural forms but also to what he called "closed" forms; "closed" forms were more "limited" than "open forms." He explained that a circle was a "closed" form as contrasted with a segment of a circle, which was more "open," and that the straight line was even less "limited" than the curve.[76] Hence he wrote: "Non-figurative art is created by establishing *a dynamic rhythm of determinate mutual relations* which *excludes the formation of any particular form."* [77] Elsewhere he wrote: "Volumes have a naturalistic expression." [78] This statement is certainly correct; his error was in his evaluation of it as a limitation, as though "natural" characteristics were a defect.

Hence he contended that the limitations of the appearances of nature cannot be eliminated in painting unless three-dimensional space is "reduced" to two-dimensional space: "In architecture and sculpture three-dimensional construction is inevitable, but in painting three-dimensional space has to be reduced to two-dimensional appearance. This is necessary not only to conform with the canvas *but to destroy the natural expression of form and space."* (emphasis ours)[79] This was more clearly and unequivocally stated

73. How essential the thick and thin layers of paint are to Mondrian's work can easily be demonstrated when this raised effect is lost or deliberately ignored in the method usually employed to reproduce his works. Many, not understanding how essential this factor is, or, more likely, never having observed it in the original, have carelessly reproduced his works by means of the cheaper zinc-plate process, which is perfectly flat and thus does not show the raised effect, to mention only this quality. Apparently they saw only straight, colored lines and so assumed that the zinc-plate method provided adequate reproduction.

74. *Cubism and Abstract Art,* preface and text by Alfred H. Barr, Jr., p. 124, Museum of Modern Art, New York, 1936.

75. Ibid., p. 126.

76. Mondrian, "A New Realism," *Plastic Art and Pure Plastic Art,* p. 18, Wittenborn and Co.

77. Mondrian, "Plastic Art and Pure Plastic Art," ibid., p. 58.

78. Mondrian, "A New Realism," ibid., p. 26.

79. Ibid., p. 19.

in an early paper: "In the New Plastic, painting no longer expresses itself by apparent *corporeality* which confers natural expression. To the contrary, it is expressed plastically by *plane within plane.* [editor's note: The action of planes within the 'picture' or surface plane.] By reducing three-dimensional corporeality in painting to a plane, *it expresses pure relationship.*" [80] This was tantamount to contending that the most complete elimination of the old content and the most complete realization of the new could be achieved only in painting. In fact, he wrote: "It is in *painting* that New Plastic achieved complete expression for the first time." [81] For Mondrian all other mediums could only approach the achievements of painting in some degree, but never supersede them.

Mondrian failed to present anything that could be considered a verifiable justification for the above theory; but we can understand from it his apparent reservations concerning Constructionist art. For he contended that both volume and closed forms or shapes, even though not imitating nature forms, never-theless had natural characteristics and hence must be avoided. This is the very opposite of the position we have adopted. For we maintain that the absence of actual three-dimensional characteristics harmfully and unnecessarily limits the Inventive artist from achieving the more adequate reality that is both possible and critically necessary for the new art. But for Mondrian sculpture, Architecture, and by implication Constructionist art, were what he called "morphoplastic," while painting arrived at the "pure plastic." Psycho-logically, since he insisted on being a painter in the new art, he was unable to realize that Construc-tionists, in assuming the "closed" or three-dimensional character of nature were thus simply acquiring an extremely important structural characteristic of reality towards the realization of *adequate reality* for the contents of the new art. This did not necessitate copying the forms of nature in any degree, as Mondrian's objections imply; the Constructionists have amply demonstrated that they can create relations of forms that are *not* the forms or relations of forms in nature; i.e., they do not have the appearances of nature objects. Constructionists *create* their art, they do not imitate nature-art; they achieve what Mondrian himself sought, only they achieve a more adequate reality for their content.

For the problem at hand is not to "conform with the canvas," as Mondrian said, but to conform with the requirements of reality. In his reasoning Mondrian was unconsciously contending that the limitations of the canvas offered greater reality possibilities than the structural example of nature, the natural process. But such a solution only reduced the structural characteristics of reality in art. This could only lead to the artist's being limited as regards the full potentialities of abstracting from the structural building method of nature. For all that Mondrian did was to reduce the *number* of characteristics which he abstracted from the Process Structure of reality: i.e., he abstracted form-space into a two-dimensional or shape-space limitation. Result: when the artist limited himself in the number of characteristics he could abstract from the reality, he was led to a particular type of "limiting form" as compared to the more adequate fulfillment possible to the new art content. Thus while Mondrian repeatedly warned against the "limited form," nevertheless by restricting himself to two-dimensional painting, he was confined to *limited invention.*

Mondrian's attempt to achieve a "neutral" content, although correct in principle, was carried to harmful extremes in practice. Thus he wrote: "We can consider all forms relatively neutral that do not show *any relationship* with the natural aspect of things or with any 'idea.'" (emphasis ours) [82] This is impossible, unless one is to believe that any artist can *exclude all* abstracting from nature. This theory of the "neutral form" only led Mondrian to the "limited form" and "limited invention," as noted above.

The great change in our century consists essentially in a reorientation of the relationships between nature and man's efforts at art. But as in his medium, so inevitably in his content Mondrian did not adequately resolve the contemporary artist's conflict with nature. He tried to resolve this conflict by speaking of "detachment from the oppression of nature," [83] and declared: "In order that art may be really

80. Piet Mondrian: *Le Neo-Plasticisme,* p. 5, Editions de l'Effort Moderne, Leonce Rosenberg, Paris, 1920; all translations from this article by Harry Holtzman and Martin James.

81. Ibid., p. 4; see also p. 6.

82. Mondrian, "A New Realism," *Plastic Art and Pure Plastic Art,* p. 20.

83. Mondrian, "Pure Plastic Art," ibid., p. 32.

abstract, in other words, that it should not represent relations with the natural aspect of things, the law of the *denaturalization of matter* is of fundamental importance." [84] This, of course, was impossible!

But for Mondrian there existed a certain kind of hostility to nature, and so inconsistencies in his theories.

Because of the conflicts between his two-dimensional, primitive medium and the three-dimensional environment of objective reality, Mondrian was forced to be in conflict with nature. In the new view of art and reality man no longer needs to be insecure before nature; rather man as an artist now sees himself as nature—not in opposition to nature—a nature ever open to greater opportunities; man-nature in harmony with the environment-nature as a ONENESS! Hence man is but a part, a particular aspect or level of nature in everything he does.

Mondrian's critical error was in not achieving all the correlation possible between his art and the Structural Process of reality. That correlation had to be not between art and the *results* of nature's Structural Process, but between the structural *methods* by which nature's results and the new art-results are produced. If artists were confronted with the task of constructing an airplane they would understand this better. For in such activities one is automatically compelled to conform to the laws of nature, or else! In art one can delude himself more easily that this is not necessary. Actually the laws of nature are as inescapable in the creation of art as in the creation of airplanes!

It is perhaps significant that Mondrian appeared to be reluctant to go beyond one direct mention of Constructionist art in his writings. In one brief reference he says of the Constructionists and Neo-Plasticists that "there always remained differences in viewpoints." [85] All further references to Constructionist art must be gleaned from the implications of his general theories. Yet in this three-dimensional art there occurred the change of medium that could give to the new content adequate reality.

It was precisely this double change, of both content and vehicle or medium, such as occurs in Constructionist art, which Mondrian advocated for the artists of music. He criticized the music which did not thus change, because "it still preserves the *old bases* in its construction," (emphasis ours) and said that the *"old tonic scale like the usual instruments must be banished from Music if the new spirit is to be plastically expressed."* Further he says that the old instruments must be replaced by *"electric, magnetic, mechanical means."* [86] These are the very kinds of criticisms we have made regarding Mondrian's own medium and his proposed objective. Hence, in one art—music—Mondrian recognized the need for eliminating the old mediums if the new content was to be achieved; but in his own field he barely mentioned by direct reference Constructionist art, which accomplished precisely such a change. Instead he continued to employ one of the oldest primitive mediums of art for what he considered the most adequate realization of the new content.

Mondrian's theoretical position like his art is in some respects between that of the Cubists and the Constructionists. The Cubists, once they had considerably eliminated nature objects, attempted a pseudo-solution of the problem of inventing the content by abstracting from recognizable man-made, invented objects (bottles, musical instruments, etc.). The "closing" of the forms, once the old nature content had been eliminated, brought to a climax the whole problem of inventing the content. For then the artist had the choice of changing his medium in order to realize adequate reality for his *closed invented forms,* or, if he continued the old primitive painting medium, of eventually being forced to return to the old macro-content in some manner and degree in order to achieve some semblance of reality for the closed content. In other words, to close the forms in the painting medium either drives one back to the old contents in one degree or another, as happened with the Cubists, or drives one out of painting to the new medium of the Constructionists.

---

84. Mondrian, "Plastic Art and Pure Plastic Art," ibid., p. 57.

85. Mondrian, "Toward the True Vision of Reality," ibid., p. 14. We limit this statement only to those writings we have been able to see—those in *Cahiers d'Art* and *Plastic Art and Pure Plastic Art* (Wittenborn) and *Le Neo-Plasticisme* (1920). Our efforts to secure his *De Stijl* articles, and many others he may have written, have been unsuccessful.

86. Mondrian, *Le Neo-Plasticisme*, p. 13.

158. Left, Piet Mondrian, Composition, 1919. Rijks Museum, Kröller-Müller, Otterloo, The Netherlands. Right, Piet Mondrian, Victory Boogie-Woogie, 1943-1944. Miller Company Collection, Meriden, Connecticut.

Significantly, Mondrian staved off the problem of closed forms until his last few works, when we see many closed *shapes,* at least a closing on the two-dimensional plane. In his very last work, *Victory Boogie-Woogie* (figure 158, right), we see a myriad of many closed shapes—where before there had only been a few—but we still find the closed shapes spilling off the edge of the canvas as unfinished shapes. In this last work the action of closing predominates, but only a two-dimensional attempt to create complete, closed relations. Mondrian was thus being driven by the force of the characteristics of reality on the way to the closed form (shape)—away from the open, the unfinished, away from the fragment of creation and fragment of reality—just as years before the Cubists were compelled to close their shapes. Hence, in the end, in his last painting, Mondrian made a desperate effort to reach a more adequate reality, a more adequate completion of his invented art content—a closed, that is, a unified, completed result.

Therefore, it would be incorrect to evaluate the last works of Mondrian as wholly regressive. For in these works, especially the Boogie-Woogie works, we see the artist making a desperate effort to further the evolution of his art. That is, he attempted to free himself from the limited reality of his previous works and move toward the further possibilities of the new. In this attempt Mondrian resorted to the old but erroneous solution of manipulating the macro-reality. Early in his career this solution had enabled him to evolve successfully from and beyond Cubism, i.e., he manipulated the macro-reality to ever higher levels of abstraction until his work reached the point where it was possible for him to invent arrangements of line-color-space directly and thus make the transition to abstracting from the Structural Process level of reality. But to resort to this method of abstracting in the last period of his art could only result largely in regression from the new to the older level of abstraction. Thus we see that during the last few years his art was again labelled as if it represented macro-reality—*Trafalgar Square, Place de la Concorde, New York City, Broadway Boogie-Woogie, Victory Boogie-Woogie,* etc. The titles of these last works form a significant contrast to his former titles, such as *Composition, Composition in White, Black and Red,* etc. In this we see a turning back toward the old method of abstracting, which *had formerly been* a stage in Mondrian's development towards the new viewpoint, but which he had left far behind. (See figures 158, 159, 160, 120a and 120b.)

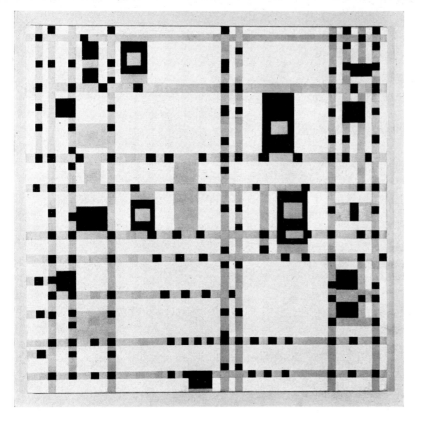

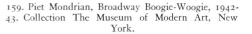

159. Piet Mondrian, Broadway Boogie-Woogie, 1942-43. Collection The Museum of Modern Art, New York.

Of course one can say, why split such fine hairs about it? Surely no one will see Trafalgar Square or Boogie-Woogie in his art. But this is not *entirely* correct; we are forgetting the identification mechanism! A very simple experiment will prove it: take the *Broadway Boogie-Woogie* painting and call it *Russian Tanks on Parade in Red Square* or *Aerial View of Traffic in Chicago,* and notice that these labels immediately change the whole character of the response to that which Mondrian called something else. And this same identificational projection operated upon the artist when he made the paintings. But this is not the important question. If Mondrian was assuming that some degree of representation of the macro-reality was now quite proper, then he had radically altered his previous theories; thus the problem of art revolved again around the question of how we should abstract from the old level, and not whether we should abstract only from the old or only from the new level. Inevitably then these last works comprised *a retreat* towards the old level of abstracting, against which he himself had so frequently and correctly warned.

Moreover, regardless of whether the artist abstracts from Boogie-Woogie, Place de la Concorde, or what not, either in a most realistic manner or in a highly "abstracted" manner, the Films can do a more useful job of recording such events and experiences connected with them. So long as we are interested in Trafalgar Square, a Film of it is incomparably more to the point than to have someone reduce that experience for us to a matter of a few lines on a canvas. If, on the other hand, we are interested in an invented arrangement of lines on the surface of a canvas, we detract from such an objective to that extent that we make these lines stand for something which they obviously are *not*! This is true even if the painting is not abstracted from nature's appearances but is labelled with the name of any aspect of nature's appearances. Similarly we detract from the experience of Trafalgar Square by making it into something which it obviously IS NOT. Under these circumstances, an artist is caught coming and going. The obvious, perhaps too obvious, fact is that an arrangement of straight lines is no more representative of Trafalgar Square than Trafalgar Square is representative of an arrangement of straight lines. To make either one representative of the other is to represent both falsely.

452

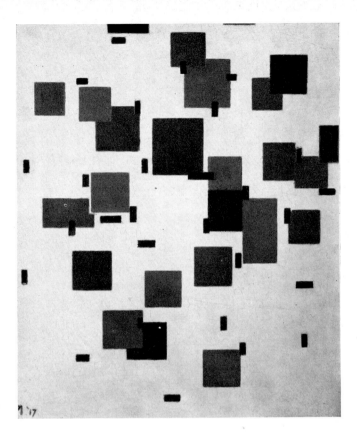

160. Piet Mondrian, Composition, 1917. Rijks Museum, Kröller-
Müller, Otterloo, The Netherlands.

We maintain that in the retreat from the direct, uncompromising action of inventing a content,
Boogie-Woogie, or whatever subject is used, operates merely to give the artist some recognizable phenomenon which excites into being some degree of invention, and at the same time retains some semblance
of reality. This is pseudo-invention, at best limited invention, because the artist in this case must again
depend upon the manipulation of nature's appearances in order to exercise his ability to invent. In this
sense, whether consciously or not, the artist is abstracting from nature's macroscopic reality. True, he is
abstracting in higher degrees than did artists of the past, but at the same time he produces greater fantasies.
But all this had been done early in the century, and to repeat it was not only useless but far more serious,
a regression.

So in his last works Mondrian abstracted merely to a higher degree from the appearances of
nature than do others who abstract from this same level. Reflecting upon this *final* stage of Mondrian's work,
one begins to realize that the regressions of his last works were inevitable, principally because he had carried
the new direction to the "abyss," to the very limit permitted by the old hand medium of paint. To develop
further it would have been necessary for the artist to discard the old medium. This he did not do, and
because he did not, there was only one course open to him, as change he eventually must. The only
change possible with the paint medium was a return in one degree or another to the old manner of
abstracting from nature's appearances. For when painters insist on retaining the old medium, there occurs
a split between the desire to invent directly and to "invent" by merely manipulating the inventions from
fields of human enterprise other than art; e.g., the Cubists' bottles and glasses and Mondrian's city streets.
In short, since life is a dynamic process which cannot be stopped at some static point, one is compelled to
progress or else one *must* regress.

Thus while his objective was one of further evolution, Mondrian's method for achieving it
forced his work in the reverse direction. Consequently it is no surprise to find great similarities not only
between the early and late theories of Mondrian but also between the early and late paintings. To avoid

these errors Mondrian would have had to change from the primitive to the advanced or Machine mediums of the present.

As a Two-Dimensionalist he could not fully accept the obvious structure of reality without realizing that his medium imposed a limiting effect upon the reality structure of his art-result. And if he assumed three-dimensional illusionistic characteristics in his medium, he would eventually be compelled to retreat to the old content, as he noted usually occurred in the case of painters who retained the third dimension. (This actually happened in his own case later, when he began to move *towards* the three-dimensional solution by increasingly employing closed shapes.) Since he insisted on being a painter, there was no alternative but to consider three-dimensional phenomena as defects or limitations, and to imply that their elimination led to results superior to the visual structure of reality. When Mondrian reached the point where he was ready to dispense with the old, he failed to do so; from there on the old inevitably increased its hold upon his subsequent theories and art, until he tended towards a Surrealist view, as is seen in works such as his *Victory Boogie-Woogie.*

Like every innovator, Mondrian was able to go so far and no further; but he has left behind him works which will remain among the great landmarks in the evolution of man's history as artist. His great importance is far from recognized, even by some of his alleged admirers. Of Mondrian we must repeat what he so well observed about the Cubists in 1931: "Logically, the cubist artists themselves could not make this last step: they would have denied their own nature. Just as they succeeded Cézanne, others had to continue cubist plastic. And that has been done." Mondrian succeeded the Cubists and developed their discoveries further. Now others must continue the work of Mondrian; and this is being done. As he himself wrote: "The past has a *tyrannic* influence which is difficult to escape. The worst is that there is always something of the past *within us.*" [87] In the end this is true of all of us!

Perhaps Mondrian's great contribution was his optimism about the future direction which he was helping to form. This was what enabled him to continue painting usefully until a few years before his life ended. In his more productive years he was able to see vaguely the need for an art which not only changed the contents but the medium as well. Thus (1937) he spoke of the need for a "more or less mechanical execution" and "the employment of materials produced by industry," and said that thereby "an art more real and more objective in relation to life than painting would arise." [88] But this had already been begun by the original Constructionists as long ago as 1913-1915. In his last writings Mondrian no longer voiced these theories.

Since he failed, in the end, to dispense with the old, primitive, two-dimensional medium, in both his works and theories he was eventually compelled to regress. Thus in 1937, when his painting and theory were still in a developmental stage, Mondrian wrote of "the *naturalistic conception* and the *descriptive or literary orientation*: both a real danger to purely abstract art." [89] But in 1941 he wrote: "It would be erroneous to limit modern plastic art to narrow frontiers. Two principal expressions exist: one of them uses more or less *naturalistic forms and colors*; the other employs more or less *purified means of expression.* These two expressions appear under different names, but all names are approximate, partial, and therefore misleading.

"It appears as though these two expressions oppose each other, but when we observe that in different ways both show the same search for freedom, then we see their unity. For all modern art reveals a *liberation from the oppression of the past.*

"Modern art rejects the methods of expression used in the past, *but continues its real content. It continues what the art of the past began: the transformation of natural vision. What the art of the past accomplished more or less invisibly due to the oppression of the epoch, modern art accomplishes more visibly.*" [90]

87. Mondrian, "Liberation from Oppression in Art and Life," *Plastic Art and Pure Plastic Art,* p. 41.

88. Mondrian, "Plastic Art and Pure Plastic Art," ibid., p. 61.

89. Ibid., p. 58.

90. Mondrian, "Liberation from Oppression in Art and Life," *Plastic Art and Pure Plastic Art,* pp. 41-42.

161. Piet Mondrian, Composition with Blue and White, 1935. Courtesy, Wadsworth Atheneum, Hartford.

On the one hand Mondrian maintains that past artists were frustrated by the "oppression of an epoch," but what could that "oppression" have been but the demands of the old content, the very content incidentally which continues to be apparent in the "Modern art," of which Mondrian finally approved. This content, however, did not oppress the *innovators* of the past; it only oppresses the *non*-Camera artists of the present! The problem is not clarified when Mondrian makes nebulous the distinction between his own so-called purified art and that of those who used "naturalistic" forms, by pointing out that "names" are misleading. After all this is not the fault of language!

Our history of painting and sculpture has shown that the earliest artists strove deliberately from the invented line towards the recording of the macro-level of reality. Ever increasing accuracy was sought until the Camera was produced to continue recording development. After that, through the efforts of the Transitional-Period artists, the transformation of the non-Camera content was begun. But the function of this transformation was at no point to destroy the old content, as some believe, since the old content was obviously continued into further development by the Camera artists. The basic function of this transformation was to reach the realization of a new content, *one created by man*. This content, however, was not *"hidden in the individual rhythm of the limiting form."* [91] Such a notion can only lead the artist to continue abstracting in some way on the old reality level. What was required was the realization of a consciousness of the new abstracting level, i.e., the Structural Process character of reality; this supplied *the method for creating man's own invented art-result.*

We repeat, the objective of past innovators was primarily *to record nature's art;* while the objective of present day non-Camera *innovators is to invent a man-art!* Such a distinction, for apparent and significant reasons, does not compel us to whittle the old artists down to "invisibles."

In the end Mondrian's position became almost indistinguishable from that of the Inbetweeners. This is seen by continuing the above quotation regarding the "two expressions" in Modern art: "All the art of the past shows an exaggeration of the tension of lines and forms, changes in the natural colors and proportions: a transformation of reality's natural aspect. Art has never been a copy of nature, for such a copy would not have been strong enough to evoke human emotion. [92] *The living beauty of nature* cannot be copied: it can only be *expressed.*

"Modern times create a greater transformation of reality; sometimes by means of freer composition, freer colors and forms (academic art, realism, surrealism) and sometimes by a more consequent transformation of forms and their relations (abstract art). Bound together by unchangeable plastic laws, the different tendencies of modern art continue the struggle for a more real establishment of the true content of art." [93] That past artists (excluding those in regressive periods and, to a certain degree, the Classicists) strove to copy nature is so obvious that there is no need to argue the point. It is of course true that *all* past artists unavoidably made "changes in the natural color and proportions," yet if one observes past art as-a-whole this is seen as a defect and not as the realization of the objective striven for. If one puts emphasis upon the impossibility of realizing a perfect copy of nature, one can then conveniently assume that artists have no other choice but to strive towards some other objective. The obvious fact is that recording perfection was sought, regardless of the impossibility of realizing absolute perfection, and continues to be sought right up to the present day by genuine Camera artists. If absolute perfection were the final criterion as to whether one should attempt *any* particular art direction, then no artist would ever be able to make *any* kind of art. Absolute perfection in any art is an impossibility. Being too perfectionist in his evaluations of the past, Mondrian arrived at certain false assumptions about it; and not being rigorous enough in his final evaluations about the present, he thus again arrived at certain false basic assumptions.

As a matter of fact, he contradicts one of the very points he continually stressed in his above evaluation of the past and the present users of natural forms. That is, he repeatedly emphasized the necessity

91. Mondrian, "Pure Plastic Art," ibid., p. 31.

92. Regarding this remark, it is doubtful if anyone would contend today, confronted with the products of the moving Film (to take the most literal record of all) that "such a copy would not [be] . . . . strong enough to evoke human emotion." But then to speak simply of "human emotion" is meaningless, since *all* art obviously does arouse "human emotion" of some kind.

93. Mondrian, "Liberation from Oppression in Art and Life," *Plastic Art and Pure Plastic Art*, p. 42.

for greater objectivity in the artist's orientation to reality. Here we submit that the artists of the past who sought to achieve ever greater realism were the ones who achieved an ever greater increase of the then objective factor in art. Furthermore, those non-Camera artists in the present, to the degree that they are tied to the appearances of nature forms (be their art called Pepsi-Cola calendar art, Picassoism, Bentonism, or what have you), are precisely the ones who are overly subjective. And this would include all the artists, in one degree or another, who Mondrian claims are pursuing the new direction. Actually, those who have properly pursued art with the Camera and in the Constructionist direction are the only ones today who are achieving an ever increasing objectivity in their orientations to reality.

But Mondrian failed to realize fully enough that the *evolution* of art had been *transformed* into the two Machine-arts of the Camera and Constructions and not into the two non-Camera directions he posits, i.e., the one in which "naturalistic" forms are used ("academic art, realism, surrealism"); and "abstract art," in which natural forms are (*sometimes*) not used. Of the two art groups which Mondrian accepts, the first is composed of impotent painters who cling to the old Aristotelian art contents; while the second group is composed of those who have only partially realized the new direction, who are held back (to borrow Mondrian's own words) by the "tyrannic influence" of the past "which is difficult to escape." There certainly exist "two principal expressions," or rather two *desirable* directions for art, but these consist of the Camera and Constructionist art. In one direction artists employ the forms of nature, but they are Photographers, not painters or sculptors; artists in the other direction employ the created forms of man, and these too are not painters or sculptors. Both reject the old, now limiting mediums. Both use Machines, the new art tools of man!

This is not to forget that Mondrian's contribution to the Constructionist direction is a major one, but rather, to point out how this contribution can be freed to its most adequate realization.

In the old way the artist abstracted from the results of nature's Structural Process, so that art and nature were similar in the sense that this method of art *recorded* the macro-level *results* of nature's building method: in the new way the artist abstracts from the structural level so that art and nature are similar in structure in the sense that the *artist's structural building method is similar to the structural building method of nature*. Thus non-Camera art is no longer an imitation (recording), in any way, of the *results* of nature's building process, but achieves results peculiar to man and not to be found in unaided nature "art."

It was this latter objective which Paul Cézanne was unconsciously referring to when he said: *"Art is a harmony parallel with the harmony of nature."*

457

Should we arrange our present beliefs and opinions on the basis of their age, we should find that some of them were very, very old, going back to primitive man; others were derived from the Greeks; many more of them would prove to come directly from the Middle Ages; while certain others in our stock were unknown until natural science began to develop in a new form about three hundred years ago. The idea that man has a soul or double which survives the death of the body is very ancient indeed and is accepted by most savages. Such confidence as we have in the liberal arts, metaphysics, and formal logic goes back to the Greek thinkers; our religious ideas and our standards of sexual conduct are predominantly medieval in their presuppositions; our notions of electricity and disease germs are, of course, recent in origin, the result of painful and prolonged research which involved the rejection of a vast number of older notions sanctioned by immemorial acceptance. 302

James Harvey Robinson

Human beings are morally and mentally lazy. They are readier to grasp the force of arguments against any radical change in their social habits than to adventure with new expedients. Consequently teaching without any bias must always maintain the status quo and obstruct the impulse to courageous and creative social effort. 150   Lancelot Hogben

Philosophy has, however, been little affected by the transformation of the ways in which men actually pursue knowledge. It has remained, as far as possible, true to conceptions formulated more than two thousand years ago in Greece, when the experimental method was not dreamed of 29

John Dewey

We very rarely consider, however, the process by which we gained our convictions. If we did so, we could hardly fail to see that there was usually little ground for our confidence in them. 302

James Harvey Robinson

As a result of modern high-pressure salesmanship many persons have come to believe that the newest is necessarily the best. This may well be true with radios and automobiles; but in religion and philosophy there still lingers on some confidence in the superiority of earlier models. It is for this reason that a knowledge of the history of human thought is invariably considered an essential constituent of a well-grounded philosophical training. This continuity of philosophy with its own past is illustrated by the fact that when a philosopher examines and evaluates an idea, he first of all goes back to the Greeks to see whether they had a word for it. 286

Oliver L. Reiser

To nothing has reverence been paid more stupidly than to the classics. We do not read them as tracts for the times, which is what most of them were, but as distillations of pure reason, and we play the game of matching one abstraction against another until all meaning is drowned in a sea of words. 293

J. A. Rice

As we proceed, we must emphasize order, considering what comes first and what next. This is semantically important, for the usual procedure is entirely different: first, we have our structurally 'preconceived' doctrines and languages; next, we observe the structure of the world; and then we try to force the observed facts into the linguistic structural patterns. But, in the new way, we start with silent observations, and search empirically for structure; next, we invent verbal structures similar to them; and, finally, we see what can be said about the situation, and so test the language. Experience shows that the old habits of labels first, objects next, instead of the structurally natural order of objects first, labels next, is semantically pernicious and harmful. 179

Alfred Korzybski

The basic assumptions of almost all art theorists of the present day, including the Moderns, go back to Aristotle. Therefore, it would seem profitable to examine the origin and general character of these theories, as well as what has since become of them, especially as concerns "Modern" art.

Aristotle's basic premises were, in brief, that nature was a sort of artist striving for, but seldom if ever achieving, an "ideal" or "universal" reality. The task of the human artist was to perceive this ideal sought by the "nature artist" and then realize this perfection of "reality" in his works. These aspects of

Aristotle's theory are clearly set forth by S. H. Butcher: [1] "There is an ideal form which is present in each individual phenomenon but imperfectly manifested." [2]

"The artist may 'imitate things *as they ought to be*': he may place before him an unrealized ideal. We see at once that there is no question here of bare imitation, of a literal transcript of the world of reality." [3]

". . . . 'imitation' which is the principle of fine art ultimately resolves itself into an effort to complete in some sense the work of nature . . . ." [4]

"By mere imagery it [fine art] reveals the ideal form at which nature aims in the highest sphere of organic existence,—in the region, namely, of human life, where her intention is most manifest, though her failures too are most numerous." [5]

"Fine art . . . . is a completion of nature . . . . it presents to us only an image, but a purified image of nature's original." [6]

"The general movement of organic life is part of a progress to the 'better,' the several parts working together for the good of the whole. The artist in his mimic world carries forward this movement to a more perfect completion. The creations of his art are framed on those ideal lines that nature has drawn; her intimations, her guidance are what he follows. He too aims at something better than the actual. He produces a new thing, not the actual thing of experience, not a copy of reality, ... but a higher reality— 'for the ideal type must surpass the actual'; the ideal is 'better' than the real." [7]

" 'Imitation,' so understood, is a creative act. It is the expression of the concrete thing under an image which answers to its true idea. To seize the universal, and to reproduce it in simple and sensuous form is not to reflect a reality already familiar through sense perceptions; rather it is a rivalry of nature, a completion of her unfulfilled purposes, a correction of her failures." [8] In these quotations we can discern two basic assumptions: (1) certain "imperfections" and "failures" exist in "actual" nature; (2) the artist succeeds where nature fails; he therefore achieves an "ideal" superior to actual nature. In brief, the artist is in "rivalry" with nature.

Our history has shown that the *natural* course of events in the development of art originally brought up the problem of the ideal. Throughout early history there had been a gradual evolution, following the natural order of recording development, as man sought to depict the general human form ever more accurately. The Egyptians had taken this development a good part of the way by the time the Greeks reached and then perfected the recording of the general. Once this "perfection" was achieved, men came to the egocentric conclusion that this particular kind of perfection in art showed that they could not only compete with but even supersede nature in its own productions. (A similar error, as we noted in chapter 7, was made when the Greeks discovered man's ability to reason about his reason, i.e., it was concluded that reason was independent of and so superior to the empirical reality.)

However, there was great difficulty in the fact that these art "creations," which were claimed to be superior to nature, were inanimate. A coherent realization of this problem was lacking, but it was vaguely *felt,* as is indicated in the many Greek stories of statues coming to life. If these stories were indications of how "real" this art was regarded, they also were in the nature of wish fulfillments; they expressed the desire to have these "perfect" forms actually live, to reach final perfection and to overcome their one very devastating defect. After all, of what use was this perfection, if it was only frozen stone? Socrates com-

1. S. H. Butcher: *Aristotle's Theory of Poetry and Fine Arts:* translated by Butcher, 4th ed., Rev., Macmillan and Co., Ltd., London, 1911. For the most part we shall quote the analysis of Aristotle's theories as given by Butcher in the book indicated above.

2. Ibid., p. 153.

3. Ibid., p. 122.

4. Ibid., p. 154.

5. Ibid., p. 157.

6. Ibid., p. 158.

7. Ibid., p. 152.

8. Ibid., p. 154.

mented on this when he remarked that the gods were greater artists than men because they created figures which actually lived. A work of art, no matter how "perfect," remained either inert stone or paint.

Plato, too, denied that the "reality" of art was superior to the appearances of nature. As Butcher puts it: "Plato had laid it down that 'the greatest and fairest things are done by nature, and the lesser by art . . . .'" [9] For Plato, however, the supreme "reality" existed only in divine "ideas," which were not in any way a part of the world of things. Whatever his intentions, he thus conveniently circumvented any competition from the actualities of nature's appearances. Under these circumstances the ideal would never take visual form and thus assume a characteristic of the empirical reality to which it could then be compared. Accordingly, Plato could well afford to see the fallacy of the theory that art was superior to nature, since with his supreme "divine ideas" he could give little value to the empirical level and even less to any imitation of it. Actually, although he quibbled on the point, he wished to eliminate art altogether. Nevertheless, Plato's theories made it possible for him to recognize, although Aristotle could not, that artists were deluding themselves with notions of perfecting the appearances of nature.

The times in which any man lives and the particular experiences he has in those times form his knowledge of and attitude towards the times in general. This no one can escape. In a very excellent manner Horace Kallen [10] has shown how Plato's experiences as he tried to practice his theories in the actual world of events—i.e., his general failure to get them across—had a good deal to do with the formation of his kind of knowledge. He was led more and more away from the real world and he came to despise it as much as he believed the world despised his "ideas."

It must not be overlooked that Plato as a thinker emerged from that state of knowledge in which religion was still the final law. Before him were the Egyptians, whose culture and art he respected. (He believed that Egyptian art was designed by the gods for the good of mankind.) Egyptian art, incidentally, was motivated by an already very developed notion of the ideal. That is, in their art the Egyptians depicted the general appearance of the human form, and their beliefs centered around the unchanging, the absolute, the permanent. It was this background which Plato crystallized into the first comprehensive system of philosophy. In doing so he achieved a system that was less theological and more empirical than any previous ones; along with Socrates he considerably extended man's discovery and consciousness of the human ability to reason.

Aristotle continued this evolution and brought the divine closer to earth, tried to fuse it with the real world into ONE. Significantly, Aristotle fitted into society with hardly a mishap until near the end of his life; where men in power refused to help Plato, they did the opposite in Aristotle's case. More scientifically inclined than his teacher, he gave more credence to the empirical observation of facts. As Butcher puts it: "Physical science, slighted by Plato, was passionately studied by Aristotle." [11] In short, Aristotle tried to tie together into one system the reality of the divine and the reality of the world, the reality of the general and that of the particular, what man "thought" and what he "observed." He tried, but failed to eliminate the Platonist split between these factors. It was the two incompatible worlds, carried over from Plato into Aristotle's system, that comprised a schism in the latter's logic about art. Thus, Aristotle made the ideal the highest reality, just as Plato did, only Plato's "ideal" was even more supreme— it was beyond the visual aspect of nature altogether. Similarly Aristotle placed the particular or individual in a lower order than the general or ideal, but Plato placed the particular even lower than did Aristotle! In other words, the views of Plato continued in Aristotle, only the latter attempted to bring them closer together.

Aristotle, however, was unable to realize that, since artists had achieved accurate depictions of the human form in general, their next step was not to try to supersede the appearances of nature, but to continue the process by which the general recording of the human form had been achieved—that is, to increase their ability to assimilate more and more of the particulars of nature's visual phenomena. Aristotle

9. Ibid., p. 161.

10. Kallen, *Art and Freedom*, Vol. 1, pp. 40–42, Duell, Sloan and Pearce, New York, 1942.

11. Butcher, op. cit., p. 160.

did not see that the legitimate objective of the artist was to achieve ever increasing correspondence with nature's appearances. He did not see that the useful historical function of the "ideal" had already been accomplished, that actually its fundamental importance lay in its being a step on the way to securing greater correspondence between art and nature at one stage in the evolution of art.

Thus Aristotle failed to comprehend the fundamental evolutionary character of art development. He, like Socrates and Plato, failed to discover that the historic emergence of art evidenced the gradually developing accuracy of man's visual functioning and of his ability to record. The following material by Kahler gives some insight into Aristotle's failure on this score: "The feeling for human history . . . . was not yet clearly developed in Greek philosophy and in the life of the ancients as a whole. Human history had just begun with these peoples. Though they made and lived history, though they even created a standard historiography, a model record of political events, ... though there was much speculation on cosmogony and evolution, an essentially historical consciousness, a realization of change and progress in human life as a whole did not yet exist. Even Aristotle's theory of evolution was mainly concerned with the recurrent evolution of beings, or of the organic world, but not with a progression of the human race. The general scheme of human events was that of perpetual recurrence, of a circle rather than a line of advance. And the general orientation was directed rather toward a better past than a better future, toward an ancestral Golden Age that was to be brought back." [12]

Aristotle was mainly concerned with what had already been accomplished particularly in the heyday of the ideal; he was making a case predominantly for the *status quo* attitude towards art. Consequently he failed to see that the next steps lay not in continuing to pursue "ideals" and "universals," which led to a static notion of art history, but in striving for more particulars.

Aristotle's attitude towards empirical reality, however, enabled him to observe that man was capable of extending the possibilities of nature; that man could utilize "nature's principles," transform them to serve more fruitfully man's needs. It was this attitude which contributed to his understanding of the function of art. Art was thus considered a kind of discourse capable of producing a healthy balance in man's morals and pleasures.

In Aristotle's theories, in short, we see an expression of a desire to release the Inventive potentialities of the artist. This is true at least in the Aristotelian sense that the artist's task is not to achieve a literal copy of nature's appearances, but rather to secure the objective towards which nature strives but seldom if ever attains. Accordingly, "The function, then, of the useful arts is in all cases 'to supply the deficiencies of nature'; and he who would be a master in any art must first discern the true end by a study of nature's principles, and then employ the method which she suggests for the attainment of that end." [13] This statement would appear, at first sight, to be in agreement with the view of Constructionists expressed in this book, particularly in its emphasis upon the point that the artist uses the *method* of nature to produce his art. Such a conclusion, however, is quickly dispelled if we consider Aristotle's views on Architecture, where the artist's dependence on the building method of nature rather than on the appearance of nature forms is quite apparent. For, even though, according to Butcher, "the method of architecture does remind Aristotle of the structural method of nature," yet we find that he denied Architecture the status of a fine-art. "His omission of architecture from the list of the fine arts may also cause surprise . . . . At the same time,—and this was the decisive point—architecture had not the 'imitative' quality which was regarded as essential to fine art." [14]

"A building as an organic whole did not call up any image of a world outside itself, though the method of architecture does remind Aristotle of the structural method of nature. Even if architecture had seemed to him to reproduce the appearances of the physical universe, it would not have satisfied his idea of artistic imitation; for all the arts imitate human life in some of its manifestations, and imitate material objects only so far as these serve to interpret spiritual and mental processes. The decorative element in Greek architecture is alone 'imitative' in the Aristotelian sense, being indeed but a form of sculpture;

12. Erich Kahler: *Man the Measure*, pp. 123–124, Pantheon Books, New York, 1943.

13. Butcher, op. cit., pp. 119–120.

14. Ibid., p. 148.

but sculpture does not constitute the building, nor is it, as in Gothic architecture, an organic part of the whole." [15] If Aristotle had understood Architecture correctly, he would have seen that this art, i.e., in its non-Mimetic aspects, was a more complete expression of his theory of art, in the sense that such art does not copy nature forms in any degree and because it does not, it achieves, of all the arts, the greatest extension of the *method* of nature. But his theories of "imitation" limited him to an erroneous "rivalry of nature" attitude, and so he failed to discover the one *major* form of art which successfully went beyond the literal imitation of nature and on a *non-competitive* and so possible basis. Aristotle was naturally unable to see that his art notions could be better achieved, not by imitating nature's macroscopics in any way, but by directly utilizing the structural building process of nature. This aspect of Aristotle's theory could not be adequately realized in the art of these times, because Aristotle's theories in general restricted man's art efforts within the confines of nature's art-results.

Historically, the recording effort, as we have seen, was more fully realized before the Inventive. So dominant did the Mimetic objective become that even in arts where invention was possible and imperative, e.g., pottery and Architecture, Inventive trends were drowned almost completely, or remained frustrated until our own century (see chapter 24).

Under the conditions of the theory of an ideal, man's efforts to be creative involved a "rivalry" with nature, and in the effort to assure success in the competition, nature was considered incomplete and imperfect. Thus Butcher points out: "If we may expand Aristotle's idea in the light of his own system,— fine art eliminates what is transient and particular and reveals the permanent and essential features of the original. It discovers the 'form' . . . . towards which an object tends, the result which nature strives to attain, but rarely or never can attain. Beneath the individual it finds the universal. It passes beyond the bare reality given by nature, and expresses a purified form of reality disengaged from accident, and freed from conditions which thwart its development." [16] Aristotle simply imposed upon the processes of nature a goal having no basis in fact. His theory was an arbitrary assumption, not an observable fact in nature, a difficulty he circumvented by resorting to metaphysical rationalizations.

Similarly, the other basic assumption of Aristotle's theory, the evaluation of the art-result as superior to nature, is also justified by a resort to the arbitrary verities of metaphysics. No empirical proof is given that nature is made more perfect in man's art. These assumptions, based largely on "pure reason," were imposed upon the observation of reality. The general becomes superior to the particular by the simple process of ignoring and thus eliminating the importance of particulars, i.e., ignoring the conditions which would permit the particulars of nature to be recognized as the criterion for the appearances of reality and/or art. Particulars (nature) represent defects, while generals (art) represent perfection.

The following aspect of Aristotle's theories played a large role in preventing a recognition of the erroneous assumptions of the theories just discussed. Butcher puts it this way: "Art addresses itself not to the abstract reason but to the sensibility and image-making faculty; it is concerned with outward appearances; it employs illusions; its world is not that which is revealed by pure thought; it sees truth, but in its concrete manifestations, not as an abstract idea." [17] According to his practice of putting various factors into isolated compartments, Aristotle here maintains that the artist (or his audience) depended upon the function of the "senses" devoid of abstract reason, as though there were something like an image-making faculty with a purely visual function. This theory, then, functioned as still another way of circumventing a recognition of the actual character of the empirical level; again the authority of metaphysics was resorted to. As a matter of fact, the notions of the "outward appearances" of the ideal in art, its "concrete manifestations," were the products of "abstract reason" and "pure thought," as explained above.

Another rationalization underlying these assumptions which isolate art from nature, may be seen in the following from Butcher's discussion of Aristotle's theories: "Art does not attempt to embody

15. Ibid., p. 149.

16. Ibid., p. 150.

17. Ibid., p. 127. Compare with previous remarks of Lipchitz, p. 348. Miro also (see fn. 19 below and p. 469) has said something similar, i.e., the "abstract" factor is denied and art is claimed to be "concrete." This is not to imply that Lipchitz, Miro, etc., are great Aristotelian philosophers, but rather to indicate how thoroughly our culture is pickled in Aristotelian logic.

the objective reality of things, but only their sensible appearances. Indeed by the very principles of Aristotle's philosophy it can present no more than a semblance; for it impresses the artistic form upon a matter which is not proper to that form. [18] Thus it severs itself from material reality and the corresponding wants. Herein lies the secret of its emancipating power. The real emotions, the positive needs of life, have always in them some element of disquiet. By the union of a form with a matter which in the world of experience is alien to it, a magical effect is wrought. The pressure of everyday reality is removed, and the aesthetic emotion is released as an independent activity. Art, then, moving in a world of images and appearances, and creating after a pattern existing in the mind, must be skilled in the use of illusion. By this alone can it give coherence to its creations and impart to its fictions an air of reality." [19] In other words, the artist cannot duplicate the objective reality; only a semblance of reality is obtained because the objects depicted are transformed by the art medium; the original object and the depiction of of it cannot be the same.

By confining himself to either-or reasoning, Aristotle was able to place a perfectionist necessity upon any attempt at seeking correspondence, a practice we have noted among theorists of Modern art. The achievement of any such perfect correspondence is obviously an impossibility, and since the art medium will not allow of perfect correspondence, the artist is thus presumably free of any such demands in that direction. (But since perfection is unobtainable in *any* kind of art, then criticism of literal imitation on this score is unjustified and so false.) In this way the art-result is severed from a strict dependence on and responsibility to the conditions of the original or objective reality. Thus the artist takes the direction opposite to that of seeking a correspondence, allegedly a direction in which perfection is obtained. That is, he follows "a pattern existing in the mind." Accordingly the "mind," not nature becomes the criterion of art. It was merely assumed, outright, that nature "ought to be" that which it was made into with man's art. The criterion was too much what arbitrarily occurred in men's minds, not enough what they observed to occur in the objective world. All this sort of reasoning was possible because of the assumed superiority of "mind over matter."

But we must consider the fact that there are actually two general objectives possible to the artist who is abstracting from the macro-reality: (1) he can strive for a strict recording by securing as much of a correspondence to the actual appearance of the original as his medium and his ability permit; (2) he can *deliberately* strive, even more than his medium or lack of ability compels him, to make nature into what it *is not*. In brief, the artist can strive *for* correspondence or for the opposite. It is the latter objective which Aristotle particularly emphasized in his theory.

True, Aristotle recognized these two forms of depiction, i.e., recording men "as they are," or as they are not (that is, depicting men as more "noble" or "less noble" than they are). However, he mentions the first type only now and then and briefly. Although he does not explicitly say that the full degree of correspondence that it is possible for the artist to achieve lacks value, his theory implies that unless perfection (the ideal) is achieved in the copying of nature, little value can be given to literal "imitation." Significantly he writes considerably about the ideal, since this is actually his main point—the great value of the ideal in art. In fact, the silent discrimination between these actually opposed views of art is so extensive that the vast majority throughout history have not been aware that Aristotle spoke of more than one kind of "imitation."

But neither way of art making here discussed, i.e., literal or ideal "imitation," can be "released as an independent activity" from actual reality, because, as we have repeatedly stressed, in making any kind of art, the artist is compelled to abstract from reality, and abstraction implies relations of some kind and so dependence. Although no art produced by either method of abstraction from reality is "*the* reality," nevertheless the important difference is that with the one method the artist attempts to *represent* the reality

18. See p. 342 where Dewey employs this very theory also for purposes of rationalizing distortions in present day art. Note similarity of the rest of the quotation with notions voiced by Picasso, Surrealists, etc.

19. Butcher, op. cit., pp. 127–128. This is precisely the reasoning that unconsciously lies behind the following remarks of Miro: "the signs that I transcribe on a canvas, at the moment when they correspond to a concrete representation of my mind, ... belong essentially to the world of reality!" (Quoted by Sweeney, *Joan Miro*, p. 13.) This is the prevailing assumption among the "Moderns."

as it appears through empirical criteria, while with the other he attempts to "create" reality as it appears with the "mind" as criterion.

Although Aristotle correctly observed that there is a difference between the mediums of the "nature artist" and the man artist, he considered this merely the indication that the supreme objective of the artist is primarily other than that of literal imitation of nature. He decided that the differences in mediums, etc., absolved the artist of responsibility for achieving correspondence; this in turn made possible the liberty Aristotle took with his logic—it allowed him to make an isomorphic objective impossible by definition. In fact, he reversed the actual state of affairs by claiming that the "ideal" in art (by which nature is actually changed into what it *is not*) is, as Butcher puts it, a "higher reality—for the ideal type must surpass the actual, the ideal is 'better' than the real."

He *reversed* the situation by arbitrarily setting a goal *for nature* which only the artist, not nature, could achieve. Then it "logically followed that the ideal depicted in art is imperfectly manifested in nature; and so the artist achieving this ideal, arrives at an art-result that is "better" than the actual. Therefore to Aristotle "imitation" meant a correction, a completion, a successful "rivalry of nature"—in short a "creative" act. Nature was ruled out as a criterion of reality; instead man's art and reason ruled as independent, superior criteria of reality. Man's art achieved what nature unsuccessfully attempted.

Had nature been recognized as the criterion of reality, then the artist would have been content to reach out for the perfection in nature as it appeared. In one sense, such a reversal of the Aristotelian theory occurred with the Invention of the Camera, but in a broader sense this was but the completion of what Aristotle had begun as he moved on from the views of his teacher, Plato, in the effort to increase the importance of the empirical level. As for man's Inventive potentialities in making his art, first formulated by Aristotle, they were not fully released from the confines of the art-results of nature until Constructionist art was realized.

If Aristotle's philosophical successors who dabbled and babbled in something called aesthetics had properly understood Aristotle's notions about art, there would have been no need to pursue this nebulous subject. They would have seen that Aristotle was expressing man's desire to be more than an imitator of nature, to be, in fact, a "creative" artist. They might have further discovered that Aristotle thought this could be done in a manner actually impossible, which accounts for his necessity to "rival" nature; that is, he wanted man to be a creator with the objects of already created nature-art.

To realize adequately the objective of Aristotle's theories would have required that the artist invent directly with the *methods* of nature, not copy the *results* of that method. But this could not yet be done in painting and sculpture. Hence the Aristotelian theories inevitably involved the artist in making fantasies of nature's reality, that is, changing nature into that which it *is not*. The theory that the achievement of an "ideal" should be the goal of the artist, resulted in a conflict between the effort to record nature's appearances on the one hand, and on the other to release Inventive potentialities. But we should not lose sight of the fact that certain aspects of Aristotelian theory are valid at least in principle, but that their originator and those after him have been frustrated in realizing the development of these theories, because they were *limited* to only a macroscopic awareness of nature's reality.

Thus we have seen that the theory of the ideal originated with the 5th century B.C. Greeks as the natural crystallization of the then entire past effort of artists to record the general form of the human figure. This theory was more precisely formulated in the 4th century B.C. by Aristotle to justify a static notion of art.

Continually since Aristotle's time there have been those who have employed Aristotle's rationalizations to justify some kind of art which deliberately changed nature's appearances. Recall, for instance, the theories of Joshua Reynolds. He wrote: "All the objects which are exhibited to our view by Nature, upon close examination will be found to have their blemishes and defects." [20] Those who are properly trained, Reynolds said, observe "what any set of objects of the same kind have in common." [21] For, "as there is one general form, which, as I have said, belongs to the human kind at large, so in each of these classes there is one common idea and central form, which is the abstract of the various individual forms belonging to that class." [22] Thus the painter "acquires a just idea of beautiful forms; he corrects Nature. . . ." [23] In this manner the artist's eye is "enabled to distinguish the accidental deficiencies, excrescences, and deformities of things, from their general figures, he makes out an abstract idea of their forms more perfect than any one original; and what may seem a paradox, he learns to design naturally by drawing his figures unlike to any one object." [24] With his logic Aristotle justified the art fantasies of the Greeks as being superior to nature; Reynolds used it to justify his fantasy portraits of the English aristocracy which made the ruling class feel they were superior beings, etc.

But it was the actual characteristics of nature which continued to intrigue the *advanced* artists; hence they sought to record more and more particulars. This, as we have shown elsewhere, was increasingly true even of the various Classical artists during post-Renaissance times. In short, the images of nature created by the "mind" and art of man were defeated by the direct image of nature. The artists who made the greatest contributions to progress were those who made no attempt to "sever" themselves "from material reality," i.e., from the "corresponding wants" of reality. Eventually their efforts contributed to the invention of the Camera.

History shows that although the *status quo* has inevitably consisted of a different, changing mentality, nevertheless, the Classical theory of an ideal has always been used by the *status quo* largely as the means of hindering further evolution in art. Thus, particularly since the Cubist decision, Modern artists and theorists have employed Aristotelian theory with all the stops out, in the indiscriminate effort to justify their particular kinds of departure from the actual appearances of reality (usually some variety of Transitional-Period art), and thereby to avert the abyss which they imagined that Cubism implied. For Cubism had made plain the necessity for removing the old contents. This the Modernists feared to do; they wanted to continue manipulating nature's appearances in some way. They were able to follow contemporary innovations only to that extent that they would not have to take too big a risk with the revered past. The implications of Cubism involved a complete reorientation to the "problem of art," to an art which must have a fully invented contents. It was then that the theories of the Classical ideal and the sameness of all "great" art came stumbling to the rescue—for they not only justified the artist in confining his abstracting to the macro-level of reality but also permitted him to distort reality.

Although, as we have seen, the Inventive potential of man was implicit in Classical theory, it was not coherently recognized because of the predominant importance attached to nature's macroscopic level. Thus we can see that it was no accident that the majority of "Modern" artists and theorists should try to keep their level of abstracting at various phases near the middle of the Transitional-Period. For in these phases artists were seemingly once more in a position similar to that of the Classical Greeks, in the sense that artists were again no longer concerned with pursuing particulars, but rather with manipulating generals.

This state of affairs is bound up with the fact already noted that the whole Transitional-Period was, grossly or symptomatically speaking, a repetition of man's phylogeny in art. That is, non-Camera art gradually moved from the accurate realism of the Camera to less and less realism, and from depictions of particulars to depictions of the generalized aspect of nature's appearances. On the gross *manifest* level, when Post-Impressionism was reached, the Transitional-Period *appeared* to be recapitulating the Classical point of phylogeny. The genuine Transitional-Period artist, however, was not, like the Idealist, striving to

20. Joshua Reynolds: *The Discourses of Sir Joshua Reynolds*, p. 40, London, 1842.

21. Ibid., p. 41.   22. Ibid., p. 43.   23. Ibid., p. 41.   24. Ibid., p. 41.

release his Inventive ability to perfect nature; rather he was employing nature as a point of departure in his efforts to create his own art. Similarly, in the first decade of the 20th century there appeared a fervent concern with Primitive art, especially African; at that time the Transitional-Period had *seemingly* reached the Primitive stage of phylogenetic recapitulation. Still later when the objects of nature were removed from the art content, the Decorative stage of phylogeny (the first period of art history) had *seemingly* been reached. However, as already explained, this phenomenon of recent arts seeming to return to past modes of abstracting was only a symptomatic aspect, and *is not basic to what was fundamentally taking place*. In other words, there are two aspects, or two levels of all Transitional-Period arts, the manifest and the latent.

In the Post-Impressionist variety of art, for example, the two levels were as follows: (1) manifestly the Post-Impressionists appeared to be primarily concerned with the depiction of the "general" rather than the particular; but (2) latently, as our observations of the historical process have revealed, the basic objective of these artists was to reach a consciousness of the Structural Process of nature in order to release their inherent ability and need to invent their art content. The Post-Impressionists were continuing the "spade work" of the Impressionists, as they analyzed the objects of reality in an effort to reach consciousness of the Structural Process level. In short, on the surface such artists appear to be returning to a variation of the old "ideal" objective of the Greeks, but fundamentally the genuine innovators were striving to dispense with the imitation of nature's appearances in order to "create" art. Accordingly, it is of crucial importance to realize that contemporary critics of the Transitional-Period, who interpret this art in terms of Aristotelian notions, have hindered a recognition of the fundamental character of these arts.

Such evaluations, however, were inevitable, since the Aristotelians of today are trying to make distortions of nature the final method of art. On the surface it might appear as if artists were once more concerned with the "great universals" and not with those allegedly inferior particulars of the Camera and Academic artists. We can now better understand why the "Moderns" generally see all "great" art, past and present, as seeking the same objective. It was indeed tempting, considering how everything was so easily solved (including the perplexing problems of history) by adopting the convenient attitude that all great art was always the same everywhere at all times. For there can be no higher order for future art if that higher order has already been achieved in the past. The "new" then becomes largely a return to some great accomplishment of the past. To borrow the words of Kahler about the Greeks, "the general orientation was directed rather toward a better past than a better future." If one reasoned in this manner, it did not appear strange that 20th century artists and critics were espousing the theories of 4th century B.C. critics.

It is not surprising, then, to find that Matisse (who was most attracted to the manifest level of Post-Impressionism) has called for a return to a "new classicism." And it is certainly no accident that Picasso, the most glorified of the so-called Modernists today, is also the one who has exhibited the strongest attraction to Greek art in his life work as a whole. The copying of Greek statues runs continuously throughout his work. It was he, incidentally, who once remarked that what art needed today was another David; it was he who tried to draw and paint like Ingres, only more idealistically, in between his other peregrinations in art.

Thus although Classical art in the old sense is no longer being made, the rationalizations that accompanied it persist fundamentally unchanged. Although sometimes encrusted with elaborations, subterfuge and disguise so as to be hardly recognizable even to those who abide by them, the basic assumptions of Aristotle remain intact, unquestioned and so unexamined in present day theory. Let us review a few examples from the writings of present day Aristotelians, who, either openly or implicitly, contend that nature is imperfect, that art is superior to nature.

Alfred Barr says that a certain Modern artist's "rearrangements" give a "clearer and more complete idea of the village than does the snapshot." Herbert Read speaks of "some plastic symbol which shall be more significant of reality than any exact reproduction can be." M. C. Cheney maintains that "the sunflowers [of van Gogh] have a dynamic and mobile life . . . . more forceful than that made by any field grown flowers." Miro says: "the signs that I transcribe on a canvas, at the moment when they correspond to a concrete representation of my mind" are "profoundly real" and "belong essentially to the world of reality!" Another critic (Kootz) claims that the "Abstract" artists, those who use nature's appearances as a point of departure, re-order "nature's chaos." It's the old story—nature is imperfect, while the artist's productions are more perfect. Kootz even uses such moralistic phrases as "the internal rightness of form," and says that: "The abstract artist has no desire to copy nature. . . . He is opposed to nature's chaos. . . ."[25] In other words, nature is very conveniently judged as chaotic, hence defective, to justify what is actually a case of the artist's defective, chaotic recording of nature.[26]

In the pre-Camera world Reynolds, for example, flatly and frankly claimed that: "The works of nature are full of disproportion and fall far short of the true standard of beauty." But most "Modern" art theorists, since they cannot claim that the art they admire makes nature "more beautiful," would find it somewhat embarrassing to claim flatly that nature had "deficiencies" (Aristotle) or was "full of disproportion" (Reynolds). The Greeks and Reynolds did strive to "perfect" the human form; they did not deliberately do the opposite as the "Moderns" do. Hence, the professional rationalist for the latter type of art, no doubt unconsciously motivated to do so, uses the Reynolds' sort of criticism of nature in a disguised form by claiming that the defects exist not in nature but in that art which literally records nature. Thus they have concluded that the most realistic period of art history was one huge mistake which has been of no great value to man. One critic says that "it is only the weak photographic-ornamental art of the 17th-19th Century period that they [the moderns] violently oppose and scornfully ridicule."[27] Another says that "The bulk, however, of those who flourished between the high Renaissance and the contemporary movement may be divided into two classes, virtuosi and dunces."[28] Still another speaks of the past "six hundred years of misdirection."[29] We also hear that "to the modern mind ["Realism" is] more shallow than art that begins with a search for order, form, revelation, expression."[30] As though all this were not enough, it is claimed that Impressionism "hastened recognition of the shallow character of all Realistic art."[31]

In all this the Modernists are inadvertently revealing that they consider nature "weak," "shallow," etc., because it is nature's appearances which the Realist's art strives to record. Some of them being more bold, or should we say careless, do speak directly of nature's imperfections. Maillol contended that "The more one departs from nature, the more one is an artist; the more one approaches nature, the more the work becomes ugly."[32] Monroe Wheeler was saying something very similar, if a little more obscurely, when he declared that "The artist who departs the farthest from the mirror viewpoint, in extravagance or stylization of his art, sometimes is most keenly concerned with the individual appearances."[33] (If Wheeler referred to the art of caricature, which was probably not his intention, then we could agree with him.) Dewey implies that nature is "unorganized miscellany"[34] and Raynal sees it as "clamorous chaos."[35] Kootz also, as we have just noted, speaks of "nature's chaos."

Those who today call themselves "Modern" should consider the fact that Whistler presented similar theories along very naive lines, which thus expose their true characteristics, something carefully avoided by the more sophisticated critics of the present. In his *Ten O'Clock* Whistler wrote: "Nature contains the elements, in color and form, of all pictures, as the keyboard contains the notes of all music.

25. Samuel Kootz: *New Frontiers in American Painting,* p. 47, Hastings House, New York, 1943.

26. For examples see Kootz's approved artists whose works are reproduced in his book, those "who work from reality," as he would put it. And "reality," of course, means for him, as is the usual case, only the macro-level, since he is not aware of any other level of reality. But he is also under the erroneous impression that an artist does not have to work "from reality" if he does not wish to; he believes what the Non-Objectivists, etc., have been telling him.

27. Sheldon Cheney: *Expressionism in Art,* p. 14.

28. Clive Bell: *Art,* p. 40.

29. J. J. Sweeney: "Picasso," *Cahiers d'Art,* p. 128, Nos. 3–5, 1932.

30. Cheney, *Expressionism in Art,* p. 31.

31. Ibid., p. 31.

32. Reported by John Rewald, "Last Visit with Maillol," *Magazine of Art,* 38:167, May, 1945.

33. *20th Century Portraits,* p. 10, preface by Monroe Wheeler, Museum of Modern Art, New York, 1942.

34. See our p. 342.

35. Raynal, *Modern French Painters,* p. 18.

"But the artist is born to pick, and choose, and group with science, these elements, that the result may be beautiful — as the musician gathers his notes, and forms his chords, until he bring forth from chaos glorious harmony. . . . That Nature is always right, is an assertion, artistically, as untrue, as it is one whose truth is universally taken for granted. Nature is very rarely right, to such an extent even, that it might almost be said that Nature is usually wrong: that is to say, the condition of things that shall bring about the perfection of harmony worthy of a picture is rare, and not common at all." [36] Whistler also said that nature very seldom succeeded in producing a picture.[37] To be more exact, nature *never* produces a picture. The absurdity is that anyone expects it to do so! To put the burden of responsibility upon nature rather than the artist, is a device not only of Whistler, but of "Modern" theorists and artists in their effort to escape responsibility for their own behavior with words or paint.

Thus we see similar theories of the ideal in Aristotle of the 4th century B.C., Reynolds of the 18th century, Whistler of the 19th, and the Modernists of the 20th. *The important difference between the Modernists, Whistler, Reynolds and Aristotle is that the latter three are more explicit regarding what is implicit in the theorizing of the Modernists.* In the Greek art of the 5th century B.C. the effort to achieve an ideal made sense; at that time it produced a useful step in the development of art, in that artists were increasing their ability to record and analyze their art. One can at least reasonably imagine a human appearing like a Greek statue, but can anyone imagine a human being looking like the individuals depicted in Modern art? Compared to its more legitimate use in earlier arts, Classical theory becomes sheer nonsense when applied to the art of the Modernists. Both the 5th century B. C. Greeks and the Modernists depict the general, to be sure, but the former idealized, the latter caricaturize nature.[38] Moreover, the Greeks had a legitimate purpose in mind with their particular generalizations of the human form, but what may the Modernists have in mind with their caricatures of reality? Just this: escape through fantasy.

In these times of confusion and change, some can no longer achieve any satisfaction from reality as it appears, as they experience it directly with their vision; they are in conflict with it. Futilely they try to dominate the reality by manipulating it, changing it to a fantasy. Thus if Aristotle, according to Butcher, claims that: "The pressure of everyday reality is removed, and the aesthetic emotion is released as an independent activity," then the Modernists, to take a typical example like Alfred Barr, say it this way: "Perhaps you feel that these pictures [Modern art] have little to do with our everyday lives. This is partly true; some of them don't, and that is largely their value — by their poetry they have the power to lift us out of humdrum ruts." [39] And Barnes writes: "To make the world over in fact is possible only within the narrowest limits, but to make it over in imagination is more feasible, and the record of this re-creation is art." [40]

36. *Mr. Whistler's Ten O'Clock*, p. 12. Note again the reference to nature as "wrong." Here, too, is the Idealist's allegation that nature is imperfect and that the artist produces "glorious harmony." The old Idealist would have frankly called this the realization of a perfection for which nature strove but could not achieve except through man's art.

37. Ibid., p. 13.

38. The term "caricature" brings to mind the many attempts to cram Daumier somewhere into the revolutionary activities of the Transitional-Period. During this artist's life and for decades afterwards, he was regarded as a mere cartoonist trying also to paint. Today, however, some critics consider him a Romantic, others a Realist. But eventually he was placed among the ranks of those who were assumed to be the forerunners of something called "Modern" art. All this confusion in the attempt to allocate this artist in his proper niche has been due to the unique circumstances which motivated his work and in turn made him unacceptable among his contemporaries as a painter. If we observe his paintings closely, we find that he is a cartoonist, a Romantic and a Realist. But he is a Modernist only by the accident of circumstances. He became a hero of Modernism in the early part of the present century because in a sense he did with the nature object what the Modernist appears also to be doing, that is, he distorted and simplified nature forms into "arrangements." But this was not his direct intention, in the sense that as a painter he was simply continuing to caricature nature objects and the caricature method naturally involves distortionist methods. Our intention is not to deprecate his art in the least, but rather to point out that Daumier was a man of social consciousness, like Millet, Courbet, and others, and that his ability as a caricaturist was used in the expression of that consciousness. As a caricaturist his intentions were revolutionary on the social level, but he was not revolutionary in his concern with the problems of art and reality, in the way that Cézanne, for example, was.

39. Alfred Barr, Jr.: *What Is Modern Painting?*, p. 3.

40. A. C. Barnes and Violette de Mazia: "Ancient Chinese and Modern European Paintings," Catalogue of the Bignou Gallery, Inc., May-June, 1943.

But this fantasy must not depart so far from the "actual" that it prevents one from projecting the actual upon the fantasy and thus finding the latter surprisingly "real." [41] For characteristic of all Modernists is their insistence upon retaining and in some degree distorting nature forms for their art content. While it is true that in these distortions the artist is concerned with fantasy objectives, nevertheless to the degree that he distorts the macro-reality he has evidenced a frustrated desire to create, to release his potential ability to invent. It makes little difference as far as our point is concerned, whether the artist is conscious of such a desire or not, because it is implicit in the very act of contemporary distortion. Our times are characterized by the general desire to "create" art by releasing the Inventive ability of the artist. The new objective is realized to that degree in which the macroscopic level of reality is eliminated, not merely distorted. But only when that level is completely eliminated, is the artist adequately freed in the new direction of the present. If artists today wish to invent their forms, they cannot expect to succeed merely by distorting nature forms; distortion is not genuine invention, but a substitute for it! We do not deny the presence of structural (Inventive) as well as fantasy factors in Modern art (the Inventive potential was, in fact, implicit in the Classical theory with which this art was rationalized); but it is the fantasy which has dominated and submerged the other. If one insists that the Inventive potentialities of the artist must be confined to the mere manipulation of nature's appearances, then one's prime interest in art can only be to make it a vehicle for fantasy experiences.

But a question of fundamental importance presents itself: is the criterion of reality what the artist makes nature into, or what he observes to be the actual case in nature? The Greeks conceived the notion that art was the criterion of nature's reality, and most artists and critics still think this way, even if they are unaware of it. They would have us believe, indeed, that they "love nature too much" to eliminate recognizable objects from their art. Actually they are the very ones who are dissatisfied with and in conflict with nature. Contrary to the genuine Photographer, they refuse to regard nature's actual appearances as satisfactory art, and contrary to the Constructionist, they refuse to regard the building method of nature as a suitable method for creating art. Instead they try to pass off a fantasy of reality as a "greater reality" than those arts—Photography and Constructions—which achieve as much correspondence to nature as possible. Their reason for insisting on "recognizable content" is their erroneous belief that without such a content there exists no relation between art and reality. Thus they imagine they have a legitimate excuse for their fantasy manipulations and distortions of reality.

It seems incredible, to be sure, that present day discussions of art are so thoroughly imbued with Aristotelian rationalizations, and yet not one of the numerous writers we have quoted has admitted the source of his theories of art. Either they are reluctant to admit it, in order to avoid the embarrassing implications of justifying their kind of art with Aristotelianism, or else they are oblivious of the fact. It must be admitted that Aristotle would sometimes have difficulty recognizing his own theories, buried as they often are under the most confused types of reasoning. The theories of Aristotle have not been improved. Each generation has merely twisted Aristotelianism a little this way or that to suit its own purpose.

Today, however, it is very important to become aware of the tremendous influence of Aristotelian logic and to appraise that influence correctly; its persistence in our culture leads only to continued confusion. We can now see how the unquestioned prevalence of Aristotelian theory has made difficult the clearer understanding of those artists who sought accurate recordings of nature before and since Greek times, and has made equally difficult the comprehension of the Transitional-Period artists whose objectives were towards the non-copying of nature's art. It has kept obscure the legitimate and scientific function of pre-Camera artists who recorded reality as accurately as possible; and it has kept obscure the reasons that advanced contemporary non-Camera artists eliminate nature's appearances altogether. In the meantime it has served to justify the changing of nature's appearances in various ways into something nature *is not*—the art of fantasy.

41. The operation is similar to the child's art activities. He also projects the reality into his art; associational devices, based on gross similarities, make it possible for him to identify his art with the objects he is trying to depict. It is a primitive level of reaction, seeing only the similarities and ignoring the differences. We have analyzed this sort of projection behavior in our discussion of Picasso's painting, *The Studio*. Thus where Aristotle was trying to make the transition from primitive, religious notions to empirical forms of reasoning, his followers in the present, now that such a transition has been accomplished, are certainly striving in the very reverse direction.

The fact that Aristotelian logic is wide open at both ends, as we have pointed out, makes it possible to justify all kinds of diverse arts past and present with these formulations. Thus we find a strange assortment of individuals who abide by Aristotelian theory, many of them actually opposed to each other.

Ultimately we find that even Mondrian was involved in Aristotelian theory. Although he criticized the tendency of "falling back into romanticism or into classicism, as happens to modern movements in general," [42] he himself committed the error of unconsciously adopting the old Classical theory of the ideal. This makes its appearance throughout his written works. Thus in 1920 he wrote of the necessity *"to determine better* the capricious and indeterminate appearance of the natural phenomenon." [43] Here we are confronted with an artist inadvertently in competition with nature; an artist who took the Idealist's view that nature was imperfect and could only reach perfection through the artist. Finally he decided to accept the two Classical views of reality, the old Academic one and the Modernist version, as well as one peculiar to his own work. For he attempts to legitimatize those who seek the various distortions (perfectionist or caricaturist) of nature's appearances, as well as those who undertake to create by "relations of lines and planes."

One of the reasons he adopted the Classical theory of art is apparent in the following aspect of his analysis of art history: "Unconsciously, every true artist has always been moved by the beauty of line, color and relationships for their own sake and not by what they may represent. He has always tried to express all energy and all vital richness by these means alone. Nevertheless, consciously he has followed the forms of objects. Consciously, he has tried to express things and sensations through modelling and technique. But unconsciously, *he has established planes; he has augmented the tension of line and purified the color*. Thus, gradually through centuries, the culture of painting has led to *the total abolition of the limiting form and particular representation*. In our time, art has been liberated from everything that prevents it from being truly plastic. This liberation is of the greatest importance for art, the purpose of which is to conquer individual expression and to reveal, as far as possible, the universal aspect of life." [44]

Mondrian is correct in his historical analysis to the extent that there have been among the painters and sculptors *some* who have unconsciously striven to release man's inherent ability to invent, who have worked *at least in the direction* of what he calls the "pure plastic expression" instead of the "descriptive expression." But none of these past artists or so-called "true artists" was concerned with *only* these qualities to the exclusion of what his forms represented. To be accurate, past painters and sculptors have "always been moved by the beauty of line, color and relationships" *not* "for their own sake" but for what they represented. The principal difference was that some used these factors to represent the real, others the ideal.

The very serious error common today is the lack of awareness that the forms of nature could and certainly did offer artists a most fulfilling objective. Today it is difficult, because of the general practice of distorting nature, to realize that "creation" in "art" could be directed to the capturing of the amazing creations to be discovered and understood in nature (see Leonardo). In our times man continues to pursue this objective in the developments of Photography, an objective as fulfilling as ever to the experience of man within nature.

42. Mondrian, in *Cahiers d'Art*, p. 41, No. 1, 1931.

43. Mondrian, *Le Neo-Plasticisme*, p. 2.

44. Mondrian, "Pure Plastic Art," *Plastic Art and Pure Plastic Art*, p. 31.

It is apparent that Mondrian was encumbered with the Idealist's insistence upon perfection, upon superiority to nature. He was willing to abide by the "laws of reality," but only in the sense that he assumed the Idealist's privilege to claim that man could alter these laws towards an allegedly superior reality. Either he refused or failed to realize that the "laws of reality" are a given framework within which we are *compelled* to operate. And we either work in harmony with them or else they frustrate us and we come in conflict with reality.

Thus Mondrian condemned the quality of "volume" because it possessed a "naturalistic expression." This was a correct observation, but his inference was incorrect. Consequently his insistence upon "denaturalization of matter" rather than upon the *naturalization of the artist's inventions* only led him to work within a limited framework of reality characteristics, which in turn *limited the framework* within which the artist could invent, create his art contents.

In short, he failed to realize that only by striving for the greatest conformity possible to the laws of reality could the Inventive artist secure the greatest freedom of possibilities to create. For the natural Process Structure revealed a building method far superior to anything man could conceive of by trying, in any case futilely, to alter it; such an effort could only lead to restricting rather than increasing the possibilities of the artist. Specifically, Mondrian was restricted to the limited reality potentialities of the canvas surface.

Hence the one serious defect of Mondrian's theory lay in his efforts towards the impossible perfection of the Idealist. The Classical Idealist, who depicted nature forms, assumed that the artist achieved a perfection which nature futilely sought. But the "ideal," the "universal" which Mondrian sought was what he called "determined relations," the creation of "purified" lines and planes achieved by the "abolition of the limiting form and particular representation." In other words, the creation of "pure" lines, planes and colors, independent of the appearances of nature objects, constituted the "true reality and true life." [45] The Classicists of Academic times spoke of "imperfect nature"; a Classicist like Mondrian spoke of "the capricious and indeterminate appearance of the natural phenomenon," and said that the true artist now transformed this indeterminate aspect of reality into a "true reality" with his "determinate relations"—the art of the "pure plastic." In short, the old pre-Camera Idealist futilely strove to create depictions more perfect than nature, to perfect the art-*results* of nature's Structural Process; whereas the Mondrian type inadvertently sought to perfect the art *method,* i.e., the Structural Process of nature itself. Both rejected the actual characteristics of reality—the results in one case, the process or method in the other. (All contemporary artists, with the exception of *genuine* Photographers and Constructionists, fall somewhere between these two extremes.)

Mondrian's idealism was further revealed in his contention that in the new art "the new man has passed beyond the sentiments of nostalgia, joy, delight, sorrow, horror, etc.," towards "a much more profound vision of sensible reality," [46] i.e., by implication a superior reality. But this is impossible so long as the living artist must live in the here-reality, a world of varied, dynamic, emotional experiences; *for it is with these experiences that any kind of an artist creates,* and it is of them that he speaks in his art. Mondrian's theory immediately brings to mind the immobile face of the ideal sculpture of Classical times, the face that was above joy, sorrow, etc. But it was only a stone face, an escape from reality to an unattainable "reality" that soon succumbed to the living actuality of existence. Art must come out of and be for this life, the here-life; there is no escape except to a more narrow life within the here-world.

It would appear, however, that Mondrian was unaware of the Aristotelian theories which were fundamental to his reasoning method. These theories, in their basic assumptions, have not, in fact, been consciously challenged by artists or scientists until more recent times. In order to understand adequately the new orientation of the non-Camera artist, it is crucially necessary to be conscious of the fact that we are passing from the limited Aristotelian view of reality to a non-Aristotelian, a more extensional view of art and reality. If a precise distinction is made between the old world of Aristotelian art and the new world of non-Aristotelian art, it is possible to begin to comprehend adequately the transformations which began with the invention of the Camera and culminated in the invention of Constructionist art. Today

45. Mondrian, "Plastic Art and Pure Plastic Art," ibid., p. 60.
46. Mondrian, *Le Neo-Plasticisme,* p. 3.

art has arrived at the stage of development which Aristotle got a glimmer of when Architecture reminded him of the "structural method of nature." At last, in Constructionist art the great aspirations of the Classical Greeks can be *properly* realized. But in order to do so it is necessary to revise the old art contents, and mediums and theories. Man can now be an artist in his own right, not by futile "rivalry" with nature, but by cooperation with it; this is the attitude that enables him to invent his own art rather than use manipulations of nature's art as a substitute for creation of art. In reaching the new view of reality and so the new art, the contemporary artist must avoid the tragic egotism of the Classical Greeks; he must not imagine that he too is now ready "to go nature one better," this time to create a better reality than nature. The new artist must seek to acquire the same reverence for nature that *all* the greatest artists of past epochs possessed.

> Systems, scientific and philosophic, come and go.
> Each method of limited understanding is at length
> exhausted. In its prime each system is a triumphant
> success: in its decay it is an obstructive nuisance.
> 358   Alfred N. Whitehead

Whenever anyone says anything, he is indulging in theories.
179
                                        Alfred Korzybski

Those who are enamoured of practice without science are like a pilot who goes into a ship without rudder or compass and never has any certainty where he is going. 212   Leonardo da Vinci

Merely to live, it is necessary to treat nature as having some order. 175   Cassius Keyser

. . . . culture is based on the existence of rules, on their recognition, and their acceptance. Such rules by and large are the essential instruments of freedom. 217   Bronislaw Malinowski

If we compare a body of criticism relating to any of the arts with an equally accredited body of remarks dealing with, let us say, physics or physiology, we shall be struck by the frequency, even in the best critics, of sentences which it is impossible to understand in the same way as we endeavor to understand those of physiologists. 246

C. K. Ogden and I. A. Richards

. . . . there are still many people in the field [of art] who . . . . continue to mumble about a vague gift which they claim is distinct and apart from "intelligence." 38

Milton H. Bird

As usually written about, and taught in colleges, aesthetics is highly abstract and conceptual, having little close contact with the works of art and the experiences of which it speaks. 241 Thomas Munro

The times are ripe for probing into our accepted canons of criticism in painting. We need to dig deep into the dust and darkness of the critical tradition and learn in what strata our antiquated beliefs belong. If we happily discover their appropriate century, it may be we will be discreet enough to quietly lay them to rest and adopt new and more appropriate ones with which to face a living art. 182

Philip N. Youtz

Moreover, we have a vague suspicion that a lot that passes for comment on painting is blithering nonsense concealed behind an iridescent screen of rare words and phrases. 182 Philip N. Youtz

It is interesting that language can state facts; it is also interesting that it can state falsehoods. 303

Bertrand Russell

Now most men do not love to think, and this is perhaps fortunate when instinct guides them, for most often, when they pursue an aim which is immediate and ever the same, instinct guides them better than reason would guide a pure intelligence. But instinct is routine, and if thought did not fecundate it, it would no more progress in man than in the bee or ant. 272 Henri Poincare

Ever since Aristotle placed the activities of the artist in a theological realm of "sensibilities," most philosophers have continued to uphold the error of the Greek by splitting "art" into two categories: "doing," the province of the artist, and "discoursing" or "theorizing," the sole responsibility, indeed the prerogative of the philosopher of art.

Aristotle's separation of the artist and philosopher was perhaps inevitable in his times. To quote Butcher: "No such conception of the artist's dignity [that the artist works for his own enjoyment] was formed in Greece, where in truth the artist was honored less than his art. . . . the painter and sculptor, approach to the condition of a manual labourer." [1] Horace Kallen has paraphrased Aristotle's views on this problem as follows: "Since taste and judgment have their natural seat in the user and not the maker of a work of art, it is the user whom the maker naturally serves. The user's enjoyment and delight is the maker's end. And thence it follows that one who lives in a house is a better judge of it than the builder, one who eats a meal than he who cooks it, one who plays a flute than he who makes it. And thence it follows that the artist belongs rather with the artizan, with the mechanic, the farmer and the slave, than with the rich, the brave, the just, free man whose leisure has enabled him to study and understand the artist's work. Nor can the arts which please the man of leisure please the laboring man. There is an art for each according to his kind, and poets and painters and sculptors and musicians bring to each, according to his kind, recreation, rest and amusement. For the purposes of their ministry, they may employ even depraved figures, provided they use such figures as parts only in a larger whole imitating the noble and the good." [2] In other words, the artist was considered incapable of being an authority in his own profession, incapable of expressing himself theoretically.

After the fall of Rome the priest replaced the philosopher as art critic and the position of the artist and his art eventually regressed to a primitive level. During the Italian Renaissance artists for the first time were recognized as authorities in art theory. From Alberti to Vasari it was the artists who produced the most qualified formulations. The Italian artist became relatively free from servility to the dictates of the Church. Ecclesiastical doctrines were replaced with the scientific attitude. After the Renaissance, however, art philosophers gradually recaptured their old position of authority as artists gradually lost theirs. Again the wordsmen of the *status quo* took precedence over the artist. By the 18th century the activities of philosophers in the field of art had been reduced to a nebulous philosophy labelled "aesthetics." Horace Kallen very ably summed up this philosophy thus: "For the most part, the authors of these works, which never or rarely came to the knowledge of poets, painters, sculptors or other craftsmen, were philosophers and dialecticians whose contacts with the actual *whats, hows,* and *whys* of artists' works and ways were also for the most part nearly nil. They could have promulgated their Science of Beauty if not a single work of art had ever been made. The long, long record of art without esthetics was about, it seemed, to be topped off by as voluminous, if greatly briefer, a record of esthetics without art." [3]

The ancient philosophers seem to have been concerned with the creative process of the artist, but subsequently philosophers have become increasingly concerned with their *own* "creative" activity, the activity of "aesthetics." This was their way of making their profession into a "creative" affair—the result of a desire to become artists too, artists in their own right. Thus we account for their almost total disinterest in actual art. So we are not surprised to hear a prominent aesthetician, Bernard Bosanquet, write in the preface of his book: "Aesthetic theory is a branch of philosophy, and exists for the sake of knowledge and not as a guide to practice. . . . Art, we are told, is useless; in a kindred sense aesthetic may well submit to be useless also." [4]

Highly suspect are the motives of present day art philosophers who are still maintaining that artists are not capable of theorizing about art; for if artists are devoid of this ability, then this field continues to be the philosopher's undisputed prerogative. Thus Curt Ducasse has written on the subject of the artist as theorist: "Indeed, an artist with a theory should be regarded *a priori* with suspicion, for such a one is likely to paint or to sing with his intellectual conscience instead of his feelings, and to give

1. S. H. Butcher: *Aristotle's Theory of Poetry and Fine Arts,* p. 206, Macmillan and Co., Ltd., London, 1911.

2. Horace M. Kallen: *Art and Freedom,* Vol. 1, p. 53. Reprinted by permission of the publishers, Duell, Sloan and Pearce, Inc. Copyright 1942 by Horace M. Kallen.

3. Ibid., p. 37.

4. From Bernard Bosanquet: *A History of Aesthetic,* preface p. xi. New York, 1892. By permission of The Macmillan Company, publishers. In the preface to one of his books, Leo Stein remarks about the subject: "There are no authorities and it is somewhat doubtful whether the subject exists." (From THE ABC OF AESTHETICS, by Leo Stein, published by LIVERIGHT PUBLISHING CORPORATION, New York, 1927.)

us, therefore, not works of art but moral documents." [5] (Actually this is as erroneous as if we were to make the claim that a philosopher with a "feeling" should be regarded *a priori* with suspicion for such a one is likely to philosophize with his emotions instead of his intellect.) According to the implications of Ducasse's theory we must henceforth look with suspicion upon all artists, for the obvious reason that all artists are unavoidably compelled to theorize the moment they talk about art. Ducasse would seem to be unaware of elementary facts about the human nervous system when he theorizes as he does about an artist who theorizes. Both artists and philosophers theorize about art, because it is neurologically impossible to avoid it.

It is not our purpose to deny the "mental" dexterity of the *art* philosopher. Most of them are clever with words and logic; but on the whole they are mere word-magicians. Their fault is not in their talent for inventing logic about art, but rather in the fact that for the most part their logic does not apply to actual art. They appear to be more concerned with theorizing about art theory than with theorizing about actual "art."

With the divorce of the art philosopher from almost all concern with actual art, in preference for something labelled "aesthetics," there appeared the art critic, who at first was largely a reporter, a describer of pictures he had seen. But in our own times this has changed also. The Modern art critic is now mainly concerned with reporting what he "feels." For him, as for the art philosopher, the subject of art has become a pretext for being a "creative" writer. On this subject Herbert Muller went to the point of the matter when he wrote: "Critics are naturally pleased to think that they, too, are artists. They are always tempted to agree with Croce, that they realize their true function by reproducing the artist's intuitive impression, in a moment of esthetic activity identical with creation. They no doubt have such moments, and may be better critics if they are also poets. Nevertheless Croce does not make clear why the great artist, with his exceptional powers of expression, should need their work at all; there is a certain conceit in the implication that they convey what he failed to, do his job for him." [6]

"Criticism is indeed whatever men have a mind to make it; but its peculiar function must lie in what distinguishes it from the creative activity. Its problem is not how to reproduce the work of art but what to do to and for this work." [7] But this latter function is not enough; the Modern critic wants to be artist, creator too. Hence one critic writes: "The only genuine constructive criticism that exists in the plastic arts is a creative act which provokes or follows upon another creative act." [8] This critic apparently not only wants to create, but presumes to provoke the act of creation in the artist.

In short, the career of the art critic has followed a course similar to that of the art philosopher. The job of both at the beginning was to explain the art of the practicing artist; but both increasingly presumed to be artists too, artists in their own right. And the more they presumed this, the more useless they became. First the art philosopher, then the art critic turned into frustrated artists. They are not content merely to have more authority than the genuinely creative artists, nor content to dominate completely the mediocre artists who actually follow the art direction they advocate—they must be artists, creators too.

The critic's profession is well explained by John Dewey: "Criticism is thought of as if its business were not explication of the content of an object as to substance and form, but a process of acquittal or condemnation on the basis of merits and demerits.

". . . . Perception is obstructed and cut short by memory of an influential rule, and by the substitution of precedent and prestige for direct experience. Desire for authoritative standing leads the critic to speak as if he were the attorney for established principles having unquestionable sovereignty." [9]

5. Reprinted from THE PHILOSOPHY OF ART by Curt John Ducasse by permission of The Dial Press, Inc. Copyright 1929 by The Dial Press, Inc., p. 2.

6. Herbert Muller: *Science and Criticism,* pp. 42–43, Yale University Press, New Haven, 1943.

7. Ibid., p. 43.

8. J. J. Sweeney: *Plastic Redirections in Twentieth Century Painting,* p. x, The University of Chicago Press, Chicago, 1934.

9. From *Art as Experience,* by John Dewey, p. 299. New York, 1934. Courtesy of G. P. PUTNAM'S SONS.

During the last four decades, as art has been undergoing tremendous, fundamental change, the critic has become increasingly impotent in his effort to explain art. With each new development of this century he has found himself falling into responsibilities that far outweigh anything he had bargained for. He is no longer able to decide specifically what is or is not important. His dilemma recalls the confusion of the King when he asked Alice:

" 'What do you know about this business?'

'Nothing,' said Alice.

'Nothing *whatever*?' persisted the King.

'Nothing whatever,' said Alice.

'That's very important,' the King said . . . . the White Rabbit interrupted: '*Un*important, your Majesty means, of course,' he said. . . .

'*Un*important, of course, I meant', the King hastily said and went on to himself in an undertone, 'important—unimportant—unimportant—important—' as if he were trying which word sounded best." [10]

We even find many critics presenting their confusion over the new directions as though it were the opposite state of mind. Regarding the conglomerate "variety" of "Modern art," one critic writes: "What is your first impression? Bewildering variety? Yes, that is true. The variety of modern art reflects the complexity of modern life; though this may give us mental and emotional indigestion, it does offer each of us a wide range to choose from." [11] Our studies, however, expose the fact that this "bewildering variety" is the reflection not merely of the "complexity" but of the chaos of "modern life." In these times when the evaluation of art has become extremely difficult, still another critic would advise us that the function of criticism is of value to the degree that it succeeds in "stripping away conscious critical attitudes." [12]

Such comments, we contend, indicate the imminent departure of the non-artist critic from the field of art. He has no specialized knowledge of any kind pertaining to his job; he is neither psychologist, nor any variety of scientist; in fact he is usually very hostile to scientific attitudes. The critic's failure to bring to art anything of much usefulness probably stimulated Oscar Wilde to make the following remark: "I think that the first duty of an art-critic is to hold his tongue at all times upon all subjects:—it is a great advantage to have done nothing—but it is not necessary to abuse it."

It is certainly no accident that the most advanced developments of the present—the arts of the Two-Dimensionalists and Constructionists—are primarily dealt with by the artists themselves. Regarding these arts the critic finds himself with little to say, one way or the other. A handful of artists have made great progress in the effort to formulate the happenings in the post-Cubist art world; these men are generally ignored and will probably be widely read and accepted when their notions are no longer up-to-date.

Many consider the critic's prime asset to be the fact that he is not an artist. The non-artists have some advantages: but the advantages of the competent artist far outweigh those possessed by the critic when it comes to *evaluating* art. Otherwise the implication is that the most inexperienced in the making of art are the most competent to evaluate it.

It should not be cause for surprise, therefore, that we find critics who apparently agree with the Ducasse type of philosopher that artists who formulate their behavior inevitably endanger their ability as artists. Thus James J. Sweeney writes: "To a plastic artist a statement of aims is a noose. Enough rope and plastic interests go hang, or at least take a secondary place. A plastic artist may, through his work, be associated with a movement as a passive illustration of certain of its aspects and survive; but a conscientious attempt to exemplify a movement's tenets inevitably paralyzes—academicises him." [13] He goes on to say that the "conscious exemplification of a theory" then becomes the subject of the artist's work. He warns the artist that the "mind fears the senses," that it is always trying to achieve "complete control by some ruse," and when this happens we see art slowly "sicken and die." [14] Such a theory ignores

10. Lewis Carroll: *Alice in Wonderland.*

11. Alfred Barr, Jr.: *What Is Modern Painting?*, p. 3.

12. Sweeney, *Plastic Redirections*, p. 42.

13. J. J. Sweeney: "Surrealism as a Public Art," *The Kenyon Review*, 1:429, Autumn, 1939.

14. Ibid., pp. 429–430.

the fact that those artists who deliberately theorize as well as those who are merely "passive illustrations" of a theory may be "paralyzed," if they make the error of becoming satisfied to repeat and repeat, consciously or otherwise, some static theory of art. All artists theorize, formulate, because they must! *Those who think they do not are simply unconscious of the theories they abide by in their art behavior.* To state that one does not wish to formulate theories of art is also a theory of art, even if a paradoxical, absurd one!

The impression one has from the entire article from which the above excerpts were taken, is that the artist is such a delicate creature that he cannot stand the strain of coping with the normal responsibilities of theorizing. But if the artist is unable to cope with that very aspect of human behavior which is fundamental to the realization of human culture, namely, the achievement of a constantly developing consciousness of mankind within a particular time-space continuum of history, then we can only regard him as an inferior specimen of humanity. Any competent physiologist, neurologist, etc., however, will assure those who may be in doubt that an artist possesses all the parts and functions of a nervous system that are possessed by Einstein and other such humans who exhibit useful, theoretical behavior. If in view of these undeniable facts, one still insists that Sweeney and Ducasse and the like are correct, then one might conclude that the practice of art has a very degenerative effect upon the human nervous system, that it prevents one from fully exercising those normal abilities which particularly distinguish a human being from an animal. But our studies of history have demonstrated that "art" does not inevitably have a deleterious effect upon the artist's nervous system. The fact that today we find so many artists who seem only too eager to agree with the critics and philosophers in their nonsensical talk about art and artists, only proves that certain *kinds* of art behavior and/or theorizing certainly do have an extremely harmful effect upon the artist's nervous system.

The majority of artists today, as we have already seen, are making drug-art, and they, like their critic-apologists, are averse to any suggestion that an artist must formulate his art in a responsible manner. A very common retort to the statement that fundamental analysis is necessary is to the effect that if an object of art gives one "pleasure," then why should one need to analyze it? Of course it is also possible to secure pleasure from taking a dose of morphine each day, yet few would contend that we need not bother to inquire regarding the consequences of taking it. In short, pleasures are of many kinds, as are also the inevitable consequences of each kind. Elementary knowledge of psychology would make one aware that "pleasure," or any sort of "feeling," can lead us to disaster or to the greatest happiness; the former will be assured if we simply live indiscriminately according to our "feelings," while the latter is more difficult to secure. It would seem to be critically necessary, then, to ferret out the consequences of our "pleasures" in "art," if we are to ascertain whether or not we are involved in undesirable or desirable forms of art behavior. In short, we must become conscious of the kind of abstracting we do as artists.

The theory that "sensibilities" and "feelings" are all the artist needs, that no analysis can be demanded of the artist to explain his behavior has been rampant to an unusual degree ever since the Cubists led the flight from Cubism. We have explained also why the Transitional-Period was necessarily of a highly intuitive character, in that artists were groping for the new direction which did not begin to come to view until 1910 Cubism. In the events since that time we have seen the tragic consequences for the Cubists and all those who chose to ignore the full implications of Cubism. In the case of the ex-Cubists, they not only failed to advance beyond the accomplishments of their youth, but even more tragic, they became the leaders of the regression, especially after 1914. The error of the Cubists was not their ignorance of what they were doing, but rather their decision to eulogize their ignorance in the unconscious effort to avoid knowing coherently what they were doing.

Thus Braque says: "To write a poem, to paint a picture, to carve a stone are unreasonable acts." Léger claims that "reasons only risk confusing rather than clarifying the issue."[15] Picasso is the most "important" proponent of the view that where art is concerned we have no right to "demand its credentials." And, as noted elsewhere, he complains that "Everyone wants to understand art." And "But still, I don't see why the whole world should be taken up with art, demand its credentials, and on that subject give free reign to its own stupidity." Of interest also is the following, which a friend of his reported he once

15. Fernand Léger: "Painting and Reality: A Discussion," *Transition*, p. 104, No. 25, Fall, 1936.

said: "All these people who always want you to explain! A picture isn't explained. When I paint I do what someone does who puts a notice in the paper to find a lost dog." [16] He has also written that he wants "nothing but emotion to be given off" [17] by his work. And he insists, "I have never made trials and experiments." [18] To have done so, of course, would have implied a definite orderly search, a definite objective; and from this would follow the dreaded responsibility of explanations.

Such is the attitude of most of those who had the courage of innovators in the early years of this century. And from this attitude the "Modern" artists have taken their cue. Today they, as well as the critics and art philosophers, are continually warning us of the danger for the artist should he make the grave error of becoming a theorist. Alexander Calder, for example, writes: "When an artist explains what he is doing he usually has to do one of two things: either scrap what he has explained, or make his subsequent work fit in with the explanation. Theories may be all very well for the artist himself, but they shouldn't be broadcast to other people." [19] According to this it would appear that theories are liable to indicate that the artist's past efforts have followed an erroneous direction, or even worse, they are liable to indicate the specific direction that future work should follow. But should an artist find that he *is* somehow in possession of these treacherous theories, then he should have the good sense to keep them a "secret" from "other people." It is this statement which reveals the primary objective of such arguments — namely, to absolve the artist from facing the theoretical implications of his work and talk.

Here are brief quotations from a number of other "Modern" artists, who in various ways make protests similar to those of Calder: "I'm afraid that those who read the following expecting to find the why and wherefore of my painting will be disappointed." Consequently we are not surprised to hear this artist conclude, "I have never been much interested in what other painters have done before me or are doing now." [20] Another starts out: "I duck when asked to explain painting or any particular one." He then informs us that he envies a certain artist who, when a critic asked him what he was doing in his art, replied, "Nothing." [21]

A similar attitude has been adopted by both artists and critics about words. The popular view is that the painter or sculptor is somehow independent of the necessity to have knowledge of the use of language-symbols. One artist says: "It's ten to one you know what art is, but maybe twenty to one you can't say it." [22] Another protests: "If one asks what the paintings mean, I can only reply that it is impossible to add with words to what has already been said with paint." [23] And another claims that, "Painting is so complete an expression in itself that I find it difficult to write about it. I never delve into the why and wherefore, but paint as I feel moved to express my reaction to life about me." [24] And Matisse is reported to have remarked that what the artist says is not important.[25] (In that case, incidentally, according to Matisse himself, his own remark cannot be considered important either, because it is something an artist said.) Henry Moore has declared: "It is a mistake for a sculptor or a painter to speak or write

16. As reported by W. Paalen in *Form and Sense*, p. 29. Series: Problems of Contemporary Art, Number 1, Wittenborn and Co., New York, 1945.

17. Christian Zervos: "Conversation with Picasso."

18. "Picasso Speaks," *The Arts*, 3:315–326, May, 1923.

19. Alexander Calder: "Mobiles," p. 63, in *The Painter's Object*. Edited by Myfanwy Evans, published by Gerald Howe, Ltd., London, 1937, reprinted by permission of John Lane The Bodley Head, London.

20. From *Americans 1942*, 18 Artists from 9 States, p. 11, edited by Dorothy C. Miller, with statements by the artists. Museum of Modern Art Catalogue, New York, 1942.

21. Ibid., p. 38.

22. Ibid., p. 60.

23. From *American Realists and Magic Realists*, p. 26, edited by Dorothy C. Miller and Alfred H. Barr, Jr., with statements by the artists. Museum of Modern Art Catalogue, New York, 1943.

24. Ibid., p. 32.

25. See Curt Ducasse, *Art, the Critic and You*, p. 23.

look like to you. In other words, SEEING and THINKING in "art" are ONE! We see, therefore, that words—i.e., the expression of what we see-think—are tremendously important in art, specifically in the *educative* field.

Actually, then, there seems to be a great need for writing and speaking about art; otherwise we must consider the constant effort in that direction, since ancient times, one great error. And for obvious reasons, competent artists are able to write and speak with the most authority about art.

One of the serious consequences of protesting the impossibility of using words about art is that the critics are thus left free to manipulate language to suit their convenience. In their writings we find such terms as "significant form," "architectonic form," "rhythmic form," "expressive form," "decorative order," "spatial order," "plastic art," "persuasive art," "social art," "proletarian art," "concrete art," "plastic vitality," "rhythmic vitality," "complete Americanization," "eternal primitive," etc., etc. Such terms are used in an obscure, ambiguous context; when a writer wishes to "prove" that some work of art has a positive rating of some kind he simply applies some such favorite label, as though that settled everything. Sheldon Cheney, beginning a chapter in one of his books, says: "Clive Bell calls *it* 'Significant Form.' Dr. Barnes calls *it* 'Plastic Form.' I have called *it* 'Expressive Form.' The aestheticians and intellectualists mostly call *it* non-existent, and Thomas Craven has implied that *it* is an imaginary plaything of a few self-deluded esoterics." (emphasis ours)[33] (In the end one fails to find out precisely what "it" supposedly represents.)

What we need is an art language of a scientific nature, in place of the present philosophical and theological word-noises. Semanticians have shown the disastrous effects of the abuse of language in all our lives. Through them we learn the paramount lesson that one *can say anything* with words, but one *cannot do anything* in the world of reality. It is only because of the flexibility of language that artists, critics and philosophers can say most of the non-sense they do. One thing is inevitable; the language we use reflects the attitude we adopt towards the objective world. In a very striking manner Alfred Korzybski has shown how this is possible. He says: "That languages, as such, all have some structure or other is a new and, perhaps, unexpected notion. Moreover, every language having a structure, by the very nature of language, reflects in its own structure that of the world as assumed by those who evolved the language. In other words, we read unconsciously into the world the structure of the language we use. The guessing and ascribing of a fanciful, mostly primitive-assumed, structure to the world is precisely what 'philosophy' and 'metaphysics' do."[34]

The important problem, then, is the way in which artists and critics use language; generally they abuse it. They hide themselves under an avalanche of word-magic.

It is highly doubtful if any artist or critic would disagree that in science and almost all other fields it is imperative to be constantly increasing one's consciousness in order to achieve useful work. But if we suggest that perhaps this responsibility also applies to the field of art, all but a very few will object. We are told that art is "always striving to be independent of the mere intelligence, to become a matter of pure perception, to get rid of its responsibilities to its subject or material. . . ."[35] This is the 20th century, and yet we are expected to accept the dogma that art is beyond the grasp of the "intellect." If we ask why, we are likely to hear various nebulous sounds indicating that art is one vast, impenetrable mystery.

Hans Arp, for instance, writes of the works of art which "seek to reach beyond human values and attain the infinite and the eternal."[36] Kandinsky claimed that art is born from the artist in a "mysterious and secret way."[37]

tion in art that a genius in art can exhibit all through his life and be ignored, while 99 per cent of the "art lovers" continue to prate about and live in the art world of the past.

33. From EXPRESSIONISM IN ART, p. 97, by Sheldon Cheney, published by LIVERIGHT PUBLISHING CORPORATION, New York, 1934.

34. Alfred Korzybski: *Science and Sanity*, pp. 59–60.

35. Walter Pater: *The Renaissance*, p. 179, Thomas Bird Mosher, Portland, Maine, 1924.

36. Hans Arp: "Abstract Art," *Art of This Century*, p. 29, edited by Peggy Guggenheim, published by Art Aid Corporation, 1942.

37. Wassily Kandinsky: *The Art of Spiritual Harmony*, p. 104, translation and introduction by M. T. H. Sadler, Constable and Co., London, 1914.

The critics are even more vocal about the mystery of art. Alfred Barr concludes, "For in the end what makes a great work of art great is something of a mystery." [38] (In this respect it is interesting to note that the term "mystery" comes from the Greek word "myein," meaning to close, especially to close the eyes.[39]) Sheldon Cheney, in one of his books,[40] begins by pointing out that the mystery of art is increasing, and warns against too exacting theories.[41] Here is one sample of his mode of "explaining" art: "Increasing numbers of people, then, *experience* in works of art an aesthetic pleasure beyond anything to be attained by sense and reason; and because those are people who experience and treasure mystic values, in other grooves of life, they are willing to speak of the form-experience in art as mystic. The revelation, communion and illumination that come with mystic apprehension—most commonly through art, love, and the religious experience—are for them the realest part of living. That the nature of the experience and the reality cannot be explained intellectually, that words cannot compass the full truth, does not nullify the existence or the importance of what we are talking about." [42] Of the mystic, Cheney writes: "He may even withdraw occasionally from the surrounding disorder of human-physical life, into blissful self-identification with the divine Spirit, experiencing the rapture of perfect realization of harmony and order." [43]

In general these attitudes have considerable in common with the behavior of the medieval thinker, so well described by James Harvey Robinson: "The medieval thinker, however freely he might exercise his powers of logical analysis in rationalizing the Christian Epic, never permitted himself to question its general anthropocentric and mystical view of the world. The philosophic mystic assumes the rôle of a docile child. He feels that all vital truth transcends his power of discovery. He looks to the Infinite and Eternal Mind to reveal it to him through the prophets of old, or in moments of ecstatic communion with the Divine Intelligence. To the mystic all that concerns our deeper needs transcends logic and defies analysis. In his estimate the human reason is a feeble rush light which can at best cast a flickering and uncertain ray on the grosser concerns of life, but which only serves to intensify the darkness which surrounds the hidden truth of God." [44]

In times of chaos—the crisis of consciousness—when so many "free" individuals are lost individuals, it is not strange that some have discovered that the whole process of art becomes in their hands a most intriguing obscurity labelled mystery, mystic secret, etc., etc. When the human organism is faced with a situation too severe to tolerate, the individual "passes out," i.e., consciousness is obliterated. This is precisely what is happening in art, where "mystery" is invoked to frustrate every attempt at analysis. In time the rude awakening will come.

In art, as in life in general, we are witnessing a throwback to primitive-like forms of orientation —magic, mysticism—as an escape from the crisis of the present. The "primitive" is glorified while science is vilified. Ancient beliefs of art as a form of inspired revelation have been revived by those who call themselves "Moderns"; they oppose the scientifically inclined with magic and religious verbal incantations.

Having no solution for the problems of the real world, the here-world, the "Modern" artists and their apologists, the critics, have turned to the escape of "religion," to the creation of another-world. In their art, implicitly or otherwise, they deny the real world and its problems (Kandinsky called it a "revolt from dependence on nature" [45]); they change what they see into that which they arbitrarily wish it to be. One "Modern" painter deplores "the spiritual breakdown which followed the collapse of religion"

38. Alfred Barr, Jr.: *What Is Modern Painting?*, p. 37.

39. Erich Kahler: *Man the Measure*, p. 83.

40. *Expressionism in Art*.

41. Ibid., p. 5.

42. Ibid., p. 100.

43. Ibid., p. 324.

44. J. H. Robinson: *The Human Comedy*, p. 134, Harper and Brothers, New York, 1937.

45. Kandinsky, op. cit., p. 91.

and contends that the "Modern" artist has become "the spiritual underground," "the last active spiritual being in the great world." [46] He further informs us that, "each artist has his own religion." [47] Another "Modern" artist writes: "As I see it, painting and religious experience are the same thing, and what we are all searching for is the understanding and realisation of infinity—an idea which is complete, with no beginning, no end, and therefore giving to all things for all time." [48] We are not surprised then to find the former artist also writing: "We say that the individual withdraws into himself. Rather, he must draw from himself. If the external world does not provide experience's content, the ego must." [49] These artists are talking in the same vein as the critic who wrote: "The ideal of to-day is that each artist should create a new art in his own image, record his own individuality in paint or stone." [50] That such non-sense is taken seriously in this century only emphasizes how serious the situation is.

The discoveries of our history have already disproved that one's response to art is essentially "unexplainable," "mysterious." The scientific attitude has proven an excellent means for penetrating mystery and for discouraging its unnecessary manufacture. This can be seen in the following series of quotations:

Critic, Sheldon Cheney:
"Linked with Spirit, with creation, with beauty beyond explanation, is the thing men call art." [51]
". . . . we have climbed, in our search for more satisfying aesthetic enjoyment, into regions intellectually mysterious, perhaps explainable only as mystic." [52]

Historian, James Harvey Robinson:
"No one need fear that the supply of mystery will ever give out; but a great deal depends on our taste in mystery—that certainly needs refining. What disturbs the so-called rationalist in the mystic's attitude is his propensity to see mysteries where there are none, and to fail to see those that we cannot possibly escape." [53]

Mathematicians, Edward Kasner and James Newman:
"High priests in every profession devise elaborate rituals and obscure language as much to conceal their own ineptness as to awe the uninitiated." [54]

Mathematician-Philosopher, Alfred N. Whitehead:
"It is a safe rule to apply that, when a mathematical or philosophical author writes with a misty profundity, he is talking nonsense." [55]

Critic, James J. Sweeney:
"The value of formal criticism to the plastic arts exists primarily in direct ratio to its efficacy at stripping away conscious critical attitudes. Neither the plastic arts in their essential nature nor the fundamentals of our response to them will be explained." [56]

46. Robert Motherwell: "The Modern Painter's World," *Dyn*, The Review of Modern Art, Mexico, p. 10, No. 6, November, 1944.

47. Ibid., p. 10.

48. Ben Nicholson: in *Unit One*, p. 89.

49. Motherwell, in *Dyn*, pp. 12–13.

50. M. C. Allen: *The Mirror of the Passing World*, pp. 32–33, W. W. Norton and Co., Inc., New York, 1928.

51. Cheney, *Expressionism in Art*, p. 4.

52. Ibid., p. 5.

53. Robinson, *The Human Comedy*, p. 140.

54. Edward Kasner and James Newman: *Mathematics and the Imagination*, p. 113, Simon and Schuster, Inc., New York, 1940.

55. As quoted by E. T. Bell in *Men of Mathematics*, p. xxi.

56. Sweeney, *Plastic Redirections*, p. 42.

Psychiatrist, Smith Ely Jelliffe:

"To say the facts are incomprehensible is a rationalization of individual ignorance.

"Ignorance, however, may be no fault. It becomes so only when the individual permits himself to rationalize it, *i.e.,* give it a disguise, which effectually blocks him in the utilization of his intelligence, which might otherwise solve the problem in hand." [57]

Mathematician-Philosopher, Bertrand Russell:

"In all these systems, however, there was felt to be something fantastic, and only philosophers with a long training in absurdity could succeed in believing them." [58]

Freud exposed the poverty of the religionists' views in a clear manner when he discussed their objections to the scientific investigation of those aspects of human behavior long considered the private province of the priest. And what he said in these matters applies directly to the field of "Modern" art, since the theories of both the Modernists and religionists rest on the same false premises. In the following quotations one could with little difficulty replace the term religion with the term art. Freud wrote: "The first objection that one hears is to the effect that it is an impertinence on the part of science to take religion as a subject for its investigations, since religion is something supreme, something superior to the capacities of the human understanding, something which must not be approached with the sophistries of criticism. In other words, science is not competent to sit in judgment on religion. No doubt it is quite useful and valuable, so long as it is restricted to its own province; but religion does not lie in that province, and with religion it can have nothing to do. If we are not deterred by this brusque dismissal, but inquire on what grounds religion bases its claim to an exceptional position among human concerns, the answer we receive, if indeed we are honored with an answer at all, is that religion cannot be measured by human standards, since it is of divine origin, and has been revealed to us by a spirit which the human mind cannot grasp. It might surely be thought that nothing could be more easily refuted than this argument; it is an obvious *petitio principii,* a 'begging of the question.' The point which is being called in question is whether there is a divine spirit and a revelation; and it surely cannot be a conclusive reply to say that the question cannot be asked, because the Deity cannot be called in question. What is happening here is the same kind of thing as we meet with occasionally in our analytic work. *If an otherwise intelligent patient denies a suggestion on particularly stupid grounds, his imperfect logic is evidence for the existence of a particularly strong motive for his making the denial, a motive which can only be of an affective nature and serve to bind an emotion."* (emphasis ours) [59] Further on, and this also applies to the general attitude in art today, Freud wrote: "And, as for the protection that religion promises its believers, I hardly think that any of us would be willing even to enter a motor-car, if the driver informed us that he drove without allowing himself to be distracted by traffic regulations, but in accordance with the impulses of an exalted imagination." [60] One could hardly put it better where the supernaturalists of art are concerned. As Freud has pointed out in regard to the religionists, these theologically minded artists and critics, in order to make it more certain that art cannot be grasped by the "intellect," refuse to submit their doctrines to verifying tests; moreover they do their best to prevent others from doing it for them.

In art times such as ours, when we are warned of the great dangers of consciousness, of "theory," where "feelings" and "instincts" are glorified to the limit, and even the behavior of the infant, the Primitive and the psychotic is seriously adopted as a guide to "normal" behavior, is it any wonder that the world of art is one chaotic mess?

According to many Modern critics and artists, however, it is only something called "society" which is at fault. Thus, for example, Herbert Read writes: "The artist, in the present unsatisfactory organization of society, has no definite status or responsible function, and until the structure of society is mended, the position of the artist must to some extent be anomalous, and his practice inconsistent.

57. Smith Ely Jelliffe: "The Technique of Psychoanalysis," *Nervous and Mental Disease Monographs,* p. 7, No. 26, 1920.
58. Bertrand Russell: *An Inquiry into Meaning and Truth,* p. 145, W. W. Norton and Co., Inc., New York, 1940.
59. Sigmund Freud: *New Introductory Lectures on Psycho-analysis,* pp. 231–232, Carlton House, 1933; permission of Random House, Inc., New York.
60. Ibid., pp. 233–234.

Meanwhile, all that the artist can do is to maintain his integrity, which means that he should concentrate on his technique and perfect his sense of form—which is precisely what the artists in Unit One are doing, to the rejection of every other irrelevant consideration." [61] We are to assume that the artist is simply waiting, in some dormant state of perfection, for an imperfect "society" to pull itself together and offer him a useful place in it. Elsewhere Read advises the artist, in the face of a chaotic world, to escape to one of his own private fabrication: "is our outer world, in its state of political, economic and spiritual chaos, one which man can face with 'universal piety', sensuous satisfaction, spiritual aplomb? Is it not rather a world from which the sensitive soul, be he painter or poet, will flee to some spiritual refuge, some sense of stability? And is he not likely, in that tendency, to desert the perceptual basis of the empirical art of the immediately preceding epoch, in favor of a fixed conceptual basis? . . . . And that is not only my belief but my experience: there is a spiritual satisfaction in such art which has nothing to do with the kind of emotional reaction to life which Rembrandt transmits. . . ." [62] Read is rationalizing a case for artists who are essentially thriving on the laissez-faire attitude that prevails today. Actually they have no desire for anything but a subjective or private world. This would seem to be clearly implicit in Read's own words: "The modern artist is essentially an individualist: his general desire is not to conform to any pattern, to follow any lead, to take any instructions—but to be as original as possible, to be himself and to express himself in his art." [63] A compulsive drive towards individuality at any cost, a sole concern with self—such attitudes are precisely those which produce and perpetuate "the present unsatisfactory organization of society." Their art is a manifestation of a chaotic world; they are a distinct part of the chaos and they thrive on it. Such artists could not assume a "responsible function" in any society, since they fail to face even the responsibilities that directly involve their own profession. Certainly if they wait for something called "society" to straighten out before assuming a "responsible function," they will wait till doomsday. History is filled with evidence that the great artists have recognized their responsibility to participate directly in the creation of an orderly, desirable culture. The great artists have never rationalized chaotic times as an excuse for an intra-uterine retreat from the world. There is no better example than the Italian Renaissance. But "Modern" artists have no solution for the critical problems of art in these times of chaos, and so they shield their impotence with obscurities.

What does all this come to? The artists and critics of Modern art are talking against the value of talking about art while they continue to talk anyway; they are theorizing against the act of theorizing; indulging primarily in analysis to do away with analysis with all the futility of paradox. It is possible to hold to such non-sense because humans can think anything they like and use words anyway they like and paint the world anyway they like. But in the world of reality one can *not do* anything he likes, and if he does assume so he is deluding himself.

But since the paradoxical situation stated above is an impossible one, then we must look elsewhere for the fundamental issues involved. That is, the opponents of theory, analysis, etc., in art inevitably are compelled to theorize one way or another, whether they know it or not. What actually happens is that the art "theorists" we are discussing fall prey to their own fears regarding the harmfulness of theories, for they are simply theorizing, reasoning in a very harmful, destructive manner. Lacking adequate

61. Herbert Read, in *Unit One*, p. 16.
62. Herbert Read: *Art Now*, p. 116, Faber and Faber, Ltd., London, 1933. Read is correct when he says that such artists have nothing to do with the kind of attitude that activated a man like Rembrandt; he faced the problems of reality that confronted artists of his times.
63. Read, in *Unit One*, pp. 11–12.

consciousness of their own theorizing, they cannot be fundamentally aware either of the harmfulness or the benefits of theories. The last thing artists who theorize in this way are qualified to judge is whether or not theorizing is a suitable preoccupation of the artist. They are not even aware of the elementary fact that they do theorize whether they want to or not. But to reason against reason obviously requires the use of reason. This, we repeat, is as much a method of reasoning as any other. Howard Jensen aptly remarks: "It is often said that man is not a reasonable creature, but it may be remarked that if this is really so, only by reason can the fact be known. And reasoners who employ reason to prove the incompetence of reason are interesting objects of study. As Irwin Edman has said, 'Reason may indeed become a fetish, but so may distrust of it.' " [64]

The problem, then, is not who shall or shall not theorize or analyze, since we all must anyway, but rather *how* we theorize or analyze—harmfully or beneficially. On this score Korzybski has written: "The process of abstracting in different orders being inherent in the human nervous system, it can neither be stopped nor abolished; but it can be deviated, vitiated, and forced into harmful channels contrary to the survival trend, particularly in connection with pathological *semantic reaction*. No one of us, even when profoundly 'mentally' ill, is free from theories. The only selection we can make is between antiquated, often primitive-made, theories, and modern theories, which always involve important semantic factors." [65]

The paradox of reasoning against the use of reason is achieved by the use of destructive second-order abstractions. What we need is to reverse this procedure, i.e., use reason to reason about our methods of reasoning. Since we all must theorize anyway to produce every speck of art we do, and since this aspect of our behavior is an obvious mess, then we have no recourse but to face the issues. We must ask if the system of reason we employ is based upon the orientational method of magic, religion or science, etc., and why. On the resolution of these problems rests the resolution of the extant chaos in the art world today.

These artists and critics we have been discussing are not so much opposed to analysis and theory as to certain kinds of analysis and theory, particularly the 20th century variety—that is, controlled, verifiable analysis. The intention is to keep art analysis in as ambiguous, nebulous a condition as possible, thus leaving each individual in a position of arbitrarily choosing to do whatever he pleases. What this amounts to is a form of psychological censorship, frustrating all methods of reason that would interfere with the general flight from reality so prevalent in art today. By avoiding a coherent consciousness of what they are doing in their work, these artists avoid the responsibilities of value judgments about the consequences of their choice of direction. As Karen Horney well put it: "Refraining from value judgments, not daring to take the responsibility for making them, is a widely spread characteristic of modern liberal man." [66]

Our times have frequently been characterized as a "retreat from reason"; to be more correct, we should recognize the present situation as a retreat from the *responsibilities* of reason. Those who are so very concerned about the dangers of theorizing for the artist, and who fail to recognize that they do theorize anyway, are essentially trying to avoid the responsibilities normally assumed in more normal times. Theirs is a program of obscurantism. Regarding this attitude, Sidney Hook has written: "Still others openly declare it to be axiomatic that every experience, every feeling and emotion, directly reports a truth that cannot be warranted, and does not need to be warranted, by experiment or inference.

"These, bluntly put, are gateways to intellectual and moral irresponsibility. They lay down roads to a happy land where we can gratify our wishes without risking a veto by stubborn fact." [67]

Until we perform an adequate examination of the modes of analysis we abide by, we cannot comprehend the nature of our objections to responsible, verifiable methods of analysis. But when this is done, it becomes possible to realize that objections of this sort are part of an effort to conceal our insecurities. These insecurities have arisen because of the vast, critical changes that have occurred in the course of art history, particularly since Cubism. Things have changed which we thought could never change.

64. Howard E. Jensen: "Science and Human Values," *The Scientific Monthly,* 53:266, September, 1941.
65. Korzybski, *Science and Sanity,* p. 279.
66. Karen Horney: *New Ways in Psychoanalysis,* p. 296. W. W. Norton and Co., Inc., New York, 1939.
67. Sidney Hook: "The New Failure of Nerve," *Partisan Review,* X:5, January-February, 1943.

During the past 2,000 years there have been periods, such as the present, when reason has been ridiculed, and periods when it has been exalted. But whichever the case, reason has always been relied upon to justify the ridicule or exaltation of reason. So long as no alternative presented itself to free men from this cage of two-valued logic (either-or evaluation), so long were men forced to flee from one wall only to run into the other. But both extremes are vitally necessary, in the sense that existence is inescapably a matter of emotion-intellect. Today we again must reinstate the "intellect," but this time we must seek to integrate not eliminate "emotion." In the words of Korzybski: "If we consistently apply the organism-as-a-whole principle to any psycho-logical analysis, we must conjointly contemplate at least both aspects, the 'emotional' and the 'intellectual', and so *deliberately ascribe* 'emotional' factors to any 'intellectual' manifestation, and 'intellectual' factors to any 'emotional' occurrence. That is why, on human levels, the *elementalistic* term 'psychological' must be abolished and a new term *psycho-logical* introduced, in order that we may construct a science." [68]

Henri Poincaré opposes the notion that "emotions," "sensibilities," "inspiration," and "intuition" are the supreme and only necessities of the "creative" process, as follows: "It never happens that the unconscious work gives us the result of a somewhat long calculation *all made,* where we have only to apply fixed rules. We might think the wholly automatic subliminal self particularly apt for this sort of work, which is in a way exclusively mechanical. It seems that thinking in the evening upon the factors of a multiplication we might hope to find the product ready made upon our awakening, or again that an algebraic calculation, for example a verification, would be made unconsciously. Nothing of the sort, as observation proves. All one may hope from these inspirations, fruits of unconscious work, is a point of departure for such calculations. As for the calculations themselves, they must be made in the second period of conscious work, that which follows inspiration, that in which one verifies the results of this inspiration and deduces their consequences. The rules of these calculations are strict and complicated. They require discipline, attention, will, and therefore consciousness." [69] To be sure, "intuition," "emotion," etc. have their necessary functions, but when we try to function with intuition alone, which is impossible anyway, the result leads to chaos; intuition is only "a point of departure."

Therefore, it is a gross error to claim that "Art may flourish in a rank and barbaric manner from an excess of animal vitality; but it withers and dies in the arid excesses of reason." [70] This over-simplifies the problem; it continues rather than resolves the split between emotion-thinking. When *either* extreme exists, the records of history show that confusion and maladjustment inevitably ensue.

The new attitude points up the defects of both the old extreme attitudes; it recognizes the interdependent nature of emotion-thinking, rather than insisting upon a split between them that can only be accomplished verbally. We deal with definite structure-function where the nervous system and environment are concerned; it is our job to search for the natural laws; ignoring them, although possible, has disastrous consequences.

Therefore, the issue in any art times has never been and is not now one of reason versus non-reason. Artists in general are simply unaware of the kind of reason they employ, unaware that their unconscious basic assumptions about art are part of an effort to ward off facing the chaos that exists.

In a sense artists and critics are correct to contend that "theory," "science," etc., are a threat to "art," because when properly used, theory and the scientific attitude will lead to the elimination of those forms of art that result from infantile irresponsibility. But if artists continue their prevalent delusion that they are different, beyond and above the level of all other forms of human life; that they have a private, telephonic communication with another-world; that they are god-like creators; that they cannot be understood except when one accepts their pronouncements as having the absolute authority of revelation; that they must be permitted the arbitrary, unlimited freedom usually attributed to gods—then so long will the rest of society leave artists to shift for themselves in their own rarefied world. If the artist wants to be recognized as an integral, indispensably important part of this-world, then he had better recognize his place in it and proceed accordingly!

68. Korzybski, *Science and Sanity,* p. 23.
69. Henri Poincaré: *The Foundations of Science,* p. 394, The Science Press, Lancaster, Pa., 1929.
70. Read, *Art Now,* p. 30.

Painting in the manner of Jack the Ripper can interest detectives, criminologists, psychologists and doctors for the insane. It is and will remain outside modern life, outside our social and artistic needs; it has no relations with our architectural spirit and our constructive intelligence. 371

Theo van Doesburg

We have the experiences of the debasers of painting to show that the dream is a false conductor
to the realm of the plastic. The goal of painting
is not to expose one's vices or to undress oneself
before the spectator. These "affecting" canvases
that are presented to you in each art shop as
modern painting are the cork on the bottle of
individualism. There is nothing in that bottle itself
but poison. 371
                              Theo van Doesburg

When we remember that in every neurosis there are contradictory tendencies which the neurotic is unable to reconcile, the question arises as to whether there are not likewise certain definite contradictions in our culture, which underlie the typical neurotic conflicts. 152
Karen Horney

These contradictions embedded in our culture are precisely the conflicts which the neurotic struggles to reconcile. . . . 152
Karen Horney

. . . . behind every rational and irrational force in human society there is a social mechanism which determines when it is to appear and what forms it is to take. 220
Karl Mannheim

If a distinction is to be made between men and monkeys, it is largely measurable by the quantity of the subconscious which a higher order of being makes conscious. That man really lives who brings the greatest fraction of his daily experience into the realm of the conscious. 110 Martin H. Fischer

The preparation of myself for future living, consciously, deliberately, purposefully, by well-chosen discipline, is a thing which apparently the rat cannot do. 148
C. Judson Herrick

Psychologically, we have to examine the relation of basic propositions to experiences, the degree of doubt or certainty that we feel in regard to any of them, and the methods of diminishing the former and increasing the latter. 303
Bertrand Russell

"Fantasy," in one form or another, has always been present in all art, but in varying kinds and degrees and for *different* reasons. In the first or predominantly Mimetic section of history, however, it *decreased* in proportion to man's *increased ability to depict nature ever more accurately*. That is, it was a *defect* gradually overcome. With the invention of the Camera the fantasy resulting from inability to depict nature accurately was to a large extent eliminated. In the subsequent Transitional-Period, however, fantasy manipulations of reality increasingly appeared in non-Camera art. This new use of fantasy was again evidence of a defect rather than an asset to the art direction which was being unconsciously sought. But even at this late date few recognize this.

The Impressionists, we have seen, began the recent tendency of changing nature into what it is not. From what they had begun there developed Cézanne, Seurat on the one hand, and van Gogh, Gauguin on the other. The former were predominantly characterized by a great effort to penetrate into the Structural Process of visual phenomena, and the latter by an attraction to the fantasies of reality, which in the Transitional-Period inadvertently arose as a result of the effort to reach the Structural Process. These two factors—fantasy and structure—flow like two overlapping streams side by side throughout the Transitional-Period, and increase in intensity right up to and beyond the advent of Constructionist art.

Let us trace these two streams further. From Post-Impressionism emerged the arts of Fauvism (or Expressionism) and Cubism. The Fauvists, we have shown, were *primarily* concerned with the fantasy factor, which they took over particularly from van Gogh, while the Cubists were *primarily* concerned with the structural factor inherited from Cézanne. At first, however, the Fauvists were greatly concerned with the problem of color-shapes and were relatively independent of the necessity to copy the *actual* shapes of nature objects. But failing to see or fearing the way in which their alleged objective could be attained, they preferred to become fascinated by the factor of fantasy which had increased considerably in their works as a result of their attempts to secure their original objective. Consequently the Fauvists eventually devoted their efforts primarily to distortive or fantasy-imitations of nature's appearances. The dream world, the fantasy, came to dominate in their works.

Whereas the symptomatic aspect of Post-Impressionism gave the impetus to the kind and degree of fantasy art-escape practiced by the Fauvists, the symptomatic aspect of Cubism offered the opportunity for still another kind and an even greater degree of art fantasy. While the Fauvists were fearful of attempting the final step entailed in their original objective, the Cubists were daring enough to continue further. The latter pursued their interests in structure to such an extent that they almost completely eliminated nature objects from their art. The intensity and extensiveness of the Cubists' breakup of nature's appearances, however, were to provide the pretext and method for the greatest degree of fantasy art-escape which has ever appeared; namely, Surrealism. The Post-Impressionists and the Fauvists had only distorted the general form of nature objects, but the Cubists juxtaposed many different views of the same object or different objects in a single painting, arbitrarily putting objects or parts of objects together which are never seen together in reality in the way these artists depicted them. In short, they appeared to break completely all the laws that previous artists had discovered and developed for the accurate recording of nature's appearances.

But it was an error of tragic proportions not to realize that the fundamental objective of Cubism was to reach a consciousness of the Structural Process of visual phenomena. Most artists, however, interpreted this breakup of nature's appearances by the Cubists as signalling their complete liberation from the dictates of nature's actual appearances. The artist was now presumably at liberty to devise any means for manipulating the appearances of reality into private symbols, the more private the greater the genius. Hence after Cubism there was no longer any question of whether one should distort the appearances of nature, nor even how one should distort; now any kind of distortion seemed justified. The only thing the Modernists refused to do was to accept Cubism as signalling the "great decision" — to remove nature's appearances from non-Camera art. They insisted on limiting the artist to the manipulation of the old content. As one Surrealist, Paul Eluard, was later to remark: "Picasso contrived to paint the simplest objects in such a way that everyone again became not only able but eager to describe them." [1] This was but another way of claiming that Picasso had succeeded in salvaging the old contents by fabricating for non-Camera artists a new interest in the old contents, which with Cubism had seemed to be distintegrating into oblivion. Thus the new conservatives, the Modernists, felt a vague relief from their fear that the old contents was coming to an end in non-Camera art.

In the diagram opposite we see what happened to the two factors of the Transitional-Period which we have been discussing. There were two general groups of artists throughout the Transitional-Period and afterwards: (1) Those who largely strove to exploit its potentialities for creating an escape art; (2) those who largely strove to exploit its potentialities for creating the new epoch of art. The Impressionists, at the beginning of the Transitional-Period, split into the two Post-Impressionist directions; the Cubists at the end of the Transitional-Period split into the two post-Cubist directions. Both the fantasy and structural factors had been considerably intensified in Cubism, because, as a greater effort was made to reach the Inventive stage, there inevitably ensued greater distortion and breakup of the arrangement of nature forms. The split between these two factors became decisively apparent after 1910 and especially after 1914.

1. Quoted by Georges Hugnet: "In the Light of Surrealism," *Fantastic Art Dada Surrealism*, p. 37, edited by Alfred H. Barr, Jr., Museum of Modern Art, New York, 1936.

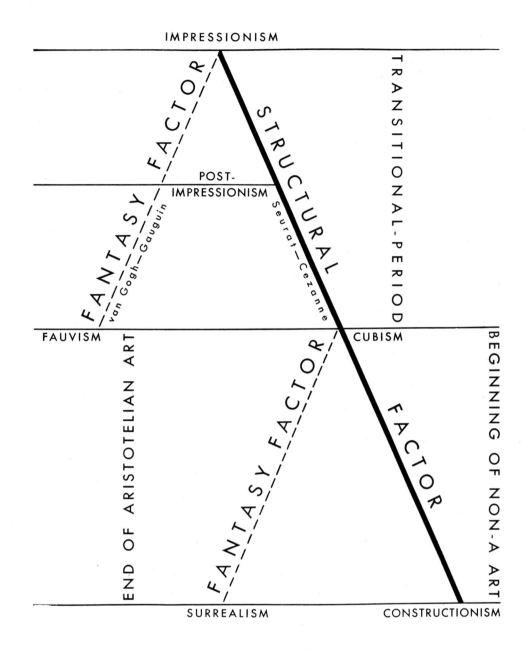

IMPRESSIONISM

FANTASY FACTOR

STRUCTURAL

TRANSITIONAL-PERIOD

POST-
IMPRESSIONISM

van Gogh—Gauguin

Seurat—Cezanne

FAUVISM

END OF ARISTOTELIAN ART

CUBISM

BEGINNING OF NON-A ART

FANTASY FACTOR

FACTOR

SURREALISM

CONSTRUCTIONISM

If we look back at our reproductions of Cubist works, we shall find that by 1910 the structural interest had already reached the highest point to which it was to be taken by the original Cubists. In that year the Cubists had concluded all their positive contributions to the future evolution of art. In the period 1910-1912 there appeared and began to dominate in their art contents those invented objects of man, such as letters, bottles, musical instruments, etc. This material, as we have seen, functioned as a substitute solution, i.e., invented forms from other fields were employed as a substitute for the artist's invention of his own man-made forms. And, as that has been explained, this material, in the sense that it was "recognizable," also acted as a back-door return to the old contents. After 1910 the original Cubists oscillated between invention and the re-introduction of the old content, as though wondering which to give up.

In this period, then, began the crisis in Western art which has continued to the present day. It was during this period, 1910-1912, that the following important, opposed events occurred:

1. Malevitch and Mondrian became Cubists, continuing where the ex-Cubists left off
2. The first Cubist sculptor (Laurens) appeared.
3. Kandinsky published *Upon the Spiritual in Art.*
4. The Futurists had their first exhibition and published their first manifesto
5. Duchamp, Chirico, Chagall, etc., began activities which were the genesis of what was later labelled Dadaism and still later Surrealism.[2]

The year following 1912 marked the appearance of Constructionist art. In short, after 1910 the "chaos of Modern art" began to spin. Certain artists—the De Stijlists and the Constructionists—continued the structural direction of Cubism, but the majority concentrated upon the fantasy factor; see diagram p. 513.

In the years immediately following the climactic events of Cubism, the general trend was to return directly to some confused form of the old kind of art. Among these we find such artists as Oritz, Weber, Rivera, Severini, and a number of other similar, minor Cubist artists. Some of these subsequently attempted to solve their personal dilemma by devoting themselves to picturizing with 19th century art techniques a crusade for the "rights of the masses." In the age of the moving Film they returned to the simple task of making what was merely an advanced form of picture-writing. Thus they thought to banish from themselves the terrifying problem of what to do. They seemed quite unaware of the fact that the Camera with all its remarkable devices for recording reality could do an incomparably better job of what they claimed to be doing.

But the majority of those who deserted Cubism and did not go directly to Dadaism or Surrealism, became Inbetweeners or Distortionists, as we have called them. The fantasy factor was nurtured by these artists until it became a major goal in art. The Dadaists and Surrealists simply gave it a final, desperate twist in their "all out" effort to overcome the deterministic implications of the "great decision" —Cubism. By 1916, just two years after the original Cubists had definitely plunged into fantasy, the Dadaists brought the extant confusion to a state of hysteria.

Rather than copy, as most artists had previously done, or eliminate nature's appearances, as the Two-Dimensionalists did, the Dadaists decided to depict nature's objects in ever more extraordinary and unexpected situations and to depict objects generally not to be met with in art. Thus they continued the older method of art, but instead of just copying or just distorting, they did both, and threw in the "unexpected" and the "absurd" as the supreme objective of art. For example, they would employ the "laws of chance" (Arp's expression), e.g., dropping all kinds of scraps of paper on another sheet of paper and pasting them down wherever they happened to land. This was considered an act of genius![3] Thus Hugnet, an ardent apologist for the Dadaists, himself a Surrealist, writes: "With Arp, on the other hand, and even more with Ernst, newspaper, wallpaper, photographs, and vignettes, picked up at random, taken ready-made and unaltered from their normal context and redistributed easily and blindly, integrate what was borrowed in a recreation of the object and transpose its superficial reality into a superior reality."[4]

Hugnet also tells us that Duchamp signed a print of Leonardo's *Mona Lisa* after painting a mustache upon it; and that Picabia nailed an empty picture frame to the ground, to which he had hoped to tie a live monkey with some strings, but being unable to do this, he produced a toy monkey and called it *Portrait of Cézanne.*[5] This sort of infantilism—Duchamp's contempt for Leonardo, Picabia's

2. The dates for these events are from the Museum of Modern Art publication, *Cubism and Abstract Art.*

3. As a result of many such antics, was it not to be expected that in time individuals by the hundreds thought they could be geniuses too, since it was that easy? Hence, business men and prize-fighters; school teachers and movie stars; housewives, carpenters, janitors, fishermen, bartenders, barbers, along with all kinds of other men and women who simply had nothing else to do, joined in with the status of professionals in the production of "Modern Art"—masterpieces all! Recently one of these amateurs wrote a book explaining that painting was a simple matter; for this assumption he is not entirely to blame.

4. Hugnet, "Dada," *Fantastic Art Dada Surrealism,* p. 17.

5. Ibid., p. 31.

contempt for Cézanne (and later the Surrealist Dali's contempt for Mondrian)—was nothing but the hostile expression of frustrated mentalities. Such behavior reminds one of some of the activities of the nazi-psychotics a few years later. The Dadaists and the Surrealists, like the swastika daubers, tried to discredit by ridicule everything that made them conscious of their own inadequacies.[6]

The Surrealists, direct offspring of the Dadaists, have carried on and perfected their heritage from their exhausted forbears. Thus they too have reinstated the old contents of art in one way or another, relying solely upon the "unexpected," the "absurd," etc. And although the Surrealists reiterate their refusal to depict the "external world," and deny it for another "superior reality," yet they cannot resist informing us that this or that work of theirs "seems more convincing than the reality of a photograph." [7] They lack the courage to give up the old art content, and as though resentful that this is so, they give vent to their frustration by literally mutilating the old art content.

Perhaps the most significant fact about the reactionary forces at both ends of the Transitional-Period is that the artists of neither group were content to be mere copyists of nature's appearances; both groups wished to be "creative" artists. Yet both opposed those who most completely did "create" their art. Thus, if the old Realists of the latter part of the 19th century represented the confusion of the conservative who wished to continue the past because he feared the new, then the present day "Realists," the SURrealists of the 20th century represent the confusion of those who at one time actually attempted the new, but lacked the courage to see it through. They decided to compromise with the old contents and thus a new type of conservative was born. (See pp. 444-445.)

The Surrealists also emulated their progenitors, the Dadaists, in their hysterical rejection of the responsibilities of reason. The Dadaists were simply among the first of that modern variety of lost, confused individuals who began to multiply rapidly after the breath-taking decisions of Cubism were stated for all to see. Lacking the courage to follow the order of development determined by the historical evolution of Western art, they therefore decided to inaugurate a program of disorder and confusion. Heretofore artists had generally striven to increase their consciousness and control of art; now the direct opposite was proposed and exalted. Being unable to face the difficult responsibilities of their times, they decided to enthrone the shirking of responsibilities as the epitome of all ambitions. Thus one of the Dadaists wrote: "What is beautiful? What is ugly? What is great, strong, weak? What is Carpentier, Renan, Foch? Don't know! What is 'I'? Don't know! Don't know, don't know, don't know!" [8] And another one said: "You do not understand, of course, what we are doing! Well, my dear friends, we understand it still less. How wonderful, isn't it, that you are right! . . . You don't understand? Neither do I; how sad!" [9]

In the following quotations we see the attempt to confuse by employing the device of contradictions—to deny and to admit *all* in the attempt to ward off *all* attacks and to justify themselves at *all* points with *all* things. (The nazi-fascist-communist behaves in this unprincipled manner in the political field.) "Dada is ageless, it has no parents, but stands alone, making no distinction between what is and what is not. It approves while denying, it contradicts itself, and acquires new force by this very contradiction. Its frontal attack is that of a traitor stealing up from behind. It undermines established authority. It turns against itself, it indulges in self-destruction, it sees red, its despair is its genius. There is no hope, all values are leveled to a universal monotony, there is no longer a difference between good and evil—there is only an awareness. Dada is a taking-stock, and as such it is as irreparable as it is ridiculous. It knows

6. True enough they ridiculed some very ridiculous conventions, but they could not stop at that; they had to ridicule everything their infantile minds touched. Their one genuine act was to ridicule even their own ridicule (for, we are told: "The real Dadaists are against Dada." Ibid., p. 30). At least the Dadaists and their successors have revealed clearly the schizophrenic split in our culture. We agree with Hugnet when he writes that "Dada was the sickness of the world." (Ibid., p. 15.)

7. Hugnet, "In the Light of Surrealism," *Fantastic Art Dada Surrealism*, p. 45.

8. Quoted by A. Breton, "Pour Dada," Les Pas perdus, pp. 93–94. As quoted by Lemaitre, reprinted by permission of the publishers from Georges Lemaitre, *From Cubism to Surrealism in French Literature*, 1941, p. 169.

9. Quoted by E. Bouvier, "Initiation à la littérature d'aujourd'hui," p. 89, Paris: Renaissance du Livre, 1928; from Lemaitre, op. cit., pp. 170–171.

only itself." [10] Hugo Ball, one of the original Dadaists, tells us in his diary of June, 1916, that: "Every kind of mask is therefore welcome to him [the Dadaist], every play at hide and seek in which there is an inherent power of deception." [11] The Dadaists also claimed: "Reason was antagonistic to the spirit: it constantly turns toward the useful and mechanically quenches any gratuitous impulse of the spirit." [12] And Duchamp has written: "What is the solution? There is no solution because there is no problem. Problem is the invention of man—it is nonsensical." [13]

The Surrealists hoped, as did the Dadaists, that by ridiculing "reason," by claiming that their world was beyond the reach of reason, they could thus keep their world from being interfered with by the use of responsible reason. Thus Hugnet speaks of Surrealism's "rôle of investigator into the *immense undetermined region over which reason does not extend its protectorate.*" [14] Breton, one of the leaders of the Surrealists, protests that: "The association of thoughts or images must not be led by the cold dry tool of logical reason which works under the control of all manner of preoccupations foreign to the normal character of expression. . . ." [15]

In this way they hoped to free themselves from everything; as Breton put it: "let your subjective being pour out its content without restraint and you shall be free, wholly free. . . . ." [16] Thus some of them claimed to be striving for the "free," direct, unconscious approach of the Primitive, of the child, etc. As one of the Dadaists put it, "To surpass oneself in naiveté and childishness—that is still the best antidote. . . ." [17] They wanted to recapture the ability of the child to slide into a world of fantasy at will. But the world of the child is reserved for only one kind of normal human being—a child. All others who attempt to adopt this fantasy world such as that possessed by the child do so at the price of giving up adult "mental" health. This is precisely why the fantasy world of the child is so greatly unlike the pathological world of fantasy that the Dadaist, Surrealist *or* psychotic fabricates. The end result of such efforts is that the individual pursuing them far enough becomes a pathological hybrid of what he futilely strives to be—primitivistic, infantile or whatnot.

In order to achieve "total emancipation" the Surrealist also "proposes automatism." [18] To submerge the consciousness of the *lost self,* to submit to the unfettered subconscious of which the self is but a fatalistic vehicle, all this is well exemplified by the Surrealists and those headed in that direction. One of the leading Surrealists, Max Ernst, writes: "Since the becoming of no work which can be called absolutely Surrealist is to be directed consciously by the mind (whether through reason, taste or will), the active share of him hitherto described as the work's 'author' is suddenly abolished almost completely. *This 'author' is disclosed as being a mere spectator of the birth of the work, for either indifferently or in the greatest*

10. Hugnet, "Dada," op. cit., p. 15. It all has a familiar ring to it; we need only recall this by the good Tertullian: "The Son of God died—this is credible just because it is folly. He has been buried and resurrected—this is certain because it is impossible." (Quoted by Kahler, in *Man the Measure,* p. 258.)

11. Hugo Ball: "Dada: 1916–1936," Fragments from a Dada Diary, *Transition,* p. 73, No. 25, Fall, 1936.

12. Quoted by J. J. Sweeney: *Plastic Redirections in Twentieth Century Painting,* p. 85.

13. Quoted by Harriet and Sidney Janis, "Marcel Duchamp, Anti-Artist," p. 24, *View,* Duchamp Number, Series V, No. 1, 1945. We have heard much about the rationalistic inquisitiveness of the French mentality in art. But after 1914 this attitude is seen definitely in reverse. In an attempt to escape their dilemma when they failed to penetrate the chaos of art, the artists of France threw the whole force of their rationalistic inheritance into the discrediting of rationality. As a matter of fact, it takes such an inheritance, gone decadent, to succeed in deceiving men as thoroughly as has the so-called School of Paris with such leaders as Duchamp and Breton. Where great artists of France once talked of problems and their solution, now their artists (the author knows of only one exception) talk of problems as "nonsensical," art as "unreasonable." (See fn. 36.)

14. Hugnet, "In the Light of Surrealism," *Fantastic Art Dada Surrealism,* p. 46.

15. Quoted by Sweeney, *Plastic Redirections,* p. 87. Of course, this, too, was "logical reasoning" of a *kind*—"cold, dry" or "hot, moist," whatever the temperature or humidity, makes little difference.

16. Quoted by Cheney, *The Story of Modern Art,* p. 517.

17. Ball, in *Transition,* op. cit., p. 75.

18. Hugnet, "In the Light of Surrealism," *Fantastic Art Dada Surrealism,* p. 52.

excitement, he merely watches it undergo the successive phases of its development. [emphasis ours] Just as the poet has to write down what is being thought—voiced—inside him, so the painter has to limn and give objective form to *what is visible inside him.*" [19] This is precisely the kind of "solution" we would expect artists to seek who are unable to face the problems of their art times; i.e., to be mere vehicles, utterly irresponsible for their behavior as artists. Since they could not face the responsibilities arising out of Cubism, they hoped to escape them by turning to the "all-powerful" *sub*conscious.

Charles Glicksberg correctly appraised the paradox implicit in this situation when he wrote: "The surrealist . . . . is essentially a practitioner of magic; his exploitation of the subconscious by means of devices learned from Freudianism, is conscious and deliberate; the will is active; the intellect bends its energies to prevent any interference with the upward flow from the depths." [20] The Surrealist did not see, because he did not wish to, that if the subconscious produced fundamental truths, it was only by adequate consciousness of them that one could fully ascertain this to be the case. The Surrealist's attraction to the subconscious and its alleged superiority over controlled, conscious reasoning, exposed the fundamental fact that he was really more concerned with consciousness as a means for evading the problems and responsibilities of consciousness. (See previous chapter.)

Closely related to their effort to return to the subconscious is the attitude of the Surrealists towards dreams. As we know, they often compare the realization of their works to the formation of the dream process as described by psychoanalysis. To look at their works from the point of view of dreams in a scientific manner, is certainly useful for comprehending them. However, we must distinguish their works from dreams, since the Surrealist, when producing his art, is not, like a dreamer, asleep, wholly in an unconscious state. His works are the result of erratic hops from unconscious to conscious decisions. Normally, however, a human being strives to realize an ever enlarging, orderly consciousness which he uses to comprehend and regulate the impulses of the subconscious.

As for the alleged relationship between the psychoanalyst's concern with dreams and that of the Surrealist, there is opposition, not correspondence, as some would lead us to believe. Freud has pointed out that in ancient times dreams were regarded as manifestations of some superior powers either demoniacal or divine, but that today it is recognized that the dream is the result of the dreamer's own behavior.[21] It is to the former of these views, the ancient one, that the Surrealist abjectly turns.

In explanations of Surrealist art its admirers often point out that such works introduce "psychological" material, as though it were unique in this respect. Actually all art introduces "psycho-logical" components. Psychological factors are erroneously identified almost exclusively with Surrealist art, because such factors are associated only with the dark, the foreboding, the insane, the cruel, the pathological, etc., of which one certainly gets his fill in the art behavior of the Surrealists. It would be more to the point if one spoke of the *particular* "psycho-logical" tendencies apparent in a particular form of "art," as differentiated from those apparent in any other form of art. Such differentiation would expose the Surrealist's aura of mystery as essentially the product of maladjustment.[22]

Charles Glicksberg, concentrating on the writers, has evaluated in an excellent manner the "mysteries" and mysticism of the new "reality" that the Surrealists would offer us. What he says applies to "visual" artists also: "The surrealists, on the contrary, dabble only in the superficial and what might be called the theatrical aspects of mysticism. Exploiting the limits of the unutterable, they cash in on the infinite possibilities opened up by the repudiation of reason; they derive a sense of heightened power from rejecting the rigid outlines of the material world and picturing the sublimely grotesque and disordered universe projected by the creative eye of the unconscious. But they are impelled by no profound and

---

19. Max Ernst: "Inspiration to Order," *Art of This Century,* p. 139, edited by Peggy Guggenheim.

20. Charles I. Glicksberg: "Mysticism in Contemporary Poetry," *The Antioch Review,* 3:242, Summer, 1943.

21. Sigmund Freud: *Dream Psychology,* p. 1, The James A. McCann Co., New York, 1921.

22. It is unfortunate that leading psychiatrists and psychologists have for the most part paid little attention to the phenomenon of Surrealism. Their neglect is partly responsible for its continuance. Most of them prefer to go roving and stumbling around in a generalization they call the artist's "creative impulse."

urgent vision of life, they possess no lofty and liberating insight into the nature of man and the fate he must undergo during his trial on earth; they are not holy seekers after salvation. *At best, they are practitioners of verbal magic, alchemists of the word, poets who make of the dream and the neurosis the secret principle of all art.* They have no unifying faith to sustain them in the anarchic universe of flux, no philosophy to guide them in their life or work. All they can do is to parade before us the bleeding pageant of their unconscious minds." (emphasis ours)[23]

Most of us are confused by the "new force" which the Surrealists acquire by their contradictions; we do not understand that it is the force of "self-destruction"; it is something like witnessing a suicide. There is little doubt that the behavior of Surrealists would be considerably less "impressive" or "amusing" if we all had the opportunity to become acquainted with "mental illness" and comprehend it scientifically in the human sense of that term. We would then become aware of the fact that the sort of behavior common with Surrealists is exactly that for which the hospital inmates are being treated. Lacking this experience, we may unconsciously possess a fear and respect for the behavior of the insane, bordering on the religious awe of the "unknown."

It is a well known fact that "insane" individuals have played important roles in the history of magic and religion. In some Primitive cultures one who is "mentally ill" is often chosen for the position of medicine man, since such a person is considered best suited to act as the connecting link between the tribe and the powerful world of the "unknown." *It is the remnant of this attitude towards the insane which continues to operate in Surrealism, both for those who make it and those who live with it.* One becomes hypnotized by the attitudes and gestures of the Surrealists, who promise escape into the protective womb of the "unknown," sheltered by the power of the occult. But they are fake medicine men. They are not trying to "heal"; they thrive upon and increase the brutality of the world.

Although the Dadaists had laid the ground work by which it was hoped to escape the despised sanity of reason, and the Surrealists had continued the direction, the climactic effort to achieve this objective was made by Dali. The Dadaists were on the right track; Dali would simply give their mode of behavior a higher, more subtle polish, in order to complete the program of confusion inherited from the Dadaists. Thus he wrote: "I believe the moment is at hand, when by a paranoiac and active advance of the mind, it will be possible (simultaneously with automatism and other passive states) to systemize confusion and thus to help discredit completely the world of reality." [24]

Speaking of the difference between Dali and the other Surrealists, James Soby writes: "What distinguishes him from established artists within the Surrealist group was his bringing to Surrealist art a new objectivity to replace the confessional subjectivity of his predecessors. He did so by changing the formula of creative stimulus. Whereas the art of the earlier Surrealists had sprung from an artificially induced and terminable state of receptivity to subconscious inspiration, Dali declared that his art sprang from a constant, hallucinatory energy. He proposed to paint like a madman rather than as an occasional

23. "Mysticism in Contemporary Poetry," op. cit., p. 236. (See also his "The Psychology of Surrealism" which appeared in the English magazine, *Polemic*, No. 8.) Glicksberg is one of the two responsible individuals who, to the author's knowledge, has had the courage to look at Surrealism for what it actually is. Most of us have been deceived, at least enough that we hesitate to maintain what we suspect is the actual case. Another author who has had the courage to speak up without compromise is George Orwell in his *Dickens, Dali and Others.*

24. Quoted by J. T. Soby, in *Salvador Dali*, p. 12, The Museum of Modern Art, New York, 1941, from *La femme invisible*, Ed. Surrealistes, 1930.

somnambulist. He added that the only difference between himself and a madman was that he was not mad. But by simulating madness he professed himself able at will to proclaim the unreasonable with extreme conviction because his reason could be made to lose its power of objection." [25]

Dali, even more than his Dadaist predecessors or any of the other Surrealists, knows the power of inconsistency; apparent consistency, above all, must be avoided if one is to be elusive. He tells us "my paradoxical tradition is the real force of my originality." [26] And when his efforts at "systemized confusion" had done their work, Dali moved on to the next deception, to have the "irrational" accepted as the rational, and the unreal as the real. Soby, in speaking of what Dali calls his "handmade photography" and "hand-painted dream photographs," says that the painter was attempting to define "appearances so sharply as to make them rival those which, recorded by the camera, were indubitably existent." [27] And, "to depict the unreal with such extreme realism that its truth and validity could no longer be questioned." [28] The same writer tells us that when Dali painted *The Family of Marsupial Centaurs,* he "inevitably reversed the whole Surrealist tendency and brought it back near its starting point. For whereas the Surrealists had eagerly brushed aside conscious thought in order to peer into the dark wells of the subconscious, Dali was now ready to scrutinize his subconscious for signs it might contain of conscious reason." [29] In all these maneuvers Dali is attempting to do precisely what we saw happen in medieval times when the religious symbols were changed from primitive to realistic forms. He is trying to "depict the unreal with such realism that its validity will no longer be questioned," in order to replace the real world with the unreal as *the reality*; the rational with the irrational as *the rational*; the conscious with the subconscious as *the conscious.* This is an irresistible gamble, something far more than any of the other Surrealists have dared to do except in a mild manner. Such ambitions will eventually result in a great service for art.

For the art of Dali carries to its inevitable end the two general types of contemporary art — that of the Modernist and that of the Academician. It is not an accident that he clothes his irrational activities in all kinds of accepted beliefs, that he lauds traditionalism, "aristocrats," Catholicism,[30] and that he denounces the artists who point to a direction contrary to the wanderings we have labelled "Modern art." So when he writes that he will save art from what he calls the "void of modern art," [31] he includes Cézanne, whom he called that "platonic mason"; Cubism; Mondrian, whose work he refers to as "little maniacal lozenges" [32]; and the Machine art of the Constructionists and Architects. In short, Dali opposes all that our history has shown as legitimate since Cézanne.

25. J. T. Soby: *Salvador Dali,* p. 12.

26. Reprinted from THE SECRET LIFE OF SALVADOR DALI by Salvador Dali, by permission of The Dial Press, Inc. Copyright 1942 by Salvador Dali, p. 394.

27. Soby, op. cit., pp. 14–15.

28. Ibid., p. 15. The general tendency has been to overrate the realism of Dali's paintings. This is because we live in times when the copying of nature with primitive methods has become a rarity both in quantity and quality. The vast majority of us today have become so canalized to the Distortionist's depiction of reality which prevails generally, that our sensitivity to the problem of realism in art has become dulled, and we are no longer exacting in our perception. For these reasons Dali's work appears far more realistic than it actually is. This becomes very apparent if we compare his works with any of the great Realists of the 19th century.

29. Ibid., p. 29.

30. See pp. 258–260 and 287 of his book *The Secret Life of Salvador Dali,* where he finds that the aristocrats are more "vulnerable" to his art than the artists. He says that the difference between him and the aristocrats was that he did not come to tradition with "empty hands." He explains that the "old gentlemen" understand him. As a matter of fact, the more observant over the past few years will have noticed that the old time conservatives are attracted to Surrealism, Dali in particular, as is to be expected. Thus, the editor of an art magazine recommends the guide of Surrealism to the American artist, as follows: "And yet, beyond these arguments [that the surrealists are clever showmen, business men and the secret of surrealism is very simple], is the more basic question: Is surrealism contributing anything of lasting value to the sum total of art history? The answer is yes. Perhaps the weakest factor in American art is its poverty of imagination, its unthinking insistence upon painting endless miles of literal landscapes, insipid still lifes, static figures. The surrealists are stimulating Americans to use their eyes less and their minds more, to develop their imagination." ("Peyton Boswell comments: The Surrealist Circus," *The Art Digest,* 17:5, May 15, 1943.) The pathological "imagination" of the Surrealists is recommended as a step forward.

31. Dali, op. cit., p. 4.

32. Ibid., p. 212.

162. Salvador Dali, Apparition of Face and Fruit Dish on a Beach, 1938. Courtesy, Wadsworth Atheneum, Hartford.

He boasts that the "Modernists" are "alarmed by the demoralizing and destructive power which I came to represent."[33] Those whom we have labelled "Modern artists" might well be alarmed, for Dali represents a complete, precise reflection of them all. In fact the Modernists in general are not at all pleased with him; he makes them all insecure and they vaguely know why he has this effect. One of their apologists calls Dali an "illustrator of dream fantasies instead of the creator of plastic fantasies"—presumably the latter is a superior product.[34] Another "Modernist" of the obvious Surrealist type, calls Dali a traitor,[35] and, from his point of view, quite correctly, since he unconsciously senses that Dali is giving the show away. The Moderns have said one thing and done another; Dali does this but he frankly admits it. He is the clear mirror image of what Braque, Picasso, Miro,[36] etc., have been doing timidly these many years in one degree or another. In Dali we see the actual objective to which every ex-radical and Surrealist aspires. He represents the extreme manifestation of the rejection of the positive aspects of Cubism.

Through Dali we can see clearly the relationship between Surrealism and other at first seemingly unrelated arts, since we can see in him the ultimate character of the direction chosen by those who have avoided or retreated from the Cubist decision. In an earlier chapter we stated that the retreat consisted

33. Ibid., p. 287.

34. J. J. Sweeney: "Surrealism as a Public Art," *Kenyon Review,* 1:435, No. 4, 1939. Fantasy has become such a widely accepted objective in our culture that it is possible to confine one's arguments to whose type of fantasy is superior, rather than to considering whether fantasy is desirable in the first place.

35. Robert Motherwell: "The Modern Painter's World," *Dyn,* p. 14, No. 6, 1944.

36. Had not Braque claimed (see p. 410) that reason could never lead to creation, that art is an "unreasonable act"? See also statements of Miro and Picasso, p. 509.

506

163. Joan Miro, Portrait No. 1, 1938. Collection Mrs. Saidie A. May. Photo, Museum of Modern Art.

of returning to the manipulation of nature objects, and that only the manner of manipulating nature into fantasies was new, however superficial that newness was. Thus when the Dadaists began to pilfer only the worst that Cubism had to offer, it was simply the beginning of those activities which were to characterize in some degree Modern art in general. In chapter 16, on the abstracting process, we noted the two general levels from which the artist might abstract—the macroscopic and the process level of reality. In chapter 20, on the dilemma of contemporary abstracting, we pointed out that the Modernists have swung from the new back to the old level of abstracting, and that, as a result of their confusion of abstracting levels, they are inevitably headed in one particular direction which leads to Surrealism. Surrealism and Dali in particular are simply the most exaggerated examples of the confusion between the old and the new which characterizes the general tendency in "Modern" art. From this point of observation it is seen that all contemporary non-Camera arts which distort reality appearances are a manifestation in some degree of Surrealism. If we realize that the epitome of Surrealism is the maladjusted effort to retain the old contents of art, no matter at what cost, then we are able to see more clearly the subtle manifestations of Surrealism in the alleged "diversity" of present day art.

507

In Matisse (figure 149) and Dali we see two extremes in prevailing efforts to retain the old content as an escape from the problems confronting artists today. Matisse tries to replace the chaotic, troubled world with a pictorial one bathed in light, bright, soft colors with figures giving the appearance of the quiet, still unconsciousness of the siesta hour. For the most part his pictures contain women quite satisfied to do nothing at all. Dali, however, makes a world out of the chaos around him; the figures in his works are shown emaciated, bleeding, cruel, cut apart, bloated, etc. For the most part his pictures contain people who seem to be undergoing some tortuous nightmare.

Comparing Miro (figure 163) and Dali (figure 162), we see still another aspect of Surrealistic efforts to escape the "great decision." Both these artists practiced Cubism; then both lost courage, as did so many others, and hurriedly looked for a way out. Dali's way out was to retain the old method of abstracting, which he had actually never given up anyway, and make the old pre-Transitional-Period of realistic art into a kind of Surrealism. Miro, on the other hand, wanted to surrealize the post-Transitional-Period of art; but the more he has done so, the more he has been compelled to rely on abstractions from the old level of reality. Therefore it was to be expected that we should eventually hear him say that "subject matter" was becoming "more important" in his work. Dali strives to present the appearances of reality in a manner which never occurs in reality. Miro makes the real world into fantasy by considerably changing the actual appearance of that reality. He abstracts less from the old level than does Dali. The latter strives to surrealize the old direction of art; Miro, the "Inbetweener," tries to surrealize the new direction of art.

Two prominent examples of Surrealist devices not generally recognized as such are Léger's use of various unexpected combinations of objects within the same canvas, and Picasso's manner of transforming particular objects in unexpected ways. These tricks upon the reality, in Léger, Picasso, and in other prominent "Modernists," are simply different aspects of devices which the Surrealists have carried to their inevitable absurdity.

This is further borne out by the now concluding character of Picasso's career. Until recently he kept up a continual but superficial "diversity" in his paintings, but gradually his work has begun to set, like concrete after it is poured, into the inevitable pattern that it was destined to assume. From about 1931 to 1939 his work took on the technique of the Fauvist Matisse, as we have shown elsewhere, to which he added the subject-devices of the Surrealists. We see here the main end results of the fantasy factor where Fauvism and Surrealism join hands, with the latter increasingly dominating the former. This was as inevitable in his case, as it was that Surrealism would appear in the general body of "Modern art."

Most unfortunately for the "Modernists," Dali has undertaken to lead them, whether they like it or not. They simply have no choice because Dali fits the position to a T. The main difference between the majority of "Modernists" and their actual leader, Dali, is that the former parade as revolutionists while deceptively hanging on to the old contents, while Dali openly hangs on to the old contents and openly contends that to be conservative is revolutionary. Dali, in fact, never did hesitate about this matter; after a few digressions he retreated directly. Others, such as Miro and Picasso, would not admit to themselves that they had lost courage in their effort to grasp the new direction; but their countryman, Dali, without quibbling, openly announced his reactionary intentions.

We see, then, that in this sense Dali was perfectly correct when he announced: "I am the most representative incarnation of post-war [World War I] Europe. . . ." [37] And as Kahler said of the nazis, so we can say of the Surrealists, and of Dali in particular: "Without shame or compunction, they have drawn the ultimate conclusions from the world situation." [38] Dali has drawn the inevitable conclusions from what we designate as "Modern" art.

Thus in his attitude towards the old art content, and in his protest against logic and his justification of fantasy, Dali, the ultimate Surrealist, is "the most representative incarnation" of the futile maladjusted effort of the majority of the "Moderns" to escape to the subconscious. The laissez-faire doctrine that each artist has the privilege of choosing whichever form of art he happens to desire, of doing whatever he wishes with the appearances of reality, was but the opening of the door to the anarchy of Surrealism in which this philosophy is carried to its ultimate conclusion.

37. Dali, op. cit., p. 399.   38. Kahler, *Man the Measure,* p. 604.

In the Surrealist tradition Miro has contended: "my painting is always conceived in a state of hallucination created by a shock either objective or subjective, of which I am utterly irresponsible. . . ." [39] And it has been reported of Picasso: "He sees overwhelming him some superior demand, he has the distinct impression that something forces him imperiously to empty his soul. . . ." [40] For these artists, as for Ernst (see p. 502) the self is merely an obedient channel for "revelations"; it is the "voice inside him" which commands his "self" to do as it does. During this period of crisis in the evolution of art, it was to be expected that the majority would retreat to the irresponsibility of the subconscious. [41]

Psychologists and others sometimes like to point out that the artist is one kind of individual who remains "free"; but actually artists in general are no freer today than anyone else, because they are in the same difficulties as the rest of us. Given the chaotic world in which we live, it would be strange indeed if artists as a group were any better adjusted than some other group. Actually the utter freedom that the Modernists claim to have, is such a liability that they must give it all to their subconscious; they have become mere automatons blindly executing orders.

But whatever "freedom" of behavior man has, has been acquired through the steadily increasing, orderly consciousness of the emotion-thinking structure of his organism within an environment; and that "freedom" is not a matter of an absolute, but always implies some kind of *limitation*. This limitation is as restricted or extended as is the degree and kind of consciousness men possess of the structure and function of their emotion-thinking behavior. The complete freedom which the Surrealists reach for is a complete delusion. All it can bring them is ever increasing ignorance and so maladjustment, which implies the loss of *human* freedom. For freedom, as we understand it, consists of those particular rules and demands of human culture, which increasingly discourage the freedom of human beings to behave like animals, and increasingly encourage the freedom of human beings to behave more and more like human beings. And those who cannot understand freedom as having some limitations, those who insist upon unlimited freedom, they are the least free of all men, for they have surrendered themselves to their unfettered subconscious—they call it deity, the divine, mystical, cosmic, and whatnot; they have about as much freedom as a cork floating on the Atlantic Ocean.

Hence, although it may appear as if artists in our times are free to roam as they please, actually it is a false freedom which has produced ever increasing confusion and insecurity. It should not be forgotten that in certain parts of the world today the artist's "mind" is, if necessary, forcibly made up for him; in other parts, individuals are "free" to the extent that each artist is left to make up his own mind as to what he thinks his stand in art shall be; but here old notions and orientations are scattered into pieces, or debased beyond recognition, leaving the majority of artists confused and fearful, confronted with the task of making a coherent decision in a world that is undergoing tremendously fundamental change. In short, the insatiable need of Surrealists and/or Modernists for an impossible "utter freedom" is the result of their fear of, their wish to escape from the world-shaking changes now in progress, of which Cubism was one of the first major signs.

The Dadaists, the Surrealists, the Modernists, all have claimed they are revolting against the stupidity of our culture. André Breton, in his defense of Dadaism, has maintained that "The despair that prevailed [following the first World War] could only be overcome by a kind of dismal jesting, a 'black humor.'" [42] But they are hypocritical in this defense, since they, more than any other type of artists have helped to perpetuate and bring to full, pathological bloom the very conditions they decry. Having evaded

39. Quoted by Cheney in *The Story of Modern Art*, p. 519.

40. Christian Zervos: *Pablo Picasso*, Vol. 1, p. xvi, works from 1895–1906, Cahiers d'Art, Paris, E. Weyhe, New York, 1932.

41. Since this was first written, this "philosophy" of Picasso, Ernst, et al, has become the general rule among the Modernists. That which each one previously kept as his own secret is now considered safe enough to state openly. So today artists repeat after each other how they begin their work not knowing what will appear, and, how once something does appear, they follow its dictates. Living with a confused consciousness, the majority of artists have made a lunge for the promised wonderland of the subconscious, only to strike a quagmire.

42. André Breton: "Genesis and Perspective of Surrealism," *Art of This Century*, p. 17.

the real issue, these lost individuals are simply trying to drag us down to their own level. Says Dali: "all men are equal in their madness . . . . madness (visceral cosmos of the subconscious) constitutes the common base of the human spirit." [43]

Today, after thousands of years during which the efforts of thousands of artists of the first rank have been expended towards gradually perfecting the vision of man and his eye-brain consciousness of it, most artists would turn their backs on the objective world of vision and retreat to the ways of the infant, the Primitive and the insane. Not since the Dark Ages have the forces of irrationality been so widespread as in our times. It was inevitable that this should happen.

This tendency to flee from the great crisis in art (*a crisis that is part of the world crisis*) has been apparent since the beginning of the Transitional-Period in that most artists and critics have sought abject recourse to the theory of the "ideal" first formulated by the Greeks. Their erroneous interpretation of the Transitional-Period led them unconsciously to exhume the old Classical theory as a justification for their art. By so doing they eulogized precisely the factor in the Transitional-Period which should have been rejected. Thus they became blind to the positive, desirable aspects they should have discovered and developed; instead they were led in a direction in which there remained only the possibility of the Idealist's maladjustment. Today all but a very few artists of the post-Cubist generation have succumbed to the escape of the "ideal," now become pathological.

In the 19th century most of the Realists had deluded themselves into believing that the Camera-Machine had not assumed the old task of the artist, that the painting artists could continue to copy nature and still "create" an art of man. (The Impressionists, whom the Realists also opposed, chose another direction, admitting the inevitable as far as the significance of the Camera artists' entrance into the art scene was concerned.) And now in the 20th century the Surrealists and/or Modernists continue the delusion of the Realists of post-Camera times. They also assume that they can "imitate" nature and still "create" an art of man. And, if the old Realists felt that they were superior to the Camera artist because they could use the factor of color, the Realists of Modern art, the *Sur*realists, feel superior to the Camera artist because they can dislocate and reallocate the various aspects of reality to suit their arbitrary desires. They feel superior to the world reality that we experience by making another world out of the pieces they break from it.

In definitely insisting on retaining the old contents in non-Camera art, the Surrealists and/or Modernists are presenting us with the last decadent remains of Aristotelian art. Like the Classical Greeks they also regard actual reality as an inferior manifestation of an "ideal" or "another world," alleged to be more real than reality; hence, *sur*-reality, meaning "over," "above" reality.

Thus it will be found that all the various shades of Surrealists, in spite of their vehement protests against reason, cannot do as they do without the aid of some process of reasoning which justifies their behavior. When we look for the justification that characterizes all the various shades of Modernism or "Surrealism," we find that it is simply the old "ideal," dusted, repainted and re-abused once more. That is, the artist perceives and achieves that "ideal" towards which nature unsuccessfully strives, and which is superior to "reality"—all to justify an escape to a world of fantasy.

The Greeks said: "But when you want to represent beautiful figures, since it is not easy to find everything without a flaw in a single human being, do you not then collect from a number what is beautiful in each so that the whole body may appear beautiful?" [44] and this was the ideal, and the ideal is a "higher reality—'for the ideal type must surpass the actual'; the ideal is 'better' than the real." Today we read of the "superficial reality" of an object being transposed "into a superior reality" [45] by the Dadaists, and that "The idea of breaking up the world of appearances into fragments and rearranging these fragments according to a new order challenging by its novelty, springing only from the mind of the

43. Quoted by Soby, in *Salvador Dali*, pp. 12–13, from "Declaration of the Independence of the imagination and the rights of man to his own madness," privately published, New York, 1939.

44. Quoted by G. M. A. Richter: *The Sculpture and Sculptors of the Greeks*, p. 20, The Yale University Press, New Haven, 1929.

45. *Fantastic Art Dada Surrealism*, p. 17 (see p. 500 for full quotation).

artist, who is striving to reveal a superior reality—that idea forms the very basis of all the most recent and astounding developments in the field of modern art." [46]

But where the Greeks talked of the "moral good," the Surrealists talk of producing "repulsion" with the "ugly." And where the Greeks concerned themselves with "laws of thought," "order," etc., the Surrealists are bent on the "denial of reason," the denial of the responsibilties of reason, and on "exalting disorder," "exalting insanity." [47]

Such individuals are taking the ideal to the opposite pole from that of the Greeks and the pre-Camera Idealists; they are fashioning a cult of the ugly. That is why some Surrealists are sensitive about the distinctions between beauty and ugliness. Thus Lemaitre writes: "Art and literature are considered merely as means designed to help us to reach a *superior, ideal state*. Literature and art should not try to draw a faithful or attractive picture of life as it is. They should take us beyond the frontiers of this life and lead us—without any concern for the trifling accidents which are called beauty or ugliness— somewhere, very far away, on the long trail to Surrealist Truth." (emphasis ours) [48] This is the state to which the notion of an ideal has finally been reduced, the decadence to which Aristotelianism has come.

In the magazine *View* one Surrealist tells us about the new standards and criteria: "The hero is the man who suddenly stands alone without anything; no principles and no parts of the universe have importance for him any longer. He became, by his deed, the universe for himself, and after his moment of triumph, there is nothing, there will be nothing save the void and the desired annihilation of every day, the wearing out of every minute." [49]

"The modern world is about ready to recognize in Narcissus one of its most beloved sons, the one of its many captives who has known himself the best and the one who has most profoundly ignored the world in which he lives. This is no ignorance cultivated through some principle, nor is it an absence of sympathy. It is rather an illness comparable to the fever which attached Narcissus to the brink of his fountain." [50] This is typical of the "ideal" they propose.

Surrealism is but the Classical notion of an ideal carried to its final termination and extinction. Thus the Surrealists unwittingly are gradually annihilating the notion of an "ideal," perhaps for all time. Because it was continued far beyond its point of usefulness, the Aristotelian system has become an un-sane method for dealing with the problems of present day art, as well as the problems of human behavior in general. Hence we should expect its most frantic proponents, the Surrealists, to be unreasonable and un-sane, and, inevitably, to seek to justify their art behavior with the art of the insane.

Dali, in flatly contending that he is "crusading" for the "defense of Greco-Roman civilization," [51] epitomizes the futile effort to continue Aristotelian notions of art, and also gives us some notion of the depths into which the Aristotelian period of culture has fallen. He exudes in his art the disintegration of a cycle of art history that is now finished. His work represents the demented cry, the "death throes of idealism."

Some of us may ask ourselves why the fantastic claims and behavior of present day art are accepted; if similar procedures of reasoning and behavior were proposed in most other fields, their proponents would rightly be considered as "mentally" ill. Recall, however, our discussion of medieval art,

46. Lemaitre, op. cit., p. 33. It would be worth the reader's time to refer again to the quotations from Butcher in chapter 21 in order to see the great similarity between the theoretical justifications of the Surrealists and/or Modernists and the theories of Aristotle.

47. All these are but further examples of our fundamental analysis; i.e., that Surrealism is pathological Aristotelianism in art —and Surrealism is but the epitome of what every non-Constructionist, non-Camera artist is bent for; whether he likes it or not changes nothing.

48. Lemaitre, op. cit., p. 202.

49. W. Fowlie: "Narcissus, an essay on the modern spirit," *View*, p. 72, Series iii, No. 3.

50. Ibid., p. 73.

51. Dali, op. cit., p. 287. This is incidentally very significantly reminiscent of the aim of two prominent American educators now trying to reinstate classicalism in toto into our university curricula.

in which we pointed out the great importance attached to art because through it the priests strove to make "visible" the other-world. And ever since medieval times certain types of artists have continued to depict some version of another-world—the Classicists, the Romanticists, and today the Surrealists. Here we find an answer to the above inquiry: that is, we tolerate the absurd theories of reality propounded in the field of art, because for most of us art is unconsciously an avenue of escape from this-world into a world of fantasy. That negative criticisms of Surrealism are few and far between indicates that most of us openly or secretly find relief in experiencing it, a relief akin to that obtained by narcotics.

It is necessary to realize that the "irrationality" of Surrealism freely breeds and multiplies its virus in our times because irrationality rules to such a great degree in our culture. In art this irrationality is simply more blatantly obvious than in most other fields. Hence the Surrealists represent in art that degeneration found in every other phase of our culture today. In failing to reach a vision of constructiveness, they have taken to a career of destructiveness. Refusing to accept the new, they attempt to destroy it with ridicule, and to rejuvenate the old with psychosis.

Karl Mannheim has written: "One has only to look at pictures like those of Bosch and Grüne-wald in order to see that the disorganization of the Medieval order expressed itself in a general fear and anxiety, the symbolic expression of which was the attention given to the underworld with its demons, and the widespread fear of the devil. In the Medieval order the luciferic element was present but had its place in the plan of the universe. When the social order goes wrong psychosis spreads, the diabolic forces are no longer integrated into the Cosmos. In an adequately functioning society the neurotic is only the borderline case. In a state of general disorganization it is he who sets the pattern." [52]

It is no accident then that artists like Bosch appeal to the Surrealists today; after all, they have a great deal in common. Thus Monroe Wheeler is correct when he writes: "But Dali's general temper and subject matter are also rather similar to those of Jerome Bosch, the sixteenth-century Italian mannerists, and Jacques Callot. Think what went on in Europe between Bosch's birth and Callot's death. It was an era extraordinarily like ours. The Reformation and Counter-reformation altered everything for everyone. Rome was sacked and Vienna was besieged by the Turks. Politicians took over the Inquisition. The Jews were herded from country to country. The Spaniards under Alva were in the Netherlands with their Courts of Blood. As a modern historian has expressed it, 'The air all over the continent blew dark from villages on fire, and resounded with screams, and stank of hungry children and sick women and cadavers of cavalry.' Dali is the type of artist who is prescient about such things and his imagination is intoxicated by them." [53] We see nothing "prescient," however, about Dali; for, as we explained, he is only an artist who, thriving upon it, has helped to foster the general chaos of our art times.

Neither is it an accident that there is considerable correspondence between the reasoning behavior of Surrealists, and that of the nazis and/or communists. The decadent ones both in art and politics act on the principle that when you tell a lie, tell the most incredible one imaginable. Thus the nazis and/or communists seek to discredit the "truth," while the Surrealists seek to discredit the world of reality. Both despise the reasoning responsibilities associated with science and forms of behavior that make humans more human. In the words of Kahler, speaking about the nazis, we can say: "Their premeditated descent from the human level is their crucial, revolutionary innovation; in this they have bared the human core of today's world crisis. They have shown that this crisis is neither purely political, economic nor social, but that it is a total crisis, a moral crisis, a crisis of the whole being of man." [54]

We see, therefore, that the loudest proponents of a future paradise for mankind in both art and politics, the Surrealists and the nazis and/or communists, are actually the foremost enemies of progress. For progress, like life itself, is only a term for them to manipulate, to twist to the attainment of their own maladjusted desires. Thus they reverse the normal process and make maladjustment the new goal of mankind.

52. Karl Mannheim: *Man and Society in an Age of Reconstruction*, p. 117, Harcourt, Brace and Co., New York, 1940.

53. Monroe Wheeler: Foreword to *Salvador Dali*, by J. T. Soby, pp. 7–8.

54. Kahler, *Man the Measure*, p. 604.

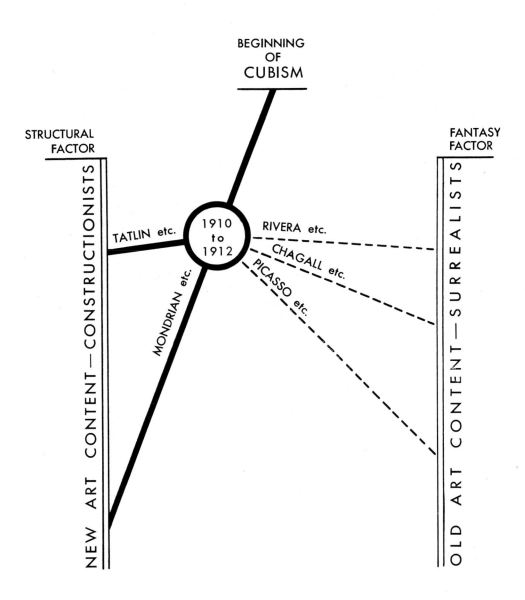

In the present world situation there are those who cannot believe that man is progressing, because they see so much that indicates regression. There are others who see man as progressing over the past, but they do so at the expense of ignoring much of a regressive nature. The adherents of both these attitudes are "either-orists," who have taken seriously the question "IS man progressing or NOT?" The former reply "No!"; the latter reply "Yes!" If we had to answer this question we would be compelled to reply "Yes and No!" For the facts clearly demonstrate that man's capacities both to regress or progress have been accelerating throughout the "evolution" of human culture. *The capacities of mankind both to destroy and to develop culture have almost uninterruptedly been increasing.* For example, man has *regressed* from the fist to the atom bomb. He has *progressed* from a scratch with a twig in the clay to the Television image, or *regressed* to the illness of Surrealism. From the intelligence of an animal man has *progressed* to the humanistic intelligence of the up-to-date scientific thinker, or *regressed* to the barbarism of a "scientific" totalitarian thinker.

In our times we see extreme opposites, representative of a schizoid split in our culture; e.g., the science of semantics and its perversion, the "science" of propaganda. In general, there exist conflicts between the forces of responsible individualism, the responsibility of international orientation by means of more "democracy" everywhere, and the forces of unlimited, irresponsible individualism and nationalism, either through the anarchy of laissez-faire democracy or the barbarism of dictatorship. In art there is the science of Constructions, and its perversion, the "science" of Surrealism.

From this point of view the fundamental issue of our art times is clearly drawn: it is a choice between Constructionist art or Surrealism, between the "reality" of the new conditions and opportunities or the flight to the past via the maladjustment of a world of fantasy. Thus the two factors with which we began this discussion, the search for structure and the pursuit of fantasy, both of which emerged from Impressionism and became increasingly manifest in Post-Impressionism and Cubism, are today separated as much as they can be in these two polar views of art. These two factors have at last come to a head, as it were. The fantasy factor has now been developed to the extreme pathological and inevitable result found in the art of Surrealism. The structural factor has been developed into the color-form-space inventions of the Constructionists. This latter direction represents a useful development from the past towards a new goal of the future, not a warping of the past towards cultural psychosis as in Surrealism. Through the utilization of nature's Structural Process artists have discovered how to invent, create their own art. They possess an interpretation of reality which parallels the most advanced notions of that reality in the advanced sciences. They agree with scientists regarding the necessity for an ever greater rigor in man's consciousness of himself and the world in which he lives. It is significant that the Surrealists maintain that reality, usually the "reality of another-world" in their kind of art, can be comprehended only intuitively, allegedly in the manner of children, Primitives and psychotics; whereas the Constructionists maintain that one must become conscious of the Structural Process level of nature if he wishes to realize a sound criterion for reality, i.e., one must observe and interpret the universe with the methods of 20th century advanced science.

It is significant also to observe the Surrealists' view of history—they are consistent, since it is impossible to evade the "deterministic" operation of human behavior. Thus, like the essentially conservative individuals they actually are, they appeal to the past for justification, and claim that they have done as others have done before them (Bosch, Blake, etc.). The Constructionists also appeal to the past, not because they claim to do as anyone in the past has done, but because they are continuing the evolution of art, which resulted from the effort of all the useful artists since the very beginning of man's art. The Surrealists appeal to the maladjustment and insanity in the past art of man; the Constructionists appeal to the sane accomplishments in the evolution of man's art. The former, true to Aristotelianism, offer us a static theory of art; the latter, non-Aristotelian in attitude, point out the asymmetrical, dynamic continuum that characterizes the historical process.

Today the issue lies between the Constructionists and the Surrealists. The Surrealists try to make of art a vehicle by which to escape to the experience of another-world; the Constructionists seek to make of art a vehicle by which to extend further our experience in this-world. The Surrealists strive to destroy our notions and values about the world which science has produced with the paranoiac excuse that they have been deceived by that adulteress, reason; the genuine Constructionists seek to contribute to our knowledge regarding these problems. The former seek the apparently easy path of escape to the subconsciousness; the latter wish to face the chaos so as to establish order, and hence they insist on a heightening not a lowering of our consciousness of the world in which we live.

The Constructionists are the only school directly advocating an entirely new content and an entirely new medium for an entirely new epoch in human history and art. These artists do not advocate an escape of any kind, but a stepping forth to continue the researches suggested by Cubism and to supply an international art for an era of international orientation among human beings. Unlike the Moderns and/or Surrealists, they are not rebelling against the evolutionary achievements of the past. The genuine Constructionists are the only genuine innovators among the non-Camera artists today; the rest are mostly rebels of various degrees and kinds—the new kind of reactionary. The Surrealists are making the supreme attempt to escape the times, while the Constructionists are making the supreme attempt to face the problems of the times that need to be solved. Let us be clear on this point: it is the one-time revolutionists, the new *status quo,* the "Moderns" in art who today comprise the greatest threat to further progress in art.

Hence we find the Modernists and/or Surrealists, the decadent Aristotelians, on the one hand, and the Constructionists, the non-Aristotelians, on the other. The former are in the gasping death throes of a no longer useful system, either for art or for human behavior in general: the latter indicate the birth of a useful progressive era of art in a world which requires a non-Aristotelian form of evaluation and behavior. So we emphasize once again that the issue is fundamentally between the representatives of dying Aristotelianism and those who are forming the non-Aristotelian attitude. The former hurl their pathological cries about the world; the latter offer the only vestige of sanity in a world ravaged a second time by World-Civil-War.

Between Constructionist art and Surrealism can be drawn *all* the shades of art that have been produced since 1914. To the degree that the artist seeks to invent the content, his work tends in the Constructionist direction; and to the degree that the artist uses the old contents, his work tends in the Surrealist direction. As we have seen, most "Modernists" are Surrealist in intention to one degree or another; even some who are erroneously called Constructionists belong in this category.

The very fact that all manifestations of "Modern" art can be placed on a scale between Surrealism on the one hand and Constructionist art on the other, is indeed an educative opportunity for those who assume that the artist is absolutely free to do as he pleases. Actually the fantasy direction is the most limited of all. Thus Matisse and his kind represent the dead-end of that fantasy which stemmed from the negative aspect of the beginning of the Transitional-Period; and the Surrealists represent the dead-end of that fantasy which stemmed from the negative aspect of the end of the Transitional-Period. But most important, the Surrealists represent the dead-end of fantasy of any kind, since one cannot go any further even in fantasy with the old primitive mediums. From here on the fabricators of fantasy will be compelled to restrict their efforts merely to repeating what has already been done, repeating and repeating until even they can bear it no longer.

In spite of what artists do, they are compelled to accept one or another course with all of the inevitable consequences. It is a truism which bears repeating, that the natural laws governing our nervous systems and the environment are not arbitrary. In short, at this present point in our history it becomes apparent more than ever that non-Camera artists today are inevitably being pommeled in either the Constructionist or the Surrealist direction. It is simply impossible to stand inbetween. Non-Camera, non-Constructionist artists and their wordsmen may talk all they want about "freedom," but while they are talking, they are being forced into one of two directions.

IX REVISED VIEW OF REALITY

Sometimes simplicity hides under complex appearances; sometimes it is the simplicity which is apparent, and which disguises extremely complicated realities.   273
Henri Poincare

The main semantic difficulty, for those accustomed to the old, consists in breaking the old structural linguistic habits, in becoming once more flexible and receptive in feelings, and in acquiring new semantic reactions.   179

Alfred Korzybski

.... Professor W. M. Wheeler . . . tells us that
"when thinking tends to congeal into two conflicting interpretations we naturally either devote
our days to showing why the one must be true
and the other false, or we seek to escape both
by adopting a new position." This is what the
"emergent evolutionists" attempt to do—escape
from the materialism-idealism dilemma by adopting
a new position. 285

Oliver Reiser

Space is only a word that we have believed a thing.
What is the origin of this word and of other words
also? What things do they hide? To ask this is
permissible; to forbid it would be, on the contrary,
to be a dupe of words; it would be to adore a
metaphysical idol, like savage peoples who prostrate
themselves before a statue of wood without daring
to take a look at what is within.   273

Henri Poincare

Up to the middle of the 19th century, art could be roughly divided into two kinds: (1) those arts in which man as a copyist of nature's appearances was compelled to be more and more *Mimetic*, particularly Painting and Sculpture (commonly called the "fine-arts"); (2) those in which it was necessary to be more and more *Inventive*, such as pottery and Architecture (commonly called "Decorative" and "minor arts"). Such distinctions as "minor" and "fine" arts rest upon the absence or presence or importance of the Mimetic factor; this factor became dominant early in man's history. The "minor" arts were necessarily and fundamentally Inventive, but the Inventive factor was not accredited a major role until the 20th century. Today, as we shall show, the labels "minor" and "fine" arts are anachronistic and erroneous.

It is no accident, however, that Constructionist and other arts with an Inventive contents are today commonly deprecated with the term "decoration." Generally both those who so use this label and those who seek to defend their art against it, are unaware of precisely what meanings they attach to it. But the silent assumptions in such uses of the term show considerable ignorance about both Constructionist and Decorative arts. In this history it is impossible to go into more than a very brief analysis of the Decorative arts; our main purpose here is to dispel the mistaken notions generally held about the term "decoration," especially when used in a condemnatory sense in reference to the new direction which advanced art is taking today.

Although the Inventive trend was in the past largely confined to "minor" (i.e., "Decorative" and Architectural) arts, even here its importance, both qualitatively and quantitatively, decreased propor- tionately as the Mimetic factor increasingly dominated the general development of art. Human beings have indeed been inventing art ever since the first artist invented the first line, but only since the appearance of Constructionist art has a more coherent consciousness of the significance and potentialities of the Inventive factor become possible.

It will be necessary to examine briefly the major manifestations of the Inventive effort in past arts. One of the earliest of these is to be seen in the development of the art of Writing.

An erroneous inference is commonly made that particular kinds of human activity began at some particular point, which turns out to be not the genesis but a stage in the course of development. Such a limited view is often taken of what is correctly called the "art" of Writing. Thus some claim that Writing began about 6,000 years ago in the Nile Valley, whereas actually this was a very advanced point in its development. The Egyptians did not suddenly begin to practice their form of Writing; it had been evolved through many difficult steps during many thousands of years and has since evolved further to the kind of Writing which we use today. If we want to find the beginning of Writing, we must go to the very beginnings of art.

To realize properly how man's ability to write evolved, recall briefly what was posited regarding the invention of art: how man began his art with the discovery of, or the invention of, the single line, and how the gradual various multiplications of these lines formed some sort of symbolical method of communication. These Symbols formed the initial stage of art and magic, what we have called the "Decorative" stage of art history. Although these lines originated as simply a discovery, eventually the various combinations of them were probably given symbolic meanings, thus forming the rudiments of magic.

In time these earliest experiences with lines led to the next great discovery. Man found that he could use them to form images or recordings of inanimate nature. But the transition to this stage was achieved slowly. The artist had to learn to discipline his use of lines in a very specific Mimetic manner. Therefore, although artists in the non-recording stage had been able to make quite complex arrangements of lines (as can be seen in the "Macaroni" examples), in their initial attempts to record inanimate nature they were *again* compelled to begin with only one or two lines. In this stage of art they learned to copy the lines left by the scraping of the great sheets of ice upon the rocks, the spiral from the seashell, and the like. Following on this stage, came the recording of the animate world, of animals in particular. Again, in tackling a new and more difficult subject, the artist started out with a single line rendition of it. In the early stages of learning to bend his lines to depict the animal form, Pictographic man would thus have produced very simple versions of the subjects, comparable to the so-called enigmatical Signs found in Paleolithic caves. He learned how to bend a line now to this contour, now to that one, gradually increasing the number of factors he was able to abstract into his record. Finally he was able to begin to record the general shape of the animal form well enough to achieve the depiction of specific types of animals.

But none of these stages—the Decorative, the recording of inanimate and then of animate reality—was evolved in quick succession, nor did there exist the delusion of art for art's sake; each stage in the Paleolithic development of art produced distinct contributions to magic symbology. That is, each stage of art had a symbolic function which the others did not, and for this reason the earlier forms were in some degree retained in later developments of art. From this point of view the "club-shaped and tent-shaped figures," and the "spirals, circles, chevrons, frets, volutes, wave ornaments and alphabetiform signs" referred to by MacCurdy and others, could have had their origin not only in the inanimate recordings and early animate recording stages (as MacCurdy points out), but some of them could have originated in the first stage of art, the Decorative or non-recording stage. Thus side by side, the different kinds of art or Symbols existed, just as we today, for example, have our highly developed Pictographs such as Photography, etc., and our highly abstracted written language as well. The one is a language largely descriptive (visual), the other largely logical (verbal). And since each type had its own unique symbological potentialities, it seems probable that each culture would revise, enlarge or delete the Symbols in each group when that was needed, just as more recent man kept on altering the alphabet. As the recording or descriptive Symbols attained a relatively high perfection in Magdalenian times, they became the chief and most important of man's Symbols, because with them man could depict the thing he actually wanted to symbolize; the earlier, more "abstract" forms that originated in the Decorative period would seem to have been retained in minor functions because they were less representative of the "concrete" world. These latter could not be exploited fully until later developments had taken place.

We assume, therefore, that although the first form of "Writing" was composed largely of non-representational Symbols, the first *highly developed* form of Writing was predominantly composed of more "concrete" representational images, because this offered the most readily comprehensible solution for the creation of visual communication. Only later were men able to invent a more complete, *highly developed,* non-Mimetic system of visual Symbols, which we today recognize as letters, words, etc., that is, a highly "abstract" form of language. The development of the abstract written language having emerged from the works of artists or image makers accounts for the fact that Writing came to be referred to as the "art of Writing," for this is what it originally was—art! (In fact, the Greeks and other peoples used the same word to mean drawing and Writing.)

We can now see why, in order to find the origin of Writing, we must go back to the very beginning, the invention of art—the first lines. For the line was the preparatory step leading up to and making possible the achievement of Pictographs, the latter in turn becoming the second major step in the development of Writing Symbols.

The first beginnings of Writing, however, involve "ear-language" as well as "eye-language." Quite probably "ear-language" came first, and first reached a high stage of development. But each must have developed more or less independently until men were able to work out an interchangeable ear-eye language. Preceding this event there were stages of interchangeable air-signs (gestures) and line-Signs (pictures), language such as was found among the North American Indians. Erich Kahler writes: "Among the Sioux Indians, gesture and picture language both existed simultaneously and corresponded closely to each other. It is known that many primitive groups, like the Sioux Indians, wrote down their gestures." [1] And W. A. Mason tells us that "the original Chinese pictures that preceded writing were called *ku-wan,—* literally 'gesture pictures,' and that many of them were retained in the later picture-writing." [2] In fact, Mason shows that: "An elaborate system of signs and gestures came into use whereby conferences were carried on and treaties enacted between the various alien tribes. This primary use of the hands in expressing emotions, actions and commands, through gestures of the sign-language, doubtless has been with many tribes and races the immediately antecedent stage—we may safely say the preparatory stage—of writing. It is more than an idle metaphor to liken this sign-language to actual writing in the air with the hands . . . . it was not so much the movements of the hands as the picture of the movements that prefigured in many cases the subsequent written signs of which they were the prototypes." [3] In the meantime, the fact that sounds could not be visually depicted and visual depictions could not be made in sound, kept these two forms of language more or less separated. Mason writes: "In the earliest stage, pictographic writing, it is entirely probable that there was no connection or at least only a loosely recognized one implied between the spoken word, the name used in the native vernacular to designate the object, and the picture representing the thing referred to. The picture recalled the thing itself to the mind, not the name of the thing, unless voluntarily called up by the reader. The employment of the ideograph to represent and recall the name of the thing as well as the corporate thing itself, or, later, abstract qualities and attributes derived from it, was a step arrived at only after the attainment of a high degree of civilization." [4]

Gradually, however, the necessity arose for a language which would be interchangeable for sound or vision, and finally the oral Symbols were associated with the visual Symbols. The former were probably composed of sounds originally derived from two general sources: (1) sounds that the human organism naturally made in response to feelings of pain and pleasure, etc., i.e., non-Mimetic sounds; (2) imitations of natural sounds. Once the visual Symbols were associated with the oral, the former began to be transformed from what probably were single Signs for single objects, to several Signs or letters that represented oral values, in order that the Symbol could be both spoken and written. Egyptian Writing can thus be seen to have been quite a highly developed stage in the process of transition from pictures of light Symbols only to light Symbols that were pictures of sound Symbols also. Mason gives the following

1. Erich Kahler: *Man the Measure,* p. 277.

2. From W. A. Mason: *A History of the Art of Writing,* p. 22, New York, 1920. By permission of The Macmillan Company, publishers.

3. From W. A. Mason: *A History of the Art of Writing,* p. 20. By permission of The Macmillan Company, publishers.

4. From W. A. Mason: *A History of the Art of Writing,* p. 51. By permission of The Macmillan Company, publishers.

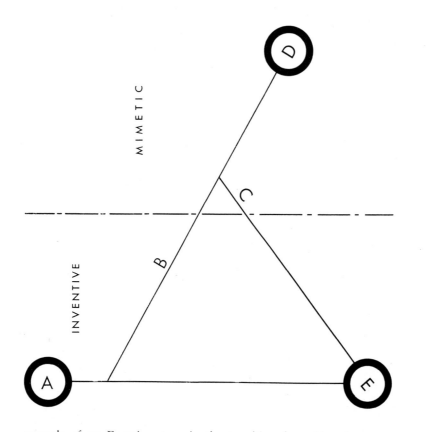

example of an Egyptian stage in the transition from idea-pictures to sound-pictures of words: "in the following words, in addition to the proper, phonetic hieroglyphs which completely spell out the word, there is a pictorial index sign set beside it more fully to define its special meaning:—as 'to dance,' by a girl dancing; 'he said,' by a man pointing at his mouth; 'to rest,' by a recumbent figure . . . ." [5]

With the help of the above diagram, we can sum up the developments discussed thus far. (1) Art and/or Writing begin with the straight line; this beginning is indicated at *a* and forms the abstract Sign direction. (2) Splitting off from *a* is *b* which develops into picture or descriptive art and/or Writing, eventually leading to the realization of Photography at *d*. (3) Splitting off from *b* is *c* which turns back towards the Inventive direction by a process of less and less abstracting from nature-appearances and gradually returns to meet *a*, the abstract Sign direction; (the latter had occupied a minor position throughout the period of picture-Writing dominance.) As *c* converges upon *a*, but before they meet at *e*, we have the various stages of Egyptian Writing, i.e., the simplified Pictograph and the abstract Sign together form the Writing. (4) Thus *e* represents the merging of the two forms of Writing, from which arises the modern type of alphabetical Symbols in use today. The invented lines that began man's art once more become invented lines. Reality is again represented by abstract rather than concrete Symbols, just as had been the case in the Decorative period.

In this regard, it is of interest to note that the Sign for "words" in the Chinese language is composed of four *parallel* lines in the upper left hand part of the following character ———. [6] The square below is the Sign for "mouth," which together with the Sign for words means "to speak," while the Sign on the right is that for "to divine." As a matter of fact, if we are correct about the lines being the first inventions of man as a linear artist, then we can as well assume that straight lines were the first written "words" in the history of human Writing. [7]

5. From W. A. Mason: *A History of the Art of Writing*, p. 22. By permission of The Macmillan Company, publishers.
6. From W. A. Mason: *A History of the Art of Writing*, p. 157.
7. Also the Sign for the first number of our arithmetical scale is simply a single vertical straight line. Hence, the single straight line could have been the genesis of (1) art, (2) writing, and (3) mathematics.

In short, "abstract" Symbols (though non-alphabetical) were present long before the Phoenicians and others made their contributions to the formation of the more recent type of written language. Judging by the extent of their use, these "abstract" Symbols played an auxiliary role to the recording type of art until the need arose for more highly abstract symbology.

The following could well be the earliest evidence of ideography in which Pictographs and the original manifestations of art—non-representational Signs—were combined: "[hand stencils or silhouettes on Paleolithic cave walls] are sometimes accompanied by signs that look like characters in a prehistoric alphabet, and may be supposed to carry out or enforce their meaning."[8] In the Writing arts of the Egyptian culture ideography develops to a higher stage, and simplified Pictographs were used together with "abstract" Symbols.

In other words, the original invented lines were developed both into "abstract" (invented) and "concrete" (picturization) symbology. The latter reached a high level of development first; the former developed at a slower pace, but eventually became predominant. For as man's experience came to include more than a concern with the simply visual, he had to widen the operation of his original *invented* Sign-lines if he was to communicate his widening experiences. This reversal of the Pictographic method of visual communication was one of the biggest steps in the *natural* evolution from the animal to the human stage. The high point of early human culture was primarily concerned with conveying information about seen things *as* seen things. In other words, early man was more "visual," he experienced the visual level in a far different manner than we do today. Primitive man was more like a Camera in his visual activity, absorbing visual phenomena more directly and completely than we do. But as man gradually developed his ability to abstract in ever higher orders beyond the gross visual level, there arose the need to convey notions and inferences which could not be conveyed by visual means alone. This led to the necessity for creating visual Signs to represent non-visual phenomena. Thus it came about that man developed a system of Symbols by which not only visual but non-visual information could be conveyed in a language that could be spoken as well as written.

If our analysis is correct, it would seem that art and/or communication by visual means, began with invented lines. Then the medium of lines was gradually used to abstract a record of the appearance of objects; thus the imitative lines. After the first period of the predominance of the imitative Signs, the former process was reversed until a point was reached where the imitative or descriptive Signs were eventually merged with and then replaced by invented lines; thus emerged the letters of an "alphabet."

Accordingly we find two general levels operating in the formation of art and/or visual communication (Writing): (1) The "subjective" level from which originated the first Inventive visual Symbols; (2) the "objective" level from which originated the Mimetic visual Symbols. The former predominated in the first stage of culture, the latter in the second, and a combination of both in the third stage. We see, therefore, that these three stages represent the formation first of man's rudimentary efforts to reason (logic), second to describe (observation), third to combine both logic and observation in a single system of interchangeable ear-eye communicational Symbols, i.e., Writing as we find it today.

After Writing reached a high state of development (i.e., the alphabet) recording art was considerably freed from non-visual, non-descriptive functions. Nevertheless recording art continued for some time to serve more than the literal, descriptive function; e.g., recall the function of the Classical portraits of Reynolds and David, to mention only these examples. But as the realistic artists freed their art more and more from non-visual loads, there finally came a time when the main drive was to achieve literal recordings of reality. Then the successful Camera was invented. Thus was perfected the major potentiality of Pictographs, namely, to describe light-rays.

Following the invention of the Photograph, invented lines again make an appearance in our own times, now to lead to still another art form, mainly Constructionist art, modern Architecture, etc., by which man can further develop his experiences in the world about him. Through the invention first of Photography and then of Constructions, non-Camera art has finally been freed completely from the old literary role, from its early task of Pictography. Much of this role was eliminated with the invention of modern Writing, i.e., non-pictorial Writing; but it remained for Photography to clear away the last

8. G. B. Brown: *The Art of the Cave Dweller*, p. 74, John Murray, London, 1928.

remnants. Such art is no longer a literary vehicle in any sense, but a recorder of visual and recently of auditory phenomena as well. With Constructions a new task for art appeared in which the artist no longer employs the art objects of nature, but creates his own objects of art.

It is a striking fact to notice that the picture-Writing of Pictographic man has twice emerged into geometric inventions: once when Pictographs were being reduced to lines, which eventually became what we call alphabetic; and once more in the 20th century in Constructionist art. Therefore, it can be said that the art of Pictography has developed into three different Inventive achievements: (1) recording-graphs of the visual-world, now become Photography and Television; (2) communicational-graphs called language; (3) man-invented or Constructionist art.

We must, however, regard the development of the art of Writing as *principally* the reversal of the evolutionary process to be found in the development of that art which records the visible world. But the development of Writing and the new epoch of Constructionist art present evolutionary parallels. Accordingly, we can say that today men are again making an effort similar to that which resulted in the invention of Writing as we now know it. Only the present effort is to invent an art of man. And just as man no longer copies the appearances of nature for communicational purposes in his Writing, so man no longer needs to copy the art of nature for the purpose of making his own art. Thus a similar process of abstracting was involved in the creation of Writing and present day Constructionist art. The evolutionary process by means of which man has already invented Writing—man's most powerful tool of evolution (or destruction)—is also the process by which man is now striving to create his own art. In the one "art," man replaces the limited Mimetic Sign method of communicating his experience in reality with Inventive Signs; and in the other "art," man also replaces the limited Mimetic method of creating art by employing Inventive forms.

In this respect it is provocative to consider the fact that today in Constructionist works man is again confronted with an art that is highly "visual," just as was the art of Paleolithic man on another level of vision. And one wonders if Constructions are to be still another form of art out of which will arise another more highly developed language, just as Pictography was the genesis of the present form of written language. This is of particular interest in view of the fact that we have become so over-verbalized in our present mode of language. The history of communicational Symbols is one of passing from over-visualization to over-verbalization; perhaps in the future the new art will lead to the discovery of forms of communication which include but do not over-emphasize either the visual or the verbal, but integrate them properly.

In addition to the significant role which Decorative artists played in the development of Writing, they have, largely unconsciously, experienced the release of their ability to invent in various other directions. Especially in the formation of the objects—the shapes of the pots, vases, etc.—the artist invented forms not to be seen in nature. The decorations incised or painted on the earliest known examples of "decorated" pottery appear to be of two kinds: (1) Invented Signs; (2) Mimetic Signs which were largely convention-alized depictions of water, rain and plants. However, as the Mimetic trend increasingly developed, it increasingly dominated in the "Decorations" painted or incised upon pottery and the like. And by the time we come to the Classical Greek period we find the human form dominating the space on the vases where formerly various types of symbolic borders had been abundantly used. The latter, from then on, occupy a very minor position, their function probably being replaced, when such Symbols were needed, by the words that were printed in the spaces around the figures. In other words, the Mimetic factor took the leading role, and the lines, zig-zags, etc., that formerly ran around and across the vase, gradually disappeared to be replaced by letters. The change is even more apparent in Roman times when the "Decorative" devices used by the Greeks in the cornices of buildings, for example, were replaced more and more by very realistic Symbols, such as leaves, flowers and fruit.

In brief, the Decorative arts, pottery and the various objects used in homes (furniture, rugs, etc.), were increasingly taken over by the picture—Mimetic art—until not only the inside and outside of buildings, but also the surface of objects placed inside are crowded with pictures. This situation increases with hardly a letup until recent times.

Since artists in the so-called fine-arts have rediscovered the Inventive factor, a new vitality has appeared in the so-called minor arts, now correctly called Industrial arts. In this field artists are no longer concerned with making ugly shapes and disguising them with Mimetic "decoration." It is now possible for utilitarian objects to be satisfactorily produced with Machine-made forms which function efficiently. There is no longer any need for covering them over with pictures or patterns of this and that in order to hide an ugly shape. The same is true of Architecture.

In its early beginnings Architecture was composed only for the direct purpose of shelter, worship and burial. In this first stage it was largely an Inventive affair. In Egyptian times Architects placed their works—the pyramid, the obelisk and the temple—securely in contrast to the natural environment. Then Architecture was treated as a problem of Sculpture; in fact the Architect was a Sculptor. Both professions used similar materials and methods of construction. The Architect was limited by the methods and natural materials of the Sculptor. The sculptured human form was an integral part of the Architecture, i.e., there was a unified organization between the sculpturing of this natural object and the sculpturing of the Architectural forms of the building on which these objects were set (figure 164).

So long as this unity existed, Architects produced great works of art—we would call them Sculpture-Architecture. But Egyptian culture marked the conclusion of *development* in this type of building. After that the medium of Architecture was increasingly taken so far afield from the *art* of building by the pressure of the Mimetic impulse that the old unity was no longer possible. As Sculpture progressed towards the *Mimetic objective,* Architecture regressed as regards the *Inventive direction.* When the Mimetic impulse reached its stride in Sculpture during Greek times, and the Mimetic objective became of supreme value, the unified participation of the human form in the Architecture was lost. It was then that Aristotle formulated his theories of "imitation" and excluded Architecture from the classification "fine-arts"; it was then that Sculpture became consciously directed towards the Mimetic objective, and the art of Sculpture-Architecture definitely decayed (figure 165). Although Roman architects brought the art of engineering to a high pitch, they failed miserably as regards the visual appearances; in fact, the visual face of Architecture became nothing but a sort of blackboard inside for making pictures, and shelves and perches outside and inside for setting up Sculpture.

With the Christian reorientation to the problem of reality, Architecture became even more muddled. The Christians made buildings into sky-rockets. Le Corbusier wrote of the Gothic products, that they were a *"fight against the force of gravity,"* [9] an apt commentary. For, as we have seen in their other arts, the Christians had a habit of defying reality. (See figures 166, 167, which show contrast between Gothic and Egyptian Architecture.)

During the Renaissance the Mimetic factor developed to even greater importance through the achievements in the medium of oil-painting. From now on the exterior of a building was literally crawling with Sculpture, particularly of the human form, and inside the Sculptor had the help of the Painter in drowning the walls with more Mimetic art.[10] And wherever the Sculptor or Painter had not placed any of their works, there the Renaissance Architect himself would take the opportunity to behave like a pastry-cook Sculptor or an embroidery Painter (figures 168, 169). One had to get far away from the building to see the actual character of the attempt peculiar to the Architect's profession; otherwise the Sculpture hid or disguised what there was of the Architecture. This was the inevitable result of considering the Mimetic parts of the building the supreme values, thus relegating Architecture to function as a mere

9. Le Corbusier: *Towards a New Architecture,* p. 30, translated from the thirteenth French edition with an introduction by Frederick Etchells, Payson and Clarke, Ltd., New York, 1927.

10. No better example of this muddle can be seen than in the four reproductions in Le Corbusier's *Towards a New Architecture,* p. 173. See especially the view of The Castel St. Angelo and the Galleria, both of Renaissance Rome. See also pp. 66–67, S. Giedion's *Space, Time and Architecture,* for Photographs of similar Architectural aberrations.

164. Egypt: the northeast corner of the second court of the mortuary temple of Ramses II, 1299-1232 B.C. The Oriental Institute, University of Chicago.

background for Mimetic objects. Beneath all this overlay, just as in the Sculpture of this period, one found the old Classical Architecture, at least what was left of it, struggling for breath. As a matter of fact, anachronistic Sculptors were often the Architects of these buildings. In short, as Architecture gradually became less and less a matter of Sculpture, and more and more a problem of engineering, the "visual" function of Architecture as a problem of art proportionately decayed.

Frank Lloyd Wright has remarked, concerning the erroneous view that Architecture was a problem mainly of Sculpture: "Buonarroti, being a sculptor himself (he was painter also but, unluckily, painted pictures of sculpture), probably thought Architecture, too, ought to be Sculpture."[11] Wright goes further to the point of the matter when he observes that: "Renaissance Architecture, being but the dry bones of a life lived and dead, centuries before, the bones were left to bleach."[12]

By the 19th century the Sculpture of the human form had lost its dominant place in Architecture, but the change that followed brought an even more destructive compromise with nature. The Architect strove to compromise his art directly with the natural environment; now it was the landscape Painter's mentality that dominated the art scene in place of the figure Painter and Sculptor. We note in this connection that the 19th century was the century of landscape Painting, the century of Turner, Constable, Bonnington in England; of Rousseau, Dupre, Daubigny, Corot in France. It might be said that the tree replaced the human form in making Architecture digestible. For if previously the human form was sprawled everywhere over the face of man's Architectural efforts, now it was the tree that spread itself all around the building. Vines and trees, in England especially, completely blotted out the buildings along the boulevards or in the small square of park. It seemed as though man wished to hide this art, as though

11. Frank Lloyd Wright: *Modern Architecture*, p. 83, Princeton University Press, Princeton, 1931.
12. Ibid., p. 49.

526

165. Caryatid Porch, The Erechtheion Athens.

he were ashamed of it. And he should have been! Of interest here is the following quotation from Sigfried Giedion: "Indeed, if the development of London may be said to follow any rule, it is an unwritten one—like so many in England which carry most weight—deriving from the democratic insistence that a man shall not be disturbed in his private life. The rule runs roughly as follows: The residential quarters of a city should, as far as possible, merge into the greenery. They should be as inconspicuous as possible." [13] We find it difficult to connect this behavior in Architecture with a desire for democracy, since one can live quite democratically without creating ugly buildings that must be hidden and visually replaced by the art of nature.

      The fact is that men, whether they know it or not, are relieved of the ugly face of their congested Architecture by the grass, vines, bushes and trees of nature. Awareness of the fundamentals involved in this problem would disclose how ridiculous nature is made when our streets are pegged with two rows of trees which hide the houses that men are supposedly so proud of. It is undeniable that our streets are more satisfactory with these rows of trees than they would be without them. The ugly forms of our houses are broken up by the forms of leaves, trunks, branches, and the ugly colors of the houses are hidden or at least considerably altered by the pleasing, dominant greens of the trees. Unconsciously we must "feel" this saving function of nature's art. For if we really thought our houses were "beautiful" we certainly would not allow them to be hidden from sight by trees, bushes, or allow vines to crawl and spread all over them. Certainly the art of nature is not improved by this use, but man's ugly houses are at least made bearable when sufficiently hidden or covered with nature-art.

      The most obvious examples of this in the United States are the clusters of university buildings

13. Reprinted by permission of the publishers from Sigfried Giedion, *Space, Time and Architecture*, p. 442. Harvard University Press, Cambridge, Mass., 1943.

166. Sanctuary of the Temple of Horus at Edfu. Photo, Jean Capart.

where the art of nature is sprayed all over the place, so that one's visual stomach will not heave at the sight of Architectural monstrosities. Just as the ugly vase was "beautified" by covering it with the Mimetic art of nature, so Architecture was "beautified" by covering it with the actual, live art of nature. But who has seen a greater monstrosity than a building covered completely with vines, giving the impression of huge, ugly, green lumps, trying to burst through the earth's surface? Look at any rock covered with vines to see the difference.

With the advent of the Machine and the new materials of the Machine, the Architect was freed technically from the old limiting medium and methods of the Sculptor. The Architect was free to develop his medium as an art of invented forms; free to develop form-organizations independent of taking on any of the forms of nature. Thus with the rise of the industrial period, two solutions faced Architects concerning buildings and the objects placed in them: (1) to return to the products of the hand and the Sculptural materials; (2) to free the new Machine materials and methods from the dead *hand* of the past and so release the inherent potentialities of using the Machine to make a new Architecture.

Few, however, realized the great importance of the Architect's new medium until recent times, so that even when the inventions of the industrial period technically freed the Architect from the limitations of the old materials and methods of Sculpture, he still insisted on covering the new materials and their new structural-visual potentialities with the old, decadent, Classical, now false front. Not only were the new structural potentialities frustrated, but also the new possibilities regarding the visual aspect of Architecture made possible by the new materials and Machines. Just as in Sculpture and Painting, so in Architecture there occurred a compromise between the old and new mediums and contents.

But the split between the old and the new eventually began; the old traditions, prejudices and authorities were criticized as an encumbrance to the new era now possible in Architecture. The fundamental impetus to the rebirth of Architecture was the revolution in the so-called fine-arts, beginning in the late 19th century, during which the Mimetic factor gradually gave way to the Inventive one. Through this

528

167. Interior of Cathedral at Cologne, Germany, looking east. Monkmeyer Photo Service.

revolution the Architect was freed from the harmful dominance of the Mimetic factor, freed to employ the Inventive factor which was essential to the success of his art. It was then that the Architect became an artist-engineer. The science of engineering became the new art method for the Architect!

Although European Architects began to sense the new possibilities—i.e., the importance of the wall surface as such, without the encumbrance of do-dads stuck everywhere, and the relation of structure to the visual problem—it was the Americans who tackled this problem first. In their works in the mid-19th century the clean wall surface had, relatively speaking, already appeared. It was only much later that the Europeans advanced to this point, due not so much to American example as to the revolution in European art. But if the American Architect was allowed relatively clean walls (no doubt because it fitted into the Machine economy) he eventually lost what was thus gained by ignoring his consciousness of being an artist of a new era of art. On the other hand, if the European Architect responded to his consciousness of being an artist forming a new period of art, European culture was hidebound by the old nature-art tradition—the limited Aristotelian view of nature—and so the Architect lacked adequate Machine-art consciousness.

Hence, the best European Architects became conscious of the Machine as an art instrument through the advanced trends in European art, which suggested the need for the Machine. The best Architects in this country became conscious of the advanced trends in art through the advances made here in the development of the Machine, which suggested the need for the new art.

If the Europeans are more conscious of what has happened in the recent innovations of art, their limitations in this respect become apparent when we find Le Corbusier getting excited about Michelangelo's dome on St. Peter's, which he says "was a *tour de force* that few men would have dared," and deploring the fact that "it has been hidden" by later additions to the building.[14] But Frank Lloyd Wright, the Architect of the Machine culture, saw all this more correctly when he wrote: "Michelangelo built

14. Le Corbusier, op. cit., pp. 170–171.

168. Farnese Palace, Interior, Rome. Alinari Photo.

the first skyscraper, I suppose, when he hurled the Pantheon on top of the Parthenon. The Pope named it St. Peter's and the world called it a day, celebrating the great act ever since in the sincerest form of human flattery possible. As is well known, that form is imitation." [15]

"Domed or damned was and is the status of official buildings in all countries, especially in ours, as a consequence of the great Italian's impulsive indiscretion. But no other individual sculptor, painter or architect, let us hope, may ever achieve such success again, or Architecture at the end of its resources may pass out in favor of something else." [16] It is not an accident that Le Corbusier admires Michelangelo's cake of sculpture and that Wright definitely does not.

One of the problems of the modern Architect is to become completely rid of the solid, block or sculptural form as necessarily basic to the building plan. This is really a hangover from the Paleolithic cave. If Architects will but turn to the Constructionists, look and live with Constructions (the art made by artists who are in a far better position than Architects to discover the manifold possibilities yet to be found in man-invented forms) then they will learn that much more how to free their works from the old sculptural form canalization.

To a degree the old function of nature-art still lingers on in the practice of most "Modern" Architects. He is basically insecure as a creative artist before the products of nature-art. He finds himself compelled to call to his aid the art of unaided nature. Few men have yet learned to build without covering or disguising the face of their art with the art of nature. Thus they put trees and bushes all over the place, so that one often observes that the Photographer who wants to make a picture of the building is compelled to wait until the autumn when trees and bushes have at least lost their leaves, if he is to avoid making a record mainly of the trees and bushes instead of the Architecture. This very operation exposes the stupidity of the whole business, for certainly if one wants his building seen, then one should not blot it out or blob it up with greenery.

15. F. L. Wright: *Modern Architecture*, p. 83.

16. Ibid., p. 84.

169. Santa Maria della Salute, Venice. Alinari photo.

But as things stand today, most Architects on both sides of the Atlantic are lacking in an adequate, up-to-date consciousness of both aspects of the problems of modern Architecture—the advances in Machine methods and in Machine art. We repeat, it is to the Architect's advantage to understand thoroughly that the works of the Cubists, the Two-Dimensionalists and the Constructionists in particular have played a leading role in restoring the Architect to the position of a legitimate artist in his own right, with his own potentialities in the field of art. Since the death of Mondrian, only the Constructionists bear the same relation to the so-called utilitarian arts as does the theoretical mathematician to the applied sciences.

Thus if the Architects from Classical times to the opening of this century permitted the Sculptor and the Painter to clutter up their walls inside and out (not to mention the Sculptural do-dads of the Architects themselves), then the Architect of the 20th century seldom makes any provisions for the works of the Sculptor or the Painter. At best he merely sticks Sculpture around much as he does the furniture and tacks up here and there the old-fashioned framed picture, as has been the practice for centuries. In short, a coordination of the Sculptural and Painting arts with Architecture is utterly lacking. Since the products of the old art mediums—paint and stone—belong in the past with the old Architecture, such art has no legitimate relationships with the new Machine materials and methods and so no relationship with the products of the modern Machine-Architect. The tendency to paint murals on the interior face of "Modern" Architecture is an attempt to overcome this problem, but this is actually a reversion to the old Classical and Renaissance method of Painting and Architecture, a substitute for the solution that is actually needed. Actually only the Constructionist can offer the Architect non-Camera art which will permit him to coordinate his Architectural plans in such a manner that art objects can be definitely planned for and not merely stuck in later, as happens when the old art mediums are used. (As far as the old mural solution is concerned, only the Photographer can supply a legitimate result.) In this way, the Architect can return to the unity of planning of the early Sculptor-Architects of Egypt, where all the arts that were employed were planned, coordinated aspects of the building. Only now he is no longer a Sculptor-Architect, but a Machine-Architect! The former used nature-made materials and the tools of the Mimetic artist; the latter uses man-made materials and the tools of the contemporary Inventive artist.

531

170. Mies van der Rohe, Model of outdoor restaurant, Indianapolis. Photo, Hedrich-Blessing Studio.

Thus we have found in the evolution of Writing, in the evolution of "Decorative" arts, in the evolution of Architecture, similar or parallel series of developments: from invention to the copying of nature forms, and once again a return to invented forms. But so far only in particular examples of "Decorative" arts and contemporary Architecture has the Inventive aspect emerged without compromise with the superannuated "fine-arts."

From Classical Greek times until this century Architects in general have had to make the building a setting for the figures and ornaments of the Sculptor on the outside and inside—and for the works of the Painter on the inside. The same thing happened to the invented objects of the potter. In this sense Architecture was a "minor" art, as was pottery and the like.

The predominance of the Mimetic factor in post-Classical times explains why the forms of the Architect, the potter, etc.—the Inventive aspect of this art—were essentially ugly. The Inventive factor was practically ignored; concentration was placed on the then considered supreme manifestation of art— that is, copying of nature's appearances. Consequently, because of the dominance of the *linear* Mimetic objective, men lost the ability or desire to work creatively in the third dimension, i.e., on the vase or building. The products of the Mimetic effort were employed to cover over and make the ugly shapes allegedly "beautiful." In brief, the products of the Architect and the potter simply supplied a setting for the "fine" or "higher" arts—the products of the Mimetic direction. It is important to note that throughout the period in which the Painters dominated the scene of art history, the period in which the greatest dominance of the Mimetic impulse occurred—particularly from the Renaissance to the opening of the 20th

171. Model of an Egyptian house and estate based on excavations at El-Amarna, Dyn. XVIII. The Oriental Institute, University of Chicago.

century—the worst Architecture, pottery, furniture, etc., ever produced by man made their appearance. For once the Mimetic factor became dominant, the fundamentally creative character of Architecture was doomed to sterility and disease. The more dominant the Mimetic factor, the more ugly the forms of Architecture became. There is no more telling evidence of this than the fact that man used the greenery, the art of nature, to hide his ugly buildings. The worse Architecture became, the more trees, bushes, vines were employed.

Consequently it is a serious error to try to make a historical case demonstrating a development of the visual characteristics of Architectural art. If one wishes to do this, one must read history backwards; in the opposite direction one finds only a series of developing monstrosities after Egyptian times. Only in one major aspect was there a development towards the present, and that was in the great developments of engineering. It was only in more recent times when Architecture was completely released from the Mimetic factor, that the full potentialities of the art were again set in motion, for it was always essentially an art of invention and not, as in Sculpture and Painting, one of recording.

With the advent of Constructionist art the Architects and "Decorative" artists again come into their own. The works of the genuinely modern Architect today again remind one of the dignity, the genuineness of the Egyptian pyramids, obelisks and ancient temples (see figures 170, 171 and 166). The Architect again creates in contrast to rather than in compromise with the art of nature, i.e., the natural environment. The genuine contemporary Architect no longer compromises his art with the human form or with trees. Today the Architect again returns to his legitimate role as Inventive artist, the role assumed by the first Architects in history.

533

172. From Top to Bottom: (1) Courbet, Coast Scene, detail of figure 78. (2) Monet, Parliament of Westminster, detail of figure 87. (3) Cézanne, L'Estaque, detail of figure 102. (4) Mondrian, Pier and Ocean, detail of figure 120 (b) below.

Man's desire and ability to invent, to make his own art, have found expression not only in the invention of Writing, the various "Decorative" arts, and Architecture, but also in certain aspects of the development of the realistic arts of Painting and Sculpture. It is important, however, to note the difference between the operation of the Inventive factor in Decorative art, Architecture, etc., and its operation in the development of the realistic direction of Painting and Sculpture. In the latter case, as that has been explained, the artist at first unconsciously used the Inventive factor as a substitute for his inability to record accurately. Thus, for example, if early man could not make a head that looked precisely like an actual head, he could invent shapes that clearly indicated such an object. All recording art previous to that of the 5th century B.C. Greeks had a large share of invented elements in the contents; but so far as the content was concerned, invention was not the actual objective. And as artists increased their ability to record accurately, this aspect of the Inventive factor diminished proportionately.[17] But as the Inventive factor diminished in one way, in still another respect it gradually increased. That is, the act of invention was gradually transferred from supplementing the inability to record perfectly, to devising more efficient mechanical methods for securing accurate recording. In the animal Paintings of Magdalenian times, for example, it can be seen that to produce a highly developed recording of an animal, less form-invention was necessary than had been the case in early Aurignacian times; on the other hand, *invention of the mechanical or technical means* by which the animal forms were made was more evident and necessary in the later art than in the earlier. More striking examples of the Inventive factor's being used to devise more efficient mechanical methods for accurate recording can be seen in the development of perspective, and finally the Camera. We distinguish therefore, between two fundamental *kinds* of invention in past art, the invention by which man unconsciously compensates for his inability to record accurately, and the mechanical means by which the art was made. Quite another situation occurs in post-Camera art.

After the Greeks achieved an accurate recording of the general human form, another kind of "invention" appears. That is, from the 5th century B.C. on into the 19th century, an "ideal" was consciously sought by some artists as an expression of man's *latent* desire to be a creative artist in his own right. The objective was "invention," and not mere literal "imitation" of nature-art. This, as other discussions have shown, was frustrated or pseudo-invention.

We have already mentioned the positive value of the Idealist in the evolution of art. But as regards his own objectives, this kind of artist (in whatever form) is essentially involved in a futile competition or "rivalry" with the "art" of nature. True, the Idealist wishes to be a creator, and, whether intentionally or not, he deceives most of us into believing that he is a creator—that he creates the perfection for which nature has striven but failed. Actually, his creation consists of no more than a working over, a mere manipulation of the "creations" of nature. He does not improve on nature forms; he distorts them. It is he who fails in his objective, not nature, as the Idealist would have us believe. He fails because his fundamental objective is impossible of attainment in the manner he seeks it. As long as this type of artist records (or distorts) the art of nature in the attempt to devise an art of man, he is frustrated, because he is actually trying to accomplish two diametrically opposite objectives within the confines of one kind—that is, nature-art. His efforts are confined to a content which is suited for the realization of only *one* of these art objectives—the recording of nature's art—the Realist's objective.

The scientist of art, the Realist, has been the only SUCCESSFUL "creator" in pre-Camera art dealing with nature's appearances. He succeeded as creator because his "creative" objective was possible. This type of artist has taken part in the evolution of achievements which eventually made it possible for man to *create,* invent a Machine by which the actual world of vision can be recorded in a highly accurate manner. Without this achievement the present human culture would be radically handicapped.

The Idealist is essentially in conflict with nature, and deliberately or otherwise expresses a basic contempt for the art of nature; whereas the Realist expresses a great regard for it, and thus is not in conflict with himself, since he functions as an adjusted part of nature. However, even some "Realists" were sometimes under the false impression that somehow they were creating a man-art by copying nature.

17. But even if the forms of nature, for example, the human form, have always remained in art the way man could make them, nevertheless, as art developed, the human forms made by the artist increasingly took on the appearances of nature's human forms.

This is precisely why a great majority of the realistic artists became bitterly opposed to the Camera when it appeared. Those who were genuine Realists simply threw their brushes out of the window and picked up the Camera.

One of the big problems for artists of the past was to realize that since their art content was comprised of nature's art, the best they could do was to try to record it as well as possible, and that to try to change the results of nature's art into a man-art, as the Classicists tried to do, was a hopeless attempt.

In other words, in the arts of Painting and Sculpture since the 5th century B.C. there has existed a schism in the abstractions from the macroscopics of nature as made by the two general opposed groups of artists. On the one hand some strove to record the art of nature, and on the other hand some wished to be "creative." But, as our studies have disclosed, from the times of the first Paleolithic artist who began the imitation of nature's art until the 20th century, no Painters or Sculptors ever created original works of art; they copied in one way or another originals which were to be found only in nature.

A more adequate understanding of many difficulties and problems in both past and present art can be gained by comprehending the fact that both the recording and inventing factors were present in past art. The schism between the two remained more or less latent, however, up to the invention of the Camera. But once the mechanical instrument was used to take over the function and task previously the prerogative of artists using the older types of mediums, the schism became ever more apparent.

Since the appearance of the revolutionary arts of the Transition-Period we have again heard a great deal of verbalization about how the artist no longer desires to be a mirror, but a "creator," and so he distorts nature's appearances in the effort to make art a vehicle which permits man to express himself "creatively." Repeated attempts are made to justify the more recent distortions of nature by pointing out that the artists of the past, especially those before the 5th century B.C., as well as the artists of the Christian, African and Oriental cultures also distorted nature. Actually the past artists who have some relationship with the general attempt among Modernists to create their own art, were not those who most obviously distorted nature, but rather the "Classicists"; that is, those who tried to *perfect*, rather than *distort*, the general visible form of the human body. While the various "Modernists" draw more on the pre-5th century B.C. *arts* for their type of nature distortions, they draw, consciously or otherwise, upon Classical Greek *theory* for their rationalizations of these distortions. This is no accident. (See chapter 21.) Neither is it an accident that the "Modern" artists and their apologists so frequently talk about "creating," and the Classicists talked about "invention." This kinship between the Classicists and the modern Distortionists lies in the basic motivations, mostly unconscious, which have prompted them both in their manipulations of nature. The latest exponents of the Classical venture are also trying to make nature *over,* futilely trying to make an art of man, meanwhile unconsciously legitimatizing their efforts with the metaphysics of Aristotle and Plato. Both types are examples of frustration and misdirection in an attempt to achieve a man-invented art content. Wendell Johnson's remarks about Idealists are very applicable to the vast bulk of artists and art verbalists today: "most, if not all, so called maladjusted persons in our society may be viewed as frustrated and distraught idealists. Distraught because they are frustrated, and frustrated because they are 'idealists,' they are living testimony of the price we pay for the traditions we cherish, and for the aspirations which those traditions encourage together with the restrictions which they tend to enforce. It is not that this 'idealism' is always immediately apparent—on the contrary, it is rather likely, as a rule, to elude the superficial observer." [18]

An invented art content is being striven for unconsciously in some degree by most artists today, but few are conscious enough of what they are striving for to be able to eliminate that aspect of their work which hinders its realization. So long as non-Camera artists abstract in ANY DEGREE from the macro-level of nature, then so long will they continue to be involved in the old schizoid experiences of the past. Today as far as the vast majority are concerned, the old conflict between the real (nature) and the ideal (man) has yet to be settled, and it is precisely this conflict which is the basis for the chaos of our generation and the one preceding us.

The schism of past art, the attempt both to record nature and to devise a man-art, was partly resolved when Photography was invented. One aspect of the double or schizoid objective of the old art

18. Wendell Johnson: "People in Quandaries," *Etc.,* 1:69, Winter, 1943–1944.

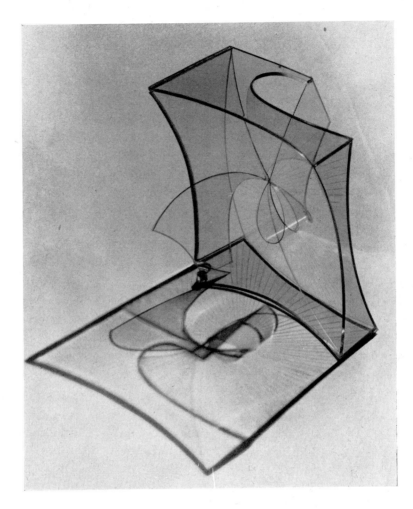

173. Naum Gabo, Construction, 1937. Vassar College Art Gallery.

174. Charles Biederman, Construction, 9/45 (1). Painted metal and wood, 37½″x28¾″x16½″.

was then directly removed. The recording factor was freed from the creative objective as regards the content, thus allowing for the full, unhampered development of recording nature-art. With Constructionist art the Inventive factor was completely freed from its frustrating confinement with the recording one. Today each of these two different kinds of art has its own vehicle and function which makes it possible for artists to release fully each kind of effort towards its specific objective.

Photography as well as Constructionist art entails the operation of man's Inventive ability. In Photography the principal act of invention lies in perfecting the accuracy of the method for recording the art of nature. The Constructionist must not only employ invented mechanical means, but he must also completely invent his art contents. The non-Camera Inventive artists have learned how man can make his own art by the *extension* of the nature-art process; this results in an extension of our experiences in the objective reality. They manipulate the *process* not the *results* of nature-art. It is true that they cannot offer the undubitably important experiences derived from nature's appearances. But the Camera artist does supply these experiences in a manner incomparably superior to the past.[19]

Thus the Camera artist in 1839 and the Constructionist in 1913, each took over one of the conflicting objectives which had operated in past art, and since then a new, as-a-whole formulation of art has been possible. Almost from the beginning of art to the present, the great achievements have been of two distinct but interrelated types; on the one hand the art created by man, on the other, the art copied from nature. But some *kind* and *degree* of the recording of nature's macroscopic level was considered (and of course still is by the vast majority) as *the only* art. All the innovations of the last one hundred years have been comprised of various conflicting combinations of what was being striven for and finally realized in the two kinds of *inventions*—the Camera and Constructions. In short, all art of the Transitional-Period was a combination in various or gradient proportions of abstracting from the macroscopic (recording) and structural (Inventive) levels of nature. In today's art neither level is eradicated; we simply understand them better and thus utilize them more profitably.

The art of nature and the art of man have become distinct but remain *interrelated* entities, whereas in the past the attempt was to make nature and man-art one and the same thing. The relationship between them is one of similarity in structure and not, as in the past, identification of contents. Today man does not stand his art next to nature (except the Camera recordings of nature's art) to see how like one is to the other, for now there are involved certain differences in objectives as well as similarities. In Constructionist art the similarities are no longer those of the past which were based on the macro-appearances of nature "art"; *the similarities are in structure, not results.* Accordingly if one wishes to argue that age-old question of which is the superior art, we find the following answer: nature-art, as nature-art, is superior to man's art; similarly, man's art as man's art is superior to nature-art. And thus we rid ourselves of the stupid question of superiority and so of the utter futility of idealism.

In Constructionist art the efforts of the Classicists both old and new, i.e., the Inventive or creative efforts, are released at last. For in Constructionist works the artist is able (without the futility of being an Idealist) to release his ability to be Inventive and thus make possible the creation of his own art contents. He no longer needs to be in futile "rivalry" with nature. When the artist is rid of the Idealist's view, nature begins to reveal new knowledge, the new possibilities of its inescapable process, the process of which we and all the art we shall ever make will always be but a part. Hence it is not the Constructionists, but the Distortionists, the incipient and full-blown Surrealists, the jugglers of nature forms—nearly all present day non-Camera artists, both "Realists" and "Modernists"—who are hopelessly competing with nature. Like the older Classicists, they too are inadvertently or otherwise involved in futile attempts to achieve an "ideal." But the 2,000-year-old argument about the "real" and the "ideal"— man's effort to record nature-art and at the same time make an art of man (actually a conflict as ancient as man's art)—all this can now come to an end. Today both can be successfully done.

19. This latter fact exposes the essential hypocrisy of those who repeatedly criticize the arts which do not offer us the experiences of nature's appearances. For if they were genuine in their demands they would not criticize arts which do not pretend to answer their demands; instead they would spend this time before those works of art which do fulfill their alleged demands, especially in the case of Photography, the most developed method of presenting nature's appearances.

175. César Domela, Composition, 1937. Collection of The Guggenheim Museum of Non-Objective Art.

In short, the Aristotelian period of art, characterized by a concern with the macro-level, the art of nature, is not abandoned, but *continued and perfected in a more adequate orientation towards reality* through the efforts of *genuine* Camera artists. But the Aristotelian period of art has now been so radically transformed, that it is necessary to regard the new epoch as a *non*-Aristotelian one if we are to free ourselves from the frustrating notions of Aristotelianism. The non-Aristotelian attitude is but a reasonable development of the Aristotelian artist's attempt to invent, create his art. The recording efforts of past artists are now continued by the Camera artist, who is no longer frustrated by the "Inventive" factor of the past, whereas the Inventive effort of past artists is now also continued by the Constructionist, who in turn is no longer frustrated by the Mimetic factor of the past. The Aristotelian attitude inevitably excludes and denies the Constructionist attitude towards art and reality, whereas the non-Aristotelian attitude includes the further, more correct development of the Aristotelian effort as that appears both in the Constructionist's and the Camera artist's direction. It is of course not surprising that Constructionist art has been so thoroughly ignored in our times, since it is essentially a non-Aristotelian art in a world laden with the fungus of Aristotelianism.

Therefore, in order to meet the new conditions of the present and future, we must adopt the non-Aristotelian point of view. Only thus can our theoretical activities correspond to the transformation which was attained with the conclusion of the Transitional-Period of art. Otherwise our theorizing will continue to be the ineffectual and aimless word-noises of those present day artists and critics who attempt to reason in a manner appropriate two thousand years ago about a world of art that has undergone two thousand years of change.

From the very beginning of art history man's art in one form or another has disclosed strivings in the very direction now *fully* taken by the Constructionist today. From the beginning of the history of his culture, man has been making geometric lines and forms, and only today can he begin to realize the basic significance behind this urge; namely, that it is an expression of man's desire to invent his own "art" for purposes peculiar to man.

The present day Jeremiahs, who lament those arts with Inventive contents, such as Constructionist art and works of Two-Dimensionalist Painters, are somewhat ludicrous when we realize that these same people generally admire similar efforts in other forms of art. As a matter of fact, many "Modern" artists are greatly attracted to and stimulated by the "decoration" placed upon the objects of past so-called minor arts, in all their various degrees and levels of abstracting from nature, because they can readily utilize the methods of this form of art in their efforts to manipulate nature forms. This attraction, however, is to the symptomatic rather than to the fundamental character of this past art in relation to the needs of the present, as we have made clear elsewhere. (Similarly the majority of present day artists have been attracted to the symptomatic and negative aspects of the innovations that occurred during the past one hundred years, rather than to the basic positive factors responsible for their development.)

Hence it is no accident or superficial coincidence, as we have already suggested, that certain innovations in present day art are called "Decorative." It is unfortunate, however, that so few realize the unconscious wisdom expressed by their ignorance in using this term, whether to praise or to condemn the new art direction. But with the rediscovery and more adequate coherent comprehension of the Inventive ability of man by the Constructionists, we can expect an ever greater rebirth in the "Decorative" arts, now become the Industrial (Machine) arts, which, from the times of the Classical Greeks until this century, have been in a state of increasing regression. Such changes, as we have noted, have begun to appear here and there, especially throughout the last three decades. Through the knowledge made possible by Constructionist and Two-Dimensionalist art it is now possible to free even more the potentialities of invention in other fields, such as Architecture and Industrial arts. Such arts need no longer simply furnish a setting for the now outmoded "fine-arts." [20]

Today, therefore, it is possible to become consciously aware of the Inventive factor and to use it consciously. If man's past efforts to invent his own visual (e.g., Writing, Decorative arts, etc.) Symbols had been properly understood, then the Transitional-Period could have been more brief and to the point.

20. Nevertheless, very few Architects today realize how much they owe to the artists who have freed the "fine-arts" from the Mimetic factor. Unfortunately so far the new attitude is more acceptable in Architecture than in Constructionist art.

176. Jean Gorin, Spatial Construction, bas relief, 1939. Photo, Marc Vaux, Paris.

But the unlikelihood of securing such an understanding of the past can be imagined, when we realize that even today what happened during the Transitional-Period remains very badly misunderstood. Then realize also that with all the historical data and evidence at our command, the birth of a new epoch of art which grew out of the art of the old primitive mediums remains unrecognized in its fundamental character except by a very few individuals. The problems could not be and were not adequately and coherently settled until the invention of the Camera was followed three-quarters of a century later by the invention of Constructionist art. Now we have the Camera to record the art of nature, Constructionists to invent the art of man!

Adequate comprehension of man's ability to invent is essential to the comprehension of our problems. It has been the primary factor which permitted man to develop out of the animal to more and more of a human stage. Animals, being definitely limited in abstracting ability, and therefore lacking in the ability to invent, are restricted to repeating the behavior of the last generation. Human beings, with their greater cortical capacity, have an ability to abstract in ever higher orders, which seems to be unlimited as far as we can now see. With this ability men have been able to transform and enlarge their comprehension of themselves and their environment. It is with this ability that mankind through the artists has been able to invent such complex and powerful instruments as Writing, etc. The Inventive factor is fundamental to the creation and continued existence of human culture. With this ability men can continue to develop human life ever further, or to increase their capacity to destroy it.

It is the ability to invent, to abstract in ever higher orders, which the Constructionists have fully released into man's art. So the issue which Constructionist art introduces is whether man, as an artist, is going to continue the useless manipulation of nature's appearances under the delusion that he is "creating" art, or whether man as an artist is going to utilize the new consciousness of his ability to abstract and invent his own art: whether man is going to utilize that very ability which enabled artists to play a decidedly major role in the invention of Architecture, and "Decoration"—that ability which is his uniquely human characteristic! The *genuine* Constructionists are showing the way.

It is the task of art to express a clear vision of reality. 232
Piet Mondrian

Everything comes from everything, and everything is made out of everything, and everything returns into everything, because whatever exists in the elements is made out of these elements. 212

Leonardo da Vinci

In dealing with ourselves and the world around us, we must take into account the structural fact that everything in this world is strictly interrelated with everything else, and so we must make efforts to discard primitive elementalistic terms, which imply structurally a non-existing isolation. 179

Alfred Korzybski

What we make of the world must be largely dependent on the sense-organs that we happen to possess. How the world must have changed since man came to rely on his eyes rather than his nose! 102

A. S. Eddington

Integration is not something that takes place merely within the organism—it is a progressive interaction between an expanding environment and a growing organism. 286

Oliver Reiser

But the power of human beings to determine their own destinies is limited by natural law, Nature's law. It is the counsel of wisdom to discover the laws of nature, including the laws of human nature, and then to live in accordance with them. The opposite is folly. 178

Alfred Korzybski

True art is always created by the reciprocal action of the surrounding world and the artist. The artist can therefore never isolate himself in a formula previously made. However, the opposition of these two factors shows us, in the course of time, an action that is not arbitrary but an evolution accomplishing itself according to the unshakable laws of nature, hidden in nature and which must be discovered through the continuous culture of life, science and art. These laws which seem to be formulas are nothing personal: being universal they are for all art. 231

Piet Mondrian

One of the great obstacles to a free consideration of the details of our human plight is our tendency to regard familiar notions as "sacred": that is, too assured to be questioned except by the perverse and wicked. 301

James Harvey Robinson

Let us note, however, that the spirit of the past was different from the spirit of our own day, and that it is only tradition which has carried the past into our own time. 232

Piet Mondrian

Our discussion in preceding chapters has shown that if artists are to progress further, they can no longer depend upon the trial-and-error, laissez-faire methods of recent years. If they fail to develop adequate "consciousness of abstracting," they will fail to achieve adequate realization of the new relationships between the artist and the world reality in which he lives. By ignoring the problem of reality, the artist is condemned to be in conflict with it, because he is not aware of the manner in which he is orienting himself to nature. From this it follows that he will be unable to utilize nature in the most useful manner possible.

Present confusions and misunderstandings among artists regarding the relationship of their art to nature stem from their failure to recognize the fact that the art attitude of the past twenty centuries has undergone a major transformation, particularly during the last one hundred years. Until fairly recently man's efforts to make art were largely confined to being some kind of mirror of nature-art. It is not yet understood that this cycle of art has now come to its inevitable conclusion as concerns non-Camera mediums. Throughout the last one hundred years one reality factor after another has been lost in the old mediums of art. First the Photographer took over the task of recording objects as they actually appeared; later the objects were eliminated altogether from advanced non-Camera art. Then the three-dimensional illusion was eliminated, and finally even two-dimensional illusion was discarded by such as Rodchenko. All this was part of an effort, to a great extent unconscious, to free art of the old reality and make way for the new.

Fundamentally, the problems which the artist throughout history has had to face have revolved around the question of how to interpret and then utilize the reality of nature for a suitable art contents. Today the artist is still faced with a similar problem (much as some may think otherwise), but at a particular and climactic phase of historical development. In short, the non-Camera artist is confronted not only with a "problem of reality," but with a radical reorientation to the problem of reality. Failing to achieve this reorientation, artists will continue to be frustrated. Yet by achieving adequate and proper abstracting consciousness, the artist can enjoy the art of nature as it appears, and the art of man, each in its own proper but *not* isolated context.

It has been widely contended, however, that if nature objects are eliminated from the repertoire of the non-Camera artist, and art is reduced to the limitations of invented forms, the possibilities of development would soon be exhausted. At the same time it has been assumed that the manipulation of the forms of nature's objects offers infinite useful possibilities for further development in the old (primitive) mediums. As for the latter contention, we have amply shown that this direction only leads to the ever increasing maladjustment which comprises the "chaos of Modern art." And as for the former contention, *we point out that the Inventive direction offers the artist the variety and complexity of nature itself!*

In some ways nature is a very simple array of forms; in others very complex, depending on one's point of view. Thus, for instance, all the forms, light, and shade possible in nature are contained in a sphere. Yet the possibilities represented by the sphere are indefinite as far as we can see. Therefore, if there are any budding Alexanders in the field of art looking for new worlds to conquer, we throw into their hands a sphere. Look at it! In it you will see the limits of the new direction; the limits are those of the Process Structure of nature! In short, the artist is no more limited than his ability to penetrate the building methods of nature's art. And that limitation, we probably can agree, is something we need not worry about now.

By employing the Structural Process of nature the artist is in the position of employing the endless possibilities inherent in this Process. With this method he will not merely copy or imitatively distort nature's art; instead he will create an art content not to be found in *un*aided nature. The "art" results of unaided nature serve needs distinct from those which can be satisfied in a man-invented art. The art process that man has discovered in nature is today extended by the creative potentialities that are inherent in man. And being no longer confined to copying the RESULTS of nature's Process Structure, but actually using this PROCESS to CREATE his own art-results, the new artist is incomparably less limited than in the past.

It is necessary, however, to have a clear notion of what we mean by the term "structure." It is commonly regarded as representing a thing in itself, but this is a very serious error. Actually there exists only the structure of particular things in unaided nature and in man-made objects. These particular things of unaided nature and man are the forms and structure we find in apples, rocks, snow, humans, etc., *and* in Constructions, Architecture, Machines, etc. And it is possible for combinations of forms which are not any of the combinations found in unaided nature to be just as complete realities as the human form, tree form, or stone form, etc.

One of the basic errors of both the Academicians and the "Modernists" is to assume that the compositional aspect of past art represents what some have called the "basic elements" of nature. It is then an easy step to adopt the popular assumption that composition and invented forms are much the

548

177. Théo van Doesburg, Composition Simultanée, 1929. By courtesy of the Yale University Art Gallery, Collection of the Société
Anonyme, Museum of Modern Art: 1920. Photo, Courtesy of Mme. Théo van Doesburg.

178. Piet Mondrian, Opposition of Lines, Red and Yellow, 1937. Courtesy of the Philadelphia Museum of Art, Gallatin Collection.

same. But to regard the new arts as simply a matter of what is "composition" in the older arts is to consider only certain similarities and to ignore the critical differences. Since in certain works of art only arrangements of forms are seen, which forms are not the forms of nature, and since forms, it is silently assumed, cannot mean or be anything unless they are the forms of nature, then all that remains is something called "arrangement" or "composition." This leads to the conclusion that such art is an arrangement of nothing; but how can one arrange nothing? "Composition" is thought of as some entity which can either be clothed with nature forms or else nothing exists but composition or arrangement.[1] Actually the case is one of nature forms and their types of "composition," and invented forms and their types of "composition," or. as in "Modern" art, confused mixtures of both. In brief, we cannot have composition without something being composed. And, as we have emphasized a number of times, it is impossible for an artist to make anything that does not mean something. If we claim that *any* kind of art does not mean anything we have simply exhibited our ignorance.

1. Thus the absurd remark of critics that Cubism is only "theory." (See p. 409.)

179. Charles Biederman, Construction, 4/39 (3). Plexiglas and painted wood and metal
rods, 32⅜"x26⅝"x3¾". Photo, Bernard Dordick.

There is a good deal of similarity between the prevalent confusion about invented forms and
that which prevented Cézanne from resolving the conflicts between his theory about the cone, sphere and
cylinder structure of nature on the one hand and on the other the results of his theory as seen in his
works. So long as Cézanne thought of nature's structure in these terms, he was bound to be limited to
the depiction of nature's appearances and so limited in his efforts to realize fully the new art direction.[2]
As he repeatedly emphasized in his last years, he did not "realize." To think of nature's structure in
terms of cones, spheres, and the like was an abstraction as yet only degrees removed from the appearances
of nature; thus Cézanne inevitably retained nature's appearances *to a proportionate degree*. He was a
Transitional-Period artist and so his theory as well as his work was of a transitional character. To put it
briefly: although Cézanne did discover that the forms of nature could be made out of a relation of cones,
cylinders or spheres, he did not realize that with this method man could make form-*relations* other than
those found in nature. Thus he could only think of spheres and cones as apples and pears, rather than

2. This criticism becomes more apparent when applied to the works of Léger.

551

as leading to the creation of man-invented art objects independent of taking on the appearances of nature's art objects. But he made a big step towards the discovery of the Structural Process of reality—a discovery he came close to finding in his last paintings and watercolors. The important point here is that Cézanne realized that he was confronted with a problem that needed a solution; he did not assume that the final solution had been found, as many of his present day adulators falsely believe.

The prevalent inadequate comprehension of Cézanne's theory of the cone, cylinder and sphere has been responsible for many erroneous arguments on this subject. We must avoid identifying nature's structure as merely a matter of cones, spheres, cylinders and the like. We are dealing with how things are put together; how they are constructed; their particular relations, order, function. By identifying cones, spheres, etc., as the basic structure of past arts and so by implication the structure of nature, we are prevented from realizing that when an artist *actually makes* such forms, he is producing relations of cones, spheres, etc., which are the *result* of employing the Process Structure of reality. Such art-results are peculiar to man, and cannot be found in unaided nature. The prevalent tendency of insisting that *any* relations of spheres, squares, etc., can be valid structural depictions only of apples and houses or whatnot, simply confines the abstracting process to some kind of a depiction of nature forms, and results in a failure to realize the potentialities of form relations peculiar to spheres and squares when employed creatively.

In other words, one *can* consider geometric *relations* of forms as merely a structural exemplification of nature forms, i.e., apples are spheres, pears are cones, etc.; this produces a Cézanne type of art. But this view is only a step in the evolution of art and is a limited view of present problems. Today the artist *can* deal with geometric *relations* of forms as structural potentialities for the creation of form relations not to be found in unaided nature, i.e., a man-invented relation of art forms. Therefore, from Cézanne to Mondrian and Pevsner we are dealing with a process of ever higher orders of abstraction from the reality of nature. It is necessary to realize that whatever the forms and relations of forms we find in art, we are always dealing with *different* levels of abstracting which result in different *relations* of forms. The difference arises from whether the artist is abstracting his form relations from nature's macroscopic level, or from the Process Structure of nature. The genuine Constructionist artist has finally reached the place where he can directly exploit (rather than partially, as did Monet, Cézanne and the Cubists) the potentialities of nature's building method.

Therefore, we are *not* dealing with a question of whether we are to be satisfied merely with depicting the "basic elements," or whether we will "add" the forms of nature. No one can paint or construct the "skeletal" or "basic elements" or what have you, which supposedly exist in past art or in nature, *without producing some kind of a nature recording*. There is simply no such thing as structure or "basic elements" or "composition" alone; there is only structure in a CONTEXT, the structure OF *something* in relation to something, of one part of something to another part of something, in one KIND of ORDER or another. There are only similarities and dissimilarities between man's art structures or form-results and unaided nature structures or form-results. All we can produce in our art are particular kinds of structural results, the kind being determined by the kind of abstracting from nature that is involved.

We can further clarify the differences between the old and new abstracting by analogy. A chemist, C. M. A. Stine, writes as follows: "The awakening of the chemical industry was the birth of a new viewpoint and of a new idea of responsibility infinitely more daring than men had yet conceived. On the one hand it recognized the imperfections in our progress, while on the other it challenged the complacency which held imperfection to be an inevitable characteristic of human effort, about which little or nothing could be done. Under the old viewpoint we believed man could not possibly improve on Nature's materials and deemed successful imitation of them the height of human achievement. Under the new viewpoint we threw attempted imitation to the winds and set out boldly to become creators in our own right of wholly new materials that Nature had failed to supply.

"Do not misunderstand me. Nature is still omnipotent in her own vast sphere. The chemist is seeking neither to paint the lily nor to perfume the rose. However, he is seeking, and finding, colors, perfumes and drugs that are far more satisfactory for man's purposes than any Nature has provided in

180. Piet Mondrian, Composition with Blue and Yellow, 1932. Courtesy of the Philadelphia Museum of Art, Gallatin Collection.

181. Théo van Doesburg. Simultaneous Composition, 1929. Courtesy of Mme. Théo van Doesburg.

flowers and plants." [3] This is precisely the attitude in the new viewpoint of art as seen in Constructions.

In the development of the airplane we can also find a good analogy of this difference between the past and present way of art. Man's efforts to fly passed through animistic and anthropomorphic stages, as can be seen in the following excerpts from *The Story of Flying*, by A. Black: "Not only the ancients but also the peoples of the Middle Ages attributed magic properties to feathers and almost every legend of early flight refers to the use of feathered wings. As late as the seventeenth century, one experimenter with this type of wing was fortunate enough to land uninjured after his first jump from a roof. Explaining the abrupt end of his experiment, he ruefully insisted that he would have been successful had he used the feathers of an eagle instead of those plucked from an earthbound barnyard hen!" [4] Further on Black continues: "Flapping-wing devices, incidentally, came into popularity among the aeronautically inclined inventors as soon as bird feathers were divested of their magic properties.

"But here again mankind was to find itself following a false trail. Several centuries more had to pass before it was realized that birds fly by flapping their wings only at the expense of relatively great muscular effort—effort that, in proportion to the weight lifted, is far beyond the strongest man's capability. Giovanni Borelli, an Italian who died in 1679, concluded from his study of the muscles of birds that man's were greatly inferior. Again, in 1655, this conclusion was propounded by Robert Hooke, an Englishman, who announced that man's muscles were incapable of exerting sufficient energy to enable him to fly like a bird. About two and a half centuries later, Octave Chanute estimated that a pigeon the size of a man would exert nearly 3 horsepower. This is something like twenty or thirty times the sustained muscular ability of an average man!" [5] The history of man's effort to fly is but another instance of his beginning with the most naive abstracting from the macro-level, then penetrating further and further until he reached beyond the macro-level to the very Process Structure of nature which was involved in problems of objects in flight.

The problem of inventing the airplane involved these factors: first, man cannot make a bird, that is, he cannot produce the materials of a bird. But even if he could, a bird would fail to meet the particular needs of man for a flying object. Therefore it is necessary to abstract in a different manner in order to obtain a different objective. The inventor studied the structure of nature by which an object can be propelled through the air under its own power, not in order to copy the RESULTS of that structure, but to utilize the structural knowledge thus derived for purposes of converting man's materials into a flying object. He then adapted man-made materials to the requirements of that reality structure and only then did he achieve an object that would fly and at the same time meet the flying needs of man. No doubt when designers of flying Machines get even further away from the imitation of nature—we still talk about "wings" and "tails"—they will be able to achieve a far more efficient Machine, safer and more desirable in visual appearance. The airplane will then look as little like a bird as trains or automobiles look like camels, donkeys, or horses (we still speak of horse-power) from which these Machines were abstracted by gradual stages.

We repeat, the invention of the airplane was not realized by simply copying a bird, but by utilizing the structural knowledge derived from birds, etc., and the structural medium in which they operated, and then transposing this knowledge to *man-made materials and needs*. But when men made their first attempts to invent the flying Machine, they did so with a methodology characteristic of the times—they tried to copy nature. And they failed because they were attempting to make man into a bird by giving him wings attached to his muscles. They were trying to make man into a bird, *just as for the last 2000 years the "Idealists" in particular have been trying to make nature's art into man's art*. The artist's problem today is similar to that of the modern inventor of the airplane, of the modern chemist, etc. He also cannot make the objects of nature, as he does not have the materials with which to make them. But even if he could, such objects would not serve his purpose, which is to invent his own art.

3. C. M. A. Stine: "Chemistry—and You," An Address, February 19, 1937, at the University of Cincinnati, before the Business and Professional Men's Group of the College of Engineering and Commerce. Permission of E. I. du Pont de Nemours and Co., Inc.

4. Archibald Black: *The Story of Flying,* p. 5, Whittlesey House, McGraw-Hill Book Co., Inc., New York, 1940.

5. Ibid., pp. 6–7.

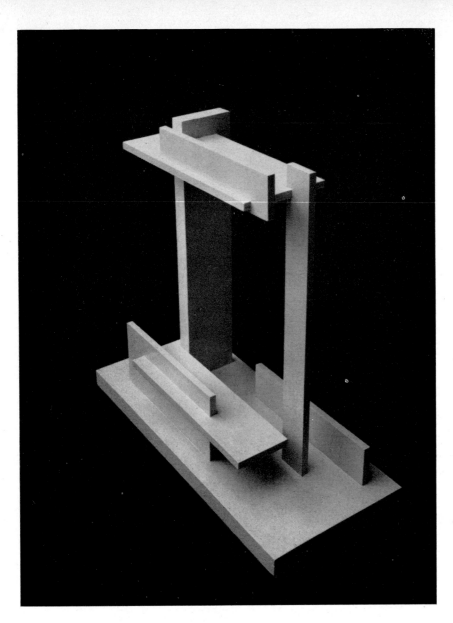

182. Jean Gorin, Architectural Plastic in Space, 1928.

Therefore, the artist investigates the structure of nature which supplies him with the *building method* and conditions for making objects of art. He then adapts man-made materials to his knowledge of that structure and only then is he able to invent through the methods of nature.

It was not until man had evolved from the copying stage, as Stine pointed out above, that it became possible to invent new materials and objects which unaided nature did not produce in that particular form. It is precisely in this manner that the advanced artist of our time proposes to abstract from nature in order to invent his own art rather than use the art-results of nature as a *substitute*. Thus the less man copies nature's appearances and the more he is able to translate knowledge of the Process Structure and function of nature into his inherent creative potentialities, the more successful he becomes in his efforts to progress.

To copy nature, for making an airplane or art, is no longer useful, except in the case of Photography.[6] The new attitude today is that whether the nature objects pertain to art or to flying, these

6. Of course the genuine Photographer is not concerned with *creating* art but rather with perfecting the creation of his Machine in its structure and function so that he can make the most accurate recordings possible of the art of nature. It is necessary

183. Charles Biederman, Construction, 12/38 (14). Clear and colored plastic sheets and painted wood. 29⅞″x21⅟₁₆″x3¾″. Photo, Bernard Dordick.

objects as particular forms belong in the context of *un*aided nature and are not to be confused with the forms required for inventing and developing a man-art or an airplane. These latter are directed towards far different purposes than the art or flying objects found in nature. Obviously, all objects of unaided nature possess certain visual characteristics which are part of the specific function and reality of those objects; just as obvious is the fact that these visual characteristics do not function as a created man-art, but as unaided nature-art. An art peculiar to man is not something that we can find ready-made in nature; man has to invent it just as he had to invent his boats (fish, etc.), automobiles (horses, etc.), airplanes (birds), and his culture in general. It is this method of art which already has had a tremendous influence upon other kinds of man-made products, such as Architecture and Industrial objects.

Nature teaches us the methods and structural conditions by which to solve problems; but to copy the *results* of those methods is futile, unless the objective is to make a record. Today, therefore, the artist either uses a Camera, if he wishes to record nature's art, or else invents his art contents if he wishes

to keep in mind the fact that the Camera artist seeks to *record;* he does not copy as do the non-Camera artists, past or present, who depict nature's appearances.

to create. He cannot abstract from nature's art and presume that he is "creating" a man-art. Nature's art, however, has been the means by which man has arrived at the notion of man-art, just as the bird suggested the airplane. And as with the airplane, man must invent his own art by studying the Structural Process of nature and not by copying its results. By abstracting from the structural level of reality, man opens up for himself all the possibilities of that level as evidenced in the phenomena of nature all about us. Nature is no longer to be regarded as something to compete with, but as something which can be *extended according to natural laws in directions useful to man's evolving needs*. Without man's great capacity to invent, human culture would be utterly impossible. The legitimate artists and scientists of today are simply continuing, i.e., extending, this process, a process of human evolution, the evolution of nature.

So far we have discussed the potentialities of the new and the old art from the standpoint of contents—unaided nature-art and man-art contents. Let us now look at these problems from the standpoint of the mediums employed in the old and in the new. We have seen that the non-Camera artist's fundamental source of abstracting from nature must now be not from the macroscopic, but from the Structural Process level, and this involves the problem of mediums employed.

Artists have given almost undivided attention to the change in art contents and exceedingly little to the medium in which these changes were after all taking place. Consequently they inadvertently made the canvas surface the criterion of reality in more ways than one, as we have explained. This went to such a point that in the direction taken by the Two-Dimensionalists the artists lost everything but the bare empty canvas. But the connecting link between man-art and nature is one of similarity in structure. This necessitates a change to a three-dimensional medium.

The new kind of non-Camera art contents makes the linear (painting, etc.) mediums not only unnecessary but frustrating. Since the new artist seeks to invent his art contents, he automatically removes the very factor which originally brought about the need for the old primitive linear medium; in fact, it hinders the realization of the new objective.

But it is as difficult to give up the old medium and learn to use the new one as it is to give up the old contents and create the new one. In short, there is compromise all down the line between the old and the new. At no time in the history of art has there been so much writing and talk about "form and space" and yet so little art which possesses actual forms in actual space! It makes little difference if the art is called "significant form," "plastic form," "expressionist form," or what not, *form is still lacking if the art is produced on a flat surface*. Many strive in the correct direction but they do not realize that actual three-dimensional forms are required for its adequate realization.

As we have already suggested, the situation in our times affords a striking parallel with that of the Italian Renaissance. Events of a similar kind occur in both periods; both are periods of medium transition. In this parallel we have an excellent illustration of the phenomenon of *similarities* in two cultures, between which, on a closer scrutiny, there will be found the even more striking and illuminating *differences* which form the apparent similarities. Such contrasts make more clear each of the cultures under consideration as well as the historical process in general.

We have already seen how the sculpture medium was the major vehicle of art up to the Renaissance, at which time it had reached the end of its usefulness as far as further progress in recording nature was concerned. With the linear medium the painter was able to enlarge the scope of the objects and phenomena in nature which could be recorded, as well as to develop further the recording of those objects which the sculptor had been able to depict. Above all the artist was now able to depict the objects of nature in their environment, e.g., figures with landscape. The artists of this period became principally concerned with transferring a world of three dimensions upon a two-dimensional surface—the canvas. This was necessary and served a useful purpose. It was the best way for man to continue developing his ability to record nature more accurately than before.

558

In other words, this change enabled artists to go beyond the recording limits of sculpture, and so continue the evolution of recording art; hence it became the major vehicle of art. However, the loss of the actual third dimension created a serious problem once art had evolved to the conditions of recent times.

After almost 500 years—from Masaccio to Mondrian—the *useful* dominance of the linear medium has come to an end in this century. Masaccio was the beginning of the last major epoch of painting art; Mondrian the end. Today, as in the Renaissance, a major medium has come to the end of its potentialities for further developments; in each period the art medium had to be changed in order that the evolution of art might continue. In the Renaissance it was sculpture which reached the end of its potentialities and an illusionistic or linear art medium had to be developed. In our times, the painting medium has come to the end of its potentialities for non-Camera art, and the three-dimensional Constructionist solution must now be employed. Thus in our generation the medium transition is the reverse of that in the Renaissance, although the transition in each case is made for quite "similar" reasons, to secure more reality (though of a different kind) for the art contents involved. The Renaissance artist was forced to switch from a three-dimensional medium to a two-dimensional one, in order to continue the progress of recording nature's appearances. Today artists are again switching mediums, but this time from two-dimensional to modern three-dimensional mediums in order to secure adequate reality for an invented contents of art.

Because art is in the process of transition back to the third dimension, the so-called "Modern" sculptor mistakenly interprets this as a new renaissance for the sculpture medium. But as we explained in a previous chapter, sculpture is an *antiquated mechanical method* for meeting the new problems facing artists today. For sculptors are tied to the old primitive methods, materials and content, just as are the painters. This is borne out by the fact that these artists increasingly return to the old content. A number of these "Modern sculptors"—Hans Arp, Henri Laurens, Jacques Lipchitz, Constantin Brancusi, Julio Gonzales—at one time in their careers could have been considered as frustrated Constructionists. They are men who thought a three-dimensional medium was more suitable for solving contemporary problems, but failed to comprehend this adequately enough. They failed to profit from Cubism.

The best that so-called Modern sculptors can accomplish is a compromise between the old and the new, just as they have compromised Cubism. Lipchitz, for example, sees Cubism merely as "a new way to represent nature"; what he actually means is a new way to depict nature's appearances, a new way to manipulate, to distort. But our historical analysis has borne out the truth of Doesburg's warning that "cubism has never been a recipe for making descriptive pictures or a mechanical method for multiplying picture motifs." Thus we find that the "Modern" sculptor's attempts to grasp the new fail in varying degrees, depending upon the individual artist's particular type of oscillation between the old and the new.

In any case, they serve as good examples of the futility of trying to invent forms under the canalizations of the old medium of sculpture with its primitive methods. Observe, for example, in the sculpture of both Arp and Brancusi, how they restrict their forms to the more or less blocked out anthropomorphic character of the old sculptural art-results—results which are derived from the old attempt to record nature objects. The forms they build are still the forms of nature-appearances; they simply manipulate the old contents to a greater degree than do most other Modernists.

The case is a little different in the work of Gonzales, who does not retain the old block effect of past sculpture. But on the other hand he uses the old romantic technique in fabricating his work. That is, he treats his surfaces and joins one piece to another in a rough, free manner, employing rusted and crudely cut pieces of metal. Where Arp and Brancusi give a perfect mechanical finish to their works, Gonzales gives his a crude handicraft finish. He uses a welding Machine as though it were a paint brush, and so superimposes the old technique upon his attempts at invented forms; the former artists obtain a Machine finish for forms which resemble far more than those of Gonzales the old macro-reality type of art. Here is another kind of confusion between the old and the new. Some artists use mechanical tools as they should be used, but retain the old sculptural materials, and the result is confined, in one degree or another, to the old content. Others who attempt to be more Inventive in the contents, use their Machines

184. Joan Barnes, Construction No. 6, January, 1947. Painted plexiglas, wood and metal rods, 20¾″x16¾″x3″. Photo, Scott Tyler.

to achieve a technique similar to that of the old arts of paint or sculpture. But the Machine was never intended to copy the technique of the old primitive art tools.

These are the kinds of maladjusted results found in "Modern" sculpture. With such a medium the artist cannot meet the demands of new conditions. And the best defense that a "Modernist" sculptor can give of his work is this by Lipchitz: "direct cutting has been frequently suggested as a remedy for the supposed ills of sculpture. But sculpture is not ill—it was never healthier. Sculpture today, following Rodin's indications, should be at its highest point. Sculptors in general have not yet understood Rodin. When they do they will once more join the Great Stream in its forward, ever-widening movement. Art cannot go back. The Royal Road leads only forward."[7] By simply denying the illness of sculpture, Lipchitz thinks to prove that it is healthy. The best he can offer is to oppose direct cutting and make obscure illusions to Rodin, a frustrated sculptor and/or painter, who tried vainly to paint with clay. Rodin, like

7. J. J. Sweeney: "An Interview with Jacques Lipchitz," Art Chronicle, *Partisan Review*, XII:89, Winter, 1945.

185. Joan Barnes, Construction No. 3, July, 1946. Painted wood and metal rods, 12″x9¾″x2¼″. Photo, Scott Tyler.

Michelangelo, made a desperate attempt to revive sculpture, but never really knew what was the matter.[8] The "Modern" sculptor, like both Michelangelo and Rodin, is living in times when another medium is more appropriate for solving the extant problems of art. He does not see that his medium, and the content that inevitably dominates it, must be radically transformed. It is the lack of this consciousness which explains why sculptors like Lipchitz have tried to leave the old content in their youth, but have held on to the old medium of that content. Under these conditions they were eventually compelled to consider the elimination of the old content as their great error, rather than their insistence upon retaining the old medium. Eventually, then, they too, like the painters, have returned to the old content that belongs to their old medium, so that in sculpture we find the various levels of abstracting that we have noted in painting, all the way from literal and Classical realism to Post-Impressionism and various disguised uses of Cubism as a recipe for distorting nature.

8. Rodin's "greatness" as an artist was not in comparison to the great artists of Impressionism and Post-Impressionism, but in comparison to the general low level of the field of sculpture. Compared to the above painters Rodin as sculptor was quite unnecessary.

Thus artists today who have insisted on continuing with the sculptural medium are just as regressive as the artists who continue with the illusionary medium. Since the Renaissance, as Spengler so well put it, sculpture has been merely "indulgence in reminiscences," a tragic affair of the sculptor's trying to recover a past that can never be recovered.[9]

As we have pointed out before, the problem facing artists today is very similar to that which confronted the artists of the Renaissance; the problem of securing a greater correspondence to that particular aspect of reality from which the artist is abstracting. The old problem, however, was to record ever more accurately the results of nature's structure; the new problem is to invent with the building methods observed in nature. And in order to gain the latter objective, three-dimensional materials, but not just any kind, are crucially necessary.

In our own times of transition, just as during the Renaissance, there is an overlapping of two- and three-dimensional mediums in the change from the old to the new. The mixtures are much more complex than in the Renaissance, when, as we have seen, sculptors tried to employ perspective in stone and other sculptural mediums, and painters tried to depict the sculptured human form with the linear paint method. By using very low reliefs the Renaissance sculptor unconsciously tried to compete with the painter's medium; instead, however, he inadvertently helped in the solution of problems that belonged to the totally flat or painting medium. In short, there were painters who sculpted and sculptors who painted. Today there are artists trying to invent their own contents, but continuing to employ the old linear medium, the very medium that came into use so that artists could better record the appearances of nature. Thus painters work with three-dimensional illusions of invented forms, unconscious that they are being stimulated by problems which require the Constructionist method for their satisfactory realization. There are some who combine the flat with the round in a single work of art, either in one medium or the other or in combinations of mediums; and there are some who are strictly painters or sculptors in each individual work of art; i.e., they waver from one medium to the other with each new work. Others have tried to eliminate the problem of three dimensions and have been caught within the dead-end limitations of the canvas surface. Still others not only paint but try to make sculpture and occasionally attempt something in the Constructionist direction. Then there are would-be Constructionists who also do a lot of painting and make trick "abstract" pictures with the Camera or the materials and methods of Photography.[10]

The current confusion over the problem of mediums, as we have emphasized again and again, has resulted from the lack of an adequate "consciousness of abstracting." Consequently artists and critics fail to realize that the painting and sculpture methods demand different kinds of abstracting from nature and that the kind of abstracting varies, depending upon the historical context involved. Although they are

9. However, according to Spengler this "indulgence in reminiscences" begins after Michelangelo; we maintain that it begins after Donatello.

10. Thus, while some artists insist on using the old, primitive mediums to record reality appearances, others use the most developed recording method, Photography, to achieve an invented content. These they call rayographs, photograms, etc.; no matter what the label, the results are primarily sought by accidental means. In doing so they reduce modern Photography to its most primitive beginnings, i.e., they simply place objects between the source of light and the recording surface. Thus merely the interception of light is recorded, rather than the appearance of light. This pseudo-method of invention, this per-version of the Camera, is comparable to Arp's method of dumping pieces of paper and pasting them down wherever they fall on drawing paper. That so many rely on such accidental methods with Photography and with the old primitive mediums is due to the lack of a genuine incentive to invent the content of art. Such artists can secure no satisfaction from the consistent, disciplined act of invention. They prefer the quick results of accidents. That is, the result happens all of a sudden with this accidental method and so a temporary satisfaction is obtained, largely dependent on the fact that the artist is invariably sur-prised by unexpected effects. This satisfaction is momentary because it was produced in this detached manner. The lack of genuine rapport between the artist and the art he does or is trying to do is further seen in the hazy character of the work, i.e., it lacks a completion and gives the effect of a fragment or fragments.

What makes the rayograms, etc., particularly attractive is the fact that the Photograph-like character of the result gives it the reality-feeling of a Photograph. Thus unconsciously the artist strives to solve the present problem of art reality in a super-ficial, back-handed manner. Instead of creating objects in actual reality dimensions, he prefers to give the *effect* of a Photo-graph of actual, real, invented objects.

unaware of these factors, artists are nevertheless living in a milieu of such a character that they are compelled to react at least unconsciously to the problem of mediums, etc. All this has inevitably led to an extremely confused art world, in which, as we have just noted, some artists are trying to be both painters and sculptors, i.e., trying to do both two- and three-dimensional work and still others are trying to combine both mediums in a single work of art.

However, it must be pointed out that in certain cases at least these overlappings of the one medium into the other have not had entirely negative results. Just as the Renaissance sculptors contributed something useful to the painters' problems, so painters, particularly the De Stijl and Suprematist schools, have contributed much that is of major value to the Constructionist solution. The Renaissance sculptors worked on the problem of perspective, worthless for their medium, yet the crux of the linear artist's problem. The Two-Dimensionalists of the present have achieved discoveries which have found a more useful and a fuller outlet in Constructionist art. These painters have done much to clarify the distinction between the old and new content. They clearly stated the initial steps to be taken, both in color-form and its organization, by those who would realize the more adequate three-dimensional resolution of the new art. Read Mondrian's writings, and observe his paintings. His works needed to be three-dimensional, and, as explained elsewhere, Mondrian employed actual three-dimensional effects, but was frustrated by the painting medium.[11] Such painters also brought into art the highly mechanical technique so essential to the new art. They used compasses and rulers—tantamount to sacrilege and regarded by others as a very low order of behavior. In short, the Two-Dimensionalists tried to show, more than all other contemporary *painters*, the necessity for securing an invented contents for man's art, independent of the appearances of nature's macro-level of reality.

We have made it very clear that so long as artists insist on making paintings of their invented forms, they will be forced eventually to insert parts of the old macro-reality into their art contents in order to give these forms some semblance of adequate "reality." We have demonstrated that the majority of those who depict three-dimensional illusions, either unconsciously abstract from nature objects, or else they return deliberately to the old content after a period of trying the new one with the old medium. The result in any case is eventually a fantasy of the macro-reality; then the artist is on his way to Surrealism. This can only be avoided by abstracting directly from the Structural Process level of nature, which, in turn, necessitates that the old mediums of both painting and sculpture be replaced by Machine mediums.

But the thought of giving up their venerated mediums is too much for the painters and sculptors. Here again we find that many artists maintain that the three-dimensional mediums of the Constructionist are very limited, that in the words of Sweeney, "The 'machine age' emphasis in the constructivists' materials was a limitation."[12] Implicitly or explicitly it is contended that the painter has more freedom with his medium and so a larger scope of possibilities. But the pertinent question is, what *kind* of "freedom" the painter has more of than the Constructionist.

While it is perfectly correct to argue that the painting medium allows far more freedom to produce form and color effects impossible to secure with three-dimensional mediums, nevertheless in so arguing, the artist inadvertently and automatically rules out the "reality" of his painting results. Since he does things that cannot be done in actual reality, with actual real forms, is it any wonder that his art lacks "reality" and that he is forced to retreat in some degree to the old art contents to secure at least a

11. As we have pointed out, Mondrian does use various high and low levels of raised paint surfaces in some of his work, suggesting the unconscious need for the third dimension; this is most obviously seen in the frames of his paintings which are comprised of a series of steps, as though pushing the painting contents out.

12. J. J. Sweeney: *Alexander Calder*, pp. 8–9, The Museum of Modern Art, New York, 1943.

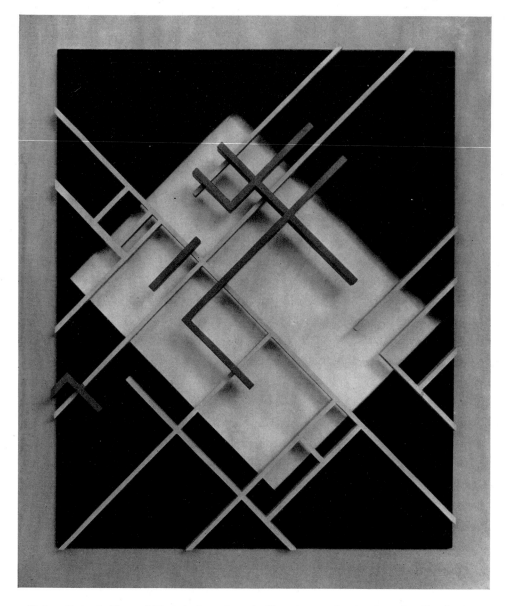

186. Jean Goria, Architectural Plastic in Space, for a dwelling place, 1946. Painted wood, 39″x30″. Photo, Yves Hervochon, Paris.

semblance of adequate reality? Even in those cases where the painter has not yet begun to retreat and insists on invented forms, the element of fantasy is present. It is true that painted illusions of non-representational invented forms are no less real than illusions of nature objects. We are dealing with *paintings* of "real" objects as much in the one case as in the other. The objects in the one are simply imitations of Inventive forms and in the other imitations of nature forms. Non-representational painting, when it is a genuine effort in that direction, is false not in the content objective, but in the medium that is employed for its *proper* realization; false because it inevitably leads to ever more fantasy of reality. In such cases the painter is inevitably attracted to the possibilities of doing things with invented forms which it is impossible to do with actual three-dimensional invented forms. The situation becomes similar to the attraction of van Gogh's sunflowers, as that was explained in an earlier chapter. The painted

564

sunflowers attract us because they are *unlike* any sunflowers that do occur in actual reality. The same principle holds true with painted invented forms. In the one case the painter makes a fantasy of nature forms and in the other a fantasy of man-invented forms. Both are appeals to fantasy of reality.

Fantasy in art serves principally as an escape not only from actual reality but from the problems of art responsibilities which face us today. In a world of confusion and great change, there are always many seeking a refuge by attempting through fantasy to make a world of their own, to make a "reality" of their own. Art, under these circumstances, becomes a substitute for actual reality.

So we see that the kind of "freedom" the painter claims for his medium as distinguished from that of the Constructionist's medium is principally the "freedom" to produce fantasies of reality, be they the forms of nature or those peculiar to man. The Inventive painter seeks a false, impossible freedom; that is, in typical laissez-faire fashion he wants to be free to do anything he wishes in the invention or creation of form; he refuses to be limited to the reality restrictions of working in *actual* form. He is like the "Realist" who refuses to use the Camera medium. He has not yet learned that absolute freedom is a myth, that the greatest degree of freedom always implies certain limitations.

Hence, it is true the painter has more "freedom" than the Constructionist, but only more freedom of irresponsibility; the Constructionist has a more desirable, i.e., *useful* kind of freedom, the freedom to adjust himself to the emerging evolutionary potentialities of the present stage of art history. So, as in other problems, the matter of "freedom" turns out to be a problem of kind and consequences, not absolutes.

In speaking about the problem of freedom, John Dewey once wrote: "All sorts of solutions have been propounded, from denial of the reality of freedom to the postulation of a realm above nature by entrance into which man's moral freedom is secured. Attention to the practical scene of contemporary human activity would have given an entirely different turn to the discussion. For every phase of techno-logical civilization shows that an advance in knowledge of natural uniformities and necessary conditions increases man's working freedom, namely, control of nature, enabling him to harness natural energies to his own purposes."[13] And Bronislaw Malinowski has written: "Those who attempt any definition of freedom in terms of negative categories and in terms of an absolute and unlimited absence of trammels, must be chasing an intellectual will-o'-the-wisp. Real freedom is neither absolute nor omnipresent and it certainly is not negative. It is always an increase in control, in efficiency, and in the power to dominate one's own organism and the environment, as well as artifacts and the supply of natural resources. Hence freedom as a quality of human action, freedom as increase of efficiency and control, means the breaking down of certain obstacles and a compensation for certain deficiencies; it also implies the acceptance of rules of nature, that is, scientific laws of knowledge, and of those norms and laws of human behavior which are indispensable to efficient co-operation."[14]

In art as in other kinds of human activity there is not unrestricted freedom to make this content or that, or use this medium or that. Every medium and every content carries with it particular kinds of either beneficial or harmful historical implications.

Men once thought that ghosts and spirits inhabited animate and inanimate objects alike. Such beliefs determined the kind of interpretations men made of reality. For the greater part of man's existence his major concern has been with the macroscopic level of reality, just as the artist's major concern has been to record and abstract from that level of reality. Today, however, we live in a world of science, not magic or religion or philosophy, and men have found that hidden beneath the macroscopics of nature are not ghosts, and the like, but different levels of reality, the micro- and submicroscopic levels. Today artists and scientists alike are striving to penetrate the macroscopic level of nature towards a more adequate com-prehension and exploitation of the world reality process in which we live. We know that the macro-level is only one aspect or level of reality. Our problems today deal with *various levels of reality*. As man evolves so does his comprehension of the world in which he lives. It is our responsibility to recognize this, to recognize the particular stage of that development in our own times and to proceed accordingly.

13. John Dewey: "Philosophy," *Whither Mankind*, p. 321, edited by Charles A. Beard, Longmans, Green and Co., New York, 1928.

14. Bronislaw Malinowski: *Freedom and Civilization*, pp. 59–60, Roy Publishers, New York, 1944.

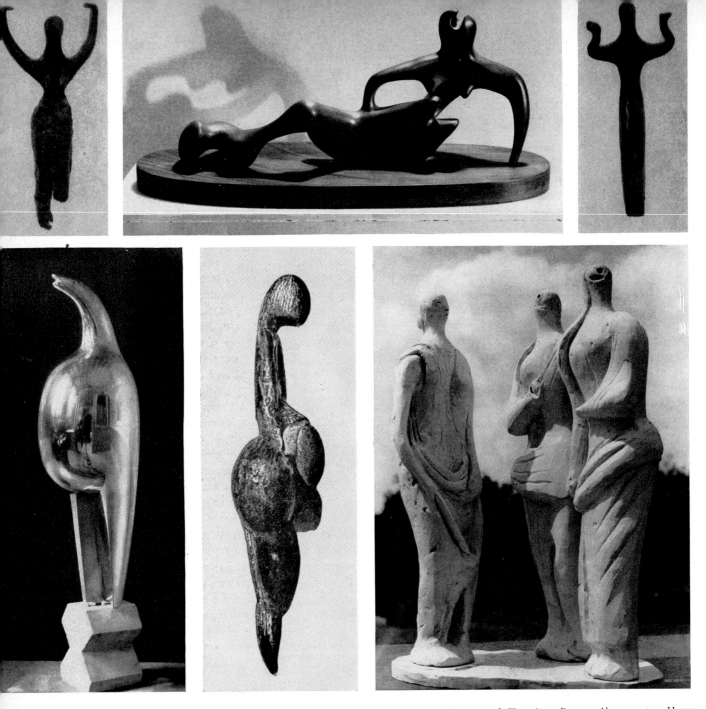

187. Above left and right, Egyptian predynastic figurines. Courtesy, Museum of Fine Arts, Boston. Above center, Henry Moore, Reclining Figure, 1938. Collection The Museum of Modern Art, New York. Below left, Brancusi, Maiastra, Courtesy, Art of This Century. Below center, Venus of Lespugue, Paleolithic. After Schmidt, after Saint-Pèrier (see biblio. No. 312). Below right, Henry Moore, Three Draped Standing Figures, 1945 (Clay model).

Yet many of us still live on a cultural level comparable to that of the men who warned Columbus that he would drop over the edge of the world if he ventured too far out to sea or of those men who thought the whole universe revolved around the earth. Such men became hysterical, then violent when a few scientifically minded individuals discovered their error, just as their counterparts do today when advanced scientists and artists state the goals towards which they are directing their researches. It is just as absurd to allocate the problems of "art" and "reality" in a past context today as it is to expect the past to have faced the problems peculiar to the present. In short, we must historically allocate the problems of art. Then we shall find interests and opportunities unheard of in the past which today await the more adventuresome.

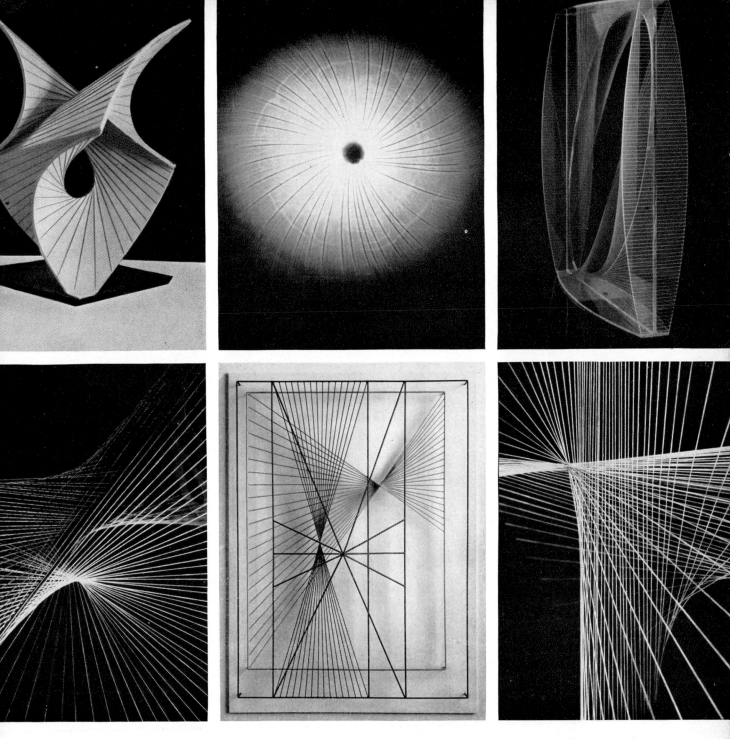

188. Above left, Pevsner, see figure 210. Above center, electrical spark pattern, see figure 225. Above right, Gabo, see figure 198. Below left and right, mathematical string model. Below center, Biederman, see figure 192.

Art history is a growing organism which today is at a particular level of development; it is from that point that we must step forward if we are not to step backward. Constructionist art is in the forward direction; IT IS THE FIRST REALISTIC ART OF MAN in the sense that *it is not an illusion of something else (nature objects) or an illusion of itself (paintings of invented art) but possesses a legitimate reality content peculiar to man's art.*

567

Hence we see how false are the accusations of Academicians and "Modernists" alike that the Constructionists have turned their backs on nature; actually they and the Photographers are the only artists of our times who have succeeded in a proper orientation to the reality of nature. They are doing as all great advanced schools of past art have done, i.e., striving for an increasingly realistic orientation to the problem of "reality" and "art." We need only remind the reader of what was made clear in chapter 16: namely, all artists of whatever kind abstract from some level of nature, as it is impossible to do otherwise. This is just as true for those artists who do not depict nature's appearances as for those who do: if artists did not abstract from reality, their resultant art would have to exclude all characteristics which could be found in nature.

Nature has always been not only the source but also the fundamental criterion of reality for all art, past or present. The artist, *any kind,* is compelled to draw upon nature as the source and the criterion of reality for whatever his art-results happen to be. True, he can manipulate these factors in various ways and degrees contrary to the laws of nature, but the operation of natural laws pursues him as much as in the case of a man who refuses to use a bridge to cross a river and yet insists on walking across anyway. Thus Mondrian was mistaken when he asserted that "art is not bound by material or physical conditions." [15] For example, everything any artist does is affected by the law of gravity. This is true even for the painter—since the linear organization of his work is determined by the influence of gravity. It cannot be eliminated.[16] The main problem, then, is not whether this kind of art or that does or does not deny nature; this is a foolish question. The problem is rather in what way is this or that art related to nature, i.e., how is the art abstracted from the reality?

Today there are two legitimate kinds of arts: (1) Recordings of nature's art with the Camera; here the artist seeks results ever more similar to the *result level* of nature's Process Structure. By such means we are able to collect and preserve visual records of nature-art. (2) Constructionist art; here the artist seeks results ever more similar in structure to the *Structural Process level* of nature. By this method man creates his own "realistic" art.

15. Piet Mondrian: "Liberation from Oppression in Art and Life," *Plastic Art and Pure Plastic Art,* p. 38.

16. If this were not true—that gravity affects the realization of a painting—it would not matter whether we hung it upside down or any other way upon the wall; in fact, it would not matter if we put the painting on the ceiling, wall or floor.

Physics, biology, psychology have each in turn passed over from superstition to science, and have each in turn demanded sacrifices dear to our human conceit. 29

Bertrand Russell

In place of the dream, the future will put art on a scientific and technical basis. 371

Theo van Doesburg

Now men are reluctant to give up such fine names as Soul. Over the centuries they have grown so accustomed to this ethereal raiment that they feel naked without it—even though rude thinkers have told them all the while that they had nothing on. 238

Herbert Muller

This assertion [that the scientific method can never ascertain a solution of the riddle of development] affords but one among very many contemporary instances of waning faith in the power of intellect; a reaction, perhaps against its overwhelming successes, which nevertheless continue without ceasing, and augment. But how curious is this confidence in intellectual bankruptcy! For the period during which the collective intellect of mankind has been consciously applied to the task of unravelling the complexities of our environment, is but a day in the epoch of humanity. Purposeful intellectual endeavor, which is science, is, as a geologist has recently told us: "but the last chapter in the last volume of a series which would fill a library." So little effort, and we are now exhausted! So brief a period, and we abandon the conflict! We declare ourselves impotent, because in a day we have not comprehended the ultimate significance of life! 297
                    T. Brailsford Robertson

However, science is curious, and this curiosity is responsible for much of the progress of mankind. It is hoped that the artist will welcome such investigations because knowledge will do no harm. 203
                    Matthew Luckiesh

But science is becoming increasingly a manner of life, a way of behaving, and is developing a philosophy which substitutes for the old conception of knowledge the new conception of successful behavior. The more scepticism seems to result from a purely theoretic attitude, the more the practical pragmatic attitude triumphs. 29   Bertrand Russell

The structure of the world is, in principle, unknown; and the only aim of knowledge and science is to discover this structure. The structure of languages is potentially known, if we pay attention to it. Our only possible procedure in advancing our knowledge is to match our verbal structures, often called theories, with empirical structures, and see if our verbal predictions are fulfilled empirically or not, thus indicating that the two structures are either similar or dissimilar. 179   Alfred Korzybski

Today "art" and "science," as far as their fundamental contributions to contemporary culture are concerned, are unintelligible or ignored by the vast majority. Many capable scientists have succeeded in producing clear explanations of the higher, more subtle achievements of their field, but few care to make the effort to grasp them. In the field of art, however, it seems (as Picasso complains) that everyone wants to understand it, yet very little that is written about it is comprehensible, even, we suspect, to those who write the "explanations." Our purpose in this chapter will be to investigate in what way the scientist's attitude is responsible for this difference, and to show that such an attitude can be adopted by the artist with equal benefits.

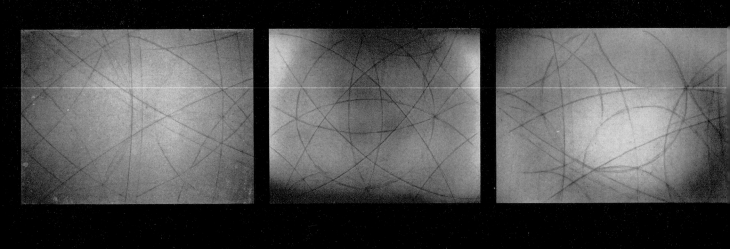

189. Kathleen Lonsdale, Divergent beam X-ray diffraction patterns from single crystals of diamond. (Reproduced from the Philosophical Transactions of the Royal Society of London, March, 1947, by permission of the Council of the Royal Society and of the author.)*

We have already noted on a number of occasions that there exists among most artists and critics today a preference for nebulous symbols, and an *opinion* that it is impossible to comprehend art with the scientific attitude. For, it is contended, art is the product not of the "intellect," as is science, but of infallible intuition.

We have seen in detail how the very nature of the Transitional-Period compelled artists to rely heavily upon the intuitive factor. It was a period of rapid developments which concluded in a tremendous revolution. Once genuine Cubism was concluded (1910), the necessity arose for discarding the now useless *over*-dependence upon intuition, and beginning the use of non-intuitive forms of evaluation in order to ascertain clearly the fundamental nature of the new period of art born in 1910. A few undertook to do this—the Two-Dimensionalists and Constructionists; the majority continued to insist upon the independent superiority of intuition. It was this insistence which led to the chaos of Modern art, the epitome of which is Surrealism. As we have stressed in a previous chapter, present day non-Camera art is headed in two general directions—the Constructionist and the Surrealist, regardless of whether artists like it or not. The Constructionist direction is characterized by increasingly non-intuitive behavior which exploits the possibilities of the scientific attitude and the Machine; the Surrealist direction is characterized by increasing dependence upon "intuition" and "subjectivism," and by blind opposition to science and the Machine.

This latter direction now appears to be in ascendance so that we are again at a point in the history of mankind when another Dark Ages threatens. In the midst of the chaos we find the soul-savers of all varieties—nazis and/or communists in politics, nationalists and various shades of Surrealists in art—who claim that their "absolute truths" are "universal and eternal." The scientists to whom we have allegedly abandoned everything are made out as "pagans" or worse. There is a general opinion that science deals only with the "externals" and not with the fundamentals of human consciousness. One "Modern"

*The arrangement of the scientific illustrations in this chapter is not intended to indicate the source of the art. In fact, the scientific illustrations were searched for and collected shortly before the book went to press. Certain schools of art like to make comparisons between their works and the art of children, primitives and the insane. Here the reader sees Constructionist art compared to quite different attitudes towards the objective world in which man lives (see also pp. 566-67).

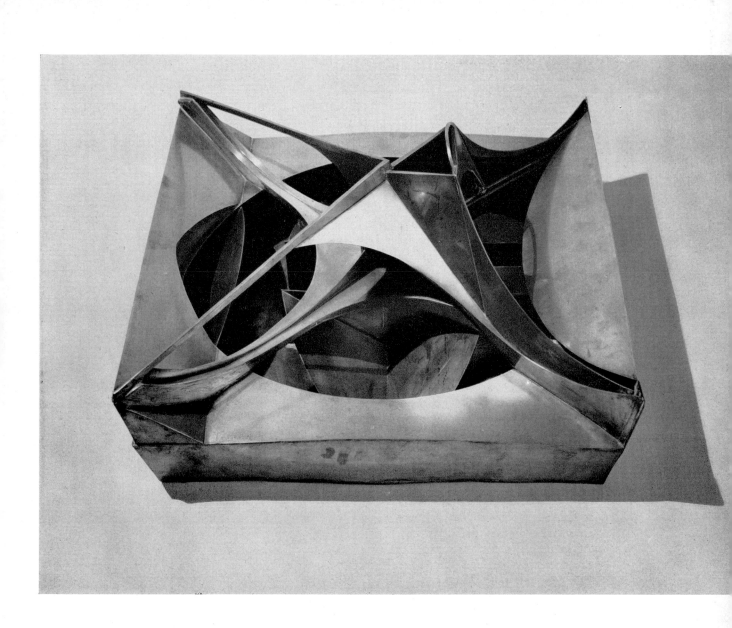

190. Antoine Pevsner, Construction in Brass, 1927. Washington University, St. Louis. Photo, Piaget.

art critic, for example, contends that science is merely the extension of the "monkey habit."[1] His reasons for this profound opinion are as follows: "curiosity" and "imitation" "are strongly marked in animals," and since he finds that these are characteristics of scientific forms of behavior, he concludes that science is the extension of animal behavior, whereas art, being concerned with the "creative" effort, is peculiar to human life, because "Creation is human."[2]

The verbalisms may differ, but in general "science," which is allegedly dominating and ruining our civilization, is regarded as dealing only with the "material" world, with Machines and inventions (notions which are survivals from 19th century popular views of science). Art, which has "defied time and space," which is "human" and concerned with "sensibilities," "the soul," etc., will save us in the end. The following, by the editor of a popular art magazine, is typical: "Truly we live in a machine age, and the wonders of science, coldly logical in its precise reasoning, are commonplace accessories in the most humble of lives. So magnificent have been the triumphs of the mind that most of us have learned to accept science as the main street of civilization, have forgotten that man also possesses a heart.

"But beneath the outward complacency, there lingers a soul-saving doubt. Somehow it is not enough that the mere touching of a button will unleash a hundred horses to solve our transportation problems, or electricity—not yet itself defined by the scientist—turns night into day. Even the atheist, who denies all that is not explained by natural laws, is not quite satisfied by material things alone."[3] In order to prove that science is merely a matter of Machines, of physical power, that it is "coldly logical," unconcerned with man's heart, the editor quotes a W. M. Dixon to the effect that "science" does not use those fine sounding words that have long been popular with philosophers. Thus Dixon: "The scientific vocabulary does not include such words as beauty or heroism, nobility or charm, resignation or despair, kindness or generosity, character or conduct."[4] The professor is quoted further on the subject of science: "Its victories have been spectacular, its successes border upon the miraculous. For some reason, nevertheless, these victories and successes do not include those for which we hoped. Wiser, no doubt, we are, yet the age of science, which made us so, has proved a disappointment. We, its children, are no happier, perhaps less happy than our predecessors."[5]

"One wonders occasionally whether our much-talked-of civilization has all the advantages our fancy paints, whether its accumulated machinery of fast and furious distractions leaves us time for thought at all, or bears any profitable relation to our inner lives."[6] And then looking back to the times of the great Greek civilization, Dixon concludes that a civilization cannot be made with machinery, and that "If we propose to look to science for our salvation, there is this to bear in mind. Science moves on the circumference of our lives. She has her being in the outer and physical world. . . ."[7]

The facts are, however, that our civilization (including the use of science) is predominantly run by those who revere ancient knowledge of human behavior—the priest and politician. Certainly it is not those who see science as a guide to human behavior who are running things today. John Dewey discusses this problem in an excellent manner: "Take the case of science as a case of 'natural' knowledge obtained by 'natural' means and methods; together with the fact that after all, from the extra-naturalistic point of view, science is *mere* natural knowledge which must be put in stark opposition to a higher realm of truths accessible to extra-natural organs. Does anyone believe that where this climate of opinion prevails, scientific method and the conclusions reached by its use can do what they are capable of? Denial of reasonable freedom and attendant responsibility to any group produces conditions which can then be cited as reasons why such group cannot be entrusted with freedom or given responsibility. Similarly, the low estimate put upon science, the idea that because it is occupied with the natural world, it is incapacitated from exercising influence upon values to which the adjectives 'ideal' and 'higher,' (or any adjectives of eulogistic connotation) can be applied, restricts its influence. *The fruit of anti-naturalism is then made the*

1. Jan Gordon: *Modern French Painters*, p. 83, John Lane The Bodley Head, Ltd., London, 1923.
2. Ibid., p. 83.
3. Peyton Boswell: "Peyton Boswell Comments: Civilization and the Arts," *The Art Digest*, 17:3, April 15, 1943.
4. William M. Dixon: "Civilization and the Arts." Reprinted from the April, 1943, issue of FORTUNE, p. 120, Vol. xxvii, No. 4, by special permission of the Editors.
5. Ibid., p. 114.   6. Ibid., p. 120.   7. Ibid., p. 120.

ground of attack upon naturalism. . . . For the view attributed to naturalism is simply another instance of a too common procedure in philosophical controversy: Namely, representation of the position of an opponent in the terms it would have *if* the critic held it; that is, the meaning it has not in its own terms but after translation into the terms of an opposed theory." [8] In another article Dewey concludes: "It [science] is taught upon the whole not with respect to the way in which it actually enters into human life, and hence as a supremely humanistic subject, but as if it had to do with a world which is 'external' to human concerns." [9]

It is no accident that those who cling to the "extra-naturalistic point of view" insist that science be restricted to certain sciences; this permits them to continue their belief that science cannot do for us what they bend every effort to prevent it from doing. Sidney Hook has stated the crux of the matter as follows: "Distrust of scientific method is transformed into open hostility whenever some privileged, 'private' truth pleads for exemption from the tests set up to safeguard the intelligence from illusion." [10] The "soul-savers" would have us continue as we are, living according to ancient knowledge that has increasingly proved unfit for the problems that face us *today*. Hence, they seek to discredit science in any way possible. One critic, representative of the "Modern" viewpoint, writes thus: "A scientific experiment is one which elucidates and makes clear to everybody. Once the intelligence has grasped the intention and the method, anyone can judge whether the experiment has succeeded or no. Once understood, the experiment can be repeated. It is not necessary for the demonstrator to have the same genius as the discoverer. But in the experiments of art these conditions are not paralleled. No amount of intelligence will empower us to judge of the rightness or wrongness of a work of art. We may *understand* the principles employed and yet our sensibilities may fail to react. A work of art which has the power of operating only upon two or three persons, if it operates strongly enough, is a great work; for the value of art cannot be measured by the extent of its audience, but by the quality of emotion which it produces in its most responsive spectator." [11] Let us examine the above quotation, since it is illuminating. It is implied that science is a rather limited form of human behavior because it merely conveys to any "intelligent" person the methods by which a conclusion was arrived at. Art, however, is presumably above this ordinary sort of behavior, precisely because it does not permit even the most intelligent to judge whether the values of a work of art are false or not. The best one can hope for is to get the right "emotion," apparently an "emotion" peculiar to the recognition of "great" art. We are told at one point that no one can "judge of the rightness or wrongness of a work of art," but it turns out that we are able to recognize a "great" work of art only if we are one of those who already happens to like the art in question. As regards such art, it is further implied, no one can justify a dislike for it, because only those who like it are justified in their reaction to it. In brief, every effort is made to obfuscate any approach that might lead to a coherent consciousness of what the artist is doing or the critic is saying. All value judgments must be avoided except one—art can be judged only on a prejudiced, "emotional" basis, never on a rational, verifiable one.

Sheldon Cheney is one of the leading exponents of another, slightly more subtle effort to discredit science. He has written: "Even our knowledge of material things is scrappy and incomplete, if measured only by the reports of the senses. It is late to be arguing for the existence of mystic elements, when leading scientists of our generation have joined philosophers and spiritual prophets in affirming that the truer life and the animating cause lie beyond anything that is measurable by the physical senses and mind." [12] In this case the non-absolute character of scientific knowledge is somehow considered as giving the green light to the pursuit of "mystical" and "spiritual" forms of "knowledge."

In a similar vein is the attempt to blame the scientist because he took away the solid world we once thought existed. Thus Georges Lemaitre points out that modern science has altered our notion

8. John Dewey: "Anti-Naturalism in Extremis," *Partisan Review*, X:33–35, January-February, 1943.

9. John Dewey: "The Democratic Faith and Education," *The Antioch Review*, 4:281, Summer, 1944.

10. Sidney Hook: "The New Failure of Nerve," *Partisan Review*, X:4, January-February, 1943.

11. Gordon, op. cit., p. 82.

12. Sheldon Cheney: *Expressionism* in Art, p. 100.

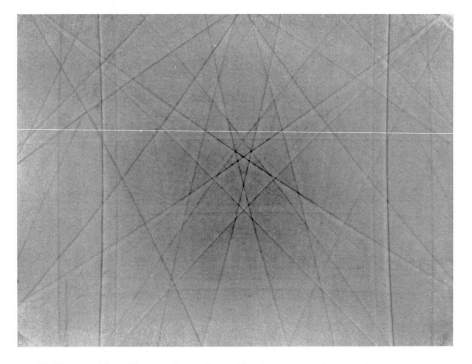

191. Kathleen Lonsdale, Divergent beam X-ray diffraction patterns from single crystals of benzophenone. (Reproduced from the Philosophical Transactions of the Royal Society of London, March, 1947, by permission of the Council of the Royal Society and of the author.)

of reality by shattering the solidity of the world we all believed in. He says that the scientists had made "Modern" artists afraid, for "the ground which their forbears had confidently trod was now giving way beneath their own feet; reality was everywhere breaking up into elusive, impalpable fragments." [13]

In the situation described by Lemaitre certain individuals in the art world saw what appeared like an opportunity to shun any further responsibility to the empirical world by placing that level of reality back into the insignificant status it once occupied in the mind of Plato, returning to that glorified, deified region of arbitrary reason that Plato called "divine madness." That we might see how very justified they really were, they recalled for us that the reason derived from the observation of reality turned out "only too often to be erroneous and misleading. . . ." [14] They were either ignorant or hypocritical or both, for what had these individuals actually lost because of the new view of reality? For that matter, what cared they whether the world was "solid" or not? That scientists, in denying absolutes, were able increasingly to secure greater accuracy in man's knowledge of himself and the reality about him was no concern of theirs. Their purpose was to escape from these very problems.

This irresponsible form of logic is referred to by Herbert Muller when he writes: "We need to protect science from the demands for orthodoxy, now coming from revolutionary as well as religious quarters—demands that would be reasonable enough if scientific truth were merely a commodity manufactured for human convenience. We need to shoo off all the genteel thinkers who have been pleased to repeat that science too is a myth, and then to add that it has no more validity than the myths of poetry and religion—that as an upstart, indeed, it has less authority. We need, generally, to dispel the fog of obscurantism that has settled about the new concepts in physics." [15]

13. Reprinted by permission of the publishers from Georges Lemaitre *From Cubism to Surrealism in French Literature*, p. 55. Harvard University Press, Cambridge, Massachusetts, 1941.
14. Ibid., p. 53.
15. Herbert Muller: *Science and Criticism*, p. 89. We highly recommend Muller's book for those who wish to pursue the subject of this chapter.

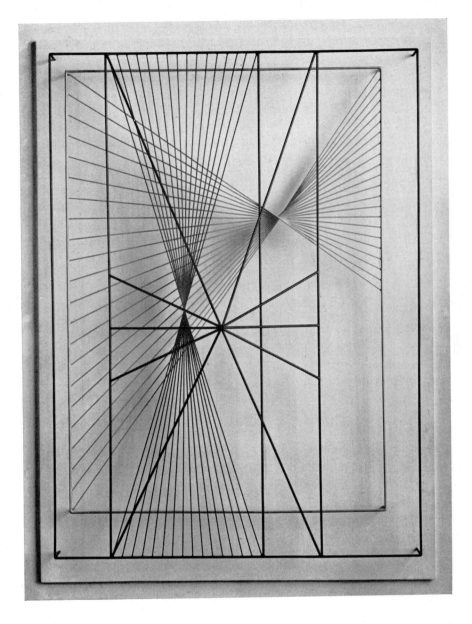

192. Charles Biederman, Construction, 2/40 (2). Painted wood and metal rods. 62½″x48⅞″x10″.

As for the scientists who have joined the "philosophers and spiritual prophets," it should at least be apparent that one cannot justifiably call upon the authority of science unless the scientist in question is behaving scientifically. For example, if a scientist responds to the problem of religion *un*scientifically, as some do, then one cannot rightly say that the authority of the scientific method justifies the religious one, although this is frequently done. Too often the scientist falls prey to the very forms of behavior outside his particular field that he warns others against when inside his field.

It is from this point of view that we reject the notion of one Modern artist, who supports his religious view of art by citing Eddington's statement that if we are to "know" anything about nature, it must be through "something like religious experience."[16] We should like to point out that Eddington made a much more intelligent observation, as regards our problem here, when he remarked that "you never know where you are with artists."[17] It is an unfortunate fact that few scientists seem to recognize their responsibilities in this problem; even more destructive are those who deliberately limit the fields in which science is permitted. On this problem Albert G. Ramsperger points out that: "there is a responsibility that falls upon all scientists alike. It is the responsibility of understanding what it is to have scientific knowledge, of encouraging efforts to increase that knowledge in every field, and, above all, of opposing all movements which hinder the scientific search for the good life on the specious ground that values, unlike other natural events, require a nonscientific certification. This last point is all the more important because scientists themselves are often guilty of discarding their scientific attitude as soon as they turn away from their special fields, and some even give addresses and write articles which give the impression that science, by its very nature and method, precludes inquiry into values. The prestige of science thus comes to be used, not to lift the study of human values out of the dark ages from which the physical sciences and biology have emerged, but to keep man in that state in which he is the master of all things except his own welfare."[18]

Just as not everything a scientist says is necessarily scientific, so also not all applications of scientific method to art are necessarily "scientific." For the scientist who judges "art" there is always the grave danger that he may supplant his art ignorance with prejudices disguised by arbitrary or convenient selections of scientific knowledge.

We find, for example, that many psychologists and psychiatrists abuse the tools of their profession when they analyze the field of human behavior in art. We shall concentrate here particularly upon the psychoanalysts, since they provide one of the most flagrant examples of the abuse of science in art. Many of them appear to imagine that knowledge of their own profession somehow offsets their ignorance about art. Too often they become so intrigued with feces, genitals, etc., that either they see little else when they observe art, or they ignore art which fails to excite them in these directions.[19] In other words, they come to art with very limited knowledge, but generally behave as though the opposite were the case.

Hence the psychoanalysts have produced little specific material by which to evaluate the visual arts. For instance, there is a great deal of talk about fantasy, but when it comes to tackling this very real problem in a specific manner, considering its desirable or undesirable sociological function in art, then little is said. In fact, few of these scientists seem to be aware that there exists a "problem of reality" in art.

16. Ben Nicholson in *Unit One,* p. 89.

17. Arthur S. Eddington: *The Philosophy of Physical Science,* p. 112, The Macmillan Co., New York, 1938, The University Press, Cambridge, 1939.

18. Albert G. Ramsperger: "The Misplaced Modesty of Scientists," *The Antioch Review,* 4:588–589, Winter, 1944–1945.

19. Harry Levey, a psychiatrist, has written: "An artist's production of a painting might somehow be psychically associated with his repressed wish to smear with feces, or to exhibit his genitals, wishes which are universal and are almost universally

Freud called the tune for psychoanalytic evaluations about art at the opening of this century, and since then most of his followers have been content merely to repeat with variations what he said. Harry Levey, in his illuminating review of psychoanalytical literature on art, points out this problem: "When one reviews the mass of reports by psychoanalysts other than Freud, and which purport to deal with artistic sublimation in a scientific manner, one is impressed not only with their patent repetition of Freud's formulations in 1905, but also with their regular imitation of the unscientific attitude Freud has accorded the subject." [20] Further on Levey writes that "instead of presenting clinical evidence," the psychoanalysts "simply repeat, or else paraphrase, Freud's earlier formulations about artistic sublimation . . . . the conclusions offered generally end with calling upon the support of authority by quoting Freud." [21] Freud is regarded not merely as an authority in his own field who is speculating about art; on the contrary his unverified speculations have been automatically transposed to the status of an indisputable source of fact. It would appear, therefore, that Freud's qualifications as an authority on art were based unconsciously upon his credentials as a psychoanalyst. Thus his ignorance in art was clothed with the prestige of the genius he displayed in his own field.

In our consideration of some of Freud's views we shall undertake to discuss them particularly at those points where they come within the area of our own knowledge about art.

Freud has stated that the artist's activity consists of a "path from phantasy back again to reality." He then says of the artist: "He is one who is urged on by instinctual needs which are too clamorous; he longs to attain to honor, power, riches, fame, and the love of women; but he lacks the means of achieving these gratifications. So, like any other with an unsatisfied longing, he turns away from reality and transfers all his interest, and all his libido too, on to the creation of his wishes in the life of phantasy, from which the way might readily lead to neurosis." [22] However, the artist is not the only one who seeks gratification in the world of fantasy, says Freud. But the rest of us suppress and repress and so limit the fantasy experience which is more fully available to the artist because he is not so handicapped. Consequently he is able to present the material of fantasy in such a manner that the usual repressive measures are circumvented. Freud then concludes: "When he [the artist] can do all this, he opens out to others the way back to the comfort and consolation of their own unconscious sources of pleasure, and so reaps their gratitude and admiration; then he has won—through his phantasy—what before he could only win in phantasy: honour, power, and the love of women." [23] Here we have a theory that certainly applies to *some* artists, but it also applies to humans generally. Such behavior is not inevitable for all who make art. Freud often enough demanded that we distinguish between genuine and non-genuine psychoanalysts. We insist that a similar discrimination be practiced, where art and artists are concerned.

Today many artists and critics are still doing their best to encourage the subjective and fantasy view of art that Freud formulated. Consider, for example, Roger Fry's two categories concerning men's reactions to reality. According to Fry, one of the early critics with the "Modern" view, there was on the one hand the "actual life," considered the imperfect reality; on the other hand there was the "imaginative" life. Both were considered independent of each other, so that in the latter one could fabricate that which he could not attain in the former. And of course we hear that these fabrications of the imagination are

repressed; but no proof is advanced by Freud, or other psychoanalysts, or by others, that it is primarily these wishes which animate the artist with an impulse to create art and not mud-pies or day-dreams, or how the artist differs from his brothers and sisters and neighbors in his specially artistic ventilation of smearing and exhibitionistic impulses common to everyone." ("A Theory Concerning Free Creation in the Inventive Arts," *Psychiatry: Journal of the Biology and Pathology of Interpersonal Relations*, Vol. 3, No. 2, May, 1940, p. 268.)

20. Ibid., p. 261.

21. Ibid., p. 262.

22. A GENERAL INTRODUCTION TO PSYCHO-ANALYSIS, by Sigmund Freud, translated by Joan Riviere, p. 327, published by LIVE-RIGHT PUBLISHING CORPORATION, 1938. A number of recent Hollywood productions about musicians reveal a similar view of the "artist."

23. Ibid., p. 328. We restrict our discussion mainly to the way in which Freud's theories apply to the visual arts. (The popularity of the Hollywood productions referred to in the preceding footnote indicates that these false portaits of the artists are actually directed towards gratifying longings of the general public.)

193. Kathleen Lonsdale, X-ray diffraction pattern. See figure 189, center.

more real than the actual reality. In 1909 Fry wrote: "I think the artist might if he chose take a mystical attitude, and declare that the fulness and completeness of the imaginative life he leads may correspond to an existence more real and more important than any that we know of in mortal life." [24]

After reading such as the following by Fry, Freud must have felt he was surely on the right track of what *all* artists strove to attain: "That the graphic arts are the expression of the imaginative life rather than a copy of actual life might be guessed from observing children. Children, if left to themselves, never, I believe, copy what they see, never, as we say, 'draw from nature,' but express, with a delightful freedom and sincerity, the mental images which make up their own imaginative lives." [25]

More than a decade after he wrote the material quoted earlier, Freud became bolder or more dogmatic, and announced that, "Art is almost always harmless and beneficient, it does not seek to be anything else but an illusion. Save in the case of a few people who are, one might say, obsessed by Art, it never dares to make any attacks on the realm of reality." [26] Our history amply demonstrates how very

24. Roger Fry: *Vision and Design,* p. 27, Penguin Books, 1940, Middlesex, England. By permission of Chatto and Windus, London. Fry was either unconscious that this is a version of the Aristotelian ideal, or else he was reticent to credit the author of the theory.

25. Ibid., p. 26. The fact of the matter is that the child does "draw from nature," unless we are to contend that the notions for the objects he draws—trees, people, animals, etc.—are taken from something other than nature. The fact that the adult does not have the same *kind* of freedom that exists on the child's level, at least in "normal" instances, does not seem to have perturbed Fry in the least. But the facts are that we cannot very well employ children's behavior as a criterion and justification for the behavior of the mature adult any more than we can do the reverse. "Freedom" towards reality, i.e., the flexibility of a human being's orientation towards the outside reality, varies at least in normal evolution, with the various age-levels. One does not have the *same* freedom as a child as one will have on becoming an adult for the simple reason that the potentialities of the adult as regards freedom are not those possible for the child. Hence the popular habit among Moderns of identifying the child with the adult serves merely as a convenient rationalization for infantile behavior in an adult.

26. Sigmund Freud: *New Introductory Lectures on Psycho-analysis,* p. 219, Carlton House, New York, 1933, permission of Random House, Inc.

580

194. Jean Gorin. Dynamic rhythms in an equilateral triangle, 1939-44. Painted copper. Photo, Yves Hervochon, Paris.

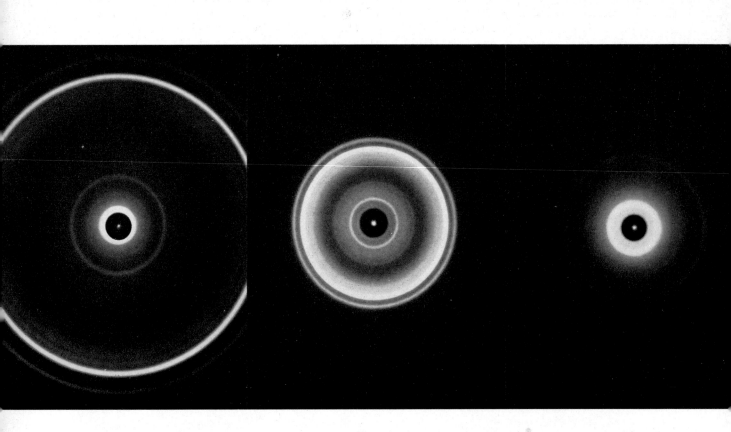

195. Frank Chesley, X-ray diffraction patterns of powdered crystalline materials; left, sugar; center, salt; right, quartz.

erroneous Freud was in such an evaluation. Art has played a major part in forming the image of reality which man possessed in each period of history. And when Freud refers to the "obsessed" ones, he refers to the greatest artists in each period of history. Furthermore, the arts which have been nothing "but an illusion" have been far from being as harmless as Freud imagined. For example, consider the Christian epoch, particularly the Romanesque period; one could hardly call these arts "harmless" illusions. The lies that have been perpetrated by means of art have been as devastating as the lies men have perpetrated with words. "Art" is essentially *a problem of reality*. The prime task of the artist has not been merely to offer fantasy escape to mankind—except in certain regressive periods.

Freud's belief that only the "obsessed" ones were ever concerned with the "realm of reality," suggests more than anything else that he had some personal difficulties with the subject of "art." For only one feeling some deep seated insecurity could possibly assume that the functions of art were merely to secure women, riches, etc. for artists, and excursions into fantasy land for non-artists. Further indications of this insecurity appear in some remarks by Brill regarding Freud's experience with music. Brill says: "Being rationalistic, or perhaps of an analytic turn of mind, he rebelled against being moved by something without knowing why; and as he could not discover the meaning of music, he was almost incapable of obtaining any pleasure from it." [27] What pleasure he achieved in the visual arts seems to have been limited to *The Prisoner's Dream* type[28] and to such religious arts as Egyptian statuettes. For obvious reasons it was the art of literature that gave him the most satisfaction. But only a man irritated and confused by the various forms of art which are so widely different in their structure and function, would dare to sum them all up with the dogmatic simplicity we find in Freud's theories. Their prime interest is that they represent Freud's attempt to dispose of, not solve the problem of, "art."

27. A. A. Brill: *Freud's Contribution to Psychiatry*, pp. 189–190, W. W. Norton and Co., Inc., New York, 1944.

28. See Frontispiece and p. 121, *A General Introduction to Psycho-analysis*.

196. Charles Biederman, White Construction with colored lights, 7/40 (9). Painted glass and wood with hidden fluorescent tubes; 54½″x52″x12½″. Waiting room, The Interstate Clinic, Red Wing, Minnesota.

Unfortunately, however, the theories of Freud passed beyond the personal psycho-logical function they served and created immeasurable harm in the process. The Surrealists are the most serious example. From Surrealists themselves and irresponsible or ignorant psychoanalysts we hear that Freud is the father of Surrealism. If this is true, then it is a case of a father who failed to meet his parental responsibilities. Actually both psychoanalysis and Surrealism were born out of more or less similar historical conditions, and not the latter from the former. Freudian theory arose in answer to an imperative need for solutions to the general chaos of our times. Freud applied his genius to the investigation of one aspect of the extant chaos. Surrealism, on the other hand, was simply a manifestation of the chaos that reached into art. This is to say that if Freud and his work had never appeared, we would have Surrealism anyhow. The chaos of our times, not Freud, fathered Surrealism. But Freud and most of his followers who concern themselves with art, have helped to preserve rather than remedy this sickness in art.

Herbert Muller, in a discussion of Freud's theories, points out that by giving the unconscious the leading role in human behavior, Freud opened the door for those who were only too anxious to go all the way with "instincts," "emotions," "the irrational" as the supreme guides to human behavior.[29] This is precisely what the Moderns and/or Surrealists did, and, as far as we know, Freud unfortunately never found it necessary to expose or denounce them. He simply served as an impressive disguise for the most severe manifestation of "mental illness" in art today. The claim of Surrealists that they are "scientific" in the psychoanalytic sense is fraudulent; they merely represent the sick, the dying remnants of Aristotelianism in art, as we have demonstrated elsewhere.

Today we read much which openly or otherwise attempts to justify neurotic behavior in the artist. We are given the impression that it is a sort of divine affliction. But neurotic behavior in the artist, as in any human being, is a manifestation of some *kind* of maladjustment. The vast majority of artists, however, are only too anxious to play the role which "Modern" critics and others have fabricated for them from the theories of Freud. In this role they hope to make tolerable their insecure orientation to our chaotic times. Indeed, the divinity of the artist's neurosis permits the buffoon to pose as the savior of culture. On this subject Lionel Trilling wrote: "Wherever the 'blame' lies, the myth of the neurotic artist grew. Both sides cherished it. The artist can find advantage in the notion—it gives him the ancient privileges of the idiot and the fool, half-prophetic creatures. That the artist's neurosis can be but a mask is suggested by Thomas Mann's pleasure in presenting his untried youth as 'sick' but his successful maturity as militarily robust and efficient.

"And the myth has its advantage for the philistine too, a double advantage. On the one hand, the belief in the artist's neuroticism allows the philistine to shut his ears to what the artist says. But on the other hand, it allows him to listen. For we must not make the common mistake—the philistine does want to listen at the same time that he wants to shut his ears. By supposing that the artist has an interesting but not always reliable relation to reality, he is able to control and modify what he is told. If he did not want to listen at all he would say 'insane'; with 'neurotic,' which hedges, he can listen when he chooses." [30]

This leads us to wonder whether many psychoanalysts are not also playing a philistine role of a kind unique to them. For they often betray an attitude towards artists similar to that of the philistines of whom Trilling speaks. The partiality of their interest in artists, when there are such excellent subjects for their professional talents, as, for instance, surgeons and psychoanalysts themselves, is a point for inquiry. But while the philistines Trilling mentions would simply like to be assured that their "security" will not be molested when they feel the urge to wander in the world of artists, the "philistines" of "mental" science seem to want to be in charge of the whole affair. Perhaps they are bent on taking the place once occupied by the old art philosopher—the man who knew all the inner workings of the child-like artist's "creative process." This is especially felt on reading their literature in which they sally forth through the world of the artist like masters with little essential respect for their contemptible charges. It is perhaps partly the artist's insecure position in our culture and partly his general disregard for most of its cherished conventions that make him an ideal target for the philistine, whether he is a psychoanalyst or some other

29. Muller, op. cit., p. 149.
30. Lionel Trilling: "A Note on Art and Neurosis," *Partisan Review*, XII:43, Winter, 1945.

type of layman. For imagine what would happen if the psychoanalyst undertook to probe the physician's, or, even more courageously, the politician's personality, with the same abandon he permits himself with the artist. "Art" seems to offer the psychoanalyst a field in which he has unrestricted freedom to indulge his particular interests without the risk of opposition; certainly he has little, if anything, to fear from the ineffectual mumblings of art "experts." "Art," however, was not made for the peculiar pleasures of a psychoanalyst.

Our objection is not to the psychoanalyst's interest in art and artists, but rather to the attitude he exhibits in his interest: to his arrogance in giving the impression that the sum total of art is being considered when he enters the field; to his lack of awareness that there is other knowledge about art that would relieve him of much of his ignorance on the subject, and thus permit him to use his own tools of investigation more scientifically and so more usefully for all concerned. In at least the following ways he does more harm than benefit to the field of art: (1) His discussions of artists' personalities generally bring out factors that are, as Levey points out, "universal" not peculiar to artists. (Artists are already considered "queer" enough without being accused of having a monopoly on queerness in the human race.) (2) He usually ignores the fact that there are many different kinds of artists, as is the case in any profession, his own included. (3) He has failed to denounce the Surrealists and their fellow-travelers; thereby he has failed to do the very thing that could help to alleviate that aspect of the world chaos that exists in art.

The psychoanalyst will have to learn that the fundamental function of art, contrary to Freud's crude impression, is that of a major tool by which man forms his notions of reality, and extends reality in various ways for his further enjoyment. He needs to realize that art as a problem of reality is not the concern of the "obsessed" ones, but of the greatest artists in every period of culture.

There is another group whose members directly consider themselves as scientists of art. They too, like the psychoanalysts, if in a slightly different way, abuse the "scientific" attitude to such an extent that they have greatly encouraged the hostility of the artist toward the scientific method. Unlike the psychoanalysts, however, they seem little interested in "theory," but concentrate on statistics, drawing up averages, norms, etc., gained from all kinds of tests with this and that for this and that. The majority of these individuals go to their task like impartial automatons, little aware of the critical necessity of being adequately aware of their own theoretical behavior. Hence they do not see the utter vapidity of the theory implicit in the conclusions drawn from their tests. They give the impression of being very proud of their ability to be purely objective—as though one could be merely objective. Lacking adequate theoretical consciousness, they are almost totally unaware of the "subjective" aspect of their own behavior. Such a scientific attitude was popular in the 19th century.

An example of this "objectivity" is the case of the testers who set about establishing the *quality* of the artists selected for the experiments on the basis of the *quantity* of "honors" won.[31] Yet it is common knowledge that in recent generations the worst artists have been the most honored, while the creative innovators have generally been honored only after their death. With much "impartiality," others spend a great deal of effort establishing the "norm" for something called "aesthetic taste," and other such verbalisms, which invariably result in reinforcing the prejudices of the *status quo*. In short, their prime interest seems to be a sort of "Gallup poll" of the whole business of "art" reactions. But, as Albert Einstein warned, "Concern for man himself and his fate must always form the chief interest of all technical endeavors. . . . Never forget this in the midst of your diagrams and equations."[32]

31. See "Studies in the Psychology of Art" by C. Tiebout and N. C. Meier, in *Psychological Monographs,* Vol. XLVIII, No. 1, Whole No. 213, 1936. "Studies in the Psychology of Art," Vol. 2, edited by N. C. Meier.

32. As quoted by R. S. Lynd in *Knowledge for What?*, p. 114.

197. Three views of a mathematical string model.

The carefree, unscientific manner in which such "art-scientists" decide that this work of art is "better" than that, or this artist "better" than that is at times amazing. They know a great deal about art tests, very little about the alleged subject of their tests. Generally they are oblivious both of their great ignorance about "art" and of the destructive role it plays in the formation of their tests and the evaluations drawn from them.

Unfortunately, however, it is these "art-scientists," along with the art philosophers, who dominate our institutions. They dutifully heed the art prejudices of the *status quo* and in return receive support for their "art" activities, which completely ignore contemporary artists who are genuine innovators.

Most "art-scientists" have much in common with the art philosophers and psychoanalysts. The "art" behavior of each group is generally found to be esoteric. Thus the works of "art-scientists" seem to be considered important only by other "art-scientists." Similarly, we have found that the works of art philosophers are usually read only by other art philosophers, and that the works of psychoanalysts, who presumably analyze art, are usually read only by other psychoanalysts. Furthermore, the boring treatises of the "art-scientists" concern them more than the otherwise interesting subject which allegedly motivates them. Similarly the philosophers and the psychoanalysts are mainly concerned with theories rather than with what the theories were supposedly made for. The philosophers tend to inhabit Plato's rarified realm of "divine ideas"; the psychoanalysts are a sort of combination of philosopher and "scientist," predominantly the former where art is concerned. At the other extreme we find that the "art-scientists" with their great concern for "facts," are over-empirical. The latter presume that they discover purely objective data in the field of art, but mostly the "data" are facts that come out of their tests rather than facts that their tests get out of the actual world of art happenings. These over-theoretical and over-empirical errors show more clearly the solution needed. Ivan Pavlov's advice on this problem is excellent: "Study, compare, and accumulate facts. No matter how perfect a bird's wing, it could never raise the bird aloft if it were not supported by air. Facts are the air of the scientist. Without them you will never be able to soar. Without them your 'theories' are useless efforts.

586

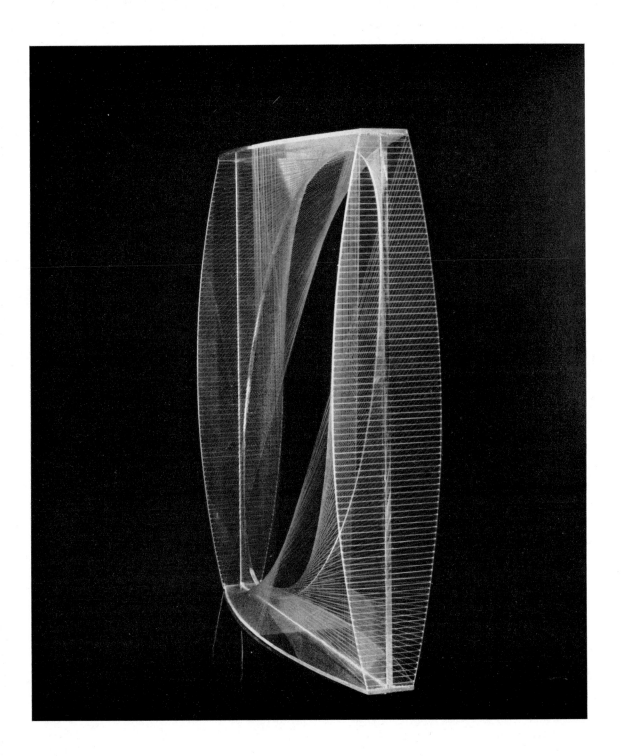

198. Naum Gabo, Linear Construction, 1942-43.

"However, the mere accumulation of facts without a general idea in mind, without a plan, is a useless occupation. . . . Try not to stop only at the surface of a fact. Don't become an archive of facts. Try to penetrate the secret of their appearance. Obstinately seek the laws governing them. The aim toward which facts are accumulated is precisely this last point—the discovery of the laws governing facts. Thus a fact is not an end in itself, but only the means toward mastery of the general laws of nature.

"When you have no ideas you can't see the facts." [33]

The fact that none of these three groups of art "experts" has any noticeable effect upon actual art, and the fact that their activities have little if any interest for those who are mainly concerned with actual art, indicate that all of them are more concerned with making a "career" than with the actual events of art. Therefore, it is little wonder that the art philosophers and psychoanalysts, and the "scientific" art testers, are completely discredited in the actual field of art. They have discredited art analysis to such an extent that artists today are only further encouraged in their beliefs that they have no need to be much concerned with the problems of logic (art philosophy) and that they do not need knowledge of the unconscious process (art psychoanalysis) and that they do not need to develop their ability as scientific observers of what they see in works of art.

To be sure, the "failure" of science in art has been noted often enough. But this failure has been looked upon as an opportunity to discredit science without any concern for whether or not such a conclusion is warranted by the facts involved. Moreover, the "failures" of science in art are only peculiar to particular times, *not to all times*.[34] And the failures result from man's failure to become an adequate or genuine scientist of the times and not from the failure of the genuine scientific attitude. No one has yet proven that the scientific *attitude* is not usefully applicable to any field in which it has not been tried or even to so-called non-scientific fields in which it has been "tried."

Actually history discloses that the orientation of humans towards the world and themselves has been passing from less and less magic and religion to more and more science, i.e., the verifiable method of behavior. This is equally true in the field of art. Thus the scientific attitude is simply a way of performing a very ancient activity in an ever more fruitful manner. Its method is the most developed outcome of man's evolution. It represents the accumulated developments of all the reasoning experiences of mankind, from the very beginning of human culture to the present. In the words of Oliver Reiser: "we find that the one general direction in which scientific thought bends is (*a*) towards an ever-increasing exclusion of the capricious, the miraculous, and supernatural powers or agencies, and (*b*) in the direction of a greater reliance upon the use of empirical method, towards the discovery and summary of observed facts in the form of uniform laws of behavior of the entities studied." [35] In short, science is *a way of life*, a form of human orientation and behavior. Generally only those aspects of science dealing with "Machine" invention are recognized and employed in our culture; those aspects dealing with "conduct," behavior of man—science as a way of living—have as yet to be tried; few are even aware that such knowledge exists. But the advanced scientists are essentially concerned with man, "heart" and all, and not merely with "Machines." Thus it is necessary to emphasize repeatedly that the scientific attitude is simply a more sane, efficient, useful *method of evaluation* than any other discovered or devised by man for living in this universe.

33. Ivan Petrovitch Pavlov: *Conditioned Reflexes and Psychiatry*, Lectures on Conditioned Reflexes, Vol. 2, translated and edited by W. H. Gantt, p. 17, International Publishers, New York, 1941. He might have added that "freedom" of inquiry is also the "air" of the scientist.
34. For example, the artists of the Italian Renaissance were successful scientists in their outlook upon living and upon art.
35. From Oliver L. Reiser: *Philosophy and the Concepts of Modern Science*, p. 221. New York, 1935. By permission of The Macmillan Company, publishers.

Although various established fields have something to contribute to the scientific-thinking artist, our emphasis is not simply upon this or that particular field of science, but upon the "attitude" fundamental to genuine science. The important point is for artists to comprehend their erroneous beliefs regarding the differences between themselves and genuine scientists.

So much verbal debris has been unloaded on this subject of the artist and scientist, often by writers who in other fields have adopted a more useful attitude, that it is little wonder that the present false knowledge persists. For example, even John Dewey, who has said some excellent things on the subject of science, nevertheless at one time distinguished between "science" and "art" by stating that the former produces descriptive information by which to reach an experience, while art produces the experience itself. He makes an analogy to the effect that science is a sort of descriptive sign-board to a city, while art is the experience itself of the city. To quote him: "The problem in hand may be approached by drawing a distinction between expression and statement. Science states meanings; art expresses them. . . . Statement sets forth the conditions under which an experience of an object or situation may be had. It is a good, that is, effective, statement in the degree in which these conditions are stated in such a way that they can be used as *directions* by which one may arrive at the experience. It is a bad statement, confused and false, if it sets forth these conditions in such a way that when they are used as directions, they mislead or take one to the object in a wasteful way . . . . scientific statement is often thought to possess more than a signboard function and to disclose or be 'expressive' of the inner nature of things. If it did, it would come into competition with art, and we should have to take sides and decide which of the two promulgates the more genuine revelation." [36] Science is presented as a purely objective affair. The scientist appears as a mere robot showing everyone the way to the experiences of life, experiences to which he is immune or in which he is apparently not interested. The scientist is thus made out as something less than a human being in his work, while the artist dives right into the very heart of human experience with his work. This view is put into even more blunt terms by De Witt Parker: "The central difference is this. The former [art works] are descriptions not of things only, but of the artist's reactions to things, his mood or emotion in their presence. They are expressions of total, concrete experiences, which include the self of the observer as well as the things he observes.

"Scientific descriptions, on the other hand, render objects only; the feelings of the observer towards them are carefully excluded. Science is intentionally objective,—from the point of view of the artistic temperament, *dry and cold*." (emphasis ours) [37]

But scientists cannot be simply "objective" in their descriptions, because like any other humans they have reactions, they are experiencing the things with which *they* deal. This business about "cold" science is so much non-sense. It is no accident that we do not find the term "hot" opposed to the term "cold"; but by doing it we expose the absurdity of such notions. The fallacy of the implicitly "hot" artist and the explicitly "cold" scientist is derived from the behavior of the average members, not from that of the most advanced members of these respective fields; that is, the over-emotional artists who rush across their canvases in emotional spasms and are confused, frustrated in their orientation to the empirical world, and those "applied" scientists who are over-empirical and so lead a confused, frustrated existence on the "emotional" level. But an island full of lepers is hardly the place to seek an average for the determination of human health. Those who consider that the artist's nervous system activity is purely an emotional paroxysm, and who see the scientist in just the opposite light, have simply never had a genuine experiential response to the tremendous world the great men of art and science are constantly discovering in the reality about us.

Actually it is among the scientists that we are more likely to find men who are aware of the subjective-objective character of human response to the reality about and within them. Relevant to our discussion, Reiser says: "There are those who say that emotion has no place in science, but this view expresses an inadequate psychology. What we need is not less emotion in science and in life, but a proper balance between emotion and reason. I suspect that the most productive and creative men of science have

36. From *Art as Experience*, by John Dewey, pp. 84–85. Courtesy of G. P. PUTNAM'S SONS.

37. DeWitt Parker: *The Principles of Aesthetics*, Second Edition, p. 20. Copyright by F. S. Crofts and Co., New York, 1946.

199. Frank Chesley, Crystal and molecular models. Left, crystal structure model of mineral Pyrrhotite; center, molecular model of 2,2-dimethyl-propane; right, crystal structure model of sodium chloride.

been those who possessed both intellect and emotion in an unusual degree. Our problem still is that of bringing the two together. In the older terminology this was the problem of reconciling the head and the heart, but in the light of our newer neuropsychiatry the conflict is really between the cortex and the thalamus, or more generally, between the new nervous system, the cerebral hemispheres (the 'specific organ of civilization,' as C. J. Herrick calls it), and the old nervous system, the autonomic nervous system and the endocrine glands." [38] And listen to this report of Alfred Whitehead regarding a meeting of some scientists: "It was my good fortune to be present at the meeting of the Royal Society in London when the Astronomer Royal for England announced that the photographic plates of the famous eclipse, as measured by his colleagues in Greenwich Observatory, had verified the prediction of Einstein that rays of light are bent as they pass in the neighborhood of the sun. The whole atmosphere of tense interest was exactly that of the Greek drama: we were the chorus commenting on the degree of destiny as disclosed in the development of a supreme incident. There was dramatic quality in the very staging:—the traditional ceremonial, and in the background the picture of Newton to remind us that the greatest of scientific generalizations was now, after more than two centuries, to receive its first modification. Nor was the personal interest wanting: a great adventure in thought had at length come safe to shore." [39] These are the people we are expected to believe spend their lives merely hanging up sign-boards, indifferent to the experiences with which they deal!

Some writers, however, have stressed the similarity between the artist and scientist. Henri Poincaré wrote: "A scientist worthy of the name, above all a mathematician, experiences in his work the same impression as an artist; his pleasure is as great and of the same nature." [40] Herbert Muller has said that scientists and artists are more like each other than anyone else. He also states: "The scientific mind is not a mere logic-grinder, turning out truths with remorseless precision. It too feels its way, has flashes

38. Reiser, *The Promise of Scientific Humanism*, pp. 23–24.

39. From A. N. Whitehead: *Science and the Modern World*, p. 15, by permission of The Macmillan Company, publishers.

40. As quoted by E. T. Bell in *Men of Mathematics*, p. 526.

200. Charles Biederman, Construction, 2/46 (1). Painted wood and aluminum. 31⅛″x25¼″x14½″.

of insight, leaps to conclusions—arrives intuitively at an intuitive goal. Although the final experimental test is all important, what is tested is a hunch, an inspiration, a dream. All the great scientific theories are great imaginative feats." [41] The scientist, however, when he is an up-to-date one, employs non-intuitive means to check his intuitions. It is on this score that most artists today balk, and to the degree that they do they are lesser artists as well as scientists.

We prefer to consider the relationships between "art" and "science" in terms of the fact that these two fields have an analogous function in human culture. Naturally there are differences between these fields, but it is precisely the interaction of these differences which goes to form the totality of human existence; because neither art nor science covers *all* factors of human concern.

Herbert Read claims that knowledge in art is superior, because its greatest examples are not only "universal" but "eternal," while in the case of scientific fact "nothing has proved so impermanent and provisional." [42] One could hardly make a more erroneous statement today. For the greatest contribution of science has been to demonstrate that quests for absolutes are invariably futile and false, that *all* knowledge in *all* fields is "impermanent and provisional." Thus man's "knowledge" remains open to revision and so improvement. And one of the main points we have shown in our history is that art, like science, has been "impermanent and provisional," because both fields serve similar, fundamental functions in the shaping of human culture; that is, they are the two major means by which man *formulates and reformulates his changing, developing interpretation of reality.* Our view of the world would be radically altered were we to adopt the interpretations of reality expressed in the "art" or "science" of the Egyptians, Greeks, Christians, etc. The values of science *and* art have been as "impermanent" as the values of reality held in the times in which they were made, because all these values are one and indivisible. In past and present ages of art and science there have always been those who sought for and eventually claimed to have found an absolute, but none of them has stood the test of *advancing* knowledge.

And the advanced artists and scientists of today are dealing with similar problems—with the big problem—the achievement of a more adequate orientation to reality, that we may utilize it to our fullest capacities and thus achieve the greatest happiness that is available for all of us. Neither field has a monopoly on the higher values of living at its best. Whatever the artists or scientists find, they both need! From this point of view John Dewey was more correct when he wrote: "The fact that science tends to show that man is a part of nature has an effect that is favorable rather than unfavorable to art when its intrinsic significance is realized and when its meaning is no longer interpreted by contrast with beliefs that come to us from the past. For the closer man is brought to the physical world, the clearer it becomes that his impulses and ideas are enacted by nature within him. Humanity in its vital operations has always acted upon this principle. Science gives this action intellectual support. The sense of relation between nature and man in some form has always been the actuating spirit of art." [43] But it is necessary to repeat that

41. Muller, op. cit., p. 257.

42. As quoted by Muller, op. cit., p. 256.

43. From *Art as Experience,* by John Dewey, p. 338, Courtesy of G. P. PUTNAM'S SONS.

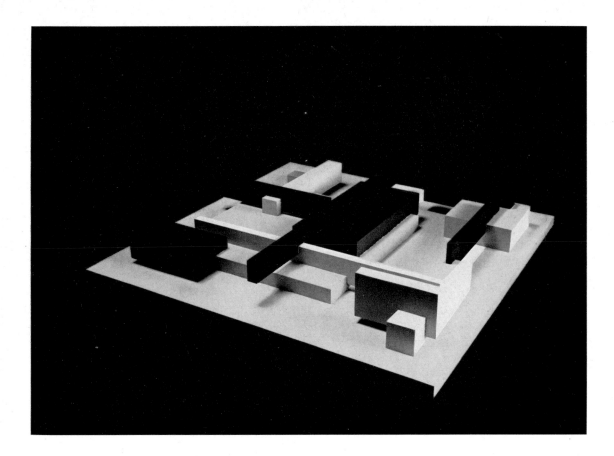

201. Jean Gorin, Etude plastique de blocs d'habitation dans l'espace, 1929.

if the artist is to learn anything useful from science, then he will first have to learn and acquire the *attitude* by which the genuine scientist establishes his knowledge. Science is not a mere convenience to be called in only now and then, as is generally done; *it is a way of life!* As A. J. Carlson put it: "The term science is sometimes limited to the fields of mathematics, astronomy, chemistry, physics, geology, biology, and their practical applications. This may be due partly to the fact that in these fields we have to-day the greatest body of verifiable data and so-called laws of science. However, one of the elements in the scientific attitude is the application of the scientific method to the entire universe, including all human experience and all human relations." [44] Freud spoke in a similar manner in regard to science and religion and philosophy; the word art could as well be substituted for religion. "It is inadmissible to declare that science is one field of human intellectual activity, and that religion and philosophy are others, at least as valuable, and that science has no business to interfere with the other two, that they all have an equal claim to truth, and that everyone is free to choose whence he shall draw his convictions and in what he shall place his belief. Such an attitude is considered particularly respectable, tolerant, broad-minded, and free from narrow prejudices. Unfortunately it is not tenable; it shares all the pernicious qualities of an entirely unscientific *Weltanschauung* and in practice comes to much the same thing. The bare fact is that truth cannot be tolerant and cannot admit compromise or limitations, that scientific research looks on the whole field of human activity as its own, and must adopt an uncompromisingly critical attitude towards any other power that seeks to usurp any part of its province." [45] In other words, the problems we are here discussing are not peculiar to certain segments of human behavior or activity, but are concerned with *the general problem of behavior in the 20th century.*

From this point of view, then, "art" is simply one of the less developed regions of "science," less developed perhaps because it is the most difficult of all. Whitehead has written: "It follows that there are an indefinite number of purely abstract sciences, with their laws, their regularities, and their complexities of theorems—all as yet undeveloped. We can hardly avoid the conclusion that Nature in her procedures illustrates many such sciences. We are blind to such illustration because we are ignorant of the type of regularities to look for." [46]

In one sense we are not at the beginning of the scientific attitude in art, but rather at the beginning of a new stage in the use of a more developed scientific attitude in art. In the first section of art history we saw that there was a predominant concern with the development of recording nature's art; this involved the ever increasing "scientific" observation of nature's macro-reality. The more "scientific" artists became, the more successful they were in attaining their objective of recording nature's art accurately; eventually a Camera was invented—a scientific recording instrument. In the second section of art history, the primary, but largely unconscious, concern of the artists was with the transformation of the content of art to a point where it became possible to realize the potentialities of the future epoch. This second section, the Transitional-Period, was in a sense the reverse of the first section in which art began with the Inventive and reached the Mimetic stage; thus non-Camera art has passed from a scientific Mimetic to a scientific Inventive stage. Today we are in the beginning of the third section of art history, and a few advanced artists are concerned with the "art" building method of nature (not its art products alone, as in the first section), in order that they may utilize it for building their own objects of art. Thus those who have chosen the genuine Constructionist direction are in a position similar to the first artists, the artists of Paleolithic times, who made the first "scientific" efforts in art. For they were the first artists who passed from the observation of nature to the task of so manipulating their materials that the results produced images having recognizable correspondence to the observed. Past non-Camera artists were largely concerned with the scientific observation and recording of nature's macro-reality; future non-Camera artists will be increasingly concerned with the scientific observation and utilization of nature's Structural Process. Art has passed from one long development of man's recording of nature-art to what will now also be another long development of man's inventing his own art.

44. A. J. Carlson: "Science and the Supernatural," *The Scientific Monthly,* LIX:87, August, 1944.

45. Freud, *New Introductory Lectures,* p. 219.

46. From A. N. Whitehead: *Adventures of Ideas,* p. 177. By permission of The Macmillan Company, publishers.

But to participate in this development artists must develop their "consciousness of abstracting," become conscious of the fundamental nature and consequences of the abstracting from nature by which they produce their art. In time, then, the extant confusion will be eliminated by artists who are coherently conscious of the needs for our art times and the most efficient methods by which to realize them. This is the only way we can create a genuine science of art for the future epoch which we are now entering.

Each new field of science is precisely that, *a new field of science.* We must create a new field of science for art; we cannot simply adopt the science of any other field. Artists in becoming the new scientists of art will eventually bring forth new scientific knowledge, and create an extension of science through art. The new art-scientists will produce knowledge of value to the other fields of science (as happens with the creation of any new field of science), and so influence the future course of science in general. Then artists will have discarded their ludicrous imaginary halos and become men who are conscious of the particular world of knowledge in which they live.

We venture to predict that when art becomes an established science, there will occur the most tremendous revolution ever to arise in the history of mankind. There will then be realized that unity within and between all the different aspects of culture which existed in the earlier stages of human evolution. When this happens again, it may well be because the science of art has been the means by which mankind in general has realized and accepted the higher potentialities of science.

And often when I see one of these men take this work in hand I wonder whether he will not put it to his nose like the ape, and ask me whether it is something to eat. 212

Leonardo da Vinci

The fact that art which is really non-figurative is rare does not detract from its value; evolution is always the work of pioneers, and their followers are always small in number. This following is not a clique; it is the result of all the existing social forces; it is composed of all those who through innate or acquired capacity are ready to represent the existing degree of human evolution. 232

Piet Mondrian

In this way there are some who stay on the terrain of pure art, that is to say, who produce painting or sculpture, and there are others who depart toward a more or less architectural realization. But all prepare the fusion of the plastic arts in a new architecture. Although there is still a great deal to do and to develop, one can already observe, as well in our palpable environment as in our social life, that the end of painting and especially of sculpture is slowly appearing, and that these arts will lose themselves in a new architecture which will contain the whole. 231

Piet Mondrian

At the threshhold of the 20th century, the great scientific discoveries, the prodigious development of machines, all the results which spring from it came to upset all technics. Life became collective, a new perspective was developed in our environment where geometry, precision mathematics triumph. The machine, by its pure functionalism, propagates in life the habit of logic, of clarity, of exactitude. 373

Jean Gorin

Another man is born from the cooperative life resulting from mechanization; the development of scientific rationalism in everything created in him a new vision of life, freed from all the dross of the past, in the sphere of culture and art; the great aesthetic revolutions occurring in the course of the last fifty years have permitted him to acquire and develop a sensibility which the man of the past did not have. 374.

Jean Gorin

Not a few stupidities in art have been justified with humanism. If a straight line cannot be drawn freehand, a ruler is used. Writing with a machine is clearer, more legible and more beautiful than handwriting. We do not want artistic handwriting. If a circle cannot be drawn freehand, a compass is used. All instruments intellectually created out of need for perfection are recommended. 372

Theo van Doesburg

Over a century ago the recording of nature-art evolved into the mass-production Machine-art of the Camera, and nature recordings became available on a large scale. How many at this late date realize the full revolutionary impact of Photography? Many would still deny the products of the Camera the status of an "art." But at least we seldom hear much objection to this "art" form today, even though the label "art" is still denied it by many. In time the Constructionist form of Machine-art will be accepted quite as naturally as the Photograph. For of all the present forms of non-Camera art that have arisen in our times, only the genuine Constructionist works are suitable for meeting the demands of mass production; they are adapted to being made from beginning to end with precision Machines, the instruments of mass production. With the Constructionist solution, non-recording art also has evolved into the mass-production

Machine stage. It is important to emphasize that Constructionists did not deliberately set out to devise an art that could be mass-produced. Art has evolved, just as have so many other fields, to a certain point in these times of mass production. Consequently painting has been transformed into the Machine-art of Photography and sculpture has been transformed into the Machine-art of Constructions.

Many insist that anything "mechanically" produced, and which can be mechanically *re*produced, surely cannot be "art" as we have "known" it in the past. But that is precisely the point—it is not "art" as we have "known" it; it was impossible in the past. It is an art for a Science-Machine culture, just as necessary for our times as past kinds of art were for past times. Lewis Mumford says something relevant to these problems when he writes: "But face to face with these new machines and instruments, with their hard surfaces, their rigid volumes, their stark shapes, a fresh kind of perception and pleasure emerges: to interpret this order becomes one of the new tasks of the arts. While these new qualities existed as facts of mechanical industry, they were not generally recognized as values until they were interpreted by the painter and the sculptor; and so they existed in an indifferent anonymity for more than a century." [1] Mondrian achieved considerable insight into this problem. Consider, for example, the following: "Execution and technique play an important part in the aim of establishing a more or less objective vision which the essence of the non-figurative work demands. The less obvious the artist's hand the more objective will the work be. This fact leads to a preference for a more or less mechanical execution or to the employment of materials produced by industry. Hitherto, of course, these materials have been imperfect from the point of view of art. If these materials and their colors were more perfect and if a technique existed by which the artist could easily cut them up in order to compose his work as he conceives it, an art more real and more objective in relation to life than painting would arise." [2]

Today we are faced with new problems for a new culture, whether we like it or not. And in this world the chisel and the brush will eventually be placed in a show case of a museum displaying various antiquated art tools of man. The Machine has become a new medium and instrument for a new art. As Mumford says further: "Expression through the machine implies the recognition of relatively new esthetic terms: precision, calculation, flawlessness, simplicity, economy. Feeling attaches itself in these new forms to different qualities than those that made handicraft so entertaining. Success here consists in the elimination of the non-essential, rather than, as in handicraft decoration, in the willing production of superfluity, contributed by the worker out of his own delight in the work. The elegance of a mathematical equation, the inevitability of a series of physical inter-relations, the naked quality of the material itself, the tight logic of the whole—these are the ingredients that go into the design of machines: and they go equally into products that have been properly designed for machine production. In handicraft it is the worker who is represented: in machine design it is the work. In handicraft, the personal touch is emphasized, and the imprint of the worker and his tool are both inevitable: in machine work the impersonal prevails, and if the worker leaves any tell-tale evidence of his part in the operation, it is a defect or a flaw. Hence the burden of machine design is in the making of the original pattern: it is here that trials are made, that errors are discovered and buried, that the creative process as a whole is concentrated. Once the master-pattern is set, the rest is routine. . . ." [3]

Similarly the "original" of a Construction is made with Machines, which in turn can repeat exactly, any number of times, each operation and result which occurred in making the *first* original. This is a most important fact—that the Machine can repeat any Constructionist object precisely as the "original" appears. Repetitions from the first "original" are indistinguishable from it. Consequently, regardless of how many times the Machine is made to repeat any Constructionist work, each repetition will be exactly as "original" as the *first original* made. Such results are incomparably superior to all other forms of art "reproduction," except those of the Camera, because in all other methods there exists only one "original," and all repetitions (reproductions) are different from it.

1. Lewis Mumford: *Technics and Civilization*, p. 334, Harcourt, Brace and Co., New York, 1934.

2. Piet Mondrian: "Plastic Art and Pure Plastic Art." *Plastic Art and Pure Plastic Art*, p. 61. We cannot, however, take seriously Mondrian's criticisms of the new materials. The great difficulty for those artists who have been using them is to possess the funds for buying and fabricating these materials.

3. Mumford, *Technics and Civilization*, pp. 350-351.

It is interesting to note some of the similarities between Photographs and Constructions. Each is a case of the Machine invading the art field. Both make "original" works of art available to everyone. Both are mass-production arts. The Camera makes it possible for everyone to achieve "original" recordings of the old content with greater precision than any of the greatest recording artists of the past could have ever achieved. Constructionist works will make it possible for everyone to have contemporary non-Camera works of art in their "original" form; heretofore this was only possible for the wealthy. *In other words, neither "originals" nor "reproductions" in the old sense occur in the Constructionist's or Photographer's art. What does occur would have seemed absolutely impossible until recent times, in that each work in the new arts combines both factors, i.e., each "reproduction" of each original results in another original work of art.* Each reproduction would be indistinguishable from any others.

Therefore, in the future no one needs to be restricted to some undersized, inadequate repro-
duction of a great work of contemporary art. Each person can have an actual original, as original as that possessed by anyone else of the same object. This will be the first time in the whole history of non-Camera art in which everyone, potentially at least, can have "original" works of the very best artists of the times, exactly as the artists intended them to appear. For the first time the non-Camera visual arts can acquire the tremendous influence resulting from mass production of "original" works of art, as is already the case with Literature, Music, Photography, Radio, Television and Architecture.

The implications of mass production of original works of art are tremendous. For one thing, it would put a welcome end to the old notion of "originals" with all the destructive, possessive behavior of many of those who own them, because in the new art it will be impossible for any one to distinguish the first "original" from any one of its hundreds, thousands, millions of "reproductions." Actually, in the old sense, original works of art cease to exist! But a new kind of "original" art comes into existence, bringing with it all kinds of needed corrective measures. For instance, the new kind of "original" art will be desired, not for the pleasure of possessing the only, expensive original, but for the experience which the art itself makes possible. Artists and laymen who put printed reproductions on their walls are often far more genuine in their appreciation than many who have an original sequestered in their homes. The former wish to *possess the experience* of the art to such a degree that they are willing to take whatever substitute they can get; the latter too often want the art because they alone possess a highly sought after original which no one else can experience unless they permit him the privilege. This has further destructive consequences in that the artists who inaugurate necessary changes in art are restricted by the efforts of dealers and collectors to maintain the value of the old in terms of money. Art thus becomes a kind of stock market.

Because of these highly destructive practices, works of art which are very important and necessary to the education of young artists, as well as of the public, are confined to a small circle, many of whom are devoid of any genuine appreciation of the art. Perhaps one day the laws of human culture will consider it criminal for anyone to possess privately any work of art that cannot be duplicated to the perfection of the "original." This would make the world's art available only to agencies which would put it where it belongs, on constant display and available to all.[4]

Today the nearest thing to public art is the museum. But these institutions, with very few exceptions, are operated by frustrated individuals who know more about society gatherings than about art education. As Piet Mondrian once wrote: "Art suffers from the ignorance of the public, educated by incompetent writers, critics, teachers, museum committees, etc."[5] Very, very few of them have ever joined the artists in the risks he takes; the rest wait, ready to abuse or praise according to what happens to the artist.

In these times of the new Machine arts it becomes apparent that the historic role of the "patron of art" is coming to a close. In fact the entrance of "government" and "business" into the field of art

4. Another desirable law would require that all such public institutions of all countries would maintain a constant series of travelling loans of all works which are movable, so that all museums would eventually exhibit nearly all existent works and keep on doing so.

5. Mondrian, "Liberation from Oppression in Art and Life," *Plastic Art and Pure Plastic Art,* p. 40.

collecting, although so far resulting in obnoxious art, indicates that the old patron of art is already pretty much a thing of the past. With him will pass into oblivion the rest of the old retinue—critics, dealers, museum officials—in short, the majority of dilettantes who are parasites upon the artist and the art public.

In the future the Machine will help to prevent money values from playing such an important role. Pecuniary differences will not determine who shall be the honored possessors of "original" works of art. As Frank Lloyd Wright put it: "The machine is here to stay. It is the forerunner of the democracy that is our dearest hope." [6] The artist should accept every genuine opportunity he has for mass-producing his work. Thus he will gradually destroy the stupid notions of rarity in art as regards money values. Lewis Mumford, writing on this problem, says: "The machine devaluates rarity: instead of producing a single unique object, it is capable of producing a million others just as good as the master model from which the rest are made. The machine devaluates age: for age is another token of rarity, and the machine, by placing its emphasis upon fitness and adaptation, prides itself on the brand-new rather than on the antique: instead of feeling comfortably authentic in the midst of rust, dust, cobwebs, shaky parts, it prides itself on the opposite qualities—slickness, smoothness, gloss, cleanness. The machine devaluates archaic taste: for taste in the bourgeoise sense is merely another name for pecuniary reputability, and against that standard the machine sets up the standards of function and fitness. The newest, the cheapest, the commonest objects may, from the standpoint of pure esthetics, be immensely superior to the rarest, the most expensive, and the most antique. To say all this is merely to emphasize that the modern technics, by its own essential nature, imposes a great purification of esthetics: that is, it strips off from the object all the barnacles of association, all the sentimental and pecuniary values which have nothing whatever to do with esthetic form, and it focuses attention upon the object itself." [7]

We would happily agree with those who claim that mass-production methods in art will make it into a mere "common" commodity, for we believe that if the value of art depends upon its rarity and great cost, then it cannot have any more value for mankind than fur coats and the like. We have had enough of that attitude towards art. Art has an incomparably more important role than that. Its function is to give humans more satisfaction to live in a more human way. So let us make it available to everyone now that we can. Let everyone have an "original" work of contemporary art as a distinct part of everyday life.

The Machine as an art tool is an accomplished fact, and rather than foreshadowing the "death of art," as so many insist, it has already been applied to the creation of a new art.

One of the problems to be solved in the new art, and one on which the new generation of Constructionists is working, is that of color for Constructions. The Constructions, figures 141, 174, 200, and 228, present one step in the solution of the problem of color in the new art. Here the artist employed the device of blended colors in order to free the Constructionist from the limitations of one color for each surface or object. See also figure 196. (Incidentally, Camera artists are also working to perfect the color factor in their art.) All kinds of colored materials are now available from the field of industry. Then there is the medium of the future, color with electric light. This has numerous potentialities, especially in the different effects such light will have on the problem of form. Matthew Luckiesh writes: "Modern artificial light is so controllable in every respect that it may be considered as a relatively new medium of expression.

6. Frank Lloyd Wright: *On Architecture,* p. 24, reprinted by permission of the publishers, Duell, Sloan and Pearce, Inc. Copyright 1941 by Duell, Sloan and Pearce, Inc.

7. Mumford, *Technics and Civilization,* p. 353.

For centuries artists have used various media, such as paints, to beautify the artificial world and to please and intrigue human beings. With the advent of bottled electric light the possibilities of the use of light as an expressive medium increased enormously. Already many uses have been made in many appropriate fields. The expressiveness of light is only limited by the knowledge, skill and taste of the user and by the capacity of human beings to enjoy this use of light. Considering that light also has the unique factor of mobility, effect can follow effect rapidly and without end. Material civilization has progressed far from a lowly beginning and artificial light has been a powerful force which in many respects has led the parade of progress. May it not be possible that the use of modern light, so controllable in brightness, color and mobility, may even evolve into a new fine art? If it does it may well be man's most abstract achievement in art, even finer and more ethereal than music. If its use attains such heights, artificial light may well deserve to be known in still another and a finer sense as the torch of civilization." [8]

Many of the potentialities of the new mediums will not be discovered until the evolution of the new art has gone far enough to make it possible to see them. But it is possible to predict some of the future steps long before we are able to attain them. And we shall acquire useful predictability, if we first learn how to make and complete each successive step properly.

One important problem facing future Constructionists is the introduction of the dynamic factor, at first with the forms, later with color, then with color produced by artificial light; eventually the dynamics of both form and color will be employed in the single work of art. In short, the eventual goal of the artist will be to exploit the factor of the four-dimensionality of time-space. [9]

Of course there have already been attempts by a few artists to pass *hastily* on to the dynamic stage; they have been in a hurry to try everything before digesting much of anything, as though desiring to avoid the various problems of any stage in order to exploit superficially the "dramatics" of every stage. They are the ones who tire easily of the discipline and experience which is necessary if the artist is to evolve profitably from the simple steps which have been by no means outgrown as yet. And so once they have exploited all the various medium potentialities, they seem to spend the rest of their lives oscillating from Constructions to painting and back again, from recordings to inventions, always trying to keep ahead of their anxieties. From such individuals we can expect little in the way of discovering the correct method for exploiting such factors as color and dynamic time-space, and the new mediums and tools of the new art. Eventually and inevitably these artists desert the Constructionist direction for one that requires far less of them.

Frank Lloyd Wright has written of the new Machine tool: "We see this adversary to the Old Order, the Machine, as—at last—a sword to cut old bonds and provide escape to Freedom; we see it as the servant and savior of the New Order—if only it be creatively used by man!" [10] This is the crucial point—the way in which the Machine as a new art tool is regarded and used!

Ever since 1839 when a successful Camera was invented, there has been a steady argument as to whether the Machine can be used as a producer of art. Today "Modernists" as well as Academicians vociferously object to the mass-production Machine methods inherent in Camera and Constructionist art. Neither group can comprehend the new arts made with mass-production Machine methods, because each is dominated by old primitive methods of experiencing-thinking-making art. Objections to the new formulations come to the same old story—ignorance and so reluctance to discard useless, harmful habits which essentially belong to other times, and a fear of adopting the new beneficial direction. Once we realize this

8. From *Torch of Civilization*, by Matthew Luckiesh, p. 14. Courtesy of G. P. PUTNAM'S SONS, New York, 1940.

9. Many critics find no difficulty in regarding the Cubists' practice of depicting objects as though viewed from many points at once, and the Futurists' practice of trying to depict objects in motion, as most astonishing and unconscious manifestations or parallels of Minkowski's discovery of the space-time principle, which was announced in 1908, the very year in which Cubism began. But actually the Cubists by their practice were trying to free themselves from the forms of the actual object, and thus release the Inventive factor; it was similar in function to the practice of turning the canvas upside down and then painting some more upon it. As for the Futurists, war and fascism interested them far more than time-space problems.

10. Frank Lloyd Wright: *Modern Architecture*, p. 62, Princeton University Press, Princeton, 1931.

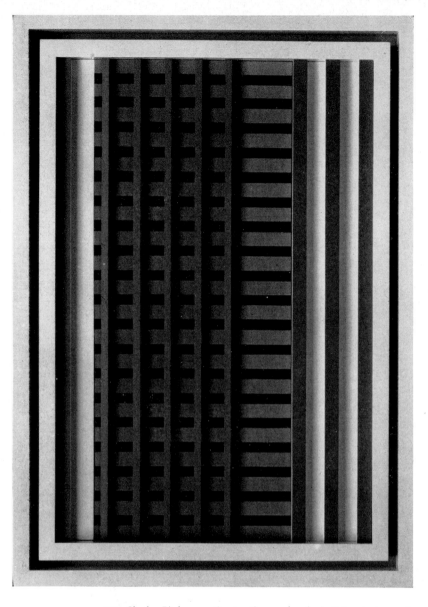

202. Charles Biederman, Construction, 11/39 (11). Painted glass and
wood, 29″x21½″x1⅞″.

fact we shall also realize that many a "radical" was never radical at all and many that were are not any
longer. It is no accident that Dali, the epitome of reaction in "Modern" art, speaks of the "hideous
mechanical civilization that is your [the artist's] enemy," and that, as Soby puts it, "wherever possible
Dali has made living organisms usurp, jeopardize or obviate the function of machinery and machine
products. . . ." [11]

The hostility towards Constructionist and even Photographic works as products of advanced
Machine, mass-production methods, and as legitimate forms of "art," is partly the result of unconscious
worship of the hand as a divine instrument of art. The products of the artist's hand are considered
majestically superior, yes, even mystic, as compared to the crudity, coldness, heartlessness of Machine
products. [12] But the premises, the distinctions upon which such arguments rest stem from false observation
and knowledge.

11. J. T. Soby: *Salvador Dali,* pp. 22–23, Museum of Modern Art, New York, 1941.
12. Thus in the book *Unit One,* devoted to the works of a group of "Modern" English artists, individual Photographs of

203. Charles Biederman, Construction, 4/40 (4). Painted wood and glass. 31″x21″x2¾″.

In the first place the problem here is not that of an art done only with the hands or only with the Machine. The issues involve semantic ignorance, which becomes apparent from the following. The only artists who used the hands alone as their art tools were those very early ones of Paleolithic times, and others at very low stages of Primitive cultures. These artists used the hand, the fingers, as an art tool, e.g., to draw through the clay or to apply the paint. But very early there began the simple handicraft methods—actually an extension of the hands. And since then artists have not only always employed some kind of "mechanical" tools to produce their art, but also have constantly sought to improve the mechanical function of their tools. In the early Oriental cultures we see the earliest forms of the Machine, used, significantly enough, in such arts as those of the potter and the Architect. In this stage the hands of the operator must be in almost constant operation with the Machine. To a large extent we are still in this stage of Machine culture, because of the limitations imposed by men, not by the Machine.

the hands of each artist are reproduced. In the case of the few Architects included in this group, the hands are not shown, for the simple reason that it would be quite ludicrous to do so. Indeed, one could write an illuminating paper on the "Modern" artist's primitive worship of the hand.

204. Naum Gabo, The Red Cavern (Space Construction). Celluloid, glass and metal.
Collection of the artist. Photo, Museum of Modern Art.

The problem then is not one of the "hand" or the "Machine" alone producing art, but one of human beings employing some kind of a mechanical aid in the production of their art. The methods for making art are no more stationary than the art itself; both pass through stages of development. Thus when we speak of a general form of art that belongs to particular times, so likewise we can speak of the tools of artists. Consequently, those who regard Machine tools as though they were independent of human contact, overlook the fact that the so-called "hand" products—painting and sculpture—are not merely "hand" products any more than a Construction or a Photograph is. Once this is realized non-sense distinctions can be avoided. Then it can be seen that the so-called hand products are the result of employing very primitive mechanical methods, and that the new arts of Photography and Constructions result from the use of highly developed mechanical instruments and methods.

So long as the Machine as an art tool is judged in terms of the old, now useless primitive tools, the full potentialities and necessity of the Machine will not be realized. In short, the third stage in man's tool development—the completely automatic Machine—is held back by men and not the potentialities of Machine inventors. In this stage man is no longer the slave of the Machine; the Machine is the slave of man.

606

Those who have nothing to offer us except warnings of the destructive possibilities of the Machine, are the ones who desire to see it as nothing else. The fact is that when the Machine is destructive it has always been because *men* have used the Machine *destructively!* As long ago as 1903 Wright put it clearly when he said: "But, I say, usurped by Greed and deserted by its natural interpreter, the Artist, the Machine is only the creature, not the Creator of this iniquity! I say the Machine has noble possibilities unwillingly forced to this degradation, degraded by the Arts themselves. Insofar as the true capacity of the Machine is concerned it is itself the crazed victim of Artist-impotence. Why will the American Artist not see that human thought in our age is stripping off its old form and donning another; why is the Artist unable to see that this is his glorious opportunity to create and reap anew?" [13]

In other words, this latest stage in the development of the Machine can only be achieved by taking the control of the Machine from the crude, undeveloped personalities who exploit the Machine as ruthlessly as they exploit the men who work them. We repeat, the Machine can *only* be what humans make it become; whatever we attribute to the Machine can only be attributed to those who employ the Machine. If the Machine is today largely regarded as the producer only of mediocre art, then we must be reminded that this is not the inevitable character of the Machine. This situation exists only because the tremendous potentialities of the Machine, in all its manifold social consequences, are left largely in the hands of mediocre, commercialized mentalities, who wilfully exploit it along with the men and materials that are involved. And this state of affairs will continue in art as long as so many hold onto the old ways with the obstinacy of ignorance.

The new Machines are producing the most remarkable materials and tools which the artist has ever had at his command. On this problem Charles Beard has said: "The machine régime does not do away with the necessity for designing or reduce the opportunities for the practice of that craft: it transfers the operation from the shop to the laboratory; and it remains to be seen whether great aesthetic powers will not flourish after the first storm of capitalism has passed. In any case, it must be admitted that the 'cheap and nasty' character of machine-made goods, so marked everywhere, may really be due to the profit-making lust and the desire of the multitude to have imitations of the gew-gaws loved by the patricians, not to the inherent nature of machine industry. Possibly what is lost in the merits of individual objects of beauty may be more than offset by city and community planning, realizing new types of aesthetic ideals on a vast, democratic basis. Certainly the worst of the aesthetic offences created by the machine—the hideous factory town—can be avoided by intelligent co-operative action, as the garden-city movement faintly foreshadows. In a hundred years the coal-consuming engine may be as obsolete as the Dodo and the Birminghams, Pittsburghs, and Essens of the modern world live only in the records of the historians. However this may be, the aesthetes of the future will have to work within the limitations and opportunities created by science and the machine, directed, it may be hoped, by a more intelligent economy and nobler concepts of human values." [14]

It might be further pointed out to those conservative individuals who abhor the notion of mass-produced, Machine art, that not only "mechanical" production of art, but even mass production is a very ancient effort. Here we need not go into the entire history of this activity; we have only to call attention to the arts of printing, woodcuts, etchings, lithography, etc. It is, incidentally, of interest to note that the natural order of development which we have witnessed throughout history regarding the linear medium—that is, development from drawing first to painting next—holds true even in our present problem. Hence, mass-production methods first appeared in the line drawing arts, such as woodcuts, etching, lithography, and only later in painting—in the shape of Photography. The old order of development is retained in other respects also; for example, the first major development in art, the art of writing, was the first to reach Machine, mass-production methods with the invention of the printing press.

There have also been printed reproductions of paintings, and mass production of plaster casts of sculpture, which have given many of us the only opportunity we shall ever have to see important works of art. More recently we have had mass production in such arts as Music, Architecture, Films, Radio,

Prior uses of machinery in art

13. Frank Lloyd Wright: *Modern Architecture*, p. 16.
14. Charles Beard: in *Whither Mankind*, pp. 21–22, edited with an introduction by C. A. Beard, Longmans, Green and Co., Inc., New York, 1928.

Television. Many who feel fortunate that they can have prints of things they cannot experience otherwise, or who enjoy without complaint the mass-produced arts of music and literature, are the first to balk at a "visual" art which solves this problem by producing "originals" on a mass scale.

Ironically enough, many of those who object to mass-produced art have been forced by conditions to make attempts in this very direction, if in a limited sense. Let us consider one example: some years ago a group of sculptors, whose objects range from nudes to donkeys, decided to "mass-produce" their art, meanwhile trying to preserve the old *business* of the "original" work of art. This was done in a number of ways: first, the artist personally scratched his name on each reproduction, just as he does on an original; in other words he autographed each piece. Next the number of reproductions of each piece of work was limited and their advertisements repeatedly emphasized the words "original" and "limited edition." In this way it was hoped to retain the coveted glamor of rarity, characteristic of original works of art and presumably to keep the prices from falling too low.[15]

Such artists compromise with the mass-production solution just as they compromise with other art problems of their times. Certainly no genuine concern with getting art to the vast majority could motivate such a pseudo-attempt at mass production. The initial motivation would appear to be that their outmoded form of art was no longer adequately supported by the old "patron" of art (now also an outmoded factor). By increasing the number of "originals" for each piece, they attempted to expand the number of buyers in the middle-class group to take the place of the old patron. In short, they were trying to preserve all the old values—rarity of original works of art along with the old outmoded content—while trying to take advantage of the new conditions in order to solve monetary difficulties. Obviously the problems and opportunities of mass production cannot be met by such art. In the older arts of painting and sculpture each work is made with the most primitive handicraft tools and was never intended to be repeated by Machines. To force the Machine to imitate painted or sculpted surfaces is to submit it to tasks for which it was never made or suited. This is not to deny the usefulness of reproductions, but rather to point out the fallacy of using Machine tool methods of reproduction for works of art which were originally fabricated with primitive tool methods. To do so is to compromise both the work of art and the potentialities of the medium of reproduction.

Perhaps the most vociferous objection to mass production of Machine-art is the claim that this direction will limit the diversity of expression, the originality in art of which men are capable. It is generally expected that the young artist will be influenced by his predecessors, that he will learn the best that has been learned by those before him. He is in fact measured at first by his capacity to acquire this learning. All too soon, however, nowadays he is expected to be "original" above everything else, to prove that he is a genius independent of the efforts of others. And since no holds are barred as to what one may do in art, in no time at all our young artist has proved himself as "original" as anyone. Thus artists attempt to pass from one extreme to another—from nothing but "influence" to nothing but "originality." If you poke around the debris of Modern art, you will certainly find plenty of "originality" and "diversity" —*but originality for what?!*

15. For one of their advertisements see the *New York Times*, Magazine Section for November 16, 1941.

205. Naum Gabo, Construction in Space, Spiral Theme, 1941.

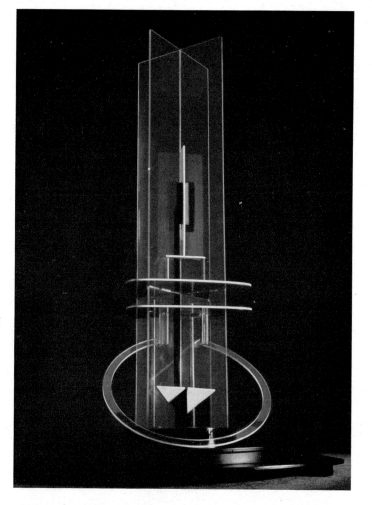

206. Naum Gabo, Column (Space Construction), 1923. Glass and metal, 38½″ high. Collection of the artist. Photo, Museum of Modern Art.

Originality & Individuality of the Artist.

What is needed today is not a suppression, but a revision of the diversity and originality potentials of artists. In order to understand the situation better, let us briefly trace the development of the problem. In the early history of man artists in a particular culture worked in a single direction more or less like each other. In those days each artist found it essential to borrow freely from the works of his fellow artists in order to contribute usefully to the art culture as-a-whole. By late Greek times, however, individuality began to be considered an important quality. But this trend was interrupted for about a thousand years by the totalitarian regime of the Christians. With the rise of the Italian Renaissance individuality was again pursued in the various aspects of life as well as in art. This change did not mean that artists were no longer borrowing from each other; they simply were not borrowing in the way of the past. They were becoming less concerned with creating an art in which all effort was funnelled into a particular mold. Although still pursuing one major direction of development, artists sought more freedom for the individual realization of that direction. Instead of each artist *primarily* striving to add to the greatness of art in general, each one now strove *primarily* to achieve the greatest art in his individual works. Artists were moving ahead on their own authority, relatively speaking.

610

The quest for individuality was, of course, a necessary and fruitful stage in the evolution of man, but it has served its purpose in the old sense. (This direction long ago reached the end of its useful development. This is clearly seen in the fact that the kind of clothes the "great individual" artist wears, whether he likes cats or dogs, his female companions, etc., etc., have at least equal news value with the artist's art.) Today the old notion of individualism has disintegrated into attitudes of despair and irresponsibility. The anarchy of the individual has been solved in some places by regression to the ancient form of totalitarian government. Where this degenerate solution has not yet occurred, we find Modern and/or Surrealist artists practicing their solution, straining every effort to achieve a world of their own, a private world of art. The majority of artists today are seeking to be unique and original merely for the sake of being unique and original, as though uniqueness and originality were the height of all accomplishment. Thus, as we have pointed out, most artists assume that "influences" are only for the young and originality only for the mature artist. Actually it is useless to be either without being usefully both. To be usefully influenced, to be usefully original, an artist must acquire and then develop the useful discoveries and accomplishments of his predecessors and contemporaries throughout his life. In short, these problems are relative.

Now we have seen that the Constructionists release the manifold potentialities of man to invent his own art, independent of taking on the specific organizations of form-color as seen in the art of nature. This does not mean a single restricted type of art—nor the elimination of the old art, since the Photographer continues that. The new art offers opportunity for originality for every artist making Constructions. But originality of artists will be exerted in a far different, more efficient, useful manner than in the past or the present.

We have traced our problem from the early collective behavior of artists to the individualistic one that is still largely extant today. It is very apparent, however, that the epoch of individual laissez-faire has long ago run its course. We can now regard the next change that is already working—the attitude that we call cooperative. Artists are approaching the end of a transition in which they will return in some respects to basic orientations of pre-Aristotelian times. That is, the art of the general culture will become more important than it has been in the previous over-individualistic period. But in the new effort to place more emphasis upon the general art culture we must avoid dictatorial methods. To imitate the collective control over artists of ancient times is to lose the opportunities for cooperative attitudes potential to the present, and end in the art sickness of every totalitarian nation.

With the new art it is possible to arrive at an orientation similar to the two previous types— collective and individualistic, but superior to both; that is, it is now possible to resolve the schism of the past and free both factors into a new and more useful kind of behavior. Once more "art" can become a product for mankind in general, as in earlier cultures, and can be spread throughout the fabric of society in "original" works of art.

In the early cultures of man *all* artists were compelled to do certain things in their art; individuality was almost completely suppressed. The new objective would be crucially different on this score. Each artist would be judged according to his own "freely" exercised capacity to exploit usefully the discoveries that occur in the general art effort. The object would be to exploit those as yet largely untouched advantages of both individualism and cooperativeness, rather than oppose one to the complete exclusion of the other. Attempts to do the latter do not eliminate one or the other; they only drive both to operate unsanely. In the long run our major objective would be to extend the horizon of life experience that is potential for each individual being. Alfred Whitehead writes: "The other side of the evolutionary machinery, the neglected side, is expressed by the word *creativeness*. The organisms can create their own environment. For this purpose, the single organism is almost helpless. The adequate forces require societies of coöperating organisms. But with such coöperation and in proportion to the effort put forward, the environment has a plasticity which alters the whole ethical aspect of evolution." [16] This holds true for the practice of art, which is a major formative factor in the environment of mankind. "Cooperating organisms" could achieve an art of the human race, not one directed towards personal, class, localized or nationalized objectives.

16. From A. N. Whitehead: *Science and the Modern World,* pp. 163-164. By permission of The Macmillan Company, publishers.

Such an objective is not only possible but essential to the survival of the new art. The individual is not over-evaluated; the new art and the very tools of the art compel a cooperative attitude. Uniqueness lies in how much one can contribute to the direction taken by a group, not in how unique one can be from anyone else.

Observation of recent events in art indicates that the views we are here advocating are not new, but have been forming for some time. In the three main streams that compose the Transitional-Period—Impressionism, Post-Impressionism and Cubism—there was an ever increasing cooperative effort and agreement upon a definite objective. By the time Cubism was completed, the works of some of the artists are so much alike that it is difficult, even for the artists who created the art, to distinguish who is the individual author of a particular work.[17] H. S. Ede gives an interesting example of this in his report of Picasso's remarks when viewing some Cubist paintings by himself and Braque: "Is that you or me?" "It's mine—no, I'm mistaken."[18] So we see the Cubists inadvertently brought still another factor to its apparent realization. Again Cubism was the signal for another new development, inaugurating a new relationship between the individual artists themselves.

The Cubists deserted this attitude, but it has been carried on by those who continued the direction set by Cubism—the Two-Dimensionalists and Constructionists in particular. Thus Doesburg in 1924 predicted that art was moving towards a "common effort and a common conception, of a collective style."[19] And Mondrian, writing of the formation of the De Stijl group, said, "We also had the idea that collective art might be possible for the future."[20] In fact this tendency is very marked in their actual art. Pevsner and Gabo, the two foremost Constructionists from the original school, have in many respects worked with similar problems and solutions, yet the differences are very apparent. The Constructionists carried further the emphasis upon the cooperative objective; the Surrealists went to the very opposite extreme.

With the conclusion of Cubism, as we have already noted, two diametrically opposed art trends appeared. On the one hand the Dadaists, and later the Surrealists, sought to achieve complete unrestricted freedom for individual behavior. They threw all restraint to the winds under the delusion that now the opportunity for complete freedom from everything was theirs for the taking.[21] From this point of view the Surrealist Max Ernst was quite correct when he wrote: "Surrealism, in turning topsy-turvy the appearances and relationships of 'realities' has been able to hasten, with a smile on its lips, the general crisis of consciousness which must perforce take place in our time."[22] On the other hand, the Two-Dimensionalists and the Constructionists have continued the emphasis upon cooperative art development which had characterized the useful part of the Transitional-Period. They strove to put order into the crisis of consciousness that ensued after Cubism. They propose to profit from the earlier past in which artists were absolutely responsible to the culture, and the more recent past in which they were irresponsible to their culture. The objective is not to force all artists into a single mold, as in Egyptian times. Each artist will be "free" to utilize whatever he finds useful in the works of others in order to accelerate not only his individual development, but also the as-a-whole development of the general art culture. The artist's major responsibility will be to contribute to the general development of "art," as opposed to the present tendency to use the art of others in various disguises in order to create one's own individual, unique world of art.

---

17. Incidentally, this complaint was made in the beginning of the Transitional-Period, during Impressionism.

18. H. S. Ede: "Georges Braque," *Cahiers d'Art,* p. 78, Nos. 1 and 2, 1933. Translated by Harry Holtzman and Martin James.

19. As quoted by Goldwater in *Primitivism in Modern Painting,* p. 132, Harper and Brothers, New York, 1938.

20. Mondrian, "Towards the True Vision of Reality," *Plastic Art and Pure Plastic Art,* p. 14.

21. In this connection J. J. Sweeney's remarks in discussing Calder's art are especially significant: "The 'machine age' emphasis in the constructivists' materials was a limitation." (Museum of Modern Art Catalogue, *Alexander Calder,* pp. 8–9, New York, 1943.) But Calder, having avoided this alleged limitation, is able to express "humor," and thus, according to Sweeney, Calder's work is "a genial development of certain aspects of the dada movement." (Ibid., p. 9.)

22. Quoted by Hugnet, "In the Light of Surrealism," *Fantastic Art Dada Surrealism,* p. 52.

207. Jean Gorin, Relief, 1937. Painted wood.

208. Charles Biederman, Construction, 5/40 (5). Painted wood and metal. 52½″x62″x19″. Waiting room, The Interstate Clinic, Red Wing, Minnesota.

Most artists today are in a state of hectic anxiety and insecurity, caught in the general anarchy fostered by the unsane scramble to be different at any cost or deception. In the new way each artist could utilize openly any of the advances made by any other artists. He would be judged on the extent and quality of his capacity to absorb the best of his own art culture. In turn, whatever inventions the individual artist thus achieved would be utilized and developed further by still others in a very great number of different ways, so that he would accomplish far more than it would otherwise be possible for him to achieve in the span of a single lifetime. Then the artist would be part of a larger organismal experience, far more satisfactory than anything secured by the present concentration upon the puny singleness of self. In the new way there need be no fear that individual potentialities will be limited; on the contrary they will be expanded beyond anything we can now imagine.

The critical difference between the cooperative attitude and the collective and laissez-faire attitudes is that the former would insist upon democratic, responsible freedom rather than complete suppression of, or unlimited amounts of, freedom. We are always involved in inescapable limitations, in the sense that men can never attain absolute freedom in anything they do. The facts of human experience amply indicate that the greatest freedom possible in any times depends upon respecting the limitations of that freedom. As Frank Lloyd Wright said: "An artist's limitations are his best friends." [23] Every kind of art offers certain kinds of freedom; it is our responsibility to inquire precisely what are the consequences of pursuing each kind of freedom. On the basis of consequences we find that it is only through the Constructionist direction that the non-Camera artist can achieve the greatest degree of useful, responsible freedom today.

The future artist will not be judged primarily on how "different" he is from anyone else, but on the degree to which his work expresses his capacity to absorb the best that is present in art as a whole, and integrate it into his "individual" achievements in the general art effort. What we are advocating is the very form of behavior which enabled all the great creative men of history to make their contributions to the evolution of human beings. Present day scientists are very dependent upon a consciousness of this attitude. In that general field it is essential to build directly upon the discoveries made by others; in fact it is a critical necessity, if one intends to stay in the running. Goethe expressed this attitude well when he said: "What am I myself? What have I done? All that I have seen, heard, noted I have collected and used. My works are reverenced by a thousand different individuals. . . . Often I have reaped the harvest that others have sown. My work is that of a collective being and it bears Goethe's name." [24]

This point may be clarified by considering briefly a fundamental mechanism involved in the realization and revision of human culture. Alfred Korzybski calls it the *"time-binding* mechanism." In the book especially devoted to this subject Korzybski writes: "If we analyse the classes of life, we readily find that there are three cardinal classes which are radically distinct in function. A short analysis will disclose to us that, though minerals have various activities, they are not 'living.' The plants have a very definite and well known function—the transformation of solar energy into organic chemical energy. They are a class of life which appropriates one kind of energy, converts it into another kind and stores it up; in that sense they are a kind of storage battery for the solar energy; and so I define THE PLANTS AS THE CHEMISTRY-BINDING class of life.

"The animals use the highly dynamic products of the *chemistry-binding* class—the plants—as food, and those products—the results of plant-transformation—undergo in animals a further transformation into yet higher forms; and the animals are correspondingly a more dynamic class of life; their energy is kinetic; they have a remarkable freedom and power which the plants do not possess—I mean the freedom and faculty to move about in *space*; and so I define ANIMALS AS THE SPACE-BINDING CLASS OF LIFE.

"And now what shall we say of *human* beings? What is to be our definition of Man? Like the animals, human beings do indeed possess the *space-binding* capacity but, over and above that, human beings possess a most remarkable capacity which is entirely peculiar to them—I mean the capacity to

23. Wright, *On Architecture*, p. 24.
24. As quoted by Otto Rank in *Art and Artist*, p. 67, Alfred A. Knopf, Inc., New York, 1932.

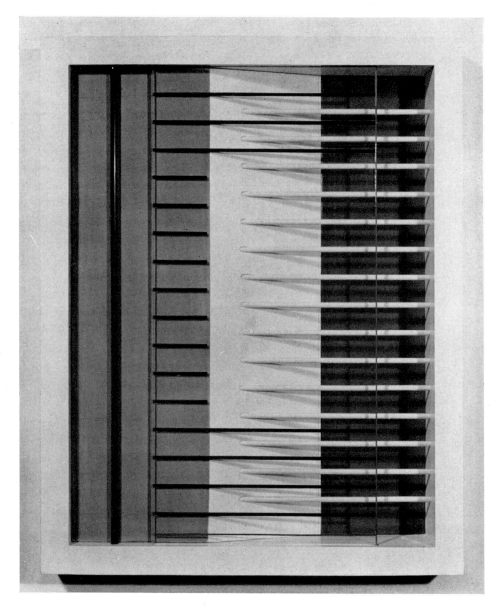

209. Joan Barnes, Construction No. 9, August, 1947. Painted wood, plexiglas and metal rods, 21½″x17½″x3¼″. Photo, Scott Tyler.

summarize, digest and appropriate the labors and experiences of the past; I mean the capacity to use the fruits of past labors and experiences as intellectual or spiritual capital for developments in the present; I mean the capacity to employ as instruments of increasing power the accumulated achievements of the all-precious lives of the past generations spent in trial and error, trial and success; I mean the capacity of human beings to conduct their lives in the ever increasing light of inherited wisdom; I mean the capacity in virtue of which man is at once the heritor of the by-gone ages and the trustee of posterity. And because humanity is just this magnificent natural agency by which the past lives in the present and the present for the future, I define HUMANITY, in the universal tongue of mathematics and mechanics, to be the TIME-BINDING CLASS OF LIFE." [25]

25. Alfred Korzybski: *Manhood of Humanity: the Art and Science of Human Engineering*, pp. 58–60, E. P. Dutton and Co., New York, 1923.

Thus while humans have certain capacities in common with animals, such as mobility, they also have capacities which are absent in the animal—*the ability to invent and progress from one generation to the next.* That is why, Korzybski points out, animals have no libraries, schools, science, art, etc., *precisely the factors which characterize humans as distinct from animals.* Says Korzybski: "In the human class of life, we find a new factor, non-existent in any other form of life; namely, that we have a capacity to collect all known experiences of different individuals. Such a capacity increases enormously the number of observations a single individual can handle, and so our acquaintance with the world around, and in, us becomes much more refined and exact. This capacity, which I call the time-binding capacity, is only possible because, in distinction from the animals, we have evolved, or perfected, extra-neural means by which, without altering our nervous system, we can refine its operation and expand its scope. Our scientific instruments record what ordinarily we cannot see, hear, etc. Our neural verbal centers allow us to exchange and accumulate experiences, although no one could live through all of them; and they would be soon forgotten if we had no neural and extra-neural means to record them." [26] We see, therefore, that animals abstract only so far and no further. This accounts for the fact that there is little or no change from one animal generation to another. Nevertheless the animal possesses the proper structure to operate naturally as a conservative organism; the human organism's structure is such that conservatism is an *un*natural form of behavior. And it is tragically harmful for humans to copy animals, for animal limitations when imposed upon humans lead to behavior which does not produce *natural, useful survival.*

Consciousness of these problems is imperative for the full utilization of the new orientations which have been forming especially during the last fifty years. Everything we have posited regarding the new behavior of the artist towards art and his relation as an individual to all other artists is simply the continuation and development of previous achievements. Constructionist art offers us the means by which we can usefully continue time-binding.

Our history-journey has now disclosed to us why Constructionist art is the only non-Camera activity pointing in a useful direction for our times. In this chapter we have noted more of its crucially civilizing functions, its necessity, if you please. We have pointed out that the range of the new direction is as wide as the range of mankind to invent; that the new art releases to ever further horizons that ability which differentiates a human being from an animal—the ability to invent on ever higher orders of abstraction, the limits of which cannot be ascertained. Thus the new avenues opened up by Constructionists to meet the demands of new conditions, the new epoch of human life, will not restrict the artist, as so many quickly assume. On the contrary, in place of the utter confused freedom in which artists do as they please, but hardly know what they please to do for more than a week at a time, the Constructionist direction offers the opportunity for more *useful freedom.* The freedom to be Constructionists has been won for us by the untold millions of artists before us who constructed the useful aspect of art history. Constructionist art offers for all of us the most satisfactory art-living possible in our times.

We have shown how this art eliminates the destructive factor of rarity in original works of art, releasing the most advanced art in an "original" form directly into the very stream of human existence. *Again* art can be for all of us. But in order to achieve this, both artists and non-artists need to realize the full implications of the fact that all levels of life are hooked up with all other levels: all of us must depend on each other for whatever life-fulfillments we may seek.

26. Korzybski, *Science and Sanity,* p. 376.

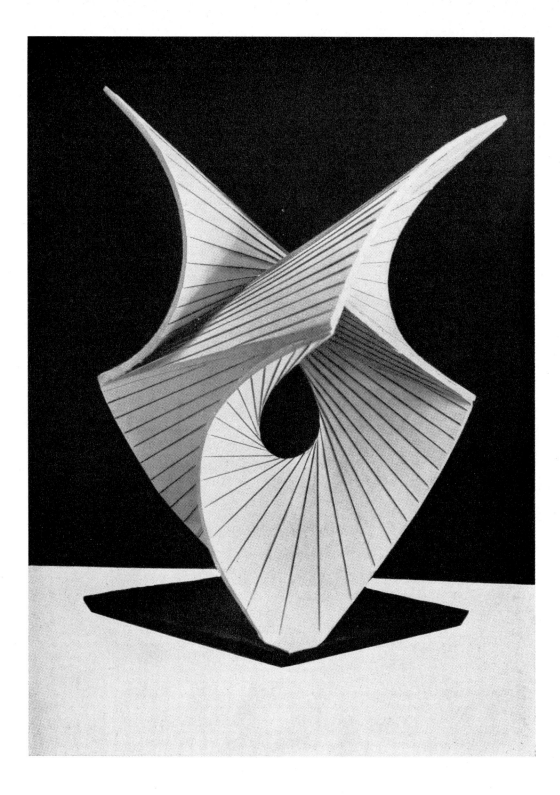

210. Antoine Pevsner, Surface Developing a Tangency with a Left Curve, 1938-39. Courtesy of The Art of This Century.

The major revisions and inventions of our times—Radio, Television, etc.—in being potentially accessible to everyone over the globe, increase tremendously the opportunities for achieving an international attitude among human beings—what Oliver Reiser has called the "world sensorium." It is in this direction that the revisions and inventions of Constructionist art move. It too is playing a tremendous role in influencing the shape of the new culture which is forming among all the peoples of the world. If we alter our outmoded attitudes, it is now possible for actual, original works of art to benefit the consciousness of all of us.

Concerning these problems, Jean Gorin has written: "Today every man may be for once a little clairvoyant and be very conscious that with the 20th century a great epoch opened, a decisive period in the evolution of humanity. Each man truly is conscious that he cannot remain indifferent before the profound revolution of values; in every domain man proceeds little by little toward his true human function; societies are going to be organized on the new rational and humane bases in which the free cultural development will be able to expand. A great current of new life animates the world today, a great current of profound forces is seething through all humanity and preparing it in spite of everything for a decisive ascent.

"To comprehend the reasons of existence of constructive art of the new times, it is necessary to be clearly conscious of all these social factors, because there are bonds which attach the artist intimately to the social life and make him one with the condition of the spirit of the epoch.

"In the face of the development of all this world-wide process the artist can no longer remain neutral, he can no longer content himself with a superb isolation in his ivory tower, he has more and more consciousness that his aesthetic activity, to be viable, must be an integral part of the great current of complete revision of values which embraces all the revolutionary activities in a strong interpenetration which is going to regenerate all social life." [27]

27. Jean Albert Gorin: "Constant Values in Art," unpublished manuscript, 1940.

An artist's limitations are his best friends. The machine is here to stay. It is the forerunner of the democracy that is our dearest hope. 366.
Frank Lloyd Wright

The old order is breaking anew, whether we subscribe to it or we do not. 367

Frank Lloyd Wright

The epoch of destruction is completely finished. A
new epoch begins—that of construction. 370
Theo van Doesburg

Now, Reality is not new except as we are new to
Reality. 365
                                    Frank Lloyd Wright

Now if vision has evolved in the past, why should
it not continue to evolve in the future? 284
                                    Oliver Reiser

We are witnessing the death-bed agonies of the
old system. (Seminar, 1941)   Alfred Korzybski

This [second world] war is only an episode in the
long series of necessary transitions from our nineteenth century liberal culture to a new social order
that has been shaping itself within the womb of
time. The old dream is fading, but a new one is
struggling for birth. 310
                                    Porter Sargent

In building a non-aristotelian-system, we have to
stress differences, build a 'non-system' on 'non-
allness', and reject identity. 179   Alfred Korzybski

Art, like all manifestations of humanity, is a function of life and its endless evolution.
Our mechanical and scientific epoch, succeeding
mystic, romantic and individualistic epochs of past
ages, demands that art fulfill a function entirely
adequate to life and the new needs of the man of
today. 374
                                    Jean Gorin

For the purposes of our discussion, we shall divide the history of man into three distinct periods—the pre-Aristotelian, Aristotelian and non-Aristotelian.[1] These encompass the principal levels in mankind's development.

In the first, or pre-Aristotelian stage, the individual as such does not exist, in the sense that a group attitude dominates. Nor are there sharp distinctions between the animate and inanimate, between man and the world outside, etc. Everything is highly INTERCHANGEABLE; there is complete identity of "everything with everything else." The structure of logic is, therefore, "one-valued." [2] In this stage man is predominantly thalamic; the cortex operates on a low level of development.

In the second, or Aristotelian stage, first formulated by Aristotle and elaborated by his followers, we find everything verbally split into isolated compartments: "body" and "mind," "emotion" and "intellect," "good" and "bad," etc. In the frequency of either-or terms there is evidence of the essentially two-valued structure of the logic. Where before no segments were fundamentally distinguishable within the whole, now there were sharp distinctions. And where in the previous stage there had been submission to the dictates of the "senses," in the Aristotelian stage the verbal level predominated. In short, men were at first primarily activated by the "old brain" or thalamus, but by Aristotle's time greater reliance was placed upon the "new brain" or cortical area.

1. The division of man's history into these periods has been made by Korzybski. See also Reiser's *The Promise of Scientific Humanism.*
2. Korzybski's term "one-valued" seems more accurate than Lévy-Bruhl's, "pre-logical." The former indicates that we are dealing with a form or kind of "logic"; the latter implies an absence of logic, an error similar to that already considered in the case of the term "pre-history."

The third, or non-Aristotelian stage, which is now forming, is characterized by the logic (psycho-logics) of the most advanced knowledge in science. In this stage the useful potentialities of the two earlier stages will be developed further. There will be a sense of unity between the self and the non-self, yet distinctions between the two will be recognized. The world and self will be regarded as INTERRELATED, but not interchangeable processes; "entities" will be distinguished, but not isolated. In other words, the Primitive's interchangeability attitude is transformed, as a result of the entity experience of the Aristotelian stage, into a non-Aristotelian emphasis upon interrelatedness of unified entities. By analogy: in the past when man viewed the phenomenon of rapidly moving objects he saw only a oneness, a unified, blurred image that spread from the beginning to the end of a particular object in motion. Today, with the extra-neural help of high-speed Cameras and other devices, we see this phenomenon as a unified series of distinct, individual images in a time-space continuum. In brief, we are now in the position of comprehending the unique, interrelated functions of the "old" and "new" brain.

Human evolution has thus moved from the one-valued "logic" of Primitive cultures, to the two- or few-valued "logic" of Aristotle, and finally to the multi- or infinite-valued "logic" (psycho-logics) of the non-Aristotelian system.

In the history of art a parallel evolution may be traced. In our examination of the Primitive's art and its functions we explained how these depictions of reality did not involve clear-cut distinctions between the animate and inanimate, life and death, man and animal, the images of sleeping and waking, etc. Everything was largely seen as interchangeable phenomena. Men became trees, stones, animals, etc. And as regards the actual act of recording reality, similarities were important, not differences. But a great transformation that had been gradually evolving in human culture during Egyptian times culminated with the Greeks. It was then that the "perfected" generalization of the human form emerged and was represented as an entity distinct from everything else. It was the age of dichotomy, when the carved human figure stood alone before nature, in art and in the thinking processes of man.

And it was then, as explained in the chapter on Greek art, that man discovered the existence of a "problem of reality"; for the Greeks this came to mean that the artist was in "rivalry" with nature. The Primitives had attributed their art and its functions to the great occult forces that inhabited nature; now the Greeks claimed to do what nature could not! The Primitive artist was one with nature; the Greek artist was in "rivalry" with nature. The Aristotelian notions of the ideal in art have flourished to the very present day.

But during this stage of the domination of the "ideal," there was also another trend; that is, there were *innovators* who strove to secure ever more accurate recordings of the *particular* rather than the general. It was these artists who achieved the greatest advances in art. Through their efforts the lone human form of the Idealists gradually became more and more real and acquired more and more of its *natural* environment. These were the scientists of art, and it was their developmental direction that finally resulted in the invention of a Machine—the Camera—for producing amazingly accurate records of the visible world.

In other words, a split existed throughout the Aristotelian period of art. On the one hand some strove to record nature as it appeared, while others changed it into what "ought to be"—a conflict between descriptive and "creative" efforts. With the Camera, for the first time, the descriptive or recording impulse was freed from the frustrating participation of the creative one. Now artists could be directly concerned with the science of recording light-rays accurately. The Photographer does not copy nature and then identify it as man's art; rather he records the light-rays which produce the image of nature's art, the art of unaided nature.

Once such recordings were achieved, the old quest for the ideal was momentarily discredited. There then appeared a new type of innovator who adopted another direction as an outlet for the creative factor. We saw the development of this effort throughout the Transitional-Period from the largely unconscious efforts of the Impressionists to the consciousness of invention with the discoveries of the Two-Dimensionalists and the Constructionists. The Transitional-Period, as we have emphasized, constituted a momentous change in the artist's method of abstracting from the art of nature. Where before the artist's consciousness of abstracting was limited to the macro-reality of nature, now he discovered that he could

211. Naum Gabo, Monument for an Airport (Space Construction), 1925-26. Glass and metal, 19½″ high x 28⅞″ long. Collection of the artist. Photo, Museum of Modern Art.

abstract from the Structural Process level of reality, and that this type of abstracting permitted him to invent, create his own art.

Thus within the last century two tremendous events have occurred, so that man as an artist is no longer alone and in "rivalry" with nature, but *again* a part of nature. With the Camera and Constructions we witness the overthrow of the Aristotelian ideal and the elimination of the schism that had existed during this stage. Today man can be either a recorder of nature-art or a creator of his own art without the paralyzing conflict engendered by the erroneous notion of an ideal, i.e., copying nature-art under the delusion that one is creating. With these events we arrive at the birth of the non-Aristotelian stage of art in which the efforts of past artists can now be more fully realized through a proper integration with the world and the laws of nature in which man lives. Thus the artist has passed from the limited Aristotelian view of reality (i.e., limited to the macro-reality level) to the more general, more fundamental non-Aristotelian view (i.e., nature viewed in terms of Structural Process).

Our contention that we are emerging into a non-Aristotelian context is not altered by the fact that the majority of artists today still continue to "imitate" nature's appearances and reason like Aristotelians. We have repeatedly demonstrated that most contemporary artists deliberately or otherwise, strive to retain the old while desiring the new. We have seen the tragic consequences of this schismatic situation which characterizes almost all contemporary art, Modern or otherwise. For most artists today what is commonly referred to as "tradition" represents security, while the changes required of the genuinely new represent insecurity; they are wrong on both counts. For they are wandering in a no-man's land that lies between two worlds, one that has passed forever, and one that is being born.

Meanwhile their theories are fundamentally based on the Aristotelian assumption that the artist perceives a "higher reality," which only he, not nature, achieves. Thus we find that all those who have opposed the main evolutional directions in art over the past 2,000 years—i.e., in the pre-Camera period, the increasingly accurate recording of the art appearances of unaided nature, and, in the post-Camera period, the invention of the art content—have rationalized their position with some variation of the Aristotelian theory of the ideal.

But it is impossible to restore the Aristotelian mode of behavior to its former effectiveness. All attempts to reverse the course of human evolution inevitably lead to cultural psychoses. In regard to this problem Korzybski has written: "The aristotelian-system was the result of the *semantic reactions* of the white race of more than two thousand years ago; it built up the doctrines, institutions etc., appropriate to this system. In those days, knowledge was very scanty; the interconnection of different peoples, vague; the means of communications, very primitive, etc. It may be considered that science, and particularly mathematics, began a non-aristotelian revolution by explicitly searching for structure and adjusting the structure of the scientific languages, which we usually call 'terminology', 'theories', etc. Modern conditions of life are, to a large extent, affected by non-aristotelian science but exploited by the thoroughly aristotelian doctrines of the commercialists, militarists, politicians, priests, lawyers etc., which results in a bewildering chaos, resulting in needless, great, and imposed suffering for the great masses of mankind, as exemplified by such cataclysms as wars, revolutions, unemployment, different economic crises, etc." [3]

It seems highly unlikely that a non-Aristotelian orientation will receive its initial impetus in Europe. For Europe is the continent across which the great Aristotelian culture of man swung with its greatest force—from Athens to Paris. It was here, during the Aristotelian period, that the depictions of the human form, trees and the natural environment in general—i.e., depictions of nature's art—reached their greatest development in the primitive recording arts. The evolution of man's visual knowledge of the human form and the macro-face of nature can be traced from the Paleolithic caves of France to the caves of the Louvre in Paris. It is extremely important for us to be aware of this situation. For thus we can see why the Europeans, submerged in this more than 2,000-year-old Aristotelian culture, find it painfully difficult, even undesirable, to struggle against it. This attitude has persisted even though that culture crashed to pieces in the last World-Civil-War. To part from this great but now completed cultural "tradition" is seen by most Europeans as a disastrous denial of it. The majority of "Moderns" in Europe

3. Korzybski, *Science and Sanity,* p. 555.

212. Jean Gorin, Sculpture No. 1, 1930.

213. Salvador Dali, Debris of an automobile giving birth to a blind horse biting a telephone. Coll., Mr. and Mrs. James Thrall Soby.

have attempted to hold onto a vanished past while trying to grasp the emerging new. The Cubists well exemplify this schizoid conflict in European culture; in their works the new was struggling to pass beyond and throw off the useless old. But the human face and body—the old content—persistently peered through and in the end dominated their art. Since then we have found the European Modernists struggling in the death embrace of the old, as they tear, twist, deform, mutilate, ulcerate the old content, and present it as worm-eaten, discolored, molding, rotting. Thus they reveal themselves as morose, prostrate, tormented with self-pity.

Too many of the best mentalities of Europe had preferred to keep on tasting the old culture to the very last tasteless drop. It became more important for them to hold on blindly to what was rapidly dying than to make a genuine effort to create the Machine culture that was inevitable in some form. Thus the Surrealist hoax—which was the "solution" of those post-Cubist European artists who lacked the necessary courage to resolve their dilemma—was palmed off as representing the inheritance of the great European cultural tradition. (Indeed, only the inheritors of a great cultural past, who themselves have become decadent, could have the "mental agility" to perpetrate such a hoax successfully.) Thus many found themselves taking very seriously the antics of these European artists. The decadence of a great culture was disguised by its unquestionably great past. The great men of Europe who had increased the extent and order of human consciousness were now but a shield for those who lauded the "irrational subconscious." Thus tradition—warped, distorted and sick—returned in full force for all but a handful of the great European innovators in art.

628

The evidence is inescapable that the European continent, the place where the first developed culture of man began in Paleolithic times, is the place where the art of nature, used as the art of man, comes to its end. The circle is complete—Paleolithic man erected the high points of his first culture largely in what is today France and Spain; and today we see this very culture end in France, with Spaniards like Picasso, Miro, Dali this time leading it backwards to complete oblivion.

It is very fitting then that Dali should warn the artist to "resist the hideous mechanical civilization that is your enemy. . . ." [4] Relevant to this is one of Dali's paintings, produced in 1938, just as Europe was poised for its disastrous plunge into the most barbaric of all wars; he called it *Debris of an automobile giving birth to a blind horse biting a telephone* (see figure 213). This painting actually symbolizes the general attitude of Europeans towards the Machine. For here we see symbolized the reversal of the evolution which has taken mankind towards the development of the Machine—i.e., the regression from the Machine and the return to the horse or animal. And so European culture is represented in the horse, blindly, madly struggling against changes that were relentlessly pushing the old culture into past history. It is the stumbling, hopeless struggle against the Machine of the once great nature-worship-handicraft culture—a culture becoming more and more transformed into a blind, mad animal—fascism-nazism-communism.

In Dali's painting we see, as in all his work, not a prophecy of the future, as his defenders maintain, but the most obvious symbol of the chaotic present to which he is certainly attuned. His work symbolizes the frantic, confused, decadent European mentality that resents the changes being forced upon human culture in the direction of the genuine, i.e., democratic, Science-Machine behavior. It is resentment run wild in an un-sane attempt to discredit and destroy Science-Machine culture.

And so the Machine culture came in the shape of the most stupendous war Machine man had ever devised. For the Europeans the Machine became precisely what they insisted it was—predominantly a barbaric tool. It became so, however, because most of the best people of Europe left the Machine to most of the worst people in Europe. Thus the Machine was *used* to smash what was left of the old European culture. Those who could see only the destructive possibilities of science and the Machine were destroyed by them.

It is possible to correct this grave error of the European intellectuals by insisting that this is precisely what the Machine must not be: by insisting that the most civilized among us exploit the Machine as a constructive tool of the new culture that is forming. Europe is a tragic demonstration of the very great danger that prevails even in this country, particularly among the blind worshippers of European culture, who wish to keep science and the Machine out of art. What they say about science is naive because their sole objective is to rationalize the ignorance of their *prejudice*. Hence they foment the notion that the Machine is inevitably "anti-human," "anti-nature," "anti-art," and the like. The danger of this is that thinking so can make it so, as the European example has clearly shown. This is also true of science. Because so many consider it as nothing but a "cold," "intellectual" affair, as something merely for creating Machines, as merely "utilitarian" etc., it remains largely nothing else. And so, if we continue to permit predatory individuals to abuse science and the Machine, we shall only further primitivize ourselves. If we do not discard our primitive evaluation of science and the Machine, we cannot achieve the increase in humanizing benefits that are to be had from a Science-Machine culture.

Along with other changes in Europe, Paris as the art center of the world is no more. The French have played a role as important as that of any other group in the evolution of man's experience through the medium of art. The dream of Colbert (pp. 205-06) did become a reality, but now it is over. Since Cubism Frenchmen have not played a leading role in the evolution of art. In fact, since Paul Cézanne, the French have had less and less of a monopoly on great artists. It is not an accident that certain French (as well as other European) artists have tried to ridicule Cézanne.

4. Quoted by Soby in *Salvador Dali*, p. 22.

In this country the conditions are ripe for starting the world out of the muck and ruin of Aristotelianism in art and the general culture, and giving the initial impetus to the realization of the non-Aristotelian attitude. For we have been mere onlookers and at best feeble participants in the old nature-worship-handicraft culture tradition of Europe. Though we have been the least envied, culturally speaking, we can today transform this situation into a major asset, for we have the great advantage of not being hampered by the dead weight of Aristotelianism to the extent the Europeans are. At least we do not have 20 centuries of Aristotelian art tradition cajoling us from every side of our daily lives, drawing us back to a past that is gone forever. Here we have been gradually evolving a culture of Science-Machine consciousness. This fact partially explains why artists in this country have failed to make any significant contributions to the former greatness of the old nature-worship culture of Europe—the limited Aristotelian view of reality. This is also why they are in the best position to initiate the Science-Machine culture that is forming toward a greater future. Artists, Architects, etc., living in the environment of this country are in an ideal psycho-logical position to give up without regret the now useless primitive mediums, the limited view of nature—in short, the tradition of the last 2,000 years—and to exploit the new tools, methods and materials of art—the Machine and Machine-materials, to build the new contents of art.

In fact, some Architects in this country have already gone far in this direction. In earlier discussions, we found that American Architects have not compromised their art with the human form and other forms of the natural environment to anything like the extent that they have in Europe. Most "Modern" European Architects have continued old attitudes in one way or another. Sigfried Giedion, a European writer, tells us that, "Modern architects often boast of the attention they pay to trees; indeed, they sometimes build a house around one." [5] If past Architects hid their works with vines, bushes, and trees, as though ashamed of them, the "Modern" Architect makes his work sit in abject worship around a tree ridiculously alone. Other "Modern" Architects have used rough, "natural" walls or marble ones here and there, etc. The split between the old and the new is further indicated in their tendency to place the old, pre-Machine, primitive-tool art products—paintings and sculptures—in the interior of their works.

The European, Le Corbusier, well exemplifies such behavior in the details of his Architecture, both inside and outside, and in his choice of environment. On the one hand he finds that the Machine has tremendous potentialities for making a new visual face for the world, yet on the other hand he has felt a need to continue being a painter, the artist of the pre-Machine age of art. Consistent with this, he employs two names, one for the painter, whom he calls Jeanneret (his original name) and another for the Architect, whom he calls Le Corbusier. This splitting of names is no mere personal idiosyncrasy; it is symbolic of the European mentality struggling to reach the new, but most unwilling to break the shackles of the old in order to reach it. Yet, for all that, Le Corbusier is one of the few European artists who has achieved basic insight into the new era of Machine culture.

Paradoxical as it may seem, it is the very insignificance of American "fine-arts" which may be our greatest asset. As we have pointed out, our lack of tradition in art leaves us incomparably freer than European artists generally to break with the Aristotelian past. We can do this because our potentialities as contributors to the progress of human culture lie in the present and future. This is true not only because we are building more directly towards a Science-Machine culture, but in many other ways also. For instance, Erich Kahler writes: "In America, fixed ranks or castes never existed, as there were no sacred monarchs and long established feudal nobility, no court or hereditary society, no guilds and no villages with their inveterate customs, their folk traditions and communal grounds. There were none of all those weatherworn, overgrown and interwoven institutions, the origins and often the meaning of which nobody knew any longer, but the magic power of which people could never actually overcome. No American-born person may be fully able to realize this European way of life under the perpetual and ever-present burden of immemorial memories." [6] It is not so much what we have done as what we have not done and what we are now in a position to do. The future that is arising is offering to artists in this country the opportunity to continue the evolution of the *art of mankind*, to make secure the evolution of international art.

5. Reprinted by permission of the publishers from Sigfried Giedion, *Space, Time and Architecture*, 1943, p. 444.

6. Erich Kahler: *Man the Measure*, p. 447.

630

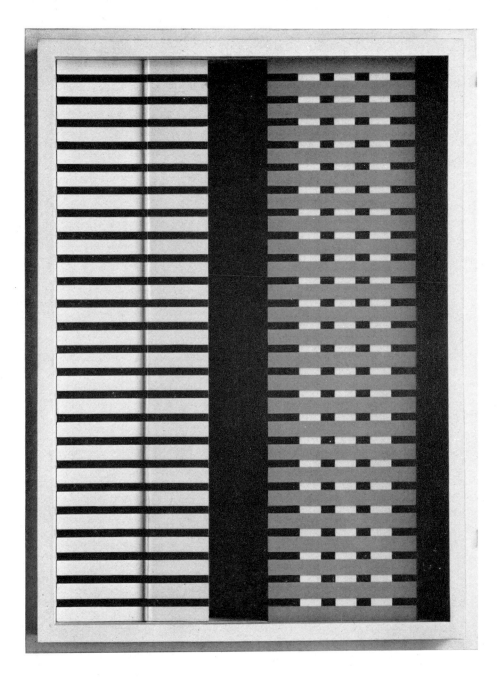

214. Charles Biederman, Construction, 10/39 (8). Painted wood and glass, 31¼″x24″x3″.

For today, art, like science, must be consciously international, if it is to survive at all. In this country we can resume the task that the first Constructionists began in Russia.

Perhaps the greatest tragedy for the development of art in our times occurred in Russia in 1922. In previous chapters we have seen how thoroughly Constructionist art meets the needs of an up-to-date integration with the general culture of mankind. In Russia, in the early part of the century, there was a tremendous opportunity for this to be realized. But five years after the revolution the rulers literally padlocked the studios of artists who insisted upon remaining Constructionists; thereafter Russian art became the most reactionary of the 20th century. The first Constructionists were interrupted in the very beginning of the crucial period of trying to work out the new direction of art. This interference of the ignorant not only drastically reduced the number of artists, but also retarded the formulation of the new art.

Previous studies have indicated that the artists of the new arts can no longer work with the comparatively inexpensive, primitive tools of the past. And it is necessary for the advancement of Constructionist art that it be made available to the vast majority. Some will contend that the future unification of art with the general culture cannot be secured without government compulsion. But compulsion, as every dictatorship in our times proves beyond doubt, produces only a constant increase in the barbaric behavior of those who control the art. The dictators recognized that a "free" art formed a major threat to their rule; they also realized that once controlled, they could use art to further their destructive purposes. And so in the dictator nations the artist was forced into a 19th century art strait-jacket, making an art for a culture of robots. The problems of art cannot be solved by forcing everyone to be a so-called "national-socialist" (Hitler and Stalin have both used these terms when speaking about art), nor by forcing anyone to be any particular kind of artist. Compulsion and its inevitable results are precisely the opposite of what we seek. But we must take art just as seriously as does the dictator, if we want to keep it from becoming a doormat for the feet of sick politicians.

However "obvious" the notion appears, it is far from popular to hold that art is a reflection as clear as a mirror image of the culture from which it springs. Much more acceptable is the romantic attitude of considering art above and apart from all other forms of human behavior. There are others who consider art as quite harmless and of no great consequence. The reading of the present history makes clear that art has always served as a major tool for constructive or destructive purposes. If we do not realize this, certainly the dictators do. They cannot afford to be as careless as we are with our laissez-faire attitude. Of course the mirror image that art produces is clearest in countries infected with dictatorships because the social fixation of the dictator is enforced completely upon artists, not to mention scientists, educators, etc. But the reflection produced by such a country as ours is not so clearly to be seen. For in this country two opposing forces—nationalism and internationalism—are struggling to replace laissez-faire with a "new order." In such a world as the present the artist must take a stand, if he does not wish laissez-faire freedom replaced with a dictatorship, if he wants to be part of building a better world than the one that is gone forever.

The lack of a great past in this country, while it can be our advantage, can also be a serious danger, in that the resulting ignorance, being mistaken for useful knowledge, can lead to isolationist, nationalist art—the solution of every totalitarian nation. Look at such art, see it alongside any of the great art of the past, and see how shabby, cheap and depraved it appears before the test of genuine products of history. But in 1945, shortly after some examples of Hitler's "taste" in art arrived in this country, a leading magazine significantly reported that it was "embarrassingly" similar to the art preferred by the United States public.[7] Joseph Davies' reactions to Russian art are also significant. Although he could not refrain from informing the Russian dictator that he was a "capitalist," this did not interfere with his appreciation of totalitarian art.[8] Most so-called "capitalists" and "communists" are usually very much agreed as to the kind of art they prefer, since the function they impose upon it is very similar in both cases. Nineteenth century nationalist methods of art are found to answer their atavistic needs.

The Germans under Hitler read: "True art is always the creation of a specific blood, and a

7. "Nazi art," *Time Magazine,* October 8, 1945, p. 67.
8. See *Mission to Moscow,* p. 313.

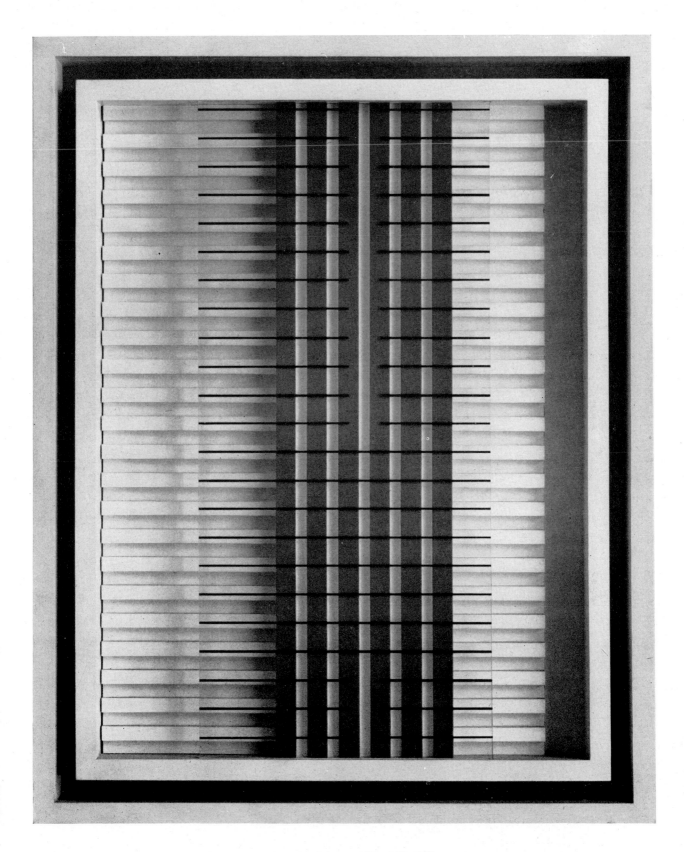

215. Charles Biederman, Construction, 10/39 (9). Painted wood and glass, 27⅝″x21⅝″x2⅝″.

216. Thomas Benton, detail of figure 148.

217. Max Ernst, The Attirement of the Bride, Courtesy of The Art of This Century.

218. Romanesque relief, detail of figure 40. Photo, Giraudon, Paris.

219. Shot from A Corner in Wheat, 1909, by D. W. Griffith. Museum of Modern Art Film Library, New York.

work of art can only be understood by creatures of that identical blood; to others it says little or nothing." [9] This statement is very similar to much that we have heard over the years in this country. And certainly it is no accident that Hitler ranted with psychotic hysteria against all art innovations from the beginning of the Transitional-Period on. For whether he knew it or not, these arts announced the end of the nationalist period of art. And what the nazi did to art is only the more obvious form of what we find in every nation under more restrained but inherently no less barbaric impulses. The question is whether we will wake up before the virus of nationalism grows into the psychotic, i.e., totalitarian stage.

It might be well to remind Americans that art was not invented by Americans, or any other national group. And probably the nearest thing to an "American art" that will ever be was that produced by the American Indians, which still remains the most important *group* manifestation of art ever produced in this country. Nor has the historical course been noticeably affected by so-called American "fine-art" artists. Most American artists have not adequately realized the fact that "art" is the product of the time-binding of the human race throughout thousands of years of human history. From this point of view it is utterly nonsensical to assume that we in this country will ever produce even a remotely worthwhile art on a nationalist basis.

So we see that even if the historical conditions now seem to favor this part of the globe, still it is a question of whether we are going to exploit our possibilities or abuse them as the majority are now doing. We must realize, as Frank Lloyd Wright remarked in connection with Architecture, that: "we are the modern Romans. Reflect that the ancient Romans at the height of their prosperity lied likewise to themselves no less shamefully, when they pasted Greek architecture onto their magnificent engineering invention of the masonry arch to cover it decently. The Romans, too, were trying to make the kind of picture or the grand gesture demanded by Culture. The Roman arch was, in that age, comparable to the greatest of all scientific or engineering inventions in our own Machine Age, comparable especially to our invention of steel. So likewise, what integrity any solution of the skyscraper problem might have in itself as good steel-and-glass construction has been stupidly thrown away. The native forests of steel, concrete and glass, the new materials of our time, have great possibilities. But in the hands of the modern Doctor-of-Appearances they have been made to *seem* rather than allowed to *be*. Sophisticated polishing by the accredited Doctor only puts a glare upon its shame. It cannot be possible that sham like this is really our own civilized choice?" [10]

In the non-Aristotelian art of the Constructionists, nationalist tendencies cannot appear, since it is an impossible vehicle for such a purpose. The new artists are striving for that greater unity, the integration of all humans on the earth. In the world today subjectivism, sectionalism, nationalism, hemispherism, etc., can be only harmful forces. On this problem Oliver Reiser writes: "The building of the world-consciousness, the international mind, that must replace the economic nationalism and patriotic motifs of present-day mentality, is the next objective of education. As we have already indicated, this means that in the coming years *the nations of the world will have to evolve for the social organism a world-sensorium,* a center of intellectual dominance similar to that which nature provided for individual organisms when she produced the cerebral hemispheres, the vehicle of highest metabolic rate and the synthesizer of reactions. Until a level of social integration, or unification of the world's cultural patterns, is attained; until we have an organ to centralize and co-ordinate the complexity of function of the emerging social organism, our humanitarian aspirations will continue to suffer defeat." [11] In this direction of orientation Constructionist art is already leading the way.

America has produced so far only three "visual" artists who stand in the ranks of the great artists of history: their names are Louis H. Sullivan, Frank Lloyd Wright and D. W. Griffith. It was Griffith who first made it clear beyond doubt that the Film was a genuine medium of and a major development in Machine-art. And it was Sullivan and Wright who opened men's eyes to a new view of nature and the great revolution possible in the proper use of the Machine in Architecture. Towards the realization of the new world in which artists will again play a prominent part, the role of the Architect

9. Ralph Rosenberg as quoted by M. C. Otto, in "The Nordic Blood Myth," *The Antioch Review*, 2:564, Winter, 1942.
10. Frank Lloyd Wright: *Modern Architecture*, pp. 95–96.
11. Oliver L. Reiser: *The Promise of Scientific Humanism*, pp. 273–274.

220. Jean Gorin, Architectural plastic in space-time, construction emanating from pyramid; model for a monument in a modern city, 1947. Photo, Yves Hervochon, Paris.

as planner and builder is of the greatest importance. His role is crucial to the entire problem of art. Hamper him and the art of the Constructionist must suffer, for then the Constructionists would have to build in an environment that would continue to reject the assimilation of such works.

It is indeed significant that Sullivan, Wright and Griffith used the Machine as their tool of art! Actually these artists represent the two legitimate art directions in the non-Aristotelian culture that is forming. Our history has revealed that three general kinds of art comprise all man's activities as "visual" artist: (1) That in which the artist's main intention is to record nature's art as literally as possible. The highest manifestation of this type of art is the work of the genuine Photographer, e.g., D. W. Griffith. (2) That in which the artist distorts nature's appearances. In this kind the artist had either failed in his desire to record nature accurately, e.g., Giotto—which is true in some degree of all Realists—or he has failed in his desire to be a creative artist, e.g., Léger—which is true of all Classicists or Idealists, including all Modern artists. (3) That in which the artist strives to create art, not "imitate" the art of nature; his main intention is to be Inventive. This is seen in Architecture, today in the works of such as Frank Lloyd Wright, and in the works of genuine Constructionists.

Each of these three very general forms of art is being practiced today, but, as we have shown, each has had a legitimate or regressive place, as the case may be, in the times when each occurred. The next evolutionary step requires that artists either continue with type one—if the Camera-Machine is used, or type three—if the Machine is employed as the medium for creating art. The Camera was the first step, as we have seen, towards the resolution of the age-old schism that had existed between the recording and the creative effort; it freed the recording impulse from the frustrating participation of the creative one. The final resolution of the schism occurred with the creation of a man-made art content. Not only has Constructionist art completed the process of freeing the Mimetic as well as the Inventive artists, but now Constructionists assume the leading role in the Inventive arts. And as a result of Constructionist art, it has become possible to discover a new view of history and nature.

We have stated that the general direction of the Constructionist is the only legitimate one for non-Camera artists today. We have also stated that our formulations for a future non-Camera art, both as to the kind of content (actual three-dimensional, invented content) and kind of "tools" employed (the Machine) are unavoidable unless we choose to regress. We expect to hear vehement protests to such statements. The artist, it will be contended, cannot be thus limited; he must have complete freedom. After almost four decades of ever increasing do-as-you-please attitudes, artists and critics will certainly find it difficult to comprehend how any worthwhile art can come from a single, non-Camera direction. Actually such an effort is neither new nor impossible for the creation of useful art.

Perhaps the following thalamic material may help to eliminate the kind of thinking that prompts the above objections. Let us imagine that, once the discovery of Mimetic art had occurred, one of the Paleolithic artists announced that future painters and sculptors would be almost entirely confined to recording the visual phenomena of nature. One can also imagine then, just as would happen now, the numerous voices calling out against such a severe limitation, protesting that previously artists had been perfectly free to invent and were not confined by any outside limitations such as the appearances of nature forms. Yet precisely such a "limited" direction of art was pursued; for many thousands of years men have been content to sculpt and paint the art appearances of nature. In fact, today the vast majority vehemently refuse to step beyond this single, limited direction of art!

221. Jean Gorin, Construction of relation of planes in space, 1930. Photo, Yves Hervochon, Paris.

Or let us suppose that Masaccio had predicted that for almost the next 500 years the greatest artists would be painters, because only by employing the painting medium could an adequate solution be found for the various problems that would arise for the next five centuries. In fact, how many during the Renaissance did protest when such a "limited" direction was explicit or implicit in the remarks of Leonardo and others? Yet who have been the greatest artists since—painters or sculptors? [12]

As for those who will ask what value an art can have that no longer presents recognizable material, one might recall to them the story told about Michael Faraday. He was demonstrating the principles of the electric current, when a woman asked him: " 'But, Professor, of what USE is all this?' Faraday, without looking up from his demonstration, shot back: 'Madam, what use is a new born baby?' " [13] Recall also that the successful Camera was greeted as "French humbug," as useless, even harmful (see p. 238).

The antagonisms one finds toward Constructionist art have their repeated parallels many times in history. It is hostility to change—hostility because habits, canalizations are disturbed. This destructive attitude has appeared every time some more alert member of the human family proposed some change or discovered some error. For instance, it probably was extremely difficult for the majority of early men to comprehend how they could ever devise a language superior to the Pictographic one. For in the abstract direction which eventually dominated, symbols were produced that obviously did not "look like" that which they represented. But although the collection of marks B I R D certainly does not in the least "look like" an actual bird, no one today would argue that because it lacks this visual correspondence it can have no relation to actual reality and so no value. Yet many find it difficult to take seriously an art which does not look like anything ever seen before in reality. Such reactions are the most deadly weapon of man, for they are wasted, destructive, energy that could have been converted to full scientific consideration of proposed changes, and then their immediate adoption or rejection, as the case might warrant.

It is true that Constructionist art is but barely begun on its way into the new era of art, that it is an effort in which only a few artists are working. But these few are hindered in setting free many of the potentialities of this future form of art, mainly because the means of communication both pictorially and verbally between the artist and the culture are in the hands of supporters of the *status quo*. Pertinent to this problem, J. E. Boodin writes: "Indeed those who are farthest in advance in the creative adaptation to the future are generally deemed unfit by conventional society. It is only when this advance in turn is conventionalized that society builds tombs to the prophets." [14]

Also involved in these issues is the problem of utilitarian versus non-utilitarian activities and the false knowledge that often gives rise to and stems from such considerations. The so-called "pure" fields of art and science (e.g., Constructionist art, "pure" mathematics) are generally regarded as useless and thus there is the least sympathy for them and the most ignorance about them. As Mondrian wrote: "It is a great pity that those who are concerned with the social life in general do not realize the utility of pure abstract art. Wrongly influenced by the art of the past, the true essence of which escapes them, and of which they only see that which is superfluous, they make no effort to know pure abstract art. Through another conception of the word 'abstract,' they have a certain horror of it. They are vehemently opposed

12. As for those who would balk at the complete elimination of the sculptors, we reframe our question as follows (but *only* for the sake of argument): "Have the greatest number of great artists employed the painting or the sculpture medium?"

13. Quoted by Willy Ley in the Newspaper *PM,* January 26, 1944.

14. John Elof Boodin: *Cosmic Evolution,* p. 264, The Macmillan Company, New York, 1925.

222. Charles Biederman, Construction, 5/41 (2). Glass, bakelite and brass. 35⅞″x31″x5¼′.

223. Calcite crystal between polaroid filters. Courtesy, Polaroid Corporation.

to abstract art because they regard it as something ideal and unreal. In general they use art as propaganda for collective or personal ideas, thus as literature. They are both in favor of the progress of the mass and against the progress of the elite, thus against the logical march of human evolution. Is it really to be believed that the evolution of the mass and that of the elite are incompatible? The elite rises from the mass; is it not therefore its highest expression?" [15]

In these more pure fields abstractions are performed that are so different from and so much more extensive than those of the majority, that few are in a position to realize their vast, fundamental importance for the maintenance of what sanity exists in our culture. Forms of cerebration or behavior that transcend problems concerned with economic gain are generally suspect. Actually this is the most impractical attitude we could possibly adopt. Consider the following example: "When Michael Faraday began his electrical researches in 1831 he gave up an assured income of some £1,000 a year as a professional witness in the English courts. He also resigned his post as consultant to the Government, which had assured him £500 more. 'I have always loved science more than money,' he said, 'and because my occupation is almost entirely personal I cannot afford to get rich.'

"That point of view was incomprehensible to his political friends. One of them berated him in his laboratory one day for wasting his time on a small copper disk which Faraday cranked endlessly between the poles of a magnet [this was the ancestor of the dynamo].

15. Mondrian, "Plastic Art and Pure Plastic Art," *Plastic Art and Pure Plastic Art*, pp. 61–62.

224. Lichtenberg figures, patterns of electrical sparks. Courtesy of A. R. von Hippel, Massachusetts Institute of Technology.

" 'What possible excuse can you give,' said the politician, 'for playing with this toy when there is so much work to be done that only you can do?'

"The scientist said softly, 'Do not be impatient with my toy. Some day you may be able to tax it!' " [16]

Repeatedly the advanced products of "art" and "science" are considered useless, and repeatedly these products have evolved into the pivotal foundations of civilization. Thus the first artist who made a linear mark; the first man who transformed the lines into signs; the first man to transform the lines into imitations of nature-appearances; the first sculptor who made a geometric form; the first to make a pot to replace the cupped hand, seashells, skulls, etc.; the first man to make Architecture; the first to record nature with a Machine—all such efforts were initially regarded as meaningless, useless, dangerous innovations. With such a mass of verifiable evidence at hand, how inept of us not to realize that in the field of art men can invent still more remarkable innovations. Our observation and analysis of art has clearly demonstrated that art has always been an indispensable necessity to man. Potters, Architects, Painters, Sculptors, etc., have all played a major role in the formation of man's tools, language, his formulation of reality, and culture in general. The achievements in art are now being carried further by the artists of the Machine—Constructionists, Architects, Photographers, Industrial artists.

16. D. O. Woodbury: *Beloved Scientist: Elihu Thomson*, p. 77. Whittlesey House, New York, London. Copyright, 1944, McGraw-Hill Book Co., Inc.

643

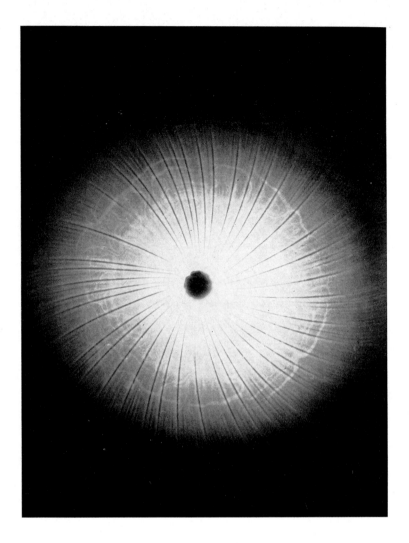

225. Lichtenberg figures, patterns of electrical sparks. Courtesy of A. R. von Hippel, Massachusetts Institute of Technology.

Actually the new art has already had a tremendous influence upon the shapes of objects that come from our industries: in Architecture, in all manner of everyday utilities—objects for clothing the body and for furnishing our homes and places of work. There are numerous indications in our times that we are gradually becoming more and more aware of the tremendous importance of "visual" order. The Industrial artists have begun to terminate the practice of "decorating" ugly objects. In one way or another they are gradually realizing that Mimetic disguises are a false solution, that the entire object can be satisfactorily invented. They are correcting the ugly shapes that used to hide under the old Mimetic curtain. For this they have the non-commercial artists to thank—the Cubists, the Two-Dimensionalists, the Constructionists, the artists of "pure" research, who freed non-Mimetic arts from the destructive participation of the Mimetic factor. In fact, the extensive visual transformation that has occurred in all the "practical" things we use—clothes, travelling bags, etc., landscaping, interiors, all the way from homes and trains to theatres and places of working, etc.—is largely due to the fact that the great artists of the De Stijl, Suprematist and Constructionist schools discovered the value of the Inventive or creative form. Today nearly all of us profit daily from these discoveries, while the artists responsible for them seldom receive the financial returns of an unskilled worker. They are honored only when properly dead.

Unfortunately, few of the "applied" artists are coherently aware of their indebtedness to and dependence upon the discoveries of these non-commercial artists. This has prevented them from taking full advantage of their opportunities, from learning and "applying" what they learn to their own work. Thus the potentialities of the new art are yet far from being fully exploited. The Industrial artist today has the opportunity to make himself a very indispensable member of industry, to become the Architect of the object, collaborating with the engineer. But there are still too many commercial opportunities in the field, both among artists and business men. As Lewis Mumford pointed out, speaking of the "arts and crafts movement," they are, "Lacking the courage to use the machine as an instrument of creative purpose, and being unable to attune themselves to new objectives and new standards . . . ." [17]

To exploit the opportunities of the present adequately there is a need for better trained men in the Industrial arts, above all for artists who realize that making a genuine "modern" object involves more than simply making something round or square or simple. There is need of artists who are less interested in money and more interested in "art," of men and women who are willing to struggle as do the artists who perform the original innovations in art history, and face their responsibilities regardless of the outcome. [18]

Yet even before the products of art and science are converted to so-called practical ends, they can offer us the highest degree of humanizing experience. In fact, to the degree that we are able to achieve the fundamental experience contained in Constructionist art, we are able to exploit its "applied" values. In this sense the so-called "pure" fields are already an applied form of behavior having immediate value. It is non-sense to consider them "useless." For in them we see the highest order of behavior in human life, without which civilization and all our prized practicality would be impossible.

But to achieve the new attitude, it will be necessary to perform drastic revisions in our educational methods, in the general field, as well as in art. We shall have to teach men that forms and their colors do not need to surround an icebox or an automobile or a fountain pen before they can produce "useful" values, that forms and colors can acquire values incomparably more important and necessary to human experience. It would be more correct, then, to point out that if we were all properly educated in these higher order experiences, we would be adopting the most practical, useful attitude that is natural for the human class of life—for these fields represent the epitome of "practicality" reached by mankind. In other words, the hierarchy of values in practicality which is generally held today needs to be *reversed*. Then it will be possible to realize the important values of Constructionist works, to realize that they have direct, immediate, "applied" value as such before they are "applied" in the more obvious sense.

These values are connected with rhythmic order, as evidenced in the normal function of the human nervous system and its relation to mind-body health. On this subject Korzybski has written:

17. Lewis Mumford: *Technics and Civilization*, p. 347.
18. As for the advertising artists, most of them are only to be deplored, for the form of "art" most of them foster is part of an extremely vicious kind of propaganda.

226. Kathleen Lonsdale, X-ray diffraction patterns from single crystal of urea oxalate. (Reproduced from the Mineralogical Magazine, September, 1945, by permission of the Council of the Mineralogical Society, London, and of the author.)

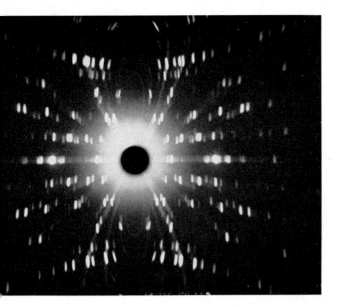

"What we have to deal with in this world and in ourselves appears as periods and periodicity, pulsations, etc. We are made up of very long chains of atomic pulsating clocks, on the sub-microscopic level. On the macroscopic level, we have also to deal with periodic occurrences, of hunger, sleep, breathing, heart-beats, etc. We know already that, beyond some limits, discontinuous times, when rapid enough, are blended into continuous feelings of pressure, or warmth, or light, etc." [19] Herbert Muller writes: "Underlying consciousness are the basic patterns and rhythms of human life in a natural environment. The temporal rhythms in poetry and music, the symmetries or spatial rhythms in painting and architecture, have their source in the pulsings and cycles of life itself; and these in turn are among the regular sequences that alone make knowledge possible. In all their doings, from their noblest creations to their games and their doodlings, men instinctively follow rhythms and make patterns. Their dissatisfaction with an unruly game, an unfinished job, an imperfect understanding, an unsettled situation, a disorderly life is as esthetic as it is moral or intellectual; for it is the dissatisfaction with a rhythm broken, a pattern left incomplete." [20] The new art can play a large part in the investigation of these fundamental phenomena of human experience in a manner similar to other already established "pure" fields of scientific inquiry and experiment. Eventually, as we have suggested, the new art will become a full-fledged major branch of science.

Much of the valuable investigation of the structure and function of the visual process which has been done by scientists can eventually be converted to the researches and experiments which the art-scientists of the future will evolve. The new changes in art, together with knowledge of the advanced scientific attitude, will make it possible for artists to enter a new field of discovery of tremendous value both to themselves and other scientists—psychologists and psychiatrists in particular.

Matthew Luckiesh tells us that: "The effects of visual stimuli can be observed upon the blood pressure, upon muscular, mental, and nervous activity, upon the mood and in various other ways." [21] C. W. Valentine has reported: "One of the most interesting and surprising things which experiments have revealed, is the fact that people can find themselves markedly pleased or displeased even with simple lines and curves, often much to their astonishment." [22] In order to exploit fully the potentialities of the

19. Korzybski, *Science and Sanity*, p. 230.
20. Muller, *Science and Criticism*, p. 35.
21. Reprinted by permission of DODD, MEAD AND CO., INC. From *The Language of Color*, p. 156, by Matthew Luckiesh, New York, 1930. Copyright, 1918 by DODD, MEAD AND CO., INC.
22. C. W. Valentine: *An Introduction to the Experimental Psychology of Beauty*, p. 39. T. C. and E. C. Jack, Ltd., 1919, by permission of Thomas Nelson and Sons, Edinburgh.

new art, one of the new tasks of artists will be to discover what reactions color-form-organizations in time-space have upon the human organism. As Luckiesh has written: "our final interest in the use of color, as in many other activities, is largely concerned with psychological effects. In other words, the ultimate object of the various arts lies largely in their influences upon human consciousness." [23] Experimental findings have demonstrated beyond question that invented color-form-organizations have very significant meanings, that the personality structure as a whole is reflected in them.[24]

As we learn more about the visual structure of nature and the imagery we produce from it, we shall increase our knowledge about everyday visual experiences and discover that our lives can be changed beneficially by the proper change in colors, lines, forms and their organizations. Since most of us are inadequately aware of our visual experiences, we fail to realize the pathological nature of many of them.

Artists can now, in cooperation with the scientists directly involved, produce knowledge and material which can be employed to restore normal rhythmic function and order in the human organism, to open new channels by which these rhythmic structures can be maintained in healthy individuals. All too little inquiry has been made into those visual levels of experience which are beneficial to human beings. There is much yet to be effected in the general field of visual therapy and visual sanity. It is up to artists to meet the situation of our ugly environment, to analyze it, to clean the air visually.

Through Constructionist research art may become a further source for discovering new knowledge of the structure of ourselves and the world in which we live. Order, structure, relations in Constructionist art are directly emphasized in man-made terms, in the sense, for example, of so-called "pure" mathematics. In fact, the outstanding characteristic that strikes the eye before the Constructionist works is the effort to achieve creative control and exploitation of "visual" stimuli. Art can thus continue to be as it has been in the past one of the major tools by which our attitude towards and exploitation of the reality about us will be realized.

It is interesting to note that experiences comparable to those the Constructionist offers on the visual level of art are readily and unquestionably accepted by many where the sound level of art is concerned, i.e., music. This is probably because sensory acuity on the verbal or auditory level usually far exceeds that on the visual.[25] This situation further suggests the need for re-education in art. It is significant that foremost investigators in semantics, such as Korzybski, emphasize the critical importance of the "visual" level. And as we suggested elsewhere, it is quite possible that the new direction of art begun by the Constructionists may lead to repercussions in the general field of linguistics, in the sense that over-verbalized Aristotelian attitudes will give way before the greater importance to be placed upon the visual level.

We have seen how "art" has played a major role in the invention and development of the "art of Writing" and the "art of Photography," and have noted the crucial role these two factors played in the realization of human culture. Now in our times "art" is making a third major contribution, namely, the therapeutic potentialities of Constructionist art. The new art can gradually help us to sanify our "visual" living, to remove the visual monstrosities which plague us all around, especially in cities and towns. Yes, the art of the Constructionist can literally open the eyes of humans and lead them to acquire an adequate consciousness of visualization.

Much that we advocate for the future is not new, in the sense that it is not an abrupt change. Art as a science is not new, the use of Machines to produce art is not new, the cooperative attitude is not new. Above all, the art of invented contents is not new. As a matter of fact, the useful innovators are invariably characterized by their success in further *extending* the Inventive enterprise that is so unique to the human form of life. Actually, everything that man has produced in the field of art has been preceded by experiments with invented lines or forms. This is true even of that art which has striven to record

23. Luckiesh, op. cit., p. 3.
24. See, for instance, "A Differential-Diagnostic Method of Interpreting Mosaics and Colored Block Designs," by Frederic Wertham, M. D. and Lili Golden; *Am. J. of Psychiatry,* Vol. 98, No. 1, July, 1941.
25. The "historical" examination of the reasons for this are of great importance and the present author hopes at some later date to write his views on the subject.

227. Jean Gorin, Contrasting Rhythms in Space, 1947. Museum of Modern Art, Paris. Photo, Yves Hervochon, Paris.

nature accurately. But all this could not become clear until the Inventive factor achieved its proper stature with the appearance of Constructionist art. Before that it was the Mimetic factor that held the dominant position. Today both the Mimetic and Inventive factors, hold their special, unique importance for man on a non-competitive basis.

Therefore the great discovery of the genuine contemporary artists and scientists is that man is able to play a tremendous role in the determination of his experience and destiny in the world of nature, because he is a part of that nature. Through art and science man's ability to experience, to reason his experiences, and to extend them ever further is gradually being freed from the myths man himself has invented — spirits, souls, gods and the rest.

When we began our studies of man as an artist we found him surrounded by the art of nature, the value of which he gradually discovered. Up until the beginning of the 20th century artists concentrated largely upon the methods by which they visualized nature-art. In the future artists shall gain ever greater consciousness and so knowledge of how to exploit that method in a "creative," extra-neural extension of the notion of art. Art thus is no longer only a problem of capturing visual experiences in the art of nature, but of producing visual experiences not to be found in unaided nature. Eventually, man will find himself in a visual environment created by man-nature. It will comprise a new "natural" environment of man — "natural" because man and all he does is a part of, a manifestation of, an extension of nature. Of course much of the natural world has already been replaced with the invented products of man, in cities and towns particularly. Long ago man replaced the natural cave shelters with man-made dwellings; the future will find him doing something similar with the environment as he already has done to a degree, but stupidly, in his cities and towns.

The attitude of the developing future will be one of non-compromise with the art of nature, the natural environment. This is not a denial of nature but a recognition of the distinction between the art of the Machine and that of unaided nature. An effort to compromise them, results only in a bastardization of both. The artist of the present has it within his ability to supplant the natural environment with inventions better suited to his purpose, as he did, for instance, when the natural cave-dwelling was supplanted by invented Architecture. This is the direction in which the Architect, and creative artists in general, must go; trees, bushes and genuine Machine Architecture simply do not *mix!*

In the future, then, man will no longer be struggling with the forces of nature, as in the past, but will be striving to his utmost to preserve great areas of nature's world which offer him experiences indispensable to his continued well-being. Unaided nature will become a living museum, as has already happened in city parks and in forest preserves.

In this great transformation of the natural world we see that it is critically important for artists to become adequately conscious of the evolution of man's visual knowledge if they are to meet the new responsibilities that face them in the future. In the past, men were more conscious of nature's art environment; the new consciousness will include a more adequate awareness of the man-made natural world that increasingly surrounds us. Then men will achieve an even more extensive consciousness, and so greater experience, of nature as such and of man as a part of that nature.

In our times, however, certain of the artists who have chosen to pursue the new art direction, i.e., away from the "art" appearances of nature towards a man-created art, have taken to repeating an old error. Just as the Classical Greeks erroneously discovered that they could "perfect" nature's human form

228. Charles Biederman, Construction, 2/47 (2). Plexiglas, painted wood and metal, 47″x39½″x8″.

and then proceeded to imagine that their recordings were superior to the nature original, so certain present day artists, upon discovering that the artist could "create" his own art independent of copying the forms of nature-art, proceeded to over-estimate their newly acquired ability. Certain of the new artists voiced their contempt for nature as "chaotic," "ugly," and the like; some even claimed that the sight of nature's art in the city (or country)—trees, bushes, etc.,—was simply unbearable. They did not seem to realize that it is not the trees, etc., that are ugly, but the ugly cities around the trees that make the latter appear ugly. Nor did they realize that men put nature-art in their cities in order to relieve the dead, ugly, gray nightmare of their cities' visual faces.

The new artists who feel a need to express contempt for nature-art are thus only expressing their great insecurity before the art of nature, perhaps stemming from insecurity before the great past art of man. Such artists are not sure of their position in the world of nature, and to compensate for it they express contempt for nature-art and the artists who have most accurately recorded it in the past. But once the new artists attain the proper perspective of art history, coherently comprehending the change from Aristotelian to non-Aristotelian art, then they no longer need be in competition with nor contemptuous of nature and/or past art. On the contrary, they will attain a new orientation towards nature, they will realize that they are just as dependent upon nature as were past artists, only in a different way. The new artists, as well as the great ones of the past, will find the art of nature indispensable for the creation of the new art of man. In fact, the new experiences possible for the new artist will be far superior to any possible for past artists. For the new artists will see nature not merely as an exhibition of art products, but as an exhibition of the Process Structure, the creative process. Artists will find the greatest joy in pursuing what are yet the "secrets" of nature, in unearthing them and then exploiting them for man-made purposes.

In this new world of art—the art of nature and the art of man—the conservatives, both "Academicians" and "Modernists," are largely irrelevant. The art "authorities" and institutions of art are encouraging the artist to do very little beyond fruitless twisting and mangling of nature's appearances with the old tools of the Paleolithic artist—sometimes under the tragic delusion that such activities are motivated by a great "love" for nature and the art of man's past. The facts indicate that their behavior results from the "superiority complex" of the frustrated Idealist. Those who claim they are too fond of nature to give up its appearance in their art, and those who imagine they are independent of nature— they are the ones who have yet to acquire a decent respect for art, both nature's and man's, the respect that the genuine Photographer and Constructionist experience and practice—the respect that all the greatest artists have had for nature.

Through the proper study of nature man can make a world of art which he need not be ashamed of in the face of nature's art. There will then be no need to hide the face of Architecture with trees, bushes, vines, etc., or have *paintings* of trees, flowers, etc., inside our houses. (Replacing the latter will be highly developed color-photos.) Man as an artist will thus have found an integration with the art of nature and no longer be in futile competition with it. The Constructionist and Camera artists, together with Architects and Industrial artists, are ready to make these contributions to the new world of man— a world in which men will grow from, not recede into the European-Aristotelian culture. It was of this future that Mondrian wrote in the following: "It would be illogical to suppose that non-figurative art will remain stationary, for this art contains *a culture* of the use of new plastic means and their determinate relations. Because the field is new there is all the more to be done. What is certain is that no escape is possible for the non-figurative artist; *he must stay within his field and march toward the consequences of his art.*

"This consequence brings us, in a future perhaps remote, towards the end of *art as a thing separated from our surrounding environment, which is the actual plastic reality.* But this end is at the same time a new beginning. Art will not only continue but will realize itself more and more. By the unification of architecture, sculpture and painting, a new plastic reality will be created. Painting and sculpture will not manifest themselves as separate objects, nor as 'mural art' which destroys architecture itself, nor as 'applied' art, but *being purely constructive* will aid the creation of a surrounding not merely utilitarian or rational but also pure and complete in its beauty." [26]

26. Mondrian, "Plastic Art and Pure Plastic Art," *Plastic Art and Pure Plastic Art,* pp. 62-63.

229. Jean Gorin, Architectural plastic in space-time, construction emanating from pyramid; model for a monument in a modern city, 1947. Photo, Yves Hervochon, Paris.

230. Jean Gorin, Bas-relief, 1948.

Our task is to lead in building the new culture to which the Europeans gave birth. Men like the Film directors, Griffith and the *early* Eisenstein; the painters, Mondrian, Doesburg, Malevitch; the Architects, Sullivan, Wright, van der Rohe, Le Corbusier; and the Constructionists, Pevsner and Gabo, have already shown us, in some ways, and in some respects, how to proceed.

Like the very first artists we also stand at the beginning of a great new epoch of human art, which can be realized if we are determined to do so. Man, not the Machine or Science, can destroy himself or create a new, more human world with the "Machine" and "Science." All the great achievements of the past are still ours to enjoy, only now we see nature with a wider, more fundamental attitude, an attitude that permits us to make art that is truly a creation of man.

And just as each innovator in the past did, when men went too far into themselves and too far away from nature, the innovators of today are calling for a rebirth in the artist's orientation to reality. They are calling for a return of the artist to his proper place within nature; for a renewal of an adequate consciousness of the artist's relation to nature. Just as Masaccio in the 15th century, Leonardo in the 16th, Velásquez in the 17th, Chardin in the 18th, Constable, Monet and Cézanne in the 19th, so in our century the Constructionist and the Photographer reaffirm the place of the artist in the world of nature; reaffirm the fact that nature is the supreme artist and teacher of art.

A great artist, he was called a mathematician, wrote: "We must understand and not forget that there was a time when there were no human beings on this globe. There was a time when humans began to be. We must try to realize, for it is true, that our remotest human ancestors did not know what they were nor where they were. They had no clothes nor houses—they were probably covered with hair and dwelt in caves. They had no language, no human history, not even human tradition, no knowledge of number, no guiding maxims, no tools nor craftsmanship. But they had a marvelous thing—a gift that enabled them and impelled them to *start* what *we* call civilization; and they were, moreover, the first of a race that had another equally marvelous and equally precious gift—a gift enabling them and impelling them to *advance* civilization. These are the gifts that make humans human.

"And so we see that civilization is the creature, not of men, but of Man. It is the product of Humanity. It is to the time and thought and toil of those remote rude ancestors, groping in the dark, and of the many generations of their descendants that you and I and our living fellows are indebted for the immeasurable riches—the material and spiritual wealth—of our present world.

"To receive that Human Inheritance as we habitually do receive it, taking it all for granted as we take the gifts of Physical Nature—land and light and sea and sky; not to realize in thought and in feeling that, though we are individuals, we are living organs of Humanity; not to realize in our heads and hearts and ways of living and not to teach in home and school, our relations and obligations to the Dead and the Unborn: *that* is what I mean by 'living in and upon our civilization like maggots in a cheese.'

"But in proportion as we learn to understand and to feel those relations and obligations, we shall emancipate ourselves from the lower ideals dominant in the world and come under the sway of the higher ones. For, as Benjamin Kidd has justly insisted, there is a hierarchy of ideals and a hierarchy of emotions begotten of them. From the power of the emotion of the ideal of self-efficiency—causing us to live and kill and die for *self*; from the power of the emotion of the tribal ideal—causing us to live and kill and die for *tribe;* from the power of the emotion of the state ideal—causing us to live and kill and die for *state*: from the domination of these we shall emancipate ourselves and more and more come under the sway of the highest of all possible ideals, the ideal of Man—causing us to live and, without killing, to die for Humanity." [27]

27. C. J. Keyser: *The Human Worth of Rigorous Thinking,* pp. 313-314, 3rd edition, Scripta Mathematica, New York, 1940.

ACKNOWLEDGMENTS

A C K N O W L E D G M E N T S

I have not commented upon relevant material in many books of recent date, because post-war publications began to appear only after I had concluded writing the present work. Even so, I could have considered many of them, had not the load of preparing this book for publication and seeing it through the press fallen upon my wife and myself (during 1946-47 the manuscript was submitted to the readers of two publishers). No radical changes, however, have occurred since the war which were not already considered or anticipated. The general "Surrealist" direction of "Modern" art, and the impotence of the Academicians are now more blatantly obvious than they were when this book was begun in 1938.

1948 saw the beginning of several attempts to re-evaluate the morass called "Modern Art." Unfortunately, however, these attempts offered no other alternative but to regress to the past. Consequently, such writers were forced to go to excess in their attacks upon the few inadequately understood faults they were able to discover in Modern art. Their solution was to reject the hysterical idealism of the Surrealists and/or Modernists in favor of the polite idealism of pre-Surrealist times—a choice between hanging and shooting.

Because my attitude towards understanding art assumed the obvious—that art is a part of everything else that goes on in this world—I have quoted from numerous authorities in numerous fields "outside" the field of art. None of them, however, must be held responsible for the correlation I have made between their writings and the field of art. Since none of them saw the manuscript of this book before it went to press, the sole responsibility rests upon myself. I hope the use of their work, however, will help to initiate a more mature attitude between artists and men and women of other fields of human activity, the lack of which is one of the most tragic defects of our culture.

I regret that the written works of three artists came to my attention too late for discussion in the text. First there was the publication of Louis H. Sullivan's Kindergarten Chats (Wittenborn, Schultz, 1947). Had I known of his remarkable writings in time, I should have quoted him extensively, for I regard his theories of art and human living as the most momentous formulated by any artist anywhere in the 20th century.

Then there were two articles by Theo van Doesburg which were made available to me by his widow shortly before this book went to press. Van Doesburg courageously stated the course of future art with a clear, uncompromising vision. He ranks as one of the great innovators of the 20th century. The recognition which he deserves is known only to a few.

Finally, there were the writings of Jean Gorin. In general, he and I, as artists and theorists, are searching along similar roads of development from the Two-Dimensionalists and the original Constructionists. In the cases of both van Doesburg and Gorin I have done the next best thing by quoting them wherever I could at the head or end of various chapters.

I regret that the work of Antoine Pevsner is inadequately represented in this book. Every effort to obtain permission from Pevsner's dealer to reproduce his works met with failure. I was therefore restricted to works outside the jurisdiction of the dealer. Of these I was only able to locate a few that were divested of the old content, and I have reproduced all I was able to secure.

I wish to express my appreciation: to John and Eugenie Anderson, for their continued interest and support which have made this book possible: to Alfred Korzybski, for the education received from his written works and a seminar in 1938; without these tools of evaluation this book could not have been undertaken: to my wife, whose assistance in revising and preparing the manuscript for publication was indispensable to completing this work: to Raymond and Elizabeth Hedin and to Frank and Jean Chesley, for their part in making publication possible: to Julia Ross, whose participation in this book, although indirect, I wish to acknowledge: to John and Joan Barnes, who contributed several months to the preparation of the manuscript for publication: to Harry Holtzman, for generously permitting me to quote freely from the writings of Piet Mondrian; toward this end he made available translations by himself and Martin James of Mondrian's French writings, while they were preparing this material for publication: to Mary Raymond, who was more than conscientious in typing the final manuscript: to Edna Steiner, head librarian, Carnegie-Lawther Library, Red Wing, Minnesota, and E. W. McDiarmid, head librarian, University of Minnesota Library, Minneapolis, Minnesota, for their kind help in making books available to me: to friends and others, who helped in some way, especially those who opposed my views; the latter were valuable not only in enlarging my knowledge of their opposition, but also in compelling me to seek ever further comprehension of my own position.

The following persons and institutions were especially helpful in my efforts to obtain photographs: Jean Gorin sent the photos of his work, as well as copies of his writings; John Rewald very kindly lent me photographic portraits of Pissarro, Monet and Cezanne from his collection; Mme. Theo van Doesburg made available for the book all but two of the photos of Theo van Doesburg's work, as well as two articles by the artist; John Anderson made many of the photos in chapter 5 and photos of nearly all my Constructions; Dr. Arthur von Hippel supplied photos of electrical spark patterns; Dr. Kathleen Lonsdale supplied photos of X-ray diffraction patterns; Dr. Frank Chesley supplied photos of X-ray diffraction patterns and molecular and crystal models; the Polaroid Corporation furnished the photo of a calcite crystal; Macmillan and Co., London, went to considerable trouble to supply me with photos of Australian Aborigines and secured permission to reproduce them from the Executors of Baldwin Spencer, Messrs. Goutley and Goodfellow; A. M. W. J. Hammacher, Director of the Rijks Museum, Otterloo, The Netherlands, supplied a number of photos of Mondrian's early works; the heirs of Dr. Gaston Lalanne made available photos from the rock-shelter at Laussel; Dr. K. Absolon and Abbe Henri Breuil, while unable to supply photographs, were extremely helpful and generous in their suggestions as to where material might be obtained; Lincoln Rothschild was helpful in directing me to the source of certain photographs; Peggy Guggenheim gave me free access to the reproductions in the catalogue, The Art of This Century; The Minneapolis Institute of Arts was very generous in supplying photographs of works in its collection; Doris Fessler and Jessie Abbott, of The Oriental Institute were most helpful in my search for Egyptian material; The Chicago Natural History Museum supplied numerous photographs of Paleolithic art; Pearl Moeller, of The Museum of Modern Art, Evelyn Grier, of The Metropolitan Museum of Art, and Margaret Bush, of The Ryerson Library, The Art Institute of Chicago, were especially helpful in my search for photographs. The photograph of Mondrian's Victory Boogie-Woogie was supplied through the courtesy of Mrs. B. G. Tremaine, Jr. The self-portraits of Leonardo and Chardin were supplied by The Bettmann Archive; the engraving of Courbet by Boucourt is from The Metropolitan Museum of Art, New York; the photograph of Louis Sullivan is from The Burnham Library, The Art Institute of Chicago; the photograph of van Doesburg by courtesy of Mme. Theo van Doesburg; the photograph of Mondrian by courtesy of A. E. Gallatin; the photograph of Mies van der Rohe is by William Leftwich; the photo of D. W. Griffith by courtesy of International News Photos. Many others have generously granted me permission to quote from their publications or reproduce visual material—too numerous to name individually, except in footnotes and captions, so I must be content to extend them my collective thanks and appreciation for their cooperation. Finally, I would like to express my appreciation to Potter Hageman, Raymond Jordan, Robert Rennie, Fred Lindahl, Edwin Charles Potter, and the other members of the Bureau of Engraving staff, for their cooperation in the production of this book.

BIBLIOGRAPHY

B I B L I O G R A P H Y

1. ACKERKNECHT, ERWIN H.: "Problems of Primitive Medicine," *Bulletin of the History of Medicine*, Vol. XI, No. 5, May, 1942.
2. ———"Primitive Medicine and Culture Pattern," *Bulletin of the History of Medicine*, Vol. XII, No. 4, November, 1942.
3. ———"Psychopathology, Primitive Medicine and Primitive Culture," *Bulletin of the History of Medicine*, Vol. XIV, No. 1, June, 1943.
4. ALBERTI, LEON BAPTISTA: *Treatise of Statues*, John Evelyn's translation, T. Roycroft for J. Place, London, 1664.
5. ALEXANDER, FRANZ: *Our Age of Unreason*, J. B. Lippincott Co., Philadelphia, New York, 1942.
6. ALLEN, M. CECIL: *The Mirror of the Passing World*, W. W. Norton and Co., New York, 1928.
7. "American Abstract Artists," Catalogue for 1938, articles by 24 artists.
8. "American Abstract Artists," Catalogue for 1939.
9. *American Abstract Artists*, distributed by Wittenborn and Co., New York, 1946, articles by 6 artists.
10. ANASTASI, ANNE and FOLEY, J. P., JR.: "Study of Populistic Painters as an Approach to the Psychology of Art," *Journal of Social Psychology*, 11:353, May, 1940.
11. ———"Survey of the Literature on Artistic Behavior in the Abnormal: I, Historical and Theoretic Background," *Journal of General Psychology*, 25:111, July, 1941.
12. ———"Survey of the Literature on Artistic Behavior in the Abnormal: II, Approaches and Interrelationships," *Annals of the New York Academy of Sciences*, Vol. XLII, Art. 1. pp. 1-112, August, 1941.
13. ———"Survey of the Literature on Artistic Behavior in the Abnormal: III, Spontaneous Productions," *Psychological Monographs*, 52, No. 6, Whole No. 237, 1940.
14. APOLLINAIRE, GUILLAUME: *The Cubist Painters*, aesthetic meditations 1913, translated by Lionel Abel. In the series: The documents of modern art: General Editor, Robert Motherwell, Wittenborn and Co., New York, 1944.
15. ARAGON, LOUIS: "Painting and Reality: a discussion," *Transition*, Fall 1936, No. 25, p. 93.
16. AVEBURY, JOHN LUBBOCK: *The Origin of Civilization and the Primitive Condition of Man*, D. Appleton-Century Co., New York, 1882.
17. BALL, HUGO: "Dada: 1916-1936; Fragments from a Dada Diary," *Transition*, Fall 1936, No. 25, p. 73.
18. BARNES, ALBERT C.: *The Art in Painting*, Barnes Foundation Press, Merion, Pa., 1925.
19. ———*Art and Education*, with articles by John Dewey, Lawrence Buermeyer, Violette de Mazia, Mary Mullen, Thomas Munro, Barnes Foundation Press, Merion, Pa., 1929.
20. BARNES, ALBERT C. and DE MAZIA, VIOLETTE: "Ancient Chinese and Modern European Paintings," Bignou Gallery, New York, May-June, 1943.
21. BARNES, HARRY ELMER: *A History of Historical Writing*, University of Oklahoma Press, Norman, 1937.
22. ———*An Intellectual and Cultural History of the Western World*, Reynal and Hitchcock, New York, 1941.

23. BARR, ALFRED H., JR.: *Cubism and Abstract Art*, The Museum of Modern Art, New York, 1936.
24. ———*Picasso: Forty Years of His Art*, The Museum of Modern Art, in collaboration with The Art Institute of Chicago, New York, 1939.
25. ———*Paul Klee*, articles by Alfred H. Barr, Jr., James Johnson Sweeney, Julia and Lyonel Feininger, The Museum of Modern Art, New York, 1941.
26. ———*What Is Modern Painting?*, The Museum of Modern Art, New York, 1943.
27. BARRY, IRIS: *D. W. Griffith*, American Film Master, The Museum of Modern Art, New York, 1940.
28. BAUMGARTEL, ELISE: *Dolmen und Mastaba*, J. C. Hinrichs, Leipzig, 1926.
29. BEARD, CHARLES A., editor: *Whither Mankind*, with articles by Bertrand Russell, John Dewey, Lewis Mumford and others. Longmans, Green and Co., New York, 1928.
30. BECKER, CARL L.: *The Heavenly City of the Eighteenth-Century Philosophers*, Yale University Press, New Haven, 1942.
31. ———"The Function of the Social Sciences," *Science and Man*, with articles by 24 authors, edited by Ruth N. Anshen, Harcourt, Brace and Co., New York, 1942.
32. BELL, CLIVE: *Art*, Frederick A. Stokes Co., New York, 1913, Chatto and Windus, London, 1914.
33. ———*Since Cézanne*, Chatto and Windus, London, 1922, Harcourt, Brace and Co., New York, 1928.
34. BELL, E. T.: *Men of Mathematics*, Simon and Schuster, New York, 1937.
35. BENESCH, OTTO: *The Art of the Renaissance in Northern Europe*, Harvard University Press, Cambridge, 1945.
36. BERENSON, BERNHARD: *The Italian Painters of the Renaissance*, Rev. Ed., The Clarendon Press, Oxford, 1930.
37. BIDDLE, GEORGE: "The Victory and Defeat of Modernism," *Harper's Magazine*, 187:32, June, 1943.
38. BIRD: MILTON H.: *A Study in Aesthetics*, Harvard Monographs in Education, No. 11, Harvard University Press, Cambridge, 1932.
39. BLOODSTEIN, OLIVER: "General Semantics and Modern Art," *Etc.*, 1:12, August, 1943.
40. BORN, MAX: *The Restless Universe*, translated by Winifred M. Deans, Harper and Brothers, New York and London, 1936.
41. BOSANQUET, BERNARD: *A History of Aesthetic*, Macmillan and Co., New York, 1892.
42. BRAQUE, GEORGES: "Reply to a questionnaire directed by Christian Zervos," *Cahiers d'Art*, Nos. 1-4, 1935, p. 21.
43. BREASTED, JAMES HENRY: *Development of Religion and Thought in Ancient Egypt*, Charles Scribner's Sons, New York, 1912.
44. ———*A History of Egypt*, from the earliest times to the Persian Conflict, Charles Scribner's Sons, New York, 1912.
45. ———*The Dawn of Conscience*, Charles Scribner's Sons, New York and London, 1934.
46. BREUIL, HENRI and CARTAILHAC, E.: *La Caverne d' Altamira à Santillane près Santander* (Espagne), Monaco, 1906.
47. BREUIL, HENRI and BURKITT, M. C.: *Rock Painting of South-*

ern Andalusia, The Clarendon Press, Oxford, 1929.

48. BRILL, A. A.: *Freud's Contribution to Psychiatry*, W. W. Norton and Co., Inc., New York, 1944.

49. BROWN, G. B.: *The Art of the Cave Dweller*, John Murray, London, 1928.

50. BRUNTON, GUY and CATON-THOMPSON, GERTRUDE: The *Badarian Civilisation*, British School of Archaeology in Egypt, London, 1928.

51. BRUNTON, GUY: *Mostagedda and Tasian Culture*, British Museum Expedition to Middle Egypt. First and Second Years, 1928-29, B. Quaritch, Ltd., London, 1937.

52. BULLEY, MARGARET: *Art and Counterfeit*, Methuen and Co., Ltd., London, 1925.

53. BURKITT, M. C.: *Our Forerunners*, Henry Holt and Co., New York, 1924.

54. ———*Prehistory*, The University Press, Cambridge, 1925.

55. ———*Our Early Ancestors*, The University Press, Cambridge, 1926.

56. ———*South Africa's Past in Stone and Paint*, The University Press, Cambridge, 1928.

57. ———*The Old Stone Age*, The University Press, Cambridge, 1933.

58. BURNS, A. C.: *History of Nigeria*, G. Allen and Unwin, Ltd., London, 1929.

59. BUTCHER, S. H.: *Aristotle's Theory of Poetry and Fine Arts*, translated by S. H. Butcher, 4th ed., Macmillan and Co., Ltd., London, 1911.

60. ———*The Poetics of Aristotle*, edited and translated by S. H. Butcher, 4th ed., Macmillan and Co., Ltd., London, 1925.

61. CAPART, JEAN: *Primitive Art in Egypt*, translated by A. S. Griffith, H. Grevel and Co., London, 1905.

62. CARLSON, A. J.: "Science and the Supernatural," *The Scientific Monthly*, LIX:85, August, 1944.

63. CARMICHAEL, R. D.: *The Logic of Discovery*, The Open Court Publishing Co., Chicago, London, 1930.

64. CARR, HARVEY A.: *An Introduction to Space Perception*, Longmans, Green and Co., New York, 1935.

65. CASTERET, NORBERT: *Ten Years Under the Earth*, translated by Barrows Mussey, The Greystone Press, New York, 1938.

66. CEZANNE, PAUL: *Paul Cézanne Letters*, translated by Marguerite Kay, edited by John Rewald, Bruno Cassirer, Ltd., London, 1941.

67. CHAKOTIN, SERGE: *The Rape of the Masses*, translated by E. W. Dickes, Alliance Book Corporation, New York, George Routledge and Sons, Ltd., London, 1940.

68. CHAMBERS, FRANK P.: *Cycles of Taste*, Harvard University Press, Cambridge, 1928.

69. ———*The History of Taste*, Columbia University Press, New York, 1932.

70. CHASE, G. H. and POST, C. R.: *A History of Sculpture*, Harper and Brothers, New York and London, 1924.

71. CHENEY, MARTHA CANDLER: *Modern Art in America*, Whittlesey House, McGraw-Hill Book Co., New York, 1939.

72. CHENEY, SHELDON: *A World History of Art*, The Viking Press, Inc., New York, 1937.

73. ———*Expressionism in Art*, Tudor Publishing Co., Liveright Publishing Corp., New York, 1939.

74. ———*The Story of Modern Art*, The Viking Press, Inc., New York, 1941.

75. CHILDE, VERE GORDON: *New Light on the Most Ancient East*, George Routledge and Sons, Ltd., Kegan Paul, Trench, Trubner and Co., Ltd., London, 1934.

76. ———*Man Makes Himself*, Watts and Co., London, 1937.

77. ———*The Dawn of European Civilization*, new ed., Alfred A. Knopf, New York, London, 1939.

78. CLARK, J. G. D.: *The Mesolithic Settlement of Northern Europe*, The University Press, Cambridge, 1936.

79. COHEN, MORRIS: *Reason and Nature*, Harcourt, Brace and Co., New York, 1931.

80. COOMARASWAMY, ANANDA K.: *Why Exhibit Works of Art*, London, 1943.

81. COWPER, H. S.: *The Hill of the Graces*, Methuen and Co., London, 1897.

82. CRAWFORD, O. G. S.: *Man and His Past*, H. Milford, Oxford University Press, London, New York, 1921.

83. CRAVEN, THOMAS, editor: *A Treasury of Art Masterpieces*, Simon and Schuster, New York, 1939.

84. CROCE, BENEDETTO: *Aesthetic* as science of expression and general linguistic, translated by Douglas Ainslie, 2nd ed., Macmillan and Co., Ltd., London, 1922.

85. DALE, MAUD: *Before Manet to Modigliani*, from the Chester Dale Collection, Alfred A. Knopf, Inc., New York, 1929.

86. DALI, SALVADOR: *The Secret Life of Salvador Dali*, translated by Haakon M. Chevalier, The Dial Press, New York, 1942.

87. DANIEL, GLYN: "The 'Dolmens' of Southern Britain," *Antiquity*, XI:183, June, 1937.

88. DANTZIG, TOBIAS: *Number: The Language of Science*, The Macmillan Co., New York, 1930.

89. DAVIDSON, D. S.: "A Preliminary Consideration of Aboriginal Australian Decorative Art," *Memoirs of the American Philosophical Society*, Vol. ix, The American Philosophical Society, Philadelphia, 1937.

90. DAVIS, STUART: "What About Modern Art and Democracy?" *Harper's Magazine*, 188:16, December, 1943.

91. DENSMORE, FRANCES: *Teton Sioux Music*, Smithsonian Institution: Bureau of American Ethnology, Bulletin 61, Washington, D. C., 1918.

92. ———*The Study of Indian Music*, Smithsonian Institution, Washington, D. C., 1942.

93. DEWEY, JOHN: *Art as Experience*, Minton, Balch & Co., New York, 1934.

94. ———"Anti-Naturalism in Extremis," *Partisan Review*, X:24, January-February, 1943.

95. ———"The Democratic Faith and Education," *The Antioch Review*, 4:274, Summer, 1944.

96. DEXTER, T. F. G.: *The Sacred Stone*, New Knowledge Press, Perranporth, Cornwall, 1929.

97. DIXON, RONALD B.: *The Building of Cultures*, Charles Scribner's Sons, New York, London, 1928.

98. DIXON, WILLIAM M.: "Civilization and the Arts," *Fortune*, XXVII: 114: April, 1943.

99. DOESBURG, THEO VAN: "Fernand Léger," *Cahiers d'Art*, Nos. 3-4, 1933.

100. DUCASSE, CURT JOHN: *The Philosophy of Art*, The Dial Press, New York, 1929.

101. ———*Art, the Critics and You*, Oskar Piest, New York, 1944.

102. EDDINGTON, A. S.: *The Nature of the Physical World*, The Macmillan Co., New York, 1933.

103. EDDY, A. J.: *Cubists and Post-Impressionism*, A. C. McClurg and Co., Chicago, 1914.

104. EDE, H. S.: "Georges Braque," *Cahiers d'Art*, Nos. 1-2, 1933.

105. EDER, J. M.: *History of Photography*, translated by Edward Epstean, Columbia University Press, New York, 1945.

106. EDMAN, IRWIN: *The World, the Arts and the Artist*, W. W. Norton and Co., Inc., New York, 1928.

107. ELLIS, HAVELOCK: *The Dance of Life*, Random House, Inc., New York, 1929.

108. ENG, HELGA: *The Psychology of Children's Drawings*, Kegan Paul, Trench, Trubner and Co., Ltd., London, 1931.

109. EVANS, MYFANWY, editor: *The Painter's Object*, with articles by Fernand Léger, Henry Moore, Jean Helion, Amédée Ozenfant, Wassily Kandinsky, Alexander Calder, Max Ernst, Pablo Picasso, Giorgio de Chirico and others, Gerald Howe, Ltd., London, 1937.

110. FISCHER, MARTIN H.: "Spinal Cord Education," *Illinois Medical Journal*, 54:428, December, 1928.

111. FOWLIE, WALLACE: "Narcissus," *View*, Series 3, No. 3, page 72.

112. FOX, D. C.: "Prehistoric Rock Pictures in Europe and Africa," *Bulletin of the Museum of Modern Art*, Vol. 4, April, 1937, New York.

113. FRANKFORT, HENRI: *Cylinder Seals*, Macmillan and Co., Ltd., London, 1939.

114. FRAZER, JAMES GEORGE: *The Golden Bough*, abridged edition, The Macmillan Co., New York, 1934.

115. FREUD, SIGMUND: *Dream Psychology*, The James A. McCann Co., New York, 1921.

116. ———*New Introductory Lectures on Psycho-analysis*, Carlton House, New York, 1933.

117. ———*The Basic Writings of Sigmund Freud*, edited by A. A. Brill, The Modern Library, New York, 1938.

118. ———*A General Introduction to Psycho-analysis*, translated by Joan Rivere, Garden City Publishing Co., Inc., New York, 1938.

119. FROBENIUS, LEO and FOX, D. C.: *African Genesis*, Stackpole Sons, New York, 1937.

120. ———*Prehistoric Rock Pictures in Europe and Africa*, The Museum of Modern Art, New York, 1937.

121. FROMM, ERICH: *Escape from Freedom*, Farrar and Rinehart, Inc., New York, 1941.

122. FRY, ROGER: *Vision and Design*, Penguin Books, Harmondsworth, Middlesex, England, 1940.

123. GABO, NAUM: "Constructive Art," *The Listener*, Nov. 4, 1936, Vol. XVI, No. 408.

124. ———"The Constructive Idea in Art," "Sculpture-Carving and Construction in Space," *Circle*, International Survey of Constructive Art, editors, J. L. Martin, Ben Nicholson, Naum Gabo. Statements, articles by numerous painters, sculptors, architects and others, E. Weyhe, New York.

125. ———"Constructive Art," an exchange of letters between Naum Gabo and Herbert Read, *Horizon*, X:57, July, 1944.

126. GALTON, FRANCIS: *Inquiries into Human Faculty* and its development, New York, 1883.

127. GAUGUIN, PAUL: *The Intimate Journals of Paul Gauguin*, translated by Van Wyck Brooks, William Heinemann, Ltd., London, 1931.

128. GIEDION, SIGFRIED: *Space, Time and Architecture*, Harvard University Press, 4th printing, Cambridge, 1943.

129. GLICKSBERG, CHARLES I.: "The Decline of Literary Marxism," *The Antioch Review*, 1:452, Winter, 1941.

130. ———"Mysticism in Contemporary Poetry," *The Antioch Review*, 3:235, Summer, 1943.

131. ———"General Semantics and Psychoanalysis: Korzybski and Freud," *Etc.*, 1:33, August, 1943.

132. ———"The Negro Cult of the Primitive," *The Antioch Review*, 4:47, Spring, 1944.

133. GOGH, VINCENT VAN: The Letters of Vincent van Gogh, 1872-1886, 2 Vols., Constable and Co., Ltd., London, Houghton Mifflin Co., New York, 1927.

134. ———*Further Letters of Vincent van Gogh*, 1886-1889, Constable and Co., Ltd., London, Houghton Mifflin Co., New York, 1929.

135. GOLDWATER, R. J.: *Primitivism in Modern Painting*, Harper and Brothers, New York, London, 1938.

136. GORDON, JAN: *Modern French Painters*, John Lane The Bodley Head Ltd., London, 1923.

137. GORER, GEOFFREY: "Themes in Japanese Culture," *Transactions of the New York Academy of Sciences*, Series II, Vol. 5, No. 5, March, 1943.

138. GRIS, JUAN: "A Lecture by Juan Gris," *Cahiers d'Art*, Nos. 5-6, 1933.

139. GUGGENHEIM, PEGGY, editor: *Art of This Century*, with articles by André Breton, Hans Arp, Piet Mondrian, Max Ernst, Ben Nicholson, Manifesto of the Futurist painters, Realistic Manifesto by Gabo and Pevsner, Art Aid Corporation, New York, 1942.

140. HAGEN, OSKAR F. L.: *Art Epochs and Their Leaders*, Charles Scribner's Sons, New York, Chicago, 1927.

141. HALLIDAY, W. R.: "The Gods of Ancient Rome," *Wonders of the Past*, Vol. 2, G. P. Putnam's Sons, New York, 1937.

142. HAWKES, C. F. C.: *The Prehistoric Foundations of Europe*, Methuen and Co., Ltd., London, 1940.

143. HAYAKAWA, S. I.: *Language in Action*, Harcourt, Brace and Co., New York, 1941.

144. ———"Semantics, General Semantics: An Attempt at Definition," *Etc.*, 2:116, Winter, 1944-45.

145. HELION, JEAN: "The Evolution of Abstract Art as Shown in the Museum of Living Art," Museum of Living Art Catalogue, New York, 1940.

146. ———"How War Has Made Me Paint," *Art News*, XLIII:17, March 1-14, 1944.

147. HERRICK, C. JUDSON: *Neurological Foundations of Animal Behavior*, Henry Holt and Co., New York, 1924.

148. ———*Brains of Rats and Men*, The University of Chicago Press, Chicago, 1926.

149. HOGARTH, WILLIAM: *The Analysis of Beauty*, J. Reeves, London, 1753.

150. HOGBEN, LANCELOT: *Dangerous Thoughts*, W. W. Norton and Co., Inc., New York, 1940.

151. HOOK, SIDNEY: "The New Failure of Nerve," *Partisan Review*, X:2, January-February, 1943.

152. HORNEY, KAREN: *The Neurotic Personality of Our Time*, W. W. Norton and Co., Inc., New York, 1937.

153. ———*New Ways in Psychoanalysis*, W. W. Norton and Co., Inc., New York, 1939.

154. HORTON, PAUL B.: "Does History Show Long-Time Trends?" *The Scientific Monthly*, LV:461, November, 1942.

155. HUGNET, GEORGES: "Dada," "In the Light of Surrealism," *Fantastic Art Dada Surrealism*, The Museum of Modern Art, New York, 1936.

156. IVINS, WILLIAM M., JR.: *On the Rationalization of Sight*; with an examination of three renaissance texts on perspective, Metropolitan Museum of Art, New York, 1938.

157. JAENSCH, E. R.: *Eidetic Imagery*, and typological methods of investigation, Harcourt, Brace and Co., New York, Kegan Paul, Trench, Trubner and Co., Ltd., London, 1930.

158. JANIS, SIDNEY: *Abstract and Surrealist Art in America*, Reynal and Hitchcock, New York, 1944.

159. JANIS, HARRIET and SIDNEY: "Marcel Duchamp, Anti-Artist," *View*, Duchamp Number, Series V, No. 1, 1945, p. 18.

160. JELLIFFE, SMITH ELY: "The Technique of Psychoanalysis," *Nervous and Mental Disease Monograph Series*, No. 26, 1918, Editors, S. E. Jelliffe, W. A. White.

161. JENSEN, HOWARD E.: "Science and Human Values," *The Scientific Monthly*, LIII:258, September, 1941.

162. JOHNSON, WENDELL: "You Can't Write Writing," *Etc.*, 1:25, August, 1943.

163. ———"People in Quandaries: and why they are there," *Etc.*, 1:69, Winter, 1943-44.

164. JUNG, CARL G.: *Two Essays on Analytical Psychology*, translated by H. G. and C. F. Baynes, Dodd, Mead and Co., Inc., New York, 1929.

165. ———*The Integration of the Personality*, translated by Stanley Dell, Farrar and Rinehart, Inc., New York, Toronto, 1939.

166. KAHLER, ERICH: *Man the Measure*, Pantheon Books, Inc., New York, 1943.

167. KALLEN, HORACE M.: *Indecency and the Seven Arts*, Horace Liveright, New York, 1930.

168. ———*Art and Freedom*, 2 vols., Duell, Sloan and Pearce, Inc., New York, 1942.

169. KANDINSKY, WASSILY: *The Art of Spiritual Harmony*, translated by M. T. H. Sadler, Constable and Co., London, 1914.

170. ———*In Memory of Wassily Kandinsky*, a survey of the artist's paintings and writings, arranged and edited by Hilla Rebay, The Solomon R. Guggenheim Foundation, New York, 1945.

171. KASNER, EDWARD and NEWMAN, JAMES: *Mathematics and the Imagination*, Simon and Schuster, Inc., New York, 1940.

172. KEYSER, CASSIUS J.: "Korzybski's Concept of Man," Chapter XX, *Mathematical Philosophy*, E. P. Dutton and Co., Inc., New York, 1922.

173. ———*Thinking About Thinking*, E. P. Dutton and Co., Inc., New York, 1926.

174. ———*Mole Philosophy and Other Essays*, E. P. Dutton and Co., Inc., New York, 1927.

175. ———*The Human Worth of Rigorous Thinking*, 3rd Ed., Scripta Mathematica, New York, 1940.

176. KOFFKA, KURT: *The Growth of the Mind*, translated by R. M. Ogden, Harcourt, Brace and Co., New York, Kegan Paul, Trench, Trubner and Co., Ltd., London, 1924.

177. KOOTZ, SAMUEL M.: *New Frontiers in American Painting*, Hastings House, New York, 1943.

178. KORZYBSKI, ALFRED: *Manhood of Humanity: the Art and Science of Human Engineering*, E. P. Dutton and Co., Inc., New York, 1923.

179. ———*Science and Sanity: An Introduction to Non-Aristotelian Systems and General Semantics*, The Science Printing Co., Lancaster, Pa., 1933.

180. KRETSCHMER, ERNST: *A Textbook of Medical Psychology*,

translated by E. B. Strauss, H. Milford, Oxford University Press, London, 1934.

181. KROEBER, A. L.: *Configurations of Culture Growth*, University of California Press, Berkeley and Los Angeles, 1944.

182. LADD, HENRY: *With Eyes of the Past*, with an introduction by Philip N. Youtz, W. W. Norton and Co., Inc., New York, 1928.

183. LATTA, R.: "Notes on a Case of Successful Operation for Congenital Cataract in an Adult," *British Journal of Psychology*, I:135, 1904.

184. LAYARD, JOHN: "Maze-Dances and the Ritual of the Labyrinth in Malekula," *Folk Lore*, XLVII:123, June, 1936.

185. ———*Stone Men of Malekula*, Chatto and Windus, London 1942.

186. LEAKEY, L. S. B.: *Adam's Ancestors*, Longmans, Green and Co., New York, 1934.

187. ———*Stone Age Africa*, H. Milford, Oxford University Press, London, 1936.

188. LE CORBUSIER: *Towards a New Architecture*, translated by F. Etchells, Payson and Clarke, Ltd., New York, 1927.

189. ———"Painting and Reality: a discussion," *Transition*, Fall, 1936, No. 25, p. 109.

190. LEGER, FERNAND: "Painting and Reality: a discussion," *Transition*, Fall, 1936, No. 25, p. 104.

191. LEMAITRE, GEORGES: *From Cubism to Surrealism in French Literature*, Harvard University Press, Cambridge, 1941. LEONARDO, see 212.

192. LEVEY, HARRY B.: "A Theory Concerning Free Creation in the Inventive Arts," *Psychiatry: Journal of the Biology and Pathology of Interpersonal Relations*, III:229, May, 1940.

193. LEVY, HYMAN: *Modern Science*, Alfred A. Knopf, Inc., New York, 1939.

194. LEVY, JULIEN: *Surrealism*, The Black Sun Press, New York, 1936.

195. LEVY-BRUHL, LUCIEN: *Primitive Mentality*, translated by Lilian A. Clare, George Allen and Unwin, Ltd., London, The Macmillan Co., New York, 1923.

196. ———*How Natives Think*, translated by Lilian A. Clare, George Allen and Unwin, Ltd., London, 1926.

197. LIPPMANN, WALTER: *A Preface to Morals*, The Macmillan Co., New York, 1929.

198. LOWENFELD, VIKTOR: *The Nature of Creative Activity*, Harcourt, Brace and Co., New York, 1939.

199. LOWITH, KARL: "The Japanese Mind," *Fortune*, XXVIII: 132, December, 1943.

200. LORAN, ERLE: *Cézanne's Composition*, University of California Press, Berkeley and Los Angeles, 1943.

201. LOWIE, R. H.: *Primitive Religion*, Boni and Liveright, New York, 1924.

202. LUCKIESH, MATTHEW: *Visual Illusions*, their causes, characteristics and applications, D. Van Nostrand Co., New York, 1922.

203. ———*The Language of Color*, Dodd, Mead and Co., Inc., New York, 1930.

204. ———*Seeing and Human Welfare*, The Williams and Wilkins Co., Baltimore, 1934.

205. ———*Torch of Civilization*, G. P. Putnam's Sons, New York, 1940.

206. ———*Light, Vision and Seeing*, D. Van Nostrand Co., New York, 1944.

207. LUCKIESH, MATTHEW and Moss, F. K.: *Seeing; a partnership of lighting and vision*, The Williams and Wilkins Co., Baltimore, 1931.

208. ———*The Science of Seeing*, D. Van Nostrand Co., New York, 1937.

209. LUBKE, WILHELM: *Outlines of the History of Art*, Tudor Publishing Co., New York, 1937.

210. LUQUET, G. H.: *The Art and Religion of Fossil Man*, translated by J. T. Russell, Jr., H. Milford, Oxford University Press, London, Yale University Press, New Haven, 1930.

211. LYND, ROBERT S.: *Knowledge for What?*, Princeton University Press, Princeton, 1940.

212. MacCURDY, EDWARD, editor: *The Notebooks of Leonardo da Vinci*, 2 vols. arranged and rendered into English by E. MacCurdy, Reynal and Hitchcock, New York, 1938.

213. MacCURDY, GEORGE G.: *Human Origins*, D. Appleton and Co., New York, London, 1924.

214. ———*The Coming of Man*, The University Society, Inc., New York, 1935.

215. MACK, GERSTLE: *Paul Cézanne*, Alfred A. Knopf, Inc., New York, 1942.

216. MALINOWSKI, BRONISLAW: *Argonauts of the Western Pacific*, G. Routledge and Sons, Ltd., London, E. P. Dutton and Co., New York, 1922.

217. ———*Freedom and Civilization*, Roy Publishers, New York, 1944.

218. MALLERY, GARRICK: "Picture-writing of the American Indians," *10th Annual Report of the U. S. Bureau of Ethnology*, (1888-89), Washington, D. C., 1893.

219. MANDER, CAREL VAN: *Dutch and Flemish Painters*, McFarlane, Warde McFarlane, New York, 1936. Translated from "Schilderboeck" with an introduction by Constant van de Wall; first published in 1604.

220. MANNHEIM, KARL: *Man and Society in an Age of Reconstruction*, Harcourt, Brace and Co., New York, Kegan Paul, Trench, Trubner and Co., London, 1940.

221. MASON, WILLLIAM A.: *A History of the Art of Writing*, The Macmillan Co., New York, 1920.

222. *Masters of Popular Painting*, text by Holger Cahill, Maximilien Gauthier, Jean Cassou, Dorothy C. Miller and others, The Museum of Modern Art, New York, 1938.

223. MAUCLAIR, CAMILLE: *The French Impressionists*, Duckworth and Co., London, E. P. Dutton and Co., New York, 1903.

224. ———*Claude Monet*, Dodd, Mead and Co., New York, 1924.

225. MICHELET, JULES: *Satanism and Witchcraft*, translated by A. R. Allinson, Walden Publications, New York, 1939.

226. MILLER, DOROTHY C., editor: *Americans 1942*, 18 artists from 9 states, with statements by the artists, The Museum of Modern Art, New York, 1942.

227. ———*American Realists and Magic Realists*, edited by Dorothy C. Miller and Alfred H. Barr, Jr., with statements by the artists, The Museum of Modern Art, New York, 1943.

228. MOHOLY, LUCIA: *A Hundred Years of Photography*, 1839-1939, Penguin Books, Ltd., Harmondsworth, Middlesex, England, 1939.

229. MONDRIAN, PIET: *Le Neo-Plasticisme*, Editions de l'Effort Moderne, Leonce Rosenberg, Paris, 1920.

230. ———"De l'art abstrait," réponse de Piet Mondrian, *Cahiers d'Art*, No. 1, 1931, p. 41.

231. ———"Reply to a questionnaire directed by Christian Zervos," *Cahiers d'Art*, Nos. 1-4, 1935, p. 31.

232. ———*Plastic Art and Pure Plastic Art*, 1937, and other essays, 1941-43, The Documents of Modern Art, general editor: Robert Motherwell, Wittenborn and Co., New York, 1945.

233. MOREY, CHARLES R.: *Mediaeval Art*, W. W. Norton and Co., Inc., New York, 1942.

234. MORGAN, C. LLOYD: *Emergent Evolution*, Williams and Norgate, Ltd., London, 1923.

235. MORRIS, G. L. K.: On the Mechanics of Abstract Painting," *Partisan Review*, VIII:403, September-October, 1941.

236. ———"Relations of Painting and Sculpture," *Partisan Review*, X:63, January-February, 1943.

237. MOTHERWELL, ROBERT: "The Modern Painter's World," *Dyn*, No. 6, November, 1944, p. 9.

238. MULLER, HERBERT J.: *Science and Criticism*, Yale University Press, New Haven, 1943.

239. MUMFORD, LEWIS: *Technics and Civilization*, Harcourt, Brace and Co., New York, 1934.

240. ———*The Condition of Man*, Harcourt, Brace and Co., New York, 1944.

241. MUNRO, THOMAS: *Scientific Method in Aesthetics*, W. W. Norton and Co., Inc., New York, 1928.

242. MURRAY, MARGARET A.: *Egyptian Sculpture*, Gerald Duckworth and Co., London, 1930.

243. NEWHALL, BEAUMONT: *Photography, 1839-1937*, catalogue Museum of Modern Art, New York, 1937.

244. OBERMAIER, HUGO: *Fossil Man in Spain*, published for the Hispanic Society of America, by the Yale University Press, New Haven, 1924.

245. OBERMAIER, HUGO and KUHN, HERBERT: *Bushman Art;* rock paintings of south-west Africa, H. Milford, Oxford University Press, London, New York, 1930.

246. OGDEN, C. K. and RICHARDS, I. A.: *The Meaning of Meaning,* fifth edition, Harcourt, Brace and Co., New York, Kegan Paul, Trench, Trubner and Co., Ltd., London, 1938.

247. ORWELL, GEORGE: *Dickens, Dali and Others,* Reynal and Hitchcock, New York, 1946.

248. OSBORN, HENRY F.: *Men of the Old Stone Age,* Charles Scribner's Sons, New York, 1915.

249. OVERSTREET, H. A.: *We Move in New Directions,* W. W. Norton and Co., Inc., New York, 1933.

250. OZENFANT, AMEDEE: *Foundations of Modern Art,* translated by John Rodker, Brewer, Warren and Putnam, Inc., New York, 1931.

251. PAALEN, WOLFGANG: *Form and Sense,* Series: Problems of Contemporary Art, No. I, Wittenborn and Co., New York, 1945.

252. PACH, WALTER: *The Masters of Modern Art,* The Viking Press, Inc., New York, 1929.

253. ———*Vincent van Gogh,* 1853-1890, Artbook Museum, Inc., New York, 1936.

254. PARKER, DEWITT H.: *The Principles of Aesthetics,* 2nd ed., F. S. Crofts, New York, 1946.

255. PARKYN, E. A.: *An Introduction to the Study of Prehistoric Art,* Longmans, Green and Co., London, New York, 1915.

256. PARTRIDGE, G. E.: *Genetic Philosophy of Education,* Sturgis and Walton Co., New York, 1912.

257. PATER, WALTER: *The Renaissance,* Thomas Bird Mosher, Portland, Maine, 1924.

258. PAVLOV, IVAN PETROVITCH: *Conditioned Reflexes and Psychiatry,* Lectures on Conditioned Reflexes, Vol. 2, translated and edited by W. H. Gantt, International Publishers, New York, 1941.

259. PEAKE, H. J. E. and FLEURE, H. J.: *Apes and Men,* "Corridors of Time" series, Vol. 1, Yale University Press, New Haven, H. Milford, Oxford University Press, London, 1927.

260. ———*Hunters and Artists,* "Corridors of Time" series, Vol. 2, 1927.

261. ———*Peasants and Potters,* "Corridors of Time" series, Vol. 3, 1927.

262. ———*The Way of the Sea,* "Corridors of Time" series, Vol. 6, 1929.

263. PEET, T. ERIC: *Rough Stone Monuments and Their Builders,* Harper and Brothers, New York, 1912.

264. PERRY, LILLA CABOT: "Reminiscences of Claude Monet," *The American Magazine of Art,* Vol. XVIII, March, 1927.

265. PETRIE, W. M. F.: *The Arts and Crafts of Ancient Egypt,* A. C. McClurg and Co., Chicago, 1910.

266. ———*Prehistoric Egypt,* British School of Archaeology in Egypt, London, 1920

267. PIAGET, JEAN: *Child's Conception of the World,* translated by Joan and Andrew Tomlinson, Harcourt, Brace and Co., New York, 1929.

268. PICASSO, PABLO: "Picasso Speaks," *The Arts,* 3:315-26, May, 1923.

269. PICKFORD, R. W.: "Some Interpretations of a Painting Called 'Abstraction,'" *The British Journal of Medical Psychology,* Vol. XVIII, The University Press, Cambridge, 1939-41.

270. PIJOAN, JOSEPH: *An Outline History of Art,* 3 vols., The University of Knowledge, Inc., Chicago, 1938.

271. PISSARRO, CAMILLE: *Camille Pissarro: Letters to His Son Lucien,* edited with the assistance of Lucien Pissarro by John Rewald, translated by Lionel Abel, Pantheon Books, Inc., New York, 1943.

272. POINCARE, HENRI: *The Value of Science,* The Science Press, New York, 1907.

273. ———*The Foundations of Science,* The Science Press, New York and Garrison, N. Y., 1929.

274. PORTNOY, JULIUS: *A Psychology of Art Creation,* Chapel Hill, 1942.

275. RAMSPERGER, ALBERT G.: "The Misplaced Modesty of the Scientists," *The Antioch Review,* 4:581, Winter, 1944-45.

276. RANDALL-MacIVER, DAVID and WILKIN, ANTHONY: *Libyan Notes,* Macmillan and Co., Ltd., London, 1901.

277. RANKE, HERMANN: *The Art of Ancient Egypt,* The Phaidon Press, Vienna, 1936.

278. RAPHAEL, MAX: *Prehistoric Cave Paintings,* translated by Norbert Guterman, Pantheon Books, New York, 1945.

279. RASMUSSEN, KNUD: *Across Arctic America,* G. P. Putnam's Sons, New York, London, 1927.

280. RAYNAL, MAURICE: *Modern French Painters,* translated by Ralph Roeder, Brentano's New York, 1928.

281. READ, HERBERT: *Art Now,* Faber and Faber, Ltd., London, 1933.

282. READ, HERBERT, editor: *Unit One,* with articles by Barbara Hepworth, Henry Moore, Ben Nicholson, and others, Cassell and Co., Ltd., London, 1934.

283. READ, HERBERT: *Education through Art,* Faber and Faber, Ltd., London, 1944.

284. REISER, OLIVER L.: *The Alchemy of Light and Color,* W. W. Norton and Co., New York, 1928.

285. ———*Philosophy and the Concepts of Modern Science,* The Macmillan Co., New York, 1935.

286. ———*The Promise of Scientific Humanism,* Oskar Piest, New York, 1940.

287. REWALD, JOHN: "Proof of Cézanne's Pygmalion Pencil," *Art News,* XLIII:17, October 1-14, 1944.

288. ———*Georges Seurat,* Wittenborn and Co., New York, 1943.

289. ———"Last Visit with Maillol," *Magazine of Art,* 38:165 May, 1945.

290. ———*The History of Impressionism,* The Museum of Modern Art, New York, 1946.

291. REYNOLDS, JOSHUA: *The Works of Sir Joshua Reynolds,* His Discourses, Idlers, A Journey to Flanders and Holland, etc., London, 1801.

292. ———*The Discourses of Sir Joshua Reynolds,* James Carpenter, London, 1842.

293. RICE, J. A.: "Fundamentalism and the Higher Learning," *Harper's Magazine,* 174:590, May, 1937.

294. RICHTER, G. M. A.: *The Sculpture and Sculptors of the Greeks,* Yale University Press, New Haven, 1929.

295. ———"Polychromy in Greek Sculpture," in The Metropolitan Museum of Art Bulletin, April, 1944.

296. ———"Greek Painting," brochure of The Metropolitan Museum of Art, New York, 1944.

297. ROBERTSON, T. BRAILSFORD: *The Chemical Basis of Growth and Senescence,* J. B. Lippincott Co., Philadelphia and London, 1923.

298. ROBINSON, JAMES HARVEY: *An Introduction to the History of Western Europe,* 2 vols., Ginn and Co., Boston, 1924.

299. ———*The Ordeal of Civilization,* Harper and Brothers, New York and London, 1926.

300. ———"The Newer Ways of Historians," *The American Historical Review,* XXXV:245, January, 1930.

301. ———*The Human Comedy,* Harper and Brothers, New York and London, 1937.

302. ———*The Mind in the Making,* Harper and Brothers, New York and London, 1939.

303. RUSSELL, BERTRAND: *An Inquiry into Meaning and Truth,* W. W. Norton and Co., Inc., New York, 1940.

304. ———*A History of Western Philosophy,* Simon and Schuster, New York, 1945.

305. SANDFORD, K. S. and ARKELL, W. J.: *Paleolithic Man and the Nile-Faiyum Divide,* The University of Chicago Press, Chicago, 1929.

306. ———*Paleolithic Man and the Nile Valley in Nubia and Upper Egypt,* The University of Chicago Press, Chicago, 1933.

307. ———*Paleolithic Man and the Nile Valley in Upper and Middle Egypt,* The University of Chicago Press, Chicago, 1934.

308. ———*Paleolithic Man and the Nile Valley in Lower Egypt,* The University of Chicago Press, Chicago, 1939.

309. SANTAYANA, GEORGE: *The Life of Reason,* 2 vols., Charles Scribner's Sons, New York, 1932.

310. SARGENT, PORTER: *War and Education,* Porter Sargent, Boston, 1943.

311. ———*The Future of Education,* Porter Sargent, Boston, 1944.

312. SCHMIDT, R. R.: *The Dawn of the Human Mind*, translated by R. A. S. Macalister, Sidgwick and Jackson, Ltd., London, 1936.

313. SHOTWELL, J. T.: *An Introduction to the History of History*, Columbia University Press, New York, 1922.

314. SMITH, G. ELLIOT: *The Ancient Egyptians*, Harper and Brothers, New York and London, new and revised edition, 1923.

315. ———*Culture*, the diffusion controversy, with essays by Bronislaw Malinowski, H. J. Spinder, Alex Goldenweisser, W. W. Norton and Co., Inc., New York, 1927.

316. ———*The Evolution of Man*, 2nd ed., H. Milford, Oxford University Press, London, 1927.

317. ———*Human History*, W. W. Norton and Co., Inc., New York, 1929.

318. SMITH, HOMER W.: *Kamongo*, The Viking Press, Inc., New York, 1932.

319. SOBY, JAMES THRALL: *Salvador Dali*, The Museum of Modern Art, New York, 1941.

320. SOLLAS, W. J.: *Ancient Hunters*, and their modern representatives, 3rd ed., The Macmillan Co., New York, 1924.

321. SOROKIN, P. A.: *Social and Cultural Dynamics*, Vol. 1, American Book Co., New York and Cincinnati, 1937.

322. SPEARING, H. G.: *The Childhood of Art*, Kegan Paul, Trench, Trubner and Co., London, 1912.

323. SPENCER, BALDWIN and GILLEN, F. J.: *The Northern Tribes of Central Australia*, Macmillan and Co., Ltd., London, New York, 1904.

324. SPENGLER, OSWALD: *The Decline of the West*, Alfred A. Knopf, New York, 1939.

325. STEFANSSON, VILHJALMUR: *My Life with the Eskimo*, The Macmillan Co., New York, 1913.

326. STEINDORFF, GEORGE: *Egypt*, Photographs by Hoyningen-Huene, 2nd revised edition, J. J. Augustin, New York, 1945.

327. STENGER, ERICH: *The History of Photography*, translated by Edward Epstean, printed by Mack Printing Co., Easton, Pa., 1939.

328. STERNER, ALBERT: "The Cézanne Myth," *Harper's Magazine*, 168:672, May, 1934.

329. STINE, C. M. A.: "Chemistry and You," an address, February, 1937, E. I. du Pont de Nemours & Co., Inc., Wilmington, Delaware.

330. STOW, G. W.: *Rock-Paintings in South Africa*, Methuen and Co., Ltd., London, 1930.

331. STRAYER, JOSEPH R., editor: *The Interpretation of History*, with articles by Jacques Barzun, Hajo Holborn, Herbert Heaton, Dumas Malone, George La Piana, Princeton University Press, Princeton, 1943.

332. SWEENEY, JAMES JOHNSON: "Picasso," *Cahiers d'Art*, Nos. 3-5, 1932, p. 128.

333. ———*Plastic Redirections in 20th Century Painting*, The University of Chicago Press, Chicago, 1934.

334. ———"Surrealism as a Public Art," *The Kenyon Review*, 1:429, Autumn, 1939.

335. ———*Paul Klee*, Catalogue for Memorial Exhibition at The Arts Club, Chicago, January-February, 1941.

336. ———*Joan Miro*, The Museum of Modern Art, New York, 1941.

337. ———*Alexander Calder*, The Museum of Modern Art, New York, 1943.

338. ———"An Interview with Marc Chagall," *Partisan Review*, XI:88, Winter, 1944.

339. ———"An Interview with Jacques Lipchitz," *Partisan Review*, XII:83, Winter, 1945.

340. TALBOT, W. H. Fox: *The Pencil of Nature*, Longman, Brown, Green and Longmans, London, 1844.

341. TIEBOUT, CAROLYN, and MEIER, N. C.: "Artistic Ability and General Intelligence," Studies in the Psychology of Art, Vol. II, edited by N. C. Meier, *Psychological Monographs*, University of Iowa Studies in Psychology, No. XIX, Psychological Review Publications, XLVIII, No. 1, 1936.

342. TONGUE, M. HELEN: *Bushman Paintings*, Clarendon Press, Oxford, 1909.

343. TRILLING, LIONEL: "A Note on Art and Neurosis," *Partisan Review*, XII:41, Winter, 1945.

344. VALENTINE, C. W.: *An Introduction to the Experimental Psychology of Beauty*, revised ed., T. C. and E. C. Jack, Ltd., London, Edinburgh, 1919.

345. VAN DER ELST, JOSEPH: *The Last Flowering of the Middle Ages*, Doubleday, Doran and Co., Inc., New York, 1944.

346. VASARI, GIORGIO: *Lives of Seventy of the Most Eminent Painters, Sculptors and Architects*, 4 vols., edited by E. H. and E. W. Blashfield and A. A. Hopkins, Charles Scribner's Sons, New York, 1896.

347. VENTURI, LIONELLO: *Art Criticism Now*, The Johns Hopkins Press, Baltimore, 1941.

348. ———*Paul Cézanne Water Colours*, Bruno Cassirer, Oxford, 1944.

349. VOLLARD, AMBROISE: *Paul Cézanne*, his life and art, translated by H. L. Van Doren, Frank-Maurice, Inc., New York, 1926.

350. WEIGALL, ARTHUR: *Ancient Egyptian Works of Art*, T. F. Unwin, Ltd., London, 1924.

351. WELLS, H. G.: *Crux Ansata*, Agora Publishing Co., New York, 1944.

352. WERTHAM, FREDERIC and GOLDEN, LILI: "A Differential-Diagnostic Method of Interpreting Mosaics and Colored Block Designs," *American Journal of Psychiatry*, 98:124, July, 1941.

353. WHISTLER, JAMES A. MCNEILL: *Ten O'Clock*, Thomas Bird Mosher, Portland, Maine, 1925.

354. WHITE, WILLIAM A.: "The Language of Schizophrenia," *Archives of Neurology and Psychiatry*, 16:395, October, 1926.

355. WHITEHEAD, ALFRED N.: *The Concept of Nature*, The University Press, Cambridge, 1920.

356. ———*Process and Reality*, The Macmillan Co., New York, The University Press, Cambridge, 1930.

357. ———*Science and the Modern World*, The Macmillan Co., New York, 1931.

358. ———*Adventures of Ideas*, The Macmillan Co., New York, 1933.

359. WILENSKI, R. H.: *The Modern Movement in Art*, Faber and Gwyer, London, 1928.

360. ———*The Meaning of Modern Sculpture*, F. A. Stokes Co., New York, 1933.

361. ———*French Painting*, Hale, Cushman and Flint, Boston, 1936.

362. WINKLER, HANS A.: *Rock-Drawings of Southern Upper Egypt*, H. Milford, Oxford University Press, London, The Egypt Exploration Society, 1938-39.

363. WORRINGER, WILHELM: *Egyptian Art*, G. P. Putnam's Sons, Ltd., London, 1928.

364. WRIGHT, FRANK LLOYD: *Modern Architecture*, Princeton University Press, Princeton, 1931.

365. ———*An Organic Architecture*, Lund, Humphries and Co., Ltd., London, 1939.

366. ———*On Architecture*, Duell, Sloan and Pearce, Inc., New York, 1941.

367. ———*When Democracy Builds*, The University of Chicago, Press, Chicago, 1945.

368. ZERVOS, CHRISTIAN: *Pablo Picasso*, Vol. 1, works from 1895-1906, Cahiers d'Art and E. Weyhe, New York.

369. ———"Conversation with Picasso," *Cahiers d'Art*, Nos. 7-10, 1935, p. 173.

ADDENDA

370. DOESBURG, THEO VAN: "Towards A Collective Construction" (Manifesto V of the 'De Stijl' group), Paris, 1923.

371. ———"Towards White Painting," in the introductory number of the group and review, Concrete Art, Paris, December, 1929.

372. ———"Manifesto on Concrete Art," Paris, January, 1930, (reprinted in "Prisma der Kunsten," Orgaan van Nederlandsche, Kunstenaars, Vereeinigingen, May, 1936).

373. GORIN, JEAN ALBERT: "Constant Values in Art," unpublished manuscript, 1940.

374. ———"The Art of the New Times," unpublished manuscript, 1946.

INDEX

I N D E X

R. W. Pickford on disguises in, 436
see also Mediums

ART CONTENT, MODERN
C. Bell's false notion of, 425
A. Barr's false notion of, 425ff
A. C. Barnes on, 425, 429
A. Barr's false notion of realism in,
 427
Braque &, 431ff
problem of consciousness &, 435
see also Art Content, Old; Modern
 Art; Modernists

ART CONTENT, NEW
crisis in, 353
Doesburg on, 353
problem of reality in, 353ff, 357,
 359ff, 361, 368ff, 390ff, 425ff, 427,
 443
two choices arising from, 357
limitations of old abstracting &,
 357ff
"Abstract" artists' regression in, 361
criterion of reality in, 361
relation of, to nature, 368ff
Mondrian on, 369
K. Malevitch on, 376
Soviets, capitalists &, 383
Constructionists achieve reality for,
 390ff
problem of structure in, 448ff
demands of Structural Process in,
 450, 457
inventive factor &, 472
problem of medium &, 558ff

ART CONTENT, OLD
Cubists' return to, 331ff
retreat to, in Post-Cubist art, 388
Gabo on Cubists &, 410, 420
problem of suppression of, 420
"Abstract" art &, 437
A. C. Barnes on function of, 442
Modernists' false view of, 442ff, 456
Mondrian's regression to, 451ff
Mondrian's false view of, 456
Surrealism &, 507
Dali &, 508
problem of removing, 548
"Modern" sculpture retains, 559, 561

"ART FOR ART'S SAKE"
fallacy of, 78ff

ARTISTS
language &, 6, 11, 485ff
status of, in Greek culture, 131, 479ff
Christianity &, 146ff
Renaissance &, 161ff
science &, 161, 162, 176ff, 514, 571,
 575, 576, 590ff, 599
freedom of, 217, 219, 509
as judges of art function, 223
historical process &, 273ff
theories &, 275, 281, 315, 410, 410n,
 480ff, 484ff, 491ff

Pissarro on, 424
reality &, 429ff
irresponsibility of "Modern," 439
 491
false view of great, 446
as part of nature, 450
Aristotelian views of "Modern,"
 469ff
as authorities in Renaissance times,
 480
H. Muller on critic &, 481
as new art-critics, 482
their abject acceptance of critic, 485
Pissarro on critics &, 485
as self-centered, 488, 489
H. Read offers escape to, 490ff
H. Read on, as individualists, 491
theorize against theorizing, 491ff
problem of individuality &, 491,
 610ff
as lost individuals, 502ff
A. Eddington on, 578
H. Levey on, as unique neurotics,
 578n
Freud's analysis of, 579
Hollywood portrayal of, 579n
R. Fry on, as mystic, 580
on neurotic behavior of, 584ff
F. L. Wright on limitations of, 615
J. Gorin on new responsibilities of,
 619
F. L. Wright on Machine &, 619

ART-SCIENTISTS
accepted ones as esoteric, 586
as frustrated artists, 588
discredit their field, 588

**ASSOCIATED AMERICAN
ARTISTS**
on American art, 10

AURIGNACIAN PERIOD
early art of, 60
ILL., Clay copy of cup markings, 52

AUSTRALIAN ABORIGINES
D. S. Davidson on art of, 64ff
art of, 69, 73ff, 92, 100
B. Spencer & F. J. Gillen on, 72ff, 100
G. Mallery on pictographs of, 73ff
Oldfield on art & vision of, 92
W. Sollas on, 100
ILL., Sacred drawings, 63; Body dec-
 orations, 64; Ground drawings, 74,
 75

BACON, FRANCIS
on medieval learning, 155
Leonardo &, 177

BACON, ROGER
Giotto &, 157

BALL, HUGO
on being childish, 502
on Dada, 502

BARNES, ALBERT C.
on difference between old & new,
 425
on Cézanne as abstract, 427
on abstract form, 429
on "Modern" art content, 429
on early Italian painters, 442
on Giotto's art content, 442
his continuity theory of history, 443
on art & the world, 471

BARNES, HARRY E.
on historical facts, 16
on historical objectivity, 18
on term prehistory, 26n
on medieval hell-neurosis, 139
on Christian intolerance, 142
on Christian language, 148
on Aristotle's writings, 157
on Leonardo's versatility, 176ff

BARNES, JOAN
ILL., Construction, 1947, 560; Construction, 1946, 561; Construction,
 1947, 616

BARR, ALFRED H., JR.
on "Modern" and "Prehistoric" art,
 91
on term abstract, 347
use of term concrete, 347
on Cubist literary devices, 411n
false notion of new art content, 425ff
on "Modern" art content, 425, 426
on Expressionists, 426
on Les Demoiselles d'Avignon, 426
on Stuart Davis, 427
on "Abstract" artists, 429
Aristotelianism of, 469
on "Modern" art, 471, 482
on art as mystery, 488

BAUDELAIRE, CHARLES
on Millet's art, 222ff
on hatred of camera, 238

BEARD, CHARLES
on Machine & art, 607

BEAUX-ARTS
attitude of, toward Cézanne, 303

BECKER, CARL
on Christianity as primitive, 138

BEGOUEN, COUNT
on Paleolithic magician, 83ff

BELL, CLIVE
false notion of new art content, 425
on pure form, 425, 434
on problem of history, 438ff
on good & bad art, 439
on Post-Impressionism, 439
on realistic art, 470
significant form &, 487

686

Mondrian's conflict with, 449ff
laws of, in art, 450, 568
artists bound by laws of, 450, 547ff, 568
Aristotle on art as rivalry of, 462ff
Plato on art as inferior to, 463
Aristotle on structural method of, 464
Aristotle's ideal imposed upon, 467
J. Dewey on, as "unorganized miscellany," 470
S. Kootz on "Abstract" artists &, 470
S. Kootz on, as chaos, 470
A. Maillol on art &, 470
Modernists' hostility to, 470
M. Raynal on, as chaos, 470
J. Reynolds on, as chaotic, 470
Whistler on art &, 470ff
Mondrian on, as capricious, 473
C. Keyser on, as order, 478
Kandinsky on art &, 488
Architecture &, 526ff
"Modern" Architecture, art &, 530, 533
idealists, realists &, 535ff
art of man &, 539
realists, Surrealists in competition with, 539
consciousness of abstracting &, 547
Korzybski on laws of, 547
problem of abstracting from, 552
C. M. A. Stine on chemists &, 552
Photographers &, 568
A. Eddington on religion &, 578
J. Dewey on art, science &, 592
L. H. Sullivan &, 636, 638
F. L. Wright on art &, 636, 638
art as extension of, 650ff
see also Reality; Structural Process

NATURE-ART
differences between man-art &, 552ff
"Modern" Architecture &, 530, 630
Modernists' confusion before, 652

NATURAL OBJECTS
G. G. MacCurdy on, 57, 59
early sculpture &, 63
magic &, 63
role of, reversed in Impressionism, 264ff, 266

NAZI
see Totalitarians

NEWHALL, BEAUMONT
on camera inventors, 234

NEWMAN, JAMES
on obscure language, 489

NICHOLSON, BEN
on art & religion, 578

NIEPCE, JOSEPH-NICEPHORE, 234
on Daguerre, 226

NON-ARISTOTELIAN
O. Reiser on semantics, 373n
stage of man, 624

NON-ARISTOTELIAN ART
Constructions as, 401ff, 515, 541, 626

NON-ARISTOTELIAN SYSTEM
Korzybski on, 623

OBERMAIER, HUGO
on cave-art, 49, 103
on early cave-art, 53, 74
on eolithic ornament, 55n
on cave sculpture, 60
on Paleolithic body decoration, 72
on early cave painting, 72
on hand silhouette, 82
on magic of cave-art, 87
on French & Spanish cave-art, 98

OGDEN, C. K.
on language, 4
on language, science & art, 479

ORIENTAL ART
its false role in Post-Impressionism, 283, 284, 294ff, 300
Cézanne &, 296
see also Japanese art

ORIENTAL INFLUENCES
H. Frankfort on Middle Ages &, 143
in Fauvism, 315
false role of, in Western art, 316ff

OSBORN, H. F.
on Paleolithic art, 71

OZENFANT, AMEDEE
on Doesburg & Mondrian, 367n
on Cubism & nature, 408

PACH, WALTER
on Impressionism, 272

PAINTERS
Renaissance sculptors compete with, 168
become Photographers, 235
E. Stenger on, as Photographers, 235
camera artists &, 235, 237
Photographers as successors to, 237
L. Moholy on camera &, 238
contribution of, to Constructionist art, 563

PAINTING
H. Obermaier on early cave, 72
of hand, 73ff
beginning & development of, 74ff
beginning of animal recording in, 76
Egyptian, 109
Greco-Roman, 132, 134ff, 171
human form in, 134

confusion of vision in Greco-Roman, 134ff
of Renaissance sculpture, 165
B. Berenson on, 166, 172, 174
perspective &, in Renaissance, 168
Renaissance sculpture in competition with, 168
ideal in Renaissance, 171
Masaccio as rebirth of, in Renaissance, 174ff
as dominant medium in Renaissance, 177ff
sculpture &, 178
Michelangelo's, 179
Michelangelo on sculpture &, 179
sculpture compared with, 182
psycho-tactile problems in, 183
of Venetians, 193ff
end of, as recording art, 229
relation of camera to, 233ff
as inferior to Photography, 240ff
post-camera color in, 263
Monet on, 275
P. Delaroche on death of, 363
Doesburg on end of, 364
usefulness of, ends with Two-Dimensionalists, 364, 366, 388
Gris on form &, 385
illusions of, & camera, 387
as inferior to Constructions, 390
Constructionists &, 393
uselessness of, in Post-Cubist art, 397
Structural Process &, 449
sculpture, Architecture &, 531
from Masaccio to Mondrian, 559
fantasy & inventive factor in, 563ff
freedom of, as art medium, 563ff
Mondrian on sculpture &, 599
see also Leonardo; Mediums; Michelangelo; Sculpture

PALEOLITHIC ART
H. G. Spearing on evaluation of, 37, 61ff, 77
H. Obermaier on, 49, 53, 55n, 60, 72, 87, 98
beginning of sculpture in, 50ff
animal as content in, 57
human form as content in, 60
G. G. MacCurdy on symbols of, 67
signs in, 67ff
art chronology of, 71
H. F. Osborn on, 71
relief character of engravings in, 71ff, 76
H. Obermaier on body decoration in, 72
human hand in, 73ff
perspective in, 76
development of mediums in, 77
N. Casteret on mask in, 83ff
G. H. Luquet on function of, 87

evaluation of realism in, 88ff
on copying of, 89
art schools in, 89, 90
Impressionism &, 91
nature &, 91
"Modern" art &, 91ff
R. R. Schmidt on end of, 97
development of Egyptian art from, 102ff, 107, 111
G. B. Brown on signs in, 523
see also Aurignacian Period; Levant Art; Magic; Magdalenian Period; Mousterian Period
ILL., Relief, horse, Cap-Blanc cave, 57; Sculpture, Venus of Willendorf, Aurignacian, 58, 127; Sculpture, Mentone Venus, Aurignacian, 59; "Macaroni" finger engraving, 66; Enigmatical signs, Altamira cave, 67; Lines, animal (?), early Aurignacian, 70; Finger engraving, animal, early Aurignacian, 70; Finger engraving, animal, early Aurignacian, La Clothilde, 70, 71; Ivory engraving, female figure, Predmost, 71; Relief, bison, Aurignacian, La Greze, 72; Reindeer engraving, Magdalenian, Limeuil, 73; Animal cave drawings, Magdalenian, 78, 79, 80, 81; Male figure, relief, Laussel, Aurignacian, 84; Female figures, relief, Laussel, Aurignacian, 84, 85; Female head, Brassempouy, Aurignacian, 86; Female torso, Brassempouy, Aurignacian, 86; Horses, engravings, Aurignacian, Hornos de la Peña, 90; Fresco, Alpera, Spain, Levant, 105; detail of Brassempouy head, 142; Venus of Lespugue, Aurignacian, 566.

PALEOLITHIC CULTURE
V. G. Childe on, 47
Leo Frobenius on Egyptian &, 102ff
see also Norbert Casteret; J. G. Frazer

PALEOLITHIC MAN
early tools of, 51ff
W. Sollas on migrations of, 102

PARKER, DE WITT
on science & art, 589

PARTRIDGE, G. E.
on genetic psychology, 20

PATER, WALTER
on art as above intelligence, 487

PAVLOV, IVAN
on facts & theories, 586ff

PEARSON, R. M.
on copying art, 10n

PERSPECTIVE
vision &, 32
in Paleolithic art, 76
in Greco-Roman painting, 134ff
Leonardo on, 161
problem of, in Renaissance art, 166ff
sculptural attempts in, 166ff
Ghiberti &, 166, 167, 388
Renaissance painting &, 168
of Pompeian painting, 171
of Donatello, 179
discovery of, 183
W. Ivins on, 183n
as problem of image-consciousness, 184ff
"Moderns'" false evaluation of, 185
Cézanne &, 303ff, 387
problem of, in Cubism, 326, 387
see also Visual Consciousness

PESTALOZZI, C.
on Photography, 238

PETRIE, W. M. F., 116
on Egyptian cave-art, 103
on Egyptian art, 113

PEVSNER, ANTOINE, 395, 552
Realistic Manifesto of, 379
Soviets &, 382, 383
new culture &, 655
ILL., Abstract Construction, 1923, 389; Surface Developing a Tangency, 1938-39, 567, 618; Construction in Brass, 1927, 573

PFISTER, O.
on Impressionism, 272

PHILOSOPHERS
as authorities in art, 479ff
as aestheticians, 480
of art, as word-magicians, 481
see also Aestheticians

PHILOSOPHY
J. Dewey on experimental method &, 460
O. Reiser on Greek, 461
Korzybski on, 487
B. Russell on absurdities of, 490
Freud on science, religion &, 490, 594
B. Russell on science &, 571

PHOTOGRAPHERS
as successors to realists, 224ff
Daguerre, 226, 229, 234, 235, 243
Fox Talbot, 231, 233, 234, 235
B. Newhall on inventors, 234
J. Niepce, 234
painters become, 235
compared to painters, 237
as successors to painters, 237
Nadar, 263
compared to Modernists & Constructionists, 472
nature &, 568

PHOTOGRAPHY
Leonardo's primitive, 176
as superior medium, 224, 237
invention of, 225ff, 263
realists &, 226
necessity for, 229
Fox Talbot on, 231
A. Lamartine on, 232
J. Herschel on, 233
G. Lussac on, 233
relation of painting to, 233ff
P. Delaroche on, 233, 235
A. Disderi on, 235
J. Janin on, 235
J. Weil on, 235
painters rebel against, 235, 238
P. Mantegazza on, 236
L. Mumford on, 236
visual consciousness &, 236, 241
Baudelaire's hatred of, 238
L. Moholy on painters &, 238
C. Pestalozzi on, 238
E. Schreiner on, 238
hostility to invention of, 238ff
C. Blanc on, 239
reduces fantasy, 239
P. de St. Victor on, 239
F. Wey on, 239
false evaluation of, 239ff
painting as inferior to, 240ff
Television &, 244ff
uses of, 244ff
as development from pictographs, 252ff, 524
O. Reiser on, 254ff
color in painting after, 263
realism, fantasy &, 288
Aristotelian ideal &, 288, 626
painting illusions &, 387
as invention, 443n
old & new realists &, 510
writing &, 523
as mural art, 531
inventive factor &, 535, 539, 541
Constructions &, resolve schism, 536ff
Modernists' primitive, 562n
as art, 599
Constructions &, compared as Machine-art, 601
see also Films; Machine-Art; Photographers; Television
ILL., Edgerton, Multiple-flash photos, 253, 255

PICABIA, FRANCIS
Cubism &, 420

PICASSO, PABLO
African art &, 316ff
Post-Cubism of, 316n, 412ff
pre-Cubist period of, 317
Cubism of, 318ff, 327, 330, 333

C. Becker on Christianity &, 138
art, reality &, 624

PRIMITIVE INFLUENCE
Pissarro on, 285
in Fauvism, 315
false role of, in Western art, 316ff

PRIMITIVE MAN
magic-of-words &, 8
E. Kretschmer on vision of, 35
H. Spearing on evolution of, 37
E. Ackerknecht on medicine of, 38
K. Rasmussen on fears of, 39
R. Linton on ghosts &, 40
problem of reality &, 40
visual experiences of, 40
dreams &, 40ff
Christian visions &, 41
E. Kahler on death &, 41
cause & effect &, 42
K. Koffka on mystic &, 42
seen & "unseen" worlds of, 42
occult forces &, 42ff
E. Ackerknecht on supernatural &,
    43
witchcraft of, 43
magic &, 43ff
validity of his assumptions, 44
attitude of, towards death, 45
creative mentality of, 45
W. A. White on vision of, 50
early tools of, 51ff
on early stages of vision of, 51ff
R. R. Schmidt on first tool of, 52
see also John Layard; Lévy-Bruhl;
    Magic; Paleolithic Man

PROGRESS
Korzybski on ideas &, 422
problem of, 513ff
see also Evolution; Time-Binding

PSYCHOANALYSIS
Surrealism, dreams &, 503
art &, 578ff
H. Levey on, as unscientific in art,
    579
Freud as art authority for, 579ff
philistines in art &, 584ff

PSYCHO-TACTILE FACTOR
in linear art, 76ff, 134
vision &, 76ff, 110, 134, 170
in Egyptian art, 110
problem of, in painting, 168, 183ff
in Greek painting, 170
see also Perspective; Tactile Factor;
    Vision

PURE FORM
C. Bell on, 425, 434
"Abstract" artists &, 433, 434ff, 441
analysis of, 434ff
theory of, as false notion of reality,
    434, 435

PURISTS
Cubism &, 332, 332n

RAMSPERGER, A. G.
on responsibilities of scientists, 578

RANKE, HERMANN
on Egyptian culture, 97
on Greeks & Egyptians, 119

RAPHAEL
Vasari on, 186, 229
Cézanne on, 298

RASMUSSEN, KNUD
on primitive's fears, 39

RAYNAL, MAURICE
on Cubists' return to old contents,
    411
on lines & colors, 433
on Cubism as rejuvenation, 440
on nature as "chaos," 470

READ, HERBERT
on distortions, 288, 289
Aristotelianism of, 469
on artists & their ideas, 485
on society at fault, not artist, 490ff
on artist as individualist, 491
offers escape to artists, 491
on art & reason, 493
on art as superior to science, 592

REALISM
O. Reiser on naive, 25, 26
evaluation of, in Paleolithic art, 88ff
problem of, in Egyptian art, 114ff,
    118, 188ff
increase of, in Greek art, 123ff, 127,
    130
of Roman art, 133
return to, in Renaissance, 157, 164
Savonarola on, in art, 164
in Renaissance sculpture, 166
Courbet on, 192, 221ff, 223, 229
various kinds of, 202ff
Diderot on, 216
of Manet, 216
of Constable, 221
Impressionism &, 270
camera, fantasy &, 288
A. Barr on, in "Modern" art, 427
Mondrian's false evaluation of, 456ff
of Dali, 505n

REALIST
Leonardo as, 181
Hogarth as, 210ff, 229
Daguerre as, 226
Cézanne as, 428, 431n

REALISTIC ART
C. Bell on, 470
S. Cheney on, 470
J. J. Sweeney on, 470

the value of today, 473
Constructionist art as, 567
see also Recording Art

REALISTS
in French art, 220ff
scientific attitude of, 223
camera as improved medium for,
    224
romanticism of, 224
Photographers as successors to, 224ff
as human cameras, 225ff
Modernists' false evaluation of, 225ff
necessity of, 226
assisted by idealists, 227
C. L. Morgan on idealists &, 280
Post-Impressionists &, 292
Cézanne &, 300

REALITY
history & problem of, 20
Freud on magic &, 37
primitives &, 40
Christianity &, 41, 140ff
Lévy-Bruhl on primitives &, 43, 43n
Lévy-Bruhl on primitive art &, 93
art as problem of, 125, 579ff
Greek generalized notion of, 125,
    126, 130
problem of fantasy &, 155ff
nature as criterion of, in Renaissance
    painting, 176, 186
two levels of art &, 187, 188, 239,
    246, 579ff
identifying art as, 188
Flemish painters &, 197ff
problem of, in Post-Impressionism,
    292ff
Mondrian on art &, 352, 368, 448,
    449ff, 456ff, 545, 547
art contents & problem of, 353ff, 357,
    359ff, 361, 368ff, 443
Two-Dimensionalist art as limited,
    359ff, 361
Constructionists &, 390ff
problem of, in Cubism, 408, 411
problem of, in Post-Cubist art, 409
fantasy of Post-Cubist art &, 411ff,
    415
primitive orientation to, in Post-Cub-
    ist art, 415ff
Dali &, 417, 504
art as harmful, 417ff
art, words &, 418
science & problem of, 418
Korzybski on progress, ideas &, 422
abstracting & two levels of, 424
problem of, & Cézanne, 428, 431
artists &, 429ff
pure-form as false notion of, 434, 435
art, history &, 443
problem of, in new art content, 443
art as criterion of, 467, 472

judges nature as chaotic, 470
ILL., Portrait of Sir William Hamilton, 211

RICE, J. A.
on classics as pure reason, 461

RICHARDS, I. A.
on language, 4
on language, science & art, 479

RICHMOND, W. B.
on Impressionism, 303

RICHTER, G. M. A. 124n, 130n, 169
on Renaissance sculpture, 165n

RICHTMYER, F. K.
on Leonardo's science, 177

ROBERTSON, T. BRAILSFORD
on science & intellectual bankruptcy, 571

ROBINSON, JAMES HARVEY
on language, 3
on history, 15
on pre-writing history, 26n
on Greek & Christian beliefs on death, 140ff
on Christian state, 141
on medieval animism, 142
on medieval art, 144
on new & old, 406
on history as weapon of innovator, 445
on ancient origin of beliefs, 459
on convictions, 461
on medieval mystic, 488
on mystery & rationalist, 489
on familiar notions, 547

RODCHENKO, ALEXANDER
on death of art, 362, 363
politics &, 382

RODIN, AUGUSTE
Michelangelo &, 233
"Modern" sculpture &, 560ff

ROHE, MIES VAN DER
new culture &, 655
ILL., Model of outdoor restaurant, 532

ROMAN ART
development of, 131ff
realism of, 133
F. L. Wright on present &, 636
ILL., Head, Emperor Caracalla, 128; *Head, unknown man,* 128; *Agrippina, the "Younger,"* 130

ROMANESQUE ART
see Christian art
ILL., Relief, Vision of the Apocalypse, 144; *details of same,* 145, 634; *Sculpture, Figure of a bishop,* 145; *detail of head, figure of bishop,* 142; *Relief, Prophets,* 146; *Sculpture, Madonna & child,* 147

ROMANTICISM
in Greek art, 131
emotion-intellect attitude of, 131, 216ff, 219
compared with idealism, 216ff
of French school, 216ff
of realists, 224
Post-Cubist end of, 409ff

ROSS, ROBERT
on Impressionism, 303

ROUAULT, GEORGES
as Inbetweener, 425

ROUSSEAU, THEODORE
realism &, 221, 223, 270

RUBENS, PETER PAUL
Italian Renaissance &, 205
Cézanne &, 300
ILL., Portrait of Old Parr, 201; *The Judgment of Paris,* 203; *detail of same,* 204

RUSSELL, BERTRAND
on language, 5
on Renaissance, 159
on language & falsehood, 479
on philosophic absurdities, 490
on basic propositions, 497
on superstition & science, 569
on science & philosophy, 571

SAINT VICTOR, PAUL DE
on Photography, 239

SANTAYANA, GEORGE
on church & world, 154

SARGENT, PORTER
on history teachers, 17
on new social order, 623

SAVONAROLA
on art realism, 164

SCHMIDT, R. R.
on first human tool, 52
on "Macaroni" lines, 69
on end of cave-art, 97

SCHREINER, EDWARD
on Photography, 238

SCIENCE
Korzybski on facts, theory &, 25, 335
Christian culture &, 157, 158
Renaissance &, 158, 162
Leonardo on, 161
Leonardo &, 162, 176ff
abstracting process, art &, 348ff
art &, 348, 569, 571ff, 589ff, 643ff, 647, 648ff
problem of reality &, 418
Leonardo on practice &, 478
C. K. Ogden & I. A. Richards on language, art &, 479
mystery in art &, 489

Freud on religion, philosophy &, 490, 594
as threat to art, 493
Constructionists &, 514
Doesburg on art as, 569
B. Russell on superstition &, 569
M. Luckiesh on artists &, 571
T. B. Robertson on intellectual bankruptcy &, 571
B. Russell on philosophy &, 571
art, intuition &, 572
function of, 572ff
J. Gordon on, as "monkey habit," 573ff
P. Boswell on Machine &, 574
W. Dixon on Machine &, 574
J. Dewey on value of, 574ff
as inferior to art, 574ff
false view of, 574, 588ff, 592
"Modern" art critics &, 574, 575
S. Cheney on mystics &, 575
J. Gordon on art &, 575
S. Hook on illusion &, 575
G. Lemaitre on "Modern" artists &, 575
Modernists' false regard for, 576
H. Muller on religion &, 576
failure of, in art, 588
from magic to, in art, 588
O. Reiser on function of, 588
J. Dewey on art &, 589
De Witt Parker on art &, 589
objective & subjective factors in art &, 589ff
O. Reiser on emotion &, 589ff
A. Whitehead on, as drama, 590
art, reality &, 592
J. Dewey on art, nature &, 592
H. Read on art as superior to, 592
relation of, to art, 592
A. Carlson on human experience &, 594
art as, 594ff
J. Gorin on Machine &, 599
art &, as useless, 643ff
use of, in art, 647
not new in art, 648ff
ILL., Electrical spark patterns, 567, 643, 644; *Mathematical model,* 567, 586; *X-ray diffraction patterns,* 572, 576, 580, 582, 646-7; *Crystal & molecular models,* 590; *Calcite crystal,* 642

SCIENCE-MACHINE CULTURE
hostility of Europeans to, 629
opportunity for American artists in, 630

SCIENTISTS
A. G. Ramsperger on responsibilities of, 578

statistical, on art, 585ff
H. Poincaré on artists &, 590

SCULPTURE
as tactile consciousness, 31, 60ff, 111, 184
first manifestations of, 50ff, 54, 58ff, 60
early development of, 54ff
beginning of animal—, 59
H. Obermaier on Paleolithic, 60
development of art &, 60, 62, 70, 111
early problems of, 60ff, 70
natural objects & early, 63
as recording art, 64
Levant culture &, 99ff
relations between linear art &, 100, 108, 111
Egyptian art &, 111
G. E. Smith on Egyptian, 113
Greeks &, 123ff
Romans &, 132ff
of Christians, as relief, 151
Renaissance painted, 165
attempts at perspective in, 166ff
B. Berenson on Renaissance, 166, 172
influence of, on Renaissance painting, 172
Giorgione on painting &, 178
Michelangelo on painting &, 179
Donatello as end of, 181ff
compared to painting, 182
realism & Egyptian, 188ff
of Rodin & Michelangelo, 233
role of, in Transitional-Period, 385, 387
abstracting differences in Constructions &, 392ff, 397ff
limited to old content, 395
N. Gabo on history of, 397
Constructions & term, 399
Architecture as problem of, 525
painting, Architecture &, 531
Machine medium &, 559ff
J. Lipchitz on ills of, 560
Rodin & "Modern," 560ff
Michelangelo & "Modern," 561
Mondrian on painting &, 599
see also Mediums; Relief Art;
   Renaissance Sculpture; Stones;
   Tactile Factor

SEEING-THINKING
interdependence of, 25, 92, 226ff
in art, 487

SEMANTICS
B. Malinowski on freedom &, 5
A. Korzybski & general, 6
O. Reiser on non-Aristotelian, 373n

SEURAT, GEORGES, 272
compared with Cézanne, 306ff
Gris &, 327, 330
ILL., Port of Gravelines, 307

SHOTWELL, J. T.
on Christianity & historiography, 153

SIGNORELLI, LUCA
Cézanne &, 300

SMITH, G. ELLIOT
on culture diffusion, 96
on Egyptian sculptors, 113

SOBY, J. T.
on Dali, 504ff
on Dali's realism, 505
on Dali & Surrealists, 505
on Dali & Machine, 604

SOCRATES
on gods as greatest artists, 462ff

SOLLAS, WILLIAM, 69, 90
on Mousterian balls, 55
on Bushman art, 86
on Australian Aborigines, 100
on Paleolithic migrations, 102

SOROKIN, PITRIM
on Greek idealism, 125
on Greek realism, 130

SOVIET RUSSIA
see Totalitarians

SPEARING, H. G., 49
on primitive's evolution, 37
on early art efforts, 61ff, 77

SPENCER, BALDWIN
on art of Australian Aborigines, 72ff
on Australian Aborigines, 100

SPENGLER, OSWALD
on Renaissance sculpture, 562

STEIN, LEO
on aesthetics, 480n

STENGER, ERICH
on Daguerre, 234
on painters as Photographers, 235

STERNBERG, A. VON
on Photography, 238

STERNER, ALBERT
on Cézanne, 303

STINE, C. M. A.
on chemists & nature, 552

STONES
development of vision &, 51ff
eoliths &, 51, 57
early use of, 54
magic use of, 54
evolution in use of, 54ff
see also Magic; Sculpture
ILL., Regular & irregular natural stones, 52; Natural stones resembling animal & human forms, 53, 56

STRUCTURAL FACTOR
Post-Impressionism &, 287ff, 292ff
Cubism &, 332
Cézanne, fantasy &, 345
Constructionists &, 514

STRUCTURAL PROCESS
Post-Impressionism &, 292ff, 301
Cézanne &, 301, 306
Cubism &, 324, 411
abstracting &, 343
abstracting demands of, 358ff
inventive factor &, 361
as new abstracting level, 368, 369ff
Two-Dimensionalists &, 376
Constructionists &, 390ff, 392, 399
art history &, 443
painting &, 449
demands of, in new art content, 450, 457
potentialities of, 548
problem of invention &, 555ff

STRUCTURE
Korzybski on language-, 4, 5, 6, 10ff, 262
as link between words & things, 7
Impressionist & color-, 261, 264, 267ff, 269, 273
Post-Impressionists & visual-, 281
Gauguin on visual-, 281, 282, 293
Impressionists, fantasy &, 314
Post-Impressionism &, 314
Cubism, fantasy &, 332
Doesburg on, 353
problem of, in new art content, 448ff
Aristotle on nature &, 464
Post-Cubist problem of fantasy &, 497ff
Transitional-Period problem of fantasy &, 497ff
problem of, 548ff
Cézanne & problem of, 551ff

STUART, EVELYN MARIE, 9n, 239ff

SULLIVAN, LOUIS H.
as one of great American artists, 244n
nature art &, 636, 638
new culture &, 655

SUPREMATISTS
as Cubists' successors, 353, 357, 358ff

SURREALISM
regression of ex-Cubists to, 408
Picasso's Cubism becomes, 413
Doesburg on painting as sickness &, 421, 495, 496
J. J. Sweeney on Cubism, Miro &, 433
"Abstract" artists &, 438n
Cubism, fantasy &, 498
reason &, 502
M. Ernst on role of artist in, 502ff
psychoanalysis, dreams &, 503
psychological aspect of, 503
subconsciousness &, 503
psychiatrists, psychologists &, 503n

on arguments about mediums, 178
on Leonardo, 181
on art & nature, 185, 187
on Raphael, 186, 229
on Titian, 194

VELASQUEZ, DIEGO
Italian Renaissance &, 205
ILL., Portrait of a Man, 201

VENETIANS
development of their painting, 193ff
Michelangelo on, 193ff
comparison of Florentines &, with
    Flemish, 194ff
Cézanne &, 300
ILL. See Renaissance Art

VERROCCHIO, ANDREA
painting &, 167

VENTURI, LIONELLO
on Cubism as only theory, 409
on representations of Cézanne, 428
on Giorgione, 441

VISION
Max Born on, 23
M. Luckiesh & F. Moss on evolution
    of, 24
art history as evolution of, 25
K. Koffka on, 25, 26, 29
art &, 26
development of, in infant, 26
pictographic man's, 26, 32
H. Carr on blindness &, 27ff
sight restored &, 27ff, 29
M. Luckiesh on restored, 29
as problem of consciousness, 29, 32
translating tactile experiences into,
    30
tactile factor &, 30, 57, 61, 74ff
as phenomenon of observer &
    observed, 31
art & sanity in, 32
low level of today, 32
perspective &, 32
time-binding &, 32
primitive man &, 40, 42, 60, 92
early tools of man &, 51ff
stones & development of, 51ff
early stages of, 51ff, 60
early tactile role in, 57, 60ff
O. Reiser on evolution of, 61, 623
psycho-tactile factor &, 76ff, 110, 134,
    170
art development &, 114
similarities & differences in, 126ff
Greco-Roman painting &, 134ff
religion &, 146
Leonardo on, 160, 161, 237
Courbet on, 223
of Impressionists, 259, 260, 264, 266,
    269, 273, 276, 314
Monet on, 259, 264, 266, 269, 276
Pissarro on, 260

Impressionist revolution in, 273
Post-Impressionists &, 281, 289
M. Luckiesh & F. Moss on, 423
A. Eddington on, 423, 547
"Modern" art & problem of, 434ff
"pure-form" &, 434ff
art as not merely, 486
Modernists' infantile, 510
C. W. Valentine on, 647
M. Luckiesh on blood pressure &,
    647
problem of, in human life, 648
the new, in art, 650

VISUAL CONSCIOUSNESS
art &, 26
image as distinct from object, 31, 183,
    184, 233, 236
non-allness of, 92, 187, 189
problem of, in art, 126
primitives &, 126ff
nature &, 181
as problem of observer & observed,
    185
of Florentines, 194ff
of Venetians, 194ff
of Flemish, 197ff
camera contribution to, 236, 241
J. W. Dunne on, 434

VOLLARD, AMBROISE
on Cézanne & Gauguin, 293
on pictures on Cézanne's walls, 300

WATTEAU, ANTOINE
color idealism of, 215

WEIL, J.
on Photography, 235

WESTERN ART
M. C. Cheney on, 284
false role of Oriental & primitive
    influences in, 316ff
Cubism, primitivism &, 317

WEY, FRANCIS
on Photography, 239

WHEELER, MONROE
on distortion, 470
on Dali, 512

WHISTLER, JAMES
on art & subject-matter, 425
on nature & art, 470ff

WHITE, W. A.
on magic-of-words, 5
on primitive vision, 50

**WHITEHEAD, ALFRED, N.,
157, 219**
on the past, 13, 14
on sociological theory, 15
on Christianity & science, 158

on F. Bacon & Leonardo, 177
on assumptions, 275
on abstraction & nature, 340
use of term concrete, 340, 348
on abstracting & progress, 423
on systems & their limitations, 475
on "misty profundity," 489
on science as drama, 590
on evolution, 611

WILDE, OSCAR
on art-critics, 482

WILENSKI, R. H.
on Colbert & Le Brun, 206

WINKLER, HANS, 103

WITCHCRAFT
primitive man &, 43

WOLFF, A.
on Impressionism, 302

WORRINGER, WILHELM
on Stone Age in Egypt, 103

WRIGHT, FRANK LLOYD
as Machine artist, 244n
on Machine & art, 381, 607
on Renaissance Architecture, 526
on Michelangelo's St. Peter's, 529ff
on Machine & democracy, 602
on Machine as creative tool, 603
on artists' limitations, 615
on artists & Machine, 619
on Old Order, 621
on new reality, 623
on Roman culture & present, 636
nature, art &, 636, 638
new culture &, 655

WRITING
relation of, to Egyptian linear art,
    111
inventive factor & development of,
    519ff
origin of, 520
pictography of, 520
W. A. Mason on pictographic, 521
Photography &, 523
recording art &, 523
two levels of, 523
Constructions &, 524

YOUTZ, PHILIP N.
on criticism & art, 479

ZANE, N. B.
on Christian music, 148n

ZERVOS, CHRISTIAN
on Picasso's compulsion, 509